The Scourge of War

The news from the Potomac and Richmond appear so favorable that I sometimes begin to think the Secesh will have to give in and submit. Indeed at the moment their Country is suffering the Scourge of War, and Peace or destruction seems their fate.—William T. Sherman to Ellen Ewing Sherman, July 15, 1863

I thank you for the expressions of confidence in me, and repeat that you do me but justice in thinking that I am not the Scourge and monster that the southern press represents me, but that will take infinitely more delight in curing the wounds made by war, than in inflicting them.—William T. Sherman to Mrs. Caroline Carson, January 20, 1865

The Scourge of War

The Life of William Tecumseh Sherman

BRIAN HOLDEN REID

OXFORD
UNIVERSITY PRESS

OXFORD
UNIVERSITY PRESS

Oxford University Press is a department of the University of Oxford. It furthers
the University's objective of excellence in research, scholarship, and education
by publishing worldwide. Oxford is a registered trade mark of Oxford University
Press in the UK and certain other countries.

Published in the United States of America by Oxford University Press
198 Madison Avenue, New York, NY 10016, United States of America.

Library of Congress Control Number: 2020933024
ISBN 978-0-19-539273-9

3 5 7 9 8 6 4 2

Printed by Sheridan Books, Inc., United States of America

To my American Cousin, Thomas Holden Reid,
for many good turns

And to the memory of three irreplaceable friends
Roger J. Spiller (1944–2017)
Curtis Roosevelt (1930–2016)
Hugh Brogan (1936–2019)

ERRATA

The Scourge of War
Brian Holden Reid

Oxford University Press regrets that there are
several errors in the art program:

PAGE 192   Caption should read: Tennessee and Kentucky—Advance
to Chattanooga

PAGE 222   Caption should read: The Vicksburg Campaign, 1863

INSERT PAGE 1   Caption should read: West Point accommodation was
deliberately hardy, all cadets rolling up their bedding on
rising and emptying the "slop bucket" positioned underneath the wash stand. US Military Academy Library,
Special Collections.

INSERT PAGE 10   Photo of P.G.T. Beauregard should appear here:

INSERT PAGE 16   Photo of Sherman in 1890 should appear here:

Acknowledgments

Historical research is best not conducted in isolation. I owe a great deal to the advice, encouragement, and enthusiasm of others. My greatest debt is to my cousin Mr. Thomas H. Reid of Parma, Ohio, who has hosted my many visits to the Buckeye State. Together we have explored the state's hinterland and massive contribution to the Civil War era. We have explored the statehouse in Columbus, discovered Major General James B. McPherson's grave at Clyde, and journeyed to General Sherman's hometown, Lancaster, through a bewildering array of weather, to visit his birthplace on Main Street, now a museum. The current owners of the Ewing residence at the top of the hill, which must have been imposing in the 1830s, have (at the time of visiting) painted it pink, but I decided not to disturb their repose. I was greeted in the most welcoming way by the staff of the Sherman House, who thoughtfully and without being asked put on an extemporized walking tour of Lancaster for us; later in the day, we discovered the town's Roman Catholic cemetery, somewhat farther out of town, and the graves of the Ewing family. These visits have done much to inform my understanding of the life and background of William T. Sherman, in spite of—perhaps because of—his naked dislike in later life of Ohio, and Lancaster in particular.

I have been treated with great courtesy and kindness by the staffs of the Manuscript Division, Library of Congress, Washington, DC; the Archives of the University of Notre Dame, Notre Dame, Indiana, where the senior archivist and curator, Dr. Kevin Cawley, was most helpful, as was Joe Smith; the Special Collections and the Archives of the United States Military Academy at West Point in Jefferson Hall, and am especially grateful to Susan Lintelmann; the Chicago Public Library (Special Collections and Preservation Division); the Chicago History Museum Research Center (formerly Chicago Historical Society); the Liddell Hart Centre for Military Archives at King's College London; and the archives held by the Hove Public Library in East Sussex. I am pleased to acknowledge permission to quote from copyrighted material.

I am indebted to a number of scholars for their advice and help. I am most grateful to Daniel Walker Howe for first introducing me to OUP New York. For discerning general advice, and sometimes critical readings of chapters or frequently the entire work, I am obliged to the late Roger J. Spiller, George Rable, Joseph G. Dawson III, Steve Weiss, Lawrence Lee Hewitt, Joseph T. Glatthaar, Richard J. Carwardine, Richard H. Kohn, and Sir Richard Trainor. I am deeply appreciative of their encouragement and hospitality— although they may not be aware of the occasion or approve of the result. In addition, I am indebted to Charles M. Hubbard for a tour of the battlefields between Chattanooga and Atlanta, the high point of which (in every sense) was a memorable visit to Kennesaw Mountain with its alluring view toward the city of Atlanta. To my former doctoral pupil Howard J. Fuller, I am grateful beyond measure for the gift some years ago of a CD-ROM that made available the complete set of the *Official Records*; although I am aware that this is no longer cutting-edge technology, even for an unreconstructed technophobe like myself, it has revolutionized my research, as complete sets of this magnificent collection are rare in Britain. Douglas Eden went to great lengths to trace the movements and activities of Theodore Roosevelt at the June 1884 Republican convention in Chicago. I am also particularly indebted to my friend and colleague Sir Simon Wessely, president of the Royal College of Psychiatrists, for finding the time to proffer so many wise injunctions on Sherman's state of mind—not just during Sherman's breakdown in the autumn of 1861, when he was judged "crazy," but throughout his life. I have found his counsel invaluable, and he has saved me from many errors. I am also obliged to another distinguished medical colleague and friend, Professor Sir Robert Lechler, who offered tantalizing insights in our discussion of Sherman's asthma.

I have also received specialist advice from Major General Julian Thompson, Major General Mungo Melvin, Dr. Harold R. Winton, and Professor Arthur Lucas. Professor Ian F. W. Beckett tipped me off about the availability of Sherman material in Britain. Their insights and knowledge have proved invaluable.

I am deeply obliged to two friends, H. J. Rogers and T. March, for accompanying me to Dedham, Essex, on a pilgrimage to explore the ancestral roots of the Sherman family. They proved very convivial company. Mr. Rogers has a claim to descend from "Roaring" John Rogers, the outspoken critic of Charles I who encouraged the Sherman family to speak out against oppression. Finally, I am grateful to four people for the completion of this book. My literary agent, Robert Dudley, has worked indefatigably in my interest and is always solicitous of my morale. My editor, Susan Ferber, has shown not only inexhaustible patience but also editorial skills of extraordinary intelligence and acuity from which I have benefited so much. My splendid copy editor, India Cooper, has also saved me from many errors and solecisms. Simon Blundell has been a significant mainstay of the whole project, offering help so cheerfully on so many occasions, and revealing much good sense. He is the best librarian in London. However, after receiving such a great deal of help so freely given, I alone am responsible for any errors on the pages that follow.

BRIAN HOLDEN REID
King's College London

The Scourge of War

Introduction

William T. Sherman has not lacked admirers. He was one of the architects of the Northern victory in the American Civil War in 1865. Yet his popular image is unenviable. What has come down to us over the more than 150 years since the end of the Civil War is a depiction of a ruthless, utterly heartless, and unprincipled destroyer. Sherman was a stern, insistent, and brutal man, so the story runs, certainly not a gentleman. He appeared happy to unleash on the South unprecedented devastation by fire and sword. During his Marches across Georgia and the Carolinas in 1864–65, the Confederate press likened his armies to the pillaging hordes of barbarians that despoiled the Western Roman Empire during its death throes. For hundreds of miles, not a house stood, not a living creature survived. This black portrait had the advantage for the defeated of placing the burden of guilt solely on the North, and one general in particular. Catastrophic Southern decisions were left out of the reckoning.

Lurid descriptions of a return to "barbarism" encouraged later generations to link Sherman's advance into the Southern hinterland with the Strategic Air Offensive launched by British and American bombers against Germany in 1943–45. Sherman's campaigns appeared prophetic—but he seemed a prophet of doom. The ever-expanding cycles of death and destruction unleashed by what came to be known as "total war" appeared insatiable. During the nuclear age, humankind appeared to stand on the brink of annihilation. When the origins of these cycles were investigated, it all appeared to begin with Sherman, and the Southern view of his wickedness appeared vindicated. Sherman's utter lack of moral sense, absence of restraint, and wild declarations appeared to have heralded all of these appalling developments. It was frequently claimed that Sherman should have been indicted for "war crimes" like the Nazis put on trial at Nuremberg. This harshly etched depiction of Sherman retains to this day many adherents. There is only one difficulty with it: this diabolical image veers drastically from the reality of the historical Sherman. It reads historical change, and Sherman's career, back to front. It distorts their outlines to a point where they become unrecognizable.

Contents

Instead, Sherman's military career should be assessed within the context of his own time. The dilemmas confronting Sherman and his peers resulted from the failure of the North to gain a quick victory during the opening campaign that culminated with the Union defeat at the First Battle of Bull Run in July 1861, in which he took part. During 1862 Northern armies occupied much Southern territory, but a decisive victory seemed as far distant as ever. In the autumn campaign of 1862, an outright Union defeat, though averted, seemed possible. Sherman discerned that Southern resistance was ferocious. Although he underestimated the strategic strength of the Northern position, he was correct in divining that the solution to winning lay in breaking Southern resistance, and that could only be done if the North showed superior resilience and will. Sherman sometimes doubted whether the North had the capacity to reveal these moral qualities and rise to the challenge, but he remained adamant that a display of Union military power was vital to exposing Southern weakness. The task that Sherman set himself was to sap Southern resistance and break the Confederacy's will to fight on. Precedents for such measures already existed in the Napoleonic Wars.

While Sherman reflected on these problems, he came to understand that the solution lay in the very nature of war—the "scourge of war." War was not a game and should not be entered into lightly, as it was inherently violent and destructive. Sherman became seized by the idea, as he wrote, that war could be "made so terrible" that not only could the South be defeated, and the war resources available to it seized or destroyed, but it could serve as a deterrent to prevent it recurring. These calculations were perfectly rational. It is an error to suppose that they represent mere mindless violence.

It is also important to understand that Sherman meant that war should be made terrible psychologically. Southern pride should not just be broken; it had to be humiliated and its boasts of martial superiority rendered false. Here Sherman's experience of living in Louisiana in 1858–61 illuminated his path. Sherman was always more concerned with the psychological impact of his more vigorous measures and long advances—not just piling up the ashes of savage destruction. In any case, the levels of destruction attributed to him were simply beyond the capacity of the two small armies that he fielded during his Marches. His method, then, was to grasp war's true nature rather than play at it, to achieve victory and not to hesitate in taking the war to the enemy. So throughout 1863–65 Sherman expressed trenchant views on the North's need to exert itself, to organize and direct its power. He wanted it to act as a "scourge" on its enemies and bring about a complete Southern collapse.

In the last year of the war, Sherman did successfully attack the Southern war economy, but more by psychological than physical means. His advances in Georgia and the Carolinas appeared unstoppable. He outthought as well as outmaneuvred his Confederate opponents, and his speed helped spread fear. He did not despise his foes. His plans were well thought-out because he respected his opponents too much. Moreover, he acted on grounds of military necessity. This concept is consistent with the laws of war and perfectly legal. The laws are not designed to prevent defeat even if the vanquished form the weaker side. Such Southern special pleading needs to be set aside. The South's sufferings were not unique or unprecedented. By comparison with the horrors of the Napoleonic Wars they were comparatively mild.

Viewed in the longer stream of Western military history, Sherman was not prophetic and did not anticipate the methods used during the two world wars of the twentieth century. He simply recognized with great clarity that warfare is cruel and pitiless—a veritable scourge—and does not provide ready-made protection for the weaker side. Here, then, is a major, arresting figure that played a significant role in the greatest drama in American history: the Civil War. But in Sherman's case, because he displayed obvious cerebral qualities, it is necessary to consider not just what he did but also what he thought and wrote.

Historians have often considered the relationship between military thought and execution, the difference between theory and practice, as puzzling, even intractable or enigmatic. What is the precise link between the intellect and the conduct of a great war? Is there one? In reappraising Sherman's military conduct, and the thinking that lay behind it, the main aim of this book is to show how these two sides of one of the most admired but also most condemned of American commanders, the thinker and the doer, intermesh. This requires an assessment of the workings of his intellect and the actions he took as a commander in response to his calculations within the appropriate military milieu. The latter is especially important because of the ingrained habit among historians, especially of the twentieth century, who viewed Sherman's writing in prophetic terms and drew connections between it and later wars of a very different character, scale, and destructiveness. In short, this work reconsiders Sherman within the context of mid-nineteenth-century warfare, its ideas, society, and politics, rather than extrapolations governed by the twentieth-century debate over "total war" with which Sherman is frequently associated.

This approach has been aided by the general direction of Civil War scholarship since the 1990s. Historians have shown a tendency to calculate downward the levels of destruction inflicted on the South during the Civil War. Mark E. Neely complains of the "strained emphasis on destructive 'modernity' in the writing on the Civil War." He rejects the notion that during the four years of the Civil War a "crescendo of violence" swept away all restraint, that "moral barriers as well as technological ones to the advent of truly and indiscriminate warfare had been breached decisively," and during that breach Sherman led the storming party, having assumed the symbolic role of the harbinger of the "return to barbarism."[1] This book is intended to contribute to the revision of a return to barbarism. Its stress on the intellectual and social context and the precise calculations that Sherman made, particularly in relation to the problems involved in the maintenance of military movement, will lead to a fresh understanding of his famous Marches.

In short, this book aims to give the main issues of Sherman's military life a different twist, combine them in novel ways, ask different questions of the material, and reach new conclusions about Sherman's Civil War based on the issues and preoccupations of his own time. It seeks to understand "levels" of work and activity—or the skills that are needed at a particular rank, those needed to command a battalion or a regiment being very different from those required to command an army, which demands greater breadth of knowledge, vision, and a different kind of imagination. The choices Sherman made were not invariably influenced by the tactical progress on the battlefield but were frequently determined by very different strategic-political factors. Operational and strategic concerns often came to the fore, and Sherman's sense of his true priorities should always be made clear. The shift in contemporary Western armed forces to a more comprehensive understanding of the nature of operational art and its vital link to strategy, the overall objectives set by political leaders—between means and end—has been of inestimable value in assessing the kind of decisions that were made in the past. The very best past practitioners of operational art had an instinctive understanding of its importance even if they did not call it that.

My argument has three essential dimensions. First, it will seek an explanation of his response to problems over which he had little direct control. It is important to remember that most of his military career was spent as a subordinate commander. His cerebral reactions are one way of moderating the interaction with the chain of command and his responsibilities both upward to his seniors, eventually to the general-in-chief and president, and downward to his subordinates. Sherman had a wide range of literary and historical interests and was a natural teacher. His pre-1861 life was happiest when he served as a college president. The conduct of war is not directly an intellectual process, and nor can it ever be. The ideas found on a page of a book cannot be immediately transferred to the battlefield. War is above all things a clash of *instincts*.[2] Ideas, however, did fertilize the solutions that Sherman arrived at; they gave his thoughts shape and a sense of proportion and permitted him to arrive at distinct solutions before his opponents could react. Like all ideas, they have weaknesses as well as strengths.

All commanders need to recognize when action is needed and also to identify the paths required to drive subordinates forward to secure their parts in the overall plan. Sherman was a hard taskmaster and sometimes expressed frustration with the comparative inertia of some of his subordinates. Such difficulties were largely the product of forces, systems, or structures beyond his control, particularly the lopsided organization of the armies that he commanded. It was only in the spring of 1865, just as the war ended, that Sherman was able to fashion a structure best suited to his requirements. These unpredictable circumstances ensured that ideas cannot leap unmodified from their pages onto the field of battle.

Second, Sherman's intellectual dexterity will be assessed, his ability to learn and adapt from experience. This requires more than anything else a discussion of *how* Sherman commanded. The book is structured around his eventual rise after one severe interruption through successive levels, regiment, division, corps, army, military division, and, finally, commanding general. Detailed coverage is offered of Sherman's relations with his subordinates and how these relations changed over time. It examines how Sherman harnessed their talents and delegated to Francis P. Blair Jr., James B. McPherson, George H. Thomas, John M. Schofield, Joseph Hooker, John A. Logan, Oliver O. Howard, and Henry W. Slocum, among others. How did Sherman harness their talents? How effectively did he delegate?[3] Particular attention is given to where Sherman placed himself on campaign to ensure accessibility, so that senior subordinates might be able to confer with him without too much difficulty. On crowded or chaotic battlefields, simply finding the commander is a task of no small difficulty. The book also explores what use Sherman made of his staff in commanding ever-growing formations.

Third, the discussion takes account of the technical sides of war, as these present significant intellectual challenges. The most immediately pressing for Sherman concerned logistics and sustainability. Armies had to be kept moving, and they had to be supplied over great distances and frequently over inhospitable, barren, poorly mapped, or even unmapped terrain. The railroads and telegraph solved some of these problems but by no means all— and often produced new ones. Sherman learned from hard experience that the more road transport that became available, whatever the means of co-ordination, the less mobile an army's constituent parts became.[4] This book explores how Sherman solved the fundamental problem of advancing over great distances in sparsely populated and poorly developed country. These challenges were fiendishly difficult and stretched his organizational and intellectual powers—but he overcame them. Much attention is given to Sherman's intricate logistical planning and preparation for his campaigns. Logistics is the all-important link between thought and practice, for any de-tailed logistical plan requires intricate preparation to sustain any lengthy campaign. This requires thorough knowledge of topography, movement, and the means of supply. Sherman conscientiously labored over all of these and was assiduous in carrying out a thorough personal reconnaissance whenever required while on campaign.[5]

However, this book is still a biography, and its starting point remains Sherman's character. Even as it rejects the assumption that Sherman's strong, vibrant, and sometimes uncomfortable personality is the source of all his actions, it does not imply that personal attributes are not critical in commanders. "They must be personally courageous to function usefully in the hazardous and chaotic conditions of the battlefield," avers Colonel Roger Nye, a scholar of command methods. "They cannot allow fatigue to cloud their minds. They must get their troops to fight. They must wage violence competently." And, of course, they must win.[6] Sherman displayed all these attributes, and his energy and stamina remained phenomenal into old age. Although earlier biographers have denied this, Sherman's ruminating imagi-nation reveals a powerful intellectual cast of mind.[7] What does the term "in-tellectual" mean in this world of soldiers and war, from which refinement and the climate of civilized values seems to have been banished? Conventional definitions stress that intellectuals live "for ideas" and are dedicated "to the life of the mind which is very much like a religious commitment."[8] The "military intellectual" may be no less preoccupied with the life of the mind but is a very distinct subspecies because its members pursue ideas in a very particular habitat of violence. Military intellectuals search out answers to very specific problems posed by war. It is important not to confuse intellectuality with academic study; they are by no means identical, especially in war, when all ultimately lies in the execution, not the conception.[9]

Of course, Sherman came from a society, especially in the American West, inclined to underrate intellectual endeavor. During the first decade of his life, the governing class of the United States, a patrician intellectual elite, was displaced by an ambitious, grasping, and ruthless group of self-made, "practical" men who served "the people"—a professional political class who evinced a high level of anti-intellectualism and suspicion of elites. Sherman spent most of his life regretting this significant social development. He was a loquacious and assertive individual, much less prone than Ulysses S. Grant to conceal both his reading and his views. At various times in his life Sherman felt himself to be an outsider, a servant, or a scapegoat. His early life appeared an irredeemable failure, saved only by the drama and opportunities offered by the Civil War. Yet in the spring and autumn of 1861, Sherman, for all his superb mental gifts, got things seriously wrong and became almost hysterical. It was at this point that he was judged "mad." Cleverness, that is, inherent mental ability, alone does not illuminate the path to success, even though Sherman enjoyed more privileges than most in what Abraham Lincoln called "the race of life."[10]

Yet though the value of intellectual attributes might be exaggerated, it can still be important for a commander, particularly if he is faced by novel, perplexing circumstances. They allow him to think his way through them, as Sherman learned to do. Consequently, if we are to understand Sherman's military achievement, his heritage, background, and formative experiences are crucial in elucidating the quality of his mind and understanding how things took shape. What did Sherman read, and what did he make of it? These are important questions, and so is the nature and influence of Sherman's West Point education.

Many doors were opened to Sherman in the 1850s, and he passed through them with high hopes that were quickly deflated, and then passed out again. He became despondent and disillusioned. Knowledge of Sherman's failures during the first four decades of his life illustrates, too, how much of this experience he naturally carried with him into the war. This is especially true of his political, social, and racial opinions and his unguarded antidemocratic bias. There can be no doubt that Sherman entertained the commonplace, midwestern racism of his generation of whites. During Sherman's time in Louisiana in 1859–60, he had quickly acquired Southern habits in referring to African Americans. A notorious letter of January 1865 encapsulated this rebarbative tone: "I profess to be the best kind of friend to Sambo, and think on such a question [the recruitment of black soldiers] Sambo should be consulted." He remarked on his popularity with the freedmen, "They gather around me in crowds . . . and it is hard to tell in what sense I am most appreciated . . . in saving him from his master, or the new master that threatens him with a new species of slavery."[11] Sherman's attitudes were not obsessive but rather ambivalent. Though he left harsh descriptions on paper, he enjoyed friendly and unaffected personal relations with all blacks wherever and whenever he met them. Toward the end of his life he wrote an essay championing the rights of black citizens in the former Confederate states, which indicates that his views had shifted 180 degrees from those he had held a quarter century earlier. Likewise, his attitudes toward the Indian tribes were a good deal more liberal than the biting language he employed would indicate. Yet Sherman never seems to have expressed any sympathy in the 1850s for the American or "Know Nothing" Party or agitators reflecting their views. Racial opinions in the mid-1850s that execrated African Americans, Hispanics, Indians, and Jews tended to come as a package that included anti-Masonry and hatred of newly arrived white immigrants, especially if they were Roman Catholic.[12] But Sherman expressed unusual sympathy for the Roman Catholic Church for much of his life, having married a Catholic. Certainly his earlier experiences in California after 1848, and the tumult he witnessed in San Francisco, left him with a lifelong abhorrence of anarchy and social revolution. In 1861 Sherman was a reluctant warrior, and the reasons for his lukewarm attitudes need to be assessed.

The other significant issue is Sherman's attitude to the South, which seems again ambivalent and complex, perhaps paradoxical. One of the few Northern generals who had lived and worked there, Sherman believed that his informed views should carry additional weight. His respect for and fear of Southern martial capabilities and organization—rather than rage— compelled Sherman to develop more punitive methods as the only way that the Confederacy could be subdued. In this interpretation, the motives that lay behind the famous Marches might be psychological and political, seeking to humiliate the Confederacy rather than instilling terror by inflicting brutal and gratuitous destruction. The distinction is a fine one, but the destruction inflicted on the South was more controlled than it has often been represented, and much of the looting was in line with that experienced in earlier wars.

A paradox lies at the very heart of Sherman's attitude to the South: he was a conservative figure, yet he sought to create havoc psychologically and break the bonds of a cohesive white society that he had in many respects admired. He freed more slaves than any other Union commander, but he was temperamentally disinclined to support the progressive measures that would prevent former Confederates from retaining power after 1865.[13]

In short, despite the flow of recent biographies, the subject of Sherman's military career is far from closed in terms of either scholarly or public scrutiny. My consideration of the post-1865 years will be attuned to this fresh context. Although he has been remembered most for his activities during the Civil War, the book will examine the approaches that Sherman adopted while commanding general of the US Army after 1869, as his reforms were largely based on the deductions that he drew from the experience of 1861–65. Sherman sought to fight future wars by enlarging the US Army's "brain" and capacity to expand itself in time for the next war and avoid the confusion, muddle, and waste he had witnessed in 1861–62. He sought a compromise of an expandable army formed around a regular core. The study of the Civil War has witnessed an unusual commingling of military thought and military history, and Sherman contributed to both. As for the latter, attention will be devoted to Sherman's methods in conveying his own historical experience and his emphatic rejection of the nostrums advanced by the Southern Lost Cause school of writers and apologists after 1880. A renewed understanding of all these links should establish a full and proper context for Sherman's mid-nineteenth-century ideas. Ideas, however, need to be reformulated for them to be translated into deeds. They need an intermediary like William T. Sherman to invigorate the "soul of an army." It is now timely to consider his formative experiences.[14]

PART I
THE FORMATIVE YEARS
1822-1861

1

Origin and Evolution of the Sherman Family to 1840

Unlike many of his fellow countrymen, William T. Sherman did not display an enduring fascination with his family tree. His treatment of it in his *Memoirs* is perfunctory. He never bothered to inspect his ancestral home, even during his European tour of 1872. Consequently, his biographers have been perplexed by his ancestry or thought better of treating it in detail. The Sherman family hailed from southeastern England and played a minor part in the upheavals that culminated in a great civil war that engulfed the British Isles from 1642 to 1651. The full context of Sherman's life is not complete without some consideration of this background and the legacy bequeathed to him by his forebears. Earlier experiences also provide parallels and contrasts with what Sherman faced during another great civil war, the defining experience of his life.[1]

The main Sherman ancestral home lay in Dedham in the county of Essex, the northeastern part of the county, five to six miles north of the city of Colchester, an important center since pre-Roman times. The picturesque landscape around Dedham has been rendered for time immemorial in the rural paintings of John Constable. Though not descended from Constable, Sherman displayed his own artistic urges, sensibility, and deep understanding of the color and layout of topography and vegetation in all his writings.[2]

Essex was a bountiful country, "most fat, fruitful, and full of profitable things," according to John Norden in 1594. The Sherman family ranked among the most prominent of Dedham's clothiers. The weaving of russet broadcloth, and its export to the Baltic, remained a Dedham specialty, and the town grew in wealth. . However, the opening decades of the seventeenth century marked a downturn in its prosperity, with high inflation, stagnation, and numerous bankruptcies. As ready money became scarce, the impositions of the Crown became more onerous.

These vicissitudes can be traced in the reaction of the Sherman family to the troubled times through which they lived. The family fortune had been built up by Henry Sherman (1510-90). His second son, Edmund (1548-1600), carried on his father's work and brought to it a humane and charitable disposition. His father's will left £20 to the poor "at the discretion of the Governors of the Free School of Dedham to take security of the principal." The school had been endowed in 1577, and Henry and his two sons, Henry and Edmund, were named as governors in the Royal Charter granted by Queen Elizabeth I. Edmund exceeded his father's generosity by bequeathing his house "at the church gate" on Royal Square opposite the fifteenth-century St. Mary's Church, plus the sale of eight and a half acres of land "to be employed for a dwelling house for a schoolmaster." This bequest grew into a school that survived until 1873. The elder Edmund had two wives who bore the same name: Anne Pallette (d. 1584) and Anne Clere. By the first he had two sons, also called Henry and Edmund, and by the second Samuel, among at least 11 children.[3]

The Sherman brothers faced financial challenges by 1620 but found ample consolation in their religious devotions. Both the senior Henry and Edmund had encouraged a Calvinist, radical, evangelical tendency in Dedham generically termed Puritanism, though its adherents never used this term. Anti-Catholic, zealous, reformative, and self-confident to the point of self-righteousness, Puritanism also exhibited a great respect for intellectuality and encouraged an introspective bent verging on self-disgust; it gained great sway among the professional business classes and the gentry. Henry Sherman had encouraged the creation in Dedham of a classis, a gathering of 16 local Puritan ministers led by the lecturer of the parish, the most celebrated of whom was "Roaring" John Rogers (ca. 1570-1618).[4]

By the 1620s the combination of harvest failure, economic depression, and overbearing royal policy stirred discontent and opposition in Essex. In 1627-28 soldiers were billeted on Dedham. The finances of the Sherman family were strained, and Edmund endured periods of indebtedness. This Edmund Sherman (1572-1643) is the first ancestor that General Sherman mentions in his *Memoirs*. He appears a stern and unforgiving critic of the king's government. The Shermans were followers rather than leaders in this impending upheaval, although they spoke out when King Charles I resolved to rule without Parliament in 1628 and levied taxes without its consent.[5]

The calamitous harvests of 1629-30 were quickly followed by demands for a new tax called ship money. The economy recovered somewhat after 1630, but Dutch competition damaged the cloth trade. Samuel Sherman was assessed at £1 13s just as his trade collapsed. Ship money hit the commercial classes hard, and it was the extension of the tax, without parliamentary sanction, that provoked fury. Simultaneously royal ecclesiastical policy sought to impose elaborate Anglican ritual on church services, plus an expensive program of repair of churches. "Roaring" Rogers, voicing the opinions of many, including Edmund Sherman, dismissed these as popish fripperies—and the ecclesiastical Court of High Commission suspended his lectureship. In 1634 Edmund Sherman, furious at this oppression of English liberties, decided to emigrate.[6]

His despairing, momentous decision had been influenced by Rogers's replacement as lecturer, Thomas Hooker, who had urged that God "begins to ship away his Noahs" and prophesied "that destruction was near." Both Hooker and Rogers's son Nathaniel fled, first to the Netherlands and then to the New World. In the years 1630–39, 565 individuals migrated to America from Essex, including 30 from Dedham. In taking this decision, the defiant parliamentary leader, Thomas Hampden, set an admired example for the Sherman family. The Sherman migration formed part of a diaspora of 21,000 souls. It was made to "a remarkable degree" by family groups. Edmund Sherman had married in 1605 and was accompanied by two sons, John (aged 21) and Samuel (16), and possibly also a daughter, either Ann or Joan. Leaving Ipswich in April 1634, Edmund Sherman was in his mid-50s, so rather old to make the journey. Most of the migrants were of the "middling sort," with 11 percent classed as "gentry." Emigration was not for the poor; the cheapest berth cost £50.

Edmund's son, the Reverend John Sherman (1613–85) had, like John Rogers, graduated from Emmanuel College, Cambridge, "a stronghold of Puritanism at the University." John Sherman learned well from his mentor, earning a reputation in New England as an "accomplished preacher." The American migrant Edmund Sherman's eldest son, also called Edmund (1599–1673), later came to Massachusetts in 1636 but returned to England the following year. In 1637 the royal government restricted passports to those who had taken the oaths of allegiance and supremacy acknowledging the king's rule; in 1637–38 proclamations were issued preventing emigration of anyone who had not gained a license from the Commissioners of Plantations and ordered all those who had failed to do so to return immediately—which might explain his sudden change of mind.[7]

In Massachusetts, Edmund Sherman and his family moved from Boston to Watertown; both he and his son of the same name were admitted as freemen before the latter's sudden departure in 1637, and John became a minister there. One son might have returned home, but Edmund remained steadfast in his decision to become a colonist. Around 1635 Edmund Senior moved on to Westerfield, Connecticut. As a respected freeman he participated in the decision taken at Hartford in May 1637 to seize the lands of the Pequot Indians by a two-pronged attack in the Connecticut Valley and stamp out their raids once and for all. In 1639 he moved to New Haven, where he died three years later. His part in the Pequot War is the only military element in Edmund Sherman's life. His illustrious descendant, General Sherman, mentions in his *Memoirs* Edmund's nephew Captain John Sherman, who served in the colonial militia, the patriarch of a distinguished line. General Sherman's own line was more modest, though not short of lawyers and judges. "I cannot claim for my ancestors superior rank, wealth or ability," writes the general's younger brother Senator John Sherman in his own memoir. They bequeathed certain moral qualities to the next generation, along with cerebral capacities of great value.[8]

The dominance of lawyers in the Sherman family tree is not surprising given that Puritans tended to display "a decidedly legalistic turn of mind," notably if a legal decision did not suit them. Colonial courts were much preoccupied with land titles and provincial boundaries; the law became crucial in establishing personal and social legitimacy and formed the prime vehicle of social mobility on the frontier. All branches of the Sherman family prospered from an acquaintance with it. General Sherman's immediate family was descended from Edmund Sherman's younger son, Samuel (1618-84), who married Sarah Mitchell, a fellow passenger on the *Elizabeth*, in 1634. He eventually resided in Woodbury, Connecticut, which he helped found, and sat on the colony's Supreme Judicial Tribunal. His fifth son, John (1650-1730), was ordained, and he, too, had a son called John, who predeceased him (ca. 1687-1727); his progeny Judge Daniel Sherman (b. 1721) begat a likeminded son, Judge Taylor Sherman (1758-1815), General Sherman's grandfather, who presided as a probate judge in Norwalk, Connecticut. Taylor, the most distinguished of the line before his three grandsons, married Elizabeth "Betsey" Stoddard and had three children, Charles Robert (1788-1829), Daniel, and Elizabeth, also called Betsey. The first child is General Sherman's father. All of these Shermans are mentioned in the general's *Memoirs*, with corroborating detail in those of his brother John.[9]

The American War of Independence (1775-83) accentuated a second wave of westward migration. When Connecticut became a state it gained 500,000 acres of the Western Reserve of Ohio in 1786, given to indemnify those Connecticut citizens who had suffered and lost property during the ceaseless Loyalist raids during 1779-82. It is a striking feature of Sherman's heritage that it is framed by the experience of civil war; both the English Shermans and Daniel and Taylor Sherman chose the winning side. The latter had been appointed a commissioner entrusted with the allocation of this land bounty—now Huron and Erie Counties, Ohio. Prosperity appeared to be guaranteed for his family when he was appointed collector of Revenue for the Second District of Connecticut and was awarded two sections of Ohio land. It was during a visit to inspect his property that he contracted typhoid and unexpectedly died.[10]

Taylor Sherman's actions set in train events that would shape the destiny of two families, the Shermans and the Ewings, who had also migrated to Ohio and whom they befriended. Taylor had sold his Connecticut holdings and provided a powerful motive for his children to migrate westward. His son Charles, the general's father, showed ability, energy, and ambition. After taking a degree at Dartmouth College, he gained admission to the bar in 1810. That year he married Mary Hoyt, a refined, affectionate daughter of a mercantile Norwalk family, who had graduated from the Poughkeepsie Seminary for young ladies. An ardent and adventurous soul, Charles set off to explore his father's patrimony. Deflected from the Great Lakes by warriors led by the great Shawnee chief Tecumseh, who had organized a coalition to resist these white incursions, he turned south and headed along "Zane's Trace" toward "New Lancaster." He liked the place enough to settle there and returned to Connecticut to fetch Mary. In the meantime, she had given birth to their eldest son, Charles Taylor Sherman. Undeterred, the Shermans shared the care of their newborn son while riding on horseback; they did not even take the stagecoach. On arrival in Lancaster, Charles opened a law office. By 1812 he acted as county attorney and had established himself as a dependable, capable, and pleasantly affable citizen of Lancaster.[11]

When in April 1812 the United States found itself at war with Great Britain again, Charles Sherman was elected a major in the 4th Regiment of Ohio Militia and charged with recruiting soldiers. Skilled at delivering rousing speeches, he was fortunate in not accompanying the regiment to Detroit. There, on August 16, 1812, the fort was ignominiously surrendered to the British commander, Major General Isaac Brock, with the loss of 2,500 prisoners, 33 guns, and a brig; the British left had been covered by Tecumseh's 600 warriors, the largest contingent in Brock's small force. "Never before had the Indians signally contributed to so great a military triumph," writes Tecumseh's biographer, "nor would they again." Though his efforts had turned to dust, Sherman attended assiduously to his commissary duties until the end of 1814. Tecumseh had fallen at the Battle of Moraviantown, or Thames, in 1813, and thereafter Sherman idolized the Shawnee chief. Sherman had also during these years forged links with the University of Ohio at Athens and been appointed as a trustee.[12]

The forebears of the Ewing clan, who would play such a dominant part in General Sherman's upbringing, had arrived in Ohio before the Shermans. Hugh Boyle (1773-1848), a Catholic Irish emigrant from County Donegal, arrived in Lancaster in 1798. Three years later he moved his wife and new-born daughter, Maria (b. 1801), there. His sister-in-law Susan Gillespie married Philemon Beecher, a prominent local lawyer and militia general, in 1803. In 1816 Beecher took into his office a promising law graduate, Thomas Ewing. Ewing had been born near Wheeling, Virginia (now West Virginia), in 1789, the son of an impoverished officer in the Continental Army. He was self-educated and paid for his legal studies at Ohio University by laboring in the Kanawha salt wells. In May 1815 Ewing became one of the university's first graduates; he had been examined by Charles Sherman, who recommended him to Beecher. In January 1820 Ewing married Hugh Boyle's daughter, Maria, who had been raised by the Beechers since her mother's death in 1805. Thereafter the two families, Sherman and Ewing, grew close, and the two lawyers traveled and lodged together on the legal circuit. They both became judges and men of influence, with Ewing becoming the most renowned lawyer in the state. Charles Sherman was generous, hospitable, and affable; perhaps too generous. In 1813 he had been appointed by President James Madison as collector of revenue for the Third Ohio District; his deputies in its six counties collected taxes in local bank notes. In 1817 the Madison administration, keen to increase its tax receipts from rural areas, announced that it would no longer accept these notes. Quite unnecessarily Charles Sherman assumed this liability and mortgaged his home and future earnings to pay the deputies. He wore himself out attempting to clear this indebtedness that he felt honor-bound to carry.[13]

The decline of his prosperity dates from this ill-advised act just as his family commitments expanded. Charles Taylor—always known as "Taylor"—had been born in Connecticut. Four more children followed in Lancaster, three daughters, Mary Elizabeth (1812-1900), Amelia (1816-62) and Julia Ann (1818-42), and one son, James (1813-64). Mary Sherman enjoyed an intimate, gossipy relationship with Maria Ewing and quickly informed her that another child had been conceived in the spring of 1819. When a third son appeared, crowned with red hair, on February 8, 1820, the first person to hold him affectionately after his mother was Maria Ewing. This boy was christened William Tecumseh by his parents, not Tecumseh, as he says in his *Memoirs*. His elder brothers' names had been easily decided, after their grandfather and Mary's two brothers, so his father got his way in commemorating his historical idol, the Shawnee chief. In 1932 Sherman's biographer Lloyd Lewis, relying solely on Ewing folklore, recycled a century later, suggested that he had been named "Tecumseh" and that "William" had been added at the insistence of a Roman Catholic priest during a christening at the Ewing mansion when he was about 10. The new name had been selected arbitrarily because the service occurred on St. William's Day. There are strong grounds for rejecting this tale, accepted by virtually all Sherman's later biographers.

It is likely that Charles Sherman intended that "Tecumseh" should have priority, as "Taylor" had for his eldest son, and Sherman was called "Cump" by his intimate family circle. His intimates confirm that he had been given the names "William Tecumseh"—conferred at an earlier christening that had occurred during his infancy. Evidence as to the date of the later Ewing christening is lacking, and it is more than likely that on this occasion the priest wanted to drop "Tecumseh" rather than add another name. Then the young Cump spoke up and asserted that he had already been named. But this incident is significant, too, for it anticipates in symbolic form certain problems in assessing Sherman's youth. There would have been no shame for the young Cump to admit that he had acquired a new name in the Ewing household. But if he held these monikers already, then biographers could take a more relaxed view of certain claims that had been inferred from the opposite portrayal. The whole atmosphere of his upbringing in the Ewing family home was far more harmonious than it has been depicted hitherto. The Ewings had not acted high-handedly by giving him a new name; they were not determined to convert him to Catholicism; finally, the "humiliation and alienation" that several biographers have insisted upon, and the anxious ambivalence that these biographers claimed he exhibited, falls away. Sherman emerges as far more contented as an adolescent than many of them have assumed.[14]

Yet a fundamental problem raised by Sherman's early life still persists. Why did Charles Sherman's "fancy" so capture him that he named his son after an enemy of the United States? Charles Sherman was hardly alone in celebrating his memory; a cult of Tecumseh developed among the communities of the Great Lakes. He had been a warrior, not a peacemaker. He pursued a dream of a confederacy that embraced *all* Indian tribes working to secure their rightful lands. He was an extraordinary figure, tall and imposing, handsome, eloquent, and a true leader. He was unusually merciful and magnanimous, and he has been romanticized as a "noble savage," the model for Uncas in James Fenimore Cooper's novel *The Last of the Mohicans*; he transcended the savagery common in these frontier wars. It is not unusual for societies to romanticize their enemies as Americans did Tecumseh and Northerners canonized Robert E. Lee by the 1890s. Tecumseh was safely dead when this admiration reached its peak in the 1820s when he could no longer pose any threat.[15]

Five more children followed Cump: three more sons, Lampson Parker (1821–1900), John (1823–1900), and Hoyt (1827–1904), and two more daughters, Susan Denmore (1825–1876) and Frances Beecher (1829–1889), always known as "Fanny." This growing brood placed more pressure on their father's wits and resources. Charles's many friends rallied around and petitioned the governor to appoint him to the Ohio Supreme Court, and in 1823 he accepted this elevation. The petition stressed his unshakable firmness and "unquestioned integrity," but this elevation, though initially easing his financial burdens, only added to his absences from home. It is significant that Sherman's most vivid recollection of his father evoked a long-awaited return. In 1827 Cump had prepared his position carefully and managed to beat the elder children in greeting his father at the gate and thus win the privilege of riding his horse into the stable. Alas, he had overlooked the stable door, which remained closed, so Old Dick trotted off to a neighboring stable but found this closed, too. Losing patience, he returned home in a rush and threw Cump into a pile of rocks. The elder children thought their brother dead rather than knocked senseless, "but my time was not yet, and I recovered, though the scars remain to this day."

To help Mary during her husband's long absences, Grandmother Stoddard came to stay. She had a stern presence: tart in expression, she snapped at the children with her tongue as she rapped their knuckles or caned their legs with a stick. Sherman's brother John often sought his soft-voiced mother's skirts as shelter from her tirades. Yet she imbued the children with reliable good sense and when in a good mood would entertain them with yarns of the Revolution and the family's defiance of the dastardly British and their Tory collaborators.[16]

There were broad fields to play in, thick green woods to hide in, the creek to swim in, and Niebling's Pond to skate on in winter. The woods were full of birds and beasts—sometimes livestock—an endless kaleidoscope of play and adventure. The talk of adults also diverted a lively and curious boy like Cump. His parents' genteel background conferred on the children manners and a style that attracted all guests, from the hungry Ewing boys to a range of worthies. The most picturesque was Bernhard, Duke of Saxe-Weimar, who accepted an invitation to tea with the Shermans. "I met with a very agreeable society," he reported, such a relief from the squalor and boorishness he had encountered earlier in Indiana. The no less grand Governor DeWitt Clinton of New York also accepted an invitation. But the most welcome and frequent as well as garrulous guest was Tom Corwin. Corwin, the most celebrated Whig west of the Appalachian Mountains, spoke with a deep, beautifully modulated voice. He often expounded Whig principles across Sherman's table and believed "that John Hampden was the first Whig. . . . *It was the opposition to the one-man power.*" Charles Sherman's heart must have burst with pride at this reference to his own family's political stance running back two centuries. Corwin and Sherman were resolute opponents of Andrew Jackson and the Democrats, whose ambitious program they considered a threat to American liberties.[17]

Young Cump Sherman might have felt that he had cheated the Angel of Death, but the hour beckoned for his father. Beset by a mountain of debt and exhausted by his labors to reduce it, he succumbed to a typhoid infection in Lebanon, Ohio. The Sherman children were called out of school, and the general would vividly recall the air of "lamentation." All the children received firm instructions to keep quiet and stay outside. At first their father had rallied, but he died quickly on June 23, 1829. He left behind a paltry estate, his house and its contents and bank stock worth $200 per year. Under these circumstances, it was traditional on the frontier for family and friends to support a widow and "take in" the children and treat them as their own. The older children were easily housed. Taylor went to work in the Mansfield, Ohio, law office of Judge Parker, who had married Taylor's aunt Betsey; James already worked in a store in Cincinnati. The older girls escaped poverty by early marriage. The eldest, Elizabeth, married William J. Reese, and Amelia married Robert McComb and took in young Julia. Susan, Hoyt, and Fanny, the last only two months old, remained with their mother. That just left Cump, Lampson, and John. Thomas Ewing, by this time a grand and wealthy figure, had not forgotten how much he owed Charles Sherman. He organized a fund to pay the mortgage on the house and then offered to take in a son. He preferred the cleverest, and Mary offered up Cump.[18]

The loss of a parent and breakup of a household was no doubt a traumatic experience, though initially young Cump Sherman did not notice
much difference in the pace of his life, or indeed the texture. It did become
more sumptuous and refined materially, but emotionally it remained awkward, rather like living with schoolfriends, as he was. He had known the
Ewings all his life and enjoyed the closest affinity with Phil; he lived as
a neighbor to his mother, brother John, and younger sisters. He enjoyed
a rather formal relationship with Thomas and Maria Ewing, but he experienced great kindness and wanted for nothing; although Maria's
zealous Catholicism ensured that an invisible line divided him from the
other Ewing children, this difference would always be respected. Still, he
owed the Ewings an inestimable debt. Thanks to them Cump went back
to school, the Lancaster Academy, which he praised in his *Memoirs*—"as
good a school as any in Ohio." To this school, whose fees would have been
beyond his mother's purse, Sherman owed his grasp of languages (Latin,
Greek, and French) and the fundamentals of mathematics and "natural
law" (physics); he also became acquainted with the plays of William
Shakespeare, which would be his constant companions through the
vicissitudes of life.

Cump appears as a sensitive, reserved, studious, sensible, and well-
behaved child. His brother John remembered him as "a steady student, quiet
in his manners and easily moved by sympathy or affection." By comparison,
John described himself as "a rather troublesome boy," full of pranks, frequently disciplined at school, and "wild and reckless": Cump and John appear almost the exact opposite of each boy's adult persona. John could not
remember his father very distinctly, although he recalled the event of his
death. The contrasting behavior of the two boys perhaps reveals their different ways of coping with their loss. In 1831 John departed to live with his
father's cousin also called John Sherman, "a prosperous merchant," although
he would return four years later.

Cump's timidity concerned both Thomas and Maria Ewing. In 1831
the former gained election as a senator for Ohio and spent much time in
Washington, DC; while there Ewing wrote to his wife that Cumpy "is disposed to be bashful, not quite at home. Endeavour to inspire him with
confidence and make him feel one of the family." Maria Ewing, after all his
godmother, oozed reassurance, kindness, and good-natured domesticity,
as Sherman fondly recalled after he had moved away. He had not been formally adopted, and the Ewings made no effort to supplant his birth family.

Sherman must have counted his blessings for having benefited immeasurably from the bounty the Ewings provided without hesitation or condition.[19]

Periodically he accompanied his nearby mother and sisters to visit the McCombs, the Parkers, and Grandmother Stoddard in Mansfield; Taylor had also launched his legal career there and had improved his mother's financial position. They would travel the 75 miles in a three-day journey, and Mary brought medicine as well as affable conversation to many households en route, for so many suffered from the "chills" and the ague. Cump's own family links thus remained firm, though Taylor was so much older (19 years) that later many assumed he was an uncle rather than a brother. Sherman profited from the two families that shared his life. His agreeable experience with the Ewings, moreover, fostered his own sense of belonging to an elite. Mr. Ewing had purchased items from the household of the former emperor of Mexico, which adorned his white mansion (by far the most impressive and prominent house in the county). The Ewings' intimate circle included other distinguished Ohio families, the Beechers, Stanberrys, Irvins, and Gillespies, all of whom had intermarried and provided useful connections. Thomas Ewing had proven a loyal follower of Henry Clay and Daniel Webster, and Cump met them both when they visited Lancaster. Inspired by the luminaries that he met, during his adolescence Cump inherited strong Whig loyalties. The Ewings also encouraged his intellectual bent. Being self-educated, nobody understood the value of reading and education more than Thomas Ewing. He often gave books away as presents and sought to encourage reading for pleasure from an early age. When he worked in the evening on legal papers or speeches, he invited Phil and Cump to read in his study while he wrote. In December 1831 he sent Maria detailed instructions, based on his own childhood experience, to sit the elder children—Phil, Cump, Ellen, Bub [Hugh], and Tom Jr.—around a table for 30 minutes "and let Phil and Cump take turns reading the stories for general information." He hoped by this means to prevent the boys "from falling into vicious practices." He enlisted his eldest daughter, Ellen, in these efforts, a role she assumed enthusiastically, for she lavished adoration on her "two big brothers," Phil and Cump.[20]

After a year or two with the Ewings, Cump began to speak up and show some spirit, bordering on mischief. He was chased out of the Lancaster Post Office for his cheek, but his much later reminiscences of his childhood and a dalliance with one Billy King seem informed by a conscious effort to recast his youth in John's mold. It is significant that John does not remember his elder brother like this at all. Though John had to endure the condescension that older boys thought necessary when dealing with juniors, he recalls that his intercourse with Cump consisted largely of sensible advice. Cump took John hunting, his preferred milieu. "I fired my first gun over his shoulder. He took me with him," John adds, "to carry the game mostly squirrels and pigeons." Of course, he blundered occasionally (especially when he tried to dye his hair and it turned green) got filthy dirty, and played the fool—and was doubtless reprimanded and punished in an age when corporal punishment was frequently resorted to. But the abiding impression is of a very sensible, thoughtful, and considerate boy. Although John recounts playing tricks on his elder brother Lampson ("Lamp"), there are none recorded being played on Cump, which suggests he did not stoop to bullying or humiliating the younger boys.[21]

At school, Cump applied himself conscientiously, and his closest friend, Phil, was equally serious-minded. Though keen to demonstrate his knowledge and love of writing, the 14-year-old was not an inky-fingered teacher's pet; he was tall, athletic, mature, and self-reliant, with quick brown eyes, and exhibited strong intellectual potential, like his father. In 1833 Thomas Ewing wrote to his wife, "Tell Cumpy I want him to learn fast that he may be ready to go to West Point or college soon. Kiss the little fellow for me." Mr. Ewing discerned that Cump had the moral qualities to excel in a West Point–type atmosphere and, further, that it might nourish qualities he did not yet know he had.[22]

Thomas Ewing nominated Cump in August 1835. In a family bereft of any military tradition, the name "West Point" meant little to Cump. He did grasp that he would need to pay attention to his French and mathematics, as these served as the twin pillars of the West Point curriculum. In 1834 Cump worked on the preliminary surveys of the canal that would connect Lancaster to the Ohio Canal at Carroll, earning a daily silver half-dollar. Ewing worried that Cump might misinterpret West Point as a consolation prize compared with attending an Ivy League college as his father had done, but there is no evidence he ever thought this then or later; on the contrary, he chaffed with impatience until his sixteenth birthday. In June 1835 William Irvin, a cousin of the Ewing children, son of Judge William Irvin, entered West Point thanks to Ewing. Cump received notification of his appointment in March 1836; two months later a letter from the secretary of war followed, listing all the clothes he required and giving him instructions to report to Mr. Ewing in Washington, DC. Maria Ewing furnished all the apparel. Cump had a long private talk with his mother before setting out, and all the Ewings waved him off on his first significant journey outside of Ohio. He traveled by stagecoach to Frederick, Maryland, without a break, arriving three days later. After an uncharacteristic hesitation to experiment with the new, he continued with the stage rather than take the train. He arrived at Ewing's lodgings on the corner of Third and C Streets in Washington on June 1, 1836.[23]

After visiting prosperous relatives in Philadelphia and New York, Cump took the boat up the Hudson River to West Point, perched on a promontory above the waters. On June 12 he arrived at the South Boat Landing, clambered up its many steps lined by thickets of trees and bushes, sought out the adjutant's office, and handed his credentials to Lieutenant C. F. Smith. He then went to the treasurer's office and handed in all his cash, which cadets were not allowed to carry.[24]

Sherman became a "plebe" and shared a room in the Old South Barracks with a Virginian, George H. Thomas, "Old Tom," and Stewart Van Vliet of Vermont, who at 20 and 21, respectively, were both a lot older than Sherman. For the years following he shared with William "Bill" Irvin, who acted as a mentor and guide and effective antidote to homesickness. The West Point regimen had been designed to harden the cadets. They rose at dawn and studied until breakfast two hours later. Classes began at 8:00 a.m. and lasted five hours; after a one-hour lunch break, classes resumed for another two hours, prior to drill on parade until sunset. Then the cadets studied again until 9:30, with lights out at 10:00 p.m. The furniture was basic and the bedclothes sparse, but the rooms were lit with roaring fires. The system of hazing that gripped West Point from the 1880s had not yet developed, apart from the odd prank or joke. Thanks to Bill Irvin, Sherman quickly befriended older cadets. Both already knew Bill's cousin Irvin McDowell, whom Sherman held in affectionate regard for the rest of his life. Although Jacksonian attacks on West Point for perpetuating a self-selecting "aristocracy" were exaggerated, there can be little doubt that a substantial number of cadets were relatives of rich, powerful, and notable interconnected families who constituted a professional elite in American socety.[25]

After the comforts of the Ewing home, Sherman found the West Point regimen a shock, and he recoiled at the constant shouting and drilling. Thomas Ewing learned that "the cadets live pretty roughly." But Sherman found the work easy. He passed the June entrance examination—designed to ensure the entrance of cadets far less privileged than Sherman—effortlessly; Lancaster Academy had prepared him well. He then formally embarked on his course, recently extended to four years. The syllabus was created by Superintendent

Sylvanus Thayer. He aimed to create a fine engineering school and succeeded; its products were to be "officers and gentlemen," smart, punctual, polite men of honor. Thayer's aim ensured that science dominated the syllabus at the expense of classics and the humanities. Mathematics served as the basis for teaching engineering, and French was the language needed to read the best textbooks. The First Class, or final year, eagerly anticipated by all and largely taught by Dennis Hart Mahan, covered dimensions of engineering, including, briefly, the science of war. Mineralogy was also featured, as were rhetoric, moral philosophy, and political science, including international and constitutional law. The last four subjects were swept up under the rubric of "the Chaplain's Course" taught by the academy chaplain, Jasper Adams. As such it often provoked derision, but Sherman thoroughly enjoyed it because it offered a rare excursion into the humanities as well as legal literature.[26]

Thayer's system required not just hard work but intense competition among the cadets, as well as the absorption of massive quantities of technical information that was recited aloud in class and examinations. Sherman was already skilled in this method, though it stifled the imagination and conferred advantage on conformity and rote learning. In his third year Sherman cursed "all Philosophers and all Chemists," as their textbooks "contain 400 and odd pages which we will be examined upon next January." There were no vacations, not even in the summer, though cadets could apply for leaves of absence. Given the burden of work and crushing routine, West Point often felt terribly dull. For Sherman, having relatives close by was a godsend. In spring 1837 his sister Elizabeth Reese and her husband visited. Sherman "was very glad to see them, and for the short time they were here I almost felt as if I were at home." Another elder sister, Julia, visited, too. But he longed to hear from Lancaster, as "home" meant the Ewings, and he urged his foster sister, Ellen, to tell Maria Ewing "that I have been for a very long time expecting a letter from her, also Ellen I shall expect an immediate answer to this." In July some relief came when his persistence gained its reward with a leave of absence, and he went back to see the Hoyts, his mother's prosperous family, who lived in Brooklyn Heights.[27]

Thayer's faculty formed his most substantial legacy to the academy. As a group they were intellectually brilliant and made enduring contributions to American science, but they presented a grim and forbidding face to the cadets. Claudius Berard , taught French and introduced them to Alain-Réne Lesage's *Histoire de Gil Blas de Santillane* (1715-35), where wanderers experience a series of adventures, and Voltaire's *Histoire de Charles XII* (1731), the latter their only slender contact with military history until their First Class. The brilliant but cold and humourless Albert E. Church taught mathematics. A distinguished artist, Robert W. Weir, guided the cadets' efforts at drawing. Their chemistry teacher, Jacob W. Bailey, showed the cadets some kindness and thus enjoyed great popularity. He also tried to stimulate their imaginations rather than stuff them full of facts and formulae. Sherman described him as "a perfect gentleman [who] renders chemistry as interesting as possible." The same could not be said of the prominent astronomer William H. C. Bartlett, who taught physics and whom most cadets found difficult to follow. By far the most influential of West Point's teachers, Mahan intimidated the cadets with his razor-sharp mind. He had a rare skill at exposing the ignorance of bluffers and the negligent. Desirous to avoid such a humiliation, Sherman worked especially hard on his engineering classes.[28]

Examinations, lasting two weeks, were held in January and June. The latter exams held pride of place because they were held under the gaze of the Board of Visitors, a group of distinguished outside citizens, and they and the faculty sat at two large tables facing three blackboards; six cadets entered at a time, with two at each board; one answered the set questions by recitation while the other prepared his answers. Sherman described how at the end of his first year he had invested 20 days in "the examination" that might last five hours; immediately after, "I have been engaged with guard duty almost every day on account of the Corps being so reduced," as one class had graduated. At West Point, youthful high jinx and rebellion often bubbled up despite— perhaps because of—the innumerable, oppressive rules. Sherman, thanks to Bill Irvin, soon grew in social confidence, emerging as a lively and sought-after companion. Irvin, though, proved a bad influence. He had a furlough in August 1837. "Bill who I suppose lived highly when he was off complains of hard times but he will soon return to old habits."

Irving had introduced Sherman to the famous Benny Haven's Tavern and its abundant oysters and beefsteak—as well as beer and whisky—that supplemented the academy's dismal, unappetizing fare. There were also nightly fry-ups in the cadets' rooms. Sherman's Ohio outdoor skills were put to good use cooking potatoes for five or six cadets; his hash was much in demand, and he catered for many of the older cadets: the lugubrious Braxton Bragg, who would become a brother officer; John C. Pemberton; P. G. T. Beauregard; Edward D. Townsend, a budding novelist; William F. Barry; and a defensive poseur, Joseph Hooker, who grated on his nerves. The first three would become Confederate generals, and the last three would serve with or under him. In the course immediately above Sherman's were three cadets whose lives and careers would be intertwined with his: Henry W. Halleck, who would become captain of a company of cadets; Edward O. C. Ord, a wealthy Roman Catholic with whom he shared a tent at his first summer camp; and the earnest and reserved E. R. S. Canby. A year below him was the rather shy but haughty and rebellious Don Carlos Buell. Another important friend in his own cohort was Stewart Van Vliet; "Van" became a loyal confidant throughout all Sherman's later disappointments and successes. With his other roommate, George H. Thomas, there occurred an attraction of opposites: Thomas, ponderous, painstaking, and steadfast, to Sherman's quicksilver brilliance, flashes of wit, and vivacity. Despite their age difference, Thomas regarded Sherman as his closest friend at West Point.

All agreed that Sherman displayed a splendid talent as a raconteur. He discovered that he liked being popular, and he would play to the gallery of sympathetic classmates in defying the endless rules. Bill Irvin encouraged him on this reckless course. In 1838 Irvin sneaked off to Benny Haven's in the dark, fell off a cliff, and ended up being treated in the hospital, but the punishment meted out for this mishap did not discourage other nocturnal expeditions in which Sherman enthusiastically participated.[29]

By far the most dramatic event that interrupted "the dull and monotonous course of events" during Sherman's time at West Point occurred when a fire broke out in the library and academic departments east of the Cadet Barracks on the night of February 17-18, 1838. A cry of "Fire!" was heard at about 3:00 a.m. "The cry was so unusual that it acted like an electric shock," Sherman recorded, "and everyone was up in a moment and ready for action." All cadets realized that they must help, especially when the hose pipe of the "useless" fire engine burst, and the cadets removed "the library and also the philosophical and chemical apparatus"; most books were saved. "The night was extremely cold and almost everyone caught a severe cold." The superintendent paid tribute "to the untiring zeal of the cadets" in limiting the damage to the building; "and for my part," Sherman reported proudly to Ellen, "I never saw so much done in so short a time."

The summer camps, run by the Department of Tactics in July and August and staffed by regular officers, were the only opportunities the cadets had to learn anything about the essentials of army life and acquire some military knowledge. From 5:30 a.m. to 5:30 p.m. they would cover dismounted drill, infantry tactics, musketry, artillery drill, and firing, plus fencing, and after 1839 equitation, or horseback riding, which greatly improved Sherman's seat in the saddle. The camp was usually concluded with a dress parade and a ball. Dancing featured in the camp syllabus; in August 1837 Sherman revealed that "we had a royal 'Stag dance' . . . on the parade ground. I think I never saw the encampment so enlivening there were about 150 cadets dancing before a double row of candles and great many ladies and gentlemen looking on and walking about." But the young Sherman shied away from learning any ballroom dancing techniques.[30]

Sherman's academic progress remained impressive. He coasted along effortlessly during this first year, and his second presented no greater challenge. "I think I will still have about the same standing as I have now in Mathematics and French, but in Drawing I will be among the first five." Robert Weir recognized Sherman's artistic talent. In November 1838 he received a privileged invitation from Weir "with three or four others . . . to visit his studio to see a landscape painting he had just finished." In January 1839, though, the gear changed, as "the course of studies we are engaged in this year," he wrote, referring to physics, "has always had the reputation of being the most difficult of the four"; consequently, "I expect to be very studious and busy." He maintained his overall position of sixth in his class, ranking seventh in physics, sixth in chemistry, and third in drawing. It is a curious feature of Sherman's cadet years that though he worked hard he did not take his military obligations very seriously. His attitudes remained resolutely "civilian": he dressed carelessly, saluted slovenly or not at all, and used his disregard of the rules as a means of winning laddish approbation from his peers. Simultaneously he lectured his brother John that "a reputation for a strict compliance to one's duties, whatever they may be, is far more valuable"— although he did not follow his own advice.[31]

In the autumn of 1838 he at last enjoyed a furlough in Lancaster. He tried to visit John, but vexatious delays frustrated him. He did see Grandmother Stoddard and his brother Taylor. But "home" really meant life with the Ewings, and he shared in their disappointment at Thomas Ewing's failure to be reelected to the Senate. After the furlough ended, his letters evinced a nostalgia for his life with them. In May 1839, though delighted by Ellen's gift of a pair of slippers, he complained, "I have almost despaired of receiving that long-wished for and expected letter from your mother." Ellen scolded him mildly in response, and Sherman admitted that although "I have rarely spoken of it," he often reflected on his "inability to repay the many kindnesses and favors received at her hands and those of her family. Time and absence serve to strengthen the claims and to increase my affection and love and gratitude to those who took me early under their care and conferred the same advantages as they did upon their own children." There is no reason to doubt the sincerity of these feelings or the powerful ties that drew him into the Ewing orbit.[32]

In November 1839 the burden of work seemed less than he had expected, and his thoughts drifted elsewhere. The 1837 Canadian uprising and subsequent filibustering over the border, plus the "Maine difficulties," seemed to prefigure a war with Great Britain around the time he would graduate, "and for my part," he assured John confidently, "there is no nation that I would prefer being at variance with than the British"; he looked forward to learning about war's essentials in his final year. The results of the 1840 examinations were "favorable towards me, as usual." He stood fourth in engineering and sixth in geology, rhetoric, and moral philosophy, but he conceded several demerits—assessments against a cadet's grade: he guessed "about one hundred," a severe underestimate.[33]

With a little more time on his hands, Sherman explored the West Point Library. Like other cadets, he took out the two volumes of Baron Gay de Vernon's *Treatise on the Science of War and Fortification* (1817). He then ranged beyond the science syllabus and checked out Louis de Bourrienne, *Mémoires . . . sur Napoléon*, written by a classmate and loyal friend of Napoleon at the Royal Military School at Brienne after he had been summarily dismissed as Napoleon's secretary.[34]

The courses on engineering run by Mahan concentrated mainly on its civil aspect, although he ranged over the "science of war" for a week. Mahan's later reminiscences of Sherman were affectionate—he described him as "eager, impetuous, restless"—but they hint at an irritating immaturity. If his back was turned and any subdued chatter or guffawing occurred, he invariably "[held] up my finger to Mr. Sherman"—who could not resist playing to the gallery. But such irritation received ample compensation in "the clear thought and energy he threw into his work." Mahan described Sherman's "mental machine" as belonging "to the high pressure class" that lets off steam and smoke "with a puff and a cloud, and dashes at its work with restless vigor, the result of a sound boiler and plenty of fuel." Praise from Mahan always meant a lot to Sherman.

Mahan's survey of the science of war was too cursory to have real impact. Flying high above the cadets' heads, his comments on strategy and generalship, on the principles of war, or on speed, maneuver, and the need for a secure base of operations were less significant than the style of thinking he instilled.

His methods were based on thorough preparation, precision of thought, and "common sense," that is, acute judgment—"what is the proper thing to be done under given circumstances." Mahan also elevated "directness of purpose," keeping the mind focused "on the great object before it" while resisting the temptation of distractions. This system constitutes Mahan's greatest gift to Sherman, enabling him, when he became more mature and intellectually aware, to bring critical judgment to any taxing problem he might face.[35]

A change of leadership in his last year changed the atmosphere Sherman had come to know. For his first three years Colonel R. E. DeRussy presided as superintendent. Colonel Richard Delafield succeeded him in 1838, and Smith, newly promoted, became his commandant of cadets. All were exemplars of the "old" army about which Sherman would wax lyrically after 1865. At the time Sherman was far less keen on the change in regime. The popular René DeRussy had taken a relaxed view on enforcing the substantial West Point rulebook. Delafield proved to be a stickler for the rules. With Christmas approaching, Sherman worried over "what particular privileges will be granted to us on those days." He concluded optimistically and wrongly, "I am confident that Major Delafield is too much of a gentleman to interfere with them." Delafield proved zealous in ensuring that all rules were properly enforced. He insisted that Christmas be treated with the same reverence as any Sunday. Fire drills were scheduled on Saturday afternoons, a precious time for recreation and parties. All cadets quickly regarded Delafield as a petty, joyless tyrant, and Sherman would suffer under the new regime.[36]

However mistaken his view of the new superintendent might be, Sherman's faith in his intellectual abilities was rarely unjustified. In his final examinations he performed most creditably. He emerged fourth in mineralogy, seventh in both engineering and ethics, eighth in artillery, twelfth in infantry tactics; his French and drawing were *très excellent*, with 96 out of a possible 100 in both. His academic class standing stood at fourth. Military conduct usually favored the best students and should have pushed him higher, but with Sherman it had the opposite effect. He had amassed 148 demerits, though he did not hold the record set by Don Carlos Buell at 193. But Sherman's tally brought him down to sixth place, while other cadets who were academically weaker advanced up the list. Sherman, moreover, could not be recommended for the *corps d'elite*, the Engineers or another illustrious corps, Ordnance. He had to be content with the Artillery. Thomas Ewing and Phil attended the graduation ceremony before hurriedly returning to the stump to speak on behalf of the Whig candidate, William H. Harrison, in the

1840 presidential election. Sherman afterward visited Ellen at the Academy of the Visitation at Georgetown, in Washington, DC, and then hurried to Lancaster. He received his posting as a second lieutenant in the 3rd Artillery a few weeks later in September and was ordered to sail for Florida from New York. Sherman foolishly visited old West Point friends en route, thus infringing a rule that serving officers should have no contact with cadets. Superintendent Delafield sought to make an example of him and pressed charges for a court-martial. A frank and forceful letter from Sherman admitting thoughtlessness persuaded the secretary of war to dismiss Delafield's request, though a further five demerits were added to Sherman's record. In his *Memoirs* he admitted to "about 150." It was hardly an auspicious start to his military career.[37]

At the age of 20 Sherman stood on the cusp of manhood, and some of his mature features were already prominent—gregariousness, affability, loquacity, wit, cleverness, and an ability to master huge quantities of information and utilize it well—though he temporarily regressed in others, appearing to lack social self-discipline. He had a tendency to develop strong opinions and demonstrated an impressive intellectuality and curiosity, and he had inherited a mastery over words, as well as an artistic sensibility initially expressed in drawing and painting. His West Point letters were sometimes awkwardly expressed, but by 1840 he began to display more than a hint of his characteristic fluent trenchancy. Humorous and full of fun, he displayed a talent for making friends; others enjoyed his company and wanted more. His father's position on the Ohio Supreme Court and his reputation gave the young Sherman a sense of being a member of a higher caste, which was sustained by the wealth and power of the Ewing family.[38]

During his time at the academy Sherman's rebelliousness became obvious—and he paid the price. It is a curious feature of his life that he spent so many of his later years proclaiming West Point's virtues, the very standards that he had ignored in his youth. But by graduating Sherman entered a self-conscious elite, and its values had a powerful influence on his opinions and military attitudes.[39]

He was primed to make use of the intellectual tools provided by West Point. Mahan had taught him to employ his method. One of the sources of Sherman's success as a leader—his empathy—enabled him to transcend the limitations of the West Point tradition: its narrow focus, obsession with detail, and preoccupation with doing things "by the book." His mind would be broadened. Sherman made an interesting observation to his brother John just before he graduated: "Whether I remain in the army for life or not is doubtful; but one thing is certain—that I will never study another profession." Sherman nonetheless continued to educate himself in the face of consistent misfortune.[40]

2

Leaping the Mark

Soldier or Civilian? 1840–1852

It appears no more likely that Thomas Ewing expected his foster son to pursue a military career long-term than that Jesse Grant did when contemplating his son Ulysses's future two years later. The luster of a West Point education, with the prospect of a lucrative career in engineering, building, mining, business, or the law, tempted many graduates to resign after serving their mandatory five years. Almost from the moment he graduated, Sherman came under pressure to think about leaving the army; his letters home gave abundant evidence that should he stay in the service, his life would be one of "tedium and genteel poverty," not to mention painful isolation from family and friends. When asked why he did not resign, he gave a forthright answer in 1842. "Why should I? It is the profession for which my education alone fits me, and as all the appearances indicate the rapid approach of action when the soldier will be required to do his proper labor, when a splendid field will be spread before him, every reason exists why I should remain." He stressed his contentment, "and it would be foolish to spring into the world bare-headed and unprepared to meet its coldness and trials." But he did not rule resignation out, only postponed it to "a more auspicious moment when he felt better prepared."[1]

The "action" Sherman referred to was the Second Seminole War (1835–42) in Florida. Sherman's posting to Fort Pierce threw him into his first taste of warfare. He had stumbled into the last phase of an indecisive and frustrating campaign. The Seminoles enjoyed a remarkably decentralized social system, and American incursions were resisted by small, elusive, independent bands that melted away into the sweltering, impenetrable, and virtually uncharted Florida Everglades. The theater of war could not have been more different than the European campaigns discussed by Dennis Hart Mahan at West Point. In October 1840 Sherman arrived at Fort Pierce, at Indian River, about 180 miles from St. Augustine, fresh from the academy. He had sailed from Savannah, Georgia, but to reach the fort, he had to take a small boat that negotiated inlets, a lagoon, and, finally, a treacherous surf and sandbar that shortly after his arrival took the lives of an entire boatful of soldiers and its pilot; thereafter he treated the journey with great circumspection. The officers' quarters consisted of "six or seven log-houses, thatched with palmetto leaves." He began service with Company A. The subsequent arrival of Stewart Van Vliet and Edward Ord quickly relieved his sense of isolation. There were other compensations, too. "I do not recall in my whole experience," he reminisced later, "a spot on earth where fish, oysters, and green turtles so abound as at Fort Pierce, Florida." Most violence erupted within the fort, not without, and shortly after his arrival an outraged husband shot and killed one Sergeant Broderick for flirting too openly with his wife. Such was the young Second Lieutenant Sherman's introduction to frontier soldiering.[2]

He very quickly grasped the nature of this war and the Seminole tactics that had defied the best military minds in America, including Winfield Scott and Zachary Taylor. "The Indians," he informed his brother John, "retreat, scatter and are safe. This may be repeated ad infinitum." He blamed the entire conflict on greedy local settlers. Writing to the Ewings, he struck a more upbeat note. "This is the kind of warfare which every young officer should be thoroughly acquainted with as the Indian is most likely to be our chief enemy in times to come"; he expressed some admiration for Seminole skill, "although those qualities have been chiefly cunning and perfidy."[3]

The failure of their initial grand strategic designs forced senior commanders to rely on small columns led by junior officers attempting to round up the leaders of the separate bands. Seminole fighting strength had been augmented by some 400 runaway slaves, so any captured blacks were treated with caution lest they lead their captors into a deadly ambush. Sherman described his dealings with one runaway who "offered to act as guide" in early 1841: he had him handcuffed, then had "a noose fixed about his neck as a gentle hint, then told [him] to go on." Later in the summer, Sherman scored a success when an emissary from a group of Seminoles offered to surrender. This deal had been arranged under the auspices of the new commander, William J. Worth. Sherman was ordered to take a detail of 10 men out and bring in this recalcitrant chief, Coachoochee, though he suspected a trick. He eventually found Coachoochee and escorted him, "decked with turban and ostrich feathers," to Fort Pierce, where after prolonged negotiations he agreed to surrender his entire band. But he strung the garrison commander along. Rapid preemptive action by Sherman prevented Coachoochee and a number of warriors from absconding, though many of the band still escaped into the Everglades.

Sherman's other experience consisted of rounding up odd families—"about as good a plan as could be adopted," though he does not mention that progress had only been made after 1838, when the runaway slaves were offered emancipation and many blacks changed sides. More bands were captured, and as Sherman recorded, the troops "destroyed everything that could not be carried with ease," which included "all the corn, pumpkins, and household stuff" and any horses and livestock. He also records other expeditions that achieved nothing. Nevertheless, exhaustion eventually prevailed, and in August 1832 Worth declared the war over. This turned out to be premature, as it had to be renewed in 1855.[4]

Sherman left Florida long before this date. November 1841 found him at Fort Lauderdale after another "excursion" and some carousing with his old classmates Thomas, Ord, and Van Vliet. While there he received gratifying news of his promotion to first lieutenant after only 17 months. He told John that he regarded himself as "exceedingly fortunate," since achieving this rank usually took five to eight years. The promotion occurred in another company, so it required a move to Fort Picolata in East Florida. Moreover, as a young officer he had not yet become accustomed to postings at a moment's notice and complained to Ellen about being "turned about and sent off at a tangent." Picolata turned out to be a pleasant posting where he had a semi-independent command, as the colonel and two other companies remained at Fort St. Augustine. In June he was posted again, this time to Fort Morgan at Mobile Point, Alabama.[5]

Historians have suggested that the punitive character of the Seminole War had an impact on Sherman's later practice. From the Pequot War onward, some argue, American settlers had attempted to negate Indian skill at fieldcraft by destroying settlements and foodstuffs, defeating them by starvation and exhaustion. But any precise connection with this and Sherman's mature methods is difficult to establish. His later response to his experiences in Florida seems lighthearted, as the forays in the Everglades "possessed to us a peculiar charm, for the fragrance of the air, the abundance of game and fish, and just enough of adventure, gave to life a relish." By 1841–42 the conditions were such, he reasoned, that it would be "absurd any longer to call it a 'war.'"[6]

An overwhelming desire to enjoy life found plenty of scope in Mobile, which Sherman believed had "the most beautiful suburbs and country seats in this country. We were invited everywhere," he delighted in telling Ellen, "and the bright button was a passport at all times to the houses of the Best." Sherman details his social exploits, but his administrative efficiency and sharp eye for detail led to the first of many appointments as quarter-master and commissary. Fort Morgan was both dirty and lacking all but the most basic amenities. Sherman negotiated with charm and assurance with "Messrs. Deshon, Taylor, and Myers, merchants," and "procured all essentials for the troops." He had emerged as truly his father's son.[7]

In June 1842 the regiment found itself on the move again, posted to Fort Moultrie, Charleston, South Carolina. They traveled by sea in two waves; Sherman's Company G and Lieutenant Martin Burke's Company D arrived first, and Braxton Bragg's Company B and Lieutenant Erasmus D. Keyes's Company K arrived shortly afterward, 250 soldiers in all. Here they remained for five years. Sherman described his service as "strict garrison duty, with plenty of leisure for hunting and social entertainments." All parades, drills, and inspections had usually been concluded by 9:00 a.m., leaving the rest of the day free. "Some read, some write, some loaf, and some go to the city." Sherman began to explore his intellectual interests, and given his success at West Point, "I took a notion into my head that I could paint." He went to Charleston, organized a studio, and assembled his brushes and paints. He got to work and "finished a couple of landscapes and faces [portraits] which they tell me are very good." Then he revealed the instinct of the true artist. "I have great love for painting and find that sometimes I am so fascinated that it amounts to pain to lay down the brush." This passion raised certain doubts in Sherman's mind, because he had always thought of himself as a soldier rather than an artist. He asked Ellen if he should "stop now before it swallows all attention to the neglect of my duties and discard it altogether or keep on—what would you advise?" Sherman made up his own mind and discarded it altogether, but his artistic instinct was apparent in his writings.

Sherman also threw himself into his social life with balls and parties most nights. "Most officers waltz but I do not," he admitted ruefully. Sherman soon discovered that invitations could not be declined without giving offense, as military men were much in demand. Somehow the air of false gaiety palled. "A life of this kind does well enough for a while," he reported to John, "but soon surfeits with its flippancy—mingling with people in whom you feel no permanent interest, smirks and smiles when you feel savage, tight boots when your fancy would prefer slippers. I want relief." What Sherman yearned for was more intellectual stimulation. He had largely accepted the white South at its own valuation as a place of elegance and sophistication, but he glimpsed its fundamental aridity and insincerity.[8]

Sherman's main duty consisted of appearing in courts-martial, as his grasp of military law impressed all; soon his services were required beyond the mundane duty of trying deserters in Fort Moultrie. In the early months of 1843 he acted "as a kind of lawyer before a Court Martial at Fort Johnston in North Carolina." This talent seemed to mark out an alternative career. The issue of his future resurfaced in the summer of 1843 when, after serving consecutively for three years, Sherman applied successfully for a furlough for three months and headed back to Lancaster, which he then called "the best of homes." Sherman's *Memoirs* are silent about the main preoccupation of this vacation. Ellen, now 17, had greeted him with such warmth on the steps of the Ewing mansion that it demonstrated publicly how their relationship had broadened and deepened. They rode together before breakfast; they visited family and friends together; Sherman loved musical evenings during which Ellen played the harp, an exquisite instrument in skilful hands, and he strained "to catch each perfect chord and a more satisfying glimpse of Ellen's face." Then there were starlit walks in the garden in the summer warmth. It is possible that Maria Ewing discerned how their relationship had altered and grasped, as Ellen's biographer puts it, "them both in a tender and approving embrace." Yet whatever thoughts Sherman entertained as he sat in the Ewings' garden and smoked a cigar—a habit acquired in Mobile and Charleston society—he could harbor few illusions about marriage just yet. He constantly reiterated the view that the army was no place for married couples.[9]

Sherman began his journey back to Charleston in November 1843 via Cincinnati, where he visited his brothers Lampson and Hoyt; he then took a riverboat to St. Louis. In his *Memoirs* he says he had been "impressed with its great future," but despite the city's merits at the time, he observed that "it has not yet that fixed and solid appearance that Cincinnati wears as an established city of business and manufacture." He then took his first trip down that great river that exerted such a pull on his imagination—the Mississippi. From its end in New Orleans he crossed to Mobile, then took the train to Macon and Savannah, where he caught the "regular steam-boat" to Charleston.

During his travels and time spent in remote Southern outposts, Sherman kept up his reading. If he could find something suitable, he would study the geography of the region where he lived or contiguous to it. With access to either Charleston or Cincinnati booksellers, he acquired at the end of 1843 a work by John L. Stephens, *Incidents of Travel in Central America,* "which I have read with infinite pleasure"; this book must have been recommended by a brother officer, because for once he recommended it to Ellen rather than vice versa. Stephens's book summed up the literary qualities he preferred: dramatic, sharply observed, and sparely written.[10]

Shortly after returning to Fort Moultrie, Sherman received notification that in January 1844 he would be required to assist the inspector general of the army, Colonel Sylvester Churchill. Churchill was to begin an inquiry examining the use of funds from a congressional appropriation for the Seminole War in Florida involving Georgia and Alabama volunteers. Sherman had been recommended by his company commander, Captain Robert Anderson, who had married the daughter of a Georgia slaveholder and was well connected in the state. Sherman feared it would "be a most disagreeable and laborious duty," but on arrival in Marietta found he only needed to take depositions and tabulate them. Although Churchill ordered that they should resume at Bellefonte, Alabama, Sherman was in no hurry to get there; accordingly, he visited Kennesaw Mountain, rode to Allatoona on the Etowah River, and visited some impressive Indian mounds located on a plantation owned by Colonel Lewis Tumlin. Tumlin took a shine to his young visitor, and Sherman accepted an invitation to stay for a couple of days. He then rode on to Rome and crossed into Alabama over the Racoon Range to Bellefonte on the Tennessee River. Work resumed in March 1844 and lasted for two months. Once it concluded, Sherman and his companions rode back to Georgia via Rome, Allatoona, Marietta, and Atlanta, where Sherman took his leave to travel to Augusta and catch the train to Charleston. But the echoes of this trip would bounce forward further in his life. Later in life Sherman observed, "Thus by a mere accident I was enabled to traverse on horseback the very ground where in after-years I had to conduct vast armies and fight great battles." It had been a good investment in time, but he also had the leisure to think over his fundamental dilemma: Should he resign or not?[11]

Sherman had agreed to work for Churchill to gain "the good opinion" of a future patron. But this aim had been pursued before the change in his relationship with Ellen the previous autumn and their informal agreement that they had reached an "understanding." In February 1844, after a long lapse, Sherman wrote to Thomas Ewing asking for his approval that his second son Hugh ("Bub") "could come and spend the winter and spring [of 1844–45] with me." Sherman had been encouraging his ambitions to enter West Point. He received a kindly answer, but it concluded "with the hope that I was studying for 'civil life.'" Sherman guessed that Maria Ewing had informed her husband of his increasing intimacy with Ellen; even if he approved, clearly

Sherman would be better able to provide for her outside the army. At the age of 24, even if he resigned, "I would have to depend on someone till I could establish myself in the practice of some profession." He found this prospect unpalatable. To resign now he thought "madness," but this consideration missed the real point. "Shall I not therefore write to your father," he asked Ellen, "and tell him of my views, see whether he approves or not and ask his permission to seek your hand for life?" Sherman did so in June 1844 and received Ewing's blessing. Indeed, the proposal pleased Ewing because it offered Sherman a firm, lifelong, unbreakable link with the Ewing family that the relationship had previously lacked.[12]

Sherman expressed his determination to "share my future life with one whom I have so long loved as a sister," but he needed an alternative plan for their future. In the summer of 1842, Congress had reduced army pay, which had cost Sherman $40 per year, and it might be reduced again. So, he informed Ellen, "after casting about," he had taken up the law. He had "seized upon a Book that young lawyers groan over—Blackstone—and have with avidity swallowed its contents and shall continue to study and read hard all summer instead of idling my time in securing and forming friends temporary and changing." Sir William Blackstone's *Commentaries* remained the ultimate legal authority, and American lawyers had to master it. Sherman had tried to discourage his brother John from studying the law several years before, and his own conversion appeared halfhearted. He doubted that he "would make a good lawyer, although I meet with little difficulty in mastering the necessary book knowledge." He had not yet discovered his natural gift for public speaking and claimed to dislike bombast. Sherman still hoped that if Ellen saw "something of the Army" she might like it—a vain hope indeed.[13]

While clinging to the profession he liked best, he developed two attitudes that underwrote his army life. The first concerned party politics. He supported Henry Clay in the presidential election of 1844 in part because he hoped he might be more generous toward the army, but his Whig enthusiasm so evident at West Point was already diminished. Henceforth, he would "never permit myself to become interested in the success of either party." When John began speaking "on the stump" for Clay, Sherman was appalled and reproved him: "I really thought you were too decent for that" and too proud "to humble and cringe to beg party or popular fervor." John would invariably ignore his elder brother's claims to moral superiority. The second matter involved religion. Since childhood Ellen had demonstrated remarkable diligence in her Catholic devotions. Sherman believed firmly in

Christian values but lacked faith—a true agnostic. Even when Ellen queried after their betrothal how he could defend her, "when you become my protector," against Protestant taunts—she faced foul slanders regularly—unless he could prove "the truth of that which I claim to be true, pure and holy," Sherman still could not convert to Catholicism. But he continued to be happy to be tolerant toward Catholics in a pragmatic way.[14]

This strong pragmatic and utilitarian streak emerged in his legal studies. Both these qualities would be needed by a successful attorney. Yet he remained an army officer, and these studies became an important part of his continuing military education. Sherman had imbibed some law, both constitutional and international, in his moral philosophy course at West Point. The ethics of any matter, the question why one choice should be selected over another, had been dealt with in his final year as a cadet, in which he learned "the obligation of every law depends upon its ultimate utility." Once budding lawyers had mastered the four volumes of Blackstone, the next step would be to read James Kent's *Commentaries on American Law* (1826). Sherman had admired Kent's book since his cadet days. Kent, sensitive to the conventional wisdom that federal unions were fragile, had asserted that "disobedience to the laws of union must either be submitted to by the government to its own disgrace or those laws must be enforced by arms." In pursuit of this course of study, in 1846 Sherman acquired his own copy of another book he had studied at West Point, Emmerich de Vattel's *The Law of Nations; or, Principles of the Laws of Nature Applied to the Conduct and Affairs of Nations and Sovereigns* (1758), a new English edition of which had been published in 1844. Whatever Sherman's assumptions about the laws of war, Vattel drew a relative distinction that transcended them. No belligerent should automatically be regarded as just; all should be treated as equally just (or unjust). Otherwise the laws of war could not have their desired effect. This distinction permitted a degree of flexibility and therefore introduced necessity as an important consideration: what needed to be done to win. Even Hugo Grotius in his famous *On the Law of War and Peace* (1625) did not regard any laws that might introduce restraint into warfare as obstructions to seeking victory, as war "will finally conduct us to peace as its ultimate goal." What Sherman stored away in the recesses of his capacious memory was the possibility that the rights, property, and privileges that citizens enjoyed in peacetime were not preserved in wartime, even though under army regulations plunder and pillage were capital offenses. At this date, thanks to growing familiarity with the white South, Sherman strongly approved of the defense of property written into American laws of war in the early Republic that strengthened the position of slaveholders.[15]

In autumn 1844 Sherman attended to a duty not calculated to endear him to all his brother officers. He visited the arsenal at Augusta, Georgia, "as a sort of peacemaker" among the officers of Company B of his regiment. Braxton Bragg had earned a reputation for being remarkably petty and quarrelsome and, separated from the rest of the regiment, had quarreled with all his officers. Sherman had managed to maintain good relations with Bragg and was able to broker a kind of compromise between Bragg and his feuding subordinates. For well-earned recreation Sherman spent the winter of 1844–45 hunting on the Poyas plantation on the Cooper River in South Carolina, until he dislocated his shoulder badly in an accident that forced convalescence in Ohio for two months. Once back at Fort Moultrie, he continued to take advantage of a kind invitation from Robert Anderson, "a man of great taste" with "a pretty collection of paintings and most expensive selection of engravings which I love to look over," to view them whenever he liked—a refuge from the endless scandalmongering, bickering, and tedium of garrison duty. Sherman remained of two minds. The congressional resolution to annex Texas spurred him to frantic activity; desperate for any chance for action and reputation, he even considered transferring into an infantry regiment in Louisiana. But by January 1846 he considered "the prospect of a peaceful year . . . strong, and it therefore behoves me to make all possible preparation to leave the service" shortly.[16]

He dismissed all such thoughts when the United States acknowledged on May 3, 1846, that a state of war, announced by Mexico the previous week, existed between the two countries. Sherman's initial experience replicated his father's in 1812, as he received a posting on recruiting duty at Pittsburgh, Pennsylvania, with an outstation at Zanesville, Ohio, which permitted visits to family and friends. Once news arrived of the early battles, "when my comrades were actually fighting," Sherman found this duty "intolerable." On returning to Pittsburgh from Zanesville, he opened a letter from Ord informing him that Company F had received orders to sail for California from New York and suggesting he might apply for a recent vacancy. He did so at once but foolishly left his post without orders and traveled to Cincinnati, hoping that the superintendent of the Western recruiting service would send him along with his recruits; of course, he did no such thing, and Sherman was ordered back to Pittsburgh with a severe reproof. Luckily, he found orders posting him to Company F. He managed to write to Ellen, and he had to work all night to clear his desk before rushing off to catch the boat from New York, leaving all his kit to be packed up and transported to Zanesville by Phil Ewing. He would soon regret this impulsive decision.[17]

On July 14 he sailed aboard the *Lexington* to Monterey, California, via San Sebastian, Rio de Janeiro, Cape Horn, and Valparaiso, Chile. This long, circuitous, wearisome, and dangerous journey would take 198 days through the winter months of the southern hemisphere. Sherman at least traveled with convivial company, as he shared a stateroom with Ord, and also enjoyed reading in the sun on the quarterdeck, over which an awning had been spread. He almost immediately gave up smoking cigars—"it hurt my breast"—but this abstinence did not last. Apart from reading, he went sightseeing in San Sebastian and Rio de Janeiro, including attending an opera. He wrote many long letters to Ellen and his brothers and sisters, though he did not find it easy to post them. Ellen received detailed, beautifully written accounts of his visits to cathedrals, churches, monasteries, and nunneries. The influence of writers like John Stephens had helped hone Sherman's written style and erased adolescent posturing. He visited the Rio aqueduct with an old West Point acquaintance, Henry W. Halleck. But reading absorbed time like a sponge. "I have read all of Washington Irving's works that are aboard, Pickwick [and] Barnaby Rudge [by Charles Dickens], Shakespeare, everything I could get, and yesterday cast about to determine which I should read next, the Bible, History of the Reformation or the Wandering Jew"—but he put the choice off. Ellen had urged Dickens on him, as had her brother Hugh.[18]

As they passed Cape Horn the weather deteriorated, "and [we] had [a] very hard time." Sherman genuinely feared that the ship would be swamped, but bravado prevailed among the young officers; "if anyone uttered a prayer to his Maker" he "would be laughed at and ridiculed." Eventually the wind and waves abated. News that San Francisco and Monterey had already been taken depressed Sherman and his friends, but on reaching Valparaiso and attending another opera, his spirits rose. "I hope the war ain't over, and I will be so selfish as to will enough promotions to make me a captain." But nothing looked more pacific than Monterey when Sherman arrived, at last, on January 27, 1847; serving again as quartermaster and commissary, he easily got his supplies ashore and under cover, plus the $25,000 fund he carried safely locked up. He occupied the Customs House, a comfortable billet that many envied. His dreams of fighting ashore and performing gallant deeds remained just that.[19]

The essential part of Company F's mission had already been rendered re-dundant. It had been originally intended that it should advance eastward and find Brigadier General Stephen W. Kearny's column that had set off from Fort Leavenworth, Kansas, in July 1846, then cover the last phase of his ad-vance into California. Rather, Kearny found them instead, having arrived at San Diego weeks earlier. He came aboard the frigate USS *Independence* while Sherman and others were dining as guests of its captain. Sherman noted that Kearny, whom he knew from St. Louis and whose energy and power of de-cision he admired, "looked haggard," understandable since he had endured a "rough march" and had been wounded; despite it all, he appeared indom-itable, and "his face wore that smile so characteristic of him. He has always been a favorite of mine and I was peculiarly glad to see him." Kearny's ar-rival triggered a tussle with John C. Frémont, the famous explorer based in Los Angeles, over who bore the title of governor of California. Frémont refused to relinquish the title, mainly on the grounds of possession, having arrived first. Frémont certainly had the more glamor thanks to his acclaim as "Pathmarker of the West," assisted by Kit Carson. He had given ample evidence of audacity and resolution and could inspire loyalty. However, his ambition outran his wit. He relied too heavily on the advice of Commodore R. F. Stockton, who had appointed him governor in January 1847. Sherman, soon appointed to Kearny's staff, favored his chief, but he felt no antipathy toward Frémont, believing his ambition had wrong-footed him. Likewise, he continued to admire Carson as a free and adventurous spirit. The resolution of the dispute in Kearny's favor occurred in February 1847 when President James K. Polk ruled that in the government of California the civil and military powers should be combined in the most senior officer, Kearny. When he de-parted in the summer, he would be succeeded by Colonel Richard B. Mason. Kearny sent Sherman to fetch Frémont so that he could be informed by the new governor personally of his abrupt demotion; Kearny rather enjoyed his humiliation.[20]

Kearny thought highly of Sherman's abilities and intended that he should accompany him on his tour of the territory. This trip never materialized, but something unexpected did. In the spring two officers who had served with Kearny on the advance from Kansas to California, Captain Henry S. Turner and his friend Lieutenant William H. Warner, met Sherman. They eyed Sherman's well-stocked chest containing three years' supply of socks, calico shirts, and underwear enviously. In a characteristic good-hearted flourish, Sherman "told them to help themselves," but they insisted on paying for the items, and ever since "Turner and I have been close friends." Warner, alas, was killed by Indians a few years later. This new friendship ranked among the few consolations offered by California. Sherman did not like its aridity; further, he briefly reverted to company duty before being brought back onto the governor's staff. Although he had been at the center of things, he had still not seen frontline action, and thus had few chances to gain promotion, missing out on the opportunities many of his contemporaries had enjoyed. He exhibited some symptoms of mild depression, "I feel ten years older," listless and saddened that "out here in California, banished from fame, from everything that is dear and no prospect of getting back . . . I must make the best of a bad bargain." He estimated that it would take three years to apply for a transfer and act on it, but he knew he had nobody else to blame for this exile but himself. "I fear that I leaped the mark in search of glory," he admitted; "such is the chance of fortune," and he had no choice but to accept it. He also nursed deep-seated Whig doubts over the morality of a war he had so intently wished to excel in.[21]

Sherman found working for the new governor, Colonel Mason, a pleasant and rewarding experience despite his stern reputation. Sherman liked men who meant what they said. He spent some time rounding up those intent on ruling their own baronies, like the renegade official John H. Nash, whom Sherman arrested in June 1847. Shortly afterward, in the spring of 1848, Mason called Sherman into his office after welcoming two visitors from the Sierra Nevada. He asked Sherman, "What is that?" pointing to a yellow substance lying on some papers. Sherman had examined some recently prospected gold in Georgia in 1844 and confirmed that it was indeed gold but thought it of mediocre quality. He underrated the significance of the discovery of gold and the massive impact on California that it would have. Although in theory Sherman always hailed the pioneer spirit, his own pioneering instincts were less sure. His instincts always sang to a cautious tune. In July 1847 he had traveled up to San Francisco (then called Yerba Buena), where he found his old classmate Captain Joseph L. Folsom. Folsom had bought up lots in the city and began selling them, offering several to Sherman. Had he accepted the offer Sherman would have become a wealthy man; but, suspecting Folsom's motives, he felt "insulted" by what he believed to be a ruse. Again, his judgment was askew: he lacked the audacious spirit to be a successful speculator, being too conventional and straight-laced.[22]

In a similar vein, Sherman did not welcome the immediate effects of the discovery of gold. All of California had been thrown into tumult. Chronic inflation, particularly the price of labor, rotted military discipline and pro-voked desertion. Curiously, Sherman had also unwittingly spurred on the crazed "gold rush" by his authorship of some official documents he had drafted for Mason's signature. After their delivery to Washington his graphic language served as the basis for official announcements publicized by the newspapers. He also wrote vivid descriptions of gold "fever" in his private letters home that had a major impact on the old northwestern states. Ellen reported six months later that "your letters . . . have been circulated in the newspapers, and all rely, about these parts, upon your testimony." Sherman urged Colonel Mason to go and see the gold fields for himself, and he did not need much persuasion. They made two trips in June 1848 to the gold mines at Sutter's Fort, and Folsom joined the party at San Francisco; the latter would be an influential voice in the decision to make San Francisco the city of northern California, rather than the official army choice, echoed by Sherman, of Benicia. Conventional authority had been usurped by those prospectors who got there first, who were literally masters of all they sur-veyed. Sherman sent Ellen vivid descriptions of the effects of gold fever. Monterey and San Francisco had been abandoned by their menfolk. "All are gone to the mines."[23]

Ellen reported that her brother Hugh and Sherman's brother-in-law Samuel Stanbaugh, the "gold diggers," as Ellen called them, were on their way to California. "Father thinks the expedition a fine one and says were he a young man he would soon be out there." Sherman's keenest insight into the gold rush was that a fortune could be made by providing necessi-ties to the prospectors rather than by joining them, as many arrived with nothing. Clothing had become scarce, and Sherman could not "afford the exorbitant prices now charged." Ellen reassured him that "I shall send as much [clothing] as the boys will be able to take with them. . . . I wish they could take you some books. You must desire some although you never complain of the want of them." Hugh wanted to restrict the load as much as possible, but Ellen still managed to tuck in Lord Macaulay's *History of England*, which Sherman devoured over the next month. Interestingly, Sherman's view of how to make money received validation when, in part-nership with his new friend William Warner and a civilian, Norman Bestor, he opened a store in Coloma. This netted him $1,500, on which he survived in 1849. His army salary amounted to $70 per month, but, Sherman complained, a servant could not be hired for less than $300 per month.[24]

Ellen also reported that her father and brother Tom were lobbying to secure him a furlough. "Then you will have time to dig gold and come home too," she wrote optimistically. At this time Sherman lived "comfortably" in the family of Doña Augustias de la Guerra, whose local magnate husband chose to reside elsewhere. The historian Michael Fellman suggests this relationship became less gallant than Sherman presents it both in his *Memoirs* and to Ellen, but the evidence is weak and can be no more than speculation. Sherman boarded with Halleck, Ord, and Dr. R. Murray, and none suspected impropriety; Sherman later asked Ord to be his best man at his wedding, and he would not have accepted if there had been, especially as Ord married Doña Augustias in 1856.

In February 1849 Persifer Smith, who had distinguished himself on the advance to Mexico City, replaced Mason as governor. Sherman requested a transfer, but Smith would not hear of it, as he needed a staff officer of Sherman's caliber, while he traveled to see as much of California as he could with his own eyes. The way these two dynamic officers directed their huge commands left a permanent impression on Sherman. In the spring of 1849 Major Joseph Hooker arrived to relieve him as assistant adjutant general, and he reverted to being Smith's aide-de-camp. Hooker's officious presence only underlined how far Sherman had fallen behind in the promotion race. His artillery company would not be relieved for another 18 months, and even if he resigned, it would take two years to conclude the process.[25]

Ellen had received no word from Sherman for some time; the infrequency of the mail had disrupted any marriage timetable. Since 1845 she had nursed the fear that she would never see him again. She became depressed and prone to psychosomatic illnesses that baffled her doctors. By May 1849 she began to believe that she was too ill for marriage and started to encourage Sherman to look elsewhere. "Do not let a thought for me prevent you marrying," she urged. Sherman could never be described as a romantic, but in a letter that brought her renewed happiness that month he offered a forthright statement of attachment. "Though my hopes in life are all destroyed, my love for you has never abated, never varied in the least and upon it you may constantly rely."[26]

Sherman had made some money—not a huge amount by prevailing California standards, but it made him feel better about life. He had earned $500 from surveying, another $500 by selling lots in Benicia, plus $6,000 from another three lots in Sacramento. Then in the spring of 1850 he received the orders he had long waited for. Smith wanted him to take a series of reports to New York and hand them to General Scott personally. He would at last return to the eastern seaboard. The Ewing family had moved to Washington, DC, in 1849 after Thomas Ewing Sr.'s appointment as secretary of the interior in Zachary Taylor's cabinet. Ewing had much patronage to dispense. Sherman's fare home cost him $600 for the shorter route established via Panama, crossing the isthmus on mules. John and Jessie Frémont were fellow passengers part of the way; Ord and A. J. Smith, another old friend from West Point who had graduated in 1838, also accompanied him. He then took ship to New York City, where Scott lived. In return for the safe delivery of the reports, he received orders to dine with Scott, who regaled Sherman with reminiscences of his triumphant campaign ending with the fall of Mexico City. These depressed Sherman because he "felt deeply" his absence from the adventure. He believed "my career as a soldier was at an end." His frantic efforts to get himself to California in retrospect appeared a rash blunder.[27]

Ellen looked forward to his "speedy return," but first he traveled to Mansfield to see his mother, John, and other relatives. Here he endured a debilitating illness. He emerged "thin, and weak in proportion" and warned Ellen that any wedding plans should be delayed. This illness is the first unimpeachable evidence of the asthma that would come to haunt Sherman. As a young man he never mentioned it, so he might have glossed over its symptoms, or they were very mild or latent. The latter seems more likely, as Ellen took a keen interest in the health of others, and in their early correspondence she never inquired about asthmatic symptoms. Asthma most commonly strikes while the patient is young, and the symptoms might ease with age, but this pattern did not occur in Sherman's case. Since he spent long periods of his pre-1861 career in hot and humid climes, that might have helped him ward off the worst symptoms. Even at this date Sherman insisted that the doctor "has long since ceased to prescribe for my lungs" and informed Ellen that he "says my tongue, appearance and symptoms indicate Mexican Dysentery." Perhaps, but after all the years Sherman had spent in the warmth and humidity of the South, the harsher, colder, drier climate of northern California had provoked serious asthmatic attacks and would continue to do so.[28]

Sherman still managed an optimistic tone despite his ailment and lack of promotion. He reminded Ellen, "The present is ours. Let us make the most of it." He also contended that he could peer along the road of life and "make a good guess" at what lay ahead. "Therefore, I hope you will not urge me to resign"; he wanted to remain an officer "till the time arrive[s] when I am compelled to act." So Sherman set a date for their wedding, May 1, 1850, even though Ellen remained unconvinced as to the wisdom of his course. "I have always rejoiced to see the flowers bloom," he wrote, and the spring always remained a special time for him. March and April were taken up with Maria Ewing's preparations for the wedding, so after Sherman arrived in Washington, he kept out of the way. Thanks to his father's old friend Senator Tom Corwin, he managed to gain access to the floor of the Senate and listened to the great speeches pronouncing on the Compromise of 1850, including on March 7 Daniel Webster's great oration in defense of the Union, but he came away less impressed than he expected.

The Ewing-Sherman wedding, one of the great events of the Washington social season in 1850, took place at Blair House, which Thomas Ewing rented. Father James Ryder, SJ, president of Georgetown College and a popular and influential cleric, officiated, assisted by his fellow Jesuit Father James Vespre, Ellen's confessor since her schooldays. Though Ellen did not meet the period's criterion for a dazzling beauty, she appeared radiant, with bright blue eyes and luxuriant dark brown hair; she moved gracefully, showing off her slim figure to good effect. Sherman stood upright, handsome and immaculate in full dress uniform, with Ord by his side. There were 300 guests, including President Taylor and his entire cabinet and all the capital's great luminaries, Webster and Thomas Hart Benton among them. Henry Clay arrived late but kissed the bride with consummate charm. Ellen got carried away and "actually kissed the President," to his obvious delight. There could be no doubt as to Lieutenant Sherman's standing in the world. For once he might have understated things when he described the wedding preparations to John as having "much pomp!"[29]

The happy couple honeymooned first in Baltimore and then Philadelphia, where they visited Sherman's elder sister Elizabeth and her husband, William Reese. The latter had given up the law to become a "merchant" but was a speculator who gambled recklessly and turned to drink when he lost money, not an uncommon occurrence. Sherman had already lent Elizabeth $250 and on this trip increased the loan by a further $1,000. Ellen resented this generosity. Given his social eminence, Sherman appeared to adopt the role of the head of the Sherman family, for he had also lent his elder brother James $135 (though, alas, he, too, started drinking heavily) and urged his younger brother Hoyt, a mere typesetter, "to improve his condition." But Sherman lacked the money to sustain this patriarchal position. From Philadelphia the newlyweds traveled to New York to visit the Hoyts, his mother's family, and spent an enjoyable day at West Point before admiring the grandeur of Niagara Falls. They then turned west to Ohio to visit other family.

Though in these early days both adopted the conventional language of marriage—Sherman called Ellen his "Adjutant and Chief Counselor"—the consummation of the most important relationship of Sherman's life concealed for only a short time that their marriage was unorthodox. Not a conventional "army wife," Ellen would emerge in many important respects as the senior partner, with a clear idea of her own interests and priorities. Not only was she a powerful influence on his evolving intellectual development, but she had patronage at her disposal and her own money; she would never be a passive or subordinate figure.[30]

Initially, Ellen appeared to give her husband's wish to remain in the army the benefit of the doubt. Officers of his rank had to wait until a vacancy appeared in their own regiment. His company, still commanded by Bragg, was stationed at Jefferson Barracks, near St. Louis. Sherman returned to regimental duty in September 1850. Soon after his arrival Congress passed a bill increasing the Commissary Department by four captains, and Sherman's name appeared on the list. He left at once for departmental headquarters in St. Louis. His joy at the promotion was increased further by news that his first child, Maria Boyle Ewing, known as Minnie, came into the world, on January 28, 1851. Sherman hastened back to Lancaster and brought his family to St. Louis for the first time, renting a house on Chouteau Avenue. The fussy Ellen deemed this "not very grand" but "pleasantly situated." Her fears of homesickness were assuaged by the rapid arrival of her parents; her brothers Phil and Charley joined them, and Maria returned for another visit in November. Captain and Mrs. Van Vliet arrived in St. Louis, too, and the Sherman residence quickly became a center of convivial hospitality.

Ellen soon became pregnant again and returned to Lancaster to give birth to her second child. Sherman traveled to Fort Leavenworth to inspect cattle, and during his journey reported to Ellen proudly how he had not contravened "my old rule never to return by the road I had come." Here was another lifelong habit firmly set. In the summer Sherman heard that he might be transferred to New Orleans. Having experienced the joys of promotion and fatherhood, he was stunned by the arrival of the "sad tidings of poor Mother's death, so sudden and unexpected to me." He believed (probably rightly) that his sweet-natured mother had turned a blind eye to the symptoms of heart disease to avoid alarming others. Ellen commiserated, "How I shall miss your good Mother." By November Sherman had transferred to New Orleans, leaving the family behind, and sang its praises by comparison with the "bleak, cold and inhospitable" North. It was a lively cultural center. "Everybody goes to shows, theatres, and operas for pastimes." Sherman rented a house on Magazine Street, "a very genteel neighbourhood," for his family. Ellen had already set out to rejoin him, accompanied by Sherman's sister Frances Moulton, Minnie, and baby Mary Elizabeth, born on November 17, 1852.[31]

So, after 12 years' service, with a long-awaited promotion to captain, Sherman remained in the army. No other alternative had quite tempted him to abandon his profession. He had seen a lot of logistic service and excelled at it, but he soon discovered that when he had nothing else to do he found it constraining and dull. He began to consider once again taking a leap outside the military.

3

Unfortunate Civilian, 1853–1861

The origins of the proposition that would change the direction of Sherman's life lay in St. Louis and the competition between two of its leading banks. Page and Bacon had been the first to open a branch in San Francisco, California; its rival, Lucas and Symonds, calculated that it could not allow Page and Bacon to steal a march on them. A niece of the senior partner, James H. Lucas, had married Sherman's close friend Henry S. Turner, who had settled in St. Louis as assistant US treasurer after leaving California and the army. Lucas consulted Turner on San Francisco conditions and offered him a partnership if he would return to San Francisco to open a branch there; Turner accepted but demurred over returning to California for the long term. Instead he recommended Sherman, who could help him set the project up and then be entrusted with its care after Turner returned to St. Louis. Turner urged Sherman to take a leave of absence from the army for six months and review his progress; not surprisingly, both Ellen and her father enthusiastically supported this opportunity for Sherman to become a civilian again. The leave of absence was quickly approved. In January 1853 Turner set off for San Francisco.

The proposal had been perfectly timed. Sherman had "tired of this dull, tame life," for he did not regard commissaries as "fighting men," and any chance to make money seemed alluring. He quickly gave up the house on Magazine Street in February 1853, returned his family to Lancaster, Ohio, and the following month began another journey to California. He traveled via Greytown (San Juan del Norte), Nicaragua, then took the riverboat up the San Juan River to Lake Nicaragua and Virgin Bay, and transferred to mules to complete the journey to San Juan del Sur. This route had been established by tycoon Cornelius Vanderbilt, who failed to achieve his aim of building an isthmus canal but found a quicker and cheaper route than the alternative Panama one.[1]

Sherman's ship, the SS *Lewis*, made excessive progress because she passed beyond San Francisco, then ran aground about a mile from the shore. All the passengers were safely rowed ashore, and Sherman pushed inland on foot and persuaded a schooner captain to take him to San Francisco to alert the authorities to the *Lewis*'s plight. Alas, on entering the harbor, the schooner became swamped and overturned, but Sherman managed to climb onto the keel. Rescued by another small boat, he made his way up to the Presidio and reported the *Lewis*'s distress. The passengers were all rescued, but they had been very lucky; a rougher sea the previous night could have been disastrous. Never one to linger over the horrors of things that had not happened, Sherman gave thanks as he retrieved his luggage that he had lost only a carpetbag. Still, he reflected, two shipwrecks in one day made an inauspicious start in his "new peaceful career."[2]

Sherman's return to San Francisco, with its gambling casinos, barrooms, and crowded streets, felt like a homecoming—though the city's population had mushroomed from 400 to 50,000 between 1846 and 1853. Sherman quickly found Turner lodging with General Ethan Allen Hitchcock on Clay Street; Turner moved out, and Sherman replaced him, "but we all get our meals together at a restaurant. This is the usual way," he reported to Ellen, "and it suits very well indeed—breakfast of tea, beefsteak, muffins and radishes, dinner according to call, fine soup, fish, roasts, stews, and all sorts of French notions—indeed I would not ask for a better table." Business proceeded promptly: Lucas agreed that Sherman could have at his disposal $200,000 and credit of a further $50,000 in New York should he need it, but he insisted the bank must be profitable. All three, Lucas, Turner, and Sherman, were affected by heady, boundless Californian optimism, but the good times could not and did not last forever. Sherman expressed himself satisfied and agreed to return to St. Louis for further discussions, then come back to San Francisco with his family. Sherman's thoughts were not directed solely toward business. The famous Irish dancer Lola Montez gave three benefit concerts, and Sherman attended one—evidence of a new interest in the dance he indulged in the 1850s.[3]

Back in St. Louis Sherman agreed to an annual salary of $5,000 and staying until 1860; Lucas, whom Sherman came to admire, committed to building Sherman a new branch at a cost of $50,000 and allowed him to design it himself. In July 1854 staff moved into the handsome building located on the northeastern corner of Jackson and Montgomery Streets. Sherman exuded pride in it: "I enjoy it," he admitted. "as much as the artist does a fine picture." Even Ellen got caught up in the sanguine mood—"I will cheerfully submit to any course you may determine upon"—and when he returned to Lancaster she and Lizzie and her nurse, Mary Lynch, were ready and waiting to accompany him westward. But there were two matters on which she expressed reservations. First, after Sherman's sleepless nights in St. Louis in the autumn of 1851, she feared that San Francisco's damp and dust would inflame his asthma; and second, she made clear that it would be a trial "for me to leave my parents, now growing old, with a certainty of not seeing them again for years and a probability of never meeting them again in this world." Consequently, on leaving so abruptly, Ellen struck a bargain with her parents in return for their blessing on her departure. She would leave her daughter Minnie with them. "Father could not live without Minnie, so we must give her up during his lifetime," Ellen candidly justified her move later. Sherman reluctantly agreed to this arrangement, though not permanently, and soon resented this enforced separation from the elder daughter with whom he enjoyed so intimate a bond. Before departing yet again from New York, Sherman sat down to write his letter of resignation from the army, to take effect from September 6, 1853.[4]

Despite Ellen's fear of ships, the only untoward incident on the arduous journey involved Lizzie's nurse, Mary. She took fright at the Pacific surf on the beach at San Juan del Sur and began screaming hysterically "like a fool," as Sherman described it sharply, which frightened Lizzie, who fainted. For months afterward both Shermans feared Lizzie had been permanently affected—an illustration of the nineteenth century's preoccupation with "nerves." Their initial accommodation in San Francisco did not prove perfect, either. Ellen did not like "roughing it," as they lived in two rooms plus full board for $100 per week. But their meager surroundings were rendered tolerable by musical evenings when Ethan Allen Hitchcock accompanied Ellen on the piano with his flute.[5]

With his customary thoroughness, Sherman studied business practices carefully. He did not embrace its ethos wholeheartedly, unlike his classmate Captain Folsom. He viewed the trust placed in him with an elevated sense of moral responsibility not widely shared by other San Francisco bankers. The system knew no regulation; laissez-faire in its most extreme form prevailed. So, in the best military fashion, Sherman laid down a series of principles to determine his conduct. These reveal the workings of his mind and broader mental affinities. His lodestone enshrined caution, particularly in loans and discounts; "there lies our profit and there are our risks." His second principle prescribed looking ahead and being alert to developments in the business environment. Third, he assumed that no transaction could ever be permanently secure. Consequently, he attempted to expand deposits and expressed pride in February 1855 when these amounted to $966,000; he also decided to operate without making use of his $50,000 New York overdraft. Furthermore, the foundations of his bank should continue to be strong if he remained steadfast in his desire not to diminish "our capital by a single cent." Finally, he remained determined "not to put myself in the power of those men" who extracted loans by false promises. Sherman's principles would be tested, yet his attitudes are illustrative of a broader code of conduct that he would follow throughout the rest of his life.[6]

Sherman had really rededicated himself to the military code he had imbibed at West Point, rather than reject it, by entering the business world. This consistency would be a source of strength, as he would be widely respected as a trustworthy soul. He had even turned down a salary increase, arguing that he should prove himself first. Turner, now a partner at Lucas and Symonds, became Sherman's immediate boss, and their relationship was governed by frankness "because it is our agreement to have no reserve." Sherman gained the trust of all serving and retired military investors. When Hitchcock departed on April 15, 1854, he granted Sherman power of attorney over all his investments, mainly real estate. Yet the limits of Sherman's embrace of business practice would also be the source of his undoing as a banker.[7]

In February 1854 the Sherman family moved into a house on Green Street. Sherman reported to Turner that though Ellen was "contented with her new house [she] still has a very poor opinion of California generally." She appeared homesick, "still pining for home," accentuated by a poor and unreliable postal service. She felt terribly isolated, disliked "economizing," and thought ill of the high cost of living. Her discontent was too obvious to be ignored. Sherman decided to let her go home in the spring of 1855 but doubted that she would return west; she did so in December. Another matter that agitated her was the decline in Sherman's health. He succumbed to recurring bouts of asthma. In April 1854 he warned Turner, "Should I at any time be short or cross, charge it to account of the asthma." It became so fearful that he expressed "little or no faith in my prolonged existence. . . . This asthma is so fixed on me and is so serious at times that I care but little how soon it terminates fatally." Every night's sleep had been disturbed; he had spent "weeks and months of nights forced to sit, breathing like a broken-winded horse, thankful for a couple [of] hours repose. . . . This climate will sooner or later kill me dead as a herring." He complained of San Francisco's damp, fogs, and winds. Fearing that alcohol aggravated his condition, he tried to avoid it.

Despite his numerous complaints, asthma did not prevent him working, so they may have given Lucas and Turner a misleading impression in St. Louis.[8]

The bank made sound progress that pleased Sherman. He hired Schuyler Hamilton, the grandson of Alexander Hamilton, who had been a year below him at West Point and enjoyed enviable social connections. Sherman appreciated his efforts. "Every little adds," he observed to Turner, though Hamilton left in September 1854 to become a street broker. A nephew of Turner's turned out less well, pleasant enough but not up to banking, Sherman judged. Then on February 8, all too aware that his doctor blamed his asthma ("the last cold settles on my lungs") on the damp walls of Green Street, Sherman decided to buy a house on Harrison Street on Rincon Hill overlooking the city and the bay; immediately, he brought in builders to extend it. His timing could not have been worse. The previous October "Honest Harry" Meiggs, president of the California Lumber Company, fled to Chile with bags stuffed with money just before his company folded. He owed Sherman's bank $80,000. The aftershocks of this failure took some months to have an impact on the city, but the tsunami hit Sherman and Lucas and Turner in the third week of February 1855.[9]

The failure that precipitated this financial crisis involved Page and Bacon's branch, the very reason why Sherman moved to San Francisco. Unlike its rivals, Lucas and Turner had fared well at first. On Thursday, February 22, 1855, its cash balance stood at a healthy $1,145,391, and Sherman had noted that "quiet people were drawing their money out"—an orderly but sustained withdrawal of $530,000. Sherman kept a reserve on hand of $65,000 "in case of a run." The news of the collapse of Page and Bacon altered this sedate atmosphere. The following morning, "Black Friday," Sherman, on arriving to open the bank, was "thunderstruck" when greeted by large, unruly crowds waiting to withdraw their money soonest. By noon Lucas and Turner had paid out $337,000 in cash. Several army friends accosted Sherman, "For God's sake, what are things coming to?!" Sherman, utterly calm and collected, reassured them his bank "would not break"; he insisted that if anxious they should take their money. "My own personal friends simply took my word." He admitted later that he trusted them too much, "but they were as true as steel." As the pressure on the other banks mounted, some friends deposited their money. "So the word went out that the run had ceased and deposits were coming in." By 4:00 p.m. the bank still had $45,000 cash available, and total deposits amounted to $781,370. Perhaps the worst had passed, but Sherman, who faced the worst crisis in his life so far, understood that he could not complacently rest on his laurels. The battle might be renewed the following day, and he had to be prepared or his reserves might give way.[10]

Sherman rode that night to see his old classmate Folsom, stricken by a fatal illness. Folsom could never be described as an altruistic man, but he owed Lucas and Turner $25,000 secured on two properties. Sherman asked him to raise $17,000, and at 10:00 p.m. he did so. Then Sherman paid a call on a friend from his days in Georgia in 1844, Richard P. Hammond. He promised Sherman $30,000 if he gave him his word he would return this money by March 1; Hammond gave him $45,000 because he knew that Sherman needed every cent he could raise and accepted no voucher or receipt, "only my word," but that was enough. A state representative, Hammond raided state funds to provide this sum. Never did Sherman's integrity earn a greater dividend than friends prepared to take such risks on his behalf. When he at last reached home, Sherman knew he had doubled the amount of ready cash he could draw upon should the storm be renewed. The bank opened on Saturday, a day of "absolute calm," and at its close Lucas and Turner's balance stood at $792,307. "So the battle is over, and we are not dead by a d——d sight," Sherman wrote to Turner proudly.[11]

It had been a sudden and dramatic challenge. The qualities that Sherman most prided himself on had been tested and not found wanting. He revealed the potential of a true leader, not least the ability to inspire trust. Hammond had risked his own reputation for him, but he had also enjoyed the support of Schuyler Hamilton and his old West Point superintendent Colonel DeRussy, who rented rooms above the bank. Both had made stalwart declarations in the bank that had "inspired public confidence" and helped turn the tide of malign rumormongering. Of the $3 million paid out by San Francisco banks over those three fraught days, $400,000 had come from Lucas and Turner. "We have resisted it well and come out safe." The triumph had been Sherman's, but he felt contempt for businessmen who "sat in their offices scared and paralyzed." By the end of February money flowed back into the bank, but Sherman knew that it would take California another three years to recover fully. The financial crisis had put him off banking: "the cares and necessary labor of my post makes it about as much as my precarious health can stand."[12]

Despite the deep recession that affected real estate values, Sherman was confident he could still turn a decent profit by paying coin for gold dust. But he was distracted from his efforts at the bank by two separate domestic issues. His family had grown when on June 8, 1854, William Tecumseh Sherman Jr.

arrived, "a boy of the reddish kind that will need a good deal of watching," he observed proudly to Turner. Ellen so feared sea travel that when she returned to Ohio in the spring of 1855 she decided to leave the children, including her infant son, in her husband's care. Lucas and Turner's attorney, Samuel M. Bowman, and his wife had befriended the Shermans, and as the lease had run out on their house in April, Ellen suggested they lease the Shermans' new house and Mrs. Bowman could take care of Sherman, Lizzie, and Willy until she returned. Sherman's impulsive house purchase, moreover, had overstrained their finances at a bad time, and the Bowmans' taking over the lease eased this difficulty. The Bowmans accepted the offer and put Ellen's mind at ease. She departed on April 16 aboard the *Golden Age*, escorted by a business acquaintance of Sherman's, W. H. Aspinall. A month later, Sherman was horrified to hear that her ship had run aground, but fortunately all the passengers and luggage had been safely removed. Sherman noted wryly that "you can now tell your tale of a traveller of shipwreck and disaster."[13]

Sherman's placid tone did not last long. A sudden crisis erupted that placed great strain on the bonds of not just law and order but freedom of expression. Sherman had already expressed annoyance at the newspapers for spreading false rumours that had led to the complete collapse of the Page and Bacon firm in St. Louis. Within weeks another newspaper editor involved himself in a further fracas that culminated in a complete collapse of civil government in San Francisco. Sherman became involved in this crisis "in spite of myself."[14]

It all began when James King of William (who since the age of 16 had used this curious appellation to distinguish himself from others named James King), the editor of the *Daily Evening Bulletin*, denounced a corrupt politician, James P. Casey, claiming he had spent time in prison. Casey sought him out on the street and on May 14, 1856, fatally shot him, though he lingered for six days. A Vigilance Committee had been organized in 1851, and the shooting resulted in strident calls for its revival to drastically change the way San Francisco was run. Within 24 hours 1,500 men stepped forward to join the movement. The San Francisco Vigilance Committee set up its headquarters at "Fort Gunnybags" on Sacramento Street. In the meantime, Casey took the precaution of handing himself in to the forces of law and order and took up residence in the city jail. Large crowds gathered outside both places and refused to disperse. Sherman's political stock had risen over the previous months, and the Democrats had offered him the nomination for city treasurer with an annual salary of $4,000, but to Ellen's disappointment, he declined it. Sherman had even made a speech, and to his surprise it "was chronicled as decidedly energetic" and enthusiastically applauded. Just prior to the shooting, California governor Neely Johnson—of whom Ellen disapproved because he was an anti-Catholic "Know Nothing," had offered Sherman a commission as major general of militia that he accepted reluctantly. He regretted this decision as soon as the commotion began in earnest. Sherman hardly rejoiced when he heard that 60 gentlemen had rallied as a posse at the jail and elected him their captain. He had been inexorably sucked into the crisis on the strength of his reputation for fine judgment and cool decision. But from the first he felt constrained by two pressing realities. First, his top priority must be his bank—when most vigilante leaders were also business leaders. Second, if he should call the militia out and it did not respond, as seemed likely, he would appear "odious and ridiculous," as Sherman conceded to Turner in his lengthy contemporary account of these events.[15]

Sherman visited the jail mainly to "sustain the civil authorities" and saw instantly that it was indefensible, surrounded on all sides by higher buildings. By then the Vigilance Committee could count on 5,000 men; its leaders were drawn from the prosperous and wealthy, headed by William T. Coleman, "one of the largest merchants of this city." Sherman and Governor Johnson conferred with Coleman, whom Sherman describes as "a man of fine impulses," although he lacked education and entertained "not the least doubt of himself, his motives or intentions." They reached a deal whereby a small group of vigilantes would join the posse defending the prisoner Casey as an "assistant guard" under the "control of the Sheriff," a crony of Casey's. Despite many proud protests that he remained determined to enforce the law, Johnson excused this concession, claiming he had treated with a series of individuals, not a group "leagued together," but Sherman could hardly have been deceived by these legalistic semantics.

Indeed, he sensed imminent violence. The sheriff had two prisoners, Casey and Charles Cora, "a low gambler," who had murdered a US marshal and whose acquittal had outraged respectable opinion. The governor then gave the sheriff permission to surrender his prisoners in extremis, and both he and Sherman repaired to the roof of the nearby International Hotel on Jackson. A crowd of about 10,000 gathered near the jail, 2,500 with muskets, with a further 5,000 people beyond. On May 20, when news arrived that poor King had at last expired, the crowd stormed the jail and carried Casey and Cora off. Sherman hoped their execution might result in the disbandment of the vigilantes; instead he noted with alarm that they took measures for the "perpetuation of their power." Further arrests followed, and the vigilantes fortified another building on Clay Street and displayed "an enmity to the free expression of opinion," Sherman opined gloomily. Ellen expressed vitriolic criticisms of the vigilantes and received a frank warning from her tenant Bowman "to suppress my views." Sherman declared government "at an end" and daily expected bloody revolution, with "immense masses of men idle in the streets watching for blood."[16]

Both Sherman and Governor Johnson agreed that their salvation lay in the hands of the regular army. On May 30 they visited the commander of the Department of the Pacific, Brevet Major General John E. Wool. Johnson asked Wool outright: If he should issue a proclamation ordering the vigilantes to disperse, would the general distribute arms and ammunition to the militia? Sherman told Ewing, "General Wool said 'yes.'" On the strength of this assurance, on June 1 the governor asked Judge David S. Terry of the California Supreme Court to issue a writ of habeas corpus in the name of one of the committee's unlawful captives, though the vigilantes ignored it. At once, Sherman gave orders to the militia indicating his intent to enforce all writs issued since June 1—an order, Sherman wrote with considerable satisfaction, that "caused tremendous excitement." Then Wool dropped a veritable bombshell. He declared to the governor that conditions were currently "unsafe" to issue arms. Sherman did not expect intervention from Washington, DC, and none materialized. He had hoped that the threat of military force would be sufficient to cajole the more respectable supporters of the vigilantes to come over to the side of the forces of "law and order." But Wool's decision completely overthrew his strategy. On June 6 Sherman resigned his commission, having been put in an intolerable position.[17]

Matters quickly deteriorated, with Sherman as a disapproving but aloof bystander. The vigilantes intercepted a schooner, *Julia*, carrying muskets; Judge Terry, a colorful and belligerent character, persuaded Governor Johnson to take firm action and seize them back again. In the subsequent altercation, Terry stabbed a vigilante. "Then arose such a tumult as I never witnessed," Sherman reported to Turner, which led to a repeat of the events of May. "The Vigilance bell pealed forth its wildest clamour, and men ran, calling 'Hang him! Hang him!'" Terry and his men surrendered and were taken to Fort Gunnybags. The deadlock was less real than apparent, and Sherman quickly realized that "the [Vigilance Committee] is tired of its position, but finds it difficult to withdraw from the complications in which they are involved." The man Terry stabbed did not die, and consequently, the judge's removal from

San Francisco could be negotiated. No vigilante leaders were arrested; indeed, to Sherman's disgust they were allowed a parade, "rejoicing at the regeneration of society." Sherman lost his faith in the Californian future that day and feared that worse conditions might yet arise. The sudden vigilante explosion would leave a deep mark on him. At all events, he assured Turner, "it is a lesson which I will never forget—to mind my own business in all time to come."[18]

Earlier Sherman had been sounded out by Lucas and Turner as to his willingness to run an agency for them in New York City, and he gave this more serious consideration after the summer of 1856. With all his other cares, he almost forgot to tell Turner in October 1856 that "Mrs. Sherman presented child No. 4 just a week ago—a boy, large 10½ pounds, fine and healthy." The baby was named Thomas Ewing Sherman after his grandfather. With four young children, the Sherman family's financial pressures continued to grow. Sherman's stewardship of the bank had been prudent and sound, but the profit margins were not great enough to persuade the partners to continue. In January 1857 Turner wrote to reveal Lucas's decision that he wanted "to withdraw from the banking business in California, but leave you to accomplish it in such time and manner as will make least sacrifice to the parties in interest." For two years he had recommended another old friend, Charles P. Stone, as "the best man" to succeed him, but there was to be no successor. He found it difficult to admit defeat when he had done so well, but this blow was less humiliating than it might have been, as it was agreed that Sherman should go to New York. He had, however, grown disenchanted with banking. He found it "too sedentary" but could not work out "what I *am* fit for." He also began to be seized by the notion that he brought misfortune to everything he touched.[19]

On July 4, 1857, Sherman met Lucas and Turner in New York City, and they opened an office at 12 Wall Street. He left his family behind again in Lancaster, and although they got on "well," Ellen reported, ". . . we miss you greatly. Poor Willy seems to feel your absence as a kind of desertion of him." Sherman had hardly set up when he was engulfed by disaster again with the severe onset of the 1857 recession. As in California panic spread swiftly, worsened by the sinking on September 11 of the steamer *Central America* in the Atlantic with the loss of several hundred lives, plus $1.6 million in gold. This calamity redoubled Ellen's opposition to Lucas's proposition that Sherman return to California to finalize outstanding accounts. She also feared that a damp California winter would aggravate his asthma; despite

Sherman's impatience with her fussing, she had helped him alleviate his suffering. In August and September 1855, while journeying through New York, she consulted a Dr. Hunter, who had pioneered "some of the inhaling remedies" for asthma. Thereafter Sherman's symptoms were eased by the fumes burned from niter paper at night. This practice reduced spasms and assisted expectoration, and his condition improved, especially after the move to New York. Another piece of health advice he accepted from Ellen concerned warding off colds and asthma "by suffering your beard to grow so as to be a protection to the chest." Certainly, by the late 1850s his persona had assumed its familiar guise; a portrait of 1860 shows a full but trimmed growth. But on the question of going back to California, her husband ignored her impassioned protests. In October 1857 James H. Lucas's firm, along with much of the whole national banking enterprise, collapsed. Sherman traveled to St. Louis, taking any portable assets and documents with him. He stayed until December, spent Christmas at Lancaster, and returned to San Francisco via New York. There he tried to settle all accounts and debts owed to Lucas and Turner. It was not a pleasant experience, as "those who owed us were not always as just." He returned on July 3 and remained in Lancaster until August 1858.

Sherman looked back with pride at his success in retaining a reputation for integrity during this whole sorry episode. Yet he felt racked with guilt at the financial losses he had inflicted on many of his old army friends, especially Ethan Allen Hitchcock. He had placed their monies in a separate trust fund and in Hitchcock's case had assumed power of attorney. He had no legal obligation to do so, but he undertook to pay them all back, just as his father had done under similar circumstances in the 1820s; the sum amounted to about $20,000. When combined with the losses sustained in the purchase of the house on Rincon Hill, this was an onerous financial burden that Sherman assumed while depressed and in poor health. With Ellen's help he paid these debts by selling property in San Francisco, Kansas, and Illinois. "I am going to quit [the commercial world] clean-handed—not a cent in my pocket. I know this is not modern banking, but better be honest."[20]

Thomas Ewing did his best to rescue his son-in-law's fortunes, first offering him a job at his salt wells at Chauncey, Ohio, which Sherman declined, and then suggesting he manage Ewing property interests in Fort Leavenworth, Kansas, which he accepted. Ellen showed real enthusiasm for living there because they could reside cheaply in a Ewing property on Third and Pottawotomie Streets. She loathed the long separations from her husband,

and at least the entire family was united. Sherman entered into a law partnership with Tom Ewing Jr., and they opened an office in Leavenworth. Sherman aimed to concentrate on business aspects, collections, agencies, and real estate. Ellen warned him that Tom's real interest lay in politics, and, being self-absorbed, he might neglect his duties.

The practice made little money, and Sherman, not a qualified lawyer, thought it best to gain a license, which he presumed would involve a course of study. He was surprised when a local judge admitted him instantly on "grounds of general intelligence." Another lawyer, Daniel McCook, joined the firm on January 1, 1859. Sherman took on additional jobs to make ends meet. His old classmate Captain Stewart Van Vliet, quartermaster at Fort Leavenworth, gave him a job auctioneering surplus army equipment at Fort Riley. Sherman expressed chagrin at the unfortunate turn of events, and Van reacted more sympathetically than Ellen. When Sherman burst out that "I regret I ever left the Army" and applied for any available field commission in 1857 and again in 1858, she wrote shortly, "Please do not mention the army to me again unless you have made up your mind that we are not worth working for." She did express pleasure that Van Vliet had "favoured you with such agreeable work," but she did not wish to resume a wandering life. Sherman also ran a farm for Thomas Ewing Sr. that, he recalled, "passed the time but afforded little profit." This phase of his career ended without success when he returned to Lancaster in July 1859, oppressed by his inability to earn a living for his family and feeling "I am doomed to be a vagabond" weighed down by debt. Ellen had also become pregnant again, adding to the pressure to provide. Another daughter, Eleanor Mary, "Elly," arrived on September 5.[21]

Then Sherman's fortunes took a turn for the better. On June 17, 1859, Don Carlos Buell replied to a query he had made concerning possible vacancies in the Paymaster's Department by sending him details of positions available at the Louisiana State Seminary (later Louisiana State University) in Alexandria in central Louisiana. If Sherman were awarded one of the professorships and appointed superintendent, he would enjoy a salary of $3,500. "If you think well of it," Buell wrote, then he would write to Vice President G. Mason Graham (to whom he was related) "such a letter as will secure you a valuable advocate at first and a useful supporter afterwards." The range of posts advertised attracted 100 applications; Sherman's for the position of superintendent and chair of engineering ranked among the shortest. Graham expressed admiration for the substance of his credentials. In an editorial he wrote for the *Louisiana Democrat*, he praised Sherman as "a man of great firmness and

discretion eminently remarkable for his executive and administrative qualities," but interestingly, the description that comes first is "a scholar, soldier
and gentleman." In his letter congratulating Sherman on his appointment in
August, Graham wrote accurately that "a great deal will devolve upon you."
In truth, this post was perfect for a man of Sherman's qualities, interests, and,
indeed, sensibilities.[22]

Graham had attended West Point, and though he did not graduate, he
had ever since expressed "unlimited admiration" for the academy and its
methods. He sought to re-create them in a college that he hoped would
resemble the Virginia Military Institute (VMI) in Lexington, Virginia.
Sherman described the seminary's newly completed building as "a gorgeous
palace," and he and Graham dedicated themselves to providing a practical
education that would equip Louisianans for their future careers and make
a positive contribution to the state's economy. Graham had considered the
seminary as "a scientific and literary institution under a military system of
government," a curious hybrid. Sherman emphasized that "we want the development of as much literary talent as possible." He simultaneously elevated
mathematics, urging that their teaching be "thorough and not superficial."
He hoped the fusion would be created by practicality.

Sherman wrote to George B. McClellan, one of West Point's most glittering
graduates and president of the eastern division of the Ohio and Mississippi
Railroad, asking for advice on building the curriculum and on textbooks.
McClellan replied that it would be impossible to have a West Point–style
summer camp in Alexandria, a view that Sherman shared. McClellan
also made some sensible suggestions concerning "practical instruction,"
with more attention being given to the precise use of instruments in sur-
veying, astronomy, topography, field sketches, and railway engineering. He
recommended Alexander Holley and Zerah Colburn's technical work on coal-
burning boilers in locomotives on European railways (1858) and Randolph
B. Marcy's *The Prairie Traveler: A Handbook for Overland Expeditions* (1859),
as it conveyed valuable information on camps and looking after animals and
equipment on the prairies. But all this only concerned the margins of the curriculum. Sherman still believed that the utilitarian approach could light his
way. He intended "to control the system of studies to make it a more practical
school than any hereabouts."[23]

While addressing some of the weaknesses of the West Point syllabus, particularly its excessive technocratic bias and neglect of the arts and humanities, Sherman advanced on a broad front. In one area he made immediate

progress. He insisted that all staff were present a month before term started to ensure a smooth opening. He also made it a priority to "impress the cadets with our kindness, justness and fairness"; he also sought to "give them a manly bearing, good ideas of truth, honor, and courtesy, and withal teach them practical wisdom." And this "good seed," he argued, would spread beyond the confines of the academy. As he had no teaching duties, "all the details of discipline and management" lay in his hands.

Sherman had not selected his staff, so he had to make the best of what he had. The most senior by far, the only member of staff with a higher degree, was Dr. Anthony Vallas, professor of mathematics, who had previously worked at the Royal University and Academy of Science in Pest, Hungary. The other scientist, "a very handsome young man of twenty-two," as Sherman described him, was Francis W. Smith, a graduate of the VMI and the University of Virginia, who held the chair of chemistry, mineralogy, and geology. The remaining staff came from the humanities: E. Berté St. Ange, formerly of Charlemagne College, Paris, occupied the chair of modern languages, and David F. Boyd served as professor of English and ancient languages. Together the academic staff formed the academic board. As Vallas and St. Ange were "foreigners," Sherman informed Boyd, "I shall, therefore, count much on your capacity of teaching and social qualities." Sherman delegated authority to him, and he served as deputy in his absence. Sherman's eye for talent did not desert him, as Boyd went on to become president of the institution.[24]

Sherman worked in a quasi-military institution with procedures concerning turnout, dress, and discipline reminiscent of West Point. He enjoyed the honorary rank of colonel in the Louisiana militia. But he did not delude himself, despite all these trappings, that he had returned to the army.

Shortly after accepting the Alexandria post he received a request from Captain George Cullum for biographical information to be included in a (much-delayed) dictionary of West Point's graduates. Sherman complied with a "sketch" of what he called "a rather checkered career"; in remarking that he had "never been badly hurt," he observed "that on the whole my career has been more Civil than Military" and saw no reason for this state to change. His cadets were more likely to enter civil professions or universities. Sherman had become an educator at a time when American social thought elevated the "practical man"; the intellect and the "speculative" provoked suspicion. He escaped this by quickly embracing the argument that science and technology afforded tools whereby Nature could be mastered and an entire continent subjugated. Sherman identified strongly with these impulses without surrendering to crude, preemptive anti-intellectualism. Such pressures persuaded him to gradually embrace a concept that recognized the intimate association of thought and action. The tension between thoughts and deeds is frequently latent: the demands of practice outrun the comfortable nostrums of thought.[25]

During the 1850s, despite many preoccupations and distractions, Sherman read two important books on the practice of war, Sir William Napier's *History of the War in the Peninsula* and Baron Jomini's *Summary of the Art of War* in the augmented French edition of 1855. Napier's book is a brilliant narrative of the drama, conceived in terms of the clash of regular armies. Although he neglects guerrilla war, the very nature of this bloody struggle requires him occasionally to acknowledge the "shameful" acts of the French armies. At the time, Sherman agreed with Napier's denunciations, but he would only grasp their significance later. Jomini's book is literally a summary, of the thinking underlying his eight-volume history of the campaigns of Frederick the Great and Napoleon. Jomini agreed that strategy could only be determined by immutable principles of war that never altered. "Military science," he avers, "rests upon principles which can never be violated"; plans might be formulated "as circumstances may demand," but their execution had to take the principles into account. "War," Jomini concluded rather enigmatically, "in its ensemble, is not a science but an art." Still, his paradoxical treatment fitted the prevailing outlook in America that accepted that "sublime precepts of revealed truth" determined mankind's actions: "those fundamental principles, which govern the affairs of states, countries and nations." Sherman thus received assurance of the validity of his notion that practical knowledge should be a lodestone and that preparation for war could be improved by scientific method. His thought here reflected French teaching that the higher art of generalship could be treated like a higher "science" or branch of philosophy.

What is so striking about Sherman's reactions to the world of the 1850s is his marked indifference to religion. The "Third Great Awakening" of 1857–58 had no effect on Sherman—unlike McClellan, who took to reading the Bible every day. Despite this indifference, Sherman recognized that life consisted of more than calculation and intricate weighing of quantities. Elucidating "certainty" always remained important to him. Sherman gave ample evidence of his skill in this regard and his grip on detail when setting up the Louisiana Seminary. In a display of logistical skill, he bought up in 1859 "blankets, brooms, glass tumblers, soap, wash basins and dippers and mattresses"; all would determine not just the comfort of the cadets but "the price of every-thing needed by us in the future." The following year he ordered 14 boxes of textbooks, 80 rolls of bedding, and 60 hundredweight of sundries and urged Boyd "to write to him very fully . . . that I might act with the greatest chance of economy and certainty." The Whig emphasis on disciplined inquiry and painstaking consideration never left him. It had never been better expressed than by a former Whig congressman, Abraham Lincoln, then making a name for himself as Republican: "Reason, cold, calculating, unimpassioned reason, must furnish all the material for our future support and defence," he said in an early speech.[26]

Yet education and leadership demanded more than just rationality and calculation. At the age of 38 Sherman enjoyed the benefit of a humane and cultured mind. Ever since attending his first dramatic production at the Park Theatre as a cadet in 1836, he had been in love with the theater; innumerable sea journeys departing from New York allowed him to maintain a close ac-quaintance with Broadway's theaterland. It is likely that he befriended the actors John McCullough and Lawrence Barrett in the 1850s; both would be-come famous. He liked opera, symphony concerts, and the ballet, describing the latter to Henry Turner as an "intellectual exhibition," and he had patron-ized San Francisco theaters as well. His literary tastes were overwhelmingly British. Above all others towered William Shakespeare, whose great works plumbed the depths of depravity in human motivation but also scaled the heights of its nobility, while offering a moral guide to the uses and abuses of power and fame. For Sherman, as for many other Americans, a knowl-edge of Shakespeare denoted a cultured and sophisticated student of human nature. Sherman also read and reread voraciously the novels of Charles Dickens, a remarkably dramatic writer, with brilliant dialogue and arresting scenes. Close behind him, with similar qualities and an acute historical sen-sibility, ran William M. Thackeray. Other English or Scottish writers he fa-vored included Oliver Goldsmith, Sir Walter Scott, Robert Louis Stevenson, and Robbie Burns. In addition to presenting the unvarnished truth, Burns also gave incomparable expression to the nature of romantic love, to which, though he often tried to hide it, Sherman was far from indifferent. Sherman did read American authors like Washington Irving and Henry Wadsworth Longfellow, for instance, but Ellen referred to British writers as his "heroes."[27]

Sherman's drive and energy made their mark in the seminary's early days. The number of cadets slowly increased from 24 to 120 by November 1860. Progress had been made on all fronts. Sherman had even negotiated a 10 percent discount on textbooks in return for cash, though the French and Latin grammars still arrived late. He had overcome inertia, as "people do not work hard down here." In February 1860 a job application that Sherman had virtually forgotten was unexpectedly revived. William F. Roelofson, on behalf of a syndicate, offered him $15,000 to move to London, England, for two years as an investment banker "to look after bonds." There could be no doubt that Sherman preferred the "certainty and stability" of the Louisiana post, but Thomas Ewing favored Roelofson's proposal and intervened on his behalf. Ellen preferred the idea of London to Louisiana. Sherman laid down his terms to stay. He asked Graham for a salary increase to $5,000 and an increase in the seminary's endowment to $25,000 for two years that would allow him to invest in projects without being dependent on income from the cadets' fees. "I can't afford to run any more risks," he warned his father-in-law, "and have been buffeted about enough." Sherman resigned on March 1, 1859, but gave himself a month before it took effect to sort out his affairs, because he no longer trusted financial proposals. Like a whirlwind he returned to Ohio to consult all parties; in the meantime, Graham worked frantically on behalf of his "irreplaceable" superintendent. On hearing the glad tidings that the board of supervisors had agreed to his terms, Sherman withdrew his resignation and turned down the London proposal. He reported proudly that the cadets "are as proud as peacocks and have hailed my return as though I was their grandfather." Alas, within a month Sherman had cause "to regret my sudden refusal of the Roelofson proposal."[28]

During 1860 Sherman's seemingly impregnable position, not just at the seminary but as a figure respected more broadly in the state, began to crumble. The first serious blow came at the beginning of the year when his brother John carelessly endorsed Hinton Rowan Helper's book, *The Impending Crisis of the South* (1859), though he had not read it. Helper's book had become notorious in the slave states because he blamed the planter class for the poverty and backwardness of the region that he attributed to slavery; it enriched the few and impoverished the many. John could not even remember endorsing it, but his act damaged Sherman, especially with the new secessionist governor, Thomas O. Moore. Sherman did not lack allies, not least Graham; Braxton Bragg, his old company commander, intervened to "vouch for your soundness in any and all ways." Indeed, Bragg had gained a further increase of $4,500 in Sherman's salary by preparing a bill to open a state arsenal at the seminary with Sherman in charge of it.[29]

Sherman's attitude to slavery and slaveholders revealed some ambivalence. He regarded the latter to be "as big fools as the abolitionists," and he assured Ellen, "I will not go with the South because with slavery and the whole civilized world opposed to it, they in case of leaving the Union," he wrote accurately, "will have worse wars and tumults than now distinguish Mexico." But he did not wish to see the slave system dismantled. "Two such races," he wrote with unjustified dogmatism, "cannot live in harmony save as master and slave." He had obviously imbibed the views of his Southern white friends. In April 1861 he declared that Southern slavery was "the mildest and best regulated system of slavery in the world, now or heretofore." Sherman had only ever met domestic slaves and not field hands, and such views reflected both the limits of his knowledge and his readiness to parrot the views of his Louisiana neighbors.[30]

In the spring of 1860 the critics of the military system and the scientific bias of the seminary's curriculum grew more strident. They found allies in Dr. S. A. Smith and Governor Moore on the board of supervisors. Though a scientist himself, Dr. Anthony Vallas emerged as Sherman's foremost critic and aligned himself with those who wished to see more attention given to the arts and humanities. Sherman responding by arguing that the military system was "the truly watchful, parental system instead of the neglectful one of common academies." Braxton Bragg wholly approved of Sherman's desire to produce a "reformation" among the spoiled, unruly, violent Southern products of the plantation. During these months Sherman had dealt with problems of insubordination, brawling—when a bowie knife had been drawn—and supposed public drunkenness, with admirable firmness and discretion. But his prompt action permitted Vallas to complain that the superintendent acted in a high-handed manner. As a colonel, Sherman retorted, he should be able to command the cadets through a system of appointed noncommissioned officers and control the staff. But at a meeting of the board of supervisors held in August 1860, the voices of Governor Moore and Smith prevailed. The board decided that it constituted a "standing court" on disciplinary matters and could overrule the superintendent's decisions. Furthermore, it agreed that the academic board also had a voice on disciplinary matters. Finally, the supervisors decided that the arts and humanities should be given more attention. In response, Vice President Graham resigned, though he remained a member of the board. In his report in January 1861 Sherman feared that the load imposed on the cadets by extending the syllabus could not be borne and was "calculated to make imperfect and superficial scholars."[31]

It could not be a coincidence that Sherman's decline in influence and authority occurred as the secession crisis became more ferocious. The crisis had begun with the unilateral secession of South Carolina on December 20, 1860, a month after Abraham Lincoln was elected president. The secession of Mississippi followed on January 9, 1861, and Alabama two days later. While Louisiana remained in the Union, Sherman reassured Graham, he would continue to serve the state faithfully, but if it seceded, "that instant I stop." Sherman followed the developing confrontation over the status of Forts Sumter and Moultrie in Charleston harbor with fascinated horror. He lamented the pusillanimity of the Buchanan administration that remained in office until March 1861. The federal commander, Major Robert Anderson, "my old captain at my old post," became a symbol of Union defiance. Anderson's decision, taken on his own initiative, to abandon Moultrie and withdraw to the more defensible Sumter on December 26, 1860, heightened the tension. Sherman feared for Anderson's safety; the forces surrounding him were commanded by P. G. T. Beauregard, who had sent his sons to the seminary and proven a friendly ally while Sherman built up its reputation. No matter: should they "hurt a hair of his head," then "Charleston should be blotted from existence." The enormity of the issues combined with a bitter sense of personal betrayal encouraged Sherman to indulge this kind of violent, exposed rhetoric. Sherman's friend Bragg understood his dilemma. He sensed the future "may throw us into an apparent hostile attitude," but the idea so appalled him that "I will not discuss it."[32]

Louisiana passed an ordinance of secession on January 26, 1861. Even before this inauspicious event, secessionists had seized federal property, including arms. Sherman considered such outrages "acts of war and a breach of common decency." But his acceptance of responsibility for the arsenal at Alexandria put him on the spot. On January 18 he wrote to Governor Moore a taut letter that conveyed his dilemma clearly. He occupied a "quasi-military position under the laws of the state," yet his reluctance to acquiesce in illegal seizures of federal property rendered it wholly "wrong in every sense of the word" for him to remain as superintendent, and he asked to be relieved. Moore's earlier maneuvers made his resignation easier. As Sherman observed pointedly, the "present professors can manage well enough" without him. The board of supervisors passed a vaguely worded resolution of "sincere regret" at his departure, but his oft-stated loyalty to the Union had left him no alternative to resignation, and they must have sighed with relief after he had departed. There could be no doubt, however, as Sherman instantly recognized, that "I will be the chief loser." He was owed $500 and had spent $200 of his own money traveling back and forth to New York.[33]

His loss could not be calculated in merely material terms, though he received some reimbursement later. Sherman had sustained a severe blow, as circumstances had again conspired against him and overthrown his hopes. With them went the dream of creating a true family home in Alexandria for all his children. "The house itself looks beautiful," he rhapsodized to his eldest daughter, Minnie, at the end of 1860. Yet he had to face the hard reality that "Man proposes and God disposes. . . . The dream and hope of my life, that we could all be together once more in a home of our own, . . . all, I fear, is about to vanish, and again I fear I must be a wanderer, leaving you all to grow up at Lancaster without your papa." Then, in reflections unsuitable for a 9-year-old child, as he acknowledged later, he lashed out at the hysterical, indiscriminate search for enemies provoked by Southern newspapers who stirred the rash stampede toward secession. This produced "blind and crazy" men who "think all the people of Ohio are trying to steal their slaves and incite them to rise up and kill their masters." After his experience in California, Sherman had developed a profound contempt for fevered accusations— "when people believe a delusion, they believe it harder than a real fact." Only years later would he understand that his portrait of slavery as "mild" was no less illusory. White Southerners sought to blame everybody but themselves for their troubles and found a bromide in secession; to turn back might invite catastrophe.[34]

Sherman's failure in Louisiana followed a long line of failures, as he saw it, as a soldier and as a civilian. He missed out on the laurels of the Mexican War and in the mid-1850s failed to embrace the business ethos wholeheartedly. In Louisiana he failed in his efforts to re-create a military life in an academic context. Sometimes he only had himself to blame, but in Louisiana he discovered that he could still fail no matter how hard he worked or how ingenious were his solutions to the problems he faced. Despite the strength of his character, the number of his connections, and the wide respect he enjoyed, something always held him back from seizing the moment; perhaps his moment had not yet come. Even in February 1861 he did not long indulge self-pity. He did become more cynical about his failures. When he considered moving to London the year before, he joked that "I think my arrival in London will be the signal of the downfall of that mighty empire."[35]

Failure toughened Sherman with a hard, protective shell that could leave the impression of brusque coldness—despite his emotional, excitable, affectionate, and voluble nature. By 1861 he could appear gruff and intolerant. Ellen noticed this tendency and did not welcome it. "And you know," she counseled in the spring of 1859, "that you always make it a point to conceal your feelings and as far as possible to have none." Sherman's aloofness did not prevent him from making new friends or keeping old ones. "No matter what happens I will always consider you my personal friend," he reassured Boyd in spring 1861, "and you shall ever be welcome to my roof." In retrospect, California served as the crossroads of his life. There he made many friends and acquaintances, all of whom would exert a decisive influence on the course of his life, including Halleck, Hooker, and his former legal counsel Bowman, who cowrote the first major book about him. California and, to a lesser extent, Louisiana also agitated his prejudices. His vitriolic attacks on the irrationality of public opinion, the irresponsibility of the press, and the venality of reporters, as well as his slight acquaintance with slavery: all would distort his opinions in the years to come.[36]

His military education did not end after he resigned from the army. After Halleck, he was probably the best-read ex-officer in civil life. He had also been a witness to the success and length of General Kearny's march across the West to California. He also recognized from the first that should war come, "superior arms and numbers are the elements of war and must prevail." But these thoughts were half formed at best. If civil war broke out he would greet it with caution and skepticism, and perhaps try to mind his own business and evade its entanglements.

PART II
WORKING HIS WAY
March 1861–March 1864

4

Brigade Commander, March–August 1861

Sherman was on the move again. On February 24, 1861, he departed New Orleans with a clear conscience but not without regret. He took a train to Jackson and Clinton, Mississippi, changed for Jackson, Tennessee, and Columbus, Kentucky, took a steamboat from Columbus to Cairo, via St. Louis, and then caught another train to Lancaster via Cincinnati. He arrived in Lancaster on March 1. The journey eroded his spirit as well as his constitution. The rhythm of the train had been disturbed by "warm discussions about politics." Sherman noticed Southern readiness for war and could only compare this adversely with Northern apathy and half measures; henceforth this asymmetry would dominate his outlook on the burgeoning conflict. While on board the steamboat, Sherman had written gloomily, "Political matters are certainly as bad as possible, and I see no immediate chances of a favorable change—I fear all the Slave States will secede, for they seem to await Legislation for which there is neither time or inclination." With virtually no chance of a successful political compromise, violence seemed inevitable. Sherman added caustically, "If the Politicians would do the fighting it would be a good thing but when that comes they are the first to run away." Like many of his contemporaries, he blamed what appeared to him as a quite avoidable crisis on the machinations of selfish and unscrupulous professional politicians.[1]

Sherman may have been contemptuous of this conniving tribe, but his own prospects were enhanced by the welcome news that his brother John would succeed Salmon P. Chase, recently named secretary of the treasury, as an Ohio senator. Sherman warned John that supporters of the senior senator, Benjamin F. Wade, were lukewarm toward him, fearing that he might damage Wade's chances of reelection in 1862. Sherman thought this opposition could be overcome, and he wished him success "because of the more honourable, dignified and less laborious position as Senator, as contrasted with your present Post [congressman]." Sherman always held that the pettiness, meanness, and skulduggery of American politics stemmed from the electoral process. As senators were then elected not by the popular vote but by a majority in a state legislature, they did not have to mount elaborate statewide campaigns. John had only to maintain his support within the party caucus in Columbus, Ohio. "Kick all platforms & old part [sic] precedents to the Devil," Sherman implored his brother, "and look the Questions that now threaten our national Existence square in the face—and generally aim to be a U.S. Statesman instead of a mere republican, a mere partizan."[2]

Sherman could give these matters only cursory attention because the restoration of his own fortunes had to take priority. He faced up to the implications for himself of the imminent political disorganization most unwillingly. He intended to leave Lancaster at the earliest opportunity and "take all the family and household Goods" to the one other place where he felt truly at home, St. Louis. Sherman's return to Lancaster exposed a continued dependence on the Ewings and underlined yet again his own failure at age 41 to make his way in the world. In January 1861 Ellen had urged on her husband "a money making thing for you" if he would take over running her father's salt works at Chauncey, Ohio, as Thomas Ewing Sr. had invested a further $10,000; they could "be happy together yet." But Sherman could not accept such an offer when still hoping for the possibility of doing what he had always hankered after—returning to the army.[3]

Sherman's plan relied on Missouri remaining loyal to the Union. If he should find himself once more in a seceded state, then he might as well have stayed in Louisiana. "I am also certain of some break-up of our present Confederacy",[4] he confided, "but to what Extent [I] cannot foresee—and violence must ensue." He considered Missouri "physically bound" to the northwestern states, then formed of Illinois, Indiana, and Ohio, "and cannot break off without sure & certain strife within her borders." A good friend, Thomas Tasker Gantt, a St. Louis attorney and former law partner of Lincoln's postmaster general, Montgomery Blair, had promised to keep Sherman informed when Missouri had rejected secession before he moved and attempted to remake his life. "I see nothing definite to do—but still," he observed defiantly with a sarcastic jab at the prospect of working in his foster father's salt business, ". . . am not willing to move my family down to the Salt Wells, where they would grow up in rudeness and without future."

Early efforts came to nothing. Sherman applied to be the treasurer of St. Louis and hoped Gantt could persuade the state's most powerful political dynasty, the Blairs, to smile on the application. But the main political power in the state, Francis Preston Blair Jr. (Postmaster General Blair's son), resented the intrusion of a representative of a rival out-of-state political clan, the Ewings, and ensured that Sherman's application would fail. Sherman resented his opposition but proved powerless to circumvent it; he would not forget this gratuitous setback. "I am the only Northern man who has declared fidelity to the Union," he grumbled to John, "in opposition to this modern anarchical doctrine of State Secession—and yet this is nothing as compared to local partizans service." Certainly Sherman had sacrificed his livelihood, but his behavior over the next two months would render this sense of high moral indignation difficult to sustain.[5]

The great national crisis worried many, but such calamities always present opportunities to those willing to remake their lives. On his return to Lancaster, Sherman faced a choice. Two letters had been awaiting him. The first letter came from his brother John. He urged Sherman to travel at once to Washington, DC, where he could introduce him to President Lincoln, who could offer him a suitable command. Ellen had urged on John the duty of finding his brother a "high position" in the regular army. She shrewdly observed that her husband would never be happy in civil life. But the second letter Sherman opened offered him the choice of remaining a civilian. This letter had been written by his friend Major Henry S. Turner and offered him the presidency of the Fifth Street Railroad, a company specializing in streetcars; he also offered a salary of $2,500, not an overwhelming sum, but one that would go a long way to covering his expenses.

Initially, Sherman accepted his brother's invitation, not slow to make use of the political connections that he condemned in others, though his experience would not be a happy one. The early days of a presidential administration could often be chaotic, and Lincoln's did not buck the trend. On March 10 Sherman arrived in the capital and could see few signs of organized preparation for war but heard much talk, some of it candidly treasonous. His brother took him to the Executive Mansion and introduced him to the president, and he came away unimpressed. Sherman noted that Lincoln's main concern appeared to be party matters, especially the distribution of the patronage to deserving Republicans. In Sherman's view the president's questions did not rise to the occasion. When John mentioned that his brother had recently returned from Louisiana and might supply Lincoln with useful information, the president asked casually, "Ah! How are they getting along down there?" Sherman replied rather shortly, "They think they are getting along swimmingly—they are preparing for war." "Oh well," Lincoln replied languidly, "I guess we'll manage to keep house." Sherman's superior manner in turn failed to impress the president, and nothing came of this ill-starred meeting. On leaving, Sherman once more blamed politicians as a class for the current crisis and wished a plague on all their houses. Lincoln might have judged Sherman's praise of the preparedness of his former associates as yet another example of the counsel of despair to which he had already been treated.

"No military man will place his life & honor in jeopardy," Sherman fulminated to John on returning to Lancaster, "for the sake of a weak temporizing & partizan Government." Lincoln seemed to Sherman the partisan-in-chief. The result could only be yet more muddle and confusion. Jefferson Davis had not made the same mistake; he hurried to enlist the services of the "very best officers—South and *North*"—and paid no attention to party affiliations. Lincoln, he thought, had made "a fatal mistake in giving the Cold shoulder to all national men, as compared with mere politicians." Sherman feared the vulnerability of party loyalties to swings in public opinion; governments were prone to follow the course of demoralizing extremes, and they abandoned too readily "the Great Centre on which must depend the Future of this Country." Sherman would write several weeks after his meeting with Lincoln that the president had intimated "that military men were not wanted"; this seems unlikely, unless it refers to regular officers rather than volunteers. It was John's reaction, too, though this notion might have become fixed by his brother's constant reiteration of it. Sherman had been repelled by the lack of order and decision in a government where "the real power [lies] in some obscure evening paper." He decided that he would abstain from the war and put his own interests first.[6]

Sherman objected to the way that officers like himself had been treated. "I will not identify myself with a Partizan Government," he repeated insistently. In actual fact, Sherman's impression of Lincoln and his administration was too hurried and too harsh. Lincoln offered many commissions to his Democratic opponents and would be criticized by his own supporters for the extent of his generosity. While Sherman castigated politicians for their selfish ways, he did not neglect to warn John of the danger he ran after failing to introduce Thomas Ewing Jr. to the president. As Sherman's brother-in-law, Tom Ewing Jr., then chief justice of the Kansas Territory, was in a strong position to secure a senatorial seat after Kansas was admitted to the Union as a state, he worried lest John had made a dangerous enemy so soon after his entry to the Senate.

Sherman also revealed to John, "All the Ewings think you have slighted me—that your mere demand would have secured me anything." Such an eruption of family tensions had its source in an offer of the chief clerkship of the War Department sent to Sherman on April 6 by Montgomery Blair after discussions with Salmon Chase. Sherman and his Ewing foster family were unanimous in regarding this invitation well "beneath my Deserts [and] certainly a shock to my pride." Another indication of the level of their disgust came a month later when Sherman wrote to Tom Ewing, who nursed his own grievance against John, "You know enough of the social status of a Washington office-holder to appreciate my feelings" and understand his wish to decline the offer. He also preferred to see his family starve than go on bended knee to Frank Blair; all the Blairs were, in any case, "a selfish and unscrupulous set of ——." This reaction again was too hasty. Blair's intention had been to place a firm, industrious, and trustworthy administrator under the careless, indolent, and corrupt first secretary of war, Simon Cameron. Blair also promised Sherman an assistant secretaryship once Congress assembled in July. Had Sherman accepted this offer, he would have been in a strong position to inherit the War Department after Cameron's removal on January 13, 1862.[7]

The Southern bombardment of Fort Sumter, in Charleston harbor, on April 12–13 triggered the civil war that Sherman dreaded. Lincoln issued a proclamation calling for 75,000 volunteers to serve for three months "to suppress" illegal "combinations." Sherman repeatedly refused to serve in the volunteers, because such a commitment to a force very distant from the great army that he thought necessary for the task would prevent him from securing remunerative employment without the salvation of permanency. "I know any foul mouth scamp of a sub editor will be preferred to any amount of professional skill." He preferred to play a waiting game. He did not blame his brother for the lack of an offer appropriate to his talents; he continued to urge him to look out for something in St. Louis that might be preferable.[8]

After various Washington disappointments, Sherman decided to accept Turner's offer of civil employment. On March 27 "off I went" to St. Louis, he recorded laconically, followed by an unenthusiastic Ellen, the children, and all the furniture. The choice finally made, he could reject Montgomery Blair's offer of the War Department chief clerkship in lofty language, as he was "not at liberty to change." He took a house on Locust Street, and his brother-in-law Charley and his new law partner, John Hunter, agreed to lodge on the third floor. Sherman had taken an important step toward restoring his family finances, though its effect was diluted by Ellen's rapid purchase of expensive new carpets and furniture to keep her in the style to which she had become accustomed. Also, Sherman's taking up a new civil job at such a time of travail could be regarded as controversial. An eminent Missourian, Edward Bates, the new attorney general, was unimpressed. He claimed Sherman was a rich man looking for further enrichment, who had succeeded in finding a comfortable billet to enjoy himself.[9]

Sherman reacted defensively when he heard Bates's denunciation of his selfishness. He argued that his act of self-sacrifice in Louisiana had not been appreciated. (He had some justice on his side here, as other Northerners like John C. Pemberton and Josiah Gorgas, who had made marriages and careers in the South, became Confederates.) John Sherman also showed signs of growing exasperation with his contrary brother, who asked him, on arrival in St. Louis, to secure a commission, preferably in the cavalry, for Turner's son Thomas. As for his own prospects, he seemed to be opting out. He sent John a detailed note on his finances to show that he was not wealthy, although he inaccurately listed his salary as $2,000. He then insisted that his new position would not allow him to accept anything less than the rank of brigadier general or the position of inspector general.

To David Boyd, with whom he continued to correspond on friendly terms, he conveyed a measure of John's annoyance. Sherman believed that John considered him "erratic in politics"; Sherman persisted in trying to retain the moral high ground by suggesting that professional politicians failed to fathom a man like himself "who thinks himself above parties and looks upon the petty machinery of party as disgusting. There are great numbers here who think like me." But a good many more could be found in the South. Sherman's last sentence might indeed be true, but his move to St. Louis had been motivated by pecuniary self-interest, not a rejection of the patronage system that had so far failed him. "Politics" for Sherman, as for so many other officers of his generation, appears as an activity that others indulged in, not him. Politicians, moreover, assumed the form of a moral scapegoat on whom he could always blame his ills, even if they were of his own making.[10]

In 1861, however, conservatives like Sherman persuaded themselves that slavery had played no part in the coming of the war, and thus its destruction should have no part in the war's conduct. Sherman feared abolitionists as the bringers of anarchy. They would hurtle the United States into a maelstrom of political convulsions. Sherman admitted that "slavery was the cause for a severance of the Union," but he still could find no fault with the peculiar institution itself. He had for several years accepted the Southern case that slavery had assumed a humane form, but he utterly rejected demands for its expansion into the territories; "the line of separation should be drawn before rather than after settlement."[11]

Accordingly, he did not believe that free labor and slavery were inconsistent. To admit this point would concede a prima facie case for secession. The United States needed a government that could reconcile and protect *both* systems of labor. It should call a halt to its further disintegration, "assert the integrity of the Nation and fight for it. The longer it is postponed the worse it will be." Sherman thus assumed that during the resultant conflict a distinction could be maintained, namely, that "on the Slavery Question as much forbearance should be made as possible, but on the Doctrine of Secession, *none* whatever. They are widely different."

At this date, Sherman believed passionately that if the two elements were allowed to coalesce, then catastrophic anarchy would result. Four million black slaves would be "turned loose," and the conflict would "become a War of Extermination a war without End." His own position was thus unambiguous, even though he had yet to commit himself unreservedly to the Northern war effort. "On the necessity of maintaining a Government and that Govt. a Constitutional one, I have never wavered—but I do recoil from a war when the negro is the only question." Those of a like mind to Sherman thought this ideology enough: they were committed to the defense of the finest system of government yet created, a beacon of liberty—even though this beacon shone only on one side, for on the other the flame had been extinguished by the muck thrown up by the defense of the right to own human beings as chattels. To this aspect Sherman turned an indifferent face.[12]

Life at Locust Street began to develop a routine. On April 1 Sherman began his new job. The Fifth Street Railroad immediately felt the benefit of his forceful presence as he cut costs by reducing the workforce and overheads. Yet though Sherman had chosen to concentrate on domestic prosperity, public affairs kept breaking in to disturb his tranquility. Sherman took no part in the dramatic events that ensured that Missouri would remain loyal to the Union. The Blairs, especially Frank Jr., and Nathaniel Lyon, a young and determined regular officer who displayed unqualified zeal for the Union cause, pushed themselves to the front of the stage. "At a moment like this the country expects every man to do his duty," Sherman pleaded feebly. "But every man is not at liberty to do as he pleases." After three weeks Sherman reported to his brother that life had been "squally" of late, with the good citizens of St. Louis "alarmed by all sorts of Reports." Both Blair and Lyon were determined to protect the nearby US arsenal that housed 60,000 muskets and a million and a half ball cartridges, various items of machinery, and some cannon; for these to fall into rebel hands would be unthinkable. Brigadier General Daniel M. Frost and 700 militia, supporters of Missouri's prosecessionist governor, Claiborne Jackson, approached the city intent on seizing the arsenal and precipitating the passage of an ordinance of secession. Frank Blair Jr. had set up an unofficial committee of public safety, in effect a counterrevolutionary body; he also enlisted 10,000 St. Louis citizens into federal service by irregular means, mostly ardent Unionist antislavery Germans, who were the bedrock of the state's Republican Party.[13]

Sherman did not entirely approve of Blair's energetic action. He thought Blair "rabid" and believed he "would not stop till the whole Country is convulsed—and slavery abolished everywhere." Such comments mirror the complaints of other conservatives who continued to serve in the army or former regulars who contemplated open warfare with the greatest reluctance. Sherman did not rally to the colors determined to do what it took to sustain the government. Instead he denigrated the efforts of "Lincoln's Vice Roy" and "his Lager Beer friends"; he had a personal grudge against Frank Jr. and was happy to hold him responsible should violence break out in Missouri. News on April 16 of the Virginia convention's vote for secession depressed Sherman because "feeling and prejudice are much stronger than Reason," yet he stood aside while Missouri Unionists acted to prevent the same happening in Missouri. If they failed, then the result could only be "Free States against Slave. The horrible array so long dreaded."

John Sherman had continued to lobby hard for his brilliant but wayward brother. The rank of major general of volunteers to organize and direct Ohio's state forces seemed perfect for him. Sherman was not so sure. He claimed that the Buckeye State had never shown him any favor or encouragement, and he had not lived there since boyhood. Understandably, John was upset by his brother's tepid reaction and his own wasted effort. It almost came as a relief to Sherman to hear that George B. McClellan had accepted the appointment. He still remained fearful in case his aloof attitude should be "misunderstood in Ohio"; indeed, a public rejection of the position might have provoked accusations that he harbored treasonous sympathies in the paranoid post-Sumter atmosphere. Sherman claimed that he could still afford to "await events," but he relied on excuses in an effort to soothe a ruffled John, such as his inability to win elections among the men he might command because of the short period of time he had spent in Ohio. At this early stage in the war, volunteer soldiers retained the right to elect their officers and non-commissioned officers.[14]

Sherman's attitude might have been prudent but was hardly heroic. The extent to which he lurked in the background as a spectator is revealed in the final, dramatic conclusion to the struggle to bind Missouri to the Union. At the end of April Sherman was summoned from his bed in the middle of the night and offered by Frank Blair Jr. the rank of brigadier general of volunteers and command of the Department of Missouri. The incumbent, Brigadier General William S. Harney, had been arrested by Confederates at Harpers Ferry while en route to Washington, DC, for consultations. Lyon, whose substantive rank was captain, had caused alarm among the Committee of Public Safety by his belligerent actions and violent opinions; Sherman seemed a more moderate and dependable choice.[15] Shocked by this irregular proceeding, Sherman turned the offer down immediately, and Lyon took over the department. He at once undertook a personal reconnaissance of Camp Jackson in Lindell's Grove at the end of Olive Street, where Frost had established himself. To do so, Lyon disguised himself in female garb, including a sunbonnet. He discovered that the Confederate militia were equipped with muskets taken from the US arsenal at Baton Rouge, Louisiana, and more were on their way. On May 10 Lyon marched upon the Confederate camp with several thousand troops, mostly militia leavened by several companies of regulars.

That day Sherman left his office on the corner of Fifth Street and Locust at 3:00 p.m. and walked home for an early dinner. Hearing the commotion, he walked the empty streets with his eldest son, Willy, reached Camp Jackson, and joined a large crowd of spectators. Sherman quickly heard the welcome news that Frost had surrendered; as the secessionists were marched away under guard, "a parcel of noisy men" cheered "for Jeff Davis" and scuffled with the accompanying regulars before they marched on. The militia then followed, and a second altercation broke out. "I heard a couple of shots, then half a dozen and soon a general straggling fire upon the crowd to my front and right. . . . I heard balls cutting branches and leaves over our heads"; his brother-in-law Charley, who had joined them, threw himself over Willy. As the militia reloaded, Sherman, Charley, and Willy ran for cover to a nearby gully and got home safely. At least five people were killed, including a woman and a child. "The whole resulted from want of discipline," a furious Sherman complained; in "Civil Strife Militia won't do."[16]

Lyon's place could have been Sherman's. The latter offers a striking description of Lyon in his *Memoirs*, this "man of vehement purpose and of determined action." He could be seen "running about with his hair in the wind, his pockets full of papers, wild and irregular"; while Sherman stood watching momentous events unfold from the sidewalk, Lyon was without question the man of the hour. By mid-May 1861 Sherman's aloofness began to redound to his discredit. As early as May 6 an impatient John warned him to get a commission before all suitable ones had been taken. Nonetheless, Sherman disclosed an unwillingness to acknowledge the gravity of the times. "It may be that sooner or later it [war] is inevitable—but I cannot bring myself to think so." Such an attitude was common among those of a conservative cast of mind—an inability to grasp the magnitude of the challenge they faced. Sherman was perhaps most candid with his Louisiana friend David Boyd. He admitted that they were now "enemies and I cannot yet recognize the fact." He had chosen to "forbear and the consequence is my family and friends are almost cold to me, and they feel and say that I have failed at the critical moment of my life." The specter of failure loomed once more over him. "It may be that I am but a chip on the whirling tide of time destined to be cast on the shore as a worthless weed."[17]

Sherman sensed that the Civil War would throw up opportunities that might occur once in a lifetime to win fame or even glory. His caution in trying to pluck these plums of good fortune arose from his deepest antidemocratic instincts. He suspected that the causes of the war were "too deepseated, and too virulent" to be settled by the inefficient and chaotic party system. He also feared the destructive influence of churlish and erratic public opinion. He feared that any man in uniform would face a second firing line—one coming from the rear. Once the federal government failed to suppress the rebellion in the first phase, "the leaders will be cast aside. A second or third set will rise, and amongst them I may be, but at present I will not volunteer as a soldier or anything else." This prediction, though self-serving, is not inaccurate.

A measure of opportunism did exist in Sherman's calculations, but they were not cynical. His support for the coercion of the South remained constant. "The integrity of the Union and the relative power of state and General Government are the issues in this war." If large-scale hostilities ensued—and Sherman could not exaggerate the conditional enough—then "of course the United States must prevail." For all such protestations of loyalty, Sherman persisted in waiting for what he wanted, though he ran serious risks of alienating the War Department, provoking John's anger, and exasperating the

Ewings. Sherman continued to make known his contempt for volunteers, "for I like not the class from which they are exclusively drawn," he snorted. Some of his earlier disappointments were blessings in disguise. Sherman could never have worked with Simon Cameron, for instance. It was a delicate balance: his worry for his own and his family's material well-being set against the need to make sacrifices in order to save the Union. The outcome depended on good luck. Sherman sought "to become independent of any body so that I cannot be Kicked about as heretofore"; if his county wanted his services, "it can call for them." Had Lyon's expedition failed while he stood idly by, Sherman's reputation might not have survived. He could have been swept aside along with the first generation of leaders and not been permitted to take his place with their successors.[18]

At his leisure Sherman pondered deeply the question of scale in any future war and the nature of the task facing any army that tried to subdue a recalcitrant South. Superior arms and numbers must prevail, but how? The war, he thought, would probably open in Virginia and Maryland, "but the Grand operations of the war will be on the Mississippi." The physical geography of its basin made separation impossible, "and all its extent must be under one government." But Sherman realized from the first that "it will take a vast power to cover so extensive a Country." He saw scant evidence that such a power could be mobilized; the task of occupation as well as fighting battles should be given a high priority. It should be carried out so "as to impress upon the real men of the South a respect for their conquerors." Sherman remained impressed by the vitality that the South had shown so far, not least the capacity to organize itself, which he rated as superior to the North's. While "the Secession Element is young, defiant and ready for action," those who sought its suppression were complacent fumblers at a loss about how to proceed. Sherman did not throw off his pessimism during the months he would spend in the environs of Washington, DC. On the contrary, his gloom deepened.[19]

Sherman first discerned a glimmer of the settled war policy that the crisis needed with the president's proclamation of May 3 calling for 42,034 volunteers to serve for three years.[20] Sherman had always preferred to serve with the regulars, and this became possible when Lincoln, without congressional sanction, increased the size of the regular army by eight regiments. The combined weight of the Sherman and Ewing lobby ensured that Sherman was offered one of these commands, and his commission was dated May 14. His *Memoirs* give the misleading impression of unwavering commitment to a military career henceforth, but at the time his view was more equivocal.

He knew that he had made a favorable impression on the owners of the Fifth Street Railroad and had "assured my influence here, so that I can fall back on it." By May 27 he had obtained only the private assurances of John Sherman and Tom Ewing Jr. that the command was his; he had received no official notification. By June 1 he feared that "they will be playing fast and loose with me" and that he would be kept waiting "dancing attendance on the Secretary [of War]."

On June 8 he departed St. Louis for the capital in a fatalistic mood. At least the journey brought some pleasure, because he stayed at John's house in Mansfield, Ohio, and visited his sisters Amelia, Eliza, and Susan. Before setting out he detailed to Ellen how he intended to handle the continuing uncertainty. If he failed to receive a "prompt answer" as to the nature of his command, "I will come back forthwith and consider my patriotic duty fulfilled unless the safety of St. Louis should call all hands to arms." If the commission was placed safely in his hands, then he would telegraph Ellen immediately with the instruction "Go to Lancaster with all things."[21]

Affairs in Washington went better for Sherman than he expected. He stayed at Willard's Hotel and met his old friend Major Turner, who had conferred with both the president and John Sherman. Turner told him with a pinch of exaggeration that he was being considered as quartermaster general with the rank of brigadier general. Although John had lobbied for him, he was never the main candidate. In any case, Sherman refused to join in the clamor for an appointment already allotted to Montgomery C. Meigs. At the War Department, he found "the same disagreeable crowd, pressing for contracts and sinecure offices," but in the adjutant general's office he saw the list containing his name and command, 13th US Infantry. Confident in his military future, he telegraphed Ellen, then visited Lincoln again to "try and see as much of the actual state of affairs as possible." He hoped to train his regiment at Jefferson Barracks, about 12 miles south of St. Louis, and thus planned to return to Missouri, as his troops would not be ready for the summer campaign. The general in chief, Brevet Lieutenant General Winfield Scott, however, had other ideas. Sherman received orders to join Scott's staff as an inspector general. He moved into John's lodgings in I Street, while the latter quenched his thirst for some frontline action by serving briefly as a temporary aide-de-camp to Major General Robert Patterson, commanding Union troops in the Shenandoah Valley.[22]

Scott worried over Washington's vulnerability to a Confederate attack. So with a blaze of his characteristic energy, Sherman had within a few days visited all the nearby sites in the Washington area, including Alexandria and Georgetown. Sherman's tours provided him with valuable background information. Within a week of his arrival to take command of the Army of the Potomac, Brigadier General Irvin McDowell asked for Sherman to be assigned to his command. Sherman had spent some time selecting officers for his new regiment, but despite all the fuss he had made over gaining his appointment, he would never command the 13th US Infantry in battle.

On June 30 Sherman received notification that he would command a brigade in McDowell's army, 3rd Brigade in 1st Division, commanded by Brigadier General Daniel Tyler. Tyler, a 62-year-old scion of Connecticut, had graduated from West Point in 1819 and resigned his commission in 1834. He managed to retain Sherman's respect, as he invariably gave him the benefit of every doubt, a benefit that he often denied others. At first Sherman thought less of his old comrade McDowell, whom he judged a "paper" soldier, with too much "service in a smooth office chair." Sherman was rightly conscious of his own lack of command experience and told John frankly that he was not mentally equipped to be a major general. "To attain such station I would prefer a previous schooling with large masses of troops in the field, one which I lost in the Mexican War by going to California." This was not false modesty but a sober self-assessment. Too many Civil War generals were promoted too rapidly and failed at high command as a result. Sherman would allow his name to go forward for promotion in the autumn against his better judgment, and he would rue the decision. The best schooling a successful commander could have was getting experience of the demands at all the important command levels and becoming accustomed to them before moving to the next.[23]

For the moment, Sherman concentrated on mastering the details of his brigade. He presided over a colorful organization of five regiments: 13th New York with 700 men, commanded by Colonel Isaac F. Quinby;[24] 69th New York, 1,000 Irish soldiers commanded by Colonel Michael Corcoran, a "most enthusiastic" Irish nationalist; the 79th New York, whose 900 men were mostly troops who claimed Scottish provenance, wore kilts on parade and were commanded by Colonel James Cameron, the brother of the Secretary of War; and 2nd Wisconsin, commanded by Lieutenant Colonel Harry W. Peck, where 900 men were arrayed in gray uniforms and were thus liable to be fired on by their own side. (Some Union regiments wore gray uniforms and Confederates blue—mainly due to the individual choices made in the 1850s when they formed as volunteers.) The brigade's first billet was Fort Corcoran, on the south bank of the Potomac opposite Georgetown. Sherman's tolerance of Catholicism might have been a factor in his being placed in charge of a force with a significant number of Catholic troops, and Corcoran's brigade went into battle flying a green banner emblazoned with a gold harp. Captain R. B. Ayres's Battery E of the 5th US Artillery, consisting of 112 men, 6 guns and 110 horses, accompanied Sherman's brigade. One other regiment, 29th New York, commanded by Colonel Bennett, would serve as Fort Corcoran's garrison.[25]

Sherman found himself weighed down with work. "Reports to receive and make—orders to give and to drill 4,000 men is hard work—My voice is now very hoarse." He had never been a model regular in his casual attitude to dress, and initially his men were rather skeptical about him, as his straw hat and disheveled coat did not fit their idea of what a commander should look like. Eventually they came to appreciate his abilities, not least a complete lack of pomposity. Each of his regiments had its own very particular problems, which all were referred to him to resolve. The trickiest involved a dispute over the muster-out date of the 69th New York, a three month volunteer regiment. It had experienced some delay in mustering into the service, and many of the men believed their time would expire in the middle of July; nonetheless, Corcoran gave Sherman a firm assurance that his regiment would fight in any imminent campaign.

At least Sherman found himself comfortably situated in a house in the countryside. From there he found it difficult to remember that war had broken out. He even counseled his daughter Minnie not to denounce as enemies "people . . . whom I used to know as kind good friends." He wrote to Ellen with some pride that the officers "feel very friendly to all the People" as "we mean them no harm—and have not disturbed a single slave"; even Robert E. Lee's slaves at Arlington sold his men milk and vegetables on behalf of their master. "This is a strange war." But the men were not so forbearing, as the destruction of fences for campfires confirmed.[26]

Sherman had to attend to other mundane details. He needed to buy another horse and saddle. As to headgear in the hot sun, he cast aside his straw hat and took up a felt hat rather than a Havelock (a kepi with a cloth to protect the neck) and hereafter always wore one. His mood also lightened with the welcome news of the birth of another daughter, Rachel Ewing, who "was flourishing." But in more somber moments he continued to worry about the financial burdens of his six children. He had recently discovered that his regular commission would lapse with the termination of the war. "I won't bother myself on this point but leave things to their natural development."[27]

The constant flurry of momentous events prompted Sherman to make a stab at predicting their course. In the first week of July he foretold a Union advance into Virginia via Vienna, Fairfax Court House, and Centreville to Manassas Junction, then on to Fredericksburg and Aquia Creek before the final onslaught on the Confederate capital, Richmond. Although he sympathized with Scott's dread of "General Impatience"—the fear that public opinion would press the army into a premature advance before it was ready—Sherman became caught in the air of confidence that imbued the army. Still, "I propose to mind my own show & allow others to do the same." He fully expected General P. G. T. Beauregard to give battle. This vain and fastidious Louisiana Creole, who had won a fearsome and unwarranted reputation by commanding at Fort Sumter, commanded Confederate forces in northern Virginia. In anticipation of an early advance, Sherman reduced his baggage to a minimum, only what he could carry in his valise and saddlebags. As for the advance, Sherman believed it would be prudent, as Scott wished to see no unnecessary risks taken. In any plan that McDowell might fashion, "all the risks should be made on the flanks."[28]

On July 16 Sherman received orders to advance on Fairfax, Germantown, and Centreville. His brigade started out at 2:30 p.m. with the men carrying three days' cooked rations in their haversacks. That night they encamped at Vienna. Sherman assumed Beauregard would make a stand at Manassas. "I still regard this as but the beginning of a long war but I hope my judgment therein is wrong, and that the People of the South may yet see the folly of their unjust Rebellion against the most mild & paternal Government ever designed for man." The seeming inevitability of a clash of arms in a few days, "no matter the result," set him thinking about his possible demise. He assured Ellen that he left their children in her care "with absolute confidence," knowing they would benefit from "the large circle of our friends and relations." He told her that he did not wish his sons to follow him into the army because their prospects would be too dependent on "blind chances."[29]

Daniel Tyler's 1st Division constituted McDowell's most powerful formation. It marched southward in numerical order, with the 1st and 2nd Brigades taking the lead under Erasmus D. Keyes and Robert C. Schenck respectively, followed by Sherman, with Israel B. Richardson bringing up the rear with the 4th Brigade. Sherman set off from Vienna at 5:30 a.m. on July 17 and took some time to reach Germantown, an impoverished hamlet. He expressed horror as the troops of 79th New York plundered the shacks and stole pigs and chickens. When Sherman sent his aides to stop them, their injunctions were rudely dismissed. "Tell Colonel Sherman we will get all the water, pigs, and chickens we want!" Their booty included a feather bed and a quilt. Sherman later likened his soldiers to Goths and Vandals. He feared "absolute national ruin and anarchy" and that armies would degenerate "into mere bands of men, struggling for power & plunder."[30]

The 3rd Brigade's path was blocked by fallen trees; the men had already marched about 30 miles and showed signs of severe fatigue. By the time Sherman's troops approached Centreville the enemy had not been seen; their commander put this elusiveness down to a superior knowledge of the roads. The newspapers opined that the rebels had a special skill at concealing their artillery in "masked batteries" and would open fire with a sudden and deadly accuracy, evading all Union efforts to destroy them. This ubiquitous notion exerted a powerful sway over the imaginations of the very inexperienced Union commanders. McDowell issued orders that divisional commanders should take every precaution to ensure their columns were not surprised.[31]

On July 18 Tyler believed that he had discovered a masked battery covered by "no great body of troops" at Blackburn's Ford on the Bull Run, immediately to the south of Centreville and divergent from McDowell's axis of advance. He sought to unmask it by what Sherman accurately termed "an unauthorized attack" on a strong position. Richardson's 4th Brigade occupied Centreville at about 9:00 a.m. with Sherman following close behind. Tyler ordered Richardson forward and lent him two 20-pound rifled guns from Ayres's battery; he also told Sherman to be prepared to advance in support when ordered. The Bull Run lay 3 miles away, and by noon Sherman heard firing. Shortly afterward a courier arrived with Tyler's orders for an immediate advance. Sherman carried them out reluctantly, as McDowell had not intended to attack at this point. But within minutes the 3rd Brigade drew up in column and began to make its way forward hastily "on a narrow Rocky road" with Sherman at its head. The men cheered, but their enthusiasm was dampened by the summer humidity and then dissipated, first at the sight of ambulances "& doctors with their appliances at work," and later at the tales of doom related by stragglers from Richardson's brigade to all who cared to listen. When Sherman reached Butler's Farm, Tyler ordered that he cover Richardson, who had gone into action some 20 minutes before. Sherman deployed for any eventuality in the trees on either side of the road and bid his soldiers to lie down.

Ayres had done well in engaging the Confederate artillery, but Tyler pulled him back to the right of Butler's Farm when his ammunition ran low. Sherman still could not see the rebel batteries, but their shots passed overhead. As these shells struck the trees his soldiers ducked, winced, and grimaced. Sherman rode conspicuously slowly over their position, saying coolly that ducking made no difference because if a cannonball could be heard it was already too late. Almost at once a ball hit the tree above him, and Sherman ducked down to his horse's neck. This immediately cheered the men up, and he responded humorously, "Well, boys, you may dodge the big ones!"

Shortly thereafter, Sherman discovered that when Richardson had attacked Blackburn's Ford, 12th New York had broken and fled, and some of its stragglers had been encountered as the 3rd Brigade approached. At about 4:00 p.m. a displeased McDowell rode onto the field and ordered the action to cease. Sherman's first brief experience of being under fire thus came to an inauspicious end. The Union force had got the worst of it, and the 4th Brigade had been spent and would play no further major part in the campaign. Sherman had exhibited a cool head, and his own loss was trifling: three gunners, one infantryman, and three horses killed.[32]

On July 19 Sherman received a summons to a meeting at McDowell's headquarters at 8:00 p.m. to receive a briefing on the final plan. He arrived early enough to scribble a line to Ellen, noting that "all the Brigade commanders are present and only a few minutes intervene before they all come to this table." Once they were all seated, McDowell explained that he had never intended to attack the Bull Run frontally; he wished to hold Beauregard to this position and then turn his flank, advance into the Confederate rear, and cut his railroad links to Richmond in the vicinity of Bristoe Station, 5 miles south of Manassas Junction. This plan depended on Robert Patterson pinning down the Confederate troops of General Joseph E. Johnston in the Shenandoah Valley; should they come to Beauregard's aid, then any outflanking move would be hazardous in the extreme, with Union columns strung out over the countryside. The risk had been heightened recently when McDowell discovered that the roads were not good enough to sustain the preferred course of pivoting on the Union left to attack the Confederate right. McDowell had no choice but to attack the Confederate left, the flank nearest to the Shenandoah Valley. The point of main effort was thus switched at the last minute: 20,000 men in two divisions commanded by David Hunter and Samuel P. Heintzelman would carry out this task, while Tyler's 1st Division pinned the Confederates to their position.

McDowell had an excellent plan, but its details still had to be worked out by his staff on July 20. He intended to attack the following day. Despite Sherman's doubts, McDowell had shown determination and resourcefulness. What McDowell did not know was that Johnston had already eluded Patterson and had begun to transport his troops to Manassas by rail. Throughout the night of July 18–19 Sherman thought that he could hear the whistles of trains arriving at Manassas Junction.[33]

"Some manoeuvering must still precede the final attack," Sherman hinted to John, but he doubted whether volunteers were capable of carrying out ambitious plans. They were easily distracted, "robbing, shooting in direct opposition to orders . . . showing a great want of Discipline—Twill take time to make soldiers of them." Probably while Sherman made these complaints, the soldiers of 69th New York decided to cool down by taking a dip in a creek near to their camp. They were at once fired on and scampered back in the nude to their lines. Sherman thought his own troops were a greater danger than the enemy because they were much closer. But during the night of July 19–20 Sherman personally led a reconnaissance of half a company in an attempt to verify reports that a masked battery lurked on his front. This incident revealed Sherman to be more vulnerable to the clamors of the press than he would later pretend.[34]

At last, at 2:30 a.m. on July 21, Sherman's brigade marched off after Schenck's to take part in the action that many participants—though not Sherman—thought would end the war. At 6:00 a.m. the 3rd Brigade arrived in the vicinity of the Stone Bridge, over which the Warrenton Turnpike, running from Manassas to Centreville, crossed the Bull Run. Sherman had his men deploy to the right of the bridge "along the skirt of timber and remained quietly in position." Apart from some felled trees, Sherman was surprised to see few signs of any rebel defensive preparations. At 9:00 a.m. he was exposed to an incongruous incident, an event that underscores the curious civilian style of this battle, the greatest yet fought in North America, but exotic and amateurish compared to later engagements. Sherman was busy studying the terrain when he "observed two men on horseback ride along a hill, descend, cross the stream and ride out towards me—he had a gun in his hand which he waved over his head, and called out to me [']You D——d black abolitionists, come on &c [']—I permitted some of the men to fire on him—but no damage was done." Indeed, one such abolitionist, Owen Lovejoy, an Illinois congressman, joined the brigade uninvited. Lovejoy's presence so infuriated Sherman that he informed his guest, with a modicum of tact, that he should go elsewhere, and he did so.[35]

Sherman "could see nothing" still but understood his mission: "to threaten and give time for Hunter and Heintzelman to make their circuit." Between 10:00 and 11:00 a.m. a delighted Sherman could see clouds of dust rising above the trees, a sure sign of a forced march. At noon he received orders from Tyler to cross the Bull Run. This stream did not constitute a significant obstacle, but his inexperienced troops thought otherwise. The creek had a bedraggled appearance with many overhanging trees, dipping branches, thick bushes spewed all over its high banks, and the water covered by a green gauze. The belligerent Southern civilian just encountered had unwittingly shown Sherman where to cross. He ordered a company over as skirmishers, and then the rest of the brigade waded over with 69th New York in the van. However, the opposite bank could not be traversed by artillery, so Ayres's battery remained on the north side. Sherman would sorely miss those guns.

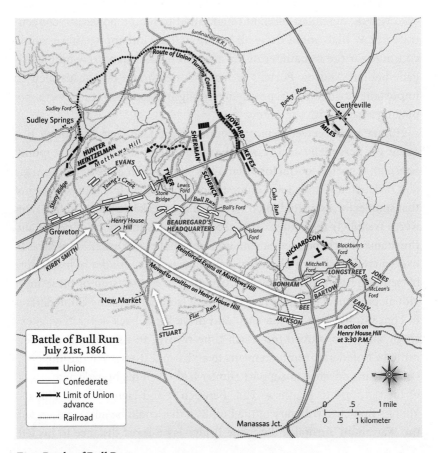

First Battle of Bull Run

The 3rd Brigade advanced slowly across the fields enclosed by a meander of the Bull Run, its commander anxious that "the regiments in succession" should "close up their ranks." At the first glimpse of a Confederate, a battalion commander of the 69th New York, Lieutenant Colonel James Haggerty, revealed the excessive keenness of the green soldier; he rushed forward unbidden in a vain effort to catch some scattering Confederate infantry. A single Confederate soldier took careful aim and, as Sherman observed, abruptly "shot Haggerty and he fell dead from his horse." The 69th New York opened fire to avenge him, but Sherman put a stop to this unwanted distraction that threatened to delay his arrival in support of Hunter and Heintzelman. When Sherman arrived before 1:00 p.m., with the colors flying to prevent his men being fired on by their own side, he got an enthusiastic reception. McDowell's plan seemed to be working well. The Union divisions had arrived safely on a weakly defended flank but had failed to land a powerful, concentrated blow that would drive all before it. This unhappy pattern would continue for the remainder of the afternoon. Sherman drew up his brigade behind Andrew Porter's. Haggerty's death had taught his men an important lesson: naïve posturing brought death, for they were not playing a game with the enemy.[36]

Hunter had received a nasty wound in the face, and McDowell had come up personally to oversee the deployment at the decisive point. Sherman reported to him for orders. His commander appeared optimistic and instructed him to join "a pursuit of the enemy," but things were not that simple, for, as he told Ellen sarcastically a week later, the Confederates were "*seemingly* retreating." This account reflects the shock of defeat and the shame of a chaotic retreat and underestimates McDowell's closeness to overwhelming victory. Sherman, alas, repeated the blunder of his seniors by sending his regiments forward singly. The overall sum of these individual, piecemeal efforts across the entire front allowed the Confederates to concentrate their fire on each and drive them back separately; every single attack consumed too much time relative to its strength and permitted Confederate reinforcements to arrive and strengthen the line.[37]

Sherman's advance to support Hunter had taken his brigade across a lip of high ground to Matthews Hill. Between it and Henry House Hill ran Young's Branch, a tributary of the Bull Run that could be jumped over, and the Warrenton Turnpike; the Stone Bridge lay a short distance to his left.

Sherman organized his brigade into a column by "divisions"[38]—that is, each regiment deployed two companies abreast at a time, with the 13th New York, his smallest regiment, in the van, followed by the 2nd Wisconsin, 79th New York, and the largest regiment, 69th New York, in the rear.

The efforts to drive the Confederates from Henry House Hill had been under way for about an hour before Sherman's intervention. "I kept to my horse and head of the Brigade, and moving slowly," he recalled, "came upon heavy masses of men, behind all sorts of obstacles." He then ordered Quinby and the 13th New York forward. As they deployed in line of battle and marched off, Sherman's sharp eye for ground discerned shelter for the remainder of the brigade along the sunken surface of the Warrenton Turnpike. Quinby initially made good progress and got off a volley but, under heavy fire, sought cover on the Union left; here the 13th New York encountered several regiments retreating that had sought unsuccessfully to support the battery of Captain J. B. Ricketts, who had gained an advanced position with the potential to enfilade the Confederate position and drive all enemy troops from it. But Confederate defenders—Stonewall Jackson's brigade—concealed behind the crest of the hill virtually destroyed this gallant but unsupported battery.

At this juncture Sherman received peremptory orders to send forward his gray-clothed 2nd Wisconsin "by the left flank" in an effort to retrieve this setback. The 2nd Wisconsin "ascended the brow of the hill steadily," he recounted in his report, "received the severe fire of the enemy, returned it with spirit, and advanced delivering its fire." But as Henry House Hill had a conical shape, the 2nd Wisconsin could not see, let alone coordinate its attack with, the 13th New York and fell back excited "by the universal cry that they were being fired on by their own men." Such apprehension featured prominently in recollections of the battle on both sides. Lieutenant Colonel Peck managed to rally his men—no mean feat considering that he chose to lead his regiment on foot and could not be seen or heard easily—but a second advance made no greater progress.

Sherman felt impelled to send another regiment forward; he could see little, as "the ground was very irregular, with small clusters of pines behind which sheltered one battery of [Confederate] artillery" that inflicted much damage on his troops. In the absence of Ayres's battery of six guns Sherman could offer no reply. He ordered 79th New York to attack, and it charged impetuously, fell back, then rallied, and as it charged again, Colonel Cameron fell mortally wounded. Then chaos reigned, as these men, too, thought that they had been fired on by their friends. The soldiers of 79th New York were not as yet accustomed to the supreme confusion of the battlefield. Just as the men rallied for one final effort, a well-timed deluge of fire struck their ranks, and to Sherman's disappointment, they "finally broke and gained the cover of the [Matthews] hill," leaving Cameron behind, although he would be brought back to die in the bosom of his regiment shortly afterward.

Aided by the intervention of Colonel J. E. B. Stuart's cavalry, Jubal A. Early's brigade of Confederate infantry had worked around the Union right flank and was enfilading McDowell's lines. A battery commanded by Lieutenant William W. Blackford directed supporting fire that began to unnerve Union soldiers. Sherman then gambled on sending the 69th New York up Henry House Hill "with shot shells and canister over and all around us." For all of Corcoran's courage and histrionics, his regiment fell back under "incessant" fire. "It was manifest the enemy was here in greater force," Sherman later explained, not entirely accurately, "far superior to us at this point." The strength of his and other brigades had been frittered away by piecemeal attacks; "first one Regiment & then another were forced back . . . by musketry and rifle fire, which it seemed impossible to push our men through." The balance of advantage lying with the Confederates was only slight. Unsupported, Sherman's regiments could achieve little tactically; neither the 79th nor 69th New York had attempted to coordinate its advances with the 13th New York, which had been in action throughout this time. It is perhaps not surprising that the novice Sherman, in his first great battle, repeated the error committed by both his seniors and his peers.[39]

Sherman had always sought to lead from the front and had ridden as far forward as the spot "where Ricketts' Battery had been shattered to fragments, and saw the havoc done." He had not been on a major battlefield before, and its grisly features shook him. "Then for the first time I saw the carnage of battle—men lying in every conceivable shape, and mangled in a horrible way," he confided to Ellen, "but," he protested, "this did not make a particle of impression on me." He felt more pained by the poor horses "lying on the ground hitched to guns, gnawing their sides in death." By comparison, he had been fortunate: he had sustained a slight wound to his knee, and a ball "hit my coat collar and did not penetrate." Several of his staff were wounded, and he reported one aide-de-camp missing.[40]

If Sherman had committed tactical errors during the attack, he more than compensated for these during the subsequent retreat. He had already discovered the fickle mood of raw troops. He first noticed the signs of their wavering at about

3.30 p.m.; thereafter "confusion and disorder" set in. Earlier in the afternoon the men "had kept their places, and seemed perfectly cool and used to the shells and shot that fell comparatively harmless all around us," but deadly small arms had unnerved them and cut down many of their officers, leaving the troops bereft of direction and vulnerable to "an incessant clamor of tongues"—mischievous and exaggerated rumors. "Men fell away talking and in great confusion." By 4:00 p.m. Sherman had decided his men would not stand even though Confederate attacks were hardly overwhelming. He pulled his brigade back from the Warrenton Turnpike to Matthews Hill, where he attempted to re-form its ranks on the ground where they had first assembled just three hours before. McDowell himself exhorted the men to stand firm. But they wavered when Stuart's cavalry, although only two companies strong, pursued stampeding Union soldiers over the Stone Bridge and up Matthews Hill. It says much for Sherman's strength of character that, with Corcoran's help, he formed the brigade into an irregular square to fend off the rebel cavalry, while other units disintegrated.[41]

Then Sherman had a stroke of inspiration, as always the essence of simplicity. Rather than risk withdrawing along the Warrenton Turnpike, where the men might be infected by panic, he decided to return the way he had come, ford the Bull Run, pick up Ayres's battery, and march to Centreville via a more indirect route. Ayres could not be found, as Tyler had ordered him to cover the withdrawal of Keyes and Schenck's brigades. So when Sherman heard reports of Stuart's cavalry on the Warrenton Turnpike, he decided to take a wider circuit avoiding the bridge over Cub Run, entering Centreville from the northwest. Shortly after his arrival at about 10:00 p.m., Tyler personally conveyed to Sherman the outcome of a council of war convened by McDowell, which had decided that the retreat should be continued until the army reached the capital. Sherman described this phase in graphic language, as the degree to which the entire army panicked was exaggerated by eyewitnesses. On his return to Fort Corcoran, he immediately strengthened the guard at the Potomac crossings to prevent those so minded from continuing their retreat. Once order had been restored, men quickly returned to their regiments.[42]

Sherman was praised by Tyler in his report and had also earned McDowell's high opinion. He had demonstrated resolve, organizational capacity, and ability to think and make decisions under pressure. He might have been as unseasoned as the men he commanded, but he had not fallen prey to the naïve illusions nursed by so many on the field of First Bull Run. Sherman saw the defeat and humiliation as confirmation of his worst fears about the Union war effort.

5

Departmental Commander—And Disaster

August–December 1861

When in 1875 Sherman reflected in his *Memoirs* on the experience of First Bull Run, he did so in a didactic mood. He wished to convey specific lessons in order to shape postwar military policy. Although by this date Sherman agreed that both sides were equally raw, the side that "stood fast" with a slight margin of resolution would win, while the other fled "in a state of disgraceful and ceaseless flight." The Union army had unraveled first, but with only a slight effort its retreat might have been prevented. Sherman blamed the Union retreat on deficiencies in four main areas: Union troops had "no cohesion, no real discipline, no respect for authority, no real knowledge of war." The men did not lack courage or enthusiasm for the cause. The casualties sustained by the 3rd Brigade were testimony to their ardor: of the 609 in combat, 111 were killed, 205 wounded, and 293 missing—almost a quarter of McDowell's entire loss. Total Union casualties were officially listed as 2,896 but were probably over 3,000.[1]

On July 21 Sherman's brigade had endured the hardest fighting. His superior officers believed that he had done well. On August 3 he received notification that he would be promoted to brigadier general of volunteers. "I have closely minded my business," he observed sardonically, "which is a bad sign for fame." This state of affairs would shortly change. Sherman might have witnessed his men's foolhardy courage, but he found little else to praise in their conduct. He focused his intellectual powers on their performance. His deductions were often correct, especially when he dilated on the need for improved organization and discipline. But he lashed out indiscriminately, and those on the receiving end of his views tired of hearing them; further recapitulation provoked questions about his judgment and worse. As his biographer Charles Vetter concludes shrewdly, Sherman revealed foresight of a high order, but "he did not know when to keep his mouth shut." He had revealed this weakness earlier, but at this time his behavior was much worse.[2]

After the completion of his judicious report on First Bull Run he could contain himself no longer. He unleashed a torrent of emotion in a long, furious letter to Ellen on July 28. "I had read of retreats before—have seen the noise and confusion of crowds of men at fires and shipwrecks but nothing like this." Sherman, like other observers, exaggerated levels of hysteria during the Union retreat. He was right, though, in thinking the Confederate pursuit feeble. "I saw but little evidence of being pursued, though once or twice their cavalry interposed between us and our Rear."

The root of the problem lay in chronic indiscipline. "Every private thinks for himself—if he wants to go for water, he asks leave of no one"; when he so chooses, he takes what he wants when he wants, even burning "the houses of the enemy." Sherman had not witnessed the conduct of volunteers in Mexico, so he was shocked and worried in equal measure. "Everywhere we found the People against us—no curse could be greater than invasion by a Volunteer Army. . . . They did as they pleased." What more could be expected, as politicians only wished to gain votes. "Our Rulers think more of who shall get office, than who can save the Country. Nobody," he thundered, "no one man can save the country." The fundamental obstacle they all faced, he argued, was the democratic system itself: the unwillingness to deny the people what they wanted. The flabby, soft, and self-indulgent soldiers he had commanded at Bull Run "brag, but don't perform—complain sadly if they don't get everything they want—and a march of a few miles uses them up." He added sarcastically a week later that he was putting in "a Requisition for two wet nurses per soldier, to nurse them in their helpless pitiful condition."[3]

Sherman doubted that a democracy could impose the system and order that produced discipline; defeats tended to be explained away by excuses such as "mismanagement" in the face of "masked batteries & such nonsense"—though he did not admit that he had believed in their existence like everybody else. Morale, including, Sherman admitted, his own, suffered. He truly believed that First Bull Run marked "the defeat of our nation"; if he was wrong and it did not, "then it is a miracle." Further advances into Virginia remained "too dangerous," and on hearing of the appointment of George B. McClellan to replace McDowell as commander of the Army of the Potomac, he praised the new commander's desire "to proceed slowly and continuously." The change at the very top could not erase harsh realities, however: "We are still on the border, defeated and partly discouraged—I am less so than most people, because I expected it." This last sentiment has the ring of a self-fulfilling prophecy.[4]

Of greater interest is Sherman's opinion of the Confederacy, as this would shape his analysis of the war's conduct for the next six months. He regarded the North as "pure bluster," but the South, he feared, exerted real potency and military muscle. The experience of the First Battle of Bull Run, in his opinion, had revealed that the Confederates enjoyed significant tactical virtues. Sherman judged them as "more united in feeling" and thought they could "always choose the ground"; at Bull Run they had made effective use of the topography and the woods, whereas federal troops had no choice but to cross open ground. The Confederate army also gained accurate information gleaned from the newspapers, enabling it to make the best possible use of the available manpower. In short, the North had committed the supreme folly of underestimating its opponent. "The Real War has not yet begun," he predicted ominously and correctly. This would begin, he had always believed, in the Mississippi basin. But the cost would be "the destruction of all able-bodied men of this Generation and go pretty deep into the next." Sherman implied that democracy was a greater handicap in waging war than slavery, as he contended that the South was better organized than the North. "Courage our people have, but no government." The power of public opinion, Sherman held, was "a more terrible tyrant than Napoleon." The Confederacy had dodged the tentacles of public opinion and had prospered. From these ideas, one-sided and not always correct though they might be, his later theory of war would evolve, especially after he turned his attention away from tactics and toward operations and strategy.[5]

For the moment his sphere of action remained restricted to the more mundane problem of how to keep the 3rd Brigade in the field. General McClellan had laid down the policy, he explained to Ellen, "endeavoring to advance so as never to make a step backwards." He had also told Sherman that the Confederate army was little better than the Army of the Potomac; otherwise Washington, DC, would have fallen. Sherman paid little heed to this opinion, though he certainly agreed that Beauregard had been a fool not to pursue after the Union repulse at Bull Run; in reality he lacked both the strength and cohesion to do so. Sherman even admitted that the Confederate failure to pursue showed "the Southern army is not much better than ours"; he consoled himself that he might not be able to accept literally Napoleon's maxim that a trained soldier took three years to produce, but at least after McClellan's arrival and introduction of systematic professional methods, he could "build up from the foundation."[6]

An immediate problem was presented by the 69th New York. Corcoran had been taken prisoner during the retreat to Centreville, and without his charismatic presence the regiment soon became restive. Quibbles over its muster-in date had surfaced before Bull Run when Corcoran had given his word that his men would fight. With Corcoran no longer among them, many of his soldiers had grown tired of war's supposed glory and agitated to be sent home at once. Sherman had instituted a program of drills and inspections that were not welcomed by the men. So he had Captain Ayres unlimber his battery to ensure attendance and gave orders that he should fire on any groups of soldiers that left camp without permission. The officers were just as mutinous as the men. After Sherman had dismissed the 69th from the parade ground, a captain followed by a crowd of soldiers intimated to his brigade commander that he was leaving for New York City. Sherman had remained in the camp deliberately to ensure that all officers stayed at their posts and did not slink off. He responded quietly that he did not recall signing a leave pass. The captain retorted that he had signed on for three months, and he calculated that they were now up. "He was a lawyer," Sherman later wrote, "and had neglected his business long enough, and was then going home." Sherman growled that such an act constituted mutiny, "and I will shoot you like a dog . . . and don't dare to leave without my consent." He could not afford to let this Captain Thomas Meagher defy him in front of the men. Meagher acquiesced in Sherman's authority and returned to his quarters.[7]

On July 23 this incident led to a memorable encounter when President Lincoln and Secretary of State William H. Seward paid an unannounced visit to the army to boost morale. They certainly confounded Sherman's belief that when things went awry, the politicians would be the first to run. Sherman met the distinguished visitors by chance while inspecting a blockhouse designed to protect the Georgetown aqueduct. For once, he even looked the part, as he had worn his colonel's uniform and carried a sword. When Sherman asked whether they were heading for Fort Corcoran, the president replied, "Yes; we heard that you had got over the big scare, and we thought we would come over and see 'the boys.'" Sherman sent word ahead that the president was coming and then, on joining him in the carriage, asked whether he wished to address the troops. When Lincoln said that he did, Sherman made his disapproval of cheering and commotion evident; then, with a typical flourish, he snapped that "what we needed were cool, thoughtful, hard-fighting soldiers—no more hurrahing, no more humbug." The president appeared rather bemused by this candor. At the first camp Lincoln delivered what

Sherman regarded as "one of the neatest, best, and most feeling addresses I ever listened to" but always stopped the men cheering. Lincoln repeated the speech at all the brigade's camps, adding at the end that if any man had a grievance, he could appeal directly to him.

When Lincoln's carriage reached Fort Corcoran, the 69th New York came out to hear his speech and promise of redress. Near the front was Captain Thomas Meagher. When Lincoln finished, he pushed forward and declared that he indeed had a grievance. General Sherman had expressed an intention to shoot him. This was the sort of incident in which Lincoln reveled. "Threatened to shoot you?" "Yes, sir, he threatened to shoot me." With a theatrical stoop and looks back and forth between Sherman and his subordinates, taking in Sherman's urgent manner, Lincoln replied with perfect comic timing: "Well, if I were you, and he threatened to shoot, I would not trust him, for I believe he would do it." The officer disappeared amid an eruption of laughter. Lincoln's clever handling of a tricky incident impressed Sherman more than he had expected. Thus began the rehabilitation of Lincoln in his watchful but suspicious eyes.[8]

Both Lincoln and Seward complimented Sherman on the order and regularity of his camps. Sherman claimed that ample evidence of presidential confidence helped him restore confidence. A watershed had indeed been crossed, but he still experienced some anxious moments. Disaffection—"a determination to do no duty"—spread to all of his New York regiments, and the 79th New York threatened to leave. Sherman feared he might be forced to order Ayres to open fire, but at the last moment the soldiers backed down. He had 100 men arrested from the 69th and 79th New York for insubordination; once the ringleaders were rounded up the obstreperous regiments fell into line. By August 19 he reported that the 3rd Brigade was in a state of "Subjugation." It was just as well. If McClellan's worst fears had been realized and the Confederates had attacked, Sherman could only have mustered his 90 gunners and the 2nd Wisconsin.[9]

This restoration of morale, good order, and discipline counts as Sherman's last though by no means least achievement as a brigade commander. By the middle of August moves were afoot to give him a more senior job. On August 17, after a meeting at Willard's Hotel in Washington, he learned that his old commander Brigadier General Robert Anderson had been appointed to command the Department of the Cumberland two days before and had asked for Sherman to be his deputy. Anderson had acquitted himself well while commanding Fort Sumter earlier in the year. He was dedicated to "reconciliation"—his wife was from Georgia. He and Sherman agreed on the fundamentals of policy: the need to resist "government by the mob"; an understanding that "in the South . . . all is chivalry and Gentility"; that the Unionist party in Tennessee and Kentucky "has [had] the worst of the fight, and our armies are too scattered." Thus rebuilding the Union cause should be the top priority, which required a firm but light touch. Sherman, conscious of his inexperience, was fearful that Union methods would make such sensitivity impossible. He extracted from Lincoln an understanding that should Anderson's health collapse, causing him to step down, he would not be appointed in his place.

En route to Anderson's headquarters he visited Ellen at Lancaster. He hoped the break would improve both his health and mood. He revealed his persistent sleeplessness, a sure sign of stress. "I have not undressed of a night since Bull Run—and the Volunteers will not allow of sleep by day."[10] Such an admission did not augur well for Sherman's service as Anderson's "right hand." Knowledge of their closeness and mutual respect since 1843 did not calm his agitated spirit. "Our Northern states deal in hyperbolic expressions of patriotism," he warned Ellen, returning to his favorite theme of superior Southern organization, "but allows our armies to be in a large minority at every point of attack." Sherman's central idea was the need to create three large armies, one in the East, another in the center, and one in the West, all with "over 100,000 effective men." Sherman's later impolitic reference to the need for large numbers of reinforcements grew out of this central insight.

Although he showed some discernment, Sherman at this stage lacked the experience and confidence to acquit himself well at the higher level of command. He admitted that "I hardly know my sphere in Kentucky, but it will be political and military combined." In short, his fears of his incapacity for "superior command" were at this date justified. His task appeared thankless, "but when danger threatens and others slink away I am and will be at my Post."[11]

Having arrived in Louisville, Kentucky, Sherman continued to be agitated by the fickleness of public opinion. In the coming months his annoyance with it would get out of control. His antidemocratic sentiment and disgust with the "apparent indifference" to the needs of the war effort were prejudices he could not overcome. The state governors of Ohio, Indiana, and Illinois were making prodigious efforts to raise troops, but he would not benefit much from these during his tenure of command. Sherman was also anxious because Kentucky secessionists were arguing "that sooner or later the war will degenerate into a war of abolitionism, and they fear the consequences." He thus urged his subordinates "to have nothing to do at all" with escaped slaves, lest Kentuckians become "estranged from our cause." The matter of run-away slaves should be left to the Kentucky state courts, as should all civilian prisoners under arrest. He admitted some grounds for optimism because of "great demands" made by Confederate leaders in reaching their levels of pre-sumed superiority. Sherman hoped "if we remain on the defense they will ex-haust themselves" so long as more Northern troops were put into the field.[12]

Sherman went so far as to warn Lincoln that the Confederates would make even more desperate efforts to seize Kentucky than they did for Missouri. But he was glad to be back in the West, which he considered of primary im-portance to the Northern war effort. The Mississippi "will be the Great field of operations"; Memphis should be taken at the first opportunity: "I think it of more importance than Richmond." Yet it is difficult to agree with his conclusions concerning the superiority of Southern organization. Shortly after receipt of orders to report to the Department of the Cumberland, he toured Indiana and Ohio and visited their governors, Oliver P. Morton and Richard Yates. He learned that the majority of the troops they were raising were destined for John C. Frémont's command, the Department of the West, which comprised all formations stationed between the Mississippi and the Rocky Mountains and was headquartered at St. Louis.[13]

Sherman resolved to visit Frémont, whom he had known in California, and attempt to persuade him that he might share some of the Indiana and Ohio troops with the Department of the Cumberland. Since arriving in St. Louis, Frémont had turned his headquarters on Chouteau Avenue, a house owned by his wife's cousin, into something resembling a castle. All visitors encountered elaborate admissions procedures and obstacles invented by pompous staff officers furnished with pretentious titles; it often took days to gain an audience.

Sherman was forewarned but "laughed at all this." He managed by bullying and bluffing to get to the front door of the Brant House. When this was opened gingerly by a staff officer, Sherman discovered he was "my old San Francisco acquaintance, Isaiah C. Woods," a rather tricky fellow who had "flummoxed and floundered" during the run on the banks in 1855. He ush-ered Sherman into Frémont's presence within 10 minutes. Although happy to see him, Frémont remained noncommittal on whether he could spare troops to "act in concert with us"—though he eagerly sought Sherman's opinion on

St. Louis's leading citizens. Sherman noticed many of his former business acquaintances, some of dubious reputation and untrustworthy demeanor.[14]

Sherman had no inkling that shortly afterward, on August 30, Frémont would issue a proclamation of martial law that also emancipated the slaves of persistent rebels. It received a surprising level of support as evidence of "war in earnest," but Sherman felt only shock at this imprudent action. He accused Frémont of completing what Lyons had started, namely, "alienating the support of all the moderate men in the city [St. Louis]" and rendering "our cause a hard one to sustain" in Kentucky. He reaffirmed that "the laws of the United States and Kentucky" required the enforcement of the Fugitive Slave Act of 1850 and all runaway slaves were to be surrendered at the request of their owners; they were not to be allowed to seek refuge in Union camps.[15]

On his return to Louisville at the end of August, Sherman found the city in a state of commotion and subject to fearful rumors. News soon arrived of a Confederate occupation of Columbus and Bowling Green, Kentucky. Anderson explained that he had attempted to delay any Confederate advance by ordering the occupation of Camp Dick Robinson under the Virginia Unionist and Sherman's old West Point friend Brigadier General George H. Thomas. A second force occupied Elizabethtown, and on October 12 Sherman ordered the newly arrived Brigadier General Alexander M. McCook to take command of it. At a meeting convened at the St. Louis Hotel, both Anderson and Sherman expressed fears that Confederate general Simon Bolivar Buckner would push on and seize Louisville itself. An air of exaggerated panic permeated the proceedings. President of the Louisville and Nashville Railroad and former US secretary of the treasury James G. Guthrie, added to the despondent atmosphere by warning that the important railroad bridge at Elizabethtown had been torched. Anderson urged that this railroad bridge and viaducts be guarded. He and Sherman agreed that Muldraugh Hill, about 40 miles from Louisville, should be held, as it enabled the vital railroad to be shielded. To occupy it, Sherman took about 1,000 Home Guards raised by Lovell H. Rousseau, a volunteer officer and lawyer, who remained active in Kentucky politics. They had arrived by night train followed by a frantic daybreak march to secure Muldraugh Hill. After the accomplishment of his mission, Sherman learned that Buckner had not advanced after all. But this success failed to lighten his mood.[16]

On the contrary, Sherman remained frantic with worry. He complained about the quality of his volunteers. Their indiscipline and pilfering seemed "calculated to turn the people against us"; their officers were hopeless. He grumbled about a lack of intelligence, but Buckner's was no better; the latter thought Sherman had 13,000 men rather than 5,000, and the Confederate movement that Sherman so dreaded was designed to deter a Union advance. Sherman fretted over the weakness of the Muldraugh position. He also believed that the morale of Confederate troops was higher than his own, because they were "imbued with a bitterness" directed at "northern hordes of Invaders." He also jumped with apprehension at any prospect of ambush, "with woods & paths familiar to them and strange to us, and we are tied down." Sherman committed a signal error: he took counsel of his fears and failed to shake them off.[17]

He tried to console himself with the thought that "fate will allow no man a choice and he must perforce drift with the Current of Events." He persuaded himself that he had been forced to take up "this humiliating position for Political reasons" in order to permit the Kentucky state legislature to take antisecession measures, as it had done, and allow the recruitment of federal troops at Camp Dick Robinson, by this point well under way. Yet the more the war intensified , the more depressed he became. Sherman's intellect had been put in overdrive, not restrained by the brake of cool military experience. He took his arguments to logical extremes; hence the mixing of insight with juddering foolishness in his views. But even at his worst, he was still capable of dazzling clarity of thought. As he wrote sternly to his brother John, "Whatever nation gets the control of the Ohio, Mississippi, and Missouri Rivers will control the Continent[.] You of the North never fully appreciated the energy of the South."[18]

Matters took a serious turn for the worse when on October 5 Anderson, worn down by stress and poor health, resigned his command. Anderson had "gone off sick," Sherman informed Ellen tersely; "anxieties of command such as this try the best of constitutions—he gave in." By dint of seniority, Sherman had little choice but to assume it, even though this act violated the condition under which he had agreed to serve in the first place. He had hoped that he might be superseded by Don Carlos Buell.[19]

Sherman was not yet temperamentally suited to assume the level of responsibility required by departmental command. His lack of judgment revealed itself just two days after assuming command when he sent the president an impertinent telegram that frankly admitted despair at the "entirely inadequate" state of his department. "All men in Indiana and Ohio are ready to come to Kentucky, but they have no arms, and we cannot supply them arms, clothing or anything. Answer." Four days later he referred to "reliable intelligence" that "Buckner has over 20,000 men" and could advance beyond the Green River and threaten Louisville. He warned his subordinate McCook melodramatically at Muldraugh Hill that "the safety of our nation depends on you holding that ground for the present." In his *Memoirs* he admitted his fundamental error: "I was necessarily unhappy and doubtless exhibited it too much to those near me"; such pessimism travels quickly down the chain of command.[20] We should be wary of attributing these views to the early signs of some mild form of mental illness. McClellan at this stage of his career was always in excellent mental health—and habitually overestimated the strength of the enemy and evinced concern that he remained lamentably undermanned, even though he outnumbered the Confederates. All of this might simply be evidence of caution or lack of command experience at the higher levels, rather than some kind of incipient breakdown.

Sherman convinced himself that Washington neglected Kentucky because all eyes were on either McClellan in Virginia or Frémont in Missouri. A visit to Louisville by the secretary of war, Simon Cameron, and the adjutant general, Brigadier General Lorenzo Thomas, offered Sherman the chance to gain redress. They arrived in the early afternoon of October 16; Cameron wished to return to Washington as soon as possible, so he at once headed for a meeting with Sherman at his headquarters at the Galt House hotel.

Sherman had already taken the precaution of warning Cameron that "things were actually bad, as bad as bad could be." So he hardly painted a rosy picture for his civilian boss, with whom he was slightly acquainted, having commanded his late brother's regiment at First Bull Run. He declined to expand on this declaration when he noticed the presence of a number of unauthorized strangers, who turned out to be newspaper reporters. Cameron replied airily that they were "family" and he could speak candidly in front of them. Sherman responded with a superfluous gesture: he locked the door so that no others could add to their number. Then he gave what the adjutant general described with a measure of understatement as a "gloomy picture of affairs in Kentucky": its younger citizens favoured secession, Sherman opined; he had only 18,000 men to cover a front of 300 miles, and he was outnumbered 3:1. He calculated that he would need 60,000 men to defend the state and, in proportion to the frontages of McClellan and Frémont, 200,000 men to advance into the Confederacy. Cameron almost choked at the size of these figures. In his *Memoirs*, Sherman emphasized the friendly spirit of the discussions, but Thomas's account includes a detail that Sherman omits, namely, that Cameron suggested that Sherman exaggerated Confederate strength and expressed discontent with yet another example of defensiveness among Union generals. Cameron urged that Sherman "must assume the offensive and carry the war to the fire-sides of the enemy"; indeed "he begged" Sherman to seize the Cumberland Gap and the East Tennessee and Virginia Railroad. On Cameron's departure Sherman felt satisfied that the meeting had served his purposes, for Cameron had promised both reinforcements and more arms and had telegraphed to ensure the dispatch of both. But over time, Cameron's recollections of this meeting eroded confidence in Sherman's judgment.[21]

For the moment, Sherman continued with his duties unaware of the gathering storm about to engulf him. A stream of complaints flowed from his office unabated. He grew weary coping with the endless difficulties raised by those entrusted with authority to raise new regiments. He visited Thomas at Camp Dick Robinson and found that efforts to frustrate the Confederate advance under Felix Zollicoffer had fumbled because Thomas "was embarrassed for transportation"; Sherman gave him "authorization to hire teams of horses," and Thomas ended up borrowing money from a Lexington bank to cover his expenses. Sherman feared that Thomas's force remained

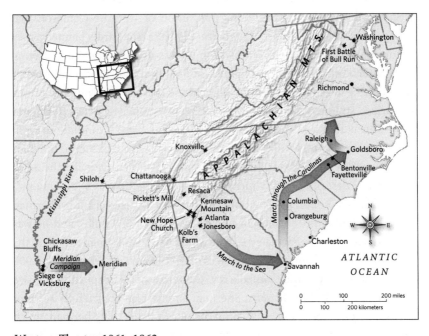

Western Theater, 1861–1862

dangerously exposed but felt powerless to influence the outcome. Convinced "that this great centre of our field was too weak," he had "begged and implored till I dare not say more." Never one to think he had overstated any argument, he warned that "our defeat would be disastrous to the nation, and to expect new men who never bore arms to do miracles is not right."[22]

All his subordinates were acquainted with his views on the impossibility of supplying his weak and scattered columns. "At a time like this men must work with the means at hand," he exhorted them. Thomas L. Crittenden received permission to equip his cavalry with lances if they could find no other weapons. Sherman's visits to his outposts were not invariably welcomed by his troops. He did not attempt to disguise his scowls and glares of disapproval at their efforts, and at Muldraugh Hill he was hooted and jeered by the very Kentucky regiments that he had led there. General McCook tried to reassure Sherman that Buckner beyond the Green River had no more than 8,000 men. But he chose to ignore this figure, as in the darker recesses of his tortured imagination he was convinced that his entire force would be surrounded. The enemy showed skill at masking his forces, so he found it difficult to verify their approximate number. He confided to Ellen the belief that the Confederates numbered 25,000 to 60,000; to his brother, 35,000. He could not even guess where they might winter. He became frantic about spies who were everywhere, peeping and noting; "to be in the midst of people ready to betray us is the most unpleasant of all feelings."[23]

Sherman's tone appeared to warn of some kind of collapse. He confided to Ellen, who had expressed "the greatest anxiety and pain" at his predicament, the full effect of his despair. He admitted a "desire to hide myself in some obscure place" but knew in his heart that he could not "avoid the storm that threatens us, and must perforce drift on to the end. What that will be God only knows." He denied that he had exaggerated the facts of his predicament. "They are so stated," he reassured the adjutant general, "and the future looks as dark as possible." Then he opined with a measure of defiant regret, "It would be better if some more sanguine mind were here, for I am forced to order according to my predictions." He had found no reason to change his mind on the central problem: the Confederates were "superior to us in numbers and equipment."

One further matter agitated what remained of his equanimity. He entertained the gravest doubts as to the wisdom of encouraging an uprising of Unionists in East Tennessee. At the beginning of November 1861 he refused to support them as they attempted to destroy lines of communication and other points; without federal military support the Unionists were easily suppressed. Two months later Sherman tried to wash his hands of any responsibility for this ill-starred adventure.[24]

The debris of Sherman's crumbling position began to scatter around him. On October 30 he was surprised to read in the *New York Tribune* Lorenzo Thomas's official report of his and Cameron's visit to the Western theater. The document had been mainly concerned with delivering a fatal blow that would ensure Frémont could not survive as commander of the Department of West, but it also revealed in unflattering detail Sherman's meeting with Cameron. By implication his own performance could be compared with Thomas's scathing indictment of Frémont's "mismanagement." One of the gentlemen Sherman saw loitering at the Galt House turned out to be a *Tribune* reporter, Samuel Wilkeson, a loyal friend of Cameron. Sherman's consistent defense of the necessity that all arrested Kentucky citizens be "dealt according to the laws" became the butt of ridicule in several Western newspapers, including the *Chicago Tribune*. Then McClellan, who had replaced Scott as general-in-chief on November 1, revealed a marked lack of confidence in Sherman by requiring him to send him daily reports via Adjutant General Lowell Thomas—under the circumstances a demeaning order. McClellan also despatched Colonel Thomas M. Key to Sherman's headquarters to check on his fitness for command. The tone of Sherman's letters confirmed McClellan's suspicions, as did Key's report that Sherman's judgment had been warped by the stress imposed by his responsibilities.[25]

On November 8, immediately after reading Thomas's report in the newspapers, Sherman asked to be relieved of his duties. Brigadier General Don Carlos Buell received the assignment, though after three days Sherman told George Thomas that he still had not heard from him. He began to adopt a tone quite unsuitable for a commanding general. His bleating, imploring manner denoted panic. He could not excuse this as the product of his subordinates' reports, for Alexander McCook and George Thomas were far more sanguine and phlegmatic than he was. McCook had assured Sherman already that "my command is improving every day, and you need have no fears for us." Sherman had, alas, lost all sense of perspective; indeed, he had started to hector his superiors, complaining that Lincoln, Chase, and Cameron had "paid no attention" to his requests. Sherman's negative message lost its edge because of his ceaseless repetition of it. And the judgment of those who persist with such an undiluted message of pessimism and hopelessness is soon called into question. On November 13 Sherman sent

George Thomas a shrill warning that he would soon face Confederate general Albert Sidney Johnston and 45,000 men—a veritable phantom army. He had persisted in this fear despite a comparatively junior member of his staff, Captain Frederick E. Prime, telling him bluntly, Sherman admitted, that he gave himself "unnecessary concern" about the range of his problems, "but then I know I do not," he snapped obstinately.[26]

A review of Sherman's performance at this point reveals that he had committed four major command errors. First, he had exaggerated the capability of the enemy while underestimating the strength of his own position. Second, he had failed to act as a calming influence for his staff and subordinates; he should have put on a brave face when faced with adversity. Third, his old problem, habitual excess of loquacity, got the better of him; he showed no great measure of tact in communicating his fears to anybody prepared to listen while simultaneously depressing confidence by conceding his powerlessness. Fourth, Sherman had overstrained his enormous resources of physical energy, had failed to take proper rest, and had left himself utterly exhausted both physically and mentally. In the summer Ellen had inquired "whether you suffer with Asthma and I have asked you so often and feel so anxious to know." He admitted that despite "sleeping in a house," he was mostly "up all night." He continued, "If I am much exposed I suppose I will suffer from cold and asthma," because Kentucky's cold, dry climate worsened his condition. He also smoked too many cigars; to make matters worse, the weather had turned "cold and wet." Asthmatic attacks and consequent sleeplessness led to extreme irritability. Chronic overwork was another symptom of command inexperience. Despite having witnessed Irvin McDowell's exhaustion and incoherence at Bull Run, Sherman had failed to learn from it, and he had worn himself out, too. His anxieties were a genuine expression of a complete lack of confidence in the overall leadership and direction of the war. As he remarked to Ellen, the Confederates "swarm at every point from Washington to Leavenworth at every point superior to us in numbers and equipment, and instead of being wiped out they propose to wipe us out." Erroneous though his views were, many Northerners shared them during this period of post–Bull Run depression. "How anybody could be cheerful now I can't tell[;] even Mark Tapley could not be cheerful," he observed of the ever-sunny character in Charles Dickens's novel *Martin Chuzzlewit*.

Worried, Captain Prime telegraphed Ellen's father asking that she and one of her brothers be allowed to come at once to Louisville to aid him in extricating Sherman from the chores of command. Ellen waited for Phil to accompany her before setting out. She arrived at 4:00 a.m. on November 9 and joined her husband at the Galt House. She conferred with the "very polite" Colonel Thomas Swords, the new chief quartermaster, and other members of her husband's staff during the day and spent the evening discussing what she and Phil had learned. She insisted that Sherman visit a doctor. Ellen then reported to John in Mansfield, Ohio, the following day that "his mind has been wrought up to a morbid state of anxiety." On the evening of November 10 the Shermans entertained Governor Oliver Morton of Indiana and his wife "and other agreeable company," including Alexander McCook, whom Ellen thought "a splendid man." An anxious John Sherman visited his brother two days later. Ellen, John, and Phil returned to Lancaster on the evening of November 15. On the following day Sherman handed over command of his department at last to Buell, an old friend, who paid Sherman compliments but advertised his friendship with McClellan, underscoring that his career enjoyed an upward trajectory while Sherman's plunged.

Sherman's failure in Missouri can be explained by a failure in style. He failed as a leader more than anything else. He admitted as much when he informed Robert Anderson that Buell was "full of confidence," while he himself had been cast down "in the midst of troubles that now envelop us. I am therefore disqualified to lead and must follow." All of Sherman's marvelous intellectual qualities—breadth of vision, command of detail, ability to see what needed to be done, and literary facility—could not compensate for his profound lack of self-confidence. Ellen urged him to come home. "I feel very unhappy on your account . . . because you are so desponding and unhappy yourself." But he did not do so.[27]

Sherman then received orders to report to Major General Henry W. Halleck in St. Louis. Sherman's relationship with Halleck had been checkered and had never truly recovered from a petulant disagreement that had erupted in 1847; since then Halleck had voiced respect for Sherman's conduct after the Californian banking crisis of 1855, but their friendship had not been renewed. At this troubled point in Sherman's career Halleck stood by him. He may have rallied around to curry favor with the powerful Ewing family, but an investment in Sherman's career did not look promising for an ambitious man at this date and probably stemmed from his recognition of Sherman's sterling qualities. He sent Sherman to inspect affairs at Sedalia, Missouri. No sooner did Sherman arrive than he took counsel of his fears again. He apprehended an assault by Confederate major general Sterling Price on the widely scattered Union forces. Halleck had given him authority to take command if he thought it "advisable for the public service"; he did so and ordered an immediate concentration. The local commander, John Pope, objected to Sherman's interference vociferously, and Halleck countermanded Sherman's orders on the grounds that they were premature.

Halleck also had Sherman examined by his department's medical director, Dr. J. B. Wright. Wright concluded that Sherman's nervous state left him unfit for command. Halleck reported to McClellan that "General S's physical and mental system is so completely broken down by labor and care as to render him unfit for duty" and ordered Sherman to take an immediate 20-day leave of absence to recover his health and restore his spirits. Halleck probably adopted this course at Ellen's request—and she was initially very grateful. She set out again for St. Louis, via Cincinnati, arriving late on November 27. Sherman arrived two days later. She whisked her husband back to Lancaster and the rented house near her parents' abode.[28]

Many previous writers have commented on the nature of this malady that hurtful rumors deemed symptoms of "madness." Ellen herself candidly admitted to John that she knew "insanity to be in the family and having seen Cump in the seize of it in California, I assure you I was transfixed by fears." Rumor, hearsay, and even direct contact with Sherman reinforced Assistant Secretary of War Thomas A. Scott's opinion that "Sherman's gone in the head, he's luny." By the middle of the nineteenth century the prognosis for any form of mental illness had become deeply pessimistic; the chances of recovery appeared to be slight, as symptoms were deemed hereditary. The experience of asylums served to reinforce the notion that most patients would not recover but continue to deteriorate. If "moral therapy" did not work it was because madness was rooted in the individual. If a member of a family demonstrated symptoms of severe mental illness, the taint of "degeneration" hovered above them all, as well as later generations. The very concept of degeneration implied that it could only get worse. "Degenerationism" held that the stresses of civilization drained the "nerve force" from constitutions incapable of resisting them. The only solution had to be isolation under conditions where patients could not beget children. No wonder Ellen was so worried.[29]

Nasty comments had percolated into Eastern newspapers and thence into the Western. A proud man, Sherman resentedIt is these imputations, finding them "unbearable." He was all too conscious that in the future "many of the officers and soldiers subsequently placed under my command" would look "at me askance and with suspicion." Even Halleck, who had offered kindness and reassurance, confided to his wife that Sherman "had acted insane." The stigma attached to mental illness was so pervasive that even highly educated men like Halleck had a very limited vocabulary and store of knowledge from which to draw their conclusions. Sherman only appeared "different" and became more so with each passing day.[30]

Sherman's biographers have not been short of explanations, despite the impossibility of making accurate diagnoses so long after the event. The biographers tend to agree with the diagnosis of depression—what the nineteenth century recognized as "melancholia"—and it certainly fits Ellen's own exaggerated fears for his mental health. But this explanation fails to explain why this breakdown remained a singular event despite even greater pressure during his wartime service. Sherman in his *Memoirs* reveals the temporary nature of the condition; it passed quickly, and he emerged from it renewed—tougher and better equipped mentally for command.[31]

Though Sherman had experienced some fitful skirmishing during the Seminole Wars, his first experience of organized violence on major scale occurred at First Bull Run on the cusp of his 40th birthday. Afterward he had categorically denied that it had affected him in any way.[32] The malady was most certainly not anything severe along the lines of post-traumatic stress disorder. First, PTSD can only be diagnosed six months after the traumatic event, and Bull Run was but three months before. Second, his own life was never seriously in danger during this battle. Third, there could be no reason why he might succumb when presumably the same conditions applied to all those who had participated in the battle, the largest major European-style battle ever fought on US soil to this date. Finally, PTSD is a chronic, relapsing disorder. If Sherman had exhibited symptoms of PTSD, he could not have subsequently behaved and developed as a commander as he did soon afterward.

Furthermore, an individual's reaction to trauma may not be a precise measurement of the experience that he suffers. There is no direct evidence between the intensity of an event, in this case, First Bull Run, and the degree of an individual's reaction to it. Indeed, a simple, seemingly harmless event is capable of producing a profound reaction, and a horrific event may produce little or no reaction. Therefore, traumatic reaction may be the result of an accumulation of events rather than a single experience. In Sherman's case, although in his own mind he had already endured a long war by November

1861, he began to learn how to function with a new set of fears and concerns, and the accumulation was arrested. His experience seems to indicate that it is more likely that he experienced an adjustment disorder.

Adjustment disorder is a condition that occurs when subjective distress and emotional disturbance interfere with social functioning and performance. This arises during the period of adaptation to significant events beyond an individual's control. Such an experience uproots a life and introduces great levels of stress. An individual predisposition or vulnerability plays an important role in the risk of occurrence of this disorder and the shaping of its manifestations, but it is nevertheless assumed that the condition would not have arisen without the outside stressful circumstances. The manifestations vary and include depressed mood, anxiety, or worry (or a mixture of these three), a feeling of inability to cope, plan ahead, or continue in the present situation, and some degree of disability in the performance of daily routines and duties. The predominant feature may be a brief or prolonged depressive reaction, or a disturbance of other emotions and conduct. As the *Oxford Textbook of Psychiatry* states, the difference between normal emotional reactions to a stressor and adjustment disorder is the presence of "impaired vocational or interpersonal functioning," which at this period Sherman amply demonstrated. The clinching piece of evidence that Sherman's condition was far from serious is that those who suffer from such disorders and who experience mild anxiety, lack of confidence, and lowering of mood recover quickly and have a good prognosis. Sherman went on to have a long and fruitful career.[33]

Sherman admitted to Ellen that the thought of his failures "nearly makes me crazy, indeed I may be so now." He felt an overriding desire to take her and the children away so "that we might hide ourselves in some quiet corner of the world." After his relief he only felt shame. "I should have committed suicide were it not for my children." The lowering of Sherman's mood had prompted these thoughts. During these months he pleaded good health, "except for the odd cold and recurring asthma," but by October he complained of unendurable sleeplessness, "though I have a headache from smoking too many cigars, and being kept down to a table writing." He was drinking too much and eating too little (though this could be said of many). His odd way of living aggravated his naturally animated manner. Louisville reporters added some color to a fraught aspect, not lessened by working 20 hours a day without proper rest and refreshment. One reporter recorded that Sherman's eye "had a half-wild expression, probably the result of excessive smoking. . . . Sherman was never without a cigar." Sherman's roughness of tongue also excited comment: his inability to conceal his thoughts in a stream of imprudent chatter. Discretion never came easily to Sherman, but during these months he lost control of his tongue. Certainly, his sense of powerlessness became all-pervading as he summoned up visions of the enemy operating with impunity in all directions. He would give approval to the schemes of his subordinates with the comment "Let the result be what it may"—hardly a strong vote of confidence. Also, Sherman did not often see what was in front of him. When he arrived back in Lancaster with Ellen, he looked through those who came to welcome him and turned to stare out of the window at unspecified points.[34]

With rest and recuperation Sherman recovered swiftly, and his demeanor improved under Ellen's care. She began to restore his appetite, he slept more regularly, and she read to him from the novels of Sir Walter Scott and Shakespeare's plays. Then on December 12 they perused a copy of the *Cincinnati Commercial* that had appeared the day before. To Sherman's horror, he found a paragraph headed "GENERAL WILLIAM T. SHERMAN IS INSANE." In a sensationalist account that embroidered actual events and invented others, the newspaper claimed that Sherman was a raving lunatic— "stark mad"—and that his subordinates had refused to obey his orders. It concluded portentously that it was only due to providence that an army had not been lost due to "the loss of mind of a general" entrusted with the defense of Kentucky. Other papers picked up the story, and their vindictive tone reveals that some reporters were paying back some of Sherman's denunciations in his own coin. Michael Fellman suggests that Sherman's reaction to these humiliating allegations was "withdrawal rather than denial" and characteristic of clinical depression, but it is the contention here that Sherman experienced in Kentucky only the mildest depressive symptoms and therefore had little to deny. Nonetheless, he endured an especially hurtful wound when young Tommy came home from school and blurted out that one of his fellows had announced "Papa was crazy!" Sherman would not be the first nor the last to experience the stigma of presumed mental illness. In his case, such prejudices presented a powerful barrier to his future military reemployment.[35]

In the face of such reported comments, Sherman reacted with energy, an indication of the strength of his rapid recovery; he did not attempt to scurry away and hide, as Michael Fellman suggests. This is not the behavior of someone with anything other than a transient mental disorder. He wrote to Halleck and his foster father, then in Washington. He admitted that he feared that the former senator "will be mortified beyond measure at the disgrace which has befallen me," but he rested his defense on the tumult of the times, when "'tis hard to say who was sane and who insane." He conceded that he had been "unable to see any solution" to the problem of fighting a more numerous and better organized enemy. Another indication of his rapidly improving state of mind is indicated by a more open-minded attitude to the problems that he had earlier grappled with. He continued to hold that the Confederates were both better organized and more determined than Union forces, but, as his sense of proportion began to return, he would "be much relieved to find I am wholly wrong."[36]

Ellen urged Sherman to go to Washington to defend his reputation, but he declined, so she mobilized her father and John Sherman to work on his behalf. Most of the Ewings initially counseled Sherman to sue the *Cincinnati Commercial* and demand an official investigation of his conduct. John thought this advice foolhardy (as it was) and offered a blunt appraisal of his brother's errors, especially his exaggeration of Confederate designs and capability and his self-defeating alienation of newspaper reporters. Thomas Ewing Sr. reached a similar conclusion and stressed that a legal case or a congressional investigation would play into his enemies' hands because of Sherman's garrulousness.

The congressional body authorized to investigate these sorts of matters, the Joint Committee on the Conduct of the War, soon determined that the kind of views expressed by Sherman were evidence of defeatism. If he had gone before its tribunal, Sherman's career would never have survived its imputations of chronic West Point feebleness. "I set a much higher measure of danger on the acts of unfriendly inhabitants," he explained, ". . . because I have lived in Missouri and the South," and he asserted that Southerners were more aggressive by nature. He informed Halleck that he intended to visit St. Louis the following week to report for duty. He had only been away 20 days but still feared that the insults of the press might "destroy my usefulness by depriving me of the confidence of officers and men." Sherman expressed here a perfectly legitimate concern.[37]

He also collaborated with Phil Ewing in writing a refutation of the *Cincinnati Commercial*'s story, as "every material statement in the paragraph is false." Phil then forwarded a copy of the letter to General Halleck and followed up Sherman's letter with his own, noting that his brother-in-law had "much improved in health and equanimity" after his stay in Lancaster. The

Ewings, and particularly Ellen, jumped to the conclusion that a conspiracy existed to destroy Sherman; she noted ruefully that the same newspapers that denounced her husband simultaneously promoted the career of John Pope. She included McClellan and even Halleck on her list of insidious plotters. In her marriage's finest hour, Ellen joined her father in Washington to fight for Sherman's career. She paid visits to the new secretary of war, Edwin M. Stanton, and to the president. Lincoln had no intention of alienating the powerful Ewings and had been making soothing noises since before Christmas. At their meeting Lincoln praised Sherman's conduct at First Bull Run and after and expressed every confidence in his ability. Throughout this crisis Ellen's performance was little short of heroic, defending her husband against accusations of madness and rallying her family's allies, playing a big role in his ultimate rescue while removing him from the public eye at the crucial moment. Sherman had a sensitive personality, and he must have felt the whole world about to collapse around him in public humiliation that December. Ellen's single-mindedness saved his career and his future. Indeed, the Ewings had treated Sherman again like one of themselves; he owed the recovery of his career to them. On December 20, when Thomas Ewing Sr. returned home, he was content that all that could be done on his son-in-law's behalf had been done.[38]

On December 18, despite or rather because of Ellen's reservations, Sherman traveled to St. Louis and placed his fate in Halleck's hands. Ellen pleaded that Sherman should stay in Lancaster until the spring and busy himself at Thomas Ewing's salt works. Sherman feared this more than dreary administrative duty in a distant garrison town. Ellen allowed her protective zeal to get the better of her judgment in decrying Halleck's efforts on Sherman's behalf. Halleck might have harbored doubts about the soundness of Sherman's judgment and his ability as leader, but he had no hesitation in thinking him a man of integrity equipped with a first-class brain who could not be spared. Halleck's actions were not entirely altruistic, as it served his own ambitions to please the Ewings; in his dealings with them (and Sherman, too) he exhibited a sense of humor at odds with his usual lugubrious manner.

On December 23 Halleck appointed Sherman to Benton Barracks, where he could train recruits. Appalled that her husband had not been restored to field command, Ellen took his assignment as further evidence of the conspiracy to ruin him, but it was just the kind of job he needed to complete his recovery. At Benton Barracks Sherman could begin the resuscitation of his military career. No other Civil War general would recover from such depths of shame and despair to rise on the strength of intellectual power and operational and strategic insight to reach such heights of fame and military success.[39]

6

Divisional Commander,
January–July 1862

In February 1862, after a surfeit of disappointment and humiliation, Sherman received the revivifying news that he would command a division. He rushed to Paducah, Kentucky, to take up this new appointment. Even the joy of imminent rescue from the military doldrums caused mishap. In his haste to leave, his path and Ellen's crossed, as she traveled to St. Louis to visit him. Sherman felt mortification at the inconvenience and disappointment that he had unwittingly caused. "Indeed do I appreciate this mark of affection and deplore the result." He had written warning Ellen that he would have to depart immediately, but she had not received the letter. Despite the confusion, Sherman's spirits were raised by news of Ulysses S. Grant's capture of Fort Donelson. "This is by far the most important event of this sad war," he assured Ellen. Yet dangers still lurked in the shadows. Sherman reported word of the "apprehension that Beauregard will cross over to this place [Paducah] from Columbus and attack." Hence the urgent need to transform his new command, which he estimated at 3,000 men, into an effective fighting unit.[1]

Sherman believed that Halleck would not be slow to exploit Grant's triumph. He owed Halleck for the enormous favor of saving his military career. His faith in Halleck's ability knew no bounds. Fifteen years later he would recall a conversation at Halleck's headquarters when Halleck rolled out a map over the table and, equipped with a heavy pencil, conducted what amounted to an exercise without troops. Halleck asked Sherman and his own chief of staff, George W. Cullum, "Where is the rebel line?" Cullum drew a line from Bowling Green via Forts Henry and Donelson to Columbus, Kentucky. "That is their line," agreed Halleck. Then he asked: "Now where is the proper place to break it?" Either Halleck or Sherman (or both) responded, "*Naturally* the center." Halleck then drew a perpendicular line from Cullum's base line that ran the course of the Tennessee River. Sherman believed this conversation took place about a month before Grant's advance on Donelson. Consequently, he was inclined to give Halleck "full credit" for grasping the strategic importance of the Tennessee River at a time when political imperatives seemed to dictate an advance directly down the Mississippi River. This conversation also reveals the unanimous approval granted by Halleck and his generals to the geometric procedures popularized by the Swiss theorist Baron Jomini, whose treatises Halleck and Sherman used to sharpen the edge of their strategic insight.[2]

Shortly afterward Halleck issued orders to Grant that required him to advance farther up the Tennessee River and destroy the railroad bridge over Bear Creek, near Westport. This stab at Confederate railroad communications, if successful, would have momentous consequences. The whole Confederate system in this region revolved around Corinth, Mississippi. Here the Mobile and Charleston Railroad that ran north-south crossed the east-west line, the Memphis–Charleston Railroad. The loss of Corinth would expose Memphis and thus permit an advance down the Mississippi. The Confederates would be forced to rely on railroads farther south that provided less direct routes: the line from Vicksburg and Meridian down to Mobile, Alabama, which would require a long detour via Atlanta, Georgia, back to Chattanooga, Tennessee. To protect the better, more northerly railroads and regain all that had been lost in the early months of 1862, the Confederates began a concentration in the vicinity of Corinth. For his part, on March 20 Halleck ordered Grant not to fight a great battle. "Don't let the enemy," he instructed his intrepid lieutenant, "draw you into an engagement now."[3]

During the following weeks Sherman threw himself into the task of bringing order, cohesion, and discipline to his division. To help him impress his own methods on his "green" troops, he asked for four companies of his old regiment, the 13th Regular US Infantry. During these hectic days he did not overlook the need to be solicitous toward Ellen. He still felt guilty about their failure to meet recently. "I ought to get on my Knees and implore your pardon for the anxiety and Shame I have caused you," he wrote. "All I hope for is a chance to recover from the Past." Ellen was agitated by what Sherman might do; she revealed a state of mind little short of terror in case he might be killed before receiving confession and absolution. At this stage, Sherman felt so indebted to her efforts on his behalf that he tolerated her Roman Catholic piety.

The miserable weather meant that he had no choice but to work "in the midst of mud and dirt, rains and thaw"; Sherman's only consolation was to view the almost 15,000 Confederate prisoners taken at Fort Donelson as they passed through Paducah. One party included Major General Simon

Bolivar Buckner, who had been required by his superiors to offer the fort's surrender to Grant. "I used to Know him well," he informed Ellen, "and he frankly told me of many things which I wanted to Know." Sherman's correspondence indicates that the meeting was quite affable, not tense or querulous. Perhaps because he had been forced to take responsibility for the surrender, Buckner argued that the loss of Donelson would not have an enduring significance for the Southern cause. In this hope he would be mistaken.[4]

By the third week of February 1862 Sherman had mustered 12 patchily armed volunteer regiments, nine from Ohio (46th, 48th, 53rd, 54th, 57th, 70th, 71st, 72nd, 77th), two from Illinois (40th and 55th), and one from Iowa (6th). Sherman trembled with anticipation that he might be ordered soon into battle. "The unparalleled success of Grant has deservedly aroused the enthusiasm of the country, and if followed up may prove overwhelming." Still, he believed that the Confederacy could not be crushed until the federal government had regained the full length of the Mississippi. Donelson might be hailed as a turning point, but Sherman poured scorn on the assumption that the war would soon be over. Paducah, he warned, was "a regular secession community" and the prisoners of war traveling through it remained recalcitrant. Sherman might still seek "obscurity" in his present duties and could not forget his "past errors," but he sensed that redemption might lie at hand in hard fighting that he expected to erupt shortly. In fending off Ellen's efforts to get her brother Charley reassigned to her husband's division, Sherman assured him directly that he would get his chance. "But who can look forward a day[?]"[5]

Sherman had been supporting Grant's advance for several weeks before he received orders to move. As a result he honed his skills as a logistician. In early March he sent cavalry to "enter" Columbus, but they arrived in time to observe the Confederate withdrawal. Sherman then promptly decided to take 900 men and accompany the gunboats leaving to bombard Columbus. They occupied the town for a day, but the retreating Confederates had already destroyed their provisions and accommodation. The following day Sherman returned to Paducah from what amounted to a training exercise to receive the long-awaited orders from Halleck to advance up the Tennessee River and join Grant's army. Sherman's division should make for Eastport, near Savannah. On the Union right flank the Confederates had withdrawn to Island No. 10 above Madrid, and thus exposed the Tennessee River to further incursions.

In urgent preparation for his new assignment, Sherman examined his finances. Having spent little of his pay since Christmas, he hoped to send Ellen money but had to bear in mind that he needed to buy two horses.[6]

In the second week of March 1862 Sherman's command, eventually styled the 5th Division, Army of the Tennessee, sailed down the Tennessee River in 50 boats full of soldiers. He had 9,000 officers and men under command, the bulk from Ohio, "but they are raw and Green," he affirmed. They traveled first to Fort Henry, where Major General C. F. Smith had taken command. Grant had ostensibly fallen foul of Halleck's fussiness over administrative carelessness, particularly slow submission of reports, and had been temporarily removed from his post. In truth, Halleck was jealous of the acclaim Grant received after his triumph at Forts Henry and Donelson. Smith busied himself forwarding reinforcements to the most advanced divisions. Smith was an important figure in the lives of both Grant and Sherman. He had been adjutant of cadets at West Point for part of their time at the academy and exerted a steadying moral influence over both commanders, but especially Grant. He was a much-admired gentleman, not perturbed by being commanded by or surrounded by colleagues who were once greatly his juniors. As a result, Smith's experience and authority served Grant well, as he acted, in effect, as deputy commander. Smith ordered Sherman to wait on the river above Fort Henry for the rest of the army.[7]

A large fleet of vessels soon came up carrying the divisions of Stephen A. Hurlbut, Lew Wallace, and Smith himself, currently commanded by W. H. L. Wallace. Smith thought he lacked sufficient knowledge of Confederate strength and dispositions, so on March 14 he ordered Sherman downriver to Savannah, where Smith intended to establish his headquarters. The weather had improved, the sun shone, and the river had risen, thus easing the task of navigation. "As I have nothing to do with the plans, I feel perfectly easy, and shall do my best," Sherman observed, revealing a sunny disposition that matched the weather. One matter did irritate him, however. One of his colonels, Thomas Worthington of the 46th Ohio, "a strange character," had been ahead of Halleck, Sherman, and Grant at West Point and continued to behave as if he were still their senior—so unlike C. F. Smith. He strutted about like a commander in chief, complained Sherman. He had thrust ahead to Savannah in front of the rest of the 5th Division. Sherman would not tolerate this competitive conceit; on arrival, he ordered Worthington to get his men back into their boats, "and gave him to understand that he must thereafter keep his place."[8]

Smith had ordered Sherman to carry out the Army of the Tennessee's mission of cutting the Memphis and Charleston Railroad below Eastport, between Corinth, Mississippi, and Tuscumbia, Alabama. Sherman made his headquarters aboard the *Continental*, and Smith told him to take two gunboats as escorts, the *Lexington* and *Tyler*. Sherman had been informed that residual Unionist sentiment would likely surface as he advanced into this part of Tennessee; indeed, his arrival in Savannah had been greeted by an applauding crowd on the shoreline. As he sailed southward such sentiment faded; "they are still far from defeated," he warned Ellen, "and being in their own country, they have a great advantage."[9]

As he steamed upriver Sherman passed a modest bluff called Pittsburg Landing and informed Smith that he thought the best way of sustaining the army's progress would be to land Hurlbut's and Lew Wallace's divisions there. Meanwhile he continued southward to Eastport and Chickasaw, both of which were defended by small Confederate garrisons and batteries. But he became anxious, because although he expected Benjamin Cheatham's division of Confederate infantry to fall back on Corinth, leaving just a regiment of cavalry at Pittsburg Landing, should Cheatham "remain" there, it "might embarrass our return." His supposition seems very sensible.[10]

Sherman assumed that either Grant or Smith would come up and take command of the advance, but Smith had been injured in a boating accident, and Grant did not appear. In their continued absence, he gave informal direction to both Wallace and Hurlbut, neither of whom was a professional soldier. On disembarking at Tyler's Landing near Yellow Creek, Sherman's troops had only to march 17 miles to reach the Memphis–Charleston Railroad near Burnsville, but they failed to cover this short distance because of the sudden, torrential rain. The Tennessee River rose by 15 feet, flooding Tyler's Landing, and all picks and shovels were lost. The neighboring houses were abandoned, as the residents assumed that Union troops resembled a cloud of locusts. Indeed, Sherman showed annoyance when "in spite of all efforts" his troops "burn Rails, steal geese, chickens &c."

With his cavalry unable to cross the swollen streams, Sherman had no choice but to abandon the expedition, unharness his teams, and drag the guns and wagons back to the boats; three men and two horses came close to drowning during this perilous if short journey. Sherman got the men, horses, and equipment reembarked and returned to Pittsburg Landing on March 14 but did not disembark. He hurriedly took a boat to Savannah to report for fresh orders from Smith personally and, if necessary, explain himself. The ailing Smith quickly instructed Sherman to take command of Hurlbut's division and land at Pittsburg Landing.

On March 18 his troops advanced inland a mile and a half, occupying the road fork to Corinth and Hamburg. Lieutenant Colonel James B. McPherson, a capable and energetic engineer from Halleck's staff, had returned with him to assist in the detailed reconnaissance the position required. Sherman spent two exhausting days in the saddle. He quickly discerned that the Confederates were "to our front from Florence to Corinth with the country full of never-ending cavalry." He then added: "We may have fights at Purdy and Corinth." He did not expect to be forced to defend his lodgement.[11]

In the light of his subsequent reputation, it is curious to find Sherman admitting to his foster father that he "was troubled in mind" due to the damage he had inflicted on the railroad around Burnsville near Yellow Creek. He experienced the occasional glimmer of optimism after this incursion. The people of Tennessee appeared more eager for peace, but he held out no hope for the spread of war-weariness to Mississippi, for there "the common people are more bitter than Ever, reckless of consequences." He reflected on these broader issues shrewdly but reluctantly. He confessed that they "are so momentous that I shrink from the responsibilities which others seem to court, and much prefer the Subordinate part I now play." Still, Sherman had given plenty of evidence of his true ability. Smith had come to rely on his judgment, and his fellow divisional commanders were content to follow his lead. He insisted, however, that among the "host of other Generals" he wished to slip into "a mixed crowd."[12]

By the first week of April 1862, Sherman's division fielded 12 infantry regiments, eight companies of cavalry and three batteries of artillery. They were organized into four brigades, the 1st Brigade, commanded by Colonel John A. McDowell, and the 2nd, 3rd, and 4th Brigades under Colonels David Stuart, Jesse Hildebrand, and Ralph P. Buckland, respectively. He kept his troops "pretty well employed and think they are gaining consistency." His staff played an important role in his success, as it oversaw the commander's orders, although some time would elapse before a cohesive team emerged. In any case, Sherman would never use his staff to assist him to command any formation, whatever its size. He envisaged the staff as solely an administrative organ. His inspector general, Lieutenant Colonel Miles S. Hascall, filled the appointment temporarily before he returned to field duty. Major William D. "Dan" Sanger would take Hascall's place; Lieutenants James C. McCoy and John Taylor were aides-de-camp, and Captain John H. Hammond, who had served with Sherman at Benton Barracks, rather reluctantly took on the job of assistant adjutant general. None of these officers were members of a trained general staff, and they often resented their staff duties. Sherman felt overwhelmed with writing; when he attempted to delegate some of it to Hammond, the latter became "sick, cross and troublesome."[13]

Sherman spent his days examining roads and streams, generally acquainting himself with the ground. He estimated Confederate strength at about 80 regiments. What were these troops for? On March 17 Grant, having been exonerated by Halleck of the charge of inefficiency, came up to take command of the Army of the Tennessee at Savannah. He and his generals gave no thought to any matter save an early and rapid resumption of the advance. A week before, Halleck had been given overall command of all Union forces in the West and ordered Major General Don Carlos Buell's Army of the Ohio to Savannah to support Grant's thrust. Once the Army of the Ohio arrived, flushed by its occupation of Nashville the previous month, Sherman expected Grant to issue the order for the drive on Corinth. Sherman also spent a lot of time on the picket line because he feared that he could not trust this sort of duty to any of his untried subordinates.

On April 3 he reported to Ellen that "the weather is now springlike, apples and peaches in blossom and trees beginning to leave. Blackbirds singing and spring weather upon the hillsides." All witnesses rhapsodized over the beauty of the region surrounding a small timber Methodist chapel called Shiloh, about 2.5 miles southwest of Pittsburg Landing. The vernal serenity of Shiloh's fields would form a mocking counterpart to the horror that would ensue.[14]

Sherman suffered from mild diarrhea but otherwise exuded rude health. On April 4 he reported "saucy" Confederate cavalry probes, skirmishes on his lines that eventually involved an infantry brigade, but he did not detect the presence of Confederate infantry. None of this activity changed his belief that the Confederates would "await our coming at Corinth"; indeed, he feared an ambush if the Army of the Tennessee delayed its departure after the trees and bushes were thick with leaves. Despite Halleck's order to do so, neither Grant nor his divisional commanders gave any priority to entrenchment in order to strengthen their positions. An ambush would indeed be sprung on the Army of the Tennessee, but under quite different circumstances than those envisaged by Sherman. Undoubtedly, he must bear some of the blame for this signal error. Nevertheless, the inconsequential operations that he conducted up and down the Tennessee River had helped Sherman to train himself and his division. This useful experience would assist him over the next few days to surmount the greatest challenge he had ever faced.[15]

The great battle of Shiloh erupted on April 6 with dramatic ferocity over this bucolic wilderness. For both sides Shiloh represented a cloaked victory—even a turning point that declined to turn. For the North, Shiloh represented one of the three decisive events that secured victory in the Western theater, along with the fall of Fort Donelson a few weeks before and of Vicksburg 15 months later. For Sherman personally, there can be no doubt about its importance. He turned a corner and emerged with his reputation enhanced: his competence as a soldier would never again be questioned.[16]

Sherman had done much to select this battlefield, though he never imagined that he would fight over it. His division's tents were pitched on the right flank around Shiloh Church, except for David Stuart's brigade, which had been placed to cover the Union left adjacent to the Tennessee River. The battlefield stretched for about 3 miles between these elements of the 5th Division. It was transected by two roads. The Paducah–Hamburg road ran north-south roughly parallel to the river, and toward the southwest coursed the Corinth road via Shiloh Church; both of these roads were connected by lesser lanes. Farther north from Crump's Landing, about 4 miles from Savannah, the road to Purdy ran roughly parallel to the Hamburg–Purdy road. Lew Wallace's division remained at Crump's Landing, and connecting roads offered the possibility that Sherman could be reinforced from this route.

The ground occupied by Sherman's men was naturally strong and ideal for encampments, drilling, and training. The Union army's flanks were secured by two tributaries of the Tennessee River, Lick Creek to the south and, shielding Sherman's right, Snake Creek; a further tributary of the latter, Owl Creek, added to the oblong shape of the battlefield. All three of these streams were deep and fast flowing; they reduced to about 2 miles the space through which an attack could be launched. Though Sherman's division was the most advanced, and thus the most exposed, it occupied the best position, a low ridge that fell away toward the river, shielded by ravines and entangled vegetation. Sherman had previously advocated placing the other divisions at scattered points, at Hamburg and possibly Eastport, as the landing at the latter he thought the "best I have ever seen" on the Tennessee River. But such suggestions were based on engineering considerations, mainly a wish to avoid the flooding that had curtailed his previous advance. They in no sense form some kind of "alternative plan" to Grant's concentration at Shiloh.[17]

The Confederates attacked the Union army at Shiloh in an effort to catch Grant unawares before Don Carlos Buell and the Army of the Ohio came up to support him. General Albert Sidney Johnston commanded the sprawling Confederate Department No. 2 that stretched westward from the Appalachian Mountains. Johnston's fumbling direction of its complex and diverse affairs had excited much denunciation and had prompted General P. G. T. Beauregard's transfer from Virginia to the West as his second in command. Beauregard drew in troops to Corinth from as far afield as Arkansas, New Orleans, Mobile, and Pensacola, as well as from Nashville and Memphis. Johnston himself did not join forces with Beauregard until March 27. On receiving word of Buell's approach, Beauregard urged on Johnston an immediate assault on Grant's army, and after initial hesitation he agreed to Beauregard's scheme. No one was in any doubt as to the magnitude of the undertaking and the degree of risk involved—nor the vital necessity for an urgent Confederate victory. On April 2 the Confederate force, temporarily named the Army of the Mississippi, left Corinth and headed northeastward in two columns, but victory appeared to be thrown away in a wearisome and chaotic approach march that Beauregard assumed must have sacrificed surprise. He attempted to persuade Johnston to abandon the enterprise; but Johnston rose to the occasion, sensing that his own reputation as well as the Confederate cause in the West could be retrieved by an audacious attack. At dawn on April 6, against the odds, over 40,000 Confederate troops drew up in line of battle unnoticed within half a mile of Grant's lines.[18]

Over these preceding days Sherman enjoyed more contact than most with the enemy. Grant, W. H. L. Wallace, and McPherson all visited Sherman's front, but the army commander took no additional precautions to strengthen his outposts or increase the frequency and strength of patrols. Sherman had received warnings that Confederate forces were close by. This was hardly news to him, but he had drawn erroneous conclusions about enemy intentions. Surprise in any war is not a panacea: its effects are not permanent, and even more important, there are various levels of surprise—its results are not uniform. At one level, it is obvious that Sherman, despite his disclaimers to the contrary, was surprised. He had informed Grant on April 5 that he did "not apprehend anything like an attack on our position." He thought that of all the Union divisions, the lonely Lew Wallace appeared the most vulnerable to a surprise attack.

One of the most unfortunate, if unintended, features of Grant's position was that the most unseasoned troops—those of Sherman and Benjamin

M. Prentiss's 6th Division—lay closest to the enemy. The troops a short distance behind Sherman, the divisions of Major General John A. McClernand, an influential Democratic congressman from Illinois, and W. H. L. Wallace, had gained experience at Fort Donelson, but they did not feel the first shock of the rebel onslaught. In the first few hours the battle would be determined by the brittle balance of inexperience. The weights of personal leadership and solid tactical sense would determine which side prevailed.[19]

On Saturday, April 5, Colonel Buckland reported the presence of Confederate cavalry—but Sherman already knew this. Buckland also reported that infantry were in the woods, but he made no effort to substantiate the claim. Similar cries also hailed from Colonel Jesse Appler of the 53rd Ohio. Appler had defied Sherman's order prohibiting regimental commanders from siting their camps at convenient sources of fresh water at the expense of tactical cohesion. Appler had allowed the 53rd Ohio to advance 400 yards beyond Sherman's line and cross a stream; he also demonstrated scant competence in marching and drilling his men. Any warning from him would be treated by Sherman with suspicion, even contempt. Indeed, Appler was told fiercely to "take his damn regiment back to Ohio." This, and other rebukes, would earn Sherman, though a Buckeye himself, a reputation for displaying consistent hostility to Ohio troops. Sherman jumped to the conclusion that Appler quivered at shadows and that no rebel force "designed anything but a strong demonstration."[20]

Sherman thus played his unfortunate part in the overall operational failure—for which Grant must assume the primary responsibility—to prepare a strong defensive response to any Confederate attack. A cohesive line had not been knitted together, as Union commanders were preoccupied with continuing their advance. But what is also obvious is that Sherman knew the Confederates were not far distant; he could not be accused of smug indifference in the face of the enemy even if he misconstrued their intent.

The sun rose at 5:40 a.m. on the morning of Sunday, April 6, but it took time to muster and align Confederate troops and launch the attack. First skirmishes broke out after 6:00 a.m. on Prentiss's front, and by 7:30 these had become severe, but he sent Sherman no warning. Sherman's troops had eaten breakfast and were preparing for morning drill. They were certainly not bayoneted in their tents asleep, as panicking reporters later alleged. The only men in his division, Sherman sniffed later, who had not eaten their breakfasts were "worthless cowards" who had scattered on hearing the first shots. Unfortunately, these included members of the exposed 53rd Ohio. As soon as Sherman spotted the "glistening bayonets" of the Confederate line of battle in the morning sunshine, he rode forward to steady this regiment. Colonel Appler issued a stream of contradictory orders, but Sherman told him firmly to stand his ground and protect the division's left. He then sent couriers to warn McClernand and Prentiss. A number of witnesses record that Sherman exclaimed in amazement, "My God! We are attacked." Such recollections might have been influenced by knowledge of the subsequent controversy, especially in a regiment that did not distinguish itself, but if Sherman did say this, then he remained very cool and collected in his reaction to the attack. His arrival at the front also witnessed another dramatic moment and brush with death. As Sherman rode forward to closely examine the Confederate line, men belonging to William J. Hardee's corps, a shot rang out, instantly killing his orderly, Private Thomas D. Holliday, who always accompanied Sherman and served as his personal bodyguard. He told Ellen after the battle that "the Shot that killed him was meant for me."[21]

The rugged ground probably saved Sherman's division from complete destruction. Confederate troops were held up negotiating deep ravines and thick undergrowth that broke up their formation. By 7:30 a.m. Sherman had got his division into line of battle, but it consisted of only three brigades, as Stuart could not be rallied to the colors. Colonel Hildebrand had got his brigade ready by 7:00 a.m., so there was no question of being taken completely by surprise. As a gunner, Sherman instantly grasped the importance of artillery in the defense of his weakest point on the left and personally sited Captain Allen C. Waterhouse's Battery E, 1st Illinois Light Artillery, on a ridge with a good field of fire between the 53rd Ohio and Lieutenant Colonel Americus V. Rise's 57th Ohio. He positioned Major Ezra Taylor's Battery B, 1st Illinois Light Artillery, at Shiloh Church; he even had to show the gunners how to cut their fuses. The Confederates concentrated on Sherman's left, despite the toll on their lines exacted by his sensible tactical alignment; resistance here began to crumble. Fortunately, McClernand had responded rapidly to the 5th Division's plight and sent Sherman three Illinois regiments to help him shore up his left; in the meantime, McClernand's 1st Division moved to fill the gap between the 5th and Prentiss's 6th Division. Under renewed Confederate pressure at about 8 a.m, alas, the 53rd Ohio collapsed, and most of the men obeyed its colonel's injunction to follow his rapid departure to the rear; the 57th Ohio soon followed them, too.[22]

The Illinois regiments were also beaten back, and the position appeared perilous, but Sherman remained calm and ordered his two remaining brigades, those of McDowell and Buckland, "to hold their ground." The latter had formed up close to Shiloh Church, advanced 200 yards from camp, and delivered a withering fire. Sherman maneuvered his regiments skillfully, not only to maintain a cohesive defensive line in a hail of fire but also to retain sufficient space to permit reinforcement from the right. His determination to stay put even though he risked the destruction of his division was motivated by more than just an obstinate reluctance to admit defeat. During Grant's brief visit to his sector of the front, just before 10:00 a.m., Sherman received word of his commander's orders to Lew Wallace to march to join the army forthwith. Sherman's grip on affairs encouraged Grant, although he reported a shortage of ammunition, which the latter immediately rectified, and an uninterrupted flow got through for most of the day. Grant must also have appreciated Sherman's quick appraisal that the Confederates were attempting to break through his left to catch McClernand and Prentiss at a disadvantage, roll them up, and reach the Tennessee River. Sherman thus revealed an ability to read the battle as a whole, rather than just concentrate on his own affairs and the welfare of his men.

But his division paid a price. By 9:30 a.m. the men had already endured attacks by six Confederate brigades. After 10:00 a.m. it became obvious that Confederate artillery had moved up behind his line, so he had no choice but to abandon this position and what remained of his camps. The division slowly pulled back to the Hamburg–Purdy road that ran across the battlefield. He had already lost three guns from Waterhouse's battery during the earlier disorder; during this withdrawal he lost more when his third battery, Morton's Battery, 6th Indiana Light Artillery, commanded by Captain Frederick Behr, came under very heavy fire while receiving its orders from the divisional commander himself to cover the brigades falling back. Behr was felled, and despite Sherman's presence, the gunners and teamsters panicked and fled on the caissons, leaving behind five of their six guns to be captured by the enemy. Sherman was not discountenanced by this setback. On the contrary, he sent McDowell's brigade forward against the Confederates surging toward McClernand's front on his immediate left.

Always in the thick of the fighting, alert to his division's needs and also to the problems of others, while deaf to the overwhelming din of battle and disregarding bullets and cannonballs, Sherman earned much praise for his conduct at Shiloh. He might appear quirky, even eccentric, nervous, and highly strung in daily affairs, but under fire he became cool, calculating, forthright, and decisive. By force of will Sherman held his command together in the unpredicted tempest of hot and grinding metal hurled toward his wavering lines. Unflustered, "I noticed that when we were enveloped and death stared us all in the face," he confided to Ellen, "my seniors in rank leaned on me"—a pointed reference to the archetypal "political general," McClernand, with whom Sherman's relations were then cordial. Sherman had been slightly wounded in the hand earlier in the morning, and an artilleryman observed him without fuss wrapping a handkerchief around it as if he had cut himself gardening. Later his shoulder was badly bruised by a spent bullet. But the decision to abandon his camps would cost him dear in every sense. He had left all his money in his tent and two horses tethered in front of it. When his horse was killed under him later that morning, he had to borrow one—and then to repeat the plea twice more, as in all, three horses were killed under him that day.[23]

The battle would continue with unrelenting fury for at least another four hours on this sector, but for Sherman the crisis had passed. He trotted up and down the 5th Division's line, urging the men to make maximum use of all kinds of cover, "trees, fallen timber, and a wooded valley to our right." Sherman and McClernand worked closely to maintain their joint position, sometimes suddenly losing their ground and then just as quickly regaining it, as the battle swept to and fro. Grant reappeared around 3:00 p.m. and immediately grasped the pressure that the two denuded divisions were under. Nonetheless, he confided to Sherman that he intended to launch a counterstroke the following morning. Grant was exasperated by Lew Wallace's inexplicable failure to come up but was pleased by the arrival of Don Carlos Buell two hours earlier; during the late afternoon the first division of the Army of the Ohio advanced on to the battlefield. As a further precaution, to protect the latter's route at Pittsburg Landing and shore up Hurlbut's buckling line, Grant placed a line of stragglers across the rear of the army that provided his divisions with additional support. Sherman still had to assume that succor would come from the right. Thus he and McClernand sanctioned one last short withdrawal to a defensive line that would be easier to hold and simultaneously protect the bridge over Owl Creek along the Paducah–Hamburg road that Wallace would surely use. As the two divisions withdrew, they were fortunate to be charged rashly by weak Confederate cavalry who could not match the firepower of infantry, and morale soared as they drove off the attackers effortlessly. On the new position, Sherman found that he "had a clear field [of fire] to about 200 yards wide in my immediate front, and contented myself with keeping the enemy's infantry at that distance for the rest of

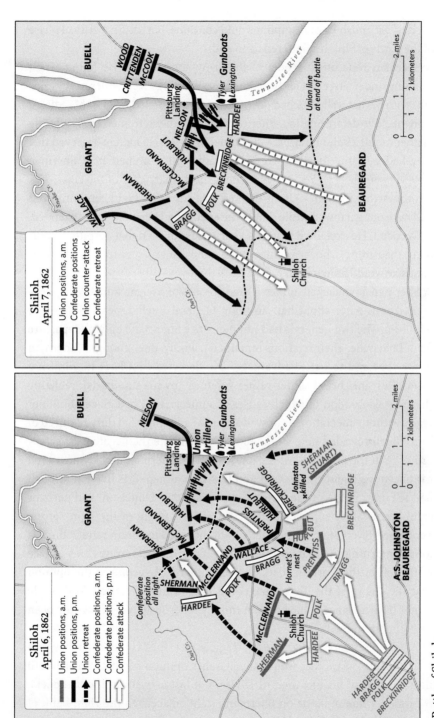

Shiloh
April 7, 1862

Union positions, a.m.
Confederate positions
Union counter-attack
Confederate retreat

Tennessee River

BUELL

WOOD
CRITTENDEN
McCOOK

Pittsburg Landing
NELSON
HURLBUT
McCLERNAND
SHERMAN
GRANT
WALLACE

Tyler **Gunboats**
Lexington

HARDEE
POLK BRECKINRIDGE
BRAGG

Shiloh Church

Union line
at end of battle

BEAUREGARD

2 miles
2 kilometers
1
0

Shiloh
April 6, 1862

Union positions, a.m.
Union positions, p.m.
Union retreat
Confederate positions, a.m.
Confederate positions, p.m.
Confederate attack

BUELL

NELSON

Pittsburg Landing
Union Artillery

Tennessee River

GRANT

Confederate
position
all night

HURLBUT
McCLERNAND
SHERMAN
WALLACE
BRAGG

SHERMAN
HARDEE
McCLERNAND
POLK

Shiloh Church
HARDEE
McCLERNAND
POLK

Tyler **Gunboats**
Lexington

PRENTISS
BRECKINRIDGE
Johnston
× killed

SHERMAN
(STUART)

Hornet's
nest
HURLBUT
PRENTISS
BRAGG

BRECKINRIDGE

BRAGG

A.S. JOHNSTON
BEAUREGARD

HARDEE
BRAGG
POLK
BRECKINRIDGE

2 miles
2 kilometers
1
0

Battle of Shiloh

the day." Skirmishing and sniping would continue, but the first, critical phase of the Battle of Shiloh spluttered to an end.

Sherman rode off to report to the army commander. He found Grant standing under a tree not far from Pittsburg Landing. Even under heavy rainfall "with his hat well slouched down and coat well pulled up," Grant radiated a pugnacious determination. Sherman instinctively refrained from offering further inquiries about retreat—his initial impulse. He merely observed that they had seen the "devil's own day." Grant replied immediately, Sherman recalled years later: " 'Yes,' he said with a short, sharp puff of the cigar; 'lick 'em tomorrow though.' " Grant divined that his army had been reinforced and his front narrowed while that of the enemy had been diffused, extended, and eroded. He explained that his experience indicated that despite the mutual exhaustion, "whoever assumed the offensive was sure to win." A counterstroke would follow.[24]

Sherman bivouacked under a tree to smoke a cigar and take a well-earned rest. After about half an hour, General Buell appeared to confer with him. The two generals had not met since Sherman's baleful departure from Louisville. Their relations remained friendly. Buell thought "Sherman never appeared to better advantage." He depicted him later in admiring terms: "a frank, brave solder rather subdued [by his standards], realizing the critical situation in which causes of some sort . . . had placed him, but ready without affectation or bravado, to [do] anything that duty required of him." Buell revealed here a tendency to accentuate the negative aspects—rather than the positive—of the day's fighting. Sherman quickly answered his questions about the ground and lent him a map. It is likely that Buell had felt envy at the praise lavished on Grant after Donelson, and perhaps exhibited a rather superior attitude toward the plight of the Army of the Tennessee. Sherman told him that Grant intended to counterattack the following morning and that it would be beneficial if Buell's troops took a place to the left of the Corinth road. Sherman guardedly ventured the opinion that the Army of the Tennessee could have won the battle unaided. He might have advanced this opinion more vociferously had his visitor been any other than Buell.[25]

At last, after dark and a series of tragicomic errors, countermarches, and interminable delays that would sour Grant's opinion of Lew Wallace until near the end of his life, the 3rd Division at last arrived on the battlefield. It formed a line of battle on Sherman's right adjacent to the right bank of Owl Creek.

Rain fell steadily during the night, but morale in his division, Sherman insisted, remained buoyant, almost sunny. Rations were found for the men and distributed; his troops were "determined to redeem on Monday the losses of Sunday." At daybreak Sherman received his orders from Grant to regain his encampment. No concerted plan with the Army of the Ohio existed, simply an agreement that an attack should take place. Most of Buell's troops took station on the Union left, though Brigadier General Alexander McCook's 2nd Division took station on the Union right flank just to the left of the Corinth road close to Sherman, as previously agreed. McCook had served with Sherman in Kentucky; Sherman was delighted to see his division and would pay handsome tribute to its performance in his report on the battle. Buell's arrival also permitted the recall of Stuart's brigade; Stuart had been seriously wounded, and although he reported for duty on Monday morning, he needed urgent medical treatment, so Colonel T. Kilby Smith took command of the brigade. Sherman's staff were ordered to round up all the stragglers in the divisional area they could find and put them into the line. The 13th Missouri Infantry did not need to be asked; its colonel sought Sherman out and volunteered to serve under his command. On April 7 the 5th Division could only be described as a collection of fragments fighting at the same time, but Sherman's presence and volcanic energy held them all together.

At 10:00 a.m. Sherman waited impatiently for the signal to advance; McCook's artillery had already opened fire. He had two formed brigades in hand, those of Buckland and Smith. At the last moment, Major Taylor galloped up with fresh ammunition and three guns that were quickly unlimbered and added to the firing line. The division advanced steadily as far as Shiloh Church but then stumbled. McCook's 6th Brigade had been held up by ferocious resistance, and it appeared to Sherman likely that the Confederates were about to throw in a counterattack. He then received a plea from McClernand for the loan of some artillery pieces; without hesitation, and despite his own shortage, he offered up Taylor's battery.

As Sherman cantered backward and forward overseeing this transfer, he spotted two other guns that seemed to lack a master. Once the staff had them brought forward, he discovered with evident delight that they were both 24-pounder howitzers. At about 2:00 p.m. Sherman ordered his division forward again in concert with McCook's 4th Brigade, commanded by Brigadier General Lovell H. Rousseau. The combined force approached a "dreaded wood" of water oaks covered by two batteries of Confederate artillery whose canister and "grape" had already devastated the ranks of Colonel August Willich's regiment, the 32nd Indiana Infantry in McCook's 6th Brigade. Sherman, however, had the unexpected solution to this obstacle already at hand and personally sited his newfound howitzers. As he later reported, "their well-directed fire first silenced the enemy's guns to the left, and afterwards at the Shiloh Meeting-House." The division's advance resumed, and by 4:00 p.m., with the enemy fleeing before them, the 5th Division reached its original front line; it had taken seven guns that made up for the previous day's losses.

As Sherman rode forward to meet Rousseau's brigade, one of the most pleasing experiences of this day greeted him. His own tenure in command of these troops in Kentucky (including three battalions of regulars) had not been a happy one. They had previously hooted him at Muldraugh Hill. On this day, though, the results of his alertness, tactical skill, and drive had saved many of their lives. They cheered him wildly, and then repeatedly, whenever he visited their camps.[26]

Faulty Confederate generalship had played its part in the Union triumph. Beauregard had forfeited the initial advantage when he unleashed unwieldy echelons of infantry across the whole battlefront, leaving no troops available to create a reserve. But Sherman's troops were too exhausted to play a major part in the pursuit on Monday evening. On the following day, during the faltering pursuit, his skirmishers and cavalry (the 3rd and 4th Battalions of the 4th Illinois Cavalry under T. Lyle Dickey) were caught unawares by the Confederate rear guard under Nathan Bedford Forrest at Fallen Timbers. But once again, Sherman's cold tactical eye saved his men from further humiliation. He quickly brought up an infantry brigade, the cavalry and skirmishers rallied, and it was the Confederate cavalry that panicked and deserted the field and their commander, who continued to ride on, unaccompanied, toward Sherman's line; at the very least Forrest should have been taken prisoner, but slashing with his saber and firing desperately with his revolver, he was wounded but escaped his pursuers.[27]

Sherman had much to be proud of in his conduct over these three tumultuous and challenging days. His report contains praise for all those who helped him: his brigade commanders, especially Hildebrand, had stayed to assist Sherman even after his brigade had deserted him; several of the commanding officers who had displayed conspicuous courage, including Worthington; Major Turner; the "fragments of men of the disordered regiments"; and finally, his staff who had carried out his bidding. But the chief reason why the 5th Division played such a prominent part in the stubborn defense on Sunday and in reclaiming what had been lost on Monday lay with its commander. Sherman's determination to hold back the tide of the Confederate onslaught, tactical insight, overall appreciation of the battle, willingness to assume responsibility, and empathy with the problems of other divisional commanders made an enormous contribution to the Union success at Shiloh.[28]

The conditions imposed by an improvised defense offered Sherman no choice but to display outstanding personal leadership so that his soldiers would be inspired to stand and hold their ground. "None of them," Sherman observed in plain language, "had ever been under fire or beheld heavy columns of an enemy bearing down on them as they did on us last Sunday." His men lacked any experience of the importance of organization and combination. Sherman threw himself into the task so recklessly that one of his biographers suggests that he may have been suicidal.[29] There is no hint of this in his correspondence—only a willingness to sacrifice himself if the cause warranted it. The truth is rather more prosaic. The enemy had defined this professional challenge for him, not the inner urges of his personality. War often presents commanders with little or, even more frequently, no measure of choice. If Sherman was to surmount his early failures, including not being prepared to receive an attack at Shiloh, he would have to persuade thousands of very nervous, callow recruits to stand and fight. In short, he behaved with a disdain for danger evident among so many earlier American commanders, like George Washington and Zachary Taylor, and many of his peers in the Civil War.

Sherman did this triumphantly over the two days of Shiloh. He laid the basis for the rapport that he would develop with his soldiers in the later campaigns. The Confederate corps commander, Leonidas Polk, admired the 5th Division's behavior, as it fought with "determined courage and contested every inch of ground." But the human cost was substantial. Over 48 hours Sherman's division sustained just over 2,000 casualties, that is, one-quarter of his initial strength, including 302 men killed.

The day after the battle, Sherman's division advanced 6 miles. Over the following weeks he would receive three new brigade commanders. Both Brigadier James W. Denver and Colonel Morgan L. Smith were received enthusiastically by Sherman and were appointed to the 3rd and 1st Brigades, respectively. They "relieve me much of the details and drudgery," he observed with relief, "where [previously] I had nothing but inexperienced colonels."

His reaction to the third, Brigadier General John A. Logan, a former Illinois congressman, was more equivocal. Initially Logan made a favorable impression, but they would come to have a tense and checkered relationship.[30]

The Battle of Shiloh might be over, but the controversy surrounding its conduct had only just begun. In the ensuing war of words, Sherman developed a number of themes that came to dominate his outlook. He clearly felt conscious that he had been criticized earlier for exaggerating "the strength, courage and determination of our enemies"; Shiloh and events at Corinth two months later gave him the opportunity to point out that he had not been wrong. The first issue that received the benefit of his forensic if frequently belligerent intellect was the success of the Confederate surprise attack that had drawn much attention in the newspapers. He offered a stout defense of his own division's conduct to all who might listen. He put most of the hyperbole surrounding the morning of April 6—graphic descriptions of soldiers being bayoneted in their tents—down to credulous fools prepared to believe "stories of butchery . . . got up by cowards to cover their Shame"; his own surgeons reported treating no bayonet wounds that day. He damned as "infamous" the attempts to single out Grant as the scapegoat; Ohio journalist Whitelaw Reid made wild claims, endlessly repeated by others, that Grant had been drunk that morning. Sherman's experience of the press at Shiloh inflamed his recollections of his own harsh treatment at the hands of reporters. Henceforward he found the sight of them insufferable and dedicated himself to denouncing them at every opportunity. "They keep shy of me," he announced proudly, "as I have said the first one I catch I will hang as a spy." He could respect Southerners, even as rebels, "but for these mean contemptible slanderous and false villains who seek reputation by abuse of others," he had nothing but scorn. Ellen warned her husband of the dangers of his unreasoning loathing, but he took no notice. He refused to "acknowledge the new Power of the Press."[31]

It is sometimes suggested that such furious opinions were the product of a post-Shiloh euphoria—an ecstatic release.[32] The dominant tone of Sherman's correspondence is rather more akin to relief. Sherman cautioned Ellen not to attack McClellan as the prime author of his eclipse. He did not forget to pick up some cannon and musket balls for young Willy. Sherman was not troubled by his wound, though his fingers stiffened, making writing difficult. He suffered "small pain" by comparison with the thousands "with all sorts of terrible wounds." Once again he identified lack of discipline as the root cause of military inefficiency. "Men run away," he lamented in a repetition of his complaints after Bull Run, "won't obey their officers, won't listen to threats, remonstrances, and prayers of their seniors, but after the danger is passed they raise false issues to cover their infamy."[33]

Sherman was already sick of war but could see no end to it. "Indeed I never expect it or to survive it," he added fatalistically. The shock of Shiloh forced him to reconsider the "horrid" nature of the war. But he did not appear to be very sensitive to the effects of the battle that reverberated through the American political and social fabric. The Army of the Tennessee had sustained a minimum of 10,162 casualties (1,754 killed and 8,408 wounded).[34] Such a weight of loss and maiming had a disproportionate effect because it was unparalleled in this martial but unmilitary society. Even the press controversy can be viewed as a reflection of revulsion against such casualties. Sherman, though, felt nothing but impatience with subsequent well-intentioned efforts by public figures to alleviate the suffering of the troops. Even members of the United States Sanitary Commission, a private charity composed of men from Sherman's own class with political opinions close to his own on many issues—the "Sanitaries"—were dismissed as bumbling nuisances. The appearance of three war governors on an errand of mercy, Louis P. Harvey of Wisconsin, Richard Yates of Illinois, and Oliver P. Morton of Indiana, received even less sympathy. Sherman stopped Morton from removing the Hoosier troops from his division. He claimed that if he allowed these men to return home he would never get them back, as he had discovered when men with slight wounds entered state hospitals.[35]

Sherman also took exception to the efforts of Ohio lieutenant governor Benjamin Stanton—"this Demagogue"—to interfere in his affairs. Colonel Rodney Mason of the 71st Ohio Volunteer Infantry had enlisted Stanton's support in a dispute with Sherman. Mason had published a letter in the *Cincinnati Commercial*, a newspaper calculated to cause Sherman maximum annoyance and embarrassment. Mason accused Sherman of favoring Illinois over Ohio troops and "exiling" his regiment to Clarksville, Tennessee. Sherman explained to his brother-in-law Phil Ewing that on Monday, April 7, Colonel Stuart (an Illinois officer), though wounded, had brought his brigade back in line with the main body of the 5th Division; the 71st Ohio, he added acidly, although "very small in numbers" was present, but its colonel was not. Later Major Sanger found Mason "crouching behind a bank of Earth," but his pleas that the colonel should return to duty only provoked him to sprint "direct to the Steamboat Landing."

Mason typified for Sherman all that was wrong with Union officers, even though he liked him personally. Sherman did not censure the men, but he wanted Mason cashiered. Such feeble leaders rotted morale because they had "impressed the men with the belief that all they had to do was to come South and the Secesh would run." Grant, possibly because of political pressure, gave Mason another chance, but Mason was "mustered out" of the service after an ignominious surrender of Clarksville. Indeed, Sherman pointed out that Grant, and not he, had ordered Mason to Clarksville. The whole affair, in Sherman's opinion, was an example of the pernicious influence of political activity on military affairs.[36]

The actual pace of military operations slowed considerably after Halleck's arrival at Pittsburg Landing on April 11. Sherman received orders to make a third attempt to cut the Memphis–Charleston Railroad. He detached a brigade of infantry and the 4th Illinois Cavalry and with these 1,000 men, in heavy rain, succeeded in destroying Bear Creek Bridge, a wooden trestle that spanned 500 feet over this swampy stream. Halleck was delighted by Sherman's success but otherwise found much to criticize in the activities of the Army of the Tennessee. Halleck had feuded with Buell before gaining the overall command in the West, but if there was one matter on which they both agreed it was to undervalue Grant. The latter had already anticipated Halleck's criticisms of what he regarded as his slipshod methods and had issued orders tightening up on, among other things, picketing and outposts. In subsequent weeks Halleck concentrated all three of his armies on the Tennessee, having transferred John Pope's thither after its success in seizing Island No. 10 on April 1, 1862. He then reorganized the command arrangements. He exercised overall command, replaced Grant with George H. Thomas, and "promoted" Grant as his "second-in-command"— a blatant vote of no confidence in his abilities as a field commander. The change of army commander presented Sherman and Thomas with no difficulty. As former "classmates, intimately connected," Sherman recalled in his *Memoirs*, ". . . it made to us little difference who commanded the other, provided the good cause prevailed." This affectionate if bland observation concealed the steady growth of resentment and tension between Grant and Thomas, with Sherman as conduit.

In the ensuing weeks Sherman made not the least of his services to the Union war effort by persuading Grant not to resign. His contemporary correspondence does not give this act the prominence he later gave it in his *Memoirs*, as his faith in Halleck's ability remained undiminished; indeed, he "rejoiced" at Grant's decision to stay because he hoped to enlist him in a joint campaign "to clip the wings of this public enemy," namely, the press, as both of them had been libeled, something that Grant had far too much political sense to attempt.[37] Such was Sherman's confidence at this date that he claimed that he would happily give himself up as the scapegoat for Shiloh. He thought the hysteria ridiculous, and "I knew it must be when the many govern the few." He taunted his brother John: "Send out an investigating committee and make it completely ridiculous." This last gibe was a reference to the Joint Committee on the Conduct of the War, which was making a fearsome reputation for itself in the East; fortunately, it showed an obsessive interest only in the war in Virginia and neglected Shiloh.[38]

Unhampered by political distractions, Halleck arrayed 100,000 men but failed to do very much with them in a sluggish, overcautious march on Corinth. Sherman took the opportunity to sharpen up his procedures and trained his division hard, emphasizing that if it was ever attacked again "no regiment should fall back without orders from the divisional commander." During the Corinth campaign, marked by the digging of extensive field fortifications on both sides, the troops of the 5th Division built seven entrenched camps, and even though his soldiers quickly moved on, they did so without complaint. He was gratified to be told by Halleck that his division was one of the best in the three armies.[39]

Halleck entrusted the right flank again to Sherman's conscientious care. He excelled at reconnaissance and the study of the ground. On May 17, in a perfectly executed operation, the 5th Division, reinforced by two regiments and a battery of artillery from Hurlbut's 4th Division, seized the Russell House, a valuable advance picket for future assaults on the heavily fortified town of Corinth. Ten days later, Halleck entrusted Sherman with an attack on the Confederate left to take a log cabin transformed into a blockhouse where the Corinth road crossed Bridge Creek in thick woods. Sherman made good use of his knowledge of artillery, aided by Major Taylor, and posted a strong reserve ready to exploit any advantage. He thus transformed an operation that Halleck regarded as a "strong demonstration" into something more important. Sherman got his guns within 1,300 yards of the main Confederate defenses. By May 29 he sensed—as Confederate officers could be overheard giving their orders—that Corinth was about to be abandoned, readied his troops, and claimed to be the first to enter it. His men then undertook sterling work in an effort to restore the Memphis–Charleston Railroad that they had earlier expended so much effort trying to disrupt and to save the rolling stock the Confederates attempted to burn. In this swampy area, alas, Sherman contracted malaria.[40]

The battle for Corinth was hardly "one of the most desperate battles of history," as Sherman expected, but the 5th Division had excelled itself. Sherman had been impressed by the efforts of both sides to reduce the risk of surprise attack by maneuvering "behind earth and timber barriers." The Confederate defenses were so elaborate that Sherman indulged a continuing tendency to exaggerate Southern numbers—although it was widespread among his peers. He put Beauregard's strength at 100,000 men. Also, the quantity of supplies that his men found in Corinth, "good bread, ham, sugar, Rice &c," indicated a well-organized force. Sherman cautioned Ellen not to believe rumors that the Confederacy again tottered on the brink of collapse—though he sometimes veered toward this opinion himself. They were facing "well trained, well clad and well fed soldiers, our equals in all respects." His admiration for the Southern martial effort would eventually determine his response as to how it might be defeated.

Whatever the solution to the problem of compelling the South to submit to the Northern will, Sherman held the North had to look with renewed energy to rectify its own weaknesses rather than continue a distracting effort to emphasize the enemy's deficiencies. Sherman displayed all the pessimism of the true conservative. He doubted at times whether the North could find this additional reserve of energy, and if this was the case, "we might as well give it [the war] up." Sherman also feared the consequences should the Confederacy resort to widespread guerrilla action—another important theme in his thinking. He criticized the policy of advancing overland toward Corinth as too slow but could not bring himself to censure Halleck. "We want the Mississippi now, in its whole length and a moment should not be lost." Such a great task would be rendered more difficult by the death on April 25 of C. F. Smith, who had served as a mentor to both Grant and Sherman and whose wise counsel would be sorely missed.[41]

Sherman felt pride in his achievements over the last five months. He had thought about the war and its character and tentatively come to certain conclusions about its nature. He worried about the North's capacity to see things through to a victorious conclusion. He feared that "our Government has gradually been tending to anarchy." The only way to arrest this process should be to demand that all obey the laws. Although not yet cognizant of this, Sherman during the spring had established the most important friendship of his maturity—with Grant. He had rallied to overturn an injustice but had failed to fully grasp the true magnitude of Grant's ability and its importance to the Union war effort. Despite his doubts about the wisdom of the concentration on the Tennessee River, he persisted in viewing Halleck as the general most able to command large armies, the commander who demonstrated "great sagacity, more than any other leader in this war," and "merits the confidence reposed in him." In these remarks, Sherman repaid Halleck's loyalty to him. Of course, his commander reposed confidence in Sherman, too, and that pleased him. Throughout the previous weeks he had continued to deny any wish for broader responsibility. In July he received orders to command both Hurlbut's 4th Division and his own and to take command of the administration of the recently occupied Memphis. A new sphere for his talents had opened up for him after all.[42]

7

Corps Commander, July–December 1862

"The trees are now in full bloom," Sherman informed his brother-in-law Phil Ewing, "oaks of various kinds prevailing—with cottonwood, willow, dogwood and plum along the watercourses—a good deal of undergrowth, fields few and scattered—people nearly all gone abandoning everything save for a few cattle and hogs running loose, horses and mules all gone." The challenge before Sherman in the summer days of 1862 lay far from such lyricism. He would find himself reluctantly searching in the sharp-edged undergrowth of Confederate resistance. On July 5 orders to assume command of the Military District of Memphis, Tennessee, arrived—a job he preferred to any other. When Sherman took up the appointment, he embraced the conservative view of the war that upheld the importance of conciliating Southerners. Alas, the realities of fighting a great war kept breaking in and disturbing his repose. After four or five months, Sherman came to realize that the irreconcilable could not be reconciled. These months proved significant in laying the foundations for Sherman's much harsher, increasingly punitive ideas about the conduct of the war.[1]

Sherman's attitudes during these months are easy to follow because his assumption of garrison command gave ample opportunity for him to correspond with his fellow officers, friends, and family without the distractions of field command. "My duties," he confided to Ellen, "are multifarious, though not laborious."[2]

Sherman passes over these five months quickly in his *Memoirs*. He arrived in Memphis on July 21, the anniversary of the First Battle of Bull Run. "I found the place dead; no business doing, the stores closed, churches, schools and everything shut up," he records. Sherman feared that the prevalence of rebel sympathy among "the whole civil population would become a dead weight on our hands." His account is informed with a measure of wisdom after the event because he does not mention his own failed attempts to conciliate the rebels or his inability to reduce their Confederate partiality. Yet Sherman did work through the contradictions and ambiguities in his view of the character of Confederate resistance.[3]

These hot, dusty months began conventionally enough. Sherman enjoyed corps level responsibilities, as command of Stephen A. Hurlbut's division had been added to his own, and he found working with his old friend a pleasant experience. Before arriving in Memphis, he had worked on building railroads and bridges. He had found seven locomotives and 60 cars that had not been burned, and all were restored to use, thanks to the ingenuity and technical skill of the men he commanded. His growing appreciation for the talents of volunteer soldiers marks another change in the direction of his earlier attitudes. But this success in repairing communications with Corinth was qualified by the ease with which Confederate cavalry disrupted this line. Sherman had to haul his stores on cumbersome, slow-moving wagon trains, and he deployed the 57th Ohio Infantry to protect them. However, the Confederate superiority in cavalry permitted them to keep a safe distance "and pick up stragglers and venturesome pillagers of which I confess our army contains too large a proportion." Tipped off by local sympathizers, they quickly withdrew before Union cavalry could catch up with them. "There is no Union feeling here," Sherman observed ominously.[4]

He attended to his garrison duties conscientiously, employing his business and legal knowledge adroitly. A measure of prosperity returned to Memphis, as the stores, schools, and churches reopened. Sherman made a point of attending services at the Episcopal church. During his first visit the minister intoned the supplicating prayer while Sherman sat head bowed, perhaps snoozing. But he was more alert than he appeared; when the customary request for divine protection for the president of the United States was omitted, Sherman stood up and supplied the missing refrain in a ringing voice. The following Monday he issued an order that the prayer be observed in full or the church would be closed again.[5]

Sherman restored the city's mayor and attended to the repair of Memphis's finances. He set up a new police force in order to reduce the number of Union soldiers on the streets while retaining a strong provost guard. "I have the most unbounded respect for the civil laws, courts and authorities," he declared, "and Shall do all in my power to restore them to their proper use, viz., the protection of life, liberty and property." To pay for these measures, Sherman encouraged commercial activities not always conducive to public order: bars and grog shops were allowed to open and taxed $25 per month. But he refused to collect state and federal taxes. He also drew the line at outright confiscation: "We deal only with possession." He envisaged his role as a kind of trusteeship, until the courts could be set up "to execute the laws."

These included the Confiscation Act of July 1862 that Congress aimed at the use of slaves by Confederates, which decreed that any slave who entered a Union encampment would be freed. Sherman realized that as Grant had not yet implemented the Confiscation Acts, he would have to rely on the laws of war.[6]

The development of Sherman's thought about war made greatest progress when he directed his energies toward dissecting its general nature. His experience in the Shiloh and Corinth campaigns confirmed his view of the magnitude of the task that lay ahead for the Federals. The war might consume "300,000 men per year for a long time. . . . To allow our armies to run down in the face & country of the Enemy invites defeat and prolongs the strife." The duration of the war would pose thorny problems when the occupiers dealt with the civil population enduring occupation, defeated but not subdued. "We tell them we want nothing they have . . . but they don't believe us, and I fear that this universal feeling will cause the very result they profess to dread." He expressed the thoughts lying behind this viewpoint in a letter to his daughter Minnie, admitting that though war demands cruelty and "even your papa has to do such acts," yet through it all, after a period living in Louisiana, "I cannot but think of these People as my old friends."[7]

Sherman's sense of duty thus presented him with a harsh personal dilemma. As he struggled to reconcile what he would have preferred to do with the way that the realities of the war were forcing him to act, three issues moved to the front of his mind: the conundrum posed by slavery, illicit trade with the rebels, and the increasingly audacious activities of guerrilla bands. The first, his attitude toward slavery and the property interests of Confederates, stemmed from an order issued initially by his predecessor at Memphis, Brigadier General Alvin P. Hovey, that required the departure south of all those subject to the provisions of the Confederate Conscription Act of April 1862. Sherman refused to modify this order, a form of compulsory eviction that would prevent Confederate irregulars from recruiting among men of military age. Sherman's main aim continued to be the transformation of Memphis into a safe base for future Union military operations. Consequently, he had no compunction in removing all "unfriendly" persons. After only ten days in the town, Sherman grasped that Memphis remained "secesh on both sides and all around. The idea of making them take the [loyalty] oath is absurd." That Oath of Allegiance, or loyalty oath, had since 1861 required former Confederates to pledge loyalty and allegiance to the Union.[8]

Sherman continued to propound his theory that the slaveholders, "the leading men are secesh," while the laborers and mechanics were at best "neutral or tired of war." Though he refused to make concessions to encourage the latter, time would reveal his interpretation of Southern resistance to be unduly optimistic. But the attack on the pecuniary interests of the Southern planter class would lie at the core of his future strategic ideas.[9]

Sherman was quicker to acknowledge that efforts to appeal to Southern unionism had been made in vain. The summer of 1862 ushered in what he called "the real struggle of conquest." Despite his fear of its "horrible convulsions," Sherman rapidly came to see that he could use emancipation as a weapon against the recalcitrant southern planter class. "Negro property and personal property are fair subjects of conquest, as also the possession of Real Estate during the lives of the present owners." Consequently, although he complained of the embarrassment that the Confiscation Acts caused him, he had by November "taken 600 houses" with rents totalling almost $150,000, "which goes to the Government." Then Sherman switched his attention to the slaves themselves, the most valuable property in the South. In General Orders No. 67 he employed first 600 and then 800 former slaves on the fortifications at Fort Pickering, being built to shield Memphis. By September their number had increased to 1,500 out of a total pool of 5,000 runaway slaves.[10]

What really embarrassed Sherman was his inability to lay his hands on any copies of the two Confiscation Acts. He had to improvise guidelines and relied on his father-in-law, Thomas Ewing Sr., for legal advice. He would feed and clothe his laborers but not their dependents. He assured Lieutenant Colonel John A. Rawlins that "I allow no force or undue persuasion in any case." He also found himself having to assure Confederate general Gideon J. Pillow, who claimed that his slaves had been forced to leave and his plantation destroyed, that he had no knowledge of any such action. He had taken precautions to prevent lawlessness or suffering and any retribution being taken against overseers; "the damage to plantations was only such as will attend all armies," of the kind that had accompanied Albert Sidney Johnston's movements in Kentucky the previous year, Sherman added.[11]

Sherman revealed his public-private ambivalence candidly when he described relations with an old school chum, Thomas Hunton, who had made his home in the South, in the following terms: "We are Enemies, still private friends." But his public duties required an ever-sterner face. He instructed his runaway slaves in the emphatic but friendly tones he always adopted toward blacks. "Boys if you want to go back to your master, Go—you are free to choose. You must now think for yourselves." Then he touched on the root of the matter. "Your master has seceded from his Parent Government and you have seceded from him—both wrong by law—but both exercising an undoubted natural Right to rebel." In fact, the Confiscation Acts rendered the last reflection invalid.

The key lesson that Sherman drew from these developments could be found hidden in the enemy's pocketbooks: "that one of the modes of bringing People to reason is to touch their Interests pecuniary or property." His historical reading, especially about the Napoleonic Wars, had taught him that punitive warfare followed a long and rightful tradition in the history of the Western world. Sherman would not permit his personal feelings ("I feel strong friendship as ever") to influence his professional judgment and his determination to employ punitive measures when they were required.[12]

Sherman also took advantage of Grant's invitation to write to him "more freely and fully in all matters of public interest" in order that he might present him with a considered statement of his views. He maintained that one way of destroying the political power of the planter class would be "universal Confiscation and colonization" by Northern migrants. He also advocated colonization of former slaves on former Confederate territory, "say Arkansas," "under some just and fair laws." After Lincoln issued the Preliminary Emancipation Proclamation in September 1862, Sherman's reaction was mild considering that he had formerly championed the slave system: it "can do no good and but little harm." What he did criticize was Lincoln's failure to create "machinery by which such freedom is assured." His views on this matter would become more astringent over the next two years.[13]

As the seizure of private property came to assume a more important place in Union strategy and policy, Sherman took the opportunity of offering Senator Andrew Johnson an emphatic codification of his ideas. The North needed to equal Southern audacity, Sherman argued, and one urgent step that needed to be taken was to force "all men" to choose their side: either to take the Oath of Allegiance, "thereby securing full rights to protection, or openly to rebel and forfeit their property and their lives."[14]

His increasingly stern view had resulted from frustrations with the burgeoning illicit trade with the Confederacy and the growing guerrilla threat. He quickly wearied of the first, which he regarded as a blight on his wartime service. The Union advance had opened up the Mississippi basin, especially since the fall of New Orleans the previous April, and made trade with the South possible again. Although the maintenance of the Union blockade remained a high priority, a semblance of internal trade offered a chance to break the self-imposed Confederate embargo on the export of cotton. In turn, these successes offered an opportunity for the Lincoln administration to improve relations with the greatest foreign customer for cotton, Great Britain. Consequently, Lincoln and Treasury Secretary Salmon P. Chase both issued licenses that entitled individuals to buy cotton. Great fortunes could be made trading with the South. Private enrichment in the public service, particularly in wartime, always enraged Sherman. And just to complicate matters, Union naval commanders viewed the seizure of cotton as legitimate "prize money" to be adjudicated by Northern courts.[15]

Sherman attempted to prohibit all Southern trade in his military district. He branded cotton "contraband of war"; if the blockade could be subverted, then the North would find itself supplying the Southern war economy and prolonging the war. He fulminated against fellow Buckeyes because he identified Cincinnati as the source of the illicit trade; it did more to prolong the war, he fumed, than Charleston, South Carolina—a rather typical Sherman exaggeration. He had no patience with the diplomatic argument; "let England get her cotton as she may," he snapped. He preferred to see cotton burned, but his minority view could not prevail against presidential displeasure. He had no choice but to allow Treasury agents to begin trading in his district, even though "it runs against the grain."[16]

By comparison, he found it much easier to deal with illicit trade in salt. He regarded this trade as "nefarious" because it aided the Confederate war effort more directly. Salt was in short supply throughout the South and was vital to curing meats that sustained Confederate armies in the field. To search for it, Sherman posted guards on the five roads radiating out of Memphis and empowered them to inspect all travelers and their vehicles. "We find clothing, percussion caps, and salt concealed in every conceivable shape," he reported, "and I doubt not that thousands of pistols reach the interior in this way." Try as he might Sherman could not stamp out this trade, though he did manage to reduce it.[17]

The spreading infection of guerrilla war he found the most troublesome of all his problems. Regular Confederate forces were no nearer to Memphis than Holly Springs or Senatobia. By the late summer, guerrilla attachments had become such a nuisance that Sherman estimated that the troops guarding the roads, and the sick and wounded, combined with patrols looking for stragglers, constituted one-half of the troops under his command. But the problems the guerrillas caused had not yet led to a resolution of his ambivalent attitudes. Even in October 1862 he still could not bring himself to regard Confederates as "the Enemy" like the British; they were still, he told his daughter Minnie, "our own People many of whom I knew in Earlier years, and with whom I was once very intimate." Such sentiment, alas, would prove valueless when Sherman confronted daily evidence of hardening resistance. Indeed, two months earlier he had been forced to admit to Grant, "All the people are now guerrillas, and they have a perfect understanding, when a smaller body gets out, they hastily assemble and attack, but when a large body move[s] out they scatter and go home."[18]

The majority of Confederate guerrillas mustered under the provisions of the Partisan Ranger Act of April 1862, which permitted the raising of guerrilla forces as part of the regular armed forces of the Confederacy. At first, Sherman had no desire to burn farms or punish the rural population, but he could not stand idly by and let such enemies strike with impunity. He became infuriated by partisan rangers as they sought to take advantage of both military worlds. They blended in "with the people and dr[e]w on them the consequences of their individual acts." Their champions, however, like Confederate general Thomas C. Hindman, claimed that they enjoyed belligerents' rights, that is, they should be treated like regular soldiers, not lawless civilians.[19]

Sherman the lawyer would have none of this and homed in ruthlessly on the contradictions inherent in the raising of "regular" guerrillas. Such discussions forced him to accept that the benefits of "conciliation" had gone unheeded. In September he had counseled moderation in case harshness provoked vengefulness. But by the following month he realized that this got him nowhere. On September 6 he mounted a guard over some rail lines in Mississippi, including parts from Jackson to Columbus, and dispatched elements of two cavalry regiments from Hurlbut's division to ride down and break up the guerrilla bands. He could not simultaneously protect the persons, property, and livelihood of those who attacked Union forces. On most days he was surrounded by Southerners who harangued him with tales of the indiscipline of Union troops who pillaged their property. Sherman remained sensitive to the dangers of succumbing to "the passions of our men" and knew that such offenses were committed. But he refused to accept that the cost of such damage as the clearing of ground for entrenchments and the dismantling of fences for firewood should not be borne by others than "those who made the war, and Generally war is destruction and nothing else." Sherman thus drew an important distinction between this kind of depredation, the by-products of military operations, and "the wanton waste committed by army stragglers."[20]

Random firing on Mississippi riverboats raised Sherman's blood pressure even more. As the miscreants could not be identified, "we punish the neighbors for not preventing them." He instituted a program of retaliation, notably the burning of houses. At the end of September, the small riverside town of Randolph, Tennessee, received exemplary punishment for shots fired at the *Eugene* and in a highly focused action was systematically destroyed by a single regiment. Sherman intended the action taken against Randolph as a deterrent, unlike his later techniques,. He warned Hindman in Arkansas that even guerrilla activity based there would not go "unnoticed." He also broached a theme that would eventually excite his imagination. "You initiated the game," he asserted harshly, with prophetic words, "and my word for it your people will regret it long after you pass from the earth." Sherman hinted at private remorse for "such acts" as the burning of Randolph, but he steeled himself for the conduct of intractable and unpleasant business; "it would be weakness and foolish in me to listen to appeals to feelings that are scorned by our Enemies."[21]

Sherman feared that a lengthening of the war would turn it into one of "extermination, not of soldiers alone . . . but the People." But his developing perspectives did not alter his earlier views on the South and the quality of Southern resistance; on the contrary, he found in them ample confirmation. The North faced 6 million dedicated Southerners; "every one of them is a keen bitter Enemy. The men are brave and trained in arms." The most vital power behind this resistance could be found in their "educated leaders, as good if not better than ours on the whole"; he had been impressed with the strength of Confederate unity, which contrasted badly with "our People and Press," who to Sherman's mind "appear more determined to ruin our army than that of the Enemy." Sherman invariably employed the South as a mirror image of all that he disliked about Northern society. But the deductions that Sherman drew from his assumptions spawned the most enduring legacy. He cautioned against relying exclusively on numerical strength in the face of such unremitting hostility. "All their people are armed and at war."[22]

By the end of his tenure of command at Memphis, Sherman had reached several significant conclusions that arouse the attention. By far the most striking relates to the duration of the Civil War. Sherman was one of the few Americans of this period who drew upon knowledge of the European military experience in an effort to explain the course of the Civil War, despite having no firsthand experience there (unlike McDowell or McClellan). When replying to a group of New York businessmen who had presented him with a sword "of great beauty in design & magnificently executed" in gratitude for his services on the field of Shiloh, Sherman remarked that wars "involving far less important principles have in Europe extended through tens of years"; in the Civil War after 17 months, "at every step of our progress we encounter the hate of a deluded people who regard us as Invaders of their soil and sacred rights." The essential challenge, he deduced, resided in countering this "bitter and determined hatred." He now agreed that it should be confronted, as all efforts at reconciliation had failed, employing "arms and arms alone." Union strategy should "be directed with a wise and united purpose," but it should be undeterred in seeking a complete victory over the insurgents. Only when federal authority was unconditionally acknowledged could "our Government . . . afford to be magnanimous to the people who in an evil hour resorted to arms in search of a Remedy provided by our Fundamental Law." Until then "we must fight it out."[23]

This insight brought him to the necessity of countering resistance to federal authority. Federal armies might "pass across & through the land, the war closes in behind and leaves the Same enmity behind." Union detachments were left isolated and vulnerable. Sherman identified one source of resistance: "all the women are secesh." Far from being peacemakers, they "inflamed the minds of their husbands & brothers" and brought "horrid" warfare on themselves. Sherman's exasperation with the women of Memphis in many ways serves as an appropriate epitaph to his attachment to conciliation.[24]

By October 1862 Sherman understood that he would play a prominent part in Grant's plans to seize the great Confederate fortress on the Mississippi River—Vicksburg. He did not underrate the challenge and expected that the Confederates might undermine Union efforts by advancing as far north as the Ohio River. But he felt "more at ease" than he had for many months now that the North had grasped "that we are in a Revolution." By the middle of November Sherman had got to work organizing, training, and equipping the "new levies" that Lincoln had called into service after the defeat at the Second Battle of Bull Run. He badly needed these troops to fill holes in his existing ranks; they also enabled him to create two new divisions, each of 24 regiments, with a further reserve of another 5 at Fort Pickering. He also had available nine field batteries, though he suffered from a cavalry shortage. But Sherman began to show a more optimistic face. "I am ready to move inland," he announced, "down the river, or anywhere." The tempo of operations began to pick up after the failure of Confederate efforts to fortify the mouth of the Yazoo River. This rendered an overland, direct approach on Vicksburg much less hazardous because the Confederates forfeited a base from which their ironclads might otherwise have challenged Union naval control of the Mississippi River. Sherman began to contemplate a plan that would enable him to land on the east bank of the Mississippi and take the Walnut Hills on which Vicksburg sits.[25]

On November 17 Sherman received a missive from Grant instructing him to confer at Columbus, Kentucky, and bring "a good map of the country south of you"—if he had one available. There Grant explained that he intended to advance and attack the troops of Vicksburg's commander, the renegade Pennsylvanian Lieutenant General John C. Pemberton, at the earliest opportunity. Pemberton's army had taken up a strong position behind the Tallahatchie River. Grant intended to take Holly Springs, Mississippi, and then Abbeville. Meanwhile, Major General James B. McPherson would join Grant at Holly Springs with a division from Corinth. Holly Springs would thus become the main supply base for his overland offensive.[26]

The detailed orders that Grant issued for the first Vicksburg campaign even before the Columbus meeting stipulated rapid preparation and celerity of movement. "I am ready to move from here any day and only await your movements," he reported. Grant's orders required Sherman to make an amphibious descent on Vicksburg and thus initiate the general advance. Grant could not have spelled out Sherman's mission in clearer language. From Memphis he should organize a combined military and naval expedition and "move on Vicksburg." Yet Grant confided a certain perplexity because he had picked up "mysterious rumours" from the newspapers of a new command being mooted for Major General John A. McClernand that would give him responsibility for a new, dynamic operation that would be entrusted with taking Vicksburg. Grant asked for official clarification of this curious arrangement. Halleck replied briskly that Grant commanded all the troops in the Department of West Tennessee, established just the month before, and should proceed with his plans as he saw fit. Hence Grant suddenly desired to talk matters over face to face with Sherman.[27]

McClernand and Sherman had last fought together at Shiloh, and the latter had never changed his initial opinion that McClernand was nothing but a bombastic, shallow glory-seeker of mediocre military judgment. Grant's exhortation for haste had more than a tactical bearing on this campaign. Both Grant and Sherman were keen to take the field before McClernand arrived equipped with an authority that might grant him additional and unearned credit.[28]

McClernand's mischievous intervention proved to be another imped-iment that brought Grant and Sherman together. Their exchange of corre-spondence in the final months of 1862 reveals that more of their friendship's warmth lay on Grant's side than Sherman's. The latter continued to be loyal, conscientious, and enthusiastic, but not outwardly affectionate in tone as his exchanges with Halleck were. In the summer Sherman confided to Phil Ewing his relative and rather surprising assessment of Union commanders. "Buell is our best soldier, Halleck the ablest man—Grant very brave but not brilliant. Thomas slow, cool and methodic. I don't think much of Pope or McClernand." Stanton he brushed aside as "a liar and coward"—though Grant would never have indulged himself in a comparable savage indict-ment of his civilian boss even in private correspondence. Sherman regretted the lack of "steady progress" that had followed Halleck's promotion. "I fear alarms, hesitations and doubt." Grant had still not taken Halleck's place in Sherman's affections and professional regard, but their joint trials with McClernand would eventually lead to a transformation in Sherman's estima-tion of Grant's true stature as a man and a general. But his growing regard for Grant would be severely tested in the following five months.[29]

Sherman had not neglected Grant's injunction on the need for speedy preparation. On Monday, November 24, he confided to his brother John, "I start on Wednesday with all the troops that can be spared from Memphis." The enemy lay about 60 miles south of the latter, and he had impressed all he could find to sustain his advance—corn, mules, horses, and wagons. Such methods had a dual advantage; they "assist us and deprive the enemy of re-sources." Ethical doubts about the program of attacks on Southern railroads that he had instituted in September had long since vanished. His immediate objective was the occupation of Chulahoma, a hamlet about 20 miles south of Holly Springs, where he hoped to "communicate with Grant," who should have arrived in its vicinity by then. He estimated their combined forces at perhaps 50,000, but more likely 40,000 men.[30]

Sherman's columns left Memphis on schedule and marched on a par-allel series of roads southwars. Grant had set a cracking pace, mainly be-cause he wanted to strike before the Confederates could reinforce their entrenched lines on the Tallahatchie River. Sherman had received permis-sion from Halleck to use troops based at Helena, Arkansas, and he contacted Brigadier General Frederick Steele, whose alacrity in cooperating in an attack on the Confederate left impressed him. Getting the formal permission of Steele's departmental commander, Major General Samuel R. Curtis, proved more of a time-consuming problem, but it was eventually proffered; thereafter Sherman opened a friendly correspondence with Curtis, keeping him apprised of developments during the campaign. Another action under Brigadier General Alvin P. Hovey, near Charleston, went ahead, forcing the enemy to hasten in their retreat eastward. Sherman faced a further obstacle getting his two divisions across the Mississippi to link up with Grant. During these vexing days he formed the highest opinion of the commander of the 6th Illinois Cavalry, Colonel Benjamin H. Grierson, a former music teacher— another indication of his changing views on volunteer soldiers.[31]

Thus by December 2 Sherman had two divisions secure on the line of the Tallahatchie, near College Hill. He conferred again with Grant near Oxford, three days later. After this meeting Grant issued Sherman a new set of orders. He should return forthwith to Memphis with one of his divisions; then he should take this and the two divisions based there and any other supporting units by water to Vicksburg. Then, with the cooperation of Rear Admiral David Dixon Porter's gunboats, he should "proceed to the reduction of that place in such a manner as circumstances and your own judgment may dictate." In like fashion, the movement and logistics of the operation, notably cooperation with the US Navy, were left entirely in Sherman's hands. Until Grant received word from Sherman, he would wait "in readiness" to cooperate with him in the defeat of Pemberton's army. In the meantime, Grant would exert pressure on Pemberton's lines to distract him and "keep up the impression of a continuous move."[32]

A rapid return to Memphis would present a number of challenges for Sherman. Simply directing his scattered land forces would be difficult. He would also have to deal with the US Navy. Before leaving College Hill, he had issued a temporary farewell to the troops he left behind. Sherman's order reassured them that "their General studies by day and night the plan which leads to victorious results at the least cost of life and treasure." During the farewell parade, some of his regimental commanders "almost cried, and the men cheered till my little mare Dolly nearly jumped out of her skin." Sherman was taken aback by this display of trust and affection and would call upon this during the ensuing weeks.[33]

On arriving back in Memphis on December 12, Sherman threw himself into his many tasks. The ensuing weeks were among the most hectic even in Sherman's tumultuous life. Despite the pressure, he took infinite care in cooperating with the capable but prickly and quarrelsome Admiral Porter, whose ironclads were based at Cairo, Illinois. Sherman had already made Porter's acquaintance earlier in the year during the operations on the Tennessee River and had taken his measure. He may also have heard comment about the upshot of the quarrels between Porter and his army colleague Benjamin F. Butler over who deserved credit for the fall of New Orleans. On the strength of his record at Memphis, Sherman briefly expressed an interest in succeeding Butler when the latter's appointment was called into question, but his interest proved a passing fancy. Sherman concentrated on developing a constructive relationship with Porter. The admiral sailed down to Memphis to visit Sherman; he seemed to prefer working with blunt, plain-speaking men like Grant and Sherman who did not provoke him, given his thin-skinned, jealous, and suspicious nature. On December 8 Sherman had taken the precaution of writing to Porter apprising him of the campaign's progress so far. He detailed Grant's advance across the Tallahatchie and the appearance of Steele's division from Helena that "utterly confounded them and they are now in full retreat"; Sherman predicted that Pemberton's forces would re-form behind the Yalaobusha River with their center anchored on Grenada.[34]

"Time now is the grand object," he stressed to Porter. "We must not give time for new combinations. I know you will promptly cooperate." He then turned to sketch in the elements of his plan. Porter and the gunboats should engage Vicksburg's batteries while Sherman's troops worked around the city destroying all "inland communications." Thereafter the naval and land forces would combine for an assault on Vicksburg. Sherman shrewdly observed, "In this I will defer much to you." Such a sentiment could not have been better calculated to engage Porter's full support.[35]

Sherman's subtle operational design rested on a concept that sought to hamper Confederate movement by attacking the railroad infrastructure yet simultaneously avoided its effects by employing waterborne transport. He hoped to drive Confederate forces back to Meridian while Grant "presses them in front." The tactical plan that he fashioned to gain these objectives required the cutting of rail and road links to Monroe, Louisiana, and Jackson, Mississippi, followed by Sherman's appearance "up the Yazoo, threatening the Mississippi Central [Rail]road where it crosses the Big Black." But he had to get the operation moving before the winter rains intervened and washed the roads away.

His whirlwind of activity resulted in the creation of a viable force designated the Right Wing of the Army of the Tennessee. He had taken Morgan L. Smith's division back with him to Memphis and around this built a force of four divisions. Those of Brigadier Generals A. J. Smith (1st), M. L. Smith (2nd), and George W. Morgan (3rd) embarked on Porter's steamboats a week after Sherman's return and sailed down to join Frederick Steele's division, which became Sherman's 4th. Thus by December 19, with commendable dispatch, Sherman, determined not to be thwarted by the unpredictability of the Mississippi, had got his 70 vessels moving downriver. They rendezvoused at Helena with Steele, whose troops were embarked, and reached Friars Point the following day.[36]

The orders and briefings he had received from Grant had impressed on Sherman that though he commanded an independent operation, it could be nothing other than a subsidiary one. Sherman's job was to get up the Yazoo River and tackle what Grant repeatedly referred to as Vicksburg's "small garrison"; Grant would confront Pemberton's army, but the subsequent course of the plan remained ambiguous. If Pemberton withdrew southward, Grant would pursue him, but as Sherman emphasized, "he would expect to find me at the Yazoo River, if not inside of Vicksburg." Sherman had not been entrusted with a great operation of war, but he had an important part in Grant's plan and had been given full responsibility for it.[37]

Sherman remarked later on the "magnificent sight as we thus steamed down the river." Porter's gunboats took up station in the vanguard and at the rear of the convoy, and others intermingled with the cargo boats. Sherman also expressed satisfaction at the degree of operational security he had achieved. He had prohibited reporters from accompanying the expedition, determined that the enemy "shall learn nothing of my forces, plans or purposes through an egotistical and Corrupt Press." Actually, a handful of crafty reporters had managed to smuggle themselves aboard his steamers. Sherman had even found time to write to Irvin McDowell, lambasting the "base and ridiculous" charges in the press that he had lately endured since the Second Battle of Bull Run the previous August, especially the absurd notion that this paragon of temperance had been drunk. Since July 1861 Sherman's own experience of high command had given him a higher appreciation of McDowell's character and ability—and the intractable difficulties he had encountered.[38]

Sherman commanded just over 30,000 men, and two of his divisions averaged 7,000 men each, but the one he rated his best, Morgan Smith's,

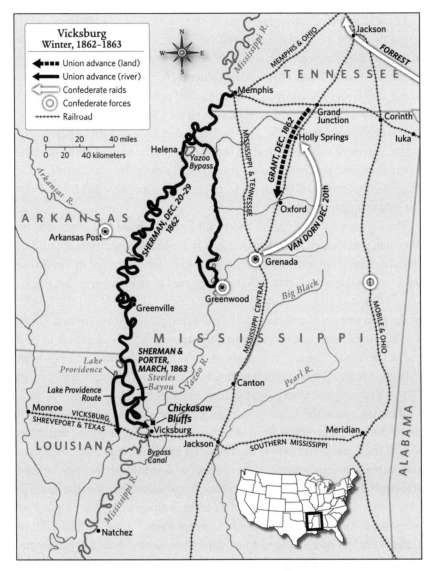

First Vicksburg Campaign—Advance to Chickasaw Bluffs

could barely muster 5,570, so the more than 9,300 men (later over 12,500) under Steele represented an invaluable supplement. Sherman could also deploy six 10-pounder Parrott guns and ten 20-pounder Parrotts; in anticipation of a siege he had requested that a further four 30-pounder Parrott guns be sent from Cairo. He also requested the forwarding of all available light batteries. "A feeble demonstration on Vicksburg," he admonished Steele's successor at Helena, Brigadier General Willis A. Gorman, "would do more harm than good." He gave the closest attention to his logistical measures and ensured that many steamers were filled half with supplies and half with coal; also, picks, shovels, and axes were loaded, the latter to chop wood for fuel once they had landed, to cut down not just trees but fences and houses if necessary.[39]

For all his forethought and energy, the great Mississippi River would determine the pace and course of operations, not the commanding general. A hint of the troubles yet to come was revealed even before Sherman had left Memphis. He might have departed earlier, but falling water levels marooned Porter's gunboats at Island No. 23 for four days. He welcomed the Mississippi's sudden rise, but eventually, alas, swelling river levels would doom the entire enterprise. His difficulties were compounded by a lack of telegraphic communication with Grant. Sherman's exercise of initiative became hampered by distance, geography, and the weather.

Sherman's first duty was to verify the threat posed by Confederate forces. He had picked up word of the fallout from Confederate president Jefferson Davis's conference at Murfreesboro, Tennessee, on December 13. This had agreed to give Mississippi a higher strategic priority than it had hitherto enjoyed. General Joseph E. Johnston received overall command of all operations in the West. On December 16 Sherman had dutifully reported a message from a spy who noted a sighting of Governor John J. Pettus and General Pemberton in Jackson, Mississippi, coordinating their preparations against Grant. Even before Sherman's force had arrived at Helena, Arkansas, an event had occurred that would dislocate the entire first Vicksburg campaign. On December 20 Major General Earl Van Dorn and 3,500 Confederate cavalry troopers seized Holly Springs and $1.5 million worth of war stores, taking the garrison completely unawares despite the warnings received. All that could not be moved and the installations were torched. This catastrophe, coupled with other crippling cavalry attacks on his supply lines, forced Grant to turn back. The next day Morgan Smith related unverified rumors of these developments to Sherman based on reports from 25 soldiers who had escaped from Holly Springs' capitulation, but such men habitually exaggerated their ordeal. Sherman realized he could not put much faith in their stories, and in the absence of confirmation or indeed any word from Grant, he relied on his instincts and decided to continue the campaign until he received further orders.[40]

Porter's gunboats had sailed on to the mouth of the Yazoo, even though the USS *Cairo* had been sunk by a torpedo (a mine). Sherman communicated his own determination to his command, and it sailed full of confidence from Gaines Landing and arrived at Milliken's Bend, 25 miles north of Vicksburg, on Christmas Day. He had fulfilled his promise to Grant that he would be at the mouth of the Yazoo by the festive season. He at once conferred with Admiral Porter on board his flagship, USS *Black Hawk*. They decided to land the army on a small island 12 miles upstream. On December 26 the fleet of transports set off with Brigadier General George W. Morgan's division in the van; Steele's division followed, with Morgan Smith behind him. A brigade of A. J. Smith's division, minus its impedimenta, got orders to destroy a substantial section of the Vicksburg–Shreveport Railroad. Smith waited for its return and did not join the main body until December 27.[41]

As soon as he disembarked, Sherman immediately realized what difficult country surrounded him. It was thickly wooded, featured dense undergrowth, and had few roads; one, which Sherman called the "main road," ran from the ruined Johnston's Plantation on the left bank of the Yazoo to Vicksburg, but it cut across a series of bayous and swamps that interrupted its course, obstacles strengthened by Confederate entrenchments. The country was dissected by deep ravines. Vicksburg lay beyond on the Walnut Hills that stretched to the northeast 200 feet or so above the average river level, but the landing ground was separated from these by a series of three bayous, the narrowest but also the deepest, Chickasaw Bayou, lay on the left. Wide sweeping maneuvers were out of the question. Two miles farther up the Yazoo River, the Confederates had placed a powerful battery at Haines Bluff. Sherman, hoping to distract attention from his broader advance, ordered Brigadier General Andrew Jackson Smith's division on the right flank to proceed along the road to Vicksburg's main defenses.[42]

On December 27–28 Sherman carried out a close personal reconnaissance of the ground that he would say in his report a week later was "as difficult as it could possibly be from nature and art." His force had in the meantime fanned out with Jackson Smith on the right flank, Morgan L. Smith adjacent to it, and George Morgan coming up on his left, reinforced by Francis P. Blair Jr.'s brigade, which Sherman drew from his most powerful division, and Steele's on the left flank. Sherman felt little warmth toward Blair at this point, but this action inaugurated their ongoing association. During his reconnaissance, Sherman had discovered that Chickasaw Bayou could only be crossed at two points, one a narrow levée and the other a sandbar; both were covered by rifle pits and batteries well dug in on the dry ground. The road from Vicksburg to Yazoo City ran behind these positions, sheltered by the "high, abrupt range of hills"—Chickasaw Bluffs—"marked all the way up" with more entrenchments, artillery batteries, and, even more ominously, signal stations on their tops. Confederate reinforcements could thus arrive quickly and block Sherman's progress; his preparations would be observed without difficulty. Sherman had only one choice: to find a way of crossing the bayou and pass through the Confederate defences and clamber onto terra firma before turning to strike directly at Vicksburg.[43]

Sherman quickly changed his mind that a tactical solution could be found on the left flank. Steele reported that on his sector the only way across the bayou lay over a corduroyed causeway (the surface was covered by sawn-off chunks of tree trunks, giving a hard but bumpy surface) well guarded by enfilading batteries supported by entrenchments that he had probed on the morning of December 28. All divisional commanders had been furnished with identical maps that they were ordered to distribute to their subordinates; they were enjoined to study these closely, so that even if they did not receive orders, they "all may act in perfect concert by following the general movement, unless specifically detached." Sherman had discovered here an insight into the command process of the first importance, but this discovery had come at an unpropitious moment. He concluded that the least hazardous course lay in the center and that he should attack there. He ordered Steele to return the way he had come and reinforce George Morgan's division, a maneuver completed that night. Logic dictated an attack on the center of his front and not on the right because this sector could be most easily reinforced by the Confederates. Yet the division Sherman rated his best—Morgan Smith's—was also his weakest numerically. Then on the morning of December 28 Morgan Smith was shot by a sniper and evacuated to a hospital ship.[44]

So Sherman had little alternative but to entrust the attack to George Morgan, previously a subordinate of Buell in the Army of the Ohio and prone to bluster. Brigadier General David Stuart, who had a commendable record from Shiloh, took over Morgan Smith's division, though Sherman took the precaution of placing it under the overall direction of A. J. Smith. Sherman ordered Stuart to carry out the orders already given to Morgan Smith, namely, that he should advance to the left, his artillery offering enfilading fire covering George Morgan's advance. A. J. Smith's own division would continue its diversionary operations close to Vicksburg. Sherman estimated the opposing Confederate force, commanded by Major General Stephen D. Lee, a general lacking tactical insight, at 15,000 men, but able to receive 4,000 reinforcements per day. Their defenses had to be hit hard and quickly. Sherman's plan aimed to give the impression of attacking all along the line when in reality he intended to strike a concentrated blow on the sector where he intended to cross Chickasaw Bayou via a sandbar and levee and drive through Lee's defenses. Sherman called this "a prompt and concentrated movement," and if he heard Grant's guns to the left he would pivot westward to link up with his commander, taking the batteries at Haines Bluff in the rear. Grant's overall plan had relied heavily on contingency, but this last part of Sherman's tactical scheme consisted of mere guesswork utterly overtaken by events.[45]

By the morning of December 29 Sherman's preparations were complete. Around midday Morgan began the assault on a narrow sector of Chickasaw Bluffs with his troops packed closely in tight formations with supporting elements close at hand. According to Sherman's *Memoirs*, Morgan offered an optimistic opinion as to the likelihood of success, but though Blair's brigade surged forward and gained a lodgement despite his troops enduring a murderous fire, Morgan lost control of his forces and failed to support Blair adequately. Sherman rode "about a mile to the right rear of Morgan's position, at a place convenient to receive reports from all parts of the line"—that is, a spot where he calculated he could best control the battle. Sherman ordered A. J. Smith to advance in the hope he could distract Confederate attention away from Morgan. The latter reported the difficulties he faced quickly but did not try to cross the Chickasaw Bayou, though Sherman claimed in his *Memoirs* that Morgan had undertaken to renew the attack 30 minutes later, action that he never took.

Once it became clear that Morgan's thrust had failed, Sherman ordered the cessation of the attack immediately, a tendency that would become habitual with him. In his report, he argued that the planned combinations were the most efficacious under the circumstances but accepted "all the responsibility and attach fault to no one." Years later in his *Memoirs*, however, he blamed Morgan for lack of tactical skill and overall grip.[46]

The repulse at the Battle of Chickasaw Bluffs cost Sherman 1,776 casualties (including 208 killed and 563 missing) to 197 Confederate. Despite the setback he persevered in finding a way around the great natural barriers presented by the bluffs. He got Porter's agreement to a joint venture, to take the batteries at Haines Bluff involving one-third of his force. Porter had initially opposed this scheme because of the torpedoes (mines) that had already cost him the *Cairo* but withdrew his opposition when a prow was fitted to a ram to clear a path for his ironclads. The gunboats would bombard the batteries, while Steele's reinforced division would land and seize them; Sherman would distract Confederate attention with diversionary attacks at Chickasaw. Should Steele be successful, then Sherman would transfer his whole force to Haines Bluff and advance around the rebel right flank. Thick fog forced the postponement of the assault on December 31, and the following day Porter resolved that the whole enterprise should be abandoned because of a full moon. Sherman concurred, as he wished to avoid a further costly repulse. He also became anxious about the weather. Water levels were rising rapidly; it was bitterly cold, and the troops were bivouacked on swampy ground that would flood after a few hours' rain. With one-third of his force already aboard ship, Sherman noticed that the trees exhibited flood marks 10 to 12 feet above their roots. He immediately deduced that he must evacuate the remainder. He made the correct decision at just the right moment, for torrential rain ensued. All troops and equipment were reembarked by the late afternoon of January 2, 1863. Sherman departed from "so unenviable a place" without regret, hoping to continue his operations from Milliken's Bend.[47]

Sherman felt depressed by his failure, though in truth he had little to be ashamed of. The newspapers soon began to publish references to "insanity" in describing the operation as if it were exclusively his, when in reality Sherman had conscientiously carried out the design of his superior, Grant. Needless to say, Sherman remained sensitive to the damage such aspersions might cause to his reputation and future prospects. Curiously, his most sympathetic biographers continue to give the impression that the campaign was his and offer harsh verdicts. Liddell Hart claimed that Sherman's plan at Chickasaw Bluffs represented a triumph of hope over "realism"; John Marszalek dubbed the whole operation a "fiasco," which it was not. These judgments, Liddell Hart's particularly, are based on the assumption that any frontal assault is predestined to fail. The odds were against it, undoubtedly, but no frontal assault is foredoomed to inevitable failure, as John B. Hood's assault on Turkey Hill during the Battle of Gaines Mill in June 1862 demonstrates.[48]

But Hood did not operate alone and in isolation from his superiors as Sherman did. The true responsibility for the failure must rest with Grant. On January 14, 1863, James B. McPherson reported to their beleaguered commander trying to pick up the pieces at Holly Springs that "General Sherman has had a severe time of it." Yet excellent commanders exhibit their best qualities under adverse circumstances. Sherman had applied himself to this tricky operation with dynamism and pertinacity. He had shown that he had the toughness required for the successful conduct of a campaign at a higher level. At Chickasaw the only thing he lacked had been good luck. Sherman had no choice but to make an unsupported attack or abandon the campaign, and he regarded the latter as unthinkable. Michael Fellman gets nearest to the truth when he suggests that no general could have done better "under such circumstances." Sherman's subordinates did less well. Of the 13 regiments he calculated should break into the Confederate defenses at Chickasaw, only 5 in one brigade, Blair's—an insufficient force—were thrust forward. The Blairs jumped to the unworthy conclusion that Sherman had deliberately sought to destroy Frank Blair's brigade, "as all those who knew him here knew him to be cowardly." This poisonous sentiment indicates the extent to which Sherman's initial hesitations about the war in the spring of 1861 continued to cloud views of his later military performance.[49]

Yet Sherman emerged strengthened by this experience, as his command technique continued to evolve. Throughout, he exhibited a keen understanding of military time: he always moved rapidly but circumspectly. He could not have disembarked on the Yazoo more rapidly than he did. After landing he gave the closest attention to reconnaissance. He also did well in devoting himself to mastering the details of the operation without allowing them to crowd out the broader perspective, which beckoned as the main priority. Finally, he employed the talents of not particularly able subordinates correctly, never asking them to do too much, while firmly resisting the temptation to do their jobs for them. Sherman failed to transcend the limitations imposed by the harsh environment and engineer a successful outcome. This failure would be valuable when he returned under different conditions to operate in harsh environments, and he overcame them—especially in South Carolina in 1865. He would always try to avoid being hemmed in, as at Chickasaw. He rationalized his defeat as a result of "the strength of the enemy's position, both natural and artificial," and not any "superior" fighting qualities exhibited by the Confederates. His switch in emphasis illuminates a change of direction in his thinking that strengthened over the next six months.[50]

At no time did he duck his responsibility for Chickasaw Bluffs; nor did he single out Morgan as the scapegoat. On January 5, having failed to make contact with Grant, he sent Halleck a copy of his report. He summed up the operation with a deft turn of phrase, an inversion of Julius Caesar's famous observation in 47 BC: "I reached Vicksburg at the time appointed, landed, assaulted, and failed." He took the precaution of starting an epistolary campaign for damage control. He was worried that the accusations of timidity that had dogged McClellan might come his way. He sent his brother John a full account and stressed, first, that "not a soldier or officer who was present but will admit I pushed the attack so far as prudence would justify" and, second, how successful he had been in extricating his command from the floodwaters.[51]

On the battlefield Sherman had revealed himself consistently positive in outlook and desirous of turning disappointments to good effect. He hoped in December 1862, despite what he had heard, that Grant might still come up and render his task easier. In the following weeks, Sherman would need every ounce of his self-assurance. On January 2 he heard that Major General John A. McClernand had arrived at the mouth of the Yazoo, probably to supersede him. Sherman rushed off to report to this man whom he held in no high regard and place his reputation in his untrustworthy hands.[52]

8

From Corps Command
to Army Command

January–December 1863

As Sherman sailed to the mouth of the Yazoo to meet McClernand on board the *River Queen* he reflected on his future. Far from succumbing to depression, he was feeling stoic. In truth, his conduct left little to be desired, and he had successfully reembarked "in the face of an enterprising and successful enemy." Once he could confirm the details of Grant's setback at Holly Springs, he instantly realized that his own small force could never have been sufficient to hold Vicksburg even if he had succeeded in breaking through and taking it. Despite his skill in managing the operation, he acknowledged that "the taking of Vicksburg by my force was an impossibility." To his dismay, McClernand had arrived to supersede him, brandishing an order from Lincoln. Time would reveal this document as rather less than it appeared. But for the moment, Sherman consoled himself, "Of course, I submit gracefully," as the president "has the right to choose his agents," and he would revert to command of a corps of two divisions; "such is life and luck." Ellen replied in much more uncompromising language: "The President ought to be impeached for such imbecile acts as placing McC[lernand] in command at the time he did or any time."[1]

Sherman had not taken much of a backward step, as he had never formally been anything other than a corps commander, though a "wing" of the Army of the Tennessee had been temporarily entrusted to his care. He had gained experience at high command, and he put this to good use. He had already come up with a proposal to dangle before McClernand's eyes at their first meeting. If Sherman had calculated that his new commander had no real ideas of his own as to how he should carry out the ambitious schemes with which he had tantalized the president, then he proved correct. McClernand talked in generalities but had no detailed plans for a systematic operational program or any preferred tactical method.

The scheme that Sherman came up with suited both their purposes. They both needed a quick, relatively easy success, Sherman to consolidate his standing before doubts could reemerge about his competence, McClernand to advance his reputation with the president and encourage recruitment. As Sherman explained the idea to Ellen, "Instead of lying idle I proposed we should come to the Arkansas and attack the Post of Arkansas 50 miles up that River"; the Confederates had used their bastion at the post, Fort Hindman, to attack federal river communications and interrupt the mails. This operation would gain the dual objectives of, first, securing the Union rear ("We must make the River safe behind us before we push too far down") and, second, offering McClernand the chance to drive on and seize Little Rock, a state capital, which would add luster to his name.[2]

After voicing some initial doubts, McClernand quickly agreed to Sherman's proposal and accompanied him to a meeting with Admiral Porter on the night of January 4. Porter had met McClernand the previous year at Lincoln's suggestion and judged him a self-seeking charlatan. He did not nurse any particular grievances against "political generals"— he would write favorably about Blair and John A. Logan—but he loathed McClernand. Once their deliberations started in earnest, McClernand presented the Arkansas Post proposal as his own and made some tactless remarks about restoring the army's morale after its demoralizing "*late defeat.*" If Porter would give him three gunboats, he boasted, "I will go and take the place." Provoked, Porter shot back that if Sherman was given command, he would sail "with a proper force and will ensure the capture of the 'Post.'" Porter suspected that all McClernand knew about gunboats was that they "had taken Fort Henry." McClernand "winced" under this assault, and Sherman walked into the aft-cabin, beckoning Porter to follow him; meanwhile, McClernand studied the wall charts in a bid, Porter thought, "to hide his temper." According to Porter's account, Sherman chastised him for his sarcastic tone toward McClernand, but the admiral protested, "He shall not treat you rudely in my cabin"; once tempers had cooled on all sides, the discussion resumed, "and the interview ended pleasantly enough." Sherman handed over command to McClernand "in the most graceful manner," Porter noted, though he rightly estimated it "a bitter pill" for Sherman to be superseded by a man for whom neither had any respect. Still, Porter agreed to command the naval flotilla himself; thereupon Sherman flattered Porter's vanity by exclaiming that this would "insure the success of the enterprise."[3]

On January 4, 1863, with the naval dimension settled, McClernand organized, without the War Department's permission, the Army of the Mississippi, composed mostly of Sherman's troops, totaling a little fewer than 29,000 men. He created two corps, the 1st under Brigadier General George W. Morgan and the 2nd under Sherman's command. Sherman's two divisions comprised that of Morgan L. Smith's (currently commanded by David Stuart) and of Frederick Steele, whom he greatly trusted. Sherman did not allow his return to equal status with Morgan to rankle, though he had little respect for his former subordinate. In practice, Sherman's conduct over the next week could leave little doubt that he was the true commander of the Arkansas Post operation.[4]

The entire force immediately sailed back up the Mississippi River in a convoy of 50 steamboats guarded by Porter's 13 ironclads, with the transports carrying Sherman and Morgan's corps in two squadrons, one following the other. On January 9 they rendezvoused at Gavin's Landing before proceeding up the White River, then turning into the Arkansas River as far as Notrib's Farm, a short distance below Fort Hindman. McClernand accompanied the force, much to Sherman's surprise, but he played only a small part in the direction of this operation. Early on the morning of January 10, Sherman issued all the orders, and the troops disembarked unopposed. Sherman later attributed the degree of surprise attained to the continuing prohibition on war correspondents accompanying the convoy. Stuart made contact with Confederates entrenched in a position dug to the Arkansas River designed to shield Fort Hindman from direct assault. McClernand ordered Sherman to take Steele's division across a "deep, ugly" swamp for about 2 miles in order to outflank it, but after interrogating some local residents and prisoners of war, Sherman realized that such a move would involve a march of 7 miles rather than 2. Probably with a good deal of satisfaction, he sent his chief of staff, Major John Hammond, back to inform McClernand that his plan would not work. In the meantime, McClernand had come forward and saw that Sherman had acted correctly and informed him that every obstacle to a direct attack on Fort Hindman had been cleared, as the breastworks on the river had been abandoned. Sherman then decided to launch a combined assault on the fort.

His plan took a simple form and bore some resemblance to Grant's assault on Fort Henry the previous year. The Union troops approached Fort Hindman along a peninsula; a road divided it in two, with Morgan on the left adjacent to the Arkansas River and Sherman's corps on the right of the road, with Stuart's division in the center and Steele on the right outer flank. At 1:00 a.m. on January 11, Sherman carried out a detailed personal reconnaissance, so close to the Confederate lines "that I could hear the enemy hard at work" strengthening their defenses. "I could almost hear their words, and I was thus listening when, about 4 am the bugler in the rebel camp sounded as pretty a reveille as I had listened to." When not charmed by the musical accompaniment, Sherman noted that the fort covered about 100 square yards and contained strong armament, with three heavy guns and four smaller 3-inch rifled guns, four 6-pounders, and six other field pieces scattered among the infantry. The fields of fire were clear and marked down so that Sherman could figure precisely its trajectory. Porter had begun a "furious bombardment" on the previous evening, lasting until nightfall, to prepare the way and cover the realignment of the Union forces. He also agreed to launch a simultaneous, combined assault the next morning. As soon as his ironclads opened fire, Sherman and Morgan's artillery would support them.[5]

At 10:00 a.m. all was ready, though McClernand began to show some impatience. Porter's gunboats did not open fire until 1:00 p.m., and about 20 minutes later Sherman's troops launched their assault, supported by covering fire provided by Morgan's corps. Sherman's men made good progress, and as Sherman followed the advance with his staff, he noticed that the Confederate artillery were getting their range and shells were landing close by; he ordered the entire party to dismount at once, but he continued to move forward and spotted a white flag unfurling on the parapet. He sent one of his staff, Captain Lewis Dayton, of whom he was particularly fond, up onto the parapet. As the firing stopped, Sherman and the others quickly joined him standing amid piles of Confederate dead. The air filled with "cheers and halloing" as men of Sherman's two divisions surged into the Confederate works.[6]

The Post of Arkansas had fallen. Its commander, Brigadier General T. J. Churchill, three brigades of infantry (over 4,500 men), and all their stores fell into Union hands; the rebel prisoners, Sherman reported to Ellen, were "clustered on the bank" of the Arkansas River waiting to be transported to Cairo, Illinois. Sherman expressed delight at the "perfect" result. He made a point of stressing the US Navy's skill (unlike McClernand, who ignored the sailors in his report): "Without them we would have had hard work, with them it was easy." The total Union casualties numbered 1,032, of which 134 were killed. His success "relieves our Vicksburg trip of all appearance of a reverse as by this move we open the Arkansas and compel all organized masses of the Enemy to pass below the Arkansas River, it will also secure this flank when we renew our attack on it." Ellen also reported the agreeable news that "people are jubilant over the capture of Post Arkansas and not a paper that I have seen refers this credit to McClernand."

Grant was less pleased. McClernand had made little effort to apprise him of his intentions, let alone gain his permission for the foray. He did not bother writing to Grant until January 11. Grant's immediate and fierce response reveals a desire to stamp on what he regarded as a challenge to his authority. He viewed the operation as a distraction and a movement made in the wrong direction and did not seem impressed by Sherman's mainly tactical arguments. Sherman became perturbed by Grant's reaction to it as "a wild goose chase." He wrote him a personal letter on January 17 in an effort to put his mind at rest, underplaying his own role in the affair while emphasizing McClernand's. Grant did not reply, though its contents were probably discussed at their later private meetings. Sherman made a persuasive case as to the practicability of the operation, given Major General Nathaniel P. Banks's failure to reduce Port Hudson. But the main reason Sherman wrote this semiofficial missive was to reassure Grant that he had not aligned himself with McClernand in any prospective tussle over command authority. He urged Grant "to come down and see. I only fear McClernand may attempt impossibilities." Grant had already decided to assume personal command of the operation and had informed McClernand. Sherman knew where his first loyalties lay, but Grant's cool response to his success did irritate him, and his loyalty would be tested over the next three months, even if it was not found wanting. Despite Sherman's self-image of the open, plain-speaking man, and his repeatedly expressed indifference to that "gnawing and craving appetite for personal fame" that so seized the likes of McClernand, Sherman could display deviousness when it suited him.[7]

Despite the minor compensating success at Arkansas Post, the great challenge of Vicksburg loomed menacingly over the whole theater of operations. Yet, Sherman contended, Arkansas Post would "have a good Effect on the Main River." He labored under no illusions: "In the end Vicksburg must be reduced and it is going to be a hard nut to crack." It was quite simply "the strongest place I ever saw" and would require much labor and even more ingenuity. Eventually, too, Grant would come to agree that the action at Arkansas Post had indeed exerted a beneficial influence on the outcome of the campaign. But at the time he resented not just the distraction and dispersal of force caused by McClernand's schemes but the strain they placed on the number of river transports and his ability to reinforce his army. In

February Grant firmly stamped on another distraction that McClernand promoted: to attack Pine Bluff, Arkansas.[8]

On leaving Arkansas Post, Sherman's convoy sailed through a severe blizzard, arriving on January 15 at Napoleon, Arkansas, where his troops disembarked. Sherman thought the town resembled "desolation covered with snow," but his mood lightened when his brother-in-law Hugh, "looking as fine as possible," unexpectedly appeared to take up command of a brigade in David Stuart's division. Sherman worried over the absence of letters from Ellen, a very conscientious correspondent, and Hugh's arrival prompted him to sit down and write to her. He urged her not to move to Cincinnati, which she had been contemplating, as he disliked the secessionist tone to be found in that city. The following day a fire broke out in Napoleon. Sherman's energetic reaction limited the damage to just one block; he suspected arson but could not find the culprit.[9]

Sherman predicted correctly that Grant would soon arrive "to command in person—McClernand is unfit" and too preoccupied with his own advancement. This required little prescience on his part, as he had urged this very course on his commander. In a War Department instruction, General Orders No. 210 of December 18, 1862, issued while Sherman was making his way to the Yazoo, the troops in the Departments of the Tennessee and Missouri, including Samuel Curtis's troops under Sherman's command, were organized into four army corps, the 13th under McClernand, the 15th under Sherman, the 16th under Stephen A. Hurlbut, and the 17th under James B. McPherson. Grant had been informed by Halleck that it was "the President's wish" that "McClernand's corps shall constitute a part of the river expedition and that he shall have the immediate command under your direction." After McClernand's return from Arkansas Post, Grant decided to exercise this direction very tightly and assume personal command. The creation of the other two corps greatly reduced McClernand's role, despite his seniority, and rendered him less influential than Sherman. A month later, on January 18, Grant arrived at Napoleon and ordered his subordinates to take their commands immediately south to the west bank of the Mississippi opposite Vicksburg at Young's Point. In private Sherman continued to grapple with the operational problem that would be Grant's primary responsibility, namely, "how a large force should somehow reach the ridge between the Black and Yazoo, so as [to] approach from the Rear."[10]

Even before Grant's arrival Sherman began to reveal more candid opinions about McClernand. Initially Sherman had consoled himself that "I certainly envy no one the anxiety of providing for so many people," meaning the five divisions under his command. On further reflection after Arkansas Post, Sherman began to consider McClernand a danger to the Union cause because of his overambitious, unsustainable plans. "I never dreamed of so severe a test of my patriotism as being superseded by McClernand," he protested to John, "and if I can keep down my true spirit & live I will claim a virtue higher than Brutus." Despite these seething tensions, Sherman and McClernand contrived to work together amicably and positively, to the credit of both. Sherman also drew an enduring lesson from the vicissitudes of the last two months. After completing an essay exploring the dangers of meddling in military affairs, written for his own satisfaction, he concluded that disappointments were mainly the product of "the condition of things. Human power is limited and you cannot appreciate the difficulty of molding into a homogeneous machine the discordant elements which go to make up our armies." This insight determined his fundamental operational caution in high command in 1864–65. He would be guided by the imperative never to endanger the cohesion, safety, and offensive efficiency of the force entrusted to his command.[11]

The more Sherman reflected on his relations with McClernand, the more his pose of diffidence revealed itself as a mask that slipped all too readily. On January 24 Sherman reported to Ellen that McClernand "is now sick in bed" after sending his "Chief of Cavalry," Colonel Warren Stewart, on an ill-conceived raid the previous day that ended in Stewart's death. Then, referring to himself in the third person, he averred, "I know one fact very well, that when danger is present, or important steps are necessary Sherman is invariably called for"; whatever it was, he attended conscientiously to numerous unglamorous chores—"unloading steamboats and repairing roads." He also reflected on his previous command experience "that when danger is present I feel it less than when it is in the remote future or in the past." Sherman evinced in these weeks a strong confidence in his own abilities, but this sense of satisfaction was marred by frustration and renewed gloom over his prospects.[12]

After Grant's arrival, though McClernand might still attempt to issue "provoking, short, curt orders," he no longer commanded Sherman—except during Grant's brief absences. On January 20 Grant stated in no uncertain terms to Halleck the universal distrust that McClernand provoked. "This is a matter I made no inquiries about but it was forced upon me." Grant later revealed that if Sherman "had been left in command," his confidence in him was such that he might have entrusted the campaign to him. Sherman, it must be said, did not reveal a comparable level of confidence in the decisions that Grant had taken since assuming command, glad though Sherman was to see him.[13]

After the Napoleon meeting Grant "hurried us back to Vicksburg on the theory that Banks might be here disappointed at our non-appearance—So here we are again but not a word of Banks." Sherman's views remained consistent over the next three months. The paramount need remained to reach dry land, "to get ashore where we can fight." The original plan developed in December 1862 he believed offered the best chance to locate terra firma. Grant should advance on Vicksburg from the northeast, Nathaniel P. Banks from the south, with Sherman operating again on the Yazoo, "but cooperation at such distances," he acknowledged with more experience than most, "and over such long lines is almost an impossibility." Nevertheless, Sherman remained dedicated to this conception, as its overall thrust resembled the form of his mature plans. It provided, he held, "the best and only" plan, because once Yazoo City had been occupied the advance could follow "Black River Bridge to the rear of Vicksburg." The fortress could then be sealed off by "a smaller force all afloat to act in front [as] the guns of the main attack be heard."[14]

Grant's General Orders No. 14 specified that the 15th Corps comprised two divisions. These were of three brigades each after Hugh Ewing's arrival, amounting to 15,909 men. The troops were encamped on a neck of low ground at Young's Plantation that ran into a levee immediately in front of Vicksburg. The town was "in full view," he informed Ellen, "and we are within range of their Rifle Guns, but thus far both [sides] are sparing of powder as the deep Mississippi intervenes, and neither can reach the other." The unpredictable waters of the Mississippi proved far more troublesome. As he recalled later, they "continued to rise and threatened to drown us." The only refuge to be found lay on the levee or on board the steamboats. Sherman reconnoiterd the area between Young's Point and Vicksburg systematically and pushed forward Stuart's division without wagons, repairing the railroad and its bridges as it marched; thereafter he ordered the preparation of a map. Frederick Steele's division then followed. Sherman instituted a system whereby each division provided alternate details of 500 men per day to dig the half-completed canal begun the previous year. Grant hoped this would turn the Mississippi on the Confederate right and allow Porter's fleet of gunboats to escort the river transports across the peninsula in front of Vicksburg and thus permit Sherman's troops to disembark on dry land.

Stuart's men began the irksome task of "widening the canal nine feet and throwing to the earth on the other side of the canal so, if it fills, it will overflow the other side first." The level of water in the canal rose a mere 2 feet. Grant meanwhile traveled to Memphis to supervise McPherson's operations at Lake Providence before hurriedly returning on January 28. Sherman thus reported to McClernand at Milliken's Bend, "The road across the swamp is now very bad, and I have ordered four of Steele's regiments to corduroy the whole distance, say two miles. I have never seen men work more grudgingly, and I have endeavoured to stimulate them by all means." Sherman busied himself drawing up rotas to ensure that his soldiers did not labor for too long, visiting camps and making sure that the men were well fed and safely sheltered. The men appreciated his efforts, and morale improved. They could not fail to notice that their commander's headquarters at Mrs. Grove's house was completely surrounded by water "and could only be reached by a plank-walk from the levee built on posts."[15]

Anxiety over the state of morale persuaded Sherman to continue a policy that had been aimed previously at reporters, namely, requiring the captains of steamboats to sign bonds stipulating that they would not carry persons unless "contracted for"; otherwise deserters would make their escape by river, and "the men will stick to the boats." Sherman also remained alert lest squadrons of Confederate transports be sailed down to Vicksburg to disturb his preparations. "No enemy," he reported, "can come through that swamp with artillery or in order, and could only act in small numbers or detached parties." He placed four 6-pounder guns below Vicksburg to prevent Confederate vessels from reaching its docks; the supply line via the Red River had been disrupted, but Sherman still fretted that due to Banks's failure to take Port Hudson, Confederates still controlled the mouth of the Red River and a long stretch of the Mississippi. Other worries included keeping Admiral Porter supplied with coal. The "foul" weather and "awful" roads rendered supply by road "a simple impossibility." His own predicament worsened when the canal suddenly began to rise and threatened his camps. He still remained positive and intent on doing all he could for the navy, and he assured Porter that coal-bearing "barges could work through the canal." Sherman was right. Those with tricky problems, especially if they involved logistics, invariably turned to him for advice or to sort the matter out for them.[16]

At the end of January Sherman embroiled himself in another frustrating affair entirely of his own making. He provoked another spat with newspaper reporters.

Its root lay in Sherman's extreme sensitivity to any hostile investigation of his conduct of the first Vicksburg campaign. He protested to Ethan Allen Hitchcock that "it is absurd to hold me responsible for not taking Vicksburg *alone* but a few weeks and months will show that double and treble any force are requisite and then not sure of success." The passage of time perhaps vindicates his argument, but as the campaign stumbled from one failed expedient to another, Sherman grew alarmed lest he become associated with continual blundering. Porter shrewdly observed that Sherman was "very sensitive and allowed things to worry him unnecessarily."[17]

"The newspapers are after me again," Sherman warned Ellen. She had already advised him wisely, "You might as well attempt to control the whirlwind as the newspaper mania so I advise you to attempt no longer to set your face against the Storm." Sherman would not listen, and she pleaded, "You cannot do anything unaided against them and there is not one man in power who will unite with you against them. So dear Cump give up the Struggle and Suffer them to annoy you no longer." He took no notice and asked the admiral to send him "a few lines" of approbation on the quality of his preparation, planning, and conduct of the operation, and generally "whether I acted the part of an intelligent officer or that of an insane fool." Sherman evidently feared a resurgence of that hateful slur.[18]

Sherman's earlier antipress measures had given journalists a pretext to attack him. In December 1862 he had issued General Orders No. 8 prohibiting reporters from accompanying his expedition. Some, including Thomas W. Knox of the *New York Herald*, succeeded in evading it, but even these intrepid souls found it difficult to make sense of what they witnessed from afar. They quickly shifted onto the attack and lambasted Sherman for a recklessness that had resulted in "another" Fredericksburg. There were numerous snide references to his "insane" disposition. Reporters could suggest quite plausibly that the denial of information by Sherman and his staff reflected deliberate conniving on their part in a complete concealment of "the truth"; the press were heroically doing their job by exposing a "cover-up." Sherman had the most to lose if he could be exposed as the chief culprit. His friend Porter commented on the "sort of freemasonry" among reporters "that makes them hang together like vampire bats" so that if Sherman offended one, he risked offending them all.[19]

These attacks were nasty, although in line with standard journalistic techniques well established by the mid-nineteenth century, especially the "pack mentality" in following with frenzied enthusiasm a story to see how it might evolve. Sherman was especially annoyed by the sarcastic tone of Knox of the *New York Herald*, who attributed Sherman's mismanagement to spending too much time thwarting the press. Certainly, Sherman's belligerent attitude had spread to his staff. Major Hammond had threatened to shoot Franc B. Wilkie, the *New York Times* correspondent. Ellen deplored her husband's wild talk of "hanging" reporters and urged him to remember that some newspapers were "only too anxious to stand by you."[20]

Sherman offered his brother a reasoned though characteristically sweeping and fiery critique of the baleful influence of an unregulated press in wartime. He argued that stress on the liberty of the press in wartime was symptomatic of a society that offered too much respect to individual liberty in a great war that threatened the existence of the whole political community. Uncensored newspapers revealed to the Confederates an abundance of information about Union strength, organizations, and intentions. They retarded the Union war effort, cost precious lives, and sapped confidence. The press, moreover, provided a conduit by which constant meddling in the Union war effort could be pursued; the newspapers encouraged "that growing and craven appetite for personal fame and notoriety which has brought our people into a just contempt with foreign nations." The lack of discipline at all levels confirmed, in Sherman's opinion, Confederate military superiority. Finally, Sherman was irked by the personal abuse, "when a malicious individual hanging about as a spy can accuse me before the world and be believed rather than me."[21]

Sherman intended to turn the tables on journalists and demand of them legal accountability. As he confided to Ellen, "I am now determined to test the question. Do they [reporters] rule or the Comm[an]d[ing] Gen[eral]? If they rule I quit. ... I will never command again an army in America if we must carry along paid spies." On January 27 Sherman ordered Thomas Knox's arrest and stated his intention to court-martial him and, he hoped, to "execute him as a spy." This last reference denotes a measure of vindictiveness, indeed obsession, on Sherman's part, but he had raised significant issues concerning the relationship of the military and the press in wartime, matters involving "a high moral and political principle." His pursuit of this principle transcends the issue of his own haunted, frenetic, and sometimes unwise conduct.[22]

Knox quickly learned of Sherman's intention and attempted to calm him with apologies, flattery, and an offer to correct the original article, after admitting its errors. On January 31 Knox was arrested and hauled before Sherman. No longer contrite, he told Sherman that he had "no feeling against you personally," which was probably true, but then boasted that as all reporters agreed Sherman was no friend of theirs, they should "in self-defense write you down." He then revealed a potentially explosive detail: Frank Blair had supplied the majority of his most damaging criticisms. To Sherman's jaundiced eye, Knox appeared "a strong, stalwart" young man "capable of holding a musket" who had chosen not to do so. His combination of servility and effrontery revolted Sherman and convinced him of the wisdom of his chosen course.[23]

Sherman intended to charge Knox at once, but first he had to satisfy himself that Blair had played no part in the imbroglio. Blair had already denied leaking information to the press, but the aftermath of Chickasaw Bluffs had spawned a good deal of poisonous gossip among the Blair family that traduced Sherman's moral character.[24] Blair sent Sherman a kind letter admiring his assumption of all responsibility for Chickasaw Bluffs, though he believed it "unjust to yourself or friends" that "the blunders committed by inferior officers ... should be laid to your charge or assumed by you." But this letter might be considered self-serving considering the controversy that had already threatened to engulf him. In a letter to his brother at the end of January, Sherman indicated a tendency to believe Knox's revelation, as he described the latter as a "correspondent Blair carries along for self-glorification." On February 2 he sent Blair a stern written interrogatory containing 22 precisely worded questions directed toward elucidating not only Blair's knowledge of the first Vicksburg campaign but also minor points of logistical detail concerning the evacuation. They included particular questions about Sherman's command technique. "Do you not know that I personally remained in our camp at the bayou till every particle of ordnance, wagons, &c., and all the troops but the rear guard had reached the river?"

Blair replied by return in a state of "mortification," denying that he had ever made a "statement" that Knox could have construed as critical. His reply, as expected, is suffused with praise for his superior, though he did concede that he thought it "unfortunate" that any major assault had been made without the aid of Porter's naval guns; that is, the assault should have been made at Haines Bluff rather than at Chickasaw, but this view fell rather short of advocating this scheme as an alternative. Blair was critical of George Morgan's slovenly methods that did not allow Blair sufficient time to carry out any kind of reconnaissance. Finally, Blair urged Sherman to consult Steele as to whether "I have not invariably expressed myself in the kindest manner toward you." Blair's was a fine legal statement that still left open the possibility that he had made sarcastic comments to Knox in private that the latter had either misconstrued or exaggerated.[25]

The emphatic but friendly tone displayed in Blair's statement and personal letter about Chickasaw Bluffs pleased Sherman and cleared the air. So Sherman followed up his earlier missive with a rather more affable letter, elaborating on his calculations at Chickasaw Bluffs. Sherman revealed that Morgan, contrary to his later justifications, "was full of confidence" in carrying out his assigned task, but Sherman reiterated his continuing lack of interest in identifying scapegoats among "any generous and brave set of men." Sherman concluded the exchange with a gracious flourish: "If at one time I did think you had incautiously dropped expressions which gave a newspaper spy the grounds of accusations against all save those in your brigade and division, I now retract that and assure you of my confidence and respect." Henceforth, though Sherman neither liked nor admired Blair, he closed the issue of his possible disloyalty, and the two men established a solid working relationship that would improve and last for the rest of the war.[26]

On February 5 Knox's court-martial convened at Young's Point, and Knox was summoned to appear two days later. He faced three charges: "Giving intelligence to the enemy, directly or indirectly"; "Being a spy"; and "Disobedience of orders." All were broad and rather vaguely framed. Knox managed to persuade Brigadier General John M. Thayer, the president of the court, a brigade commander in Steele's 1st Division and lawyer by profession, to drop a specification in the second charge that his false statements aided the enemy. Sherman offered testimony on February 10–11, but when he claimed that material from Knox's articles appeared in Southern newspapers, Knox's defense counsel retorted that this was irrelevant supposition. The latter also scored a success by eliciting an admission that Grant, not Sherman, commanded the overall force at Chickasaw and that Knox carried a pass signed by Grant. Concluding statements were delivered on February 14. Four days later the court issued its verdict: Knox was found not guilty of the first two charges, guilty of the third charge; the court found that he had disobeyed Sherman's orders "but attribute[d] no criminality thereto." Knox was ordered out of army lines. A mighty explosion occurred inside Mrs. Grove's house when the 15th Corps commander received news of the verdict. Both Ellen and her father worried that Sherman might insist on resigning, but his fury passed, and he did not do so. For one thing, Ellen warned him that his old enemy Benjamin Stanton, the lieutenant governor of Ohio, had threatened to revive the "charges of insanity," and "nothing would please him better than your resignation at a time when you are pressed and worried." At last he heeded Ellen's sensible advice.[27]

Sherman had failed to gain the legal precedent he wanted, namely, "that a nation and army must defend its safety and existence by making all acts militating against it criminal regardless of the mere interest of the instrument." Eventually such safeguards and priority would be achieved, but not in the Civil War. Throughout the trial the newspapers had offered little criticism of Sherman's action; indeed, some, like Sherman's nemesis, the *Cincinnati Commercial*, were sympathetic. Dissatisfied with the outcome of the court-martial, Sherman petitioned Grant's headquarters demanding that the judgment be reviewed by higher authority, but Grant and Rawlins, his chief of staff, were content to let the matter drop. Two months later, when Knox tried to return, Sherman gained the point tacitly, supported by Lincoln and more forcefully by Grant, that reporters could not accompany military formations unless they enjoyed the support of the designated commander. A willingness to follow orders, Sherman maintained, was "vital" against an enemy with "advantages of ... position and means of intelligence." Sherman thus seized authority over reporters, and he would use it sensibly and in the best interests of the forces he commanded. He had gained a further advantage: Knox's court-martial had frightened all reporters, and they would henceforth treat him warily.[28]

Sherman's aggressive manner has provoked overblown arguments that suggest his attitudes toward the press reveal a penchant for dictatorship. Sherman expressed skepticism about the value of democratic institutions; he never embraced any ideology that sought their overthrow. His views at this time were directed exclusively toward waging the war effort more efficiently. He took the presumption and irresponsibility displayed by the press as a symptom of the prevailing "spirit of anarchy" that he found "more alarming than the batteries that shell us from the opposite shore." The latter sentiment is typical of Sherman's exaggerations and exposed rhetoric. Still, he was right in condemning the search for scapegoats that the press encouraged. In a brilliant metaphor, he likened popular opinion to a "drunkard whose natural tastes have become so vitiated that nought but brandy will satisfy them." He argued that the press should be held accountable for its conduct. To a large extent he succeeded: for the rest of the war, reporters covering his operations were tamed, and their stories did not endanger Sherman's progress.[29]

The Knox court-martial occurred in February and March. With the arrival of spring, thoughts had to be focused exclusively on the reduction of Vicksburg. "In all controversies," Sherman mused, "there is a time when discussion must cease and action begin," for the Vicksburg campaign could wait for no legal pronouncements. The slothful course so far merely accentuated Sherman's sense of gloom over its dismal prospects. He never made a secret of his lack of faith in the canal scheme; it would fail to "draw in a volume and depth of water sufficient"; even if it did work, he believed, the Confederates would simply withdraw their guns to Warrenton on the Mississippi River, which lay below the mouth of the canal. At one point he confessed to John very pessimistic sentiments: "It is expecting too much of us to capture the place"—but this outburst merely illustrates his tendency to use correspondence as a means of discharging frustration. A further setback occurred when the new ram *Queen of the West*, sent by Porter at Grant's urging, attacked Vicksburg's wharves and river commerce and damaged the CSS *Vicksburg* but then ran aground in the Red River, fell into Confederate hands, and was quickly turned against its former owners. The incident confirmed Sherman's worst fears: it offered "ominous" evidence that the Confederates controlled "the river below free and unobstructed," and he gloomily expected the enemy at any time to make his "appearance in boats from that direction." Outposts were equipped with signal rockets to warn Sherman in the event of a Confederate naval foray.[30]

In the early days of February 1863 Grant confided in Sherman, proposing a new plan. It required entrance to the Yazoo and would attempt to turn the Confederate right flank above Haines Bluff again so that the gunboats could reach Yazoo City, "turn the main river into Lake Providence," and thence allow access to the Tensas River, and then the Black, Red, and Atchafalaya Rivers, "without approaching any bluffs or ground easy of defense." As the plan was based on the 1862 concept, Sherman hailed it enthusiastically as "admirable." "Cover up the design all you can," he advised Grant, "and it will fulfill all the conditions of the great problem. This little affair of ours here on Vicksburg Point is labor lost." Feeling the warmth of a little optimism, he wrote to his old friend Edward O. C. Ord, currently recuperating from wounds, suggesting he report to Grant as an alternative to McClernand. Ellen had grown to dislike Ord because of his regard for McClellan, but he remained one of Sherman's closest friends. But confirmation of the loss of the *Queen of the West* slowed down the pace of operations. Attempts were made to build two further canals, one at Yazoo Pass and the other at Lake

Providence; the latter "is the only one in which I feel an interest." Sherman felt such renewed despair, especially late at night, that he urged Ellen to find "some quiet place" to take the children "and prepare them at least for the better future that must be." Although she had recently recovered from illness, he warned her to "brace yourself" for the possible loss of his reputation. In these moods Ellen tried to cheer him up with news of his children: "It would do your heart good to watch them at their plays."[31]

The multitude of setbacks forced Sherman to rethink the nature of the war he was fighting. "The further we penetrate, the further we remove from home the less we are esteemed or encouraged." The occupation of increasing swathes of the Confederacy raised fundamental problems not just of procedure but in the style of fighting that the Union employed. "We get all the Knocks and rarely see one grain of Encouragement from 'home,'" he complained. He had in mind one recent letter from the secretary of war notifying him that he had received complaints from a Mrs. Jane Seymour about one of Sherman's best regiments, the 8th Missouri, which she claimed had despoiled her property in Memphis. "They are no worse than other volunteers," Sherman observed, "all of whom come to us filled with the popular idea that they must clean out the Secesh, must waste and not protect their property, must burn, waste and destroy." Sherman still regarded this as a "foul doctrine." Yet the paradox in Sherman's views at this date lay in his statement of what the North needed to do to achieve final victory.[32]

Sherman stressed a need for a coherent sense of purpose. "The Army growls a good deal," he informed John, "at the apathy of the nation, at home quiet, comfortable, and happy yet pushing them forward on all sorts of desperate expeditions." The Confederacy respected the Union more than it had two years previously, but it still remained irreconcilable. Hence the resort to punitive methods, as "our armies are devastating the land"; it might be "sad," but "we cannot help it" so long as the rebels remained defiant. Sherman still could not glimpse the beginning of the end of the appeal of this "ardent" cause, let alone victory. "Now you must see," he admonished John, "that to subdue the Rebellion you must obliterate a whole Race, our equals in courage, resources and determination." The North still had to take the war really seriously, which meant setting aside its preoccupation with individual rights and constitutional niceties. The central priority should be to organize itself to fight a great war efficiently. If the government failed to do this, the North would "continue groping in the dark ... [and] as a people we must pay the price." The recent conscription act Sherman thought "the first sensible move I have yet seen." He sent a well-rehearsed case to Ohio governor David Tod pleading that new troops be sent to sustain existing regiments rather than used to create new, inexperienced formations that would be forced to start from scratch. "Since the first hostile shot," he recapitulated a favorite theme, "the people of the North must conquer, or be conquered." The Union must therefore harness its military strength—"we must outnumber them, if we want to succeed"—but, he cautioned, the task would not get any easier. "We are forced to invade—we must keep the War South till they are not only ruined, exhausted, but humbled in pride and spirit." The latter was an especially important point. But Sherman queried whether Union armies were "equal to the occasion." His answer was no, for "our lines of communication are threatened by their dashes, for which the country, the population and character of the enemy are all perfectly adapted." Sherman could see what needed to be done, but amid the Vicksburg despondence he could not yet see how it could be done.[33]

A temporary gap thus emerges in Sherman's thinking. He was prepared to accept the need for punitive measures, especially against Southern guerrillas, so long as they were controlled by legitimate military authority rather than released in a vengeful, spontaneous, undisciplined outburst by the men in the ranks; such outbreaks should be discouraged at all costs. For example, he instructed Fred Steele to ensure that "all the people understand that we claim the unmolested navigation of the Mississippi River and will have it, if all the country within reach had to be laid waste"; such threats, however, should remain constrained, for Southerners should "be spared the ravages of war as much as we can consistent with our own interests." But for the time being, Sherman conceived such threats as responses to very specific tactical questions, not as reflecting a general outlook on the war as a whole.[34]

Sherman complained of the "vacillating Policy of our Government and People"; he again threatened to resign if Lincoln exhibited any "want of confidence" in Grant, though he wished Halleck would return to take up command of the West for a second time. He began to wonder whether Grant would ever find a way out of the quagmire, and he admitted that he was "sorry that I ever embarked in a voyage so sure to be disastrous to the first actors." Ominously he reported to Ellen on March 13 that the water continued to rise. He took his mind off his worries by penning a delightful letter to his daughter Minnie. He reflected on the art of written style, as "now is the time to learn to write plain and well and habit will make it Easy." He also revealed that he had received many kindnesses in recent weeks from the Sisters of Charity on board a hospital ship with Porter's fleet. One had sent him a can of preserves, but he did not reveal whether he had shared this with the admiral. Sherman concluded by assuring Minnie that she was fortunate in being born to such a good family "and will not want for friends in this world."[35]

On March 16 Grant confided to Sherman that he wanted to more fully explore the Yazoo route via Haines Bluff. He ordered Sherman to carry out a reconnaissance in force, "and I shall go up in a tug tomorrow morning"; Sherman expressed delight at the prospect. Grant issued his orders the same day: Sherman should take the Pioneer Corps and the 8th Missouri, as "many of them [were] boatmen." Sherman ordered their commanding officer to take 300 axes and a keg of spikes with which they could make rafts to aid the men who hacked away at the top of the overhanging tree canopy. His orders specified that he should gauge "the feasibility of getting an Army through that route to the East bank of that river and at a point from which they can act advantageously against Vicksburg." Sherman probed forward via Steele's Bayou and Black Bayou, then accompanied Admiral Porter as he sailed into Deer Creek. As this seemed wide with few obstructions, Porter indulged a sanguine mood. He asked Sherman to return and "clear out" Black Bayou while he sailed on. Porter lent Sherman a tug, the *Fern*, and he duly did so. Black Bayou, he reported, was "about a mile long, narrow, crooked, and filled with trees." He failed to find a suitable route. Provisions were "abundant" but the communications lamentable: "You know," he cautioned Grant, "the difficulty of managing detached boats in small, crooked streams, where overhanging boughs and submerged trees obstruct their progress at every quarter of a mile." Sherman also warned Grant that the Confederates could sail their boats to the Rolling Fork Bayou far more quickly than Porter, as they enjoyed the benefit of a more direct route of a mere 7 miles. Porter estimated that he needed 10,000 men to hold the country through which he passed and clear all obstructions. Sherman presented a gloomy report but left it up to Grant to order a continuance of the mission.[36]

At midnight on March 19–20 the dramatic pace of the operation suddenly quickened. While writing dispatches and issuing orders, Sherman received an urgent appeal for help from Porter written on a piece of tissue paper and hidden by a slave in a piece of tobacco. The admiral's progress up Deer Creek had been more tortuous than anticipated, but his withdrawal was endangered by Confederate infantry, which had worked around behind him and felled trees, blocking his escape route. Their musket fire killed sailors who attempted to steer the gunboats away from the bank or to remove obstacles.

Porter feared the worst and pleaded with Sherman to rescue him. Otherwise he might be forced to abandon his vessels and blow them up, which would constitute a disaster for Grant's campaign. As ever in an emergency, Sherman was energy incarnate: he paddled a canoe down Black Bayou, ordered forward elements of Giles Smith's brigade, and then rounded up men from various work details, as well as troops of Kilby Smith's brigade who had just arrived. He got them aboard ship and sailed as far as they could on a dark night, then disembarked and marched through the canebreak "carrying lighted candles in our hands, till we got into the open cotton fields at Hill's Plantation, where we lay down for a few hours' rest." At daybreak on March 21 Sherman ordered them on. "Being on foot myself, no one could complain, and we generally went at the double-quick, with occasional rests." By noon they had marched 21 miles.

After Sherman sat down for a well-earned rest, he received word from a picket that a rebel force with 6-pounder guns had got between the fleet and relief, but no larger force lay between Sherman and the gunboats. Spurred to action by the sound of musketry, "not three hundred yards off," he ordered an advance of two battalions of Kilby Smith's brigade, mounted a horse lent by an officer of the 8th Missouri, and then rode bareback and melodramatically along the levee to be greeted by a great cheer from Porter's sailors as Union troops drove off the Confederates. Sherman deployed his men to screen Porter's withdrawal as he sailed hard astern back down Deer Creek, a "slow and tedious process," Sherman recalled. It still took three days to extricate the five gunboats from the waterway and return them to Hill's Plantation. Not surprisingly after this experience, Sherman concluded that Rolling Fork Bayou was impassable and Deer Creek "useless to us in a military way." Grant had by this time received Sherman's pessimistic reports and ordered both Sherman and Porter to return to their camp at Young's Point. Sherman had repaired there by March 27. Grant expressed bitter disappointment at this setback. He candidly admitted to Sherman "that I had made really but little calculation u[p]on reaching Vicksburg by any other [route] than Hain[e]s Bluff." But the disaster could have been of a greater magnitude, as Porter had contemplated scuttling his ships when escape seemed impossible. By his extraordinary display of personal leadership and energetic action, Sherman had saved the campaign. But to what end?[37]

After the excitement and challenges posed during the previous week, the return to Young's Point cast an anticlimactic and depressing pall over the proceedings. Sherman warned John not to jump to the conclusion that the South was teetering on the verge of exhaustion. "I get deserters and other informa-tion daily and I see not one symptom of relaxation, on the contrary quite the reverse. The war in Earnest has yet to be fought." A series of brilliant insights then followed on the Civil War's general character. "People must learn that war is a question of physical force and courage," he reminded John. As the as-sailant, the North had no choice but "to overcome not only an equal number of determined men, however wrongfully engaged, but the natural obstacles of a most difficult country." It had to wear down the South and "should fight on all occasions even if we get worsted—we can stand it longest—We are killing Arkansas and Louisiana—All the lands are overflown and they cannot cultivate." But Sherman discerned that Northern numerical superiority had to some extent been negated by the chaotic system of raising troops. Military strength must be conserved even amid societies with a plentiful supply of men; resources are never limitless. These audacious insights into the war's character increasingly bolstered the cautious conclusions that Sherman drew about the operational design that urgently needed to be fashioned for the Vicksburg campaign. This paradoxical combination of audacity and caution would grow stronger as Sherman's command style matured.[38]

Grant had reacted to the Yazoo disappointment with characteristic te-nacity. He issued orders for work to begin on digging another canal to link the Mississippi River at Duckport with Willow Bayou, which abutted Milliken's Bend; he hoped it would create a route through which troops and supplies could be transported to New Carthage and thence to the river port of Grand Gulf. The canal would improve the chances of making a suc-cessful junction with Banks to the south; 3,000 men toiled on this project. "Though it is a plan," Sherman observed disapprovingly, "it is not a good plan." Sherman persisted in the belief that the campaign's decisive point lay in the north and east, not the south, and to go southward was to "commit a great mistake, but I am not going to advise one way or the other." He remained loyal to Grant and dutifully carried out his orders irrespective of his per-sonal views. He confided doubts only to his father-in-law and Ellen, issuing stern instructions that the former should not write to the War Department mentioning them in case his doubts should leak out. Yet he remained less than impressed by Grant's capacity as a planner. He made indirectly worded allusions to Ellen about Grant's "slow but sure" propensities; she could not mistake his meaning. Many others shared these doubts. Secretary of War Stanton had heard alarming gossip about Grant's alcohol consumption. He sent Charles A. Dana, a former newspaperman who had been appointed assistant secretary of war in March 1863, to check on progress and assess Grant's capacity to meet the challenges that lay ahead. Dana soon came to admire Grant, and Sherman reported that Rawlins told him Dana "was better pleased with me than he could have possibly expected."[39]

In the first week of April, Grant held a series of informal discussions concerning the campaign's future. Once these had concluded and he had thought matters over, he issued his new plan. His concept of operations shifted the entire weight of the offensive even farther southward. He required Porter's naval squadron and transports to sail past Vicksburg, and once this had been achieved, the three corps of the Army of the Tennessee were to march southward on the left bank of the Mississippi and then cross to the right bank. It was a quite extraordinarily audacious conception because Grant defied conventional wisdom that held it a blunder to leave an inviolate fortress astride his supply lines, with an unbeaten army between him and shelter. In reaching this decision, Grant had deliberately encouraged what the historian Sir John Keegan dubs "a sort of barbershop meeting" atmosphere. All his subordinates, Sherman recalled, "talked over all these things with absolute freedom." Sherman and others did not hesitate to voice their opposition, but the discussion took place against the background of McClernand's disloyalty to Grant. McClernand did not hesitate to denounce his superior's supposed incompetence behind his back or to send Lincoln an account of a drunken spree the previous March. Sherman feared that McClernand had made headway in his scheming to supplant Grant. On April 8 Sherman sent Rawlins, Grant's chief of staff, a letter suggesting that all corps commanders present their commander with "their opinions, concise and positive, on the best general plan of campaign." He then outlined his preferred alternative. He later claimed that the real point of the letter lay in the possibility that in the event of another failure, ambitious subordinates—he meant McClernand—would claim that their advice had been ignored, but if it had been followed defeat would have been avoided. His proposal would ensure that McClernand's views, or lack of them, would be on the record.[40]

Sherman promised his "zealous cooperation and energetic support" whatever course of action Grant selected. In his *Memoirs* Sherman is sensitive to any accusation that this letter constituted some kind of "protest" against Grant's new plan. He insists that he sought to smoke McClernand out and force him to put his ideas on paper so that he could be held to account. Such a move would also demonstrate the poverty of McClernand's military ideas. Perhaps, but Sherman privately exhibited little real confidence that Grant's plan would succeed. The letter had the secondary objective of ensuring that should Grant fail, Sherman's objections, too, were a matter of record.[41]

The turbulent atmosphere in Mississippi was further unsettled when news reached Sherman that "war between Ellen and Elizabeth," his sister, had broken out again over the Sherman house in Lancaster. Ellen worried, he confided to John, "lest Elizabeth attempt to come between me and her," but this could never happen. Another piece of irritating news arrived informing Sherman that David Stuart had failed to gain Senate confirmation as a brigadier general. He quizzed John as to why. "He was one of the best of the whole lot ... constantly at the Front. ... His military record was perfect." Sherman put Stuart's failure down to "some old affair in Chicago"; he had committed adultery, though he eventually married the lady in question. Sherman appears justified in thinking it extraordinary that Stuart was chastised with adultery when two generals, Daniel E. Sickles and Philip Kearny, had committed the same act and escaped congressional wrath. Ellen informed him that her father's inquiries had revealed that Senator Edgar Cowan of Pennsylvania had agreed that the "pharasiacal" members had indeed voted against him on these grounds. "Did you ever hear of a greater absurdity?" she asked. Stuart resigned his commission as colonel, and his departure caused a reorganization of the 15th Corps. On April 3 a division commanded by Brigadier General James M. Tuttle was allotted to Sherman, although it received the official designation of the 1st Division. The following day Stuart was replaced by Brigadier General Frank Blair of the 2nd Division. Sherman was less than enchanted by this appointment. "I am afraid of that class of men," he admitted to John; "they are so treacherous." It would appear that Sherman had not taken Blair's protestations of innocence at face value when he accused him of spiteful gossiping to Knox of the *New York Herald*. "Pray do not offend him Cump," Ellen implored sagely, for Blair was a brave and doughty fighter.[42]

"The trees are in full leaf—the black and blue birds sing sweetly," Sherman rhapsodized to Ellen, "and the mockingbird is frantic with Joy—the Rose and the violet, the beds of verbena and Mignonette, planted by fair hands now in exile from their homes occupied by the Rude Barbarian"—but this pastoral repose would soon be disrupted by equally frantic military activity. On April 20 Grant had made his preparations and had certainly made up his mind, and so issued his orders: he would move south. McClernand's 13th Corps would form the right flank and vanguard, McPherson's 17th Corps the center, and Sherman would follow McClernand: his 15th Corps would compose the left flank and would come up last, "the movement being by the right flank." "I don't object to this," he confessed to Ellen, "for I have no faith in the whole plan." Porter's seven ironclads and three transports cast off after dark on April 16; his flag flew on the *Benton*, but even Porter's ebullience could not disguise the rising tension. He had to escort the transports past Vicksburg's guns, with each transport towing 10 barges. They were an inviting target.

As a precaution Sherman had ordered that four yawl boats be hauled across the swamps below Vicksburg to enable his men to intercept any disabled vessels and rescue their stricken crews. As soon as Porter's ships were spotted, Confederate artillery opened fire in what Sherman called "a desperate and terrible thing," as the transport ships were "floating by terrific Batteries without the power of replying." Despite his gloomy sense of foreboding, as usual danger inspirited Sherman. He sailed out aboard a yawl into midstream and watched the federal gunboats return fire as the Mississippi's left bank was set ablaze by Confederate shells, silhouetting the vessels against the dark backdrop. Sherman jumped aboard the *Benton*, offered Porter a few breezy, uplifting sentiments, "and remained to witness the scene" until they neared Warrenton. Then, on the admiral's insistence, he leapt back aboard his yawl. In the meantime, the *Henry Clay* caught fire, though one of Sherman's yawls picked up its pilot.

On the night of April 22 another half-dozen transports passed Vicksburg carrying stores and equipment to enable Grant's troops to cross the Mississippi. These movements were not made without loss. The *Tigress* sank, taking with it most of the army's medical supplies. "I look upon the whole thing," Sherman confided to Ellen in a troubled mood, "as one of the most hazardous and desperate moves of this or any war." He was not heartened by having to discharge from the 15th Corps a significant number of officers whose terms of enlistment had ended.[43]

The roads south were overcrowded, and on April 26 Grant asked Sherman to delay his march southward until they had cleared, or perhaps to make use of the canals on which so much fruitless labor had been lavished. Grant had gone to Carthage to supervise McClernand in response to Porter's insistent call for another commander to be present that he could trust. Grant's initial objective was Grand Gulf, to serve as a base for crossing the Mississippi and as a shield for his right flank as he did so; as the campaign developed, he could then anchor his rear and left on the river port as he advanced obliquely behind Vicksburg. Grant and Porter carried out a personal reconnaissance and agreed Grand Gulf could be taken quickly, but both became alarmed by the falling river levels that threatened the safety of the gunboat squadron and diminished the chances of making the most of river transport while the roads were so bad. Grant turned to Sherman for insurance and ordered him to build new roads where he could. When Sherman received these orders, they provoked another outburst of private complaints. Yet Sherman set to, conceding, "I can aid him by building a road back to Willow Bayou, so that he could exploit water transport, too." But with a touch of self-fulfilling prophecy, he maintained that this line would be insufficient to sustain Grant's entire army. He judged Porter's squadron "in a fatal trap." And with a touch of pique that his advice to return north and base operations in Memphis or Helena had been ignored, he predicted: "I say we are further from taking Vicksburg today than we were the day I was repulsed."[44]

Grant wrote again three days later, giving Sherman more details of the intended Grand Gulf operation but saying he needed him to conduct a feint to distract Confederate attention away from it. Grant habitually used a subtle technique that ensured a measure of harmony among his troubled subordinates. All three of Grant's corps commanders were sensitive to being ordered to carry out operations that might end in tactical failure even if they contributed to a successful outcome. If Grant suggested such a course when he felt it appropriate, he would not order it, as such an operation would have to be done without any "ill effect on the army and the country"; he did not mention officially an unpalatable fact, either (though he did in a short private letter), but Grant had invited Sherman to carry out an operation that might result in a repulse or at least "the appearance of a repulse." He asked Sherman to mount "a simultaneous feint on the enemy or the enemy's batteries on the Yazoo, near Haines Bluff' as "most desirable." Grant evidently realized that Sherman would be very sensitive on this point. An implied encouragement for Sherman to defy the press earned his immediate assent.

A display of zealous public loyalty then ensued. Sherman drew 10 small regiments from Blair's 2nd Division and placed them on 10 transports. By 10:00 a.m. on April 29, he had sailed once more to the mouth of the Yazoo River and joined a small squadron of ironclads under Admiral Porter, supported by several wooden vessels. The following morning, they sailed within range of the batteries at Haines Bluff and then opened fire for four hours—"and they gave us back as much as we sent." The *Choctaw* was hit 46 times, "but," Sherman observed, "strange to say, no men were hurt." During the evening Sherman ordered an ostentatious diversion and gave the impression that he was about to launch an assault. "Keeping up appearances till night, the troops were re-embarked," Sherman reported tersely. During this successful enterprise only one man was slightly hurt. Porter praised Sherman's moral courage for returning to "the scene of his earlier repulse." Sherman had succeeded brilliantly in prolonging "the diversion as much as possible in your favor," as he informed Grant. Ellen warned him that the newspapers had nevertheless reported his efforts as "another failure."[45]

Before Sherman could repeat this repertoire the following morning, he received orders to immediately bring two of his divisions, Tuttle's 1st and Steele's 3rd, to Perkin's Plantation, some 40 miles downstream. But Blair's 2nd Division continued the demonstration until nightfall, when it boarded for Young's Point. On May 1 Sherman accompanied Blair's 2nd Division to Milliken's Bend, where it remained as a garrison while Sherman set off with his other two divisions to march the 63 miles to Hard Times Plantation, about four miles above Grand Gulf. When he arrived on May 3, he found that Grand Gulf had been abandoned by the Confederates that day and had been quickly occupied by Union forces. With these two divisions of 15th Corps, Sherman then began to cross the Mississippi River during the night of May 6–7 by means of transports used as ferries and an improvised, temporary "floating bridge," passage being completed by the evening of May 7. At long last Sherman and his men, after trials lasting six months, placed their feet firmly on terra firma. Such progress began to alter Sherman's attitude toward the campaign; he still entertained private doubts as to whether Grant could actually take Vicksburg "but shall be agreeably surprised if we do."[46]

Sherman noticed during the march to Hard Times that the countryside overflowed with foodstuffs. Not everything could be taken from the countryside, so "[we] must learn to live on corn and beef ourselves," he observed to Ellen perceptively. Although he was prepared to take food from civilians, he recoiled from "this universal burning and wanton destruction of private property [which] is not justifiable in war." In his *Memoirs* he mentions entering a plantation mansion that he later discovered belonged to the brother-in-law of his foster father's friend Maryland senator Reverdy Johnson, a stout Unionist. He found in the drawing room a soldier lounging on the piano stool with his feet on the keyboard and with the contents of the library strewn about. "I started him in a hurry to overtake his command," Sherman wrote with satisfaction. He tried his best to rescue and protect the house's contents, but the pressure of the campaign distracted him, and the mansion eventually succumbed to arsonists. Sherman was probably right in assuming that stragglers were most to blame for such depredations rather than the fighting troops.[47]

Sherman revealed to Ellen on May 6 that "Grant is calling for me very impatiently and I will probably push out to him with my advance Guard tomorrow." Sherman's troops marched 18 miles to Hankinson's Ferry, crossed the Big Black River on a pontoon bridge swiftly constructed by his engineers, and advanced on Big Sandy. On May 11 Sherman entered Auburn, Mississippi, and at last encountered Grant, who accompanied him and the 15th Corps for the next three days. Of course, Grant and Sherman had exchanged letters in the meantime. Grant had ordered Sherman to establish lines of communication with Grand Gulf and fill a wagon train with rations of hardtack and coffee, plus ammunition, and send it northeast. The Army of the Tennessee could not live off the country entirely, but to a skeptical Sherman, Grant stated firmly that he could draw necessities from Grand Gulf, "and we can make the country furnish the balance." Such logistical constraints merely added to the urgency of achieving the campaign's operational goals in the shortest possible time. Grant underlined "the overwhelming importance of celerity in your movements"; Sherman, ever loyal, hastened to do Grant's bidding. So far, he had only been delayed for three hours by a cavalry skirmish at Fourteen Mile Creek, unlike McPherson's troops, which on May 12 had defeated a small Confederate force at Raymond, 10 miles from the Mississippi state capital, Jackson. On Sherman's arrival at Raymond, Grant personally ordered the 15th Corps to change places with the 17th Corps and occupy the right flank while McPherson's command shifted to the center. The latter would advance on Jackson forthwith from the west on the Clinton road while Sherman's 15th Corps advanced roughly 30 degrees to it and approached Jackson from the southwest.[48]

Sherman and McPherson conferred through the night of May 14–15 and decided to advance on Jackson simultaneously. The roads had previously been dust laden—Sherman indeed thought the dust over the previous few days "the worst"—but it rained torrentially on May 13–14, and the going became arduous and sticky. Less than 3 miles from the city's center the Confederates occupied a position adjacent to an intact bridge. Sherman reconnoitered personally, and at the first sign of an assault, the Confederates "opened [fire] on us briskly." Sherman ordered forward three of Tuttle's brigades and two batteries of artillery; the latter quickly silenced the Confederate guns, whereupon the Confederate force withdrew about half a mile into a line of entrenchments. The Union infantry crossed the bridge and

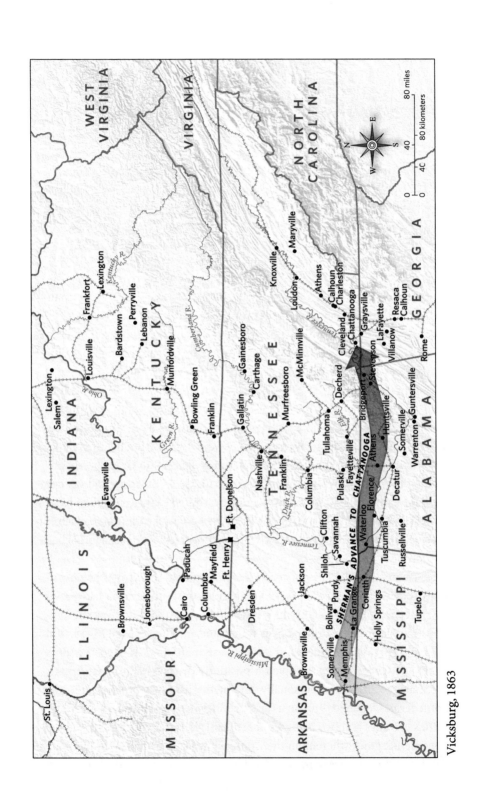

Vicksburg, 1863

deployed beyond it, but the Confederate position still looked formidable. Sherman ordered Captain Julius Pitzman, an engineer on his staff, to take the 95th Ohio Infantry to the right flank to discern whether a way around existed. In the meantime, Steele's 3rd Division came up, so when Pitzman returned and reported that the defenses were "abandoned at the point where they crossed the railroad," Sherman ordered Steele to advance and take advantage of this weakness. As soon as Sherman heard the cheers of Steele's men, he threw Tuttle's division forward, and it entered Jackson by the main road. The Confederate garrison, commanded by General Joseph E. Johnston, withdrew hastily to the north, but Sherman captured 250 prisoners and the entire stock of Confederate artillery (18 guns), plus much ammunition and stores. The biggest prize yet in the campaign had fallen.

Once Jackson had been neutralized, Grant's thoughts shifted to switching the advance westward in order to defeat the Confederates outside Vicksburg's defenses. He also aimed to prevent any junction between Johnston's troops and Pemberton's. Combined they could equal Grant's strength, but divided they remained weak fragments. Grant summoned his corps commanders to a meeting at the Bowman House Hotel opposite the statehouse. He ordered McPherson and the 17th Corps to join McClernand and occupy Bolton to the west, while Sherman was given the task of occupying the former Confederate entrenchments. On May 15 Sherman received orders "to destroy effectually the railroad tracks in and about Jackson, and all the property belonging to the enemy." Steele's division was given the latter mission, and as Sherman noted, "The work of destruction was well accomplished." Combined with specific demolition of Jackson's military infrastructure by Brigadier General Joseph A. Mower's brigade, the state capital was rendered useless to the Confederate war effort for some six months. Sherman's report includes a detailed tally: among the resources destroyed were all foundries, arsenals, gun carriage workshops, all stables, carpentry and paint shops, and a cotton factory; the railroad track had been torn up 3 or 4 miles beyond the town but up to 10 miles on the all-important line west to Vicksburg.[49]

During the first occupation of Jackson, Sherman reaffirmed his ambivalent attitude toward general destruction. He had received appeals from a Mr. Green, the owner of a factory manufacturing cotton cloth, claiming that as his factory offered valuable employment to the poor, it should be spared the torch. Sherman was by no means immune to this appeal, but he decided that it should be burned down, though he made provisions for feeding any unemployed workers. He also received blandishments from the owner of the

Bowman House that he had always been a loyal Union man (a frequently made, often deceitful claim). Having known this hotel during his travels back and forth from Louisiana before 1861, Sherman replied sardonically that he could gauge his loyalty by the condition of his sign, where "United States" had been hurriedly and inadequately painted out and "Confederate" scrawled over it. The building had not been placed on Sherman's list for destruction, and he said as much. This building and a nearby Catholic church, however, were set on fire "by some mischievous soldiers." Sherman condemned the "many acts of pillage ... arising from the effect of some bad rum found concealed in the stores of the town."[50]

On the morning of May 16 Sherman received a letter from Grant indicating that Confederates were advancing from Edwards Depot and that he should send a division forthwith westward to Bolton Station on the Pittsburgh–Jackson Railroad. He should follow with the other as soon as it completed the task of destruction of war materiél. These movements signaled the imminence of Grant's victory at the Battle of Champion Hill that day, fought largely by the 13th Corps and supported by elements of the 17th Corps. By 10:00 a.m. Sherman had Steele's division on the road, and Tuttle's followed two hours later. Sherman paroled his prisoners of war in order to safeguard the wounded left by McPherson in Jackson's hospital, as he was sure that Johnston would reoccupy Jackson as soon as he abandoned it. His two divisions covered the 20 miles to Bolton that day, so Sherman decided to press on to Bridgeport on the Big Black, where at noon on May 17 he rendezvoused with Blair's 2nd Division and the pontoon train, thus completing the concentration of his corps. The following day Grant inflicted a sharp defeat on Pemberton's troops on the Big Black; the arrival of the entire 15th Corps permitted Grant to consummate his two recent successes by giving the necessary momentum for a complete and final investment of Vicksburg. Sherman had the pontoon bridge laid speedily and on the night of May 17 ordered Blair's and Steele's divisions to cross. The boats lashed together were made of India rubber, and as darkness fell, the crossing troops were illuminated by fires of pitch pine. "General Grant joined me there," Sherman recalled in his *Memoirs*, "and we sat on a log, looking at the passage of the troops by the light of those fires; the bridge swayed to and fro under the passing feet, and made a fine war picture." Tuttle's division then followed on the morning of May 18. Sherman decided that Blair's rested division would bear the brunt of any fighting needed to finally take Vicksburg.[51]

From 9:30 to 10:00 a.m. on May 18 Blair's division advanced to the crest of the high ground above the Yazoo and cut the Benton Road, thus "interposing a superior force between the enemy at Vicksburg and his forts on the Yazoo." As it approached Vicksburg the Benton Road divided into two forks, and, careful to ensure that both forks were held until elements of McPherson's 17th Corps arrived, Sherman had hastened to carry out Grant's orders that he should advance on the right, with McPherson in the center and McClernand on the left flank. Sherman's 15th Corps advanced in echelon with Blair's division in the vanguard, Tuttle's 1st Division in support, and Steele's 3rd Division "to follow a blind road to the right till he reached the Mississippi." Early on May 19 Tuttle seized the works at Haines Bluff that had defied Sherman several times but were at long last in his hands. Sherman then dispatched the 4th Iowa Cavalry to seize the battery and magazines, which that afternoon were handed over to one of Porter's gunboats. Communication was thus opened with the fleet at Young's Point and on the Yazoo; ammunition and supplies could henceforth be transported via the mouth of the Chickasaw. In the meantime, the 15th Corps pickets had closed up to Vicksburg's defenses.

Grant and Sherman rode together ostensibly to check whether the Benton road along which hardtack, salt, and coffee would be carried was up to the task, but really to view the scene of the latter's repulse the previous December. They could also observe the continuing panicky Confederate retreat back into Vicksburg's works. As they looked over the Chickasaw battlefield, with its marshy and uninviting ground that had caused Sherman so much anxiety in December and for months afterward, Grant remained silent. Suddenly Sherman, in a burst of that impulsive candor that endeared him to his friends but annoyed many who were not so fortunate as to be included among them, declared the full extent of his previous doubts. "Until this moment I never thought your expedition a success; I never could see the end clearly till now," he admitted. "But this is a campaign; this is a success if we never take the town." At long last, Sherman had taken the full measure of his commander. Grant was too easily underrated even by the more perceptive. That remorseless, taciturn, enigmatic man never took counsel of his fears. He had got Sherman to Vicksburg after all, and Sherman, despite his quicksilver intelligence, had taken too long to understand his methods. Yet once convinced he always learned quickly.[52]

Sherman's opinion on another matter is also significant because it contradicts the doubts expressed by some authorities as to the degree that Grant abandoned his lines of supply during the culminating phase of the

Vicksburg campaign. "Up to that point," Sherman wrote forthrightly in his report, "our men had literally lived upon the country, having left Grand Gulf [on] May 8 with three days rations in their haversacks and received little or nothing till after our arrival here on the 18th." As the line of the Yazoo had been secured, he assured Ellen, his troops would "soon have plenty to eat."[53]

Despite the easing of some problems, others had worsened. Sherman observed that although he could see the enemy easily, for they were only 400 yards away, this space constituted "very difficult ground, cut up by almost impracticable ravines, and [their] line of entrenchments." Grant, keen to take advantage of Confederate demoralization, ordered a general assault all along the line at 2:00 p.m.; both he and Sherman underrated how much the morale of these poorly commanded Confederates revived once they had found shelter in Vicksburg's defenses. Sherman brought forward Blair's 2nd Division. He intended it to advance on Pemberton's fortified line with two brigades (those of Charley Ewing and Giles Smith) to the right of the Benton road running to the Yazoo, and Kilby Smith's brigade to its left. Sherman supervised the siting of his artillery carefully both right and left "to cover the point where the road enters the entrenchments." He also placed Tuttle's 1st Division close behind to exploit any opportunities, with Buckland's brigade deployed parallel with Blair's rearguard; the other two brigades were kept back under cover.

Four hours after the battle began, Blair reported that no progress had been made in piercing the Confederate defences running perpendicular to the road. The attack had started in fine order, but cohesion had been broken up by deep chasms. On the left of Sherman's sector, the 13th Regular Infantry in Giles Smith's brigade got up onto the Confederate works first and planted their colors on the parapet, supported by two further regiments; although other regiments rushed to support them, they failed to break into the Confederate position. "As soon as night closed in," Sherman explained, "I ordered them back a short distance, where the shape of the ground gave them partial shelter, to bivouac for the night." These plans indicate that Sherman anticipated a renewal of the attack.[54]

That night he quickly wrote to Ellen to assure her that both her brothers were safe. Charley had been wounded in the hand while successfully rescuing the 13th Infantry's colors after he had taken command of the regiment. Hugh had been "also under fire and had a hard time yesterday," but he was now safe. As for himself, "I must go again to the Front amid the shot and shells which follow me but somehow thus far have spared me." He had witnessed a near miss the previous day while he and Grant watched the deployment of Steele's division when a man standing next to them was felled by a random shot. Sherman did not dwell on the caprice of fate, but his casual references to such dangers provoked in Ellen "fearful apprehensions." He was actually enjoying himself and had slept on the ground the last two nights, much to the disgust of his servant, John Hill, who showed even less enthusiasm for accompanying Sherman to the front.[55]

The speed with which Grant had ordered the attack had prevented any detailed preparation. On May 20 Grant conferred with his corps commanders. Sherman did not consider this meeting a "council of war," more an act of consultation. They all agreed that the initial failure could be explained by the necessity in such a short time to attack the strongest part of the Confederate line where the three roads entered the city. All were confident of breaking it if weaker points were selected and the artillery could be placed in locations where the weight of shells could count for more. All were keen to exploit the assumed demoralization of Pemberton's troops. They expressed unanimity as to the practicality and prospects of success for the renewed offensive. On May 21 Grant issued orders for an assault the following day; he did not specify the tactics to be employed, though he summarized the consensus by stressing that a speedy assault by heads of columns "with bayonets fixed" covered by heavy artillery would increase the chances for success and reduce casualties. Roads were improved, new trenches dug, supplies and ammunition stockpiled, and the artillery moved to "new and commanding positions." The Confederates had done the same, however, though harassed by Union pickets.[56]

Sherman employed what were by now his customary techniques. He carried out a detailed personal reconnaissance of his entire front. He noted that the forts were built to command the roads, for the hills and valleys "are so abrupt and covered with fallen trees, standing trees and canebrake that we are in a measure confined to the Roads." He drew up a plan based on careful thought even though he could hardly disregard the pressure of time. He decided to attack either side of the bastion covering the road, rather than assault it directly, and confuse the Confederates by mounting a strong feint on Steele's front about a mile to the Union right. Artillery batteries were well placed and concealed. In addition, he had asked Porter to contribute to the bombardment even though he had only a single gunboat available, the *Cincinnati*. Blair's division was better concealed at the head of the road this time, with Tuttle's division well in hand for support. A select, volunteer storming party of 150 men would carry boards and poles to enable the ditch to be crossed. Ewing's brigade should follow after a short interval, then Giles Smith's and finally Kilby Smith's. Once more Sherman had attempted to anticipate every contingency in a plan that envisaged a "connected and rapid" advance.[57]

It was the best plan under the circumstances. Sherman took the precaution of devising a flank march so that the men would remain under cover for as long as possible. Confederate infantry could not be seen, but Sherman knew they were lying in wait. At the hour specified by Grant, Blair's storming party raced up the road with Ewing's brigade close behind, and five batteries of guns opened fire on the bastion. As the storming party approached the salient of the bastion and the sally port into the line, two ranks of Confederate infantry suddenly stood up along the entire position and delivered a devastating series of volleys that decimated the attackers. The head of the column sought cover; those behind followed suit. On the left face of the bastion the troops climbed up its exterior slope and attempted to dig down into it. Giles Smith's brigade turned down a ravine and found cover by taking this wide circuit, but it failed to circumvent the bastion. Kilby Smith deployed between his and Ewing's brigade, but none of these formations could get into, let alone through, this position.

At 2:00 p.m. Blair informed Sherman that though his brigades could make no progress in the vicinity of the road, Giles Smith's brigade had nonetheless linked up, thanks to his detour, with Brigadier General Thomas E. G. Ransom's brigade of the 17th Corps "and was ready to assault." Sherman had selected for his command post a position about 200 yards from the Confederate front, where he could see what was happening and also be close enough so that his subordinates could consult him if necessary—but not be so close that he might be tempted to interfere in their business. He ordered a further heavy bombardment to support a renewed infantry assault. Despite this precaution, the brigades of Ransom and Giles Smith endured what Sherman called a "staggering fire" before which they recoiled and fell back under cover of the hillside.[58]

Very shortly after the repulse, Grant rode up to Sherman's command post and dismounted. Sherman immediately reported that, despite individual acts of high courage, his troops had been thrown back; Grant responded that the troops on the fronts of the other two corps had met a similar fate. Grant's visit was indicative of the growing intimacy between the two generals, now fully reciprocated by Sherman. While they conferred, Grant received a handwritten note from McClernand claiming in melodramatic terms that he had gained "part possession" of two of the bastions on the Union left. McClernand assured Grant that one more push would be sufficient to take them. According to Sherman's account, Grant gave these boastful claims scant credibility, but he persuaded Grant that McClernand's message could not be ignored—perhaps sensing the danger to Grant's position if he failed to take advantage of any opportunity suggested by McClernand. Whatever the precise wording of McClernand's claim, this was an example of how his incorrigible self-glorification rebounded against him, even when right was on his side. Sherman offered to attack again. He ordered Tuttle to bring up Mower's brigade and Steele to continue with his feint on the right flank of the 15th Corps. Mower's brigade advanced "bravely and well," with Blair's division moving forward once more in support. Although a regiment got its colors fixed by the side of those of Blair's initial storming party on the Confederate parapet, no significant advance was achieved. At nightfall Sherman ordered the colors taken down and the troops withdrawn. In describing these assaults to Ellen three days later, which could hardly have lessened her fears for her husband and two brothers, Sherman used even more arresting language, saying that during the attacks "the heads of columns are swept away as chaff thrown from the hand on a windy day."

McClernand had indeed made more progress than the other two corps, but he had exaggerated its broader operational significance and potential for exploitation. In a rare understatement, Sherman observed that McClernand's claims had been "premature." Steele, despite the riven country over which his troops were forced to advance, had actually reached the Confederate parapet but could not carry the works, though he maintained control of the high ground around them until night fell, whereupon he retired to his own lines. Sherman's total casualty bill was slightly above the 600 claimed in his report submitted two days later. Grant's total casualties were 3,052.[59]

In the days following, 15th Corps skirmishers continued to operate close to the Confederate breastworks, while the infantry withdrew into the ravines to take advantage of the cover. Sherman ordered the working parties to continue to improve the roads up to the front. He argued that the remainder of the campaign should take the form of a siege by "regular approaches." He believed that by better use of the topography he could advance his own works as close as 100 yards from the Confederate redoubt that commanded the road. Saps—trenches dug toward the enemy's position and usually covered—were to be started on Blair and Steele's front. "Our position," Sherman declared, "is now high, healthy and good. We are in direct and easy communication with our supplies." Despite their setbacks, Sherman commented on the "cheerful spirit" of his troops. Perhaps as a reward for its courage on May 22, Mower's brigade was sent back to the left bank of the Mississippi to complete the encirclement of Vicksburg. The river port was now surrounded on all sides. But losses still mounted. Five days later the *Cincinnati* was sunk.[60]

Sherman selected as his headquarters a new position in the center of the corps line. "I have a nice camp and Grant is near me," he informed Ellen. Grant had indeed placed his own headquarters on the other side of a ravine behind Sherman's and visited regularly. "McPherson is a noble fellow but McClernand is a dirty dog," Sherman snapped. The even more vituperative language he used in this comparison reflects the intense and widespread resentment felt at the senseless cost of lives that resulted from McClernand's note to Grant on the afternoon of May 23. "Blair and I are on very good terms," Sherman revealed to John, and he benefited, too, from his brother-in-law Charley Ewing's presence, as he could keep a watchful eye on his superior's activities. Sherman and Blair now had a common enemy in McClernand. Blair had been infuriated by the unnecessary loss sustained by his division as a result of McClernand's intervention. Sherman might have sensed that McClernand had committed a self-inflicted wound by his actions on May 22, but it was Blair who initiated the series of moves that resulted in McClernand's dismissal.[61]

On the evening of June 16 Sherman had just returned from inspecting new entrenchments at Snyder's Bluff when he met a very angry Blair, who asked him whether he had seen a copy of the *Memphis Evening Bulletin* that had appeared three days previously. This contained a bombastic "Congratulatory Order" in McClernand's unmistakable florid style. Sherman read it and sat down to write Grant a letter of complaint, enclosing a copy of the paper for information. Sherman complained of the self-serving flattery of the order; rather than just confining himself to reciting the efforts of the 13th Corps on May 19 and 22, McClernand went further and slighted the efforts of the other two corps in snide asides. Sherman's letter conveyed two essential points. First, it was unusual to issue such orders after a repulse. He had not done so after Chickasaw Bluffs—though he does not refer to this example—and they were "only resorted to by weak and vain men to shift the burden of responsibility from their own to the shoulders of others." Second, and crucially in this case, General Orders No. 151 forbade the publication of all official orders and reports. McClernand's order "was not an order or a report" but, Sherman argued brutally, a "publication for ulterior political purposes." He was out-raged at the imputation that he and McPherson had disobeyed Grant's orders to support the 13th Corps on the afternoon of May 22. McPherson soon be-came acquainted with the contents of McClernand's "Congratulatory Order" and also wrote a letter of complaint, remarking sarcastically that McClernand had forgotten one of the essential qualities of the warrior, namely, justice to others.[62]

Grant wrote to McClernand immediately to verify whether what he had been sent was a "true copy." McClernand was absent when the letter arrived but on returning agreed that it was "a correct copy. ... I am prepared to main-tain its statements," he wrote defiantly. McClernand only regretted that his adjutant had failed to send Grant a copy two weeks before "as I thought he had." McClernand had earlier attempted to preempt criticisms of his conduct on May 22 by condemning the "false reports" that were "finding their ways from the landings up the river"—perhaps a swipe at Sherman. McClernand had then urged Grant to issue a "conclusive" statement that would clear the air, but wisely Grant did not do so. On June 18 Grant coolly relieved McClernand of his command and ordered him to hand over his corps to Ord, who had been urged by Sherman to be available to assume a senior po-sition. A month later when Grant reported on the controversy to the adju-tant general, he branded McClernand's order "pretentious and egotistical." McClernand tried to make a fight of it and sought reinstatement on the grounds that he had been appointed by the president under "a definite act of Congress"; he misguidedly tried to enlist the support of Stanton and Halleck. He asked for an investigation of Grant's military conduct since the Battle of Belmont. Stanton did not answer until August, by which time the Lincoln ad-ministration had no interest in any sort of inquiry. McClernand languished unemployed for the remainder of the war, apart from a brief period when he commanded elements of the 13th Corps in a Texas backwater before he resigned due to ill health in the spring of 1864.[63]

According to Sherman, "McClernand played himself out and there is not an officer or soldier here but rejoices he is gone away." Sherman cer-tainly rejoiced. Commanders do not have to be liked to succeed, and McClernand showed some soldierly skill: he was not as bad a commander as Sherman claimed. But to succeed fully, commanders must enjoy a moral appeal and earn respect. McClernand was neither stupid nor in-competent, and Sherman exaggerated his vices. Yet he exhibited a fatal flaw. As a commander he never inspired trust, even when he did well, and thus represented a disruptive influence. Sherman at least summarized this weakness well. McClernand "could not let his mind get beyond the limits of his vision and therefore all was brilliant about him and dark and suspicious beyond."[64]

After this flurry of excitement, military events lapsed back into the intricate routine of siege warfare. Sherman had his artillery well covered by earthworks, and his saps and parallel trenches had advanced very close to the Confederate line; his sappers and miners were hard at work "undermining the chief work to our front." Then on June 22 Sherman received a summons to Grant's headquarters to hear of the army commander's fears as to the import of Joseph E. Johnston's activities east of the Big Black River. He ordered Sherman to "go and command the entire force" and prevent any crossing of this river should Johnston seek to relieve Vicksburg. Sherman decided to take two brigades of Tuttle's division of his own corps and Brigadier General John McArthur's division of the 17th Corps. The 9th Corps had arrived at Haines Bluff, commanded by Major General John G. Parke, and elements of it were placed under Sherman's command, joining him at Templeton's, about a dozen miles northeast of Vicksburg. The rest of Sherman's force marched on Birdsong Ferry, which Sherman calculated would be Johnston's most likely crossing point.[65]

Our retrospective knowledge of Vicksburg's eventual fall gives these operations an overcautious and anticlimactic character, but this should not conceal the trickiness of the task that Sherman had been set. "I hear nothing of Johnston at all; no trace of him or signs of his approach," he reported. "The numerous fords in and near us will enable the enemy to get over and our first business is to divine his real points." His only consolation lay in the likelihood that "a small force can oppose a large force," though such an advantage could be turned against him. He also had no choice but to be cautious so as not to jeopardize the propaganda effect of the Union glory at Vicksburg, in which he now could not share. He would wait for Johnston "on this side of the Big Black," but he lacked reliable intelligence and had to find it quickly. "I take it for granted," he verified, "you do not want me to attempt to follow him across that river [Big Black] unless after a defeat." So Sherman pushed out a cavalry screen and soon discovered that Johnston had made no attempt to cross at any point. Grant reported intelligence that claimed that Confederates had made their appearance at Hankinson's Ferry, which Sherman doubted, but he emphasized to his subordinates that they "ought to be wide awake and ready to move in that direction."[66]

Sherman's vital job in safeguarding the gains Grant had made over the last two months by holding the line from the Big Black to the Yazoo was another important measure of Grant's trust in him, even though carrying it out deprived him of sharing in Grant's moment of triumph when he entered Vicksburg on July 4. During the interval Sherman visited more Southern friends. He ate at the Klein household near Markham's, about 90 miles northeast of Vicksburg; Mrs. Klein was related to the sister of his brother-in-law Judge T. W. Bartley. He also helped the mother of a former Louisiana State Seminary cadet visit her son after Vicksburg's fall. Yet not finding Johnston did not solve Sherman's problems, because the Big Black could be crossed easily at numerous points. The activities of pro-Confederate informers led Sherman to conclude that they expected Johnston's imminent arrival. Yet by June 27 Sherman had "not a sound, syllable, or sign to indicate a purpose of crossing Big Black towards us." Sherman felt very isolated and three days earlier had written to Grant asking him to confirm whether Port Hudson had fallen, as he had heard. On July 3 Grant warned Sherman that Vicksburg was on the verge of surrender. He ordered that when confirmation arrived, he should cross the Big Black and, as Sherman put it tersely, "drive Johnston away etc." Sherman did not feel downcast by his absence from Vicksburg. As he assured Grant, "I did want rest, but I ask nothing until the Mississippi River is ours, and Sunday and 4th of July are nothing to Americans till the river of our greatness is free as God made it." The revelation of such generosity of spirit must have fortified Grant's trust in his wayward, mercurial, and invariably loyal subordinate.

July 4 celebrations, alas, did slow down Sherman's concentration of force. He asked for the remainder of his corps and Parke's 9th Corps, as well as Ord's 13th Corps—in effect a small army of 34,000 men—that operated independently but still under Grant's control and general direction. The heat and dust, as well as hangovers, delayed his usual brisk movements. The heat was so torrid that his troops marched at night and slept by day.[67]

On July 6 Sherman crossed the Big Black and advanced eastward toward Jackson once more, this time via a more northerly route. The latest intelligence revealed that he faced "four strong divisions" of Confederate infantry—those of Major General William W. Loring, Major General Samuel French, Major General William H. T. Walker, and Major General John C. Breckinridge, plus Brigadier General William H. Jackson's division of cavalry. Sherman rated Confederate cavalry "so much better than ours, that in all quick movements," he informed Ellen, "they have a decided advantage." For some time Sherman was unsure of Johnston's strength, but by July 17 he concluded that he commanded 30,000 men; this was an exaggeration, for within a week Sherman had before him the remarkably accurate estimate of 22,000. On July 9 Sherman's force closed up on Johnston's defensive line across the Clinton road. Sherman's personal reconnaissance revealed that Johnston had "his whole army, and that he had anticipated [a] siege, and had prepared accordingly." By July 14 he noted that Johnston "has manifested no intention to rally, and has permitted us to surround him with parapets"—a striking early example of Sherman's use of entrenchments in the offensive.[68]

Sherman at once decided to hold Johnston in Jackson while his cavalry and light infantry fulfilled the second part of Grant's instructions, namely, the destruction of the railroads that would greatly reduce the Confederacy's ability to wage war further in this theater. In a design that he would replicate on a larger scale the following year, he would work around "one flank or the other" while threatening to cross the Pearl River and cut Johnston's line of retreat. On the right Ord's 13th Corps and Parke's 9th Corps on the left extended their lines to cut the railroad north of Jackson, while Ord menaced the Pearl River crossings. The 15th Corps, currently commanded by Steele, harried the Confederate lines ceaselessly, pushing Johnston's infantry back into their lines while the bulk of the Union infantry remained under cover. As an investment in security, as Sherman struck at Confederate communications, he asked Grant for a further division to shield his lines back to the Big Black more effectively. Sherman supervised all details very closely, as he had no wish to tarnish the shine of Grant's great victory by any careless error. The only serious mistake occurred on July 12 when Brigadier General Jacob Lauman's division of the 13th Corps moved beyond the cover provided by skirmishers close to the Confederate defenses covered by thick woods. It endured a battering from field artillery and musketry as it tried to move into line and suffered about 400 casualties. Sherman concluded that Lauman "either misunderstood or misinterpreted Ord's minute instructions." Ord relieved Lauman immediately; Sherman recognized instantly the need "to support his corps commanders in their authority" and approved this action "for the time being."[69]

On July 14 Sherman reported that although a raid on Canton to the north east of Jackson had come to nothing, raids on Calhoun Station over 120 miles to the northeast had resulted in the destruction of two locomotives, 14 boxcars, and 20 platform cars, precious and irreplaceable assets lost to the Confederate war effort. Five bridges were also destroyed within a circumference of 15 miles from Jackson; troops entrusted with the task of railroad destruction set about it with enthusiasm at the rate of 10 miles per day. Sherman intended to open a gap in the railroad of some 100 miles. "We are absolutely stripping the country of corn, cattle, hogs, poultry, everything," he reported "and the new-grown corn is being thrown open as pasture fields or hauled for the use of our animals." Though Sherman conceded the awfulness of this "scourge of war," he qualified it, effectively by abdicating responsibility for the suffering. He blamed "ambitious" Southern men who had appealed to the decision furnished by war rather than by the "learned and pure tribunals which our forefathers had provided for supposed wrongs and injuries." The Southern people had brought their suffering on themselves. Jackson had endured a further bombardment since his last visit, amounting to 3,000 artillery rounds from 10- and 20-pounder Parrotts and 12-pounder Napoleons. Then on July 16 Johnston conducted a deftly organized withdrawal during the night, concealed to the last minute by work on his entrenchments, escaping over the Pearl River with 23,000 men and 400 wagons under cover of darkness. Sherman hastened on July 17 to occupy Jackson with Blair's division once Johnston's escape had been discovered. Sherman found the state capital "one mass of charred ruins" but decided not to pursue. He would be required to march across a waterless plain in the summer heat until he reached the Mobile–Ohio Railroad, "which would be more destructive of my command than fruitful in results," so he issued an order to complete the destruction of the railroads. Thus began an enduring pattern first etched before Jackson. In total 20 platform cars and 50 boxcars and passenger cars were torched, plus 4,000 bales of cotton; numerous artillery pieces (including 32-pounder siege guns), muskets in profusion, and substantial quantities of ammunition were either destroyed or completely incapacitated.[70]

Sherman had thus cut his teeth as an army commander. He had perhaps been too slow to realize that Johnston had already planned his escape as he closed in for the kill, but his mission had been successful. His troops had attended to these additional duties with diligence and enthusiasm, which says much for his powers of leadership given that they could have been at Vicksburg and his command had been thrown together hurriedly. "We came together suddenly and have scattered as suddenly." He asked permission to give the citizens of Jackson 200 barrels of flour and 20,000 pounds of pork to feed the populace of the town and the contiguous rural areas—so long as it was not passed on to Confederate troops. Sherman did everything in his power to "encourage the people to rebel against a Government which they now feel is unable to protect them or support them." But the defeatist wailing Sherman had initially encountered subsided once food became available again.[71]

So Sherman advised Grant that Jackson had lost all military value and that he favored a concentration on the Big Black. The troops of his makeshift army were rested, and by July 21 the 9th and 13th Corps were back on the road to Vicksburg; by July 26 the 15th Corps and Sherman were encamped near Blair at Fox's Creek about 20 miles from Vicksburg. All the camps were chosen because they were deemed "healthy, near good water for washing and bathing," and Sherman could cover the bridges over the Big Black but be able to reach Vicksburg or Jackson swiftly.[72]

The following weeks would resonate in bittersweet discordance for the remainder of Sherman's life. Things started well. On August 14 Sherman received a commission as a brigadier general in the regular army that guaranteed a future regular salary and pension, thus permanently solving the issue of his postwar livelihood. He wrote at once to his father-in-law expressing the "hope that I have made some amends for deep anxiety which I know I have caused you at times." He had also, at long last, arrived at a just estimate of Grant's true ability and stature as a commander. His praise of Grant became fulsome and genuinely admiring, and he described himself as an "ardent friend" who took the opportunity of warning his companion in arms against sycophancy. Sherman hoped that he would "serve near and under you, till the dawn of that Peace" for which they were both striving. He revealed to Lew Wallace that he thought one of Grant's best attributes was the rare talent "of using various men to produce a common result." Wallace had complained of Grant's coldness, and Sherman offered him some excellent advice, which he had allowed himself to take in varying degrees. "Avoid all controversies, bear patiently temporary reverses, get into the current events as quickly as possible, and hold your horses for the last stretch."[73]

At the end of July, Ellen and the four children, Minnie and Willy (with whom his father had the closest rapport) and Lizzie and Tom, agreed to visit him in camp. This was a project that both Ellen and Sherman had long contemplated and worked for; as a result, both would be tortured by guilt by its consequences. Though Sherman joked with his brother-in-law Phil that Ellen would have to get accustomed to "Hard tack and Canvas," actually he thought the accommodation quite comfortable—"one of the most beautiful camps I ever saw." He waited impatiently for their arrival at the end of August. Sherman overflowed with good cheer, and there were parades, sightseeing, and calls on his friends, including the Grants (as Mrs. Grant had come to visit her husband, too). His headquarters guard, the 13th Regular Infantry, adopted Willy, just 9 years old, a clever, forceful little character, as a mascot, and he was delighted to receive a uniform as an honorary sergeant. Sherman and Ellen were housed in two hospital tents and the children, amid much excitement, in "two common wall tents." "All are well and really have improved in health down here," he wrote proudly and prematurely to John. "It makes me old to see her [Minnie] and the others growing so fast," as he had not seen them for over 18 months. Ellen conceived another child during these weeks.[74]

Disaster then struck. As the Shermans were about to begin their journey back to Ohio, Sherman noticed that Willy looked unwell. Although Ellen would later blame herself for taking the symptoms insufficiently seriously, she immediately put him to bed. A military surgeon diagnosed typhoid, but as the river level fell they made slow progress on their steamer as far as Helena and did not arrive at Memphis until October 2. Willy's condition, which he bore "with unassuming patience," deteriorated, and the doctor warned that his life was endangered. He was moved at once to the Gayoso House, where he died on the evening of October 3. Grant was one of the first to receive notification of the appalling news on October 4. That night Sherman, in shock at the loss of the son that Ellen knew he "idolized," burst out, "God only knows why he should die thus young. He is dead, but will not be forgotten till those who knew him in life have followed him to that same mysterious end." The loss of the boy that he would describe 12 years later as the "most precious" of his children represented a blow from which he and Ellen would never recover. Ellen had experienced a premonition "that he would not live to grow to manhood" the previous February but was inconsolable when the awful event came true. Though Sherman thanked the commanding officer of the 13th Infantry for the regiment's kindness to his late son, he asked for no sympathy because he would busy himself with his duty—"I must go on till I meet a soldier's fate." But he felt a needling guilt at inviting his family to "so fatal a climate." He resolved to "try and make Poor Willy[']s memory the cure for all the defects which have sullied my character."

His beloved son's sudden death shattered any residual religious belief that he may have casually entertained, and he ignored all of Ellen's subsequent entreaties to embrace the Catholic Church. He could not share pious Ellen's redemptive, symbolic sense of Willy's loss, however much it pained her, though he did join his wife in deep, prolonged and elaborate mourning rituals. Sherman never tired of memorializing Willy or inviting discussions of the enormity of the loss of one so young or the "might-have-beens" of his life. "Now that he is past all panic and sorrow his Memory must be a strange link in the chain of family love that binds us altogether." When his new son was born in June 1864, Sherman agreed with Ellen that he should not bear his brother's name, then a fashionable practice: "Though dead to the world he [Willy] yet lives forth in our memories." Whether Willy, who so resembled his father, could have continued indefinitely to carry the weighty responsibility of his parents' hopes wrapped in the "virtues of a manly nature and Christian soul," without tension, resentment, even rebellion or rejection, can never be known. What is clear is that Willy would always remain for his father a haunting presence who would be riding by his side in the next campaign.[75]

To Sherman the triumph of Vicksburg, including all the successes notched up since Arkansas Post, represented "the first gleam of daylight in this war." All of his biographers agree that it represents an important learning experience for this commander. But this experience must be set within the context of the disappointments of the first Vicksburg campaign. They distorted Sherman's judgment and account for the development of his essentially cautious outlook, mainly a product of the great distances that needed to be traversed in this theater. As Sherman explained to Ellen, "The moment an army moves in this country, it draws itself out in a long thin string exposed to all manner of Risk." Despite his characteristically gloomy prognosis that emphasizes continuing Southern resistance, especially "the deep and bitter enmity" of Southern women, he admitted that Vicksburg "looks to a conclusion."[76]

Of course, Sherman remained anxious lest complacency set in again. In July 1863 he became alarmed by the violence and anarchy of the New York draft riots, though he was pleased by how quickly they were suppressed. He fretted that even greater efforts would be required in the future to finally slay the beast of secession. "The war is not over yet," he warned Lew Wallace. The North needed to make a supreme effort; hence the need for energetic recruiting as the end of three-year enlistments approached. The simplistic idea that these views were an expression of Sherman's "fury" at the South, or that, as he embraced the elements of "total war," he desired the unleashing of expanding and indiscriminate quantities of destructive force on the South, should be set aside firmly. Such a conclusion reads too much of the future into his views. Despite the welter of distractions, during the spring he had studied General Orders No. 100, known as the Lieber Code, which clarified "military necessity," defined as "those measures which are indispensable for securing the ends of the war" and yet remain lawful.

True, Sherman upheld the "display of force" as a means of eroding Southern morale further. "It is more honorable to produce results by an exhibition of Power," he concluded, "than by slaying thousands." Certainly, he admitted that more killing would be required, but he placed an increasing emphasis on deterrent power rather than unfocused destruction for its own sake. "We must make this War so fatal and horrible that a Century will pass, before new demagogues and traitors will dare to resort to violence and war, to achieve their ends." Sherman concluded that policy should "make this War as severe as possible ... till the South begs for mercy." But the means he sought to create such conditions were altogether more subtle, based increasingly on the demonstration of superior military force rather than on its naked and brutal application. His ideas had passed the formative stage by the summer of 1863.[77]

9

Army Command

October 1863–March 1864

By autumn 1863 Sherman had arrived, after a comparatively short period, at the summit of military activity, according to his contemporaries. Sherman would go higher in rank, but to the Civil War generation army command would count for more than anything else. The kind of man he became would determine Sherman's style as a commander, so it is important to review the evolution of Sherman's personality, and the sum of his mental and moral qualities that mark out his individuality. Also relevant is the impact of his character on others, that combination of psychological traits and moral, intellectual and social qualities, which can be acquired as well as inherited. In his classic works on the Civil War, General J. F. C. Fuller argued that the constituent parts of generalship embraced strategy, tactics, and logistics, but the manner in which these elements combine to create military success varies due to circumstances often beyond the general's control.[1]

Sherman's own career demonstrates more than most the essential humanity and frailty of all commanders, even though they might present to the world a tough and unforgiving mien. In November–December 1861 Sherman had recovered strongly from a setback, his descent into despondency that might have crippled the career of a less resilient person. He then endured the death of a child, the most grievous loss any man could experience. "I can hardly compose myself enough for work but must," he confided to Grant on October 1863, "and will do so at once." He had little choice. The Confederate victory at Chickamauga on September 19–20 appeared to throw the Union war effort into convulsions and threatened to reverse consistent Union advances in Tennessee since Shiloh. His overall performance in the Chattanooga campaign could not help but be affected by his colossal burden of grief—despite the imperturbable front he presented to the world.[2]

Throughout his life, despite the early loss of his father, Sherman enjoyed numerous advantages and remained very conscious of his obligations, character, and station as a gentleman. One of the reasons for his dislike of

McClernand was the latter's uncouth treatment of others and his uncontrollable outbursts of bad temper and foul language, especially toward those who were his juniors. Sherman's own behavior was generally more restrained and courteous than his correspondence would suggest. During the Vicksburg campaign he first met "a singular," flamboyant, and intrepid individual, Corporal James Pike, whom he encouraged to gain a regular commission; when Pike much later complained about the dullness of postwar garrison duty, Sherman advised him to "become a gentleman as well as an officer, apply himself to his duties, and forget the wild desires of his nature." Sherman had not always taken his own advice, though he had succeeded in dedicating himself to the gentlemanly code.[3]

Sherman's personality remained nothing less than very strong, vibrant, quirky, strikingly individualistic, and sometimes defiant of authority or prevalent opinion. He attracted many close, fast friends and in no sense could be described as solitary; he was consistently gregarious and clubbable, with agreeable manners. He contrasted with his brother John, who tended to be aloof and gave the impression of arrogance. Sherman could be very proud and was far more volatile and irritable than John. Fury ignited very quickly, and he also nursed grudges; his good opinion, once lost, could never be regained. Sherman's fieriness exacerbated a tendency to demand immediate action to solve any problem. He could not leave things alone. Only at a later stage would he think in more dispassionate terms. He always blurted out whatever was foremost in his mind, and he could sometimes be selfish and thoughtless—a combination not always advantageous in a senior commander.[4]

Still, these mercurial and effervescent attributes aided his leadership abilities. Those who follow tend to respect commanders of a sharp, distinct profile, who speak to them, as Sherman did, bluntly with eloquence and wit. A sense of humor is an invaluable aid to any American leader from the West, with its vital humorous tradition, and Sherman was blessed with a shrewd sense of irony and mordant wit. He had also belatedly come to appreciate the qualities of the volunteer soldiers he commanded, despite persistent attachment to the regulars. Accordingly, he adapted his leadership style to act more avuncular and less nagging. Sherman enjoyed an arresting and charismatic presence, as he was handsome, lean, and wiry, capable of strenuous feats of physical exertion. He could also appear rather scruffy and careless in his dress, and he frequently forgot to comb his hair. Curiously, this distracted, absent-minded elitist matched the civilian and casual ethos of the

Western armies in which deference was offered only if it was earned, an ethos from which Sherman benefited as much as he disapproved of its spirit. As he grew more senior in rank, Sherman grew ever more popular with the men he commanded because they trusted his judgment and respected the painstaking care he devoted to his plans.[5]

Men followed Sherman readily and willingly. His peers, who might otherwise have insisted on attaining their own narrow priorities, did so, too. "But I am no grumbler," Sam Curtis assured Sherman. "I despise fault-finding, bickering, whining officers, and stood ready to lead or follow or fall back, just as circumstances seem to require or commanders arrange." He then added, "I shall cooperate cordially with anyone, you especially, having confidence in your zeal and fidelity."[6]

Sherman displayed a quite remarkable appetite for work and such conscientious application, as Curtis suggested, that was (and is) vital for commanders at all levels to establish their prestige and gain the loyalty of their troops. He carried out his duties from the early months of 1862 in a selfless (and not self-conscious) manner. Sherman did not know the meaning of indolence. Throughout his life, he had been a remarkably restless person; he could never sit still, and words poured from his lips and fell onto the page in profusion. Sherman "never ceased to talk," his subordinate Oliver Howard recalled, in an "offhand, hearty, manly way," usually in short sentences. He was consistently dynamic and highly strung and quivered with nervous energy. His niece Elizabeth Sherman Cameron, writing 40 years after his death, described him as "an electric wire which threw off sparks in quick succession." Sherman was imaginative and innovative, up to a point, but he also fell victim to an enduring weakness. He would jump to logical extremes and could draw erroneous conclusions. His profligate expression of ideas both in speech and in writing could lead to such an abundance that the result often appears contradictory. For all his cleverness, consequently, Sherman succumbed to exaggeration; he did not invariably display good judgment on the battlefield but more often off it. An articulate, passionate, and sometimes fascinating talker and a brilliant writer, Sherman was temperamentally incapable of seeking refuge in ambiguity. At his best, he demonstrated penetrating insight that reveals a profound understanding of the nature of warfare in the nineteenth century.[7]

Education, refinement, and the gentlemanly code are inseparable. Sherman's views on the place of the intellect in planning and conducting war did not subscribe to the fashionable anti-intellectualism of the mid-nineteenth century, to which Grant occasionally paid lip service. Far from it: Sherman had already developed by 1863 a technique by which he sought to master and control the progress of the operations under his command. He would exert an intellectual grip on all their proportions and ramifications. He had been blessed with a swift intelligence and memory of formidable recall; his synthetic powers were vast in range, and his reports were composed quickly yet impressively arrayed and argued. But intellect in this respect should not be confused with academic study. Sherman had the talent to be a successful scholar, teacher, and writer, but success in war cannot depend on intellect alone. In later life he himself drew a fascinating distinction between "*virtus*" and cognition, courage, and intellect. He considered courage "the motive power which knowledge must guide." Knowledge could only be acquired by study and reflection. He therefore believed that officers should strive to become students of war, and soldiering should be regarded as a lifelong vocation. Knowledge, however, could hamper courage. In January 1863 during the debate at Milliken's Bend over the future of the Vicksburg campaign, Sherman attempted to enlist the aid of a member of Grant's staff, Lieutenant Colonel James Harrison Wilson, in persuading Grant to withdraw from the city's environs and return to Oxford, Mississippi, to renew an overland offensive. Wilson admired Sherman's "earnest and impassioned" expression of his views, and he "quoted Jomini [the military thinker] in favor of the policy of concentration." Other members of Grant's staff, not having read Jomini, found it difficult to resist these arguments. Wilson felt all this "was in accordance with the books and precedents" but somehow did not meet the needs of the crisis. In ultimately rejecting Sherman's case Grant and his staff were right, and Sherman was wrong, despite the weight of his learning.[8]

Of course, Sherman would make better use of his reading than on this occasion, but it is appropriate to indicate that military thinking could mislead as well as inform command judgment. His conviction as to the crucial, intimate relationship between judgment and intellect led him to become a lifelong champion of West Point. "I have read of men born as Generals peculiarly endowed by nature: but have never seen *one*," he remarked pointedly twenty years after the outbreak of the Civil War. He read very widely throughout his life, especially military history, revealing in 1881 that he read recently the *Memoirs* of both Prince Eugene of Savoy and Wellington.[9]

Simultaneously Sherman revealed himself as a man of strong prejudices. Although not conceited, he certainly knew his own worth. Yet like many other forthright and able people, he also harbored a deep sense of insecurity, self-doubt, and fears of a nemesis. Given Sherman's previous checkered fortunes, nobody was more surprised than he that he had managed to evade, so far, doom's death knell. In the autumn of 1863, mainly as a result of the guilt he felt as the architect of Willy's demise rather than his own, Sherman experienced "more than ever my natural desire to slide out into obscurity."[10]

A combination of Sherman's highly strung nature and his desire for intellectual control over the conditions under which he waged war bred a cautious operational outlook. Although he threw off the defensive habits bequeathed by McClellan and Halleck, his aggressive skill in maneuvering armies did not carry over onto the battlefield. Brigadier Shelford Bidwell once observed that commanders must be belligerent, "relish" conflict, and show "an urge to outwit their opponents, to dominate and to overcome them." Sherman displayed the first and second qualities but not the third. He revealed the toughness of mind and determination to carry out complex operations successfully, though his blood-curdling rhetoric was often just that; his bark was worse than his bite. Throughout the war, Sherman believed that whatever moral challenges he faced, he remained loyal to the values he had imbibed at West Point. These had "impressed on the Military Service of our Country a sense of responsibility of honor and integrity which have reflected quite as much credit to the country at large as by achievements in war."[11]

The impulse of loyalty and pride beat strongly in his heart—as did a commitment to old values and attachment to new enthusiasms, especially to the troops he commanded, whom he had originally derided and shown scant respect. But even Liddell Hart admitted that his "deeply ingrained sense of loyalty" was "both his strength and weakness." He, too, openly showed partiality to West Point graduates, the 15th Corps, and later the Army of the Tennessee. The latter was invariably entrusted with the most important and exacting missions; it may have been the most consistently successful of all Union armies, but such overt favoritism excited jealousy. It is usually wiser for senior commanders not to treat their old formations with reverence, but to do the very opposite. Sherman's most relentless critics were often those who felt slighted by his overweening, sometimes tactless sense of loyalty.[12]

He had so far experienced both success and failure, and, though he had been thrown into high command too soon, he had learned both the importance of intricate preparation and the value of setting attainable tasks. His later successes were based on his industry, his dedication, and the trust these earned that would inspire confidence in him and his judgment, even amid setbacks. Sherman's military methods implied centralization, but the direction of armies in the mid-nineteenth century had been complicated by their increasing size. A Napoleonic system in which armies were directed by a single individual, no matter how competent, gradually broke down because even Napoleon's "span of command" became too great. Such developments raise important questions for Sherman's practice less because of the numbers he commanded than because of the vast geographical span of his command.[13]

One solution might have been found in an extension of Sherman's staff to help him with his multifarious tasks. Sherman's staff, formalized in General Orders No. 10 of December 1862, consisted of 13 officers, the majority of whom would remain with him for the rest of the war. Hammond was conscientious, loyal and reliable, as were Major Ezra Taylor, his chief of artillery, and his chief quartermaster, Condit Smith; Captain Lewis M. Dayton would grow in stature over the next year. Captain Julius Pitzman had played an important part in the Vicksburg campaign. Sherman, like all the best Civil War commanders, undervalued the potential of his staff as an aid to command his forces rather than just administer them. Such efforts, however, would require an increased scope for and broader interpretation of staff duties, as well as more intense professional training for which the American military system was quite unprepared.[14]

All these sources of his later success pertain to his inherent gifts or to the structures around him. A further reason for his success can be identified. He gave unsparingly of himself and proved a remarkably loyal, zealous and energetic subordinate regardless of private doubts he entertained about the course chosen by his chief. Those above him in the chain of command readily urged his promotion because his "management" qualities and efficiency "all attest his great merits as a soldier."[15]

The weaknesses of the North's war-making machinery were all too apparent to Sherman. He would quote a remark of Polonius to Laertes in Shakespeare's *Hamlet* (1.3.64–66) : "Beware / Of entrance to a quarrel but, being in / Bear't that the opposed may beware of thee." How could the North make its presence felt? Sherman had no doubts. The disagreements over the conduct of the Vicksburg campaign had made a significant impact on his thinking, and he now realized the strength of Grant's case. "I would make this War as Severe as possible and make no Symptoms of tire, till the South begs for mercy ... [for] the end would be reached quicker by such course, than by seeming yielding on our part. ... The South has done its worst and now is the time for us to pile on our blows thick and fast." Sherman concluded with an observation that had a direct relevance to his next campaign. "Still no matter what my opinion, I can easily adapt my conduct to the plans of others, and am only too happy, when I find theirs better than mine."[16]

As ever, he was not short of opinions or the capacity to present them well. On September 17 he had completed a "private and confidential" memorandum on the subject of the reconstruction of the South. In its blending of geography, history, sociology, and personal observation in less than 3,000 words, it is both cogent and compelling. Sherman held that "the valley of the Mississippi is America," a sentiment that prompted the historian Lloyd Lewis to call his paper "a prose poem." It was also informed by the realization that all his earlier efforts to reconcile the South had turned to dust. "The South, though numerically inferior, contend they can whip the Northern superiority of numbers, and therefore by natural Law are not bound to submit." He reasoned shrewdly that the South could not be reconstructed until "all idea of the establishment of a southern Confederacy" was given up. "This issue is the only real one, and in my judgment all else should be deferred to it. War alone can decide it, and it is the only question left to us as a People." The notion of "a People" here is racially exclusive, but Sherman opposed the revival of any kind of state government in Louisiana or Arkansas. He preferred "the continuance of the simple military Rule till long after *all* the organized armies of the South are dispersed, conquered and subjugated." He did not think the South could be reconstructed "as we conquer it" in a cumulative process. "The South must be ruled or will rule," he repeated. "We must conquer them or ourselves be conquered. There is no middle course." Halleck showed Sherman's essay to the president, who took little notice of it in drawing up his Proclamation of Amnesty, which permitted the creation of state governments when 10 percent of voters took the oath of allegiance.[17]

Halleck still hoped that Sherman would publish his paper. The latter feared that to do so would "impair my usefulness." He preferred the role of "silent actor." He maintained this stance in declining to write a letter of support for Don Carlos Buell, who still sought vindication after being relieved of command of the Army of the Ohio on October 30, 1862. Buell planned to write a history of this army, but Sherman replied that contentious publications were counterproductive. "I never see my name in print," he informed the cantankerous Buell, "without a feeling of contamination and will undertake to forgo half my salary if newspapers will ignore my name." Buell refused to accept this advice, and his staff continued to bother Sherman in subsequent months when he had far more pressing matters to attend to.[18]

The lull in operations that followed Vicksburg's fall came to an abrupt end with the rout of William S. Rosecrans's Army of the Cumberland at the Battle of Chickamauga and the resulting crisis as it languished, besieged, in Chattanooga in eastern Tennessee. Sherman managed to keep abreast of the flow of communications pouring out of Washington, DC, thanks to his friend Stephen Hurlbut, commanding 16th Corps in Memphis. This river port would once more be the staging post for Sherman's operations. "Urge Sherman to act with possible promptness," read an early appeal from Halleck to Hurlbut— and he never needed a second urging. On September 27 Sherman set out for Memphis aboard the river steamer *Atlantic* "followed by a fleet of boats" carrying the divisions of Peter J. Osterhaus and Giles Smith; their progress was slowed not just by shallow water but by a shortage of coal and wood. John E. Smith's 2nd Division, drawn from the 17th Corps, began its journey to support Sherman, and that of John M. Corse arrived two days later. The railroad continued to be in disarray, with the rolling stock in the wrong position; it took a week to sort this mess out and push the 2nd Division on.[19]

Sherman also made it his urgent business to comprehend Halleck's orders, which he construed to be that he should advance with 15th Corps and any other cooperating elements to Athens, Alabama, and then report to Rosecrans at Chattanooga for further orders. Sherman was under no illusions that he should "look to my own line for supplies, and in no event to depend upon General Rosecrans for supplies, as the roads to his rear were already overtaxed to supply his present army." On October 10 Sherman assured Halleck that he would advance as quickly as he could toward Chattanooga, but already the 15th Corps lay "stretched out as far as Bear Creek." Confederate cavalry lurked to the south around Salem and had already made its presence felt, delaying progress "in making this road a safe line of supply." Halleck replied in the early hours of October 14 and stressed that the logistical question was the "important matter to be attended to"; he suggested that Eastport might be reached by boats, and thereafter "the railroad can be dispensed with; but until that time it must be guarded as far as used." These orders determined Sherman's course thereafter. Even if he failed to reach Athens, Halleck assured him, he would have played a significant part in the campaign "by drawing away a part of the enemy's forces." The later Chattanooga campaign had yet to take firm shape, and Sherman's dispositions during these early days explains a certain sluggishness. At this point, Sherman traveled to Corinth determined to carry out his orders as quickly as he could to the best of his ability.[20]

On October 11 Sherman hurried off on a special train and, after traveling about 26 miles, passed Colliersville; on the other side of it his escort clashed with a sizeable force of some 3,000 Confederate cavalry and eight guns commanded by Brigadier General James R. Chalmers. As shots rang out Sherman was awakened from a nap and jumped into life, ordering the train back to Colliersville, which Sherman and his staff plus other senior officers, including Hugh Ewing, resolved to defend. Sherman had succeeded in getting off a message, ordering Corse's division to come to his aid. Despite being outnumbered, Sherman's escort managed to keep the Confederates at bay, though they did succeed in breaking into the back of the train and purloining five horses, including Sherman's favorite mare, Dolly. By dusk, Corse's division came to their rescue and the Confederates fled. The following day, after making some repairs, he continued his journey, but not before he scribbled Ellen a hurried pencil note. "I suppose you will be in constant apprehension of my personal Safety," he sighed. But he assured her that he would take all necessary precautions, "for now that Willy is dead my life is more necessary to you." He considered his attackers mere amateurs who had difficulty putting together a combined mounted infantry and artillery attack and failed to use enfilading fire. Although Sherman gained consolation from the knowledge that Dolly would "break the neck of the first Guerrilla that fires a pistol from her back," he was very annoyed that Union cavalry failed to "obliterate Chalmers." But Sherman's death or capture at Colliersville would have been an incalculable blow to the Union war effort.[21]

In the meantime, Grant traveled to Cairo to receive orders and passed through Memphis after Sherman had already left. Sherman had got wind of "a project to give him command of the Great Centre," which Sherman had advocated for two years. He urged Grant not to hesitate to accept such an offer. "By your presence at Nashville you will unite all discordant elements and impress the enemy in proportion. All success and honor to you." Sherman also reported to Ellen proudly that Grant had confided that he owed Sherman a debt, as "I stood by him in his days of dejection and he is my sworn friend." Grant did not offer his friendship easily, and Sherman had perhaps not embraced it unconditionally until May 1863. Over the next two months he would benefit immeasurably from Grant's sense of moral obligation.[22]

On October 16 Sherman had departed for Iuka, Mississippi, confident in the knowledge that the railroad had been repaired as far as Bear Creek. He planned to shift his corps to Tuscumbia, Alabama, and from there to Athens, Nashville, and Chattanooga. He initially calculated that Halleck had been correct and that he could "use the Railroad for supplies," but this proved too optimistic; he was becoming aware of the fragilities of this combination of iron and wood. Alas, he had found the bridge at Bear Creek destroyed. So Sherman added this to his list of repairs, a project of at most five days. James Harrison Wilson's suggestion that Sherman should have shifted the 15th Corps to Cairo, and on to Louisville, Nashville, and Bridgeport, contradicts two important aspects of the orders that he had received, which explain his choice of overland route. First, the river levels of the Mississippi were at unprecedented lows, and parts of Sherman's corps might have become stranded or dispersed; second, Wilson's route would have taken him across the overtaxed supply lines of the Army of the Cumberland that he had been instructed not to impede. Halleck had permitted Sherman to use his discretion, but only in the execution of his orders. Sherman emphasized in his report his adherence to these orders in his concentration on railroad repairs and, moreover, in sending Blair and two divisions to push the Confederates "beyond Tuscumbia." This objective was achieved, "after a pretty severe fight at Cane Creek" and the occupation of the former on October 27. It was fanciful for Wilson to infer that the general-in-chief's orders could be ignored.[23]

Sherman had suffered recently at the hands of the Confederate cavalry himself, and, with the aid of Hurlbut's 16th Corps, he attempted to create a Union cavalry screen south of Tuscumbia to protect his troops from Confederate depredations. "I am impatient to get forward," he reported to Rawlins, "but the capacity of the railroad is far less than I estimated and it works very slowly indeed." He added, "Rains, too, have set in, making it hard on our marching and on the [wagon] trains." A further difficulty was a shortage of forage. He had requested aid from Admiral Porter, who had promised to send some light-draft boats to Eastport. Sherman had intended to draw his supplies from them once the waters rose again. He worked hard to push Corse's division up in support of Osterhaus, but the former fell foul of "very slippery" roads; Osterhaus reported also that the Tennessee River could not be forded at Eastport.[24]

The knotty challenges of this advance tested Sherman's mettle as a logistician, but his resourcefulness was not found wanting. "The railroad has a kink somewhere," he wrote lightheartedly to Grant, "and it seems our horses and men eat up rations and forage as fast as they come forward. But I will manage to stop the leak somehow." If one idea did not work, then Sherman tried another, ordering Osterhaus to locate all the boats he could at Eastport, build them if he could not find them, and borrow cavalry from Hurlbut. Osterhaus responded that if Sherman had in mind the building of a floating bridge, then small anchors should be found at Columbus. Constantly, Sherman reminded Corse of the need for solid, ordered progress without excessive haste. "Don't fatigue your men; there is no urgent necessity for your arrival here tomorrow. ... Make the march according to the road and weather."[25]

On October 16 the dynamics of the campaign altered when Grant, as Sherman had anticipated, received orders placing him in command of the Military Division of the Mississippi, comprising the three departments east of the river, namely, the Tennessee, Cumberland, and Ohio (which also included Arkansas), with "headquarters in the field." Grant assumed command of the military division two days later and received the option of replacing Rosecrans with George H. Thomas, which he took immediately. "Grant don[']t like Rosecrans," Sherman told his brother-in-law Phil confidentially. "Rosecrans may be Grant's superior in intellect, but not in sagacity, purity of character and singleness of purpose. Rosecrans is selfish and vainglorious," he concluded, not unjustly. "Grant not a bit so." Sherman obviously preferred to work under Grant. "I confide in him my innermost thoughts and when we think differently, which we have on many minor occasions each respects the motive of the other." Sherman gained a reward for his loyal service when on October 19 he received notification of his appointment to command of the Army of the Tennessee.[26]

The new orders that Sherman received from Grant that day via Rawlins required him to "increase to the greatest possible strength your moving column, and at the same time secure your communications as to your base of supplies." Admiral Porter, Grant hoped, should play an important role in fulfilling the latter instruction, with "the convoying of supply-boats and protection of navigation." He was also "to disperse and drive out of West Tennessee" contiguous to the Memphis and Charleston Railroad, "any considerable organized body of the enemy that may be there." These orders did little to change the priority of the campaign. In some ways, Sherman's problems had got worse. The day before, he had received word that a million and half rations had been lost "between Cairo and Columbus." Furthermore, local logistical problems could not be alleviated because the railroad lacked the capacity to carry horses. The Tennessee River could not provide alternative supply routes, so Sherman had no choice but to rely on the Nashville, Decatur and Stevenson Railroad; despite its deficiencies, he empowered his chief commissaries "to draw direct on the base at Saint Louis." Hectic activity had taken its toll on the men. Hurlbut warned Sherman that "quite a number of straggling sick" of the 15th Corps had gathered at La Grange. Sherman addressed this at once. "The real sick can come in the cars, but the dodgers must march, if not more than 10 miles per day, for the cars are overtaxed. Horses must come on their own legs."[27]

Sherman could not wait for them. McPherson received delegated powers in Mississippi, Hurlbut in Tennessee, and Blair received command of the 15th Corps—a move that Sherman had anticipated by appointing Blair second-in-command three days before. A force of 8,000 men that had been extracted from the 16th Corps and placed under command of Grenville M. Dodge also struggled to join him. He ordered Dodge to repair and guard the bridges over Richland Creek and the Elk River to ensure supplies for an advance on Athens; he also ordered him to take meat and corn from the country, "leaving barely enough for the inhabitants, and let them feel and know that by breaking our communications they force us to eat them out." By October 27, with Blair at Tuscumbia, Ewing received orders to ferry his division over at Eastport. Sherman had all but a fraction of his army command available for operations and thus made adjustment to this level much more difficult. Grant by this date had arrived at Chattanooga and grasped the scale of his task in reversing the initial defeat and subsequent siege. He sent a messenger with an abrupt command: "Drop all work on the railroad east of Bear Creek; push your command toward Bridgeport till you meet orders." Sherman instantly obeyed even though this required a reversal of the order of march and leaving Dodge behind at Pulaski. He then busied himself directing his four divisions through the mountains, as if he were still a corps commander, and hurried on, arriving with his staff at Bridgeport late on November 13.[28]

Sherman felt some pride in these operations, traversing some 300 miles of treacherous and stark country so rapidly. "The Road was rough," he informed Ellen, but the weather mainly good, and "the Command came through it all in fine Condition and looking fine as they marched ... colors flying and the Band playing." On November 14 he obeyed a summons to confer with Grant. "I have not had time to study things and can therefore gain no opinion of the future," he revealed—and much had to be taken on trust. Sherman at last arrived at Chattanooga on November 15; Grant was delighted to see him. Officers of the Army of the Cumberland who had judged Grant as stern and aloof were astonished by the banter between him and Sherman over the "chair of honor," a rocking chair that Grant insisted Sherman should take because he was a year older; he even offered Sherman a cigar. Thomas rather resented his exclusion from this agreeable conviviality, as he had known Sherman far

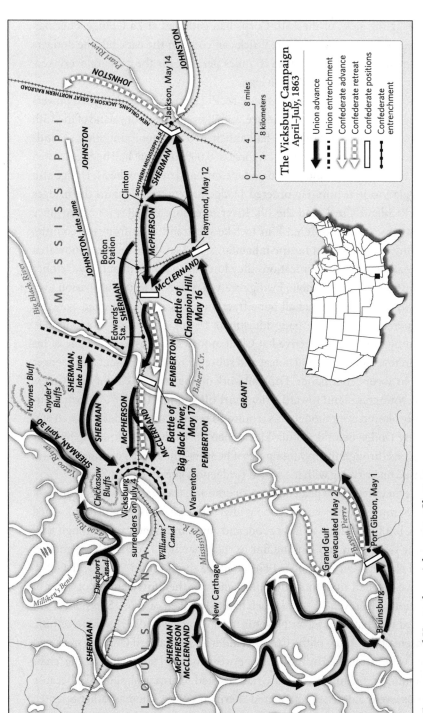

The Vicksburg Campaign
April–July, 1863

Union advance
Union entrenchment
Confederate advance
Confederate retreat
Confederate positions
Confederate entrenchment

0   4   8 miles
0   4   8 kilometers

Tennessee and Kentucky—Advance to Chattanooga

longer. After familiarizing himself with maps, on November 16 Sherman rode with Grant and the other senior commanders to inspect the terrain. "From the hills we looked down on the amphitheatre of Chattanooga," he wrote in his report, "as on a map, and nothing remained but for me to put my troops in the desired position."

Matters were not, of course, so straightforward. What sort of battle would it be and over what ground, and what part would Sherman come to play? Soon after his arrival on November 15 all the generals had walked to Fort Wood and stood on its parapets, from which Sherman had gotten his first sight of the Confederate entrenchments. The impact of this initial exposure proved more enduring than later studies. "Why General Grant," he exclaimed, "you are besieged." Grant replied instantly, "It is too true." Indeed, in his report, Sherman had observed that Union forces "were practically invested" from the Tennessee River above Chattanooga to Lookout Mountain. From this impression Sherman would draw several erroneous conclusions that would adversely affect his conduct at the Battle of Chattanooga.[29]

Generalship cannot be counted as just the sum of a commander's psychological tendencies or his prejudices; nor can it be divorced entirely from the vicissitudes of his life and the pressures these impose upon him. It is important, therefore, to review his state of mind on the eve of this campaign. Sherman's determination to concentrate on his duty and push his loss a few weeks earlier into the furthest recesses of his mind, however laudable, had one unfortunate by-product: he had no proper time to grieve for his son, and that grief kept bursting through. He habitually recalled the events of those hurried and terrible days. Ellen felt terrible guilt because she might not have "given him [Willy] the attention he ought to have had." Sherman responded, "It seems to me a dream and I still think of him as a baby, toddling on the sand hills, and clinging to me. I must not think of him so much and yet I cannot help it."

Sherman inwardly—though not outwardly because he acted as if nothing perturbed him—became increasingly distracted and careless. His failure to concentrate and focus his mental energies helps to explain the errors that he committed, which baffled friends like Grant. To critics like Wilson, who rushed to judgment, they reflected Sherman's weaknesses as a leader. But the latter's indictment is excessively harsh. During October and November pressure from home intensified: Minnie was continually ill, and Ellen vexed herself lest their daughter fall "into a decline." Fortunately, she began to recover slowly, but as she made progress, Ellen's mother's health deteriorated;

by November 30 the doctor had given up all hope "except for life beyond the grave." Ellen's letters convey an endless mournful litany of doom; "my health is too bad to Stand any more sorrow than I feel at present. But I will not write of Willy—it nearly kills me." Her blandishments that Sherman should seek conversion to the Roman Catholic Church became more insistent, though always ignored.[30]

For all his pervasive sadness, Sherman did not lack enthusiasm for the task before him. He rushed back to Kelly's Ferry, a staging post on the Tennessee River near the Union supply depot at Bridgeport, to get his troops moving forward. Not dismayed by missing the ferry, he had himself rowed down the river, occasionally taking a turn at the oars to rest a weary soldier; he changed boats and crews at Shell Mound and arrived back at Bridgeport by daybreak. After his visit to Grant's headquarters Sherman observed that he had "seen enough," but in fact he had not conducted the kind of pains-taking reconnaissance that had marked his earlier operations. It is true that he had followed the line of the Tennessee River near the mouth of the North Chickamauga Creek opposite Missionary Ridge, where Grant ordered he should cross. Sherman even "crept down behind a fringe of trees that lined the river-bank" at the exact crossing point and remained there, but he could not see what he needed to see. Still, he labored under the illusion that he had and ordered forward three divisions along the main thoroughfare via the Big Trestle at Whitesides and Wauhatchee in Lookout Valley, arriving at the latter on November 20. A fourth, Ewing's, peeled off in the direction of Trenton to feint toward Bragg's left on Lookout Mountain and give the impression that all of Sherman's troops were heading there. Sherman's army was thus straddled all the way back to Bridgeport, handicapped by heavy rain, thick mud, primitive roads, steep climbs, and treacherous descents, plus a fragile crossing point at Brown's Ferry. He took a further three days to reach his allotted point on the Tennessee River, advancing north of Chattanooga care-fully shielded from view by Stringer's Ridge.

Wilson recounts Grant's irritation with this further delay. He criticizes Sherman's approach march because he failed to detach his trains from the fighting formations, thus preventing the troops from forging ahead while let-ting the wagons catch up as best they could. Wilson himself had never carried out an operation of this complexity with a force comprising all arms of the service, and if Sherman had taken the measures he suggests, he would have undoubtedly have sped up the march. By not taking it, Sherman ensured that his troops, already wearied after long forced marches, did not arrive exhausted at the point of rendezvous. He managed to keep "the column closed up," as he had promised on November 19, but this rendered an attack on November 21 an impossibility. On that day Grant issued an order that Sherman's troops should "pass your transportation and move up at once, leaving only a sufficient force to guard your trains." At this point Sherman had only two divisions to hand, but that included Ewing's, and he needed to attack Bragg's right in greater strength. He had hoped to assault with Blair's 15th Corps, which included the divisions of Osterhaus and Charles R. Woods. "I need not express how I felt," he confessed, "that my troops should cause delay." On November 22 Grant wrote impatiently to Sherman that he would rather he attacked without Woods than "delay yet another day." But such hasty action was impracticable, and Grant had no choice but to agree to another postponement. By his action, Sherman had preserved his troops' stamina despite their prodigious efforts—and they would need every ounce of it.[31]

Yet what had been agreed? No unambiguous, contemporary statement of Grant's plan survives. In his *Memoirs* Sherman describes the triumph of Chattanooga as "a magnificent battle in conception, in its execution, and in its glorious results," but this presupposes an agreed grand design that was followed to the letter by all parties. Grant might not have lost this battle, but he won it clutching at the skirts of fortune. The Army of the Cumberland's amazing feat in seizing Missionary Ridge at the first attempt could never have been relied upon in any sober calculation. Sherman disingenuously sums up his part in the battle as a subsidiary operation, one of two assaults on Bragg's flanks, so "that he would naturally detach from his centre as against us, so that Thomas's army would break through his centre." This claim is nothing more than sleight of hand. [32]

Brigadier General William F. "Baldy" Smith, then chief engineer of the Department of the Cumberland, emerges as the true author of the plan. Smith was a talented staff officer, and despite vanity and tactlessness he truly shone in this role. Throughout these weeks, Grant shouldered the burdens of coping with the intense anxiety manifested in Washington over the deteriorating state of affairs in East Tennessee, especially Ambrose E. Burnside's loose hold on the crucial railroad junction at Knoxville. Free from distraction, Smith operated as a freelance executive chief of staff. Grant also had to tackle another urgent difficulty, namely, how to rejuvenate the offensive capacity of the Army of the Cumberland. He freely admitted to Halleck, "I have never felt such restlessness before as I have at the fixed and immovable condition" of Thomas's army. Such tasks were appropriate to the level of command that Grant exercised, as he presided over a military division. He took a serious gamble by postponing offensive operations until Sherman rode onto the field. Smith and Thomas worked together on the plan, though the latter remained doubtful as to its practicability. Grant had also ruled that Sherman's approval had to be gained, as he, after all, had to carry it out. The fundamental concept depended on an assault on Bragg's right flank on the north end of Missionary Ridge, which would permit a complete envelopment and allow Sherman's divisions to get between Bragg and Knoxville. Sherman, with Grant's blessing, had thus been allotted the primary, not a subsidiary, attack. If he pushed along Missionary Ridge and then cut the railroads running east from Chattanooga (the Chattanooga–Cleveland Railroad that ran to Knoxville and the Western and Atlantic Railroad that connected Dalton with Atlanta, Georgia), Sherman's onslaught might break Bragg's lines of communication with his base at Chickamauga Station.

Smith succeeded in persuading Sherman of his plan's utility. He had accompanied Sherman on his reconnaissance along the banks of the Tennessee River. The north end of Missionary Ridge did not appear strongly defended. Sherman assured Smith that he could occupy it by nine o'clock on the morning of the crossing. Further proof that his attack would be the point of main effort was provided by the significant preliminary preparation that Grant sanctioned. The roads north of Chattanooga were improved, and the trees were cleared on the banks of North Chickamauga Creek. Grant expected to see rapid and decisive action that justified the risks he had taken, and his annoyance at the initial pace is wholly understandable. Thomas, not Sherman, had been given the secondary task of pinning the Confederate Army of Tennessee to Missionary Ridge. Grant had also decided to reduce Joseph Hooker's strength on the Union right; Howard's 11th Corps received orders to move north of Chattanooga and marched contiguous to the Tennessee River in order to support Sherman and Thomas as required. Sherman's troops were encamped on the Union left outer flank on the west bank of the Tennessee River. Smith planned to reuse a technique that had worked well the month before, using guile to cross the river in the presence of the enemy, in order to reestablish Union supply lines at Brown's Ferry, west of Chattanooga. Sherman posted a brigade commanded by Giles Smith near North Chickamauga Creek; the pontoons would be assembled there also, and the brigade would float down to South Chickamauga Creek. After it landed, the engineers would build a bridge, and then Sherman's troops would cross the Tennessee River. Their immediate tactical objective would be the seizure of Missionary Ridge between Tunnel Hill and South Chickamauga Creek.[33]

At his first meeting with Sherman, Oliver Howard, recently arrived from Virginia, had been impressed by the "much previous knowledge and thought" he displayed. Howard must have discerned residual rather than new knowledge and evidence of a capacity to absorb detail quickly and integrate it into a preexisting framework, because Sherman had admitted to not having much chance to study the obstacles before him. Sherman had fallen back on the experience he had gained from a technique that enabled him to "bone" his campaigns, as Grant referred to it, that is, "study them hard from morning till night." Chattanooga is an exception to his customary habits, however, because on this occasion he accepted a detailed plan worked out by someone else. This scheme did contain a flaw, or at least a misunderstanding.

Sherman had available for the operation three divisions of the Army of the Tennessee, all from the 15th Corps: those of Morgan Smith, Peter Osterhaus, and Hugh Ewing, and one from the 17th Corps, that of John E. Smith. The latter had responded promptly to a warning order issued by Sherman that he should be ready to join the rest of the 15th Corps beyond Chattanooga and cross what Sherman described as the "frail" pontoon bridge at Brown's Ferry; his men had rejoined the order of battle by November 23. The river level then rose, and the increased swell combined with Confederate rafts, broke the bridge, stranding Osterhaus's division, "one of my best," on the west bank of the great meander of the Tennessee River at Moccasin Point below Raccoon Mountain. Grant ruled that if Osterhaus failed to get across by 8:00 a.m. on November 24, he should return to Lookout Valley and participate in an attack by Joseph Hooker on Lookout Mountain, which Grant had previously canceled but now revived. Grant instead reinforced Sherman with a division from the 14th Corps, Army of the Cumberland, commanded by Brigadier General Jefferson C. Davis. Grant also calculated correctly that if Bragg spotted this northward movement, he would deduce erroneously that Sherman's troops were heading for Knoxville.[34]

The operation got off to a propitious start. At midnight Giles Smith's brigade boarded boats and rowed to a point close to the mouth of South Chickamauga Creek, landed two regiments, and took the Confederate pickets by surprise, capturing them all. Below the mouth of the creek, the remainder of the brigade landed and then sent the boats back across the river to bring more men over. Brigadier General John M. Brannan, who commanded the Artillery Reserve of the Army of the Cumberland, moved 40 pieces of artillery that actually belonged to Sherman's army to cover the ground where it would cross. At about 2:00 a.m. the men crept down to the bank in pairs and boarded the boats. A young officer noticed "a tall man who stood on the bank near us who suddenly in firm but considerate tones announced: 'Be prompt as you can, boys, there's room for 30 in a boat.'" It was Sherman, ever the effective leader present with his men. "Few of us had ever before heard the voice of our beloved commander," the officer recalled later. "Sherman's kind words, his personal presence, his attention to every detail of the dangerous venture, waked confidence in everyone. He was with us, and sharing the danger." The initial wave got across safely and rushed into the thickets on the distant bank.

Such complex operations never go without a hitch. When the boats returned to pick up more men, they had difficulty in the pitch darkness identifying the landing ground. The commander, Major Charles Hipp of the 37th Ohio Infantry, shouted out for the 2nd Division but got no reply. In exasperation he bellowed, "Where in the hell is General Sherman!?" To his surprise, back came the authoritative reply, "What do you want?" Sherman himself stood about 50 feet away. Hipp said in rather meeker tones that he hoped the boats could be filled as quickly as possible. "Did you make the landing?" Sherman queried. Hipp confirmed that he had, "and captured the pickets." This information produced a whoop of joy from Sherman, who waved his hat. The operation no longer needed to be carried out in silence.

With the assistance of the river steamer *Dunbar*, the remainder of Morgan Smith's division crossed, followed by John Smith's. By daybreak, the two divisions were secure and entrenched. Thereafter work on the bridge across the Tennessee River, 1,350 feet long, commenced and was completed by midday; a secondary bridge over South Chickamauga Creek was also finished, thus linking the two regiments left on its further side to protect Sherman's left flank. By 1:00 p.m., accompanied by horses, artillery, and other impedimenta, Sherman's divisions began their advance. The auspices seemed to indicate that he was on the cusp of the greatest triumph of his military career thus far.[35]

Sherman took command of the three divisions of the 15th Corps as if he had never left them. Civil War historians are so accustomed to assume that the most senior commanders are the fount of all military wisdom that they have not asked where their commander, Frank Blair, was, or pointed out that commanding this corps was not Sherman's proper task.[36] In his report Grant noted that the 15th Corps was "under the command" of Blair, so where was he? At the time he was in Washington, DC, attempting to tackle a political problem; his dual career as congressman and general had begun to collide. In December 1862 he had been reelected to the 38th Congress, but only by a small majority. His opponent contested the election result, and accusations flew back and forth, some involving Grant. After the Vicksburg campaign Lincoln granted Blair a leave of absence, which he devoted to denouncing his critics, mostly radical admirers of John C. Frémont, whom Blair had played a key part in removing from his command in Missouri. In August Blair's leave was extended by Lincoln to October 1. Blair at once wrote to Grant insisting that he would not take this leave unless "it meets with your and General Sherman's approbation." Yet Blair was back in the field by October 4 and played an energetic part in the advance from Memphis to Chattanooga.

In early November Blair received an urgent letter from the president suggesting that he return to Washington to sort out his affairs because they were beginning to damage the prospects for Lincoln's Reconstruction policy. Blair unwittingly became entangled in the Etheridge Conspiracy, in which the acting clerk of the House of Representatives was suspected of scheming to deny the validity of Republican congressmen as the 38th Congress assembled in December 1863. If their number was reduced Blair would be faced by a tricky problem, because his brother, Postmaster General Montgomery Blair, had again advanced his candidacy for the speakership after a failed bid in 1861. Blair was reluctant to leave the Army of the Tennessee and had reached Maysville by November 14. Yet he could not ignore Lincoln's request. Blair might have been an ambitious and opinionated man, but his loyalty, once given, remained steadfast. Sherman's unusual discretion in dealing with this matter signaled that he had begun to repay it. He had already assumed responsibility for the 15th Corps' approach march to Chattanooga that had provoked Grant's impatience. Though he mentions to Ellen his meeting with Grant on November 15–16, where Blair's difficulties were discussed in the margins, a leave of absence granted, and John A. Logan named to command 15th Corps, he makes no mention of Blair's reasons for leaving the army. On November 18, Sherman mentioned to Hugh Ewing, "Logan is appointed to command of Fifteenth Corps and Blair will go to Washington." Logan, unfortunately, could not be made available to take up his new command until December 11.[37]

Sherman assumed Blair's duties without hesitation, although it would have been preferable to have appointed an acting corps commander from among the divisional commanders. Sherman was guilty of the sin of overcommand.

He became engrossed in battlefield tactics instead of concentrating on the broader problem of rolling up and completely enveloping the Confederate right flank—his proper task and where his true talent lay. Blair's solid tactical experience would be sorely missed. So Sherman ordered the 15th Corps forward, the three divisions in echelon from the left: Morgan Smith following the line of South Chickamauga Creek; John Smith, "the column of direction ... doubled on the centre at one brigade intervals to the right and rear"; finally, Ewing on the right and farther back, as Sherman anticipated an attack on this flank. The heads of columns were covered by a cohesive line of skirmishers. As the troops advanced, they were shrouded by low cloud and drizzle, concealing their movement from the Confederate observation posts on Lookout Mountain. By 3:30 p.m., after "chasing the enemy," the 15th Corps arrived on top of what Sherman called in his report "the desired point"; he called up his artillery, which had to be hauled up the ridge by hand, and a further promontory beyond was taken. Sherman felt justified pride in taking Bragg so completely by surprise. He issued an order to entrench; as the troops set to with shovels, Confederate skirmishers put in a harassing attack, and the artillery had to open fire before they were driven off. The Confederates did score a success, though, as one of the brigadiers, Giles Smith, fell wounded and had to be carried from the field.[38]

Over the next hour Sherman slowly realized that his success had been deceptive, even illusory. He had not captured Tunnel Hill at all but two hills in front of it, the largest known locally as Billy Goat Hill. The source of the error lay in Sherman's too-hurried reconnaissance with Baldy Smith on November 15 and reliance on Smith's word, though he was no wiser as to Missionary Ridge's true character than the new arrivals. "From studying all the maps," Sherman admitted in his report, "I had inferred that Missionary Ridge was a continuous hill, but we found ourselves on two high points, with a deep impression between us and the one immediately over the tunnel which was my chief objective point." His reconnaissance since gaining this success had been patchy and ill coordinated. After this discovery Sherman took counsel of his fears—further evidence of how his grief had eroded his mental toughness, capacity to concentrate, and focus on his proper task. The image of a siege brought back memories of Vicksburg, and Sherman resorted to siege craft.

He argued in his report that the ground already taken was so important that it justified his decision to entrench—it "was so important that I could leave nothing to chance"—but this ground lacked any intrinsic tactical value except to offer a safe harbor from which he could sally forth, a hardly

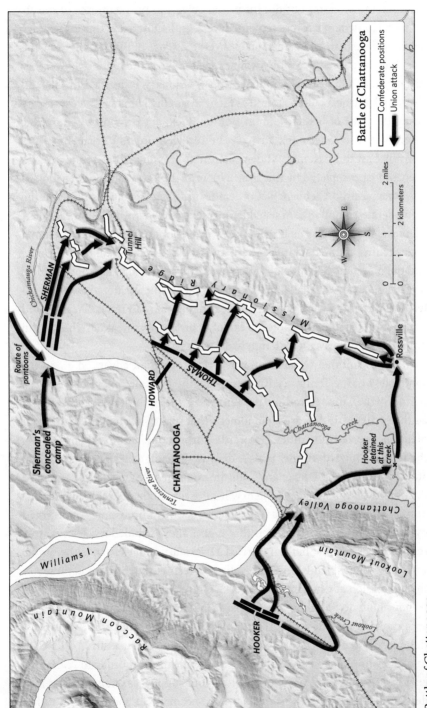

Battle of Chattanooga

inconsiderable reason but not his prime objective. In the middle of the afternoon Confederate forces remained weak and scattered with rudimentary defenses. Sherman had gained an exaggerated sense of their strength by the assault ending in Giles Smith's wounding. As late as the night of November 23 Sherman's Confederate opponent on Missionary Ridge, Major General Patrick Cleburne, could be found as far away as Chickamauga Station supervising the shift of his and Simon Bolivar Buckner's division to Knoxville. Later warned of Sherman's advance, he received orders to place his division adjacent to Missionary Ridge. Sherman's crossing of the Tennessee had been almost completed by this time. Not until 2:00 p.m. on the afternoon of November 24 did Cleburne get orders from Bragg to take his place on the Confederate right flank. Assisted by Lieutenant General William J. Hardee, Cleburne brought up one brigade to occupy Tunnel Hill, but nothing more. By switching to the defensive, Sherman thus forfeited the value of surprise and the march he had already stolen over Bragg. Sherman had only a single brigade of cavalry available for reconnaissance, which frittered away the afternoon burning Tyler's Station and tearing up railroad track. Sherman did not know and could not know the extent of the enemy's weakness, but he did not act in such a way as to attempt to discover it.[39]

In the meantime, Oliver Howard's 11th Corps had advanced along the south bank of the Tennessee River to strengthen the alignment between the Armies of the Cumberland and the Tennessee, and by midnight on November 24 the 11th and 15th Corps had joined. That night Sherman notified Grant of his unexpected difficulties. "Howard's Corps should unite with mine along the railroad toward Tunnel Hill. A deep ravine still exists between my hill and that occupied by the enemy." It is by no means clear that Grant grasped the import of this signal, and he may have assumed that Sherman had taken Tunnel Hill, "my hill," after a hurried perusal; this impression is confirmed by orders that Thomas received that night. They included a reference to a report that "General Sherman carried Missionary Ridge as far as the tunnel with only slight skirmishing. His right now rests at the tunnel and on top of the hill; his left at Chickamauga Creek." Grant continued to delegate a lot of responsibility to Sherman, merely requiring him on November 25 to launch an assault on the enemy "at the point most advantageous from your position at early dawn." Thomas had received orders, Grant assured Sherman, to attack simultaneously "early tomorrow morning" in order to "carry the enemy's rifle pits ... or move to the left to your support as circumstances may determine best." Thomas would support Sherman "in cooperation," rather than launch a decisive attack that Sherman would support. Sherman also received a briefing on Hooker's loosening of Bragg's grip on the anchor of the Confederate left flank, Lookout Mountain.[40]

Sherman thus faced a vexing tactical predicament. His campfires gave his position away; as the night wore on, the skies cleared, and a sharp frost denied his men much sleep. Sherman's confused command role on the next day is confirmed by his reference to 15th Corps as "mine" in his signal to Grant, and he plunged into minor tactical detail. Before dawn, he recalled, "I was in the saddle, attended by all my staff, rode to the extreme left of our position near Chickamauga"; he then explored Billy Goat Hill and crossed to the right held by Hugh Ewing's division, "catching as accurate an idea of the ground as possible by light of morning." There were few solutions to the problem he had brought upon himself. The troops would have to traverse the steepest saddle on Missionary Ridge, and running perpendicular along it were various ravines that would break up any formation marching along the narrow ridge. "Quite a valley" was how Sherman described it in his report, with "steep sides, the one to the west partially cleared, but the other covered with the native forest. The crest of the ridge was narrow and wooded." In a phrase, Sherman found himself boxed in and confronted by "a breastwork of logs and fresh earth, filled with men and two guns." Behind this first line, Sherman claimed, deployed "a great force on a still higher hill beyond the tunnel." These "masses" proved to be two of Cleburne's brigades, Mark P. Lowrey's and Daniel C. Govan's, the latter pulled back to protect Cleburne's right flank and line of retreat across South Chickamauga Creek. Sherman consistently exaggerated the number of Confederate troops blocking his path; this was a superfluous effort, as in truth the terrain increased their defensive firepower and diminished his comparative offensive power.[41]

Cleburne had quickly grasped that Tunnel Hill dominated all points "within cannon range." He could negate Sherman's numerical superiority because, in the restricted space, he could bring to the same point the same number of men as Sherman; he could also move them more quickly and enjoyed a better field of fire for his artillery. Sherman found mounting any kind of closely coordinated, simultaneous assault that pinned Cleburne's men to their position while moving around it immensely difficult. Union brigades quickly lost sight of one another as they advanced down into the ravines. Having lost cohesion, they became vulnerable to ambush piecemeal, while the defenders remained concentrated.

As the initial assault assembled, Sherman took the precaution of issuing orders to all his principal subordinates himself. He intended his right center to pivot on the brigades of Joseph A. J. Lightburn and Joseph R. Cockerill of the 2nd and 4th Divisions, respectively, and push Corse's brigade of the latter forward, which in turn would be supported by two brigades of John E. Smith's 2nd Division of 17th Corps. Both the plan and the way it worked out illustrates how the terrain disrupted formation integrity. Sherman had personally ordered Lightburn to send a regiment forward to support Corse. Though the latter's bugles sounded "forward" before dawn, Lightburn's regiment arrived at the Confederate line first and attacked but was too weak to exploit its success. Cleburne's line was restored by the time Corse's brigade arrived on the scene; his troops became tightly packed together as the ridge narrowed, and his assaults failed to strike home as their cohesion quickly disintegrated. The presence of Govan's Confederate brigade on a jutting spur blocked the remotest chance of any kind of envelopment. The attack concluded as a stalemate in which Corse's troops occasionally broke into the entrenchments but were driven out and then pursued by Confederates who got behind them. At 11:30 a.m. Corse was slightly wounded and left the field. An attempt to advance around the Confederate left flank by John M. Loomis's brigade of Ewing's 4th Division was frustrated by enfilading fire from the Confederate second line.[42]

Sherman thought he detected an opportunity on Cleburne's right flank. Two more brigades were sent to support Ewing, and he sent Smith forward with them to bring some order to the chaos, but troops stumbled about in confusion, unable to see, let alone find, the units they were supposed to support. Smith sent up two further brigades, but they could not join the great crowd assembled on the crest of the ridge and sought shelter on its west side. At this point Union and Confederate lines were only 20 yards apart. Cleburne chose this moment to launch an audacious counte-attack because under fire the Union brigades dispersed and opened up gaps in their lines. He concentrated three regiments against two wavering Union regiments and took them by surprise; they fled and re-formed under Union artillery cover. It was now past 3:00 p.m., and after seven hours' fighting it had become clear that Sherman could not take Tunnel Hill before dark.[43]

That afternoon Sherman did not react well to failure. He barked at his subordinates—and lacking a corps commander, he was dealing with too many of them—when he should have been offering overall direction and advice and keeping his mind fresh. He had assumed too much responsibility for this operation. He had chosen to command his beloved 15th Corps once more and allowed sentiment to warp his judgment and obscure his proper role. He rode forward to the very edge of Billy Goat Hill, behaving like a brigadier. "This is no place for you, General," a soldier warned. "The enemy's batteries sweep this ground with canister." A shrewd observer, Major General Carl Schurz of the 11th Corps, noticed Sherman's "unhappy frame of mind" and his battered and frustrated appearance. Grant had offered to send reinforcements, but Sherman still had two divisions of the 11th Corps at hand and no space to deploy any more.[44]

It was this last repulse in the middle of the afternoon that Grant, Thomas, and another distinguished visitor, Quartermaster General Montgomery C. Meigs, witnessed from Orchard Knob—a boss of high rocky ground in the Union center. "General Sherman seems to be having a hard time," Grant mused out loud. After a few minutes, he commented, "We ought to help him." Sherman had always calculated that Bragg would attack him and convinced himself that "our attack has drawn vast masses of the enemy to our flank"; this proved to be a self-serving illusion.[45] The historian Steven Woodworth is surely right in arguing that the solution to Sherman's problem lay in the operational, not the tactical, realm. Sherman should have sought clear ground on which to maneuver, pivot on the 11th Corps, brought up Davis's division, moved down and around Missionary Ridge, and attacked Cleburne's left rear. But this idea never occurred to Sherman, who had become fixated on the idea of a "siege"; he dissipated what energies he had on minor tactics. He did not conduct himself as an army commander should.

The Army of the Cumberland only accidentally discovered the solution shortly afterward when its troops exceeded Grant's orders. Rather than halt at the base of Missionary Ridge, four divisions continued up it and shattered Bragg's line. Thomas, replying to Sherman's queries as to his location, had signaled, "Am here. My right is closing in from Lookout Mountain toward Mission Ridge." Then Grant hurriedly signaled, "Thomas has carried the hill and lot in his immediate front. Now is your time to attack with vigor." Nobody had intended that the troops should attack in this way and solve Sherman's problem for him; they had decided to do so among themselves— "like bees from a hive," in Grant's memorable phrase. Sherman was hardly effusive in their praises.[46]

Sherman did not see the charge of Thomas's men, but he had noticed that Confederate guns on his immediate front were falling silent or turning around. By nightfall he realized that his attack could be renewed. Morgan

Smith's division probed toward the tunnel; Jefferson C. Davis received orders to cross South Chickamauga Creek by an old bridge that Howard's 11th Corps should have repaired, after which Howard's troops should follow; Howard had, however, found the repair of this fragile structure so challenging that he erected a new bridge 2 miles upstream that all units of the Army of the Tennessee were forced to use. Consequently, the pursuit was slower than anticipated, with Davis not arriving at Chickamauga Station until 11:00 a.m. on November 26, and Sherman joined him at midday. "The depot presented a scene of desolation that war alone exhibits," Sherman mused in his report. "Corn meal and corn in large burning piles, broken wagons, abandoned caissons, two 32-pounder rifled guns with carriages, burned pieces of pontoons, balks, chesses, &c. ... and all manner of things, burning and broken." Yet contentment prevailed that night, as the Confederates had abandoned a good stock of forage for the horses and meal and beans for the men.

After a pause for rest, Sherman ordered the pursuit to continue and switched his attention during November 26–27 to cutting the communications between Bragg and Longstreet at Knoxville. He ordered Howard's 11th Corps to occupy Parker's Gap and destroy the railroad between Dalton and Cleveland. Meanwhile Hooker had been held up by Cleburne at Ringgold Gap, and he requested Sherman to turn the Confederate position, unaware that the latter had already done so at Parker's Gap. Sherman rode to Ringgold to confer, but by the time he had arrived Cleburne had extricated himself and escaped to Georgia. On November 29 Grant suspended the pursuit. Anxious about the state of affairs at Knoxville and the "imperative necessity" for its relief, he initially dispatched Gordon Granger's 4th Corps of the Army of the Cumberland to undertake this important task, but as insurance ordered Sherman to seize the railroad crossing on the Hiwassee River to the north in order to protect Grainger's left flank or, if necessary, act as an alternative spearhead. For Sherman the Chattanooga campaign, with its highs and lows, was concluded.[47]

There are substantial grounds for criticizing Sherman's conduct during this operation. The historian Peter Cozzens refers scathingly to "a degree of incompetence that bordered on gross negligence," which seems excessive. The difficulties presented by the ground more than canceled out Sherman's numerical superiority. All had started well, though the key moment would appear to be his decision to fortify Billy Goat Hill instead of continuing the advance. Its significance is retrospective, for the decision is consistent with the orders he issued on November 22 that once he had "possession of the end of Missionary Ridge" his troops should "hold and fortify." Indeed, Edward Hagerman has praised the "revolutionary" features of Sherman's advance, especially the use of entrenchments in the offense. It was entirely legitimate that Sherman should expect a powerful counterattack by Bragg's army that would attempt to drive him off the ridge he had seized so brilliantly. He could not possibly know that Bragg had weakened himself in the middle of the campaign to be rid of his "enemies" among his generals—including Cleburne and Buckner. Sherman's determination not to be caught by surprise explains the defensive order of his attacking forces, described as odd by Cozzens.[48]

Despite what might be declared in Sherman's favor, his decision to stop and fortify did sacrifice first the tactical and then the operational initiative. He forfeited the opportunity to win the campaign with one devastating blow that thereafter remained beyond his grasp. A combination of partiality and circumstance misdirected him toward minor tactics. Instead of acting like an army commander, he became absorbed in detail and failed to concentrate on his true duties. His predicament would have taxed the ingenuity of other great commanders. Field Marshal Viscount Montgomery once argued that great commanders require a dual nature. They should exhibit an "infinite capacity for taking pains and preparing for every conceivable contingency ... the foundation of all success in war." Yet they should also display "a faith and conviction" when presented with dazzling opportunities "to throw their bonnet over the moon. When that moment comes," he asked, "will you soar from the known to the unknown?" Montgomery regarded this quality as "the supreme test" of any commander. Sherman did not reveal this instinctive sense at Chattanooga.[49]

Sherman's defensive tone during subsequent weeks is also an indication that he felt he had somehow failed. He expressed sensitivity in correspondence with John, to whom, as usual, he put his case in detail to cover his back. He certainly felt provoked that Meigs "should report me repulsed" and that Stanton should have this report published in the *New York Tribune*. In this letter Sherman experimented with the version of events that he would sanction in his *Memoirs*. This derived from a letter received from Grant immediately after the battle had concluded on November 25 that stressed that Sherman's army had drawn off Bragg's strength to permit Thomas's breakthrough. Sherman elaborated this to mean that "the whole philosophy of the Battle" revolved around Sherman distracting the enemy, who would be "forced to drive me, or allow his depot at Chickamauga Station to be in danger." Liddell Hart accepts this version, mainly because it suited his own defensive-offensive concept of warfare. Sherman's report written quickly after the battle was designed to counter any aspersions that might be cast on his conduct or the troops of his beloved 15th Corps. He paid tribute to the latter in glowing terms and extolled their "patience, cheerfulness and courage," avowing that "there is no better body of soldiers in America"; he offered as evidence of these qualities the casualties he had sustained. The 15th Corps lost 1,726 men (238 killed); the 11th Corps, 263 (37 killed). In his report he referred to 211 "missing," though Cleburne claimed to have taken "about 500 prisoners"; this was probably an exaggerated figure, though his casualties were slight by comparison with Sherman's, 220 (with 42 dead). Sherman's casualties constituted more than one-third of Grant's total loss of 5,475.[50]

November 25 might be one of the blackest days in Sherman's military career, but very quickly Sherman rose to the occasion and showed he might soar in the future. Grant had quickly regretted his decision to allocate the all-important Knoxville relief expedition to Granger, whom he thought too slow, unpredictable, and lackadaisical. On November 29 James Harrison Wilson carried a letter from Grant to Sherman in which he entrusted Sherman with the task. Grant warned him that according to the best estimates available, Burnside could not hold out beyond December 3. Sherman would reveal brilliance in overcoming all the obstacles in his path to mount an advance of immense strategic import. His review of his position was as pessimistic as the timetable he had been given, and a good deal more justified. "Officers and men had brought no baggage or provisions, and the weather was bitter cold." He would have to march 120 miles to relieve a garrison of 12,000 men in just over three days. Yet he cast these doubts aside and resolved: "This was enough and it had to be done." With the same determination that he had exhibited when going to the rescue of Admiral Porter the previous spring, he drove everybody forward. Even Wilson praised Sherman's efforts, though with the snide references to his "unusual facility in getting through an unfamiliar region" that he habitually used when he described Sherman's successes.[51]

Sherman had available for the expedition two divisions of the 15th Corps, back under Blair's command as he had returned to the army temporarily, the 11th Corps under Howard, and Granger's 4th Corps, which was accompanied by a steamboat and thus took the river road. Sherman was under no illusions about the task before him. "Recollect that East Tennessee is my horror," he reminded Grant on December 1. "That any man should send a force into East Tennessee puzzles me. Burnside is there and must be relieved, but when relieved I want to get out, and he should come out too."[52] Sherman eventually issued orders for Granger's force to join him at Philadelphia, Tennessee; lacking cavalry, he hurried up the one brigade allotted to him, commanded by Colonel Eli Long. The cavalry joined him at Athens and then pushed forward in the van advancing toward Loudon. Sherman hoped to seize the pontoon bridge there across the Tennessee River. Long's troopers tried to seize it valiantly, but the Confederate defense was too strong, and the rearguard withdrew in an orderly fashion, destroying the bridge as it departed. Despite this disappointment, Sherman was pleased to see three locomotives and 48 cars that had been dumped in the river by the retreating Confederates, which he had quickly hauled out.

Sherman was desperate to get word to Burnside that it was now vital for him to mask the bridge at Knoxville if Sherman was to have any chance of getting over the Tennessee River. Wilson then rallied to Sherman's cause and improvised a bridge built from timber taken from the houses at Morgantown. Blair began to cross it with the 15th Corps, but it collapsed before the remainder could cross. Sherman's aide, Captain Joseph C. Audenried, accompanied Long's troopers along a "villainous" road to Knoxville and got word to Burnside, and on December 4 the 15th Corps came up. It was at a house near Marysville, 15 miles from Knoxville, that Sherman and Howard the following day waited impatiently for the arrival of Granger—who eventually appeared "later in the day"; then a message arrived from Burnside announcing that Longstreet had given up his siege and withdrawn toward Virginia. Sherman ordered all troops to rest except Granger's two divisions, which he ordered to enter Knoxville.

Sherman joined them on December 6, looking with disapproval at a comfortable scene not much ravaged by war. He had been misled by faulty intelligence. He noticed the pens of "a fine lot of cattle which did not look much like starvation." This was not Burnside's fault, and Sherman did not blame him. On meeting they agreed that with "the emergency having passed," Burnside did not need the bulk of Sherman's force, except Granger's corps, which Sherman allocated to Longstreet's pursuit. Granger at once protested on the grounds that his men were worn out; his response made a bad impression on Sherman, who retorted that they had covered less than one-third of the distance traversed by the 15th Corps. His ill temper lifted, though, after Burnside invited Sherman and his generals to join him for a splendid turkey dinner at his luxurious headquarters "in a large fine mansion," an occasion that spurred Sherman to make numerous jokes about the state of "starvation" prevailing in the Army of the Ohio. His humor managed to conceal his annoyance that he had demanded such exertion from his men, all for nothing, as Longstreet's attempts to invest Knoxville had never succeeded. But the movement had been necessary, and he had carried it out well.[53]

The letters Sherman received from home failed to lighten the gloomy atmosphere. Ellen had sunk into a severe depression and feared all manner of "evils ... likely to come upon us"; she had lost her appetite and "scarcely [ate] one good meal in a week." She pleaded with Sherman to give her brother Hugh leave of absence to serve as her father's "companion accompanying him on his journeys etc. ... Please hurry Hugh on for he must come in a few weeks." Hugh did not receive an indefinite leave of absence, though he could make use of some free time before taking up an appointment to command the garrison at Louisville, Kentucky, which he held for a year before he was recalled to serve with Sherman again in February 1865. As her mother lingered on her deathbed, Ellen envied "her the privilege of seeing our lost darling before I do." Ellen's lack of appetite and reluctance to enjoy life did not diminish her extravagance. She asked for more money, and Sherman complied with $250. He urged her to "manage as cheap as possible"—always an impossibility. He reminded her that though his pay had increased as a departmental commander, "still also expenses are increased."[54]

Sherman hurried back westward from Knoxville to begin planning for 1864, arriving at Memphis on January 10. His concept for renewed Mississippi operations returned to ideas he had been forced to abandon the previous summer. On January 10, 1864, in anticipation of Grant's approval, he returned to Memphis in order to begin his preparations. Grant's letter received five days later outlined a general scheme of operations, including those on the Red River, as a prelude to a general offensive to be launched in the spring; Sherman assured him that "my acts thus far are perfectly in accordance with this unfolding series of actions." What did he intend to do? His aim is lucidly stated in his report: "My object was to break up the enemy's railroads at and about Meridian, and do as much damage as possible in the month of February, and to be prepared by the 1st of March to assist General [Nathaniel P.] Banks in a similar dash at the Red River country, especially Shreveport"; such movements would extend "our domain along the Mississippi River" and reduce the numbers of troops required for garrison duties. Meridian, Mississippi, in 1861 was a small settlement of less than a thousand people. Over the last three years it had acquired warehouses, repair shops, and an arsenal, plus barracks and a military hospital. It sat on a railroad junction that connected the Confederate hinterland with the port of Mobile and Selma, Alabama, the latter a new center for the production of munitions. Meridian was thus an important focus of distribution and bulged with Confederate war materiél.[55]

Over the following weeks Sherman was ceaselessly active and in constant motion as he attempted to reorganize his command and put a suitable force in the field. He had endured two grueling and frustrating campaigns over the last three months but gave no hint of their strain—perhaps preferring activity as a refuge from his inner sorrow. His first act was to sort out which troops he would take with him to Meridian. He ordered the weary 15th Corps to stand down and welcomed its new commander. In General Orders No. 5 he thanked Blair for his "zeal, intelligence, courage, and skill," yet another sign of their rapprochement. Logan, his replacement, would also serve Sherman well.[56]

Sherman decided to deploy the two corps of his army that had had the easiest time since the fall of Vicksburg, namely, the 16th and 17th Corps. The former had enjoyed the sedentary comforts of garrison duty for even longer—since Shiloh. It had chased guerrillas but done nothing more arduous than provide replacements for other formations of Sherman's army. Its commander, the bibulous Stephen Hurlbut, was a good administrator but did not react well to the physical discomforts and dynamism required of field command. Sherman complained to Grant "that it was like pulling teeth to get them started." To Ellen he complained that the 16th Corps was "good for Nothing as Soldiers." Still, Hurlbut produced three divisions rather than the two that Sherman had asked for, fielding 9,231 infantry and an even greater bonus of more than 7,600 cavalry. Added to the 2,500 brought by his chief of cavalry, Major General William Sooy Smith, Sherman could field a respectable cavalry force for once. As the 16th Corps had provided the vital mobile arm, McPherson's 17th Corps was asked to provide the artillery as well as two divisions.[57]

During the approach march to Chattanooga and Knoxville, he had shown how fast he could move; he subsequently improved on them. Special Field Orders No. 11, issued on January 27, 1864, stressed that the field force of about 27,000 men would be "lightly equipped." Tents and baggage were forbidden, and officers and men could take only what they could carry. All space and wagons should be reserved for food and ammunition; each regiment was permitted only two wagons, with one mule per company. The sick and wounded were to be left behind, with field hospitals being set up in houses and sheds. Sherman reduced the artillery complement by half and permitted only 200 balls per gun. By reducing the "tail" of his two corps, Sherman hoped to increase their mobility. "The expedition is one of celerity," he declared firmly, "and all things must tend to that end." His thoughts also began to dwell on the possibility of "a grand envelopment and swing round by Georgia and the Carolinas. This will take a year." With his Meridian campaign, Sherman took the first step in realizing this great scheme.[58]

Sherman's plan had been well thought out. More than 7,000 of his cavalry under Sooy Smith would leave Memphis on February 1, preferably before, and then advance via Colliersville, Pontotoc, and Okolona and move between Sherman's infantry and Mobile. Smith should disable the railroad "as much as possible," live off the country and break the connection with Columbus, Mississippi, and after a raid of 250 miles "reach me at or near Meridian" by February 10. Smith's prime aim should be to contribute to Sherman's "greater object": "strike quick and well," that is, hit Forrest hard and avoid unnecessary skirmishes. Since Sherman last encountered Nathan Bedford Forrest at Shiloh, the Confederate had attained an impressive reputation as an aggressive and crafty cavalry raider who indeed hit hard and quickly. Smith received orders to "respect dwellings and families" but destroy everything that contributed to the Confederate war effort. Sherman made it plain that the mission with which Smith had been entrusted would make demands on his initiative and require "great energy of action on your part," yet he expressed faith in his judgment. Despite the size of Smith's force, Sherman's faith in his subordinate was misplaced.[59]

Sherman succeeded in concentrating his two corps of infantry at Vicksburg in complete secrecy—with no embarrassing revelations in the press—by February 1, 1864. He intended to travel with Hurlbut's 16th Corps so that he could keep a watchful eye on both. McPherson was entrusted with the pontoons and all bridging equipment. As he prepared to leave Vicksburg, Sherman mounted another feint, in cooperation with Admiral Porter, toward Yazoo City that would distract the Confederates and "obtain forage on the Sunflower or on the Yazoo [Rivers]." Sherman ordered brusquely that if Confederate guerrillas offered resistance or the big planters protested, Union forces had "a perfect right to produce results in our own way, and should not scruple too much at the means." Such determined ruthlessness would figure prominently in the weeks ahead.[60]

Sherman gained a complete surprise on February 3, 1864, when the advance began at 4:00 a.m.; the two corps advanced on six roads, and brushed aside the small forces before them, and reoccupied Jackson. From there they moved to Morton, Hillsborough, and Decatur, entering Meridian at 3:30 in the afternoon of February 14. He had received no word from Sooy Smith. After a day of rest, Sherman turned to the task of destruction. He divided Meridian in quarters, with Hurlbut given the north and east and McPherson the south and west. Their troops set to with relish, "work[ing] hard and with a will" to complete their assignments "with axes, crowbars, sledges, chambons and with fire." Five days later, he noted with satisfaction, Meridian's military infrastructure "no longer exists."

Sherman's subordinates reported the destruction of 105 miles of railroad and 61 bridges destroyed and—equally if not more important—the burning of 10 locomotives and 28 cars; the latter figure is probably an underestimate, as a more thorough survey carried out by the engineers of the 17th Corps discovered 21 locomotives and 45 cars permanently disabled. The Confederate forces, two divisions of infantry and one of cavalry, commanded by Leonidas Polk, had been outmaneuvered or defeated when they made a stand: Sherman took 4,000 prisoners and large quantities of wagons and horses, with thousands of refugees both black and white attaching themselves to his columns. He was well pleased with these achievements and hardly underestimated them in his report. To John A. Rawlins his tone was almost exultant—"the most complete destruction of railroads ever beheld," he wrote—but he still felt perplexed by Sooy Smith's silence.[61]

On February 20 Sherman's force withdrew back toward Canton. The 17th Corps took the main road while Sherman, accompanying the 16th Corps and the remainder of the cavalry, probed to the north in the hope of making contact with Smith, but to no avail. The two corps joined hands again at Hillsborough on February 23; he crossed the Pearl River on February 25–26 and then left the army at Canton in fine fettle to rush to New Orleans to confer with Nathaniel Banks. En route he picked up word of Smith's dithering; the latter had not left Memphis until February 11, then immediately lost his nerve when confronted by Forrest at Okolona, where he suffered a defeat. He then withdrew back to Memphis quicker than he had advanced from it, a movement "being too rapid for a good effect," as Sherman noted acidly. He complained to Ellen bitterly, "Had that Cavalry reached its destination ... we should have bagged Polk's army." As to the destructive work, "I did it absolutely and Effectively." Sherman did not spare Smith's blushes and never forgave him for his failure at Okolona.[62]

Sherman pressed strong claims for his achievements during the Meridian venture, declaring, "The enemy cannot use these [rail]roads to our prejudice in the coming campaign." Sherman's march had indeed depressed morale in Mississippi, but virtually all arguments made for this kind of sustained destruction during the Civil War have proved exaggerated. Indeed, the historian Albert Castel believes that the long-term military effect of his depredations was much less enduring than Sherman asserted. The Confederates had got the railroads working again in about six weeks because they found methods of straightening the rails quite quickly; some rolling stock had been spirited away from Meridian before Sherman's arrival. Certain of these arguments are valid to varying degrees, but the difficulty with the way they are framed is that they imply that Meridian continued to work as if nothing had happened. Moreover, the effects of attrition are incremental, and lost rolling stock could not be replaced, leading to premature exhaustion of that which remained in service while increasing the strain on other parts of the transportation network, especially the roads. In this important sense, Sherman's successful operation made a signal contribution to the Union war against the Southern communications network.[63]

The Meridian campaign brought Sherman's short career as an army commander to an end. His success had been mixed, and on the field of Chattanooga highly controversial. The burden of much earlier criticism has been misconceived. His real fault lay in a tendency to overcommand and to persist in a corps command style, working well below his threshold, the responsibilities of which he had very recently taken up. But in the approach march to Chattanooga and in the relief of Knoxville, plus the drive on Meridian, Sherman had exhibited great skill in maneuver. He had also shown other qualities: drive, imagination, and an ability to husband and deploy his formations even under the most arduous conditions—when he managed to preserve their fighting fettle through it all. The success of the Meridian campaign, Sherman held, did not reside in the level of destruction inflicted on the Confederate war economy but in the moral sphere: "The great result attained is the hardwood and confidence imparted to the command which is now better fitted for war." He had also grasped a harsh reality of war's conduct over the last six months. In the advance on Chattanooga, when he repaired railroads, and at Meridian, when he ripped them up, he became conscious that far from being a panacea, "a Railroad is a weak machine in war, and is easily broken." It was as well that his troops had been battle hardened, and his judgment tempered by adversity, for at the end of the second week of March 1864, he got new orders conferring upon him even greater responsibilities in the next great campaign.[64]

PART III
COMMAND OF THE MILITARY DIVISION OF THE MISSISSIPPI

10

First Contact, March–May 1864

The year 1864 allowed Sherman to step forward and mount the steps of the podium of greatness. For the first time he could operate not as a subordinate commander but as director of a series of armies in the field. His contribution to overall Union strategy would be significant, and thus he began to exercise command at the level military analysts currently refer to as the operational level of war. Such a level links tactics and methods of fighting with strategy, in the overall scheme. It defines the manner in which armies organize in discrete campaigns and seek to fulfill the object of strategy by winning victories. It conceives of campaigns as coherent entities carrying out a distinct part in the overall plan.[1]

Sherman's performance overall needs to be considered by taking all aspects into account. As he began to work at the higher levels of the military art, he began to change the way in which we think and talk about war, and he propounded an individual philosophy of war. He thus entered a very small and select group of military individuals who succeeded both as commanders in the field and as thinkers, who combined talents wielding both the sword and the pen. The higher he progressed, the more Sherman could not avoid confronting the harsh realities of political life, for his campaigns increasingly had an impact not just on American political discourse but indeed, in 1864, on the outcome of the presidential election. Despite his frequently reiterated contempt for politicians and disdain for election techniques, Sherman expressed clear-cut political views and expounded them perhaps too forcefully. This complex mix worked as a catalyst in developing his ideas about war and his ability to put them into practice.

The year 1864 was pivotal in determining Sherman's philosophy of war, meaning his overall outlook, the assumptions he brought to bear on the planning process, the coherent efforts in thought he oxxxxffered, and the manner in which he applied his solutions to the conundrums he faced. In January 1864 he declared his major premise forthrightly: the South's "peculiar institution" was dead.. "The question is settled. Conventions cannot revive Slavery. It should be treated as a Minor Question." From this position it was thus easier to justify the deductions that Sherman drew from it. The most important relates to his interpretation of the laws of war, buttressed by his close reading the previous spring of General Orders No. 100, Francis Lieber's famous "code," which had been drafted as a field manual. These orders, issued with presidential sanction, determined how Union commanders should conduct themselves in wartime. Sherman's historical reading had first set him on the path to realize that the American interpretation of the laws of war had granted protection of private property a sacrosanct status and also considered any effort to emancipate slaves a breach of the laws. He now considered this approach untenable in a civil war, especially one involving a society that owned slaves.[2]

Sherman reflected on Britain's Nine Years' War against Louis XIV (1688–97). The authority of the Protestant Succession of William III and Mary II in 1688–89 was secured in Catholic Ireland by the suppression of rebellion and then military occupation. "The inhabitants were actually driven into foreign lands and were dispossessed of their property and a new population introduced." Sherman envisaged the Civil War along similar lines and dubbed it "a war of Races"—that is, "a species of separate existence with separate interests, history and prejudices." The Lieber Code justified the taking of private property in this American war as well as an emancipation policy. Sherman's own experience, notably in the Vicksburg campaign but also in Tennessee, revealed how great operations conducted over huge expanses of territory could be facilitated by supplying forces from the countryside.[3]

Recalcitrant resistance forced such action on commanders otherwise inclined to treat Southerners kindly. "[The] People of the South having appealed to *War*," Sherman declared vigorously, "are barred from appealing for protection to our Constitution which they have practically and publicly defied. They have appealed to War and must abide [by] *its* Rules and laws." No more special pleading could be permitted: the South could not simultaneously employ organized violence against the US Constitution and federal government *and* appeal to constitutional protection for their private property. Therefore, Sherman held that their provisions could be seized legitimately; "otherwise they might be used against us." In this spirit he joked with Ellen that as he was "short of cavalry horses" he would follow "Forrest's example and help myself from friend and foe." Abandoned houses, too, were "clearly our Right" for quarters or for use as hospitals or storehouses. Noncombatants should remain in their houses, but if they emerged and caused mischief they should be "punished, restrained or banished." He repeated his call for the "prompt" execution of guerrillas and their supporters—especially those who worked as spies. In short, the federal government could exert "the highest Military prerogatives."[4]

The high-flown claims made by Southerners for states' rights Sherman dismissed as "political nonsense" whose "deluded" appeal had seduced the Southern people into "War, Anarchy and bloodshed and the perpetration of some of the foulest Crimes that have disgraced any time or any people." Slavery could have been saved, Sherman speculated not unjustly, but by 1864 could no more be revived "than their dead Grandfathers." He predicted that next year their lands would be taken, and he then pressed his logic recklessly, "for in a war we can take them and rightfully, too, and in another year they may beg in vain for their lives, for sooner or later there must be an end to strife." The South must therefore confront the harsh reality of beckoning defeat. But, Sherman recognized, "a people who will persevere in a War beyond a certain limit ought to know the consequences. Many, many People with less pertinacity than the South has already shown have been wiped out of national Existence." Those who submitted to national authority could expect "gentleness and forbearance," but to those of a "petulant" disposition, that is, "persistent secessionists, why death or banishment is a mercy, and the quicker he or she is disposed of the better"; still, Sherman feared rightly that "years must pass before ruffianism, murder and Robbery will cease to afflict this region of our country."[5]

Sherman did not claim for himself any great ability to divine the future, for as he revealed to Ellen, "I feel that whilst my mind naturally slights the events actually transpiring in my presence, it sees as clear as any one's the results to be evolved by Time." In truth, Sherman's synthetic powers were formidable in their range and lucidity. They enabled him to express complex issues simply, clearly, and often eloquently; these qualities gave his views added punch and authority. His brother John had succumbed during the early months of 1864 to a pessimistic mood despite the great Union successes of the previous year; the state of Union finances especially caused him anxiety. Sherman responded to his despondency forthrightly. "We have no choice," he wrote. "We must fight out this War. Reason is silent and impotent and men in arms listen to nothing but force. The South must govern us, or we them. There can be no division, and finances must adjust themselves to facts." The war should be won "without reference to cost."[6]

Having clarified his governing framework, Sherman reapplied himself to developing the concepts that underlay his plans for the spring of 1864.

He made a pioneering contribution to the American interpretation of strategy and the operational level of war that would gain in authority after his death and determine a revised version of the American interpretation of the laws of war. Sherman wanted his spring onslaught to be powerful and overwhelming—and thus an important secondary thrust to the campaign in Virginia. "If they want Eternal War, well and good," he consoled himself, for the more stubborn the resistance, the greater the ultimate defeat. Sherman's language was graphic, but it is important to qualify the terms as he used them at the time rather than the meanings they were given later. Despite Sherman's need for a quick and complete victory, he did not regard his operations as an exercise in untrammeled violence and brutality, a ruthless expression on his part of emotional self-indulgence. "The war is not yet over, and I do not see its end," he mused to Minnie. He reminded her of his previous affection for the South. "I lived much in South Carolina and afterwards in Louisiana," so "in every Battle I am fighting some of the very families in whose houses I used to spend some happy days." His knowledge of the country of course influenced his operational conduct. He was prepared to "fight when the time comes, but whenever a result can be accomplished without Battle I prefer it." Sherman did not systematically avoid battle, but he did exhibit a tendency to do so, though it is not an omnipresent strand of his thought and practice.[7]

He had no choice in the first week of March 1864 but to devote his thoughts to the practice of war. In early March he received a letter from Grant that changed the terms of reference of the spring campaign. Grant notified Sherman that he had been called "to report to Washington, *in person* immediately" in regard to significant changes in the command structure. He stated frankly that though "I have been eminently successful in this War," he wanted to thank Sherman and through him McPherson, too, for their enormous contribution to his victories. "No one feels more than me," he wrote gratefully and modestly, "how much of this success is due to the energy, skill and harmonious put[t]ing forth of that energy and skill, of those who it has been my good fortune to have occupying a subordinate position under me." Grant had always placed a priority on gaining subordinates who were loyal and to whom he could entrust his orders, regardless of their personal inclinations. Consequently, he saluted Sherman and McPherson "as *the men* to whom, above all others, I feel indebted for whatever I have had of success." Although Grant alluded to the advice that Sherman had proffered, it is significant that he underlines more emphatically Sherman's diligence in "execution of whatever has been given to you to do," and in Grant's opinion, how much this "entitles you to the reward I am receiving you cannot know as well as me." Such generosity served to increase further Sherman's sense of loyalty to his chief.[8]

He replied in fulsome terms, remarking that Grant did himself an injustice. "I know you approve the friendship I have ever professed to you, and will permit me to continue as heretofore to manifest it all on proper occasions." Sherman's tone was initially self-effacing, but he went on to make one of his most famous and eloquent pronouncements on Grant's likely prospects. He considered Grant George Washington's "legitimate successor" who occupied "a position of almost dangerous elevation"; he admitted to Ellen further trepidation over Grant's "dazzling height" that would "require more courage to withstand the pressure than a dozen battles." But Sherman assured Grant that if he continued "to be [him]self, simple, honest, and unpretending," his position could be consolidated, indeed rendered impregnable, by "the homage of millions"; Sherman divined that Grant's secret lay in his "simple faith in success": the will to win. He candidly admitted still nursing doubts as to the extent of Grant's "knowledge of grand strategy and of books of science and history; but I confess your common-sense seems to have supplied all this." Sherman had got into the habit of underrating Grant's intellectual attainments and would never break it.

Sherman then reverted to a deep-seated and enduring notion of depicting Washington, DC, as a cesspool of intrigue, backstabbing, and corruption. "For God's sake and for your country's sake, come out of Washington!" Remarking that Halleck was better suited to cope with "the bullets" dealt out by the capital, Sherman exhorted Grant to return to the West and ensure a victory there, and then "we will make short work of Charleston and Richmond, and the impoverished coast of the Atlantic." Sherman's pleas were rounded off with a grand flourish. "Here lies the seat of the coming empire." Once the heartland had been secured, "I tell you the Atlantic slope and the [P]acific shores will follow its destiny as the limbs of the tree live and die with the main trunk!"[9]

Only a man of the most elevated spirit could write such a letter. The mystical appeal of the Mississippi basin and its relationship to burgeoning American power has been reiterated many times since, though none of these statements can match Sherman's verve and power. On one issue it must be admitted that Sherman was mistaken. The two coasts are the mainspring of American power; indeed, they are a pair of trunks from which, like a great branch, the Mississippi grows and contributes to the nation's well-being. The letter, too, has more prosaic, though no less important, meanings. The exchange reveals a true partnership of mutually dependent and trusting parties. Sherman urged his brother to give "Grant all the support you can." The lack of empathy and cooperation so evident during offensive operations in 1863 was gone. Grant and Sherman had arrived at a personal accord, not an institutional arrangement; both realized that they stood and fell together.[10]

As he departed for Washington, Grant issued orders for the preliminaries for the spring campaign. Sherman should protect the line of the Mississippi with one corps, employing black troops on the west bank; all of Grenville M. Dodge's troops in the 16th Corps should be taken into the field with him. He expected to return "in the course of ten or twelve days"; he did so, but only fleetingly, as he could not afford to neglect the president. He hurried back to Washington, though he must have assured Sherman that he had no intention of remaining there.[11]

When on March 15, 1864, Sherman took over command of the Military Division of the Mississippi from Grant on his return from the Meridian campaign, his headquarters were in Memphis, which aroused unfortunate memories of Willy's last days. "Though Willy died here, his pure and brave spirit will hover over this the Grand Artery of America." He had also heard more sad news. Ellen's mother, Maria Ewing, had previously rallied, but not this time, and she had passed away on February 26. Despite this upset and Ellen's urgent and numerous pleas, he would not grant her brothers undue favor and resolved not to recommend them for promotion unless "they win it fairly and manfully."

Sherman's incorrigible restlessness also got the better of him. In the early months of 1864 he seriously considered serving in the ill-fated Red River campaign, so long as McClernand was not involved. "If he [Banks] offers me the command I will go. ... I suppose Grant will soon move and will want me there." Fortunately, Banks insisted on commanding personally, so Sherman withdrew. The episode makes little sense given Sherman's prospects in Georgia. Any association with the Red River expedition, even if approved, would have taken Sherman away from a major operation and involved him in a subsidiary one—assuming that he might manage to improve its outcome.[12]

Sherman now commanded a military division, a structure unknown outside the United States.[13] As it was not a formation, it did not take the field. It was a conglomeration of departments and thus constituted an expanse of territory that needed to be garrisoned and defended; in other words, it comprised a geographical mode of command. In a real sense the commander did not command anything; his army and departmental commanders did. Sherman controlled and coordinated, unless, like Grant, he made his headquarters in the field. When comparing Grant with Halleck, Sherman observed that Grant was "better suited to act with soldiers." Sherman showed similar qualities. He thus became a superior form of army commander. His senior subordinates needed little advice on running their departments, and he did not involve himself in this level of detail; nor should he have done.

The prime duty of each level of command is for the commander to attend to his job and not to those of his subordinates—a rule that Sherman had broken in the past. As the commander of a military division he did not interfere in the tasks of others and consulted more than he had done previously. He found the task congenial, preferring it to any other command that he had held. Even in the midst of intense planning and discussion, he reported to Ellen that "I have really less labor here than I used to have and I ride out daily." He may have had less administrative responsibility and oversight, but he enjoyed more authority. He thus moved swiftly to emasculate "Prying Correspondents." He attributed the success of the Meridian campaign "to the secrecy and exposition with which it was planned and executed." In this "beautiful excursion" he had succeeded in baffling "the sharp ones of the press." "Am I not right?" he queried Ellen. Sherman did not consider soldiers' mail a threat to military security, but he came down on any senior subordinate whom he suspected of chatting indiscreetly to reporters. Brigadier General Mason Brayman, commander of the District of Cairo, a former newspaperman, emerged bruised from such an encounter. "If my dispatches to you reach the public and the enemy again," Sherman barked, "you will regret it all the days of your life."[14]

A determination to conceal his plans was all very well, but in the first place he needed to form plans to hide. The planning process emerged in two stages. First, he evolved the concepts on which the operation rested, then explained some aspects of them to his senior subordinates so that they understood how they would work together. Second, he took measures to ensure that all formations could be supplied adequately and the entire campaign sustained; otherwise disaster would ensue. As he had promised, Grant returned to Nashville to complete the handover to Sherman, and then he departed as swiftly as he arrived to give impetus to his great and numerous responsibilities, "but more particularly," as Sherman noted keenly "to give direction in person to the Armies of the Potomac and James," for his own methods were shaped by Grant's model. When Grant left on March 18, Sherman traveled with him as far as Cincinnati so that they could explore together in private conversation "many little details" incidental to the planning process. The likely place of George B. McClellan and Don Carlos Buell under the Grant regime had become a more pressing issue. Buell's loyal lieutenant James Fry, now provost marshal, had been urging Sherman to give Buell a senior command. Grant remained optimistic that both of these senior generals, plus a group of corps and divisional commanders purged after Chickamauga, could be accommodated.

In his *Memoirs* Sherman attributed the failure to reappoint them to Edwin M. Stanton's "notoriously vindictive ... prejudices," but this reflects Sherman's later unforgiving animus toward Stanton. McClellan and Buell were often their own worst enemies, being divisive, controversial, and high-handed. Sherman felt happy to give Buell command of a corps assigned to the defense of the Mississippi, but this was not good enough for him; Buell would accept nothing less than an army. The only possible solution lay in removing John M. Schofield, commanding the Army of the Ohio, to make way for Buell. Sherman recognized that this would not be welcome to the governor of Ohio, David Tod; he also expressed reluctance to take this drastic step because he feared that an intractable individual like Buell might add pressure on the rickety structure over which he presided. Buell's behavior might provoke rivalry and insubordination or even cause the complete breakdown of good order and discipline. The Army of the Cumberland was more fractious than the other two, and Sherman was more likely to find a vacancy for Buell there. But Sherman warned Buell bluntly that he needed to return to duty "and then rise to his proper station" by his own exertions. His friends should not stir matters up by briefing reporters on his behalf "to sow dissensions whenever their influence is felt." Buell could not bring himself to display a modicum of the humility that Sherman recommended.[15]

After wishing Grant all good fortune, Sherman returned to his major advanced supply base at Nashville. Initially Sherman had been ordered to concentrate "at or near Memphis," but Nashville recommended itself as the logistical point of departure for any advance into Georgia; it must also have been a relief to escape Memphis. "I cannot bear even to think of you passing over the same way where our darling suffered," Ellen sobbed. Shortly after arriving Sherman received his remarkably concise and cogent orders from Grant. The objectives of the campaign, he decreed, "were to move against Johnston's army, to break it up and get into the interior of the enemy's country as far as you can, inflicting all the damage you can against their War resources." These two aspects Grant had linked together intimately, and the linkage would shape Sherman's conduct. Although Grant's earlier letter had stressed the need to concentrate the strongest force "for the field," and his current instructions urged Sherman to "get ready as soon as possible," Grant left Sherman mainly to his own devices and thoughts, trusting a reliable subordinate to carry out his mission after his own fashion. "I do not propose for you a plan of campaign," the general-in-chief concluded, "but simply to lay down the work it is desirable to have done and leave you free to execute it in your own way." Grant acknowledged that Sherman would "have difficulties to encounter getting through the mountains to where supplies are abundant," but he made no effort to prescribe Sherman's course, merely expressing his faith "you will accomplish it." For Sherman's information he sketched out other elements of his grand plan for 1864, the one of greatest interest to Sherman being the orders he had given to Banks to complete the Red River campaign swiftly, return Sherman's troops previously loaned to him temporarily, and thence assault Mobile, Alabama.[16]

Sherman at once embarked on a hectic tour of his command, via Pulaski, Tennessee, to see Dodge, before proceeding to Huntsville, Alabama, where members of his personal staff were still stationed after Meridian, and where fortuitously James B. McPherson had arrived to assume command of the Army of the Tennessee. Sherman and McPherson traveled by train together to Stevenson and Bridgeport before returning to Chattanooga to discuss matters with Thomas; they then proceeded to Knoxville to confer with Schofield. En route Sherman met Granger, commander of the 4th Corps, who "as usual" voiced a long list of complaints, including that he had a great deal of leave owing. Sherman did not discourage him from taking it all. Schofield returned with Sherman and McPherson to Chattanooga for a meeting of all the senior commanders involved in the spring campaign. Sherman characterized this gathering in his *Memoirs* as "nothing like a council of war, but [we] conversed freely and frankly on all matters of interest then in progress or impending." This description is accurate: Sherman did not ask for their approval or suggest that they offer ideas—a symptom of the weak-minded commander.[17] Much of the discussion focused on the technique of the advance and the areas of concentration, and Sherman neither disclosed the underlying ideas of his plans to his subordinates nor involve his staff in the creative process, save to issue administrative orders, many of which he drafted.

In accordance with Sherman's meticulous methods, "we discussed every possible contingency like to arise," but he only gave each man as much information as he needed for his own advance. Interestingly, given his reflection on his own role, he recorded, "I simply instructed each army commander to make immediate preparations for a hard campaign, regulating the distribution of supplies that were coming up by rail from Nashville as equitably as possible." In the area of logistical management Sherman quickly sensed that he could make a decisive contribution to the overall direction of the campaign. As a first step, and "according to the programme of Lieutenant General Grant," Sherman ordered a concentration of the three armies "at and near Chattanooga by May 5"; although Sherman traveled back to Nashville to sort out the logistical tangles, he intended to return to Chattanooga on May 1 to orchestrate a concentrated and simultaneous advance, as laid down by Grant on May 5.[18]

Sherman predicted that the Union armies would face ferocious resistance in this campaign and went to great pains to disillusion those who believed that an imminent Confederate collapse was likely. The "Devils seem to have a determination that cannot but be admired. ... Some few deserters—plenty tired of war, but the masses determined to fight it out." So Sherman did not envisage a short, sharp operation—though this does not mean that he did not hope to pull one off. As Grant had placed pressure on all his subordinates to forward their plans quickly, Sherman reported proudly that "after a *full* consultation with all my Army commanders" he had reached "the following conclusions for which he needed presidential sanction and Grant's approval before he could issue the necessary orders. He hardly underestimated the logistical challenges he faced: 30,000 animals had died; organizations were shriveling; he did not yet know how he could obtain enough food "for mules and men in time." But he concealed these anxieties from Grant. He informed the general-in-chief that the 23rd Corps, all that remained of the Army of the Ohio, would act as "the Left of the Grand Army." Its core, the Army of the Cumberland, would be organized into three corps, the 20th (four divisions under Hooker, an amalgamation of the 11th and 12th Corps of the Army of the Potomac), the 4th, now to be commanded by Oliver O. Howard, whom Sherman rated highly for diligence and initiative, and the 14th. The latter was commanded by John M. Palmer, whom both Sherman and Thomas agreed in rating as "not equal" to such a responsibility. Sherman, ever loyal to Grant's hopes, suggested that Buell, "or any tried soldier," be given the 14th Corps.[19]

In some respects, his worst organizational problem could be found in the Army of the Tennessee. It remained significantly under strength. McPherson lacked the 17th Corps, mainly due to "veterans on furlough," but hoped to draw on two divisions, though not their commander, Blair, who remained on leave of absence. In order to expedite the possible return of this formation he asked the War Department for authority to "control" the furloughed veterans and via the state governors order their punctual reassembly. Two other divisions under A. J. Smith had been rashly loaned to Banks to go "up Red River" when he had flirted with commanding that ill-fated scheme. He had insisted on their return by April 10 and on April 3 wrote to Banks imploring they start back, as agreed, even to the degree that they should remain aboard the boats "they have used up Red River, as it will save the time otherwise consumed in transfer to other boats." But even after arrival at Vicksburg they would still be 200 miles away. Sherman became perturbed at the rumors circulating "thick and fast of defeat in that quarter"—alas, all too true. Smith's troops would not serve again under Sherman's immediate eye and would not be extricated until the following November.

In Smith's continuing absence, Sherman hoped to field 30,000 men in his old army: the 15th Corps under John A. Logan, the 17th Corps under Frank Blair Jr., and the 16th Corps under Grenville M. Dodge "as the right flank of the Grand Army." His old friend Stephen Hurlbut "will not resign and I know no better disposition of him than to leave him at Memphis." Indeed, he was a competent administrator and logistician placed in charge of a vital supply network.[20]

Sherman summed up the instrument at his disposal in sanguine terms. "With these changes this army will be a unit in all respects, and I can suggest no better." This praise was exaggerated. His army would clank along awkwardly; the great variation in its constituent parts would cause endless problems in organizing a concentrated blow in short order at the most propitious moments. In his *Memoirs* Sherman writes proudly of his three principal subordinates, Thomas, McPherson, and Schofield, as "three generals of education and experience, admirably qualified for the work before us." He had designed this praise for public consumption. In private he sometimes nursed doubts about Thomas's drive and skill at maneuver. The man he trusted most, McPherson, commanded a force too weak for decisive operations.[21]

These three predominantly infantry armies also exhibited an unmentioned weakness in cavalry. Sherman could assemble from his three departments only four cavalry divisions; two remained in reserve, and only two passably competent cavalry divisions were deployed in the field: one under Major General George Stoneman for the Army of the Cumberland, and the other under Brigadier General Kenner Garrard, neither a particularly impressive commander. Stoneman did not lack certain qualities for high command, especially loyalty, but was wholly deficient in luck. McPherson had no cavalry of his own. Sherman thus faced an insoluble problem, because the lack of cavalry aggravated existing weaknesses in reconnaissance, and in the anticipation of concentrating Union strength against Confederate weakness, that could only be achieved with good intelligence.[22]

The last requirement assumed prominence in Sherman's conduct of operations. He thoroughly approved of Grant's essential aim: simultaneity of advance. "That we are now all to act on a Common plan, converging on a Common Centre looks like Enlightened War." It also had significant implications for the way Sherman obeyed his orders. He submitted his plans for Grant's approval in less than a week. "Like yourself you take the biggest load," Sherman immediately discerned, "and from me you shall have thorough and hearty cooperation. I will not let side issues draw me off from your main plan." Sherman's part in it was designed to facilitate Grant's operations against Lee's Army of Northern Virginia—the point of main operational effort. Sherman had already given Rawlins and Orville E. Babcock on Grant's staff some indication of his thinking. What he made abundantly clear to Grant was that he had not sought the approval of his army commanders for his plans; he had only briefed them on the outline—that is, the process by which the design should be implemented, "which I inferred from the purport of our conversation here and at Cincinnati."[23]

Sherman then proceeded to outline his detailed operational design for Grant's benefit. Thomas would advance from Ringgold "straight on Johnston where he may be, fighting him cautiously, persistently and to the best advantage." In a phrase, Thomas would fix the Confederate commander to his position, the formidable Rocky Face Ridge. In the meantime, McPherson's Army of the Tennessee based at Lee and Gordon's Mills on the Chickamauga, "will cross the Tennessee at Decatur and Whitesburg march towards Rome and feel for Thomas." But, Sherman pointed out, "McPherson has no cavalry," and any probe would be deficient if faced by a powerful Confederate cavalry force. Sherman reflected further on this matter. He had earlier concluded that this "large and dangerous force" would enjoin a certain caution, "and I must be careful." If Johnston withdrew to the Chattahoochee River, "I would feign to the Right but pass to the Left and act on Atlanta or on to its Eastern Communications according to developed facts." Sherman here lays out his concept of operations, shifting from one flank to another in concerted envelopments, retaining the initiative despite the difficult country he had to

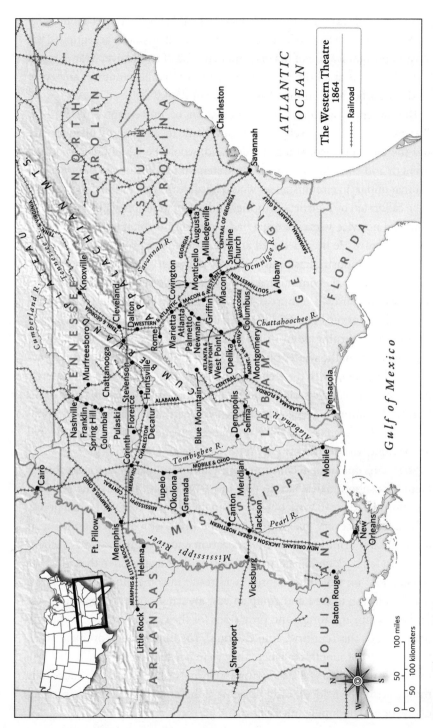

Western Theater, 1864

pass over, while keeping Johnston uncertain and at bay. "This is about as far ahead as I feel disposed to look," Sherman ruminated, but he accentuated the most important feature of his plan, namely, that "I would ever bear in mind that Johnston is at all times to be kept so busy that he cannot in any event send any part of his Command against you or Banks."[24]

The sweeping advances and articulation of movement envisaged by Sherman, shifting his weight from one flank to another of unequal size and therefore of unequal logistic demand, would be wholly reliant on the strength and efficiency of his supply system. It was clear even before he set out that under no circumstances would he allow his operational mainspring to be calibrated by logistical priorities and calculations; the latter must serve him, and not vice versa. Georgia had a million inhabitants, Sherman concluded bluntly. He then deduced another simple but profound insight into the nature of industrialized war: "If they can live we should not starve. If the enemy interrupt my communications I will be absolved from all obligations to subsist on our own resources, but feel perfectly justified in taking whatever and whenever I can find." From his major premise, Sherman reached an important turning point in his military conduct, one that would shape his campaigns in the winter of 1864–65. "I will inspire my command if successful," he joked, "with the feeling that Beef and Salt are all that is absolutely necessary to Life." In a serious afterthought, he revealed the influence of his historical reading and reflection. He remembered that "parched Corn [had] fed General Jackson's Army, once, on that very ground." If necessary he would do the same with an army twenty times the size of "Old Hickory's."[25]

Sherman's operational concept represents a formidable personal achievement. His subordinates had no part in its evolution. But in some respects, the efforts he made to work out its sustainability were worthy of equal praise. "The interest of every man in America," he wrote with a typical flourish, "is to sustain our armies that have organization and strength for if all else fails, you must fall back on it." Sherman expressed the hope to Ellen that "the base preparation" on which he labored "will result in something decisive. It is a mammoth task to feed and equip so vast an army as we are rearming," especially acquiring "forage and provisions for the Cavalry and Men who will have to cross the Tennessee into Georgia." The fundamental problem lay in the transport of supplies to where they were needed, and he aimed above all to "enable the military railroads running from Nashville to supply more fully the armies in the field." In order to achieve this aim Sherman took a number of drastic and unpopular measures.

In General Orders No. 6 he prohibited the movement of private freight or civilians on the railroads; the only civilians permitted were those traveling with the express permission of the war governor of Tennessee or departmental commanders. Needless to say, reporters, "mere traders in news like other men," were not excluded from the prohibition. Sherman also restricted the movement of any military personnel on routine business, including furloughed soldiers. "Bodies of troops will not be transported by railroads when it is possible for them to march," unless senior officers decided otherwise. The same was true of horses, cattle, and other livestock. Local posts around Nashville up to the limit of 35 miles and 20 miles from Stevenson, Bridgeport, Chattanooga, Huntsville, and Loudon were required to haul their supplies by road.

Sherman made a number of concessions permitting the movement of one car per day for the transport of sutlers' goods (those who sold nonmilitary merchandise), officers' stores, and the goods for officers' messes, and for the use of express companies. Only when "the rolling-stock of the railroads is increased, or when due accumulation of stores has been made at the front," Sherman warned, would private passengers and freight again be transported. In search of such a buildup Sherman also issued General Orders No. 8, which stopped the feeding of Southern civilians south of Nashville or the sale of provisions, except to "hired men" who worked for quartermasters. This measure was designed to limit the frittering away of prestocked provisions that had been accumulated so painstakingly to those "who were not military."[26]

At a conference with his senior logisticians, Sherman estimated that the advance would involve 100,000 men and 35,000 horses and mules, and these had to be supplied daily by 130 cars (allowing for damage or destruction) that carried 10 tons each to Chattanooga. This permitted the issue of five pounds of oats or corn per day for each animal, which was barely adequate. Sherman wrote later that "I was willing to risk the question of forage ... because I expected to find wheat and corn fields and a good deal of grass, as we advanced into Georgia at that season of the year." Sherman had to face the unpalatable fact that should he use all the rolling stock of the Louisville and Nashville Railroad, 60 locomotives and 600 cars, he would still not have enough supplies. He needed 100 locomotives and 1,000 cars. Thanks to a patriotic appeal he enlisted the support of the road's president, James Guthrie, who developed a ferryboat system that permitted the movement of rolling stock from all over the North. Sherman later attributed his success in sustaining his campaign to this measure, because the level of transportation it generated allowed the shift of stores "with all possible dispatch in a systematic fashion."[27]

Sherman's insoluble logistical difficulties could only be alleviated if Banks won a rapid victory on the Red River and then shifted eastward, as ordered, to take Mobile. Possession of this Alabama port on the Gulf of Mexico would enable a new line of supply to be established from the sea to the south of Sherman's advance; as Sherman advanced from the north, his lines of communication would shorten. His current arrangements required hauling supplies over hundreds of miles of vulnerable rail track—and these lines lengthened as he advanced. Sherman's logistical ingenuity would be tested to keep the supplies running. There is no evidence to suggest that Sherman expected Banks to act in a way that had not been conspicuous in his previous campaigns and thus conjure up a solution rather than create problems for others; in any case, Sherman was not a gambling man.[28]

Even before the campaign had begun Sherman had to look to his rear to fend off not just Confederate cavalry but vested interests on his own side. Those denied railroad transportation or wherewithal raised a ruckus that came to the president's attention. Lincoln wrote to Sherman to inquire whether he could make any efforts consistent with military success on behalf of "those suffering people." He stressed this was not an order. Sherman reacted no more sympathetically than to the pleas of any other politician. When a team of preachers requested special treatment and transport on the grounds of their holy mission, Sherman barked in response: "200 pounds of powder or oats are worth more to the US than that amount of bottled piety." As all regiments were furnished with chaplains, he could see no need for "these wandering preachers," whom he dismissed as "a positive nuisance." He esteemed charity workers no more highly; they "eat bread and meat which we need there. ... They simply aggravate the trouble." Sherman's orders should be judged by their results. On May 1 his chief quartermaster, Colonel R. Allen, reported proudly that "five months' supplies of all kinds are at Nashville. The great work on this side is nearly done, but done in vain if not followed up with the greatest possible energy and discretion." Supplies still needed to be moved even if stockpiled, and the logistic risk remained not inconsiderable.[29]

Grant's Vicksburg campaign had taught Sherman the necessity for sizable Union armies to operate vigorously at the very end of their logistical line of communications and not hesitate to reach out. He intended to do the same, if necessary. Initially, he hoped to avoid this by seeking an early decision in the vicinity of the main Confederate defensive works shielding Dalton, Georgia, anchored on the Rocky Face Ridge. Sherman aimed to envelop Johnston's position along what he described as "a gravelly range of hills covering the mouth of the famous Buzzard Roost Pass through Rocky Face Ridge," a position secured by spurs that ran down to a stream on either flank. The immediate priority lay in settling the distribution of his three armies in order to advance to contact with the enemy according to the timetable laid down by Grant—a simultaneous advance on May 5.[30]

Before leaving Nashville, Sherman wrote to Ellen warning her of the impending advance. He complained that he was 20,000 men short and deplored the effects of the furloughs permitted in 1863. Indulging in a fit of gloom, he wrote, "Our armies are now weaker than at any former period of the war." During these weeks Ellen became alarmed by his tone: "You are evidently allowing yourself to be too much annoyed by the disagreeable consequences and attendants of your present position." Still, he pulled himself up and recalled that "combined it is a big army, and a good one, and it will take a strong opposition to stop us once in motion." His family always took a strong interest in his staff. He told Ellen that he intended to take three ADCs with him, J. C. McCoy, Lewis Dayton, and J. C. Audenried. The total number of officers in the field who served on his staff numbered no more than 12. This was hardly a large number to administer his entire command. He justified its small size to his father-in-law on the grounds that he needed no more "because I deal only with the heads of these large armies which have a complete organization." None of his staff officers had executive authority to take decisions in his name. They were employed purely on administrative tasks; Lieutenant Colonel R. M. Sawyer, who issued most of the headquarters orders, pleased Ellen because he "saves you so much labor." The formal chief of staff, Brigadier General J. D. Webster, who took no part in the planning process, remained in Nashville to take care of "current business."[31]

He sent his Minnie some wildflowers so she could press them in her books. "I gathered them in the very spot where many a brave man died for you," he commented pointedly. On May 4 he struck a somber note in a letter to Ellen. He predicted accurately the onset of "some of the most desperate fighting of the war, but it cannot be avoided, deferred or modified." This fatalism, though, did not reduce his indomitable spirit. "My love to the children and let what fate befall us, believe me always true to you and mindful of your true affection."[32]

George Thomas's Army of the Cumberland received orders to concentrate at Ringgold, then the advanced logistical base, from which Schofield's Army of the Ohio would also draw its supplies, as the latter had received orders to head for Catoosa Springs on Thomas's left. On the right, McPherson's Army of the Tennessee, based at Chattanooga, was ordered to Rossville and Lee and Gordon's Mills near the old Chickamauga battlefield, before proceeding to Villanow. Sherman's subordinates had yet to be apprised of their detailed roles as the campaign developed. To Grant Sherman confided his fears that the enemy already had "a general idea of our plans." His fears were unfounded and evidence of his nervous state. The fine weather held, and the roads remained firm. Sherman could not have made his aim clearer to the general-in-chief: "Next move will be battle." There might be distracting maneuvers beforehand, but Sherman hoped to strike an early, decisive blow. He reiterated his intention to Grant: "We will all go out on the 5th [May]." When Grant stressed the paramount need yet again, "All will strike together," Sherman reassured him. "We will be on time."[33]

On May 7, after his armies had moved off, Sherman issued an order to Thomas for execution the following day: Thomas should feint toward the Buzzard Roost Pass by occupying the Tunnel Hill Ridge, to which Sherman intended to extend the railroad and which he meant to make his advanced logistical depot. Thomas's operation amounted to an aggressive feint, and it should not "lead to battle unless the enemy comes out of his works;" Schofield should guard Thomas's left and probe the Rocky Face Ridge. McPherson received the point of honor on the right of the line "to move through Villanow and occupy Snake Creek Gap to its strongest point"; once joined by Garrard's cavalry division the Army of the Tennessee should advance and cut the railroad at Resaca between Dalton and Atlanta. Should the Confederates leave Buzzard Roost Gap, then Thomas should follow immediately and Schofield advance to the east side on Dalton. Thomas had occupied Tunnel Hill by the morning of May 7. Sherman intended Thomas and Schofield to serve as the anvils to McPherson's hammer. These initial fixing operations, Sherman hoped, would grant McPherson the time to "strike and threaten the railroad." He ordered Schofield to continue harassing tactics—"I want to guard against the possibility of Johnston turning on McPherson"—but he repeated the injunction, "Don't be drawn into a battle." The battle should be fought to the south once Johnston had been forced to vacate his entrenchments.[34]

Sherman's headquarters and personal staff traveled fully packed in about six wagons accompanied by a guard composed of just one company of Ohio sharpshooters. "No wall-tents were allowed, only the flies," Sherman wrote sardonically. His austerity was driven less by an indifference to personal comfort than by a desire "to set the example"; he wished "gradually to convert all parts of that army into a mobile machine, willing and able to start at a minute's notice, and to subsist on the scantiest food." Sherman made his headquarters close to Ringgold, nearest to Thomas, who commanded his largest army, but also near to Schofield, who commanded by far the smallest.[35]

At about 2:00 p.m. on May 9 Sherman received word that McPherson had not only gained entrance to Snake Creek Gap but had also been opposed by only a single Confederate cavalry brigade. Garrard's cavalry division had yet to reach him; with increasing frustration, Sherman ordered up a brigade of Judson Kilpatrick's cavalry division in reserve to be sent to McPherson's aid. Having previously exhibited nerves in case Johnston might slip away, and because his prejudices against his slothful cavalry were once again being confirmed, Sherman expressed unalloyed delight at this good news. "Johnston had no idea of that movement." He instructed Thomas and Schofield to provide "the earliest possible information from all points" of Johnston's reaction to the discovery that he had "a large, strong army within five miles of Resaca." The two armies facing Dalton were to engage the enemy vigorously "to give McPherson a chance."[36]

That evening Sherman's mood dampened when shortly after 8:30 p.m. Captain Audenried, who had accompanied McPherson through Snake Creek Gap, delivered another dispatch containing less welcome news. McPherson's letter expressed anxiety lest Johnston turn and strike him while so exposed; he did not command a "strong army" but a force that equaled a Confederate corps. Though McPherson had gone forward to examine the ground around Resaca—which lay at his mercy, defenseless—he lacked the cavalry needed to verify the position. McPherson also became alarmed by reports that a strong force of Confederate cavalry was heading for the entrance of Snake Creek Gap to block his escape. Instead of pushing forward to destroy the railroad and any military infrastructure, McPherson took counsel of his fears. He presumed the enemy would react decisively and ferociously and underestimated the effect of his own audacious and successful movement. Given the information available to him, he was not wrong to make the decision to withdraw before destroying the railroad—but that does not render it correct. A commander with greater steel, like Grant, might have "soared into the unknown" and pushed forward.

McPherson's rearward move might also be justified as consistent with Sherman's orders. McPherson had been enjoined, once he had broken the railroad, "to retire to the mouth of the Snake Creek Gap" and then prepare to attack Johnston's army once it began to withdraw southward. He did not receive orders to seize and hold Resaca at all costs, as Sherman implies in his *Memoirs*. In short, some of Sherman's innate caution rubbed off on McPherson, whose move is reminiscent of Sherman's conduct at Chattanooga when he stopped short of Tunnel Hill. The Army of the Tennessee fell back and fortified its position on some high ground in Sugar Valley at the Resaca end of the gap's exit. At this crucial juncture McPherson felt the true cost of Sherman's manpower problems. If his missing four divisions had been present, he might have shown more confidence and pushed on.[37]

Earlier that day Sherman had telegraphed Halleck reporting his progress. He hinted at the direction in which his mind was working, namely, that he would "swing round through Snake Creek Gap" with his entire force "and interpose between him [Johnston] and Georgia [Resaca]." When on the morning of May 10 Thomas suggested sending two corps to support McPherson, he received a directive to "rapidly move your entire army ... to Snake Creek Gap, and join McPherson"; Hooker's 20th and Palmer's 14th Corps should move simultaneously "to make the game sure." These troops should also be furnished with axes and spades so that they could widen the roads to accommodate the wagon trains.[38]

Sherman depended on the luxuriant foliage and the absence of dust, thanks to rain showers, to conceal his advance. He also was very firmly against any attempt to seize a prominent, steep ridge called the Buzzard Roost, which, even if successful, would "push Johnston more compact" while the division of his own forces would be accentuated. Schofield feared that a reckless dispersal of the army would "be little more than throwing away my command," and Sherman would not countenance such a loss for no discernible gain at the beginning of the campaign. Schofield received orders to follow Thomas by May 12, though he should leave Stoneman's cavalry division behind "to keep up the delusion as long as possible." Sherman and Schofield, two clever and articulate men, had developed a warm relationship in a short time. "I am glad to have you at all times give me your unqualified opinion freely and frankly," Sherman assured his ambitious and eager-to-please subordinate.

With McPherson he was less pleased, though his disappointment did not affect their intimacy. "I regret beyond measure you did not break the railroad, however little and close to Resaca," he lamented, "but I suppose it was impossible." In his *Memoirs* Sherman mused that "such an opportunity does not occur twice in a single life." McPherson had been offered the chance to seize "half his [Johnston's] army and all his artillery and wagons at the beginning of the campaign"—as Sherman had hoped for. Certainly the seizure of Resaca would have altered the operational balance of the campaign and permitted an easier deployment of Sherman's three armies toward the point of main effort, namely, pivoting on Resaca to block Johnston's southward retreat and taking the maximum advantage of the bewildering muddle that accompanies every hasty withdrawal. With this chance forfeited at the outset, any later effort to turn Johnston's left flank would have to be made under more hazardous circumstances and under his watchful gaze. Sherman warned McPherson of the paramount need for the road through Snake Creek Gap to be kept open "and all unnecessary wagons to be kept to the rear."

He also instructed McPherson to order Blair's 17th Corps to urgently make for Chattanooga; his troops should march due to the continuing pressure on railroad capacity. Finally, Sherman issued an unequivocal order: "Should he [Johnston] attack you fight him to the last and I will get to you." Had Sherman displayed a pinch more aggression and self-confidence and issued such an order when McPherson had first set out, perhaps he would have garnered more from his envelopment. Yet the disappointment so far was only tactical, and all the advantage still lay with Sherman, but each delay compounded the difficulty in gaining a more complete victory. Both Thomas and Schofield had preferred Sherman's earlier, narrower plan, to envelop Johnston's left by marching the two armies to Snake Creek Gap via the base of John's Mountain along the Mill Creek Road rather than "cut loose from the railroad altogether." Schofield summed up the advantages of this plan thoughtfully: "If you can carry supplies enough to last while you defeat Johnston in [the] open field, and then re-open your communication with Chattanooga, your success seems more than probable."[39]

The Army of the Cumberland completed its march to Snake Creek Gap by the night of May 12, and the Army of the Ohio the following day. Sherman had no choice but to adapt his tactics to the changing operational environment. The distribution of his command remained the same. McPherson's Army of the Tennessee lay on the right, the Army of the Cumberland in the center with Hooker's 20th Corps in support of McPherson at Resaca, and Schofield's Army of the Ohio on the left. Two Confederate divisions commanded by Leonidas Polk had arrived at Resaca from Mississippi on the night of May 10. Johnston evacuated the Rocky Face Ridge in the early hours of May 13 and arrived later that morning in the nick of time. His position still faced north and west, and he occupied ground along Camp Creek to shield the railroad, though he fought with both the Conasauga and Oostanaula Rivers at his back. Sherman rightly entertained doubts as to how long Johnston could sustain this position; he might continue his retreat, for if Sherman crossed the Oostanaula he would be trapped. The weather was cold for the time of year, windy, cloudy, and with heavy showers.

This phase of the battle took the form of a meeting engagement: each side probed its respective position, collided with the enemy, sought advantage, and shuffled in one direction or the other as its flanks became exposed. Sherman arrived at the front on the afternoon of May 12. On his first encounter with McPherson, he said breezily, "Well Mac, you have missed the opportunity of a lifetime." His initial conception took the form of a turning movement mounted by the Army of the Cumberland to cut the railroad north of Resaca and encircle parts of Johnston's army still marching through the mountain passes. But this scheme was rendered moot when intelligence reported that the entire Confederate army had now reached Resaca. In any case, Thomas had to regroup northward as his left became more exposed, and Hooker's 20th Corps had to be sent to support Howard's 4th Corps as it arrived to join the army from feinting before the Rocky Face Ridge, having occupied Dalton on May 13—close cooperation that neither relished. All who witnessed this frantic fighting remarked on its severity, but the Confederates were driven back into their entrenchments around Resaca.[40]

Sherman had succeeded in fixing Johnston to his position. During the night of May 14–15 he worked almost continuously on issuing orders for the following day, an arduous duty better done by an executive chief of staff, which would have allowed him to conserve his energies. Like the Duke of Wellington he catnapped and slept by the roadside. A soldier saw him and shouted out, "A pretty way we are commanded!" Disturbed by the noise, Sherman sat up. "Stop, my man," he exclaimed, "while you were sleeping, last night, I was planning for you, sir; and now I am taking a nap"—a remark that caused much cheering. "Thus, familiarly and kindly," Oliver Howard recalled, "the general gave reprimands and won confidence." Sherman's new plan required a shift of emphasis: the point of main effort would return to the Union right flank, and he would attempt to turn Johnston's left again. But the task would be more difficult because his troops would have to cross water barriers. He gave orders that a division be sent with a pontoon bridge to Lay's Ferry on the Oostanaula, three miles south of Resaca. Its task was to build two bridges and threaten Calhoun, another crucial railroad junction; as Garrard had arrived, he, too, was dispatched down the Oostanaula to interdict Johnston's rail communications as far south as Kingston. Sherman did not envisage this force as one to block Johnston's escape but as a harassing force on his flank as he withdrew before the arrival of the main body.[41]

It is testimony to Sherman's rather anomalous position, and indicative of how he catered to public expectations about his actions, that he often presented himself in his *Memoirs* as if he were the army commander, issuing orders to divisional commanders rather than through McPherson, his usual practice. His tone remained operationally cautious. He warned McPherson, wrongly, that Johnston "moves in too much order for a retreat. Therefore be duly cautious, but prompt to engage."[42]

Thomas's role in the evolving scheme was secondary. Sherman believed his forté to be the set-piece battle, so during the night of May 14–15, he received orders to begin a major assault on Resaca. He still had to reorder his line, as the previous day's fighting had left the Army of the Ohio in his center. Schofield's troops retired from the line "to take post on the left" where they properly belonged, but at 11:00 a.m. on May 15, despite these complicated maneuvers, Thomas's line advanced a mile and half toward Resaca. The Army of the Tennessee gained high ground south of the town on which McPherson could place his artillery and bombard Resaca and its all-important railroad bridge over the Oostanaula. On the night of May 15–16 Johnston decided to make use of his escape route south while he still could, and his army slipped away, though the retreat was far from neatly executed. The following morning Sherman's troops occupied Resaca. His pride in its fall was qualified by knowledge that he had failed to severely damage Johnston's army. Any second attempt, alas, was more likely to fail than the first.[43]

The Battle of Resaca was a great battle won by Sherman, not simply a series of maneeuvers or raids, and he had designed it as such. The cost was comparatively light, about 600 dead and 3,375 wounded. The following week he wrote to Ellen proudly, "The whole movement has been rapid, skilful and successful, but will be measured by subsequent events." He also assured her that Grant's battles in Virginia were "fearful but necessary. Immense slaughter is necessary to prove our northern armies can and will fight." The Union could then intimidate its enemies by "an immense moral power." Sherman had tried to avoid "immense slaughter" in Georgia, but he had labored under significant topographical handicaps. "We were compelled to grope our way through forests, across mountains," he wrote later, "with a large army necessarily more or less dispersed." His strength was less than he had hoped for, and he had to conserve it. He wished to avoid at all costs what he called "the terrible door of death" that Johnston had prepared for his troops along the Rocky Face Ridge, but that did not involve a habitual avoidance of battle. To the contrary, at Resaca he etched a subtle design, and "by catching the strong and weak points I enabled the army to fight at as little disadvantage as possible, and following up quick and strong we gave Johnston no time to fortify though every pass was barricaded all the way down."[44]

Sherman feared Confederate cavalry the most; he could not fail to be conscious of the weaknesses of his own, a weakness that accentuated his logistical vulnerability. He failed to realize that the solution to the Union's cavalry problem lay in the centralization of its command and its concentration into a separate corps. Consequently, his ability to follow up "quick and strong" could only be faltering and puny. Still, Sherman expressed delight at the repair of the Oostanaula railroad bridge and having "the telegraph cars to the very Rear of our army." "Of course," Sherman candidly admitted to his brother John, the farther he advanced with Johnston's army largely intact, "our labors & difficulties increase as we progress, whereas our enemy gains strength." Banks's humiliation down the Red River had doubled these problems.[45]

Despite the disappointments, Sherman had not been repulsed, and henceforward he would never relinquish "the initiative, and the usual impulse of a conquering army." In one of his brilliant, prescient passages, Sherman revealed to Ellen that Resaca "was the first step of the Game. The next is to force him [Johnston] behind the Chattahoochee and last to take Atlanta and disturb the peace of the Inhabitants of Central Georgia and prevent Reinforcements going to Lee." Sherman thus turned to pursuit.[46] After a brief rearguard action at Adairsville—where Sherman and his staff were forced to scatter when a Confederate artillery battery found their range—Johnston paused to launch a counterstroke at Cassville. "But on our approach in strength," Sherman recorded crisply, "he retreated south to the Etowah River by the Allatoona Pass. The country along the Etowah is rich in wheat fields and in minerals." Sherman would have to give further painstaking consideration to the problems entailed in catching Johnston in open country and completing his destruction on the battlefield. He did not regard himself as a prophet, but he did believe that thinking about war aided his effort to fight it.[47]

11

Over the Chattahoochee, May–July 1864

In the closing weeks of May 1864 Sherman encountered a problem that had perplexed all successful commanders: how to complete a devastating pursuit. In particular, he needed to figure out how to prevent the escape of an enemy that might seek refuge in another position as formidable as the one previously vacated. On May 16 Major Dayton issued Sherman's orders that covered operations until Joseph E. Johnston had been driven "beyond the Etowah River." Thomas in the center would "pursue by the line of the railroad to Kingston," securing the bridge across the Etowah; McPherson on the right would thrust forward via the Rome road; Schofield on the left would advance on Cassville. His orders also revealed a concern for logistical matters and the organization of the transport of prisoners of war; the latter Sherman decided should be sent back to Nashville. "The repairs of the railroad and telegraph lines must be pushed forward with all possible rapidity," he declared, "but troops must not wait for them." Thomas's army as the "stable element" of Sherman's command received the vital task of "guarding all railroads to our rear"; McPherson, by contrast, was urged only to leave "small guards" behind and instructed to "call forward" all his effective troops as quickly as possible. Sherman planned to leave the protection of his lines of communication eventually to the militia, so that he could concentrate the largest possible force against Johnston's army.[1]

The three armies fanned out southward over a broad front, "by as many different routes as we could find"—a dispersal that might invite a Confederate riposte. Such an act required Johnston to demonstrate audacity, but that prudent and anxious soul had found reasons at Cassville for declining to attack. By contrast, Sherman, as his troops occupied Kingston and pushed beyond, believed this "ground comparatively open and well adapted to a grand battle." Sherman's thoughts revolved around the challenges another big battle involved; his correspondence reveals that far from spurning the necessity of fighting battles, he looked for opportunities to fight them. He intended to break Johnston's "right and left, and fight him square in front." The first phase would consist of a logistical campaign of attrition; the second phase, a staggering blow. But as Johnston fell back from Cassville and his lines of supply shortened, Sherman had to pay attention to repairing his own. "I think everything has progressed ... as favorably as we could expect; but I know," he warned Halleck, "we must have one or more bloody battles, such as have characterized Grant's terrific struggles." Sherman did not conceive his methods as an alternative to Grant's. They were based just as much on intricate, hardheaded logistical calculation as on strategic and operational inspiration.[2]

As his troops broke camp to resume the advance, Sherman remained keen that only the boldest commanders be placed in the vanguard. If he could catch parts of the Army of Tennessee unawares they should "be attacked frontally," he instructed; as Sherman reminded Thomas, "A real battle tomorrow might save us much work at a later period." Also, during these weeks, Sherman returned to stress the psychological factor. If Thomas's efforts to strike Johnston's army continued to be thwarted, he would use Schofield's Army of the Ohio to hit the right rear of the Confederate army—employing Brigadier General Edward McCook's cavalry brigade to cause mayhem along the Confederate lines of communications. McCook was told "to impress the enemy with fear of him, as it will be one element of strength in our future operations." Union cavalry had to behave more like their Confederate counterparts and spread terror and inflict destruction wherever they went. George Stoneman received orders with a similar import.[3]

Sherman's attempts to galvanize his cavalry had already earned an unwitting dividend because the unexpected movement of Schofield's cavalry had helped dislocate Johnston's preparations at Cassville. He continued to keep a viselike grip on the initiative and think in terms of pursuit. "Let all your troops be in advance of all wagons save ambulances ... and order the enemy to be attacked if found." "If we can bring Johnston to battle this side of the Etowah we must do it," he reminded Schofield, "even at the hazard of beginning a battle with but a part of our forces." Sherman enjoined Schofield to come up on Thomas's left even if he heard the sound of battle.[4] McPherson had been given a secondary role, namely, "to occupy the whole attention" of the Confederate left flank. But Stoneman quickly realized that Johnston would not allow himself to be brought to battle "in the comparatively open ground this side of Cartersville." From May 19, Sherman reported, the Army of Tennessee held Thomas at Cassville and withdrew across the Etowah, setting fire to the rail and road bridges at Cartersville, though Sherman retained use of two other good bridges and "an excellent ford" to cross this great river.

Although he had issued several injunctions to "crush or capture any force that is ... caught between General Stoneman and you," Thomas had failed to do so. He had been given the primary role during this phase of the campaign, and Sherman began to doubt his drive in the attack.[5]

The failure of the initial pursuit required a new plan so that operations could be sustained as far as the Chattahoochee River. "The railroad passes through a range of hills at Allatoona," he confided to Halleck, "which is doubtless being prepared for us; but I have no intention of going through it." Sherman joked grimly that he worried more about the vulnerability of his long wagon trains than the ceaseless fighting, but he faced a knotty problem in maintaining his existing fighting strength.

Back in Nashville, Webster received instructions to "back us up with troops in the rear" and make the most effective use of the proposed 20,000 militia promised by Halleck. Troops from both of these sources would allow Sherman to avoid the requirement "to drop detachments as road guards" as the columns advanced. He ordered Webster to announce to the newspapers that the line of the Etowah had fallen. He also took the opportunity in a general circular to assure officers and men that his prohibition on reporters' communications did not affect their mails, and he renewed his assault on reporters and their supposedly corrupting effect on gossiping, "idle and worthless officers" who boosted themselves at the expense of their industrious, modest, and meritorious colleagues.[6]

Then, while working at his papers late into the night, he received an important missive from the secretary of war, Edwin M. Stanton, which delivered a hard knock to his delicately arranged combinations. Although Stanton lavished praise on the "vigor and success of your operations," he warned that 27,000 veteran reinforcements had been sent to Grant at Spotsylvania and that urgent help would be needed to succor Benjamin F. Butler and Franz Sigel after their setbacks at Bermuda Hundred and at New Market in the Shenandoah Valley, respectively. "There appears to be a danger," Stanton concluded in his circuitous style, "that you may count too much on the new troops for your support." With manpower once more jostling to the top of his anxieties, Sherman decided on a brief pause to allow himself to take stock, a pause that pleased Thomas.[7]

Although in previous months Stanton had ordered a new draft designed to raise a million volunteers, among the Western states only Ohio had met its quota. Stanton feared that only 25,000 troops might be raised by four other states, Indiana, Illinois, Iowa, and Wisconsin. The root causes of this problem were that men were reluctant to volunteer due to war-weariness and the state governors were unwilling to press their constituents during an election year. Yet they realized they needed to take further action if the war was to be ended at the earliest date. In April 1864 the five governors visited Washington and promised to raise 85,000 militiamen for 100 days; those who volunteered would be exempted from the draft. Though it was a desperate, short-term expedient, Sherman had no choice but to take advantage of militia service to maintain his frontline strength.[8]

Stanton suggested two days later that a communication from Sherman to the governors with unfilled quotas "might stimulate their action." Sherman agreed to write to them at once because he needed men "to cover our communications while we are in the heart of Georgia."

Disappointing news of Grant's progress in Virginia impelled Sherman to demand that his entire command undertake "something now." He constantly stressed that his efforts always had to be related to the broader context of the war, especially what was happening during Grant's Overland Campaign in Virginia. Grant sought, in Sherman's opinion, to "impress the Virginians with the knowledge that the Yankees can and will fight them fair and square"; he adopted a didactic tone in correspondence with Stanton: such methods "will do more good than to capture Richmond or any strategic advantage." As for his own operations, "the enemy knows we can and will fight like the devil; therefore he maneuvers for advantage of ground." Sherman had seized the initiative, and he intended to keep it.

Sherman addressed the governors that day detailing where he wanted the militia to serve and the tasks they would be allotted. He hoped that the militia sent to Tennessee would cooperate in a movement "to prevent cavalry under [Nathan Bedford] Forrest and [Stephen D.] Lee from swinging over against my communications." He implored the governors to display "superhuman energy" to ensure he would not need to break up his "superb" army "into small fragments to guard railroads." Thereafter Halleck kept a close check on the movements of militia regiments and kept Webster in Nashville informed about their progress.[9]

The other manpower measure that Sherman needed to take required the movement of Blair's 17th Corps to the battlefront as quickly as possible. He reiterated an earlier order that it march from Decatur to Rome, which Sherman had garrisoned with a brigade (another was placed at Kingston). The logistical demands of three armies took precedence over the transport of troops, as Webster explained, and there were no cars available even for the movement of brigades, let alone divisions. The 17th Corps had no choice but to put its collective best foot forward.[10]

The problems of manpower and cooperation with politicians were two of the difficulties that engaged the attention of a commander of a military division; another was imposing a new concept of operations on his unwieldy command. Sherman had impressed on Stanton the supreme importance of gaining a "moral result" over the enemy, which "must precede all mere advantages of strategic movements"; he quickly decided how such an effort could be achieved. In a telegram of May 20 he had informed Halleck that he intended to make full use of the two bridges and a ford in crossing the Etowah. He did not consult his army commanders, though he did explain parts of his logic to Schofield. Earlier he had expected "to catch a part of the army retreating before us, but I take it for granted that it is now impossible"; consequently, he simply sought an assurance from Schofield that Johnston's army "awaits an attack through the difficult pass at Allatoona. I do not propose to follow him ... but rather to turn south ... leaving Allatoona to the north and east." Sherman had in mind a great outflanking movement that would abandon the railroad and turn the Confederate left by advancing into the thickly wooded country to the west and south of Johnston's immensely strong position at Allatoona.

Sherman exposed more of the detail to Halleck. "If Johnston remains at Allatoona I shall move on Marietta; but if he falls behind the Chattahoochee I will make for Sandtown and Campbellton, but feign at the railroad crossing." The concept of switching between two objectives and confusing the enemy as to which one he had chosen as his priority had already begun to dominate his thoughts. He wished to employ surprise and maneuver to catch Johnston off balance and dictate the course of the campaign, a stratagem Liddell Hart terms a "baited gambit." Sherman also underlined to Halleck another strategic dimension: "Notify General Grant that I will hold all of Johnston's army too busy to send anything against him."[11]

During his operational pause, while the staff labored on issuing the orders for this difficult shift southward away from the railroad, Sherman still found time to write to Ellen, saying, "You will no doubt recognize this very country as the one I was in 20 years ago, and to which I took such a fancy." Certainly, Sherman's knowledge of northern Georgia played an important part in his final selection of Dallas as his objective as he shifted away from the railroad that ran through Allatoona; it injected confidence into his calculations— though audacious, his maneuver could not be described as a leap in the dark.

Amid such pressures—perhaps as an escape from them—he reminisced with Ellen; his columns had "passed quite close to Colonel Tumlin's place," where Sherman had stayed during a visit in 1844. He recalled in his *Memoirs* that he "had noted well the topography of the country" and Tumlin had taken him to see "some remarkable Indian mounds on the Etowah River, usually called the 'Hightower.' " The activities on this more recent visit 19 years later were less diverting. Sherman noticed that the country had emptied on the approach of his armies and the majority of dwellings had been abandoned. Tumlin had returned in January 1864 from six months' service in the Georgia Mounted Infantry of the Georgia State Guards, but in May the Tumlin family found good reason not to be at home—though their property was not despoiled.[12]

As Sherman's staff began to prepare to pack up his camp in anticipation of a prompt departure, their commander's lined features lit up with delight at the welcome news that the Resaca bridge had been repaired within three days and thus supplies could be shifted to his advance base at Kingston, where Sherman had established his headquarters, and from there to formations in the field. A flurry of activity followed. Major Dayton issued an order on May 20 that specified that the armies should be ready to recommence the advance "stripped for battle, but equipped and provided for 20 days." The improvement in communications made such a stockpile possible. Anticipating later orders, this one also stipulated that all the wounded and infirm, plus all "worthless men and idlers," should be shunted to the rear to reduce the number of mouths that needed to be fed. Sherman's intricate care in logistical matters is conveyed in the order's detail. The troops should receive one pound of bread, flour, or meal, beef on the hoof, and two days' measure of bacon each week, as well as sugar, coffee, and salt; horses and mules were permitted four pounds of grain. "All else," the order states bluntly, "must be gathered in the country." Animals should graze and troops forage, "but indiscriminate plunder must not be allowed."[13]

While the armies rested, Sherman urged on their commanders the paramount need for reconnaissance and mapmaking to ease their passage. The country they were about to enter was "very rugged, mountainous and densely wooded," denuded of good roads, meandering and entangled with undergrowth where they could be found. Sherman allowed three days to move his armies through this difficult country when the weather was already hot and the roads enveloped in clouds of dust. Once they were concentrated around Dallas, an obscure hamlet, he could "strike at Marietta, or the Chattahoochee according to developments." On May 23 McPherson crossed one bridge over the Etowah at Kingston and headed for Dallas, and Thomas did likewise southeast of the town and advanced on Burnt Hickory; Schofield crossed farther east, endeavoring to mask Thomas's left. Sherman closely monitored this final movement, which began on the Union right, with Schofield on the left crossing last in the late evening. Sherman urged that the mules should not be overstrained, as supplies could be moved up to the scattered encampments by wagon train.[14]

Sherman harbored no illusions that his armies remained in pursuit mode. His new envelopment of the Confederate left flank formed an approach to a new line of battle—one that he hoped would catch Johnston's army at a signal disadvantage. In Special Field Orders No. 11, which Dayton issued the day before the operations began, Sherman stated that "the objective point" would be the railroad at Marietta, but he warned his subordinates of the continuing potency of Confederate cavalry still lurking behind the Etowah. "Henceforth," he enjoined, "great caution must be exercised to cover and protect trains"—otherwise the whole campaign might still be jeopardized. Johnston did indeed hope to inflict a defeat on Sherman in these tangled and murky woods, where his troops were distant from the railroad, which could only be picked up again at Marietta. If Johnston got his timing right, Sherman's logistical calculations might yet collapse, and he could be forced to retreat. Confederate cavalry soon spotted signs of Sherman's southeasterly advance; on May 24 the Army of Tennessee marched frantically southward and then west on a looping road from Allatoona to Dallas via Pickett's Mill and New Hope Church. Johnston's men arrived before Sherman's on this line of minor road junctions and hurriedly entrenched.[15]

Sherman thus confronted severe difficulties in concentrating his fighting power. The paucity of roads had ensured a wide dispersal, with the Army of the Cumberland alone occupying three different roads. By comparison, Johnston's troops were reasonably concentrated, though tired by their hectic march. A series of meeting engagements—which occur when armies collide—resulted along this line of obscure road junctions and points. Sherman had been forewarned of the battle's prospective shape when Thomas's vanguard skirmished with Confederate cavalry at Burnt Hickory and intercepted a courier carrying a letter from Johnston detailing his decision to block Sherman's advance at Dallas.[16]

Sherman remained optimistic that he could still bring Johnston to battle on his terms. Though he had taken a severe logistic risk with this turning movement, he had several times expressed pleasure at the efforts his logistic staff had made to supply him. "We are now all in motion like a vast hive of bees, and expect to swarm along the Chattahoochee in five days." But could Sherman get the swarm to the point where it most mattered with enough strength? This remained the fundamental problem. With his armies scattered it became more difficult to anticipate when and where he needed to concentrate and to predict what steps were required to achieve a desired concentration without starting a premature movement or sacrificing surprise.[17]

As the troops made their way along narrow roads, often drenched by heavy spring rainfall, on May 25 Joseph Hooker's 20th Corps thrust forward. Its vanguard, the division of John Geary, crossed Pumpkin Vine Creek, drove Confederate cavalry back, and advanced a further 2 miles beyond the bridge. Hooker assumed this road would take him to Dallas, but it headed toward another road junction to the north and east, New Hope Church, a small timber chapel by the roadside. While he was following this circuitous route, Confederate resistance strengthened, and Hooker ordered his troops to entrench. Throughout the day Sherman fretted at what he considered to be Hooker's laggard and overcautious movements. "I don't see what they are waiting for in front now," he murmured crossly. "There haven't been 20 rebels there today." That evening Hooker put in an attack with all three of his divisions; though it made progress, a thunderstorm erupted at 7:30 p.m. and rendered the going very glutinous. Hooker brought the attack to a close without decisive results, and Sherman's anger simmered. When he arrived on the field, he treated Hooker curtly and complained that because he had wasted hours waiting for his two other divisions to come up, he had frittered away an opportunity to damage Johnston's army before it could entrench. Hooker resented this reproof, which was followed the next morning by a "peremptory" order from Sherman to prevent his men straggling, "going back for rations" when their knapsacks should be full. Sherman thus concluded in his most brisk tone: "Schofield is now advancing by the left and McPherson by the right. Be ready for battle." Thereafter his relations with Hooker deteriorated rapidly.[18]

Over the following weeks Hooker indulged in one of his favorite pastimes, caustically belittling the abilities of his immediate superior. He likened Sherman to McClellan, a commander who held all the cards in his hands but refused to play them; Sherman had become too fond of "maneuver." The 20th Corps, he added, had done all the fighting so far and got no thanks for it. Daniel Butterfield, one of his division commanders and formerly his chief of staff, warned him to desist, but to no avail once Hooker poured himself another whisky. Sherman, as higher commanders always do, quickly picked up on these vicious accusations from the gossipy exchanges of staff officers.[19]

Sherman and Hooker resembled one another in certain respects. Their long, checkered relationship reaching back to West Point is an example of similarities clashing. They were not friends but enemies. Both were politically well connected, restless, ambitious, exuberant, petulant, and cautious. Both were tactless and expressed strident opinions; both were good haters. Neither man submitted to temperance, though Sherman was much more guarded in his consumption of alcohol than Hooker. Sherman was more loyal than Hooker and did not regard him as a gentleman. Mutual recrimination among distinguished men nearly always has its roots in earlier tussles, and the clash between Sherman and Hooker is no exception. Sherman's knowledge of Hooker's many broken pledges in California years before were the true source of their antipathy, exacerbated by later rivalries and tensions. Sherman viewed Hooker as insufferably self-important and a scoundrel. He was certainly a troublemaker.[20]

It should be recalled that Sherman's prime task was to direct rather than to command his three armies. As stalemate gripped his affairs at New Hope Church, or "Hell Hole," to use the soldiers' grim name, Sherman wrote urgently to McPherson informing him of the latest developments. He warned McPherson that the Army of the Cumberland lay three miles north and east of Dallas. He also indicated that he would renew the battle there early on May 26 as Schofield approached the Union left. He quickly sketched a concept of double envelopment even though "we are in dense woods, and see but little," though the sounds of digging "hastily-constructed log barriers" were unmistakable. Undeterred, he continued his instructions to McPherson crisply: "I wish you to move into Dallas, and then along the Marietta Road till you hit the [Confederate] left flank."

With McPherson's army striking the Confederate left, Schofield the right, and Thomas gripping the center, Sherman believed he could land a strong blow on Johnston's chin. He hoped a significant gap might be found, "but still Johnston may have his whole army, and we should act on that hypothesis." Meeting engagements are notoriously difficult to control, though Sherman went to great lengths to ensure his subordinates knew his location in case they needed to confer hurriedly. "Try and communicate with me early," he urged. "I will be near the battle-field along the road we are traveling."[21]

McPherson's Army of the Tennessee occupied Dallas by 2:00 p.m. on May 25 and advanced three miles beyond it but then ran into strong Confederate defenses; over following days the Confederates attacked the 15th Corps, attempting to exploit a gap between it and the neighboring 16th Corps. Sherman passed the rainy night of May 25–26 "on the ground, without cover, alongside a log, got little sleep," and he spent the next day in an irritable mood. In the middle of the afternoon he wrote frantically to McPherson, "I don't hear of you at all. What are you doing? I have heard no firing in your direction." Later that night he at long last received word from McPherson of an encounter with "the enemy apparently in strong force," but though he intended to attack on the 27th, "the direction of my advance and the nature of it will depend very materially upon the enemy."[22]

Such had invariably been the case in this protracted meeting engagement. At midday on May 26 Sherman stressed to McPherson that he intended to persevere with what he termed in his report "dispositions on a larger scale." He doubted whether the Confederates would remain in position. Sherman presumed that Johnston would withdraw to the Chattahoochee River—not an unreasonable assumption, given his record so far and the danger that Sherman's advance presented to his flanks— especially should Sherman strike both simultaneously. If the enemy was found, "my orders herewith will govern. I will expect to hear of you on General Hooker's right by ten (10) a.m." The orders enclosed, Special Field Orders No. 12, issued that evening, required a preliminary artillery bombardment until 9:00 a.m., followed by Thomas's assault an hour later on Pickett's Mill, a "commanding promontory" covering the Marietta Road. Sherman stressed he would be at or near General Hooker's position and wanted reports sent promptly to him announcing the fulfillment of his general plan.[23]

However imaginative the commander, directing a meeting engagement is a risky venture, and this was no exception. McPherson's slow progress, plus his desire to avoid heavy casualties that might worsen his manpower problems, persuaded Sherman to cancel the attack on Pickett's Mill, but the order failed to arrive in time to prevent a badly managed attack by two brigades of Howard's 4th Corps that cost 1,600 casualties, including 800 dead. The historian Albert Castel is highly critical of this series of operations, but they were hamstrung by "the difficult nature of the ground and dense forests," and as the Army of the Cumberland lacked cavalry, reconnaissance was shoddy. These complex and hazardous battles, despite intense difficulties in communicating between the three disjointed armies of varying size while using execrable maps, were conducted no less skillfully than Grant's during the Spotsylvania Campaign. They exhibited similar weaknesses to his, not least the high level of guesswork required to divine enemy intentions.[24]

Despite all these pressures, Sherman found time to send a telegram to Ellen reporting his progress. His main purpose, however, was to report the sad death of a family friend, Major Henry Giesey of the 46th Ohio Volunteers, who had served with Sherman since the spring of 1862.[25]

Sherman's armies had spread out with ominous cavities between their constituent parts, especially toward the ill-defined Union right flank. During the later morning of May 27 Sherman began to address this problem, suggesting to McPherson that if he failed to penetrate the Confederate entrenchments he might "work to [his] left, so as to connect with Hooker." Sherman apprised him that as the rest of the army shifted toward the left, he could not permit the gap between McPherson and Hooker to widen because it would jeopardize an opportunity he wished to exploit "to march around their extreme right and reach Marietta or Acworth." This entire maneuver had its origins in Hooker's misapprehension as to the direction of the roads around Dallas, but Sherman was keen to turn it to his benefit. Even so, he became anxious about McPherson's lack of progress, for "if you don't keep up, our line will become attenuated and liable to disaster."

By the early afternoon this suggestion had been sent as an order to "put our concentrated army between him [Johnston] and the railroad of which we want to make use." McPherson was to advance along the Marietta road "and then reach for Hooker's right. All the rest of the army are north of this road." This order, though, presented McPherson with a problem. The latter had gained intelligence that the Confederates were concentrating on his right flank and any leftward lurch would expose his trains. Sherman estimated the distance that needed to be filled at about 5 miles, so he instructed McPherson to send his trains back over Pumpkin Vine Creek, where they would be shielded by the Army of the Cumberland. The pressure could also be taken off the Army of the Tennessee by a punch at Johnston's right.[26]

In the early hours of May 28–29 the leftward shuffle began, a process during which Sherman (like Grant in Virginia) became absorbed in the tactical detail of improving fields of fire and avoiding the danger posed to the wagon trains. This involvement was not surprising as the movement did not go as easily as Sherman suggested in his report. That night he informed Halleck of his plans, and once they were passed on to the secretary of War, Stanton expressed "great satisfaction" at his ceaseless advance. All seemed contented and quiet at 3:00 a.m. when McPherson appeared personally at

Sherman's headquarters to report the repulse at Dallas of a substantial attack by three Confederate divisions on the Army of the Tennessee's right flank. Sherman quickly rose and got back to work. Though Confederate casualties numbered as high as 1,500 for a Union loss of 30 killed and 400 wounded and missing, the assault complicated McPherson's alignment with Hooker's corps; Sherman agreed that McPherson's could remain in position for a further day.[27]

When reporting to Halleck on the development of his plans, Sherman observed with a characteristically arresting phrase, "Both sides duly cautious in the obscurity of the ambushed ground." The Confederate assault at Dallas revealed this view unduly sanguine, but it proved a costly error. It made no difference to the course of the campaign. Sherman's major problem continued to be keeping his armies moving. The threat of traffic jams along these narrow and congested roads overgrown with vegetation might yet leave his formations vulnerable to a better-directed riposte. At 3:00 a.m. on the same night he ordered Schofield to build more bridges across Pumpkin Vine Creek and clear more roads through the woods. While standing with a group of officers, Sherman's party was fired upon, and a bullet passed through John Logan's coat sleeve and hit Colonel Ezra Taylor, formerly Sherman's chief of artillery in the 15th Corps, "square in the breast." His life was saved by a proudly owned and frequently brandished memorandum book securely housed in a breast pocket, which stopped the bullet and left Taylor only very slightly wounded. Sherman observed of his many visits to the front and of this ceaseless, almost Indian-style warfare of a semiguerrilla character: "I rarely saw a dozen of the enemy at any one time; and these were always skirmishers dodging from tree to tree, or behind logs on the ground"—or occasionally peering over the top of entrenchments. Such visits did encourage Sherman to play an expanding role, prescribing detailed instructions concerning the movement of McPherson's individual corps that were not his business, while simultaneously working on the logistical arrangements for the following week, which certainly was.[28]

As his armies pivoted to the north and east, Sherman placed his headquarters close to Thomas's, as the Army of the Cumberland remained the axle around which all else moved. He certainly did not shy away from the possibility of fighting a major battle if necessary in order to permit the maneuver to continue. Schofield received instructions to "hold firm to your line, even to the hazard of a general engagement. We can fight an attack here as well as we can fight anywhere. Don't yield to the enemy any ground." These instructions, though, indicate a defensive mode that would grow in importance in the coming weeks. He telegraphed Halleck again on May 29 informing him of McPherson's success at Dallas: his men, "covered by log breast-works, like our old Corinth lines"—a reference to Halleck's tortoiselike advance in May 1862 from the Shiloh battlefield to Corinth, Mississippi—"were comparatively unhurt." He declared forthrightly that Johnston had concentrated "in my front every man he can scrape," so he urged a revival of the Mobile operation that should dislocate Johnston's rear and transform his logistical prospects. Still, no great battle had been fought. "We have had many sharp and serious encounters," he informed his chief of staff, "but nothing decisive yet."[29]

Sherman's troops slogged onward, drenched once more by heavy rain and thunderstorms that lasted for three days. On May 29 Sherman prepared to receive Blair's 17th Corps, ordering him to pass Allatoona and then entrench. Once secure, Blair was to carry out Sherman's order to repair the railroad as far as Allatoona. Stoneman and Garrard's cavalry were to prepare Blair's way by occupying both ends of the pass. With a renewed railroad link Sherman would continue the maneuver to the left, the new line facing south and southeast. By June 2 he had skirmished within half a mile of Acworth. He still hoped to inflict a sharp defeat on the Confederate left during these complex maneuvers. On June 3 he urged McPherson, "All I ask is that when we do come in contact with the enemy on anything like fair terms and proportions we whip them more fully." In an interesting variant on his offensive use of entrenchments, Sherman instructed his army commanders to build their defenses around a series of fortified points rather than rely on long lines.[30]

All his hopes were pinned on Blair, and he took longer to arrive than expected; every minute of delay offered Johnston the chance to guess his intent. Sherman detailed the location of his headquarters to McPherson, at Burnt Church along the Burnt Hickory road to Marietta. He warned McPherson that as soon as he heard from Blair, the Army of the Tennessee would be shifted to Acworth, "moving you to the rear of Thomas. Study the movement and be prepared for it." He also became worried by levels of absenteeism. His headquarters issued Special Field Orders No. 17, but it shows unmistakable signs of being drafted by Sherman, presumably bored while waiting to hear from Blair. Commanders were ordered to tighten up measures against "skulking," that is, seeking safety by lurking in the rear areas without permission. All those found "loafing" should be put to work digging entrenchments and redoubts. Their officers were warned that if they hoped for promotion, those with "loose, straggling" commands could not expect "any favor."[31]

On June 5 Sherman got word from McPherson that Johnston had abandoned his position at New Hope Church. Sherman apprised Halleck that he expected Johnston to engage him at Kennesaw Mountain, near Marietta, "but I will not run hard on his fortifications." He drew sustenance from the local wheat fields and was well stocked in bread, meat, and sugar. Sherman had decided after a brief visit that Allatoona should be his new secondary base, and Resaca should be closed down; as soon as the railroad had been repaired, he would resume the advance on the Chattahoochee via Marietta, just 6 miles away. Yet he had to order McPherson to carry out this maneuver behind Thomas without a murmur from Blair. On June 6, losing patience, he telegraphed Rome. "Where is General Blair? I want instant answer." Later, at long last, Blair reported that he had arrived at Kingston; he was ordered to Acworth forthwith.[32]

Thus ended the second phase of the Atlanta campaign. Its conclusion was perhaps expressed too neatly in his report. Sherman claimed that his occupation of Acworth "thereby accomplished our real purpose of turning the Allatoona Pass." He had always intended to undertake this operation, and his correspondence stresses its primary purpose. Yet like Grant in Virginia, he invariably hoped for a bonus: to drive Johnston back to the Chattahoochee and, having gained momentum, "bounce" his army across the last river line before Atlanta. Sherman had not achieved this end and was careful to present it not as a primary but as an alternative objective. Albert Castel presents an excessively negative, perhaps hypercritical verdict: "Sherman plunged blindly and bloodily" into the Georgia woods, Johnston "foiled Sherman's plans," and he "suffered severe defeats" at New Hope Church and Pickett's Mill.[33]

Such criticisms from such an authority merit respect but are open to interpretation. Sherman's weakness in cavalry rendered all maneuvers to some degree a gamble—and did not encourage a timorous attitude in a commander increasingly prone to tactical caution. As to the progress of the campaign, success at the operational level should not be gauged as the sum of the tactical actions fought. By such a criterion Grant's handling of Spotsylvania could only be viewed as an unmitigated disaster. Throughout Sherman retained the initiative, and Johnston gained nothing from these battles. Sherman had three clear tasks: first, to know what was going on across a wide battlefront covered by a variegated conglomeration of formations; second, to confer with his subordinates and staff, and issue orders promptly; and third, via these orders and discussions, to oversee the plans he put together and rectify them when they went wrong, as they usually would. Sherman proved brilliant at adapting his plans and never lost sight of the key objectives that had been laid down by superior authority. A commander is in the wrong place if he cannot carry out all three of these tasks, and Sherman's technique appears hard to fault.[34]

Even if judged as Confederate "successes," actions like Pickett's Mills could not overcome the inexorable course of attrition that worked in Sherman's favor. He had advanced 80 miles into Georgia, crossed two great rivers, and turned six immensely strong defensive positions—and avoided a heavy casualty bill. By the end of May Sherman's total casualties were 10,528 sustained from an effective strength on April 30 of 110,123; Johnston had lost 9,187 from a smaller "effective" force of 66,089. Sherman's losses were proportionately lower than Johnston's. He continued to set the pace and direction of this campaign; Johnston remained helpless to stop him.[35]

Sherman only claimed his due when he declared confidently to Webster in Nashville, in relation to progress in the theater of war for which he had overall responsibility rather than the conduct of local engagements, "In all encounters we had the advantage. All is working well." McPherson now occupied Sherman's left, with Schofield on the right; Thomas remained in the center. Sherman thought Johnston had withdrawn across the Chattahoochee but warned that "all must be prepared for battle at or near Kennesaw Mountain." He initially preferred to maneuver around Kennesaw if Johnston made a stand. He was, however, distracted by organizational and manpower problems arising from Alvin P. Hovey's decision to resign his command in a fit of pique over the composition of his division; he wanted to command all ten of the regiments he had recruited the previous winter rather than only five. Sherman also had to deal with the administrative complications arising from three armies constantly moving across each other's lines of communications, so that garrisons got mixed up.[36]

The advance resumed on June 10 toward Kennesaw Mountain in an attempt to probe the Confederates' distribution and provoke them to give away their artillery positions. The rain continued to fall in torrents—"villainously bad," Sherman called it in his report—and the ground became marshy, impeding maneuver. "One of my chief Objects," he reported to Halleck but really to reassure Grant, "being to give full employment to Johnston, it makes little difference where he is, so he is not on his way to Virginia." Sherman hoped to entice Johnston to spread out as much as possible, particularly on his right—the point of greatest vulnerability, in Sherman's view. His own maneuvers were circumscribed, partly because of his weakness in cavalry, but mainly because he could not advance eastward, where the roads were wider and the ground less entangled, because he needed to shield the Western and Atlantic Railroad and his new supply base at Allatoona. Logistics dictated that his axis of advance should run along the Sandtown road via Acworth to a junction at Gigal Church between Pine and Lost Mountains, along the west side of Kennesaw to Sandtown on the Chattahoochee. For several days, Sherman anticipated anxiously a Confederate thrust around the Union left into his rear areas.

Kennesaw Mountain actually comprises three linked hills. "Big" Kennesaw to the northeast side rises to about 800 feet and offered an uninterrupted view of every Union movement. "Little" Kennesaw in the center is only half the size, and Pigeon Hill on the southwestern edge at 200 feet half the size again. This chain of high hills presented a powerful but by no means insurmountable barrier to his advance.[37]

The weather improved, and spirits rose. Although Sherman believed dislodging Johnston by a full-scale assault might prove too costly, over the course of the next seven days a series of events began to change his mind. The Confederate lines were broken successively between Pine and Lost Mountains. Then on June 17 Pine Mountain itself was evacuated—but not before Leonidas Polk was killed three days earlier in an artillery exchange ordered by Sherman, who had no idea Polk was present.[38]

When the weather deterred personal reconnaissance, Sherman renewed his habit of carousing with the officers of the 15th Corps. His empathy with his old corps provoked counterproductive jealousy and niggling from formations in other armies. Sherman too readily broke a senior officers' rule that they should always keep a distance between themselves and the formations they had commanded previously.[39]

The topographical scene impressed Sherman as "enchanting; too beautiful to be disturbed by the harsh clamor of war; but the Chattahoochee lay beyond," he announced with a flourish in his report, "and I had to reach it." He ordered a closing up on the Confederate position at Kennesaw and proposed an advance down the Sandtown Road pivoting on the left. Once more he hoped a decisive action might develop rather than yet another major skirmish. If the Confederate line could be broken, he reasoned, then he could defeat Johnston north of the Chattahoochee, and the woods might "mask our movements." Schofield received instructions to "try to draw to your extreme right flank as much of the enemy as you can first." To reduce the pressure on Thomas, "force the enemy to strengthen that part of his line at the expense of his center." The cavalry defeat at Brice's Cross Roads (June 10, 1864) had heightened Sherman's sensitivity to the length and vulnerability of his supply line, which would be extended further if he bypassed Kennesaw Mountain; another force had to be sent out "to get on Forrest's tail" before he could turn back to give his full attention to this taxing campaign. He urged his subordinates not to be overanxious about maintaining "connected lines." All should "invite the enemy out." Overall, he aimed to shield his own supply line and bases and get between Johnston and his. He had noticed also, as he told Halleck, how his men were "timid in these dense forests of stumbling on a hidden breastwork." He was thus after all inclined to seek a decisive action at Kennesaw Mountain, particularly when he received news that Thomas's troops had crossed Noyes' Creek and seized a hill on its southern side at the base of Big Kennesaw, but its form as yet remained unclear. First, though, the Confederates intervened.[40]

Sherman's long-term thoughts were fixed on a drive to the Chattahoochee River. Major Dayton issued an order to Schofield that reflected his chief's increasingly sanguine mood: "It is manifest the enemy is retreating, act according to your discretion." Hooker's 20th Corps was sent to support Schofield's Army of the Ohio. Quite unexpectedly on June 22 three Confederate divisions of John B. Hood's corps "suddenly sallied" and attacked the Union right over open ground. When Sherman inquired as to what was going on, he received a melodramatic reply from Hooker. No less than three "entire corps," he cried, "are in front of us" at Kolb's Farm, and he expressed "apprehension" as to "our extreme right flank." As usual the missive smacked of Hooker's irritating combination of exaggeration laced with implied aspersions on his seniors, this time Schofield, plus boasts of his own resolution and success. His message caused Sherman much anxiety just at the moment when he believed that he had Johnston on the run. This anxiety should not be underrated. His armies were distributed along a front of some 12 miles, and Schofield's small, vulnerable force lay 7 miles from its railheads; should the advance grind to a halt Sherman's armies might be logistically compromised—especially if Johnston should envelop his vulnerable right and strike directly at Big Shanty, a railhead on the Western and Atlantic Railroad about five miles north of Marietta. He would then have maneuvered between Sherman's armies and Allatoona. This reference to "three corps" suggested a movement of Johnston's whole army.[41]

Sherman was relieved to hear that a "terrible repulse" had been inflicted on the Confederates at Kolb's Farm on June 22, who had lost a thousand casualties for no gain, with Union losses barely a third of the attackers'. Sherman nonetheless remained determined to stamp on what he regarded as Hooker's attempt at stirring up dissension among the senior ranks of his command. Hooker had a proven record in this last vice, and when they next met on the field that day , Hooker received from Sherman an upbraiding before his peers rather than praise for his victory. Even Howard, who disliked Hooker, judged that Sherman "was unaware of his own severity." Most historians consider Sherman's actions as either mean or personal, or at the very least unsavory. Certainly, Sherman could be vindictive, but superior commanders are perfectly entitled to take severe action if they believe the efficiency of the forces under their command are jeopardized by truculent, self-serving subordinates. Thereafter Hooker could hardly fail to understand where he stood.[42]

Sherman's conduct over the next two weeks is among the most controversial episodes of his entire career. It would appear that he had resolved to attack an immensely strong position at Kennesaw Mountain—an action foredoomed to failure.

The tactical success at Kolb's Farm actually had exacerbated, not relieved, Sherman's operational problems and thus complicated his strategic dilemma. Should he be checked or worse, Johnston might yet reinforce Lee in Virginia. Grant had by this date crossed the James River, but his advance had been stymied at Petersburg. Would Lee launch a counterstroke? Sherman quickly reached the conclusion that Johnston could not be relied upon to launch another attack like Kolb's Farm. Union troops were tantalizingly close to their objective, the next railhead at Marietta, which lay only 2 miles behind Kennesaw Mountain. But Sherman could no longer assume that Johnston would continue to retreat; he could not know that Hood's attack had not been authorized by Johnston. Yet he had to confront the possibility that if he risked another turning movement around the Confederate left, Johnston might ambush it, with disastrous consequences. Sherman could not mount a dual envelopment of both Confederate flanks—they were simply too distant for the force at his disposal. An observation in Sherman's report thus acquires an added significance. He wrote shortly after the battle that "I perceived that *the enemy* and our own officers had settled down into a conviction that I would not assault fortified lines. All looked to me to outflank." Sherman thus worried that Johnston counted on it, too.[43]

The numerous obstacles that continued to impede the sustainability of the campaign formed another formidable pressure on Sherman's range of choice. His logistical reserve had been depleted. His staff issued a series of orders that attempted to reduce consumption and lay in a fresh reserve. Sherman needed a return to conditions when 130 railroad cars delivered supplies each day. Forrest's depredations handicapped these efforts, even though Lovell H. Rousseau, the commander of the District of Tennessee, continued to send an account of the measures he intended to take to entrap him. But the incessant rain meant the roads would not dry out quickly. In three weeks, Sherman counted 19 days of rainfall. In the meantime, Sherman's staff calculated that logistical consumption "issued daily [was] equal to from 50 to 75 per cent over the effective strength." "All other persons dependent on our supplies," an order continued, evidently dictated by Sherman himself, "are useless mouths" his armies could not afford to feed, and these "should be sent north of Nashville." All teamsters should have muskets "in easy reach"; the sutlers (an old enemy) had their shops at Big Shanty shut down because of their "outrageously" high prices and their temerity in bribing the conductors and managers to get their stocks transported instead of ammunition, provisions, or horse feed. Consumption of the first continued to be prodigious. The 92nd Ohio fired 24,000 rounds in one day. "Useless animals" were to be sent to the railroad garrisons; all remaining horses were to graze in the river valleys, as no more forage would be issued. Yet Sherman's armies could not stand still while logistical resources were refreshed. They had to move somewhere.[44]

In an important letter sent to Grant on June 18, Sherman still indicated no change of mind. He had gained, he wrote confidently, "all the high and commanding ground, but the one peak near Marietta, which I can turn." The dispatch of this letter, more reflection than reportage, had been encouraged by its recipient during their earlier frank discussions. Sherman thus offered a candid appraisal of all his subordinates. McPherson and Schofield received conditional praise. Garrard he considered "over-cautious"[45] and Stoneman "lazy"; the latter verdict was perhaps too harsh considering his health problems, though neither man was dynamic or aggressive. "My chief source of trouble," he confided, "is with the Army of the Cumberland, which is dreadfully slow." Sherman had few specific criticisms of Thomas, whom he had known intimately for many years, but disapproved instead of the lethargic, quarrelsome atmosphere that prevailed under his command.

Despite his own imperative orders, a series of opportunities had been squandered: "The whole Army of the Cumberland is so habituated to be on the defensive that, from its commander down to the lowest private, I cannot get it out of their heads." Sherman mentioned Hooker's delay at New Hope Church and then an unseemly squabble between two of Howard's divisional commanders the day before, just when he had got the line moving again. Alas, Marietta had not been seized, and the failure "gives time to fortify a new line"—and the whole process had to begin anew. Thomas's army appeared to him flabby, disputatious, and inert.

Thomas set a poor example, being overweight and fond of comfort. He defied Sherman's orders and persisted with large, lavish tents "and a baggage train big enough for a division." Thomas also tolerated too much whining and failed to push his troops with vigor. This letter would strike a chord with Grant, and not just because he disliked Thomas; he had faced similar problems in dealing with the Army of the Potomac's inertia. Castel's imputations that the letter represents an ignoble effort to blame his subordinates for his own failures—or worse, reveals Sherman's mental state to be comparable to his breakdown in November 1861—can be rejected with confidence. Sherman had already received confirmation of the Lincoln administration's satisfaction with the rate of his advance. Grant's own offensive had stalled. "I know you believe me too earnest and impatient," Sherman wrote warmly, "to be behind time."[46]

The tactical successes achieved by the Army of the Cumberland during the advance toward Kennesaw—and it did seize Confederate entrenchments that were "a thorn in the side of the enemy"—did not contribute to anything decisive. The opportunities frittered away allowed Sherman's problems to grow ominously: the strategic situation seemed to point to stalemate; the deteriorating logistical position was compounded by raiding Confederate cavalry, which "sweeps all around us, and is now to my rear somewhere"; he was dissatisfied with his sluggish lopsided series of armies. All these factors pushed Sherman to change his mind. At some point around June 23 he deduced that he could attack Johnston to advantage rather than turn his position; such maneuvers had become "routine."[47]

Sherman argued after the battle that an army "to be efficient must not settle down to a single mode of offence"; it must be flexible. He sought to force a decision and "for the moral effect to make a successful assault," and to prove to his troops that they could seize positions like Kennesaw Mountain. Sherman's error lay in the direction of the assault rather than in the decision to assault

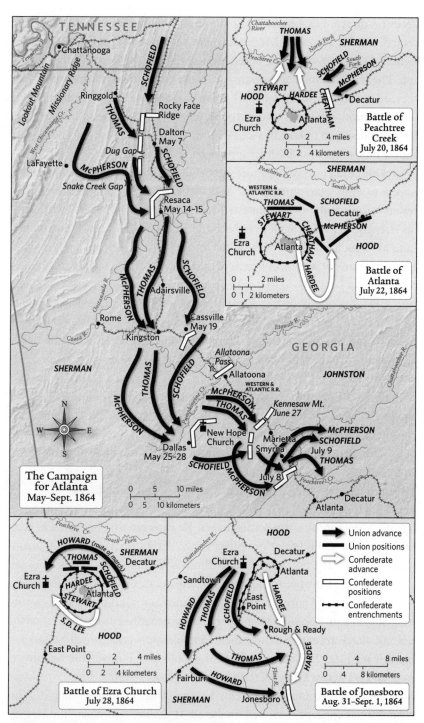

The Campaign for Atlanta
May–Sept. 1864

TENNESSEE

Chattanooga
Lookout Mountain
Missionary Ridge
West Chickamauga Cr.
Ringgold
LaFayette
SCHOFIELD
THOMAS
McPHERSON
Rocky Face Ridge
Dalton May 7
Dug Gap
Snake Creek Gap
SCHOFIELD
Resaca May 14–15

Oostanaula R.
McPHERSON
THOMAS
SCHOFIELD
Adairsville
Rome
Coosa R.
Kingston
Cassville May 19
Etowah R.
Allatoona Pass
Allatoona
WESTERN & ATLANTIC R.R.

GEORGIA
JOHNSTON

SHERMAN
McPHERSON
THOMAS
SCHOFIELD

Pumpkinvine Cr.
McPHERSON
THOMAS
New Hope Church
Dallas May 25–28
SCHOFIELD
McPHERSON
Kennesaw Mt. June 27
Marietta
Smyrna
July 8
McPHERSON
SCHOFIELD
July 9
THOMAS
Peachtree Cr.
Decatur
Atlanta
Chattahoochee R.

N
W   E
S

The Campaign for Atlanta
May–Sept. 1864

0   5   10 miles
0   5   10 kilometers

Battle of Peachtree Creek
July 20, 1864

Chattahoochee River
North Fork
THOMAS
SHERMAN
Peachtree Cr.
SCHOFIELD
McPHERSON
South Fork
STEWART
HOOD
HARDEE
CHEATHAM
Decatur
Ezra Church
Atlanta

0   2   4 miles
0   2   4 kilometers

Battle of Atlanta
July 22, 1864

Peachtree Cr.
SHERMAN
South Fork
WESTERN & ATLANTIC R.R.
THOMAS
SCHOFIELD
Decatur
McPHERSON
STEWART
Ezra Church
Atlanta
CHEATHAM
HARDEE
HOOD

0   1   2 miles
0   1   2 kilometers

Battle of Ezra Church
July 28, 1864

Peachtree Cr.
South Fork
HOWARD (route of march)
SHERMAN
THOMAS
Decatur
SCHOFIELD
Ezra Church
HARDEE
Atlanta
STEWART
S.D. LEE
HOOD
East Point

0   2   4 miles
0   2   4 kilometers

Battle of Jonesboro
Aug. 31–Sept. 1, 1864

Chattahoochee R.
HOOD
Ezra Church
Decatur
Sandtown
Atlanta
HOWARD
THOMAS
SCHOFIELD
East Point
HARDEE
Rough & Ready
THOMAS
Fairburn
HOWARD
HARDEE
Flint R.
SHERMAN
Jonesboro

0   4   8 miles
0   4   8 kilometers

Union advance
Union positions
Confederate advance
Confederate positions
Confederate entrenchments

Atlanta Campaign, May to September 1864

itself. He directed that his subordinates find a way to break Johnston's "left centre" that lay closest to Marietta, where he hoped to "cut off the enemy's right and centre from its line of retreat, and then by turning on either part it could be overwhelmed and destroyed." Such an advance was most likely to succeed toward Johnston's left flank down the Sandtown road; here Schofield, on the Union right, occupied ground about 5 miles from Marietta. But Sherman declined to take this axis of advance. In short, Sherman needed to show a little more of an indirect approach that he supposedly favored.[48]

Lacking cavalry, reconnaissance was fitful and mostly guesswork. Sherman hoped to gain both operational and tactical surprise, but his ambition rested complacently on the untested assumption that Johnston had shifted his strength to his left flank in order to deal with a Union envelopment. On June 24 Major Tom Taylor of the 47th Ohio led his skirmishers up Kennesaw Mountain and got within 150 yards of the top on the Union left with 15 companies; he was convinced that with support from the 17th Corps "we could have taken the mountain." Sherman was not informed of this development, an indication that his frustration with the lack of responsiveness of the chain of command was not misplaced. Kennesaw Mountain was not invulnerable. Schofield's advance also looked promising, but his one corps remained too weak to strike hard, and Sherman played with the idea of transferring the bulk of the Army of the Tennessee to the Union right. The move had one signal disadvantage. It would expose his base at Big Shanty to a Confederate riposte that would have utterly dislocated his logistical calculations. The line between logistical prudence and overinsurance is always fine. On this occasion Sherman took a circumspect view not to jeopardize all that had been previously gained—but at the cost of a greater operational success.[49]

On June 24 Sherman issued Field Orders No. 28, initially restricted to distribution among the army commanders. He directed that both McPherson and Schofield should feint on either flank, but McPherson should "make his real attack" at a point adjacent to Thomas with the 15th Corps. Thomas should attack "at any point" close to the Confederate center "to be selected by himself"; all would contribute to a simultaneous assault on June 27 beginning at 8:00 a.m. Sherman later amended the order to ensure that Schofield did not attack recently strengthened Confederate works, which he saw for himself on June 25. Instead Schofield should probe down the Sandtown road and get across Olley's Creek; "all dispositions," he instructed firmly on June 26, were "to induce the enemy to strengthen that flank tonight." The fundamental concept remained unaltered. "I shall aim to make him stretch his line," Sherman explained to Halleck, "until he weakens it and then break through."[50]

During the battle Sherman positioned himself on Signal Hill, a prominence in the center of the Union position about a mile in the rear, "where I will have a telegraph post." This position had many advantages, but there were dark mutterings that it was too close to the Army of the Tennessee. The telegraph wires were spread over trees and enabled Sherman to be in close contact with his three subordinates, thus unifying his direction, "spreading rays in fan-shaped order," as Howard puts it perhaps too lyrically. Patrols had to be sent out to prevent the trees carrying the wires from being chopped down. Sherman might have been the first commander to communicate via electrical current, but on this occasion the technological innovation conferred no advantage. Kennesaw Mountain might be "the great Battle" that he sought "on or near the Chattahoochee the passage of which he [Johnston] must dispute"—but it turned out very differently from how he hoped. Three divisions from three corps, Howard's 4th, Palmer's 14th, and Logan's 15th, were organized into tightly packed brigade columns. The ground over which they advanced endorsed Ambrose Bierce's claim that "no country is so wild and difficult but men will make it a theatre of war"; the soldiers clambered over steep and jaggedly etched terrain covered in rocks and brambles in the suffocating summer heat. Bierce, a veteran of this campaign, captures their valiant but superfluous efforts as Sherman's inflated hopes were burst by artillery fire and rifled-musket volleys. "When one fell, another, looking a trifle cleaner, seemed to rise from the earth in the dead man's tracks, to fall in his turn." Though they could close on the Confederate defenses, breastworks 6 feet by 9 feet, they could not fight through them, let alone break through.[51]

All Union attacks were repulsed. Thomas reported 1,580 casualties for the gain of a small bridgehead 75 yards from the main Confederate line. Total casualties were 2,051, the remainder falling on the 15th Corps. The proportion of officer casualties was high and included Dan McCook, Sherman's old law partner. In his report Sherman put the best face he could on losses that were small by comparison with Grant's and claimed the battle had "good fruits."[52]

He was right, for the battle conferred an operational success on Sherman's armies despite the tactical failure. Sherman's grip on the initiative remained unbroken; Johnston's local success gained him nothing. Schofield's brigades got across Olley's Creek and advanced 2 miles down the Sandtown road overlooking the Nickajack Valley and prevented Johnston from extending his line further. Sherman had taken some persuading that the attack on the Kennesaw line should not be renewed; he had told Webster on June 28 that he would "persevere," but once he grasped the full import of the chance that Schofield had conjured up, he jumped at it. He had no intention of brooding "under the influence of a mistake or failure." Thomas, the loudest of the voices arguing for cessation, contended that offering Schofield support was "decidedly better than battling against breastworks"; Sherman cautioned him, "The question of supplies will be the only one."[53]

On the afternoon of June 28 Sherman received a welcome missive from Halleck notifying him that Grant no longer thought it important for him to fix Johnston and "that the movements of your army may be made entirely independent of any desire to retain Johnston's forces where they are." Grant deduced that Lee could no longer sustain any reinforcements that might be sent to Richmond. Sherman's operations were therefore lent a greater flexibility. It is doubtful whether receipt of this order 24 hours earlier would have altered Sherman's decision to assault Kennesaw, as it did not materially influence the factors that led to his change of mind.

Sherman rode over to see Thomas to discuss matters in greater detail. He then issued orders to McPherson to pack his wagons with food and ammunition and be ready to move to the Union right. The whole process was speeded up by the telegraph, though couriers were still used. Thomas agreed to shore up Schofield's advance by sending another division to his right. It took longer to resupply the Army of the Ohio, and Sherman was under no illusions as to the risks he was taking. He hoped to cross the Chattahoochee and "destroy all his railroads before he [Johnston] can prevent it which will be a dangerous game for us both." But he calculated that with a further division arriving at Chattanooga, his lines of communication were secure. "I am aware of all the chances, but we must take the initiative and risk something or else attack him where he is now." If Johnston gave up Marietta, then Sherman could regain the railroad swiftly and sustain his operations south of the Chattahoochee more easily. Hence his fury when he discovered that DeB. Randolph Keim of the *New York Herald* had revealed in his column that Union forces could read Confederate signals. Keim was arrested as a spy.[54]

One of Sherman's most admirable qualities was his resilience, an ability to turn refreshed from setbacks and prepared to forge ahead and exploit any opportunities that awaited him. Each of his armies became infused with his energy, and depression was brushed aside. He managed each "as a unit" because all three could hold the Confederates while the others rallied to strike.

McPherson's entire army would be replaced in the line by Garrard's cavalry, move behind Thomas, support Schofield, thrust to the right, and thence close on the Chattahoochee via Sandtown. McPherson's preparations were not completed until July 2; he also had to check that the length of his pontoons was sufficient to cross the river. A further complication was an outburst of scurvy in the Army of the Ohio, quickly solved by the dispatch of fresh vegetables. Johnston atop Kennesaw espied McPherson's maneuver and quickly abandoned both Kennesaw and Marietta, withdrawing 10 miles to the south. At first light on July 3 Sherman peered through the spyglass he had erected close to his headquarters and saw Union skirmishers clambering up onto the summit of both Kennesaws.[55]

Sherman had warned Thomas, "Go where we may we will find the breastworks and abatis," unless they could move more rapidly. But at least his logistical problems were eased by Thomas's occupation of both Marietta and Big Shanty; his main bases could thus be shifted to Allatoona and Resaca. Even so, he still expected to lose up to six trains every week from guerrilla action, so he warned James B. Steedman, the garrison commander at Chattanooga, to give the security of the line to Allatoona the highest priority.

The next stage in his carefully wrought plan was the strengthening of Schofield's position. The buildup of his supplies had been delayed, and he lacked bread. In the meantime, Stoneman's cavalry division had made good progress and got across the Chattahoochee at Campbellton. Sherman rode to Marietta to supervise the logistical arrangements. Instead of finding rapid movement and urgency he found chaos and confusion; he was not pleased. He knew that Johnston had deployed slave labor and that it was likely that he would make a stand on the western bank of the Chattahoochee. Schofield received orders to continue pushing down the Nickajack Valley but received warning of Sherman's intention "to move you again over to the left" if a secure crossing point could be found.[56]

"You both see the whole game as well as I do," Sherman wrote to McPherson and Schofield while hinting at his displeasure with Thomas's sedentary performance. He intended Thomas to press "steadily down on the enemy" while McPherson enveloped the Confederate right flank by heading for Turner's Ferry on the Chattahoochee. Sherman encamped about 5 miles south of Marietta on the Sandtown road. "Let me hear every chance," he enjoined his subordinates, for he was close enough to keep a check on Thomas while simultaneously monitoring progress on the right. These broad maneuvers turned Johnston's first fallback position, crossing the railroad at New

Smyrna. He then withdrew back into even stronger works, the celebrated *tête-de-pont* constructed in a rectangle created by the flow of the Nickajack Creek parallel with the Chattahoochee before flowing into it. Resting on the west bank of the Chattahoochee, it was designed to cover with a single corps both the railroad bridge south of Vining's Station at Pace's Ferry and parry an assault at Turner's Ferry. The other two corps withdrew to the east bank of the Chattahoochee and were free to maneuver against any crossing point that Sherman might choose. Sherman deemed Johnston's works "one of the strongest pieces of field fortification I ever saw." Johnston boasted he could hold Sherman there for a month.[57]

Sherman's armies closed up, their commander determined that Thomas should keep Johnston's attention fixed firmly on the center. This scheme worked well because Johnston extended his lines; that sucked in more Confederate troops from his two reserve corps. Sherman undertook a close personal reconnaissance and narrowly escaped injury when a house he sheltered in on the picket line came under heavy bombardment and caught fire. He escaped in time, running "from tree to tree toward the rear." On July 5 Sherman started Garrard on a reconnaissance in force to the east toward Roswell Factory at the mouth of Rottenwood Creek, upstream of the *tête-de-pont*. Schofield was ordered to return via New Smyrna and Ruff's Station, 5 miles south of Marietta, and thence proceed to Roswell Factory as well. Sherman was greatly cheered during these tense moments by news of the sinking of the Confederate commerce raider the CSS *Alabama* off Cherbourg in France.[58]

"Atlanta is in plain view, nine miles distant," Sherman informed Halleck on July 5. By 9:00 p.m. McPherson reported that he had driven the enemy away from the opposite bank of the Chattahoochee at Howell's Ferry and secured it with a brigade. He then moved upriver to the mouth of Nickajack Creek. Sherman ordered McPherson not to attempt a full-scale crossing "except it be certain of success"; so sure was he that the initiative remained in his possession that he predicted "that the enemy will preserve this order of things until we develop our game." He was so pleased about the game's progress that he even had kind words for Stoneman, whose cavalry division appeared to be making a positive contribution. "Keep up the delusion of our crossing below Sandtown [on the Union right] as long as possible," he instructed, "and I have reason to believe the enemy expects it. We have a nice game of war and must make no mistakes." For once in this campaign, the cavalry divisions were producing excellent intelligence. "Write again," he ordered tersely.

The crossing of the Chattahoochee River moved toward its climactic phase. Sherman concealed his forces skilfully, presenting to the Confederate army only a skirmish line and making effective use of the parallel valley eroded by the creeks. On the evening of July 7 he briefed Halleck on his concept, one that had come together during the previous week by careful thought and adaption to circumstances. He had no intention after Kennesaw Mountain of assaulting any of Johnston's fortified lines—"we must maneuver some." Nor did he intend to assault Atlanta directly, for he intended "to make a circuit, destroying all the railroads." "This is a delicate movement," he declared, "and must be done with caution." Not the least of the obstacles he faced was the "turbid and swollen" waters of the Chattahoochee, gushing with heavy spring rains, but he expected the level to fall over the next week.[59]

Anxious, therefore, to strike "before the enemy made more thorough preparations or regained full confidence," he was delighted to receive a detailed report from Garrard in the vicinity of Roswell. He was confident that Johnston's cavalry had moved to the Confederate left and that all was quiet. He also detailed the destruction of several textile factories containing six months' supply of cotton that produced uniforms and ropes for the Confederacy. One factory owner had the temerity to fly the French flag over his property in a desperate effort to preserve it—to no avail, for all were put to the torch. Sherman was delighted once more. Garrard made a rare entry into Sherman's good books; he would later attest "not only respect but affection" for him—though this feeling would not endure. Garrard received further orders to "watch well the crossing" and to conceal his force but seek out any usable fords. In the early hours of July 6, the Army of the Ohio set off for Roswell via Ruff's Mill and Ruff's Station. Sherman's duties as a military division commander extended well beyond Georgia. On that same day he was busy with operations in Tennessee against Forrest, urging A. J. Smith to crush him. As the campaign developed Sherman was content, as he informed Grant, "that all my people are well employed."[60]

Schofield's crossing could not be straightforward because he had to use Thomas's pontoon train, and this had to be brought up from the Army of the Cumberland's rear areas. Thomas meanwhile feinted toward Pace's Ferry, according to Sherman's instructions, with much fuss and bustle, "as if you were making preparations to cross there." Consequently, the location of the pontoon train required careful coordination. On the morning of July 7 Sherman ordered Schofield to secure a foothold, then fortify it "anywhere about Roswell or [the] mouth of Soap Creek." Schofield preferred the latter because the ford there was shallow and lightly guarded—the higher up the river, the weaker the Confederate presence—though this crossing point lacked a decent road for egress, despite the good defensive ground on the east side. Simultaneously McPherson was instructed to feint toward Turner's Ferry "and give it thunder." But he was cautioned to "keep your masses ready to move to the real quarter when required." Sherman pondered every contingency. If McPherson could not support Schofield, then Thomas should send him a division from Howard's 4th Corps. In the event, Schofield's crossing went without a hitch. Jacob Cox's division crossed covered by a heavy artillery bombardment; the Confederates fled; Cox entrenched, and a pontoon bridge was quickly laid. Sherman then sought information as to the quality of the roads heading for Stone Mountain.[61]

Such complex, intricate operations do not go completely to plan, and never have. Sherman had to endure an interruption of the telegraph beyond Dalton that cut him off from news of operations mounted by A. J. Smith and Rousseau in defense of his lines of supply. As a precaution Sherman decided to put further pressure on Johnston. All previous intelligence had pointed to a Confederate corps shifting north and east of Atlanta; he sent orders to Stoneman to shift south and west of the city, as far as Campbellton, "appearing suddenly" and then crossing to the east bank of the Chattahoochee. "Don't be absent more than four or five days," Sherman cautioned, "and keep me advised on all possible occasions."[62]

Despite irritating distractions, Sherman felt increasingly confident that he could disperse his line along the Chattahoochee and detach when required because the Confederates had burned their bridges and therefore could not cross back to the west bank to attack in force. Already by July 9 Sherman could utilize secure points of passage. Indeed, Stoneman queried via McPherson whether the commanding general wanted him to force another passage over the Chattahoochee and hold it near Sandtown Ferry, which McPherson "inferred you did wish done at present." Sherman in the meantime issued orders to Thomas to cross the Army of the Cumberland on July 14 at either Pace's Ferry or Power's Ferry. He had to wait with increasing impatience for the last piece of the jigsaw puzzle to be inserted on the board. A few days before, on the night of July 10, he decided to brief McPherson on his pivotal role in the operation. He first assured him that, although his mind was made up "as to the next move," he would welcome any suggestions that he might make. He reiterated his desire that McPherson "feign strong" at Turner's Ferry. Then, once Stoneman and McCook's cavalry had the front covered, Sherman would "cross all the balance of the army and advance its right [the Army of the Cumberland] on or near Peach Tree Creek, and the left (you) swing toward Stone Mountain." Operationally McPherson would cross the Chattahoochee by going back the way he had advanced toward it. In short, he would maneuver to persuade Johnston to weaken either his center or his flanks, "when we can attack."

He hoped to seize the Augusta Railroad if Johnston weakened his right or center; if Atlanta was denuded of troops "we take it." He also aimed to greatly reduce the likelihood of Johnston being reinforced by destroying the railroads around the city. If Stoneman failed to cut the railroad to the west before he withdrew eastward, it did not matter, as Lovell H. Rousseau, a fellow veteran of Shiloh, who had been ordered to strike at Decatur and thence go on to the Montgomery–Opelika Railroad in Alabama, could do so.[63]

At 8:00 p.m. on July 10 Dodge sent word that he had crossed the Chattahoochee, having completed a road bridge at Roswell with a 650-foot span—"a pretty big job," he reported with justified satisfaction. The imminence of a river crossing on a broad front required Sherman yet again to look to his rear, and he issued further instructions to Steedman, commanding the Military District of the Etowah. He urged Steedman to instill in his subordinates that infantry could defeat cavalry; if the Confederates did launch a large cavalry raid, it had to be defeated. Further, he must deal with the guerrillas severely. All efforts should also be made to stockpile forage and foodstuffs in case Allatoona was besieged. Fortunately, Sherman knew that the new garrison commander there could be relied upon, as John E. Smith was given the appointment. He warned Smith that Allatoona would assume "the first importance" in his future projects; because of its natural strength, it could be transformed into a "second Chattanooga" capable of sustaining operations south of the Chattahoochee. If at any point the local civilian population proved a nuisance, then they should be deported. No impediment should block Sherman's advance—the all-consuming object.[64]

Sherman advanced on a front of 30 miles with his three armies firmly in between the enemy and his lines of communication—but progressively endangering those of the enemy. Sherman had played an operational zero-sum game with Johnston based on superb logistical understanding. Marietta he designated the "grand depot," though stores were also delivered to Ruff's Station or Vining's Station to be picked up en route. All quartermasters were ordered to have ten days' supplies at hand to sustain the advance and were enjoined to be prepared for "prompt movement." He told Halleck he held the advantage—the initiative—and sought to keep it. In a letter to Grant on July 12, Sherman praised the logistical work that had sustained his campaign. Much of its excellence was due to his detailed care and attention.[65]

Maneuvers prior to a river crossing are invariably intricate and complex and require close supervision. Sherman ordered McPherson to ensure that his pontoon bridge arrived safely at Power's Ferry by July 12 so that Thomas could commence his crossing, which might take two days. "I only await news from Stoneman," he confided to Thomas, "to put General McPherson in motion." Thomas had also seized a Confederate pontoon bridge, which provided Sherman with a "spare one, which I want very much." Thomas was given control over all the pontoons—a major feather in his cap at a time when McPherson threatened to seize all the glory.

But word from Stoneman was slow in coming. In the early hours of July 12 Sherman felt he had no choice but to authorize McPherson to send the 15th Corps to Roswell; Blair with his 17th Corps remained behind to shield Stoneman, whom Sherman implored to report his activities "to me direct," but he had yet to receive from Dodge intelligence on the roads east toward Augusta and Macon—so the risk to both flanks was hardly insignificant. McPherson's troops were to travel back to the left flank via Marietta, swinging north and then turning south to Roswell, in all a march of 55 miles. McPherson should spare "men and animals as much as possible by marching in the early morning and evening." The men should forage in the countryside, "abounding in grass, grain and cornfields," as much as possible. Sherman hoped McPherson might visit Turner's Ferry briefly to confer and compare maps with Thomas and himself.[66]

At last, on July 13, Sherman received word from Stoneman, who had taken a "roundabout way" but reported that he had captured all Confederate scouts along the banks of the Chattahoochee. The 15th Corps had arrived at Roswell at 9:00 p.m., and Sherman hastened to order Logan to cross the river the following morning and advance 2 miles to the Brewer House. Garrard was to drive down the road east of Stone Mountain. Overnight Sherman found a release for the increasing tension by venting to Halleck over the order to allow civilian recruiting agents into his rear. The Sanitary Commission, a private relief agency for soldiers founded by federal legislation, he fulminated, was "enough to eradicate all traces of Christianity out of our minds, much less a set of unscrupulous State agents in search of recruits"—a gloriously impolitic and pungent opinion he would reiterate over the next month.[67]

On July 14 Sherman issued through Dayton Special Field Orders No. 35 codifying the whole plan and reminding his subordinates of their respective roles. Much of the special order repeated individual orders already received; but it stressed the importance of the war against the railroads in order to reduce Confederate operational and strategic mobility while increasing his own. Sherman still hoped that Stoneman might be able to use the extra pontoon bridge, cross to the east bank of the Chattahoochee, "and break the Atlanta and West Point railroad and telegraph." The general alignment would be "concave," each army remaining a discrete entity connected by pickets. If attacked, "the neighboring army will at once assist" any beleaguered force. Sherman did not expect Johnston to react until Thomas crossed Peach Tree Creek miles beyond the east bank of the Chattahoochee. To increase speed of movement he decreed that all wagon trains should be parked at the bridges or at Marietta.[68]

As Sherman's troops started to cross the surging waters of the Chattahoochee, he began to receive disquieting word from Grant both directly and via Halleck. The former was anxious that after Lieutenant Jubal A. Early's Army of the Valley had withdrawn from Washington, DC, it might be transferred by rail to Atlanta. Grant also expressed concern at the length of Sherman's supply lines and ordered that he rely more on subsistence from the countryside. On July 16 Grant telegraphed Sherman directly ordering that once he besieged Atlanta he should "set about destroying the railroads as far to the east and south as possible"; should Sherman be attacked, he should take up a strong defensive position and resist until Grant came to his aid. By July 15 Sherman had already picked up word of the sudden and ominous arrival of General Braxton Bragg in Atlanta two days earlier, presumably "to consult" Johnston. Bragg had been sent on a fact-finding mission by President Jefferson Davis to determine whether Johnston's plans were realistic and he the suitable general to carry them out. His conclusions would prove fatal to Johnston's position.[69]

On July 16 Sherman moved his headquarters to Power's Ferry, close to Thomas and toward the center of his command. On McPherson's front advancing from the Union left, all had gone well, with Logan and Dodge across safely. Blair was closing up, and Sherman ordered McPherson to ensure that all advanced in tandem to draw attention away from Thomas's crossing; on no account was he to advance on Decatur without Blair. In the event, Thomas's crossing went forward without incident. At 10:00 p.m. on July 17 Sherman reported proudly to Halleck that his entire command had got across safely and advanced from the Chattahoochee to Nancy's Creek in a "general right wheel." with Thomas on the Union right advancing toward Atlanta, Schofield in the center close to Cross Keys, and McPherson on the left heading for Decatur. Thomas had received instructions to make a "vigorous demonstration at Peach Tree Creek" but should not pause, as this might permit Johnston to shift eastward and increase resistance "on the other flank"—or even link up with succor sent from Richmond, Virginia. Three days before, Sherman had assured Halleck he did not quiver at the possibility of a Confederate attack, but his supply lines continued to be vulnerable to raiding Confederate cavalry. The latter were superior "in numbers and audacity" to his own. Stoneman reported he had failed to hit the railroad at West Point, fearful if he crossed he might not be able to return. This placed greater onus on Garrard to get east of Decatur—and he succeeded with the aid of Morgan Smith's infantry division and destroyed 4 miles of the Augusta Railroad.[70]

In a gossipy letter of July 16 Halleck expanded a little on his difficulties, stressing that he could take no responsibility and offer no advice except on administrative matters without Grant's approval. Grant, Halleck emphasized, displayed no "petty jealousies", but he was not sure of his staff; he probably had Grant's overprotective chief of staff, John A. Rawlins, in mind. Halleck was full of praise for the "energy and skill" of Sherman's operations, which pleased the recipient, as Sherman still held Halleck's military acumen in high regard. With the conclusion of the third phase of the Atlanta campaign, Sherman indeed had much to be proud of, even though—as always—things did not invariably go according to plan.[71]

Sherman described the campaign so far to his old friend E. R. S. Canby, then in New Orleans, as "one immense skirmish with small battles interspersed." Still, his impressive mental grip on the overall scheme of operations was such as to limit the harmful effects of miscalculations or misfortune: Sherman grasped the initiative and dictated the course of the campaign; his logistical understanding remained brilliant. With the crossing of the Chattahoochee, virtually without loss, Sherman brought this phase of the campaign to an end with a stunning feat for which he has received insufficient credit. There is one cardinal rule for river crossings, as for amphibious landings: cross or land where the enemy is not. In some ways, Sherman's achievement is even more impressive than Grant's crossing of the James the previous month, because of the close proximity of the enemy determined to resist his forays and superior in cavalry. Sherman outthought and outmaneuvered Johnston. And for once, in this series of intricate movements, his cavalry played a creditable role. But the Army of Tennessee remained intact and dangerous. The toughest fights were yet to burst unexpectedly on Sherman's three armies over the next few days and would test their commander to the uttermost. He was ready for the challenge whenever or wherever it came: "At all events you know I never turn back."[72]

12

Slogging on to Atlanta,
July–September 1864

Having gotten his armies safely across the Chattahoochee, Sherman made their coordination his immediate priority. Under his own signature he issued new maps—a pressing duty that would have to be repeated. Old roads, he averred, ran to Decatur, new roads to Atlanta. The country was "very hilly and stony"—"hollow lands and hilly lands," in the words of the poet W. B. Yeats—but would improve on the approaches to Peach Tree Creek and Atlanta. He had to gain the main road from Buck Head that crossed Peach Tree Creek at Moore's Mill, as this would serve as the main line of concentration for Thomas's Army of the Cumberland. This army, Sherman instructed, should drive on the city, "press close on Atlanta, but not assault real works"; Schofield's Army of the Ohio, the center, should advance toward Decatur; McPherson's Army of the Tennessee, covered by Garrard's cavalry, should meanwhile destroy all rail links between Decatur and Stone Mountain. Here Sherman obeyed Grant's orders on this matter. Once all lines of communication were broken, "all the armies will close on General Thomas, occupying the main roads east of Atlanta"; in effect his line would swing "across the railroad near Decatur." McPherson and Garrard would "risk much" in cutting the railroad links, and these operations should be completed by July 20.[1]

Sherman once more underlined to his subordinates the importance of speed, and phrases such "I want that railroad as quick as possible," or "Tell Garrard that it will be much easier to break the telegraph and [rail]road today and night than if he waits longer," litter his correspondence. Special Field Orders No. 37, issued by Dayton, enjoin that all units "not lose a moment's time until night," when the Union line should anchor on Pea Vine Creek and Decatur. Indeed, he assured Halleck that "I am fully aware of the necessity of making the most of time and shall keep things moving." Proceeding in pursuit mode toward an unbroken enemy entailed risks, as Sherman willed his armies to make "a bold push for Atlanta or very close to it" before they had linked up. "It is hard to realize that Johnston will give up Atlanta without a fight, but it may be so. Let us develop the truth."[2]

He ensured that McPherson, being most distant, knew his location at the "Sam. House, a brick house well known, and near Old Cross Keys"— about 11 miles from Atlanta and 11 from Roswell. On the evening of July 19 he contemplated a "move tomorrow directly on Atlanta." Yet on the same day he noted a headline in an Atlanta newspaper, "Hood succeeds," dated the day before Johnston's farewell order to his troops. He at once ordered Thomas to cross Peach Tree Creek. "This is very important, and at once, as we may have to fight all of Hood's army east of Atlanta." He also noted that Rousseau's raid into Alabama had caused deep alarm in the Confederate rear areas and might put pressure on Hood. This response is significant because it undermines the notion that Sherman was surprised operationally over the ensuing days.[3]

Sherman had certainly been under strain. Not only did he feel the burden of his responsibilities, but he was also harassed by worries at home. He had written to Ellen in July, but as he explained to Phil, "I really feel very uneasy about Ellen. ... I hear from all parts of the world daily, but can get nothing from Lancaster." If she was seriously ill, he wanted to know, "for I really have enough care and responsibility here without the uneasiness naturally resulting from absolute silence at home." He assured his favorite brother-in-law that "my health is good. I live out of doors under a tent fly, have good rations & ride a good deal," though "my office labors are not as great as the details fall upon army commanders."[4]

Ellen had been very heavily pregnant when they had last met in Cincinnati in the spring. She had actually written on July 7 detailing the birth of a son, Charles Celestine, in the early hours of June 11, which had been followed by chills and "such a raging fever that my life was in great danger for about a week," but thereafter she recovered fitfully. The child was named after both their brothers. Ellen proudly reported that Charles "thrives grows & fattens & is very strong and healthy" and very intelligent. "I have not told you how very strongly he resembles you in form face & shape of head. The likeness is striking & I am delighted to See it." Alas, this child did not live to see the end of his first year. Amid so many distractions, Sherman could not grieve for a lost child that he had not even seen, let alone held. This further loss, coupled with the death of her mother, provoked in Ellen psychosomatic fears for her own health, leading to a search for reassuring and better medical attention and a desire to live with her children in South Bend, Indiana, rather than with her elderly father. Sherman could not spare the time to strenuously oppose a desire he had previously encouraged.[5]

During the campaign Ellen had struggled to get word to him of the death of his elder brother James in Cincinnati. Ellen managed to attend his funeral. "Poor Jim" was Ellen's way of describing this alcoholic. "Poor Jim," Sherman echoed, "he was a good fellow," but then came to a matter-of-fact summation, "but John Barleycorn was too much for him."[6]

Sherman dutifully returned his thoughts to solving the military riddles before him. His new opponent, John B. Hood, nursed a laudable aim. He wanted to seize back the initiative by offensive means and drive Sherman back in disarray. He hoped to defeat him outright in the field, as his hero, Robert E. Lee, had managed to achieve many times in the past in Virginia though outnumbered, but Lee made this look deceptively easy. To paraphrase General de Gaulle, Hood's ambition was "greater than his discernment." Hood did not give much careful thought as to how he would achieve his aim except by imitating Lee's dazzling maneuvers and lightning combinations. Hood proved to be "a slippery customer," difficult to catch and capable of pushing "rapid rapier thrusts," but he also proved to be no Lee and lacked the services of a Jackson or a Longstreet. Moreover, Hood gave no thought to the effects of the Georgia heat on his troops marching back and forth. He therefore committed two "deficits of command," namely, "lack of balance" and "setting tasks which are outside the ability of troops to accomplish"; nevertheless, he could disturb the delicate balance on which Sherman's plans rested. Sherman did not know his new opponent and consulted his former classmate Schofield, who had graduated from West Point with Hood. What sort of man was he, Sherman inquired? Courageous, Schofield replied, "bold even to rashness." Brains are not everything in war, and Hood could certainly create "sparks," but his failure cannot be put down to fickle ill-fortune. His planning was not so subtle or clear-headed that he could make his own luck. Still, Sherman could not afford to underestimate him.[7]

An abiding anxiety was Schofield's numerical weakness, and Sherman ensured that Howard's 4th Corps remained in support "in case of need." As the third week of July approached, Sherman made the perfectly logical deduction that with "the whole of the rebel army ... about Atlanta," with its strongest fortifications positioned along Peach Tree Creek, the best approach to the city lay from the east in order to get "within cannon reach of the town"—but simultaneously Sherman had to ensure that he could link up with Thomas's Army of the Cumberland. "If Hood fights behind forts close to the town, I will swing in between Atlanta and the river; but if he fights outside, we must accept battle." Thomas reported that the crossing of Peach Tree Creek would

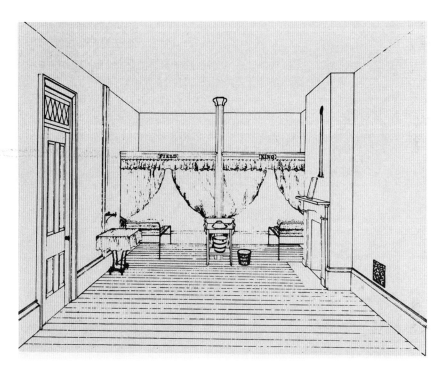

West Point accommodation was deliberately hardy, all cadets rolling up their bedding on easing and emptying the "slop bucket" positioned underneath the wash stand. US Military Academy Library, Special Collections.

Sherman climbed these steps on arrival at the United States Military Academy at West Point in June 1836. They were built through an overgrown garden laid out in 1798 and used as a refuge from the overbearing routine. US Military Academy Library, Special Collections. Photo from Jeffrey Simpson, *Officers and Gentlemen: Historic West Point in Photographs* (Tarrytown, NY: Sleepy Hollow Press, 1982).

Sherman, here assuming a Napoleonic pose, though as a commander he spent most of his time at a desk writing. Library of Congress, LC-DIG-cwpb-07136.

Sherman and his staff in May 1865. Library of Congress, LC-DIG-ppmsca-34053.

Henry W. Halleck, Sherman's closest wartime friend, who he felt betrayed him at the Civil War's close. Library of Congress, LC-DIG-cwpb-06957.

John A. McClernand might have been ambitious and bad-tempered but was not as incompetent as Sherman claimed. Library of Congress, LC-DIG-cwpb-01085.

George H. Thomas was a loyal friend and subordinate who guarded Sherman's back on the famous Marches. Library of Congress, LC-DIG-cwpbh-01069.

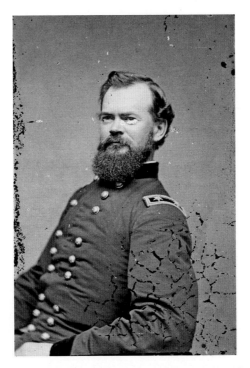

James B. McPherson, for Sherman always the "knight without fear and without doubt." Library of Congress, LC-DIG-cwpb-07051.

John M. Schofield was the most junior of Sherman's army commanders in 1864 but the cleverest. Library of Congress, LC-DIG-cwpbh-05934.

Edwin M. Stanton, Lincoln's Secretary of War, who came to personify for Sherman the vicious, unscrupulous party politician. Library of Congress, LC-DIG-cwpbh-00958.

Ulysses S. Grant as general-in-chief. Sherman admired his quiet confidence and calm good sense. Library of Congress, LC-DIG-cwpbh-00971.

Joseph E. Johnston, Sherman's wily opponent in Georgia, who proved reactive and lacking in enterprise. Library of Congress, LC-DIG-cwpb-06280.

Wade Hampton, Confederate cavalry commander, who set a pattern by accusing Sherman's soldiers of being "more savage than the Indian." Library of Congress, LC-DIG-cwpb-07541.

P.G.T. Beauregard had supported Sherman's prewar effort to create a cadet academy at Alexandria, Louisiana, but was his enemy at Shiloh, in Georgia and South Carolina. Library of Congress, LC-DIG-cwpb-05515.

Sherman's brother officer and friend Braxton Bragg, who opposed him on the fields of Shiloh, Chattanooga, and Bentonville. Library of Congress, LC-DIG-cwpb-07427.

"The Peacemakers," G.P.A. Healy's later reconstruction of the Conference of March 28, 1865, aboard the presidential steamer, *River Queen*. Sherman is doing most of the talking. The White House Historical Association (White House Collection).

Sherman, mounted on Duke, before Atlanta, a photograph he liked more than any other. Library of Congress, LC-DIG-cwpb-03628.

The Bennett Place, near Durham, NC, where Sherman negotiated his ill-fated armistice with Johnston on April 17–18, 1865. Library of Congress, LC-USZ62-108506.

Sherman succeeded U.S. Grant as general-in-chief in 1869, but his tenure brought him much frustration. Library of Congress, LC-DIG-cwpbh-00593.

912 Garrison Avenue, St. Louis, where the Shermans moved in August 1865, remained their first and only family home until June 1886. Courtesy of the Missouri History Museum, St. Louis. http://collections.mohistory.org/resource/146899.

This engraving from the 1870s reveals why Sherman remained for many an attractive presidential prospect. Library of Congress, LC-USZ62-112190.

The sheet anchor of his life, Ellen Ewing Sherman, who saved his career in 1861. This is the 1866 portrait by G.P.A. Healy. Smithsonian American Art Museum, Gift of P. Tecumseh Sherman, 1935.10.2.

The sculptor Vinnie Ream, , Sherman's mistress before she married in 1878. She failed to revive the relationship in 1885. Library of Congress, LC-DIG-cwpbh-03864.

Sherman in 1890 beginning to show the strain of old age, though only 70. Library of Congress, LC-DIG-ppmsca-46577.

be completed by the night of July 19–20. With his forces reunited Sherman considered he had "ample [men] to fight the whole of Hood's army, leaving you to walk into Atlanta, capturing guns and everything." Sherman had a big role in mind for Thomas's army for this battle because "with Schofield and McPherson alone, the game will not be so certain." He therefore decided to order the "universal movement" the following morning, instructing Thomas to communicate frequently—he would remain in the vicinity of Schofield's army in the center of his line—but also the point of greatest vulnerability should Hood attack. On July 19 Special Field Orders No. 39 was issued. Its most important instruction emphasized that "each army commander will accept battle on anything like fair terms," but if they reached "cannon range of the city" they should halt rather than assault, as at Vicksburg, "form a strong line, with batteries in position, and await orders." When reporting to Halleck, Sherman expressed optimism but not swaggering overconfidence.[8]

Sherman undoubtedly expected "a heavy battle," as he informed Thomas. He was pleased that the war of attrition against the Southern railroads to the east had made such excellent progress, because "as Atlanta is threatened the enemy will look to it rather than the river." What Sherman could not have predicted was that tactically Hood would try to have his cake and eat it, too. At 4:00 p.m. on July 20 Hood launched an attack on Thomas's Army of the Cumberland along Peach Tree Creek: the "blow was sudden and somewhat unexpected," Sherman admitted. Yet it was decidedly odd that Hood should choose to attack the strongest part of Sherman's line from his own stoutest defenses. He could have used these to create a reserve and shield a concentrated assault on Sherman's weaker lines to the east. Instead he carried out, with virtually no reconnaissance, two separate, costly, and unsuccessful assaults when a more carefully judged, concentrated blow might have enjoyed a greater chance of success. Resident in Schofield's sector, Sherman could not and did not play any direct part in these battles. Their conduct, in any case, lay in the hands of his army commanders. In his report he considered Hood's casualties at "just short of 5000" and his own at about 1,500. The first figure based on reports by subordinates was exaggerated, the true figure being closer to 2,500. The second is a slight underestimate, as Union casualties were nearer 1,600. These losses were not high by the standards of the bloody year of 1864.[9]

Hood's attack completely discredited Stoneman's earlier reassuring intelligence reports, namely, that the Confederate "army is utterly demoralized and easily frightened." Clearly, the absence of numerous and effective cavalry played an important part in the miscalculations made over these three days, as Union commanders were forced to make guesses. On the evening of July 20 Sherman confided to McPherson, "I think our only chance of entering Atlanta by a quick move if possible is lost." But he still urged McPherson's army to press forward, "for it will leave the enemy in a pocket whence they should not escape." On July 21 McPherson became increasingly cautious in carrying out these orders, convinced that Confederate infantry lurking behind Joseph Wheeler's cavalry were determined to attack him. This was a perfectly logical deduction and a realistic fear, as they would indeed attack him the following day, but on July 20, lacking Union cavalry to verify his fears, he could not know that his 25,000 men faced only 2,500 cavalry and one battery of artillery. Both Sherman and McPherson have been criticized for their lassitude on that day when opportunities to take Atlanta appeared obvious in retrospect. The real problem lay in communicating authoritative information in a timely manner and in its verification, a slow process despite technological advances.[10]

In accordance with Grant's earlier orders, Garrard had been sent to destroy the railroad for some 30 miles beyond Decatur, and the shift of Hood's troops to the east of Atlanta had not yet been reliably detected. At first Sherman jumped to the conclusion that "the enemy had resolved to give us Atlanta without further contest"—as rebel lines along Peach Tree Creek had been abandoned. His cavalry commanders had, after all, predicted this eventuality. Orders were issued that required a "vigorous pursuit." The Army of the Tennessee should pass "to the south and east of Atlanta, without entering the town. You will keep a route to the left of that taken by the enemy," McPherson instructed Logan, whose 15th Corps formed the vanguard, "and try to cut off a portion of them while they are pressed in rear and on our right by Generals Schofield and Thomas."

At 10:00 a.m. on July 22 Sherman and Schofield were examining "the appearance of the enemy's line" on some open ground opposite the distillery; "we attracted enough of the enemy's fire of artillery and musketry to satisfy me the enemy was in Atlanta in force and meant to fight," Sherman wrote, so the two generals repaired to the headquarters he had established at Thomas. C. Howard's house, the home of a well-known whiskey distiller, a prominent white building sitting on a knoll. Shortly afterward they were joined by McPherson and his staff. Though Sherman had expressed some dissatisfaction with the speed of his advance earlier, McPherson appeared in "excellent spirits," and the topic of Hood's character came up again. Sherman and McPherson agreed an "unusually cautious" approach was required since Hood, though of no "great mental capacity," displayed courage, determination, and impetuosity. As these views chimed with Schofield's, Sherman adopted them as his own. He did not meet Hood until some years later.[11]

McPherson had another, more specific matter he wished to discuss. Grant had already warned Sherman that Johnston's dismissal indicated "that Atlanta will be defended at all hazards," though in the event this order took several days to arrive. Intent on determining that Hood could receive no reinforcements, Sherman had ordered that Grenville Dodge's 16th Corps should aid Garrard in destroying railroads. McPherson disapproved of this order and sought to transfer the 16th Corps to shore up his exposed left flank. That morning Logan had reported taking prisoners from Cheatham's corps of Hood's army, spotted advancing in that direction "in order to attack [later] in the morning." Sherman indicated that he would be amenable to offering McPherson discretion as to when the change of orders could be implemented. The pair took a short walk to the tree where Sherman kept his map. It was here that he took the opportunity to brief McPherson on a plan that he had mentioned to Halleck two days before. He intended to swing the Army of the Tennessee back to the Union right "around between him [Hood] and his only source of supplies, Macon." An outbreak of firing from the direction of Decatur disturbed this discussion, which indicated that it had not occurred a minute too soon. In his *Memoirs* Sherman presents a memorable description of McPherson "in his prime," handsome and well groomed in his uniform and gauntlets—no doubt a striking, dashing contrast to his usually slovenly chief. McPherson gathered up his papers, called the staff to order, and quickly mounted and rode off to investigate.[12]

The Special Field Orders No. 40 issued by Dayton on July 21 had stressed the renewal of the attack on Atlanta, not resuming a defensive stance. McPherson and Schofield (supported by Howard's 4th Corps) were to advance their lines but were enjoined to "keep their men well in hand to repel assault, or to follow to the enemy's main line of entrenchments." With Garrard absent, Hood had indeed succeeded in almost enveloping McPherson's left. With a little more planning and careful supervision, Hood might have succeeded in dislocating McPherson's advance. Still, as he had already been repulsed by Thomas, it was a legitimate assumption that he lacked the resources to make a second effort in the opposite direction. On the morning of July 22 Sherman had apprised Thomas of his intention to "throw McPherson again on your right to break the Macon [rail]road." Sherman's thoughts, quite correctly, were focused on the operational level and the overall framework of the campaign; they were far distant from the tactical challenges about to face the Army of the Tennessee.[13]

Given his forces available and the errors made in their deployment, it seemed unlikely that Hood could overturn Sherman's operational design by tactical means, but he came close. Confederate troops emerged suddenly in waves from the woods and caught Blair's 17th Corps unawares, but thanks to good luck, the line was sustained by Dodge's 16th Corps, which had been marching parallel to the defenses and turned 90 degrees to shore them up. During this crisis at about 11:00 a.m., McPherson had sent his staff back and ridden off unaccompanied down a narrow road, where he ran into a party of Confederate infantry. They signaled him to surrender, but McPherson refused, raised his hat in salute, and galloped off in an effort to escape; the Confederates opened fire and hit him, and he fell from his horse. The bullet entered McPherson's back and lodged close to his heart. He may have lived for 45 minutes, and his possessions, including his pocketbook and papers, were rifled through, though later retrieved—to Sherman's relief. His horse, riderless and bloody, returned to the Howard house, so Sherman was forewarned of McPherson's fate.

Lieutenant Colonel William T. Clark, McPherson's adjutant general, hastened to warn Sherman, as increased fire rained down on the Howard house. Sherman was, of course, appalled to hear his news but immediately diverted him to tell Logan that he should assume command and continue the fight regardless—orders that Logan carried out with exemplary courage and vigor. Within the hour McPherson's body had been recovered and brought back to the Howard house. It was placed on a door taken from its hinges; Sherman was visibly upset by its sight, passing up and down as it was examined by a doctor, but he remained—as ever at the critical moment of crisis— sufficiently possessed to bark out a series of orders as a stream of exaggerated, doom-laden reports and predictions flooded in. The assault on the Howard House grew to such intensity that it seemed likely it might catch fire; he ordered the body to be taken back to Marietta and thence to Chattanooga for burial near the McPherson family home.[14]

The battle raged for the remainder of the day and became fiercest during the afternoon along a line anchored on Bald Hill. At one point the Confederates pierced the Union center. Sherman watched this action with mounting consternation from the Howard house. He personally ordered Charles R. Woods's division of Howard's 4th Corps to advance, throw back the Confederates, and plug the gap. This reinforcement arrived at a timely moment for the Army of the Tennessee. Logan—"a human hurricane on horseback"—with his charismatic ability to rally his formations, organized a counterstroke. Sherman had immediately ordered Thomas to mount a diversion, but he was reluctant to do so in case he provoked attacks on his own front. In the early hours of July 23 Sherman ordered him "to relieve it [the Army of the Tennessee] by an actual attack or strong demonstration on the right." But Thomas made no attack on this sector, and his dispositions "remained unchanged" for the rest of the week. Further offensive movement would have to wait until "we get our cavalry in hand and position." The readjustment could be made thanks to Rousseau's arrival on July 22 with 2,500 men and two artillery pieces at Marietta, having destroyed 35 miles of railroad, a number of bridges, and other installations and supplies at the cost of a dozen men killed and 30 wounded. Rousseau received orders to relieve Stoneman, who, in turn, could relieve Garrard, who could be assigned to operations before Atlanta. The Confederate onslaught abated. Despite the urging of Schofield, supported by Howard, Sherman failed to launch a counterstroke after Hood's repulse. Confederate cavalry had broken into Decatur but then been driven out, and only a handful of wagons had been lost. The Army of the Tennessee had sustained 1,989 casualties but had inflicted about 7,000 on Hood's troops. The erosion of Confederate strength would enable Sherman's ambitious maneuvers to be carried out with less risk and thus played to his operational strong suit.[15]

The days after the Battle of Atlanta were taken up with the backwash of McPherson's sudden and untimely death. Sherman's first task was to report formally to the adjutant general, Major General Lorenzo Thomas. "I, his associate and commander," he admitted, "fail in words adequate to express my opinion of his great worth"—but of course he did find them. Sherman described McPherson as a "Gallant Knight and Gentleman," a theme of all his communications thereafter. He could think of "few who so blended the grace and gentleness of the friend, with the dignity, courage, faith and manliness of the soldier." Sherman had consciously groomed him to take his and Grant's place, but it might be doubted, despite his nobility of character, whether he was equal to their abilities or even those who eventually succeeded them. McPherson was a sound but not brilliant tactician and cautious to a fault; he lacked Grant's political subtlety and Sherman's operational inspiration. His loss also released tensions and sorrow in Sherman repressed since Willy's death. Ellen discerned the intimate connections between Willy's demise and

McPherson's. "He is associated in my mind with dear Willy," she revealed frankly, "because of our visits to his house which was the last house that ever Willy was in—his table was the last at which he sat." Ellen's letter contained a warm but painful reminiscence of Willy and his red hair that concluded with a reiteration of guilt: "I hate myself when I think of it and it grieves me to death to think what I might have done had I been more keen sighted and more anxious."[16]

This recollection was no less painful for Sherman, who brooded over his own fated end. He stressed to Ellen that McPherson's death was an unfortunate accident, not the result of fecklessness: "With all the natural advantages of bushes, cover of all kinds we must all be killed." It is doubtful that this remark gave Ellen any reassurance. But his mind continued to work ceaselessly despite his grief. "These fellows continue to fight like Devils and Indians combined, and it calls for all my cunning and Strength." As the forts around Atlanta were "really unassailable," he would "gradually destroy the [Rail] Roads which make Atlanta a place worth having." To carry out this maneuver, he needed a man he could trust. "I think I shall prefer Howard to succeed him [McPherson]." And this disruptive, final decision could be delayed no longer. He did not agonize over this matter.[17]

Indeed, Sherman had already requested Howard's services two days earlier in a letter to Halleck. He conceded that Logan had done well in the Battle of Atlanta. Yet his detailed instructions to Logan prior to the shift of the Army of the Tennessee to the right flank betray not distrust of his military judgment so much as distrust of his military knowledge and ability to direct his army in its entirety. There also existed a natural competition between Blair and Logan, both politicians, and Sherman feared an outbreak of complaint and recrimination if Logan took command. Sherman put it plainly in his *Memoirs* when he claimed that if he needed to create "a perfect understanding among the army commanders," that is to say, cultivate an atmosphere of mutual trust, this could be best attained by the appointment of a regular. George Thomas did not believe that Logan should be confirmed in his appointment, and his opposition was important if Sherman veered toward his confirmation, though there is no evidence that he did. The other candidate was Hooker, who believed that the command should be his by natural right by seniority. His record as a corps commander had been good despite his propensity to stir up trouble. Daniel Butterfield had been forced to take sick leave on June 29, an unfortunate occurrence because he usually acted as a sobering influence on Hooker's wilder pronouncements.[18]

Howard's *Autobiography* is rather discreet on the matter, only concerned to acquit himself of self-seeking or adherence to a supposed West Point clique or distinct military class. Grant indicated that, as Sherman had "conducted his campaign with great skill and success," his recommendations for senior commanders should be accepted without demur. "No one could tell so well as one immediately in command," he concluded, "the disposition that should be made of the material at hand." Lincoln and Stanton followed his guidance, but his intervention offers no evidence of a West Point conspiracy, only standard practice. Halleck informed Sherman that Howard should assume the command on the afternoon of July 26. Sherman notified him immediately for, as he told Thomas, "I want him in his new command at once"—as important tasks were impending. Howard was called to his headquarters to hear the good news, and on departing, Sherman added, "I will ride with you and explain my wishes."[19]

Hooker could not abide this news—to be passed over in favor of the former subordinate whom he had always blamed for his defeat at Chancellorsville. "Justice and self-respect alike require my removal from an army in which rank and service are ignored," Hooker wrote tartly in a letter of resignation he had threatened and Sherman did nothing to delay. Hooker had too hurriedly mounted his high horse, because he had not yet been placed under Howard's command. He was ordered to leave forthwith to avoid any "delay in filling the vacancy." Sherman wrote to a sympathetic Halleck that he had not dreamt of replacing McPherson with Hooker, for "he is not qualified or suited to it. ... He is not indispensable to our success. ... He is welcome to my place if the President awards it"—though Sherman knew there was no chance of this. He had recently participated in correspondence with Lincoln over the promotion of senior officers who had left the front for reasons other than wounds, their number now augmented by both Butterfield and Hooker; Sherman feared that his subordinates would gain the impression that promotion "results from importunity and not from actual service." Lincoln reassured Sherman on this matter and offered his "profoundest thanks" for the campaign to date. Thomas suggested David Stanley to replace Howard, and Sherman wanted Henry Slocum, then commanding at Vicksburg, to replace Hooker. Slocum was tough, sensible, and cooperative, and he had worked well with Canby sorting out the jurisdictional tangles along the Mississippi River. As for Hooker, he did not command in the field again.[20]

How would Logan take to being commanded by another? Hooker probably expected Logan to behave as petulantly as he had done. Logan did ask to remain in command of the army until the campaign concluded. Sherman considered this administratively impossible, as decisions had to be taken on discharges, furloughs, and other detailed business that could not be neglected and could only be approved by the departmental commander. Logan, who was merely "commanding the Army of the Tennessee in the field," had to revert to corps command. He took this disappointment stoically and continued to serve conscientiously. Sherman wrote him a kind personal note of thanks, urging him to take a rest and commiserating with him on his disappointment. He insisted that "I will not fail to give you every credit for having done so well" and tried to let Logan down as gently as he could. Indeed, three weeks later he wrote to Halleck stressing how much he had admired Logan's conduct and determination to "do his duty like a man." He wanted to reward him further but felt at a loss as to how he could do so, except in the one way he had to deny. He hoped that Logan would be content with the approbation showered on his noble acts "gracefully admitted by his superiors in authority," but was this enough? Behind Logan's dutiful front, however, lurked festering resentment; he suspected a West Point conspiracy to deprive him of his rightful command. What Marcus Cunliffe calls "an almost obsessive grievance" grew in proportion with the passage of time.[21]

Preparations had already been set in motion for the ambitious transfer of the Army of the Tennessee back to its former position on Sherman's right as the drama over Hooker's resignation played itself out. While the position was reviewed, Sherman instructed Logan, "we cannot be better employed than in rendering the Atlanta and Augusta [rail]road useless," and one division continued this work 24 hours a day. Logan also needed to mount a demonstration to prepare for Garrard's return. Once that was completed, Logan should send his wagons behind Thomas's formations back across the Chattahoochee at Pace's Ferry and Buck Head, drawing his supplies over the railroad bridge. Then he should drive "to the extreme right, to reach, if possible the Macon [rail]road, which you know to be the only road by which Atlanta can be supplied." Logan was ordered to be audacious and confident "to show him [Hood] that you dare him to the encounter." If Hood should sally out, this could only add to Sherman's overall advantage. "I would rather Hood should fight it out at Atlanta," he briefed Grant, "than retreat towards Macon." Sherman intended to leave "a strong line of circumvallation and flanks" so as to build up as large an infantry column as possible; then, with the cavalry, the Army of the Tennessee would "swing round to the south and east" to gain control of the railroad at East Point.[22]

The operational objective was twofold: first, the seizure of the railroad emanating from Macon that would render Atlanta untenable, or at any rate force Hood to choose between them—or perhaps fight for both at a disadvantage. As Sherman explained to Halleck, "The cavalry will have to fight the enemy's cavalry, and we can hold the infantry and artillery to Atlanta and force them to extend and choose between Atlanta and East Point." And even more pointedly to Schofield: "I took it for granted the enemy would shift to this flank"—after all, it remained Hood's strongest position, but could he be dislodged? Out of this dilemma emerged the second objective. Sherman intended to make it as difficult as he could for Hood by frustrating him at every turn, so that he would be unable to choose a straightforward course of action and always confronted by an agonizing choice. Sherman intended to exploit the Turner's Ferry road, 4 miles from the Chattahoochee and 4 from the city, to "extend on a ridge due south, so that by facing left the right of our line will be a strong threat to East Point." In short, in an exercise of operational art of the highest order, the Confederates would be forced to "shift to this flank, but gradually we can make him extend till he is out of Atlanta." In the meantime, Schofield distracted Hood's attention to the center, reporting that Confederates were still there "in force."[23]

The campaign now entered a critical phase and assumed an increasingly political significance once Grant's operations were bogged down in front of Petersburg. Sherman's front continued to display movement—at least in the right direction—and the president looked for it desperately during this miserable summer. Given the length of Sherman's line of communications and the area of enemy territory traversed, it was vital that Sherman did not lose. He continued to win by not losing. Sherman had grasped this relationship by the summer of 1864. Its political value to the Lincoln administration continued to grow in significance during the month of August. At the beginning of this month it seemed impossible that Lincoln could win reelection—an eventuality totally dependent on the course of military events. Sherman did not need to win tactically, because such actions were pregnant with risk, could turn out to be pyrrhic, and could worsen his manpower and logistical problems. Far from halting Sherman's progress, the Battle of Atlanta was in reality a series of tactical successes and in total an operational triumph—clearer cut than anything won by Grant in Virginia.

Sherman's campaign demonstrated the value of an offensive strategy and operational plan combined with defensive tactics—notably in trench warfare. He had not set out to mount operations of this kind, but he had quickly grasped how such a combination aided his purpose. He exploited the tactical defensive so that he might take greater operational risks. What Sherman wanted to avoid was fruitless attacks on Atlanta's defenses or being repulsed in the field; by this date a setback of any order might not only endanger the integrity of his armies but would certainly seal the doom of the Lincoln administration. This attitude explains Sherman's reluctance to gamble everything on a single throw of the dice. Two examples are noteworthy. He passed up the chance to assault—Castel claims "enter"—Atlanta on July 22. Thomas had made no plans or preparations for such an operation and displayed a marked lack of enthusiasm for carrying it out. Sherman was right to err on the side of caution and refrain from insisting that such an attack be carried out. The second concerned Sherman's indifference that day to the urgings of both Schofield and Howard that he smash the Confederate left on Bald Hill with the 23rd and 4th Corps. Without thorough reconnaissance and better intelligence, both operations were inviting but hazardous; it could not be guaranteed that they would have been more "decisive" than anything carried out at Vicksburg, where Grant had been repulsed twice despite assurances that glittering success awaited him. Besides, it was essential for the morale of the Army of the Tennessee that it fight and win its victory unaided before setting out on the ambitious operation he already had in mind for it.[24]

Such considerations demanded of Sherman tactical caution; he needed to guard his freedom of maneuver as an alternative to the set-piece siege that had been forced on Grant. He lacked the support of the US Navy that had given Grant such valuable assistance at Vicksburg and would do so again at Petersburg. Sherman's ceaseless manpower problems and the degree of logistical risk he had taken persuaded him to put his dice away. Another danger he wished to avoid at all costs, far from the sea and alert to the possibility that Hood might require reinforcements, was the threat that the besieger might be put under siege. Any miscalculations on his part could lead to this disastrous transformation very rapidly. Sherman had to be sure, in Thucydides's words, that he could "accomplish something for the furtherance of the war that would be worth the risk." Temperamentally, Sherman shied away from tactical risk and preferred operational risk. "If you can keep away [Confederate] reinforcements all [will be] well," he assured Grant.[25]

The Army of the Tennessee's advance had already begun in the early hours of July 27, and Howard, accompanied by Sherman and some of his staff, caught up with it later that day. At the limit of Thomas's right flank, guarded by a series of small forts, Sherman directed Howard on "to a high point" and indicated a "wooded ridge" where he wanted Howard's army to take up position on a perpendicular line to Thomas. "This ridge ran nearly north and south," Howard recalled. Sherman believed that occupation of this long extension would enable Howard "to get hold of Hood's railroad there before Hood could extend his trenches." Sherman predicted that his previous defeats would deter Hood from launching more attacks. Lacking cavalry (which had departed on raids on the railroads to the southeast of Atlanta), Howard was less sure. He offered an alternative plan that would leave his right flank less exposed—the reminiscence of the painful loss at Chancellorsville was rarely distant from his thoughts. He would deploy his divisions in echelon, "moving up in succession, so that each successive division would protect the flank of the proceeding." Sherman thought this unnecessary but gladly allowed Howard to "deploy [his] army in [his] own way."

Howard proved right and Sherman wrong. A Confederate corps attacked Howard's temporary works at Ezra Church in their customary style: uncoordinated and piecemeal waves that were driven back by admirable fire discipline. Union casualties were 632 but Confederate almost five times as great, at over 3,000. This was a ratio of loss that Sherman could sustain without difficulty. On the field and in his report, Howard's generous spirit made many friends. He paid tribute to Logan's drive and skill. After the battle the men cheered him, Sherman noted, "in the most affectionate manner, and he at once gained their hearts and confidence. I deem this a perfect restoration to confidence in themselves and leader of that army."[26]

Over the next week Sherman paid close attention to the brittle morale of the Army of the Tennessee. Ambrose Bierce once remarked sagely, "An army has a personality. Beneath the individual thoughts and emotion of its component parts it thinks and feels as a unit." The whole was indeed greater than the aggregate of its formations, and in it "lies a wiser wisdom than the mere sum of all that it knows." He also remarks sardonically on how a commander's visits were accompanied "by their retinues of aides and orderlies making a great jingle and clank," but Sherman's visits were more low-key than was customary. Tom Taylor received one on July 23. "Reported twice that the rebels are coming. Under arms but no one came. ... Gen'l Sherman came around, talked with the boys & I and gave me some useful hints." Sherman the teacher was never far distant, but the very informality of these visits provoked jealousy among the armies that felt they did not receive comparable attention.[27]

In the last days of July, the movement of the right continued. Sherman sought to "draw the enemy out of Atlanta or force him to attack, which is to be desired." His operation was remorseless, but the wear and tear began to take its toll on his armies and himself. After a close inspection of his line Sherman discerned that the right flank after Ezra Church was "too refused to be a threat"—that is, pulled back. The Confederates had to be drawn out to East Point because the Atlanta works were too strong to be assaulted and he lacked the ammunition for a long bombardment. He thus ordered the augmentation of the right flank by Schofield's Army of the Ohio. Sherman also hoped to engage Hood's attention while the cavalry pushed south and east to strike the railroads and release Union prisoners of war from the camp at Andersonville. Things did not go well for the cavalry: McCook became heavily engaged, but a large proportion of his command escaped; Garrard was surrounded but broke out when he lost contact with Stoneman, who had himself been trapped and forced to capitulate. Sherman looked around for a more audacious commander than Garrard and selected Judson Kilpatrick, who had recovered from a wound sustained at Resaca, though Thomas was less keen about this choice. Sherman had also received notification that reinforcements lately arrived in Atlanta were mainly dismounted cavalry. He had to act energetically, "as the enemy will surely be on our railroad very soon."[28]

In the next phase of operations, Thomas would comprise the left, Howard the center, and Schofield the right. Sherman stipulated that two divisions, one from the 20th and the other from the 14th Corps, would serve as a reserve to protect the right flank "and during the action obey General Schofield's orders." Great difficulty would later stem from this brief order. Battle losses and sickness had accentuated the lopsidedness of his command, and he had to rely on detachments from the Army of the Cumberland to augment the other, smaller elements. These were resented, as service with other "outfits" was not always welcomed. Sherman stretched every sinew to keep existing forces in the field and reequip whenever necessary. On August 2 Sherman decided to allocate the 14th Corps to support Schofield. He sent a telegraph operator to the latter's headquarters, "so that he will have telegraphic communication from right to left." Alas, the communications the lines conveyed were not welcome.[29]

Overseeing this advance proved a frustrating experience. To begin with, on August 2-3 Sherman unusually complained of being unwell, but he ignoredthe symptoms and carried on working. Sherman wanted Schofield to cross UtoyCreek about a mile and a half from his initial position, occupy the Sandtown road, and cut the railroad. He worried over the unsettling quiet that seemed to accentuate the oppressive heat and humidity. Operations on August 4 advanced dreadfully slowly; he judged Palmer's 14th Corps "immovable" but he ordered their continuance the following day. The root of the inertia lay in Palmer's stubborn irritability. On the 4th Sherman had ordered Palmer, "Obey his [Schofield's] orders and instructions." Back came the rapid reply, "I am General Schofield's senior. We may cooperate but I respectfully decline to report to or take orders from him." "Cooperate heartily and the same result will be obtained," Sherman shot back. But much time was wasted in numerous, fussy exchanges between Schofield and Palmer. That night, quite exasperated, Sherman snapped, "I regard the loss of time this afternoon as equal to the loss of 2,000 men." In an effort to galvanize Palmer, he urged the seizure of his objectives "if it costs half your command." Given the weight of his manpower problems, Sherman did not mean this literally, but it is a measure of his annoyance.

Palmer might have been tired out by the incessant heat, or he might have longed for home and respite, but that was true of every man at the front. Palmer's pernickety preoccupation with status and his self-respect in the midst of important operations constitutes a severe neglect of duty. He even refused another direct order from Sherman to obey Schofield after the former had ruled that Schofield was indeed the senior. Neither Sherman nor Thomas thought Palmer equal to his duties. After a convoluted, legalistic exchange, Palmer resigned. The whole business could hardly have improved Sherman's opinion of the generals of the fractious Army of the Cumberland. He had already consulted Thomas, and Jefferson C. Davis received orders to take Palmer's place. After so much wasted time, Schofield's renewed assault on August 6 was repulsed with 300 casualties.[30]

After these frustrations a lull ensued. Sherman had already set in motion a refit of the cavalry; in addition, he initiated a whole series of measures to protect his supply lines, including alerting garrisons to the danger presented by Confederate cavalry and building blockhouses to defend bridges. Stanton wrote congratulating Sherman on his campaign "as successful beyond our expectations." He informed Sherman that Lincoln, at his request, had taken military control of the Northwestern Railroad from Nashville to Reynoldsburg. "Take your time," said Stanton, an unusual instruction devoting great approbation, "and do your work in your own way." Sherman still worried about the weakening of his armies as enlistments ended; losses ran from 300 to 1,000 per day. "Whilst mine dwindles thus," he warned his brother John, "that of the enemy constantly grows and may in the End over-reach me." Hood had used the Georgia militia cleverly, enabling him to concentrate his fighting power in the field. Sherman stressed the irritation caused to veterans by recruiting agents. "Our soldiers do not feel complimented that such stuff shall go into the count as par with them." This "stuff," he commented bitterly, "was the kind of trash [that] mainly fills our Hospitals and keeps well to the Rear." Sherman criticized "greed after gain" and crass commercialism, and some parts of his indictment carry weight. But his views also reflect his obsession that the South remained superefficient and committed while the North continued to be selfish and short-sighted and frittered its great resources away. "I sometimes think our people do not deserve to succeed in War. They are so apathetic."[31]

Sherman also snatched the opportunity to write a letter of condolence to Miss Emily Hoffman, McPherson's fiancée, whom Sherman had disappointed previously by his insistence that McPherson remain at the front. If he had permitted their marriage, then McPherson would have been by her side rather than laying in a makeshift coffin. This could not have been an easy letter to write, but he still managed to combine powerful yet controlled emotion and nobility of utterance. Admitting that nothing he could write could "Elevate him in your mind[']s Memory," he hoped that the detail he could add because of their long and intimate friendship "would form a bright halo about his image." He quickly returned to his favorite theme, with echoes of Geoffrey Chaucer, of McPherson as "the impersonation of the Gallant Knight." In Chaucer's fourteenth-century English: "He was a verray parfit gentil knight." Sherman also embellished a persistent theme in Civil War literature that remained dominant for nearly a century after the war's conclusion, namely, that extremists of both sides "by falsehood and agitation raise the Storm which falls upon the honorable, and young who become involved in its Circles." Sherman feared the proximity of his own end in 1864, but "while Life lasts I will delight in the memory of that bright particular star which has gone before to prepare the way for us more hardened Sinners who must struggle on to the End."[32]

Sherman made some similar remarks in a letter of condolence he wrote to William Harker, whose son, Brigadier General Charles G. Harker, had been killed at Kennesaw Mountain. After extolling his virtues, Sherman observed, "Death, you know, chooses a shining mark; and this has been exemplified in this campaign, for I have lost some of my best brigadiers and commanders." The ghost of Willy wafted once more over this vivid expression of heartfelt sympathy.[33]

Sherman had good grounds for thinking by the end of the first week of August 1864 that he had been more sinned against than sinning. He was under no illusion that the movement west of Atlanta had been temporarily stymied operationally. The war of attrition against Hood's communications had ground to a halt. Sherman had also received alarming news that the Confederates were repairing the Augusta Railroad now that he had shifted to his right. Most days he spent consolidating the lines. There had been few serious setbacks; even the initial repulse at Utoy Creek had been reversed the following day, and Schofield had managed to turn the Confederate left flank. Yet no overall breakthrough had been achieved. Sherman still calculated that "the enemy may attack us, or draw out," but of this there were as yet few signs. In a frank assessment sent to Halleck, he reiterated the central points that underlay his attritional outlook at the operational level. "We keep hammering away here all the time, and there is no peace inside or outside of Atlanta." He had closed up to the Confederate works in an attempt to probe for points of weakness and force Hood to commit his reserves in their defense "while we contract and strengthen." "I am too impatient for a siege," he continued, "but I do not know but here is as good a place to fight it out as further inland." On August 9 he intended to bombard Atlanta with two 30-pounder Parrotts and four 4.5-inch guns hauled up from Chattanooga, but the latter did not arrive until the following day. Once the Confederates were distracted by this weight of firepower, Sherman intended to make one last effort to attack Hood's railroads without recourse to his infantry. This required relying on the cavalry once again. "One thing is certain, whether we get inside or not, it will be a used-up community by the time we are done with it."[34]

Sherman reassured Grant that he would not be deflected by any of his problems, for "perseverance will move mountains." But he did admit that he felt isolated and should "be better advised of your plans and movements." In response Grant telegraphed to brief Sherman on the latest crisis in the Shenandoah Valley and promised "I will telegraph you in future more frequently than heretofore." In his turn Grant assured Sherman that his "progress, instead of appearing slow, has received the universal commendation of all loyal citizens"—for he still made *progress*. Sherman's positive spirit, buoyed up by Grant's praise, emerged toward the end of his reply: "Let us give those southern fellows all the fighting they want, and when they are tired we can tell them that we are just warming to the work." And with a nod to the vital political dimension during the presidential election nomination season, he wrote wisely, "Any sign of let up on our part is sure to be falsely construed, and for this reason I always remind them that the siege of Troy lasted six years, and Atlanta is a more valuable town than Troy."[35]

Sherman did admit one error in his correspondence, and one that earns admiration rather than exact censure. Sherman was not just a narrow, calculating technocrat, poring over railroad timetables and load estimates. In some ways, he revealed a deeply romantic nature. He had consented to Stoneman's ill-fated raid on Andersonville. "Nothing but the natural and intense desire to accomplish an end so inviting to one's feelings would have drawn me to commit a military mistake, at such a crisis, as that of dividing and risking my cavalry, so necessary to the success of my campaign."[36]

He was to repeat the exercise, as he had anticipated correctly that Joseph Wheeler's cavalry would attempt in August to strike at his communications. As the Confederate cavalry surged northward, Sherman relied on Rousseau to support the garrison commanders; the cavalry under his direction was to find Wheeler's flanks and hit them hard. Grant telegraphed from City Point to assure Sherman, "I think no troops have gone from here to Hood." He also praised Sherman's positive attitudes as "the same I have often expressed. We must win if not defeated at home." Grant thus dropped a strong hint as to the immense political importance of Sherman's campaign for the future direction of the war that depended on Lincoln's reelection. In this respect the "Glorious news" of the success on August 5 of Admiral David Farragut's exploit in entering Mobile Bay and closing the port offered a portent of things to come, though its practical alleviation of his logistical difficulties proved disappointing.[37]

Much of Sherman's attention continued to fall on the cavalry. He had eased Garrard out as too timid, but would Kilpatrick be an improvement? In any case, these changes were only marginal to his central operational problem. Communications were hampered by Wheeler's cuts to the telegraph lines. He preferred to have Wheeler in Tennessee than in Georgia, so long as the garrisons held fast. In the few quiet moments he could snatch, Sherman formulated a solution. He fell back on an idea he had expressed at the campaign's inception in the spring. He would advance around to the west of Atlanta and then push south to strike at Hood's communications. Such an audacious advance would depend on the defense of his logistical bases such as Allatoona. He explained his plans to Grant on August 10. His lines were now 10 miles long, and he could not extend them further without offering hostages to fortune. He needed to concentrate, shield the railroad bridges over the Chattahoochee with an entrenched corps, "and cut loose with the balance and make a desolating circle around Atlanta." He did not in-tend to assault Hood's defenses or even begin a regular siege. He only needed reinforcements because of the numbers of troops whose service had expired after three years.

He still expressed doubts that he could pull off this operation and complained to Schofield that he was in "despair of making a quick move. It takes two days what ought to be done in one." Schofield took offense when Sherman appeared to accuse him of lack of enterprise. What lurked behind Sherman's complaints was the fear that conditions might yet deteriorate, and "we are more besieged than they." He could not sit idly by and allow this to continue. So at the meeting held at 10 a.m. on the morning of August 13, Sherman informed his army commanders of his decision to swing around Atlanta to the west, advance south, and strike at the Macon Railroad below the city, cutting the West Point line en route. Three days later Dayton issued Special Field Orders No. 57 detailing how the advance should be executed.

Some of the measures would anticipate his later techniques. All super-fluous transport, materials, sick men, and horses were to be shunted back north of the Chattahoochee. The vital crossing points were to be guarded by the 20th Corps, which occupied Johnston's abandoned *tête-de-pont*. The Army of the Tennessee would advance on Fairburn, with the Army of the Ohio in support, in a great turning movement that would cut the West Point Railroad between Red Oak and Fairburn. The trains would advance be-tween the Army of the Ohio and two corps of the Army of the Cumberland, advancing as far as Camp Creek. The movement of six corps from three armies, a total of 60,000 men, would begin on the night of August 18, and the wagons would carry sufficient stores to last 15 days. Sherman did not spell out their operational objective, but the intention was to cut the Macon and Western Railroad around Jonesboro, 15 miles south of Atlanta. Once this line had been severed, Atlanta could no longer be held.[38]

Sherman wished to spare his armies such a hazardous and wearisome march in the summer heat if he could. He viewed the tactical task of cut-ting the railroad as "comparatively easy," whereas moving a large army even with reduced "paraphernalia" would not be; he had issued the orders for such a movement but would not undertake it "unless forced to do so." Joseph Wheeler's sudden though not unexpected thrust toward Dalton seemed to offer "the very opportunity we seek." The Union cavalry would thus be both unopposed and superior in numbers and if audaciously commanded might yet discharge its task. A Union cavalry victory might even force Wheeler's retirement and thus offer a bonus of eradicating the threat to his lines of communications. Sherman also thought he had found a suitably intrepid commander in Kilpatrick. Hardly one of Sherman's most intelligent subordinates, he was energetic, determined, eager to please, and inclined to bluff; Sherman saw through him, but he was always partial to likable, malleable rogues. Kilpatrick convinced him he could strike south to West Point and then proceed to dislocate the Macon line and return safely. Although preparations for the great culminating phase of the Atlanta campaign continued apace, he suspended it and gave Kilpatrick his chance. In addition, Garrard should mount a diversion toward Decatur and Stone Mountain to switch Hood's attention to the Confederate right. Thomas received instructions to supervise Garrard "minutely," as he lacked perseverance.

Kilpatrick broke camp on the Sandtown road on August 18 and headed south. Sherman issued his orders via Schofield. He wanted Schofield to carry out "a deliberate attack," not yet another cavalry raid; he tried to give Kilpatrick 12 hours "of uninterrupted work," as his "real task is not to fight but to work." Howard also mounted distractions "so that [Confederate] infantry cannot be spared to go out to protect the railroad." Kilpatrick lacked staying power to destroy substantial lengths of railroad track, as he had to keep dodging pursuers. On August 22 he returned to Union lines via Decatur, and Sherman summoned him to report that night. The outlook was at first favorable because trains had been seen reversing into Atlanta, presumably unable to complete their journeys. Never one to underestimate his achievements, Kilpatrick tried to convince Sherman that the damage he had inflicted on the Macon line (only complete for 3 miles and in parts for another 10) would take 10 days to repair. Sherman remained skeptical, and on August 23 several trains were spotted entering Atlanta from the south; any damage had already been repaired. "I expect I will have to swing across to that road in force to make the matter certain," he had written in resigned fashion to Halleck the day before. Orders were at once renewed for the swing around Atlanta, heading for Jonesboro.[39]

When he took this decision, Sherman had been left in no doubt as to the weight of responsibility resting on his shoulders. It is doubtful he had ever aspired to be a man of destiny, but he bore the hopes of all those who wished to see the war brought to a successful and utterly victorious conclusion— a man who had once been halfhearted in participating in it. Grant had telegraphed with his customary succinctness: "No division or brigade has gone from here west, and I shall endeavor to keep the enemy busy that none will go." Grant's fundamental plan had been turned upside down. At the outset Sherman had conducted a subsidiary operation designed to prevent Confederate reinforcements from going east. By the last week of August he was conducting the primary campaign with Grant supporting his efforts and not vice versa. Before setting out he received a note from Stanton congratulating him on his promotion to major general in the regular army. Though Sherman replied that he would rather it had been deferred until the campaign had been concluded, it was a tacit admission by the president that his future lay in Sherman's hands. Stanton also wrote to confirm that the Confederates were concentrating in the Shenandoah Valley. Grant wrote on August 18— again subtly and reassuringly, but as a word of warning, too—that unspecified Confederate military luminaries had predicted in the newspapers that Atlanta could hold out for another month. "If you can hold fast as you are now and prevent raids upon your rear you will destroy most of that army." Grant also gave his blessing to Sherman's chosen course. He urged him never to go back "even if your roads are cut"—advice that resonated with Sherman's deepest instincts. Grant recommended he build up all the supplies he could, "and if it comes to the worst move south as you suggested."[40]

As early as August 23 Sherman had inquired of Schofield how quickly he could resume his advance. As soon as supplies were at hand, Schofield replied. Sherman spent most of August 24 on reconnaissance and moved his headquarters to Utoy Creek. A simultaneous advance, he announced to the army commanders, would begin on the night of August 25. New maps had to be completed showing the precise location of the roads between Red Oak and Jonesboro. All temporary telegraph wires placed on trees should be gathered up and removed. Stanley of the 4th Corps would be employed to support Howard's Army of the Tennessee and later Schofield's Army of the Ohio. Sherman intended nothing less than a repeat of Grant's maneuver south of Vicksburg, which placed a city between his army and his line of supply. Initially the advance went without a hitch and caught Hood completely by surprise. Sherman's advance stole at least 48 hours' march on him. On the afternoon of August 28 Sherman reported proudly that the Army of the Tennessee and the 14th Corps had cut the West Point Railroad at Fairburn and Red Oak, respectively. "Enemy has made no serious opposition to our movement." Schofield on the left shielded the arc of the advance skilfully. The only Confederate troop movements reported were "a considerable body of rebel cavalry" pressing down the Jonesboro road in search of Union cavalry raiders.

Sherman then committed a serious error. He informed Thomas and Howard, "I wish the railroad thoroughly destroyed as far as possible"; he prescribed in detail how this should be done. The process he outlined came to be known as making "Sherman's neckties," lighting a bonfire and twisting the rails, once hot in the middle, so that they "cannot be straightened without machinery." All cuttings were to be filled in and laced with "torpedoes" (mines). Thomas's troops were to stay at Red Oak the following day, and Sherman stayed with them and inspected the efforts of both armies personally. He was determined to ensure that the war against Atlanta's railroads could not be lost, but these exertions smack of overinsurance. Sherman had got his priorities wrong. He should have concentrated on what he intended to do once Hood caught up with him, which would be sooner rather than later given the loss of a precious day. Now that significant operational advantages had been accrued, he could no longer afford to forfeit tactical opportunities.

Hood had completely lost touch with Sherman's thrust, and on the night of August 30–31 he rushed two of his corps, commanded by William J. Hardee, southward. Hood, however, wrongly gauged both the ambition and direction of Sherman's advance. He believed that Sherman had simply shifted to the west of the city in order to mount renewed cavalry raids on Atlanta's railroads. He failed to realize that Hardee's force faced Sherman's entire army. By delaying at Red Oak Sherman unwittingly sacrificed the chance of catching this substantial part of Hood's army outside Atlanta's fortifications. He did not issue orders for a resumption of his advance until the night of August 29. The following day the Army of the Tennessee struck out for Jonesboro; it reached Renfrow only to discover that no water could be found, and Howard ordered a crossing of the Flint River. Logan's 15th Corps pushed on ahead of the other two corps and entrenched on a wooded ridge just half a mile short of the Macon and Western Railroad. The other two corps hastened after nightfall to join their comrades; Thomas's Army of the Cumberland advanced via Shoal Creek and the Long Plantation, while Schofield and the Army of the Ohio headed for a small railroad junction at Rough and Ready. Sherman's entire force could only be described as "well in hand."

Yet Sherman had not considered how to employ it. He issued orders for Schofield and Stanley to advance down the railroad from the vicinity of Rough and Ready, destroying the railroad as they moved. This combination raised the specter of seniority again, and Sherman asked Thomas to reissue the orders to David Stanley, who had succeeded Howard in command of the 4th Corps, as he had done so through Schofield, a time-wasting but necessary procedure. Sherman wasted time also—discussing alterations in the boundary between the Departments of the Ohio and Cumberland that Halleck had raised at this unpropitious time. He had indicated to Halleck the drift of his plans. He wished to press the Confederates "at all points" but sought "a lodgement" near Jonesboro: "I propose to swing the whole army upon it and break it all to pieces." Hood's grip on Atlanta would at once be broken. Yet this plan remained tactically defensive and reactive because the stress placed on railroad destruction rendered it insufficiently flexible to launch a shattering attack.[41]

Hardee's force had taken up position just west of and thus covering the Macon and Western Railroad. After resting his men during the morning, he launched at Jonesboro yet another hurried, ill-directed, and piecemeal attack on the Army of the Tennessee, like so many that had preceded it, too late to capture Howard unawares, and it was repulsed with severe loss. Howard inflicted 1,725 casualties for the loss of 179. He decided against throwing forward a counterstroke, unaware that Lee's corps had been hurriedly recalled to Atlanta. He preferred a prudent waiting game, confident that Sherman and Thomas would arrive soon, even though less than half of his army had been engaged. But Howard's army remained too small for truly decisive operations. One more opportunity to fatally damage Hood's army thus passed, mainly as a result of the structural weaknesses of Sherman's command and the Army of the Tennessee's small size compared with the decisive operations of the spring of 1863. Howard could not fulfill Sherman's sentiments "that my hope of success rests mainly with you." On hearing of Howard's success, Thomas hurriedly wrote to Sherman urging him to permit him to leave Stanley to support Schofield in destroying the railroad and to take the remainder of the Army of the Cumberland "and throw it on the railroad east of Fayetteville, say at Lovejoy's, or some point below." Such a stab deep into the Confederate rear "would be eminently beneficial."

Sherman declined to change his orders. Instead he wanted to send Kilpatrick's cavalry division "hanging on Hardee's flanks," but this could not deliver a decisive blow. Sherman still wanted most of his troops to brandish crowbars and staves to upend rails rather than fall in with their muskets loaded. His orders mention "pursuit" of Hardee's force and operations "on its flanks." Something deep in Sherman's psyche inclined him to dodge the intermediate task—the shattering stroke against the enemy's main body—even when his skilful maneuvers provided the conditions for him to carry it out. He did not choose to avoid it because he had found an alternative way of conducting war, as Liddell Hart believed. He consciously sought out battles and unconsciously found ways of avoiding having to fight them. His aversion had been heightened by his previous reverses at Chickasaw, Chattanooga, and Kennesaw Mountain, though none of these proved decisive or fatal to his career. But at Jonesboro all the cards were held by him, not, as before, by the enemy.

As so much time had been consumed tearing up track and lighting fires and perfecting "neckties," the Army of the Cumberland did not start to arrive on Howard's left until the afternoon. At 4:00 p.m. Davis launched the 14th Corps, under Sherman's immediate eye, in an assault on Hardee's right flank, which proved successful, shattering a Confederate brigade and taking 1,000 prisoners and two batteries of cannon. Sherman hoped to mount a double envelopment and capture the entire Confederate force, but such a complex operation demanded more time, and so much had already been expended prodigiously. He needed at hand Stanley's 4th Corps, and this had become distracted by its initial task. Thomas rode off to find Stanley after messages from Sherman's staff did not get through: "That is the only time during the campaign I can recall General Thomas urge his horse into a gallop," Sherman observed in an affectionate but also pointed reminiscence. Stanley arrived too late and began a fastidious deployment that allowed Hardee to escape. Union casualties were 1,169, an economical success. The waste of time had been Sherman's fault. He could and should have destroyed and captured Hardee's entire force if only he had put his mind to it 48 hours earlier—and brought his mission to a triumphant and complete conclusion.[42]

Hardee withdrew to Lovejoy's Station, as Hood desperately sought to reunite his army on the night of September 1–2. The noise of numerous explosions coming from Atlanta again engaged Sherman's attention. At 11:00 p.m. he ordered Thomas to send a message to Slocum at the Chattahoochee railroad bridge instructing him "to feel forward to Atlanta, as boldly as he can," with the assurance "that we will fully occupy the attention of the rebel army outside of Atlanta." Sherman admitted restlessness and sleeplessness; after a pause the great explosions and flashes were renewed at about 4:00 a.m. Only a few hours before, he had declared that Jonesboro no longer had any intrinsic value now that Atlanta had almost fallen into the bag. Belatedly, he turned to the other part of his mission, as "we are now trying to cripple and destroy the army now there." He stopped the destruction of the railroad and ordered his armies to follow Hardee, who could not contact Hood because Sherman had ordered the cutting of the telegraph wires. By 1:00 a.m. on September

2 Hood evacuated Atlanta. Five locomotives and 81 freight cars, including the reserve ordnance train, had been torched, along with huge quantities of war materiél. The mayor surrendered the city that morning, and at long last elements of the 20th Corps entered it shortly after 11:00 a.m. Slocum sent Stanton a brief message notifying him of Atlanta's fall, and he then passed to Sherman a note informing him of his triumph. Sherman forwarded this note to Thomas, who confirmed that it was genuine. A decade later he presented a modest and affecting scene in his *Memoirs*. Thomas repeatedly examined the note. "The news seemed to him too good to be true. He snapped his fingers, whistled, and almost danced"; the news spread quickly to the troops, who shouted and whooped joyfully, and Sherman reflected that "the wild hallooing and glorious laughter, were to us a full recompense for the labour and toils and hardship through which we had passed in the previous three months."[43]

Having received the joyful news, Sherman at once issued orders to protect his trains and rear should the Confederates strike while beating a retreat. Desultory skirmishing occurred at Lovejoy's Station, but as Hardee had hastily entrenched, Sherman decided not to put matters to the proof. He seemed to sense that any demand he might make for the ultimate sacrifice from his men once Atlanta had been taken would not be well received. Without cavalry at hand, Sherman had tried but failed to locate and entrap Stewart's corps, which escaped in a southwesterly direction toward McDonough. Sherman paid a price for not surrounding Atlanta, for no sizeable portion of Hood's army fell into Union hands. Early on September 3 Sherman sent Halleck a brief account of these concluding operations, noting that he would return to his prize. "Since May 5 we have been in one constant battle or skirmish, and need rest." The letter ended on a strong, resounding note that would shortly be heard all over the North: "So Atlanta is ours and fairly won."[44]

Sherman's capture of the city at that date—and not a month later, which was likely if he had relied on the slow methods of siege—was worth more than two corps of the Confederate army. It was Sherman's single biggest success and illustrates the intersection of military and political events at this stage of the Civil War. He would later become aware of a certain agitation that he should be offered a nomination to run for president, which he did not take seriously. "The people of the US have too much sense to make me their President." In a private letter on September 4 Sherman divulged his understanding of that correlation between war and politics when he wrote,

"I hope the administration will be satisfied, for I have studied hard to serve it faithfully." Atlanta presented the North with a decision in a war with few turning points. It presented a clear-cut portent of ultimate victory. The president needed a decision in his favor by the autumn. Signs were evident that military events and therefore opinion had begun to swing in his favor earlier, notably at Mobile on August 5, but this naval success did not lift the pall of gloom that had descended on the Republicans. The fall of Atlanta did.

The political consequences were immediate: seizing Atlanta reshaped the political terrain and transformed opinion to such an extent that Lincoln's "momentum" during the presidential election proved irresistible. It produced a result on November 8 that most seasoned professional politicians in August thought impossible. Philip H. Sheridan's subsequent victories in the Shenandoah Valley cajoled the shift along, but Sherman's actions made it all possible. Lincoln's order of thanks to Sherman acknowledged his single-minded contribution. Sherman's *Memoirs* mention that "it was all-important that something startling" should occur before November 1864. The formal and informal exchanges between president and general assumed a new warmth and empathy, and gradually Sherman fell under Lincoln's spell. The *Memoirs* also take on the guise of a commentary on the testament according to St. Abraham. At the time, though, Sherman could not have offered a gesture more calculated to earn Lincoln's respect than the simple unvarnished statement "We as soldiers best fulfill our parts by minding our own business. I will try to do that." Alas, he did not invariably succeed.[45]

Grant, moreover, had taken a great gamble in lending his strategy an attritional emphasis from June 1864 onward when Lincoln needed a striking success. Sherman provided this in a timely manner, which vindicated Grant's trust in his old friend. Without the fall of Atlanta and Lincoln's subsequent comfortable reelection, taking 58 percent of the popular vote, including 77.5 percent of the soldiers' vote and 212 votes in the electoral college to the Democrat George B. McClellan's 21, it is difficult to see how the punitive war of attrition on the South could have been continued. Sherman did more than any other man apart from the president in creating this climate of opinion. His ingenuity, pertinacity, and prudent calculation were vital elements in his triumph. Strategically, operationally, and logistically his handling of the Atlanta campaign was superb. Significantly, he revealed to his father-in-law that "for 100 days not a man or horse has been without ample food, or a musket or gun without adequate ammunition." He esteemed this achievement "greater than any success that he has attended me in Battle or in Strategy."

But it was not true, as he claimed in this rather vainglorious letter to a man in whose company he had been forced to eat humble pie on more than one occasion, that he had committed only one error (he regretted sanctioning Stoneman's raid on Andersonville). Like all other successful commanders he made several errors, though none grave. He also revealed a significant flaw commented on by several previous authorities. He failed to profit tactically from his brilliant maneuvers and campaign plans, notably at Jonesboro. He failed to grasp that battle plans required the same preparation and application as campaign plans. In many ways it could be claimed that he had gained Atlanta precisely because he did not suffer from a tactical fixation that hazarded the greater gain for a smaller success. Even so, the main element of his timely victory lay in his intellectual grip over all operations for which he carried responsibility. As he mentioned to his father-in-law, "to the Extent of my ability, nothing has been undone that could be foreseen," and he would bring similar striking qualities to bear as he contemplated the future direction of his operations.[46]

13

Marching on to Savannah, September–December 1864

One of the first orders that Sherman issued after the fall of Atlanta concerned the civilian population. "Move all the stores forward from Allatoona and Marietta to Atlanta," he instructed Slocum. "Take possession of all good buildings for Government purposes, and see they are not used as quarters." He then continued in a benevolent tone, "Advise the people to quit now. There can be no trade or commerce now until the war is over." It would be best for Unionist parties to "go to the North with their effects, and secesh families move on." His armies were badly in need of rest, refitting, and recuperation— "and even more important, pay." That day he issued orders that the Army of the Cumberland return to Atlanta, the Army of the Tennessee to East Point, and the Army of the Ohio to Decatur; Garrard's cavalry would serve as the rear guard. To assault Hood's current position along Walnut Creek would not be profitable. "Besides, there is no commensurate object," he informed Halleck, "as there is no valuable point to his rear till we reach Macon, 103 miles from Atlanta." To turn Hood's position "would carry me too far from our base at this time." He also reaffirmed his desire to remove the civilian population of Atlanta "so that we will have the entire use of the railroad back, as also such corn and forage as may be reached by our troops." He sensed that his decision might be misrepresented. "If the people raise a howl against my barbarity and cruelty I will answer that war is war and not popularity-seeking. If they want peace they and their relatives must stop war."[1]

On September 7 he wrote to inform John B. Hood formally of his intention to expel Atlanta's population, allowing them to take their personal possessions (including "reasonable furniture") to Rough and Ready. He did not insist on the emancipation of all slaves, as he should have done, and allowed those who wished to travel with their masters to do so; all who wished to stay "may be employed by our Quartermaster." Sherman's tone again was helpful rather than punitive. "Atlanta is no place for families or non-combatants, and I have no desire to send them north if you will assist in convoying them south." If

Hood agreed, he would order a truce around Rough and Ready for about two days. Far from gaining Hood's accord and cooperation, this comparatively benign letter provoked what Sherman described to Ellen as "some sharp correspondence with Hood about expelling the poor families of a brave People." His attitude was quite straightforward: Atlanta had become "a conquered place" to be used solely for military tasks, "which are inconsistent with the habitation of families of a Brave People." He suspected rightly that Hood "no doubt thought he would make Capital out of the barbarity etc." However, Sherman proved to be wrong in predicting that "he will change his mind before he is done."[2]

Two days later Hood, to the contrary, dipped his pen in an inkwell overflowing with hyperbole. He admitted that he had no choice in the matter and would accept the state of truce for 48 hours, then denounced Sherman's course as an "unprecedented measure," one that "in studied and ingenious cruelty" surpassed "all acts ever brought to my attention in the dark history of war." Hood's stance, not based on any wide reading or deep reflection on the matter, as Sherman would expose rather brutally over the next few days, aligned himself with current Confederate thought and propaganda. Rather than define what the Confederate cause stood for at this crisis-laden juncture in its fortunes, its leaders depicted in rather graphic terms what it stood against: the Confederacy was placed in apposition to Yankee barbarity, ruthlessness, cruelty, and sheer wickedness.[3]

On September 12 Sherman received a more judicious statement from the mayor and two members of the Atlanta City Council emphasizing the distress his act would cause the populace. He admitted the distress but would not rescind the order because he wished "to prepare for the future struggles in which millions . . . of Good People outside of Atlanta have a deep interest." Peace was desirable throughout America, but war would only cease once rebel armies were defeated. Such military actions "make it necessary for the inhabitants to go away"—indeed, he claimed that the want of wherewithal "will compel the Inhabitants to go." He only sought to reduce the discomfort of this movement.

Sherman then issued one of his most famous declarations. "You cannot qualify war in harsher terms than I will. War is cruelty, and you cannot refine it: and those who brought war into our Country deserve all the curses and maledictions a people can pour out." He then went on, "You might as well appeal against the thunderstorm as against these terrible hardships of war"—they were inevitable and could only be stopped "by admitting that it [the war] began in Error and [was] perpetuated in pride." He dealt with Hood in a more peremptory fashion, chiding him for his exaggerations, hypocrisy, and ignorance. "In the name of common sense I ask you not to appeal to a just God in such a sacrilegious manner." He concluded eloquently, "God will judge us in due time, and he will pronounce whether it is more humane to fight with a town full of women . . . or to remove them in time to places of safety among their own friends and People." In both missives the weight of the case lay with Sherman. He grounded his interpretation not just in historical precedence but in the rejection of any Confederate claim to legitimacy based on the presentation of the worst-case view of Union action compared with the best-case view of their own.[4]

Sherman's analysis was mainly based on his interpretation of "military necessity" in seeking victory in this war—a central feature of Francis Leeber's famous code enshrined in General Orders No. 100, which he had read the year before. Sherman had understood only too well that if the traditional American views of the laws of war were taken as literally true, victory for the Union would be virtually impossible and the Confederacy would win by default. According to the historian of Lieber's Code, Sherman's actions during the final phase of the Atlanta campaign and immediately after its conclusion were "the practical embodiment of the code's unsettling critique of the orthodox laws of war." In Hood's niggling response to Sherman's broadside, he remarked that "it opens the wide field for the discussion of questions which I do not feel are committed to me." Sherman retorted that the ensuing correspondence was indeed "out of place and profitless," but Hood began it "by characterizing an official act of mine in unfair and improper terms." One of the few points of substance in Hood's second letter related to his sarcastic criticisms of Sherman's bombardment of Atlanta, which killed 20 civilian residents and wounded 100 to 200 others. Sherman responded crisply: "I was not bound by the laws of war to give notice of the shelling of Atlanta, a 'fortified town, with magazines, arsenals, foundries, and public stores'; you were bound to take notice. See the books." One feels that Hood would have needed a little more detail to locate the titles of the recognized authorities than this terse instruction. Sherman then signaled the end of the exchange, "which I did not begin, and terminate with satisfaction."[5]

Sherman's further reflections on this propaganda war in which he had unwittingly got caught up were not likewise terminated. "These fellows have a way of leaving us to take care of their families," he complained, "but when

I took Atlanta I ordered them all to quit and a big howl is raised against my Barbarity—Butler is the Beast—Sherman the Brute and Grant the Butcher." Such name-calling appeared to have an ulterior motive. "This is somewhat on the order of the school bully who if he can't whip you, can call you hard names or make mouths as you listen."

Other name-calling resulted from the reaction to the rather abrupt and tactless letter Sherman sent to John Spooner at the end of July. Spooner, the provost marshal for Georgia, Alabama, and Mississippi responsible for the recruiting of black troops for Massachusetts in these states, had received the benefit of Sherman's hostile views on the nature of his duties. Sherman had succeeded in his aim of securing a virtual news embargo on the movement of his armies toward Atlanta, and he had gotten overconfident. Sherman stated baldly, "The negro is in a transition state and is not the equal of the white man." He also referred to agents "buying up the refuse of other states" and disapproved of their peddling methods. He considered their "unwise and unsafe" tactics as frustrating the introduction of "the universal draft which I firmly believe will become necessary to overcome the widespread resistance offered us"; only such a measure would differentiate those "citizens [who] will fight for their country" from those who "will only talk."

Sherman hastened at the end to stress that it should not be inferred "that I am not the Friend of the negro as well as the white race"; rather, he explained, "I would not draw on the Poor race for too large a proportion of its active, athletic young men, for some must remain to seek new homes, and provide for the old and young, the feeble and helpless." His criticisms are not without merit and are the fruit of wide experience, as freed slaves were subject to forced impressment, kidnapping, and fraud, and no provision had been made for their families and dependents. Alas, Sherman had a rare talent for making kindly sentiments sound offensive. Spooner immediately sensed the inflammatory character of the missive and leaked what Sherman called his "negro letter" to the newspapers, just after the fall of Atlanta, a time calculated to embarrass him the most. "They did not appreciate its hasty and ironical tone," he complained. Perhaps they did, because that was what made it such good copy. Sherman had followed it up with another, written to Ellen, saying that "this kind of trash" recruited by men like Spooner "mainly fill our Hospitals and keep well to the Rear." The publication of the Spooner letter raised Stanton's hackles and aroused his suspicion that Sherman did not support the administration's policy on black troops, but he did nothing for the moment. Sherman could not understand why Spooner had leaked it and "give[n] it notoriety." He always failed to take into account the effect of his written asides that too often hit home for his readers.[6]

His pen forever twitching, Sherman had written one other long, revealing letter after the fall of Atlanta, one with an altogether more congenial effect. He had sent to "My Dear Friend" Halleck a heartfelt note of thanks, beginning with a long statement of his sense of obligation. "I confess I owe you all I now enjoy of fame, for I had allowed myself in 1861 to sink into a perfect 'slough of despond' and do believe if I could I would have run away and hid from the dangers and complications that surrounded us." He thanked Halleck again for his confidence, vision, and calm; "you gradually put me in the way of recovering from what might have proved an ignoble end." He still expressed doubt that he should have received a major general's commission in the regular army, "but now that I have taken Atlanta as much by strategy as by force, I suppose the military world will approve it." Of course, this had not been Sherman's intention, but this was how it had turned out. "I ought to have reaped larger fruits of victory. A part of my army is too slow, but I feel my part was skilful and well executed." His report would be dedicated to this theme, and though in toto his belief expressed so confidently to Halleck was far from unjustified, Sherman glided gently over his responsibility for the failure to crush Hardee at Jonesboro. He did pay tribute to the "untold labor" of his troops, for "we have achieved success by industry and courage." The result: "many stragglers fleeing in disorder, and the town of Atlanta, which, after all, was the prize I fought for." Crucial though this proved to be, he had also fought for another prize, and this had eluded him: Hood's army. It would continue to do so and would prove to be a major distraction over the next few weeks.

Even at his greatest moments events somehow conspired to spoil them. Sherman admitted to Halleck that he feared that his "negro letter" had antagonized both Lincoln and Stanton, as it had never been "designed for publication, but I am honest in my belief that it is not fair to our men to court negroes as equals." Privately, knowing that Halleck shared his skepticism, he doubted he could have taken Atlanta with an army composed of significant numbers of African Americans, whose mental abilities to learn and become tactically proficient he grossly underestimated, as he had once doubted the abilities of white volunteers whom he currently lauded to the skies. One point on the recruitment issue, though, is sound. Sherman asserted forthrightly that "it has been very bad economy to kill off our best men and pay full wages and bounties to the drift and substitutes."

In his letter to Halleck Sherman proffered a memorable passage on the clamor that now lapped around him to nominate him on either presidential ticket. It would not be the last attempt to seduce him with such ambitions. "Some fool seems to have used my name." With delicious wit he protested, "If forced to choose between the penitentiary and the White House for four years . . . I would say the penitentiary, thank you, sir."[7]

During the following days Sherman worked on his report, which he completed by September 15. He proudly reported his promptness to his father-in-law, noting with satisfaction that "the Grand Outlines contemplated these Grand Armies moving on Richmond, Atlanta & Montgomery, Alabama, & Mine alone has yet reached its goals. So that in fact I am now at a loss for the 'next.'" He exaggerated for effect because, within days of Atlanta's fall, he proposed a cooperative venture with Edward R. S. Canby toward Macon, Alabama, when the latter gained Montgomery and the upper reaches of the Alabama River above Selma; once Canby could drive on to Columbus, Georgia, Sherman could drive southwestward and use Columbus as a base for an advance on Macon, Georgia, relying on "the corn of the Flint and Chattahoochee [Rivers] to supply forage." Sherman could pinpoint no major objective beyond Atlanta worth the risk of a long approach march through difficult country. He feared that his troops and their commanders might become too fond of "breakfast, dinner and supper" if allowed to relax for too long. He worried that "the world will jump to the weary conclusion that because I am in Atlanta the work is done." This he deemed a terrible error. Sherman insisted that the 300,000 ardent secessionists that he had warned Ellen about many times must still be killed, "and the further they run the harder for us to get them."[8]

Grant sent Sherman a telegram on September 10 briskly expressing his desire that "as soon as your men are properly rested and preparations can be made it is desirable that another campaign should be commenced." He initially thought of a drive on Augusta in tandem with an amphibious occupation of Savannah mounted by Canby's troops. "I should like to hear from you however in this matter." But Grant made his own preference clear. "We want to keep the enemy continually pressed to the end of the war. If we give him no pause whilst the war lasts the end cannot be distant." As the most progress had been made in Sherman's theater, Grant wished to invest more in Georgia to maintain that relentless pressure he demanded.

Sherman made an initial appreciation that evening. He argued against a further advance "dependent on the railroad; it takes so many men to guard it, and even then it is nightly broken by the enemy's cavalry that swarms about us." The country was rich in forage and foodstuffs "but not enough in any one place to admit of delay." This logistical factor would again prove to be crucial in his calculations. He envisaged the advance in terms of occupying geographical points. For instance, he could take Milledgeville, the state capital, "and compel Hood to give up Augusta or Macon and could turn the other." He fumbled for an anvil on which to strike Hood but could not envisage striking without one. "Otherwise I would risk our whole army by going too far from Atlanta." The only other promising point of departure, on which he briefed the president—"a magnificent stroke of policy"—lay in persuading Georgia to secede from the Confederacy and surrender in an act of "separate State action." This venture seemed to promise much but produced a meager dividend. Sherman certainly exaggerated both the audacity and credibility of the initial Georgian emissaries who knew his brother John; furthermore, he exaggerated the extent of the Unionist sympathies of Georgia's governor, Joseph E. Brown, and other leading citizens, including Confederate vice president Alexander H. Stephens, all of whom had quarreled with Jefferson Davis.[9]

On September 20 Lieutenant Colonel Horace Porter arrived in Atlanta carrying a letter from Grant written eight days earlier soliciting Sherman's views on future operations. Grant congratulated Sherman on his "gigantic undertak[ing]" most skilfully executed and went so far as to claim it "as unsurpassed, if not unequalled." He continued warmly, "It gives me as much pleasure to record this in your favor as it would in favour of any living man, myself included." Sherman at once conveyed his thanks for Grant's "honorable and kindly mention of the services of this army in the great cause in which we are all engaged." Porter's memoirs offer a wonderfully graphic description of the appearance and striking mannerisms of the man he later dubbed "one of the most dramatic and picturesque characters of the war." On reaching Sherman's headquarters at Judge Richard F. Lyon's house, he immediately espied the general sitting on the porch "tilted back in a large arm-chair, reading a newspaper." He appeared typically disheveled, "coat unbuttoned, his black felt hat slouched over his brow, and on his feet were a pair of carpet slippers very much down at heel." Slippers were Sherman's preferred footwear when not riding, and he became attached to his favorite pair. Porter also captured Sherman's physical fitness, despite his asthma. "With a large frame, tall gaunt form, restless hazel eyes, aquiline nose, bronzed face, and crisp beard, he looked the picture of grim-waged war." He greeted Porter in the most enthusiastic and cordial manner, and Porter recognized traits that Grant had often referred to when describing his friend.

Grant had authorized Porter to inform Sherman that he had ordered operations to seize Wilmington, North Carolina, and its guardian bastion, Fort Fisher. Most of Grant's letter explained this operation in more detail. He seemed to welcome Sherman's initial thoughts and, like his friend, believed initially that the next phase of operations would involve cooperative advances between Sherman and E. R. S. Canby. The Confederate general Sterling Price's incursion into Arkansas that autumn, as Grant hinted, might disrupt such a scheme, as this fell under Canby's list of responsibilities. The tenor of the letter fitted Grant's habitual dealings with a reliable subordinate. He did not wish to give detailed instructions as much "as to get your views and have plans matured by the time everything can be got ready." Porter echoed these sentiments, though Grant's letter indicated a start date of October 5, 1864. But once Sherman formed a plan, its startling nature required a postponement.[10]

At lunch Porter concluded that Sherman's headquarters mess ran along "democratic" lines similar to Grant's, with a minimum of fuss and formality. During his later "animated discussion" with Sherman, Porter could hardly fail to observe his nervous fidgety energy. "He twice rose from his chair, and sat down again, twisted the newspaper into every conceivable shape, and from time to time drew one foot and then the other out of its slipper, and followed up the movement by shoving out his leg so that the foot would recapture the slipper and thrust itself into it again." Porter was especially impressed by Sherman's forceful lucidity, "crisp words and epigrammatic phrases which fell from his lips as rapidly as shots from a machine gun." Sherman announced his intention, or so Porter recalled, "to cut a swath through to the sea," and much discussion concerned how such an advance could be sustained. Sherman also warned Porter that if he carried out such a drive he could not keep up even minimal communication with Grant's headquarters. Porter might anticipate much in this retrospective account, but it is clear that Sherman had already considered, even in crude form, the techniques of his celebrated Marches of 1864–65.[11]

In his considered response to Grant's request, Sherman surveyed the war against Confederate ports in support of the blockade, covering Mobile, now isolated, and Wilmington and Savannah, where operations were pending. Sherman remarked that Columbus, Georgia, might "become a magnificent auxiliary to my farther progress into Georgia," but he would have to rely on

Canby being "much reinforced" in order that he could "subdue the scattered armies west of Mississippi," which he thought unlikely. So Sherman concluded "that much cannot be attempted as against the Alabama River and Columbus, Georgia."[12]

Sherman already had a plan formed in his mind, a significant development of previous methods already tried, most notably in the Meridian campaign. In his initial thoughts he elevated geographical objectives as a priority; these are important in providing sustenance, shelter, and indeed protection to advancing armies. Places and armies literally feed off one another and should not be placed in false antithesis. Thus a traditional component of American military thought, geographical objectives, resurfaced in Sherman's mind at this point—which is hardly surprising, as armies need infrastructure, and much of North America still remained primitive and underdeveloped. Perhaps, as T. Harry Williams concedes, Sherman "was guilty of pursuing a geographical rather than a military objective, of judging the occupation of place more important than the destruction of an enemy army." As Williams avers, Sherman stressed geographical objectives because he had no interest in chasing Hood's army himself, but more significantly because he wanted to pursue a completely different kind of operational and strategic design—one that would have resounding effects.[13]

This initial plan depended on taking Savannah by amphibious action first, as with "the river open to us, I would not hesitate to cross the state of Georgia with 60,000 men, hauling some stores and depending on the country for the balance." With Union ironclads on the Savannah River he could move rapidly on Milledgeville, "where there is an abundance of corn and meat, and would so threaten Macon and Augusta"; advancing between them would force the Confederates to concentrate to cover one while he took the other. "Either horn of the dilemma would be worth a battle." Sherman thus made clear his understanding of the hazards of the operation. He remained confident that amid such plenty "my army won't starve," but he admitted that because there were "few [rail]roads and innumerable streams, an inferior force could so delay an army and harass it that it would not be a formidable object"; therefore he faced the risk of being harried and, at last, forced to retreat or, at worst, capitulate.

At this point Sherman began to expose and expound the central theme of his thinking. He understood that simply marching about and taking small towns had in itself little to commend it. "But the more I study the game," he informed Grant, "the more I am convinced that it would be wrong for me to penetrate much further into Georgia without an objective beyond. It would not be productive of much good." It would be possible, as at Meridian, to "make a circuit south and back, doing vast damage to the State," but he feared such a sweep would result "in no permanent good; but by mere threatening to do so I hold a rod over the Georgians who are not over loyal to the South." Here lay the kernel of his strategic insight: he hoped to launch a preeminently psychological assault that would widen the fissures of social and political disunity that were already evident. In short, he still hoped to force Georgia's withdrawal from the Confederacy. He concluded by telling Grant that "I will have a long talk with Colonel Porter and tell him everything that may occur to me of interest to you." Then he stressed his admiration for Grant's dogged perseverance and pluck" before Petersburg. He likened Grant to "a Scotch terrier. Let him alone, and he will overcome Lee by untiring and ceaseless efforts." He did not believe for a second that his new plan presented an alternative to Grant's fixing operations in Virginia. With a wonderful witty flourish, he quipped, "If you can whip Lee and I can march to the Atlantic I think Uncle Abe will give us a twenty days leave of absence to see the young folks."[14]

About September 20 Hood began to make a nuisance of himself. He preferred not to cover the remainder of Georgia but plunged northward along Sherman's lines of communication. The Army of Tennessee had been damaged by the Atlanta campaign but remained dangerous. During the next month his series of stabs and dashes west of the Chattahoochee engaged popular attention. The siege of Allatoona especially became undeservedly famous in the war's folklore. Sherman paid lip service to this fuss by issuing a general order congratulating those involved in the garrison's relief. On September 25 he sent back two divisions to cover Chattanooga and Rome. Three days later he warned Lincoln that Davis had delivered indiscreet speeches at Columbia, South Carolina, Macon, and Palmetto Station in which he had revealed that Hood's troops would soon join Forrest in Middle Tennessee. He also warned the president frankly that "it would have a bad effect if I were forced to send any material part of my army to guard roads so as to weaken me to an extent that I could not act offensively if the occasion calls for it." Sherman worried lest he be forced to relinquish the initiative he had gripped so tightly since May 1864.[15]

Privately he remained calm, telling Ellen that if Hood's army remained in his rear "we can make him suffer." He amplified the point by emphasizing that it presented him with an opportunity. "Georgia is now open to me, and steps are being perfected at other and distant points that will increase the value of my position here." On October 1 he asked for Grant's approval to send the reserves to Nashville under Thomas, destroy Atlanta, "and then march across Georgia to Savannah or Charleston," wreaking havoc and inflicting damage on Confederate war resources that would have a disproportionate effect on Southern morale. "We cannot remain on the defensive," he reminded Grant tersely. Hood's departure from the theater of operations would enable Sherman to march on a distant objective without either city falling to Union arms before he set out.[16]

Another frustration lay in the difficulty of gaining reliable intelligence about Hood's precise movements while rumors proliferated. Given worries prevailing in Washington, Sherman had taken four corps in pursuit (though both Logan and Blair were absent campaigning for Lincoln's reelection). Hood refused to fight Sherman and kept slipping away. Sherman's heart was not in the affair, as he had to return the way he had already traversed. The Army of the Tennessee had marched 300 miles by the time of Allatoona's relief. Then on October 22 Hood shifted south and westward toward Gadsden on the Coosa River and Tuscumbia, both in Alabama, to begin his ill-fated odyssey to Nashville. Throughout Sherman had succeeded in preventing Hood from gaining a cheap victory at his expense.[17]

Even while these desultory and inconclusive operations distracted attention, Sherman had successfully and slowly acquired creeping approval for his Georgia maneuver. As early as September 27 Grant had authorized that all reinforcements sent to Nashville should receive their orders from him. Sherman then dispatched Thomas to Nashville to take immediate command, and the 4th and 23rd Corps arrived to reinforce him. While in the field he wrote to Grant warning that "it will be a physical impossibility to protect this [rail]road now that Hood, Forrest, Wheeler and the whole batch of Devils are turned loose without home and habitation." Here Sherman turned the consequences of his own errors and misfortune to his advantage. Occupying Georgia would be "useless . . . but the utter destruction of its roads, houses and people will cripple their military resources." He then followed up his advantage by arguing that with a saving of 1,000 men per month from garrison duty, "I can make the march and make Georgia howl"—another of his most resounding declarations. He had 8,000 cattle and 3 million pounds of bread; he lacked corn but felt confident he could find this by foraging.[18]

Sherman had come up with an incredibly daring and hazardous plan but quickly took steps to secure it and entrusted their execution to the reliable

Thomas, "slow but true as steel." His action served as a means of mollifying, even reassuring Grant, who sensibly counseled that it would "be better to drive Forrest from middle Tennessee as a first step." In response to Sherman's dispatch arguing that he should cut loose from the railroads, Grant responded, "If there is any way of getting at Hood's army, I would prefer that, but I must trust to your own judgment." Sherman drew up a detailed assessment of "the whole Field of the Future," which should determine Thomas's conduct for the next three months. He briefed Thomas that he intended to "organize an efficient army of 60–65,000 men with which I propose to destroy Macon, Augusta, and it may be Savannah and Charleston," keeping in view as alternative objectives either the mouth of the Apalachicola River or Mobile Bay. He then formulated for Thomas's benefit a theme that had been implicit in his earlier prognostications: "By this [March] I propose to demonstrate the vulnerability of the South and make its inhabitants feel that War and individual Ruin are synonymous terms." To play Hood's game was "folly," since it would dissipate manpower, "for he can twist and turn like a fox"; small garrisons could be picked off easily, "forc[ing] me to make countermarches to protect lines of communication."

Sherman argued that he must concentrate and maintain the initiative. He briefed Thomas that he intended to take the Army of the Tennessee and two corps of the Army of the Cumberland (14th and 20th), and initially the Army of the Ohio—though he changed his mind about the last later on. Thomas with the 4th and eventually the 23rd Corps would "retain command in Tennessee" plus "delegated authority over Kentucky, Mississippi, and Alabama, and there will be unity of action behind me." He was keen to underline the latter point because his operation by definition, a prolonged absence combined with being out of direct communication for long periods, required that he virtually make Thomas the de facto deputy commander of the military division, though Sherman never used these terms. He would be more explicit nearly three weeks later when he explained that "I want you to remain in Tennessee and take command of all my division not actually present with me." Here is striking evidence of his trust in Thomas and appreciation of his real abilities, even if he lacked drive. Thomas should hold the line of the Tennessee against Hood and also Chattanooga and Decatur in force. After Sherman had departed, Thomas should "watch Hood close." At this stage Sherman calculated erroneously that Hood would follow him. He insisted on secrecy but also flexibility: "I may actually change the ultimate point of arrival but not the main object."[19]

After Hood's change of direction had been confirmed, Sherman urged Grant again to "execute the plan of my letter sent by General Porter," as Thomas would be left with "an ample force when the reinforcements ordered reach Nashville." A day later Sherman returned to the charge, obviously keen to gain a final decision in his favor, having already made progress step by step. He stressed to Grant how the measures he had taken to relieve Allatoona and defend his railroads had reduced his field army. By contrast, he emphasized the advantages of an offensive movement. He intended to "send back my wounded and worthless and with my effective army move through Georgia smashing things to the sea." To Grant he repeated the erroneous view that he expected Hood to follow him once the initiative had been regained, but then added an argument that he realized would have a powerful appeal for his chief: "Instead of guessing at what he means to do he would have to guess my plans. The difference in war is fully twenty-five per cent."[20]

Though Sherman played with vigor on Grant's offensive inclinations, much less enthusiasm could be found in Washington for this plan. Halleck recoiled from it as far too risky, as it took many things for granted. His fears reinforced those of Lincoln, who disapproved of allowing Hood to rampage in Tennessee unchecked but still capable of winning a local victory against isolated forces; Hood might yet place a firm spoke in the wheel of the band-wagon of Lincoln's reelection "momentum." Grant saw the strength of these arguments and nursed severe doubts in private, preferring that Hood's army be utterly defeated before Sherman set out. Nonetheless, he could see no sense in holding Sherman back, as his only subordinate to succeed and the one farthest forward. Sherman did not know for another 23 years that one of the most vocal critics of his plan was John A. Rawlins, Grant's chief of staff. "Rawlins and I were always good friends and I cannot recall any expression of mine in speaking or writing inconsistent therewith," he observed in 1887. "Rawlins was always vehement in expression of assent or dissent," which Sherman relished, preferring it to "the flatterer to one's face and a back-biter after." Other critics claimed that Rawlins supported the idea in principle up to the moment the March was about to begin and then urged it be postponed. As Sherman knew in the 1880s that the decision had gone in his favor, he could afford to be indulgent. "I don't think I ever objected to Rawlins or any-body else differing with me in opinion before the event—but I do object to the croakers who foretell disaster and after belittle the Result."[21]

Rawlins had lost influence with Grant since May 1864. The commanding general found his presumptious manner irritating and had granted him a leave of absence beginning July 25 on the pretext of his deteriorating health, as tuberculosis had weakened his stamina. Grant continued to send Rawlins on special missions when it suited him, though the latter kept abreast of outstanding issues via his subordinates. He returned to Washington especially to denounce Sherman's errors. Yet harsh criticism of Sherman's plans by a staff officer who had never commanded in battle might have served to guarantee their adoption by Grant. In any case, Halleck and not Rawlins served as the intermediary between Sherman and his friend Grant. The very fact of the Sherman-Halleck friendship guaranteed, too, that Sherman received a sympathetic hearing; though Halleck did not accept Sherman's logic, his empathy helped Sherman deal with skeptics, especially the president. On October 12 Grant received word from Stanton that Lincoln "feels much solicitude in respect to General Sherman's proposed movement and hopes that it will be maturely considered." However, Stanton qualified this hope with the somber warning that any "misstep by General Sherman might be fatal to his army." Lincoln still feared that last-minute disasters might fatally derail his reelection.[22]

Grant reassured both Lincoln and Stanton that Sherman's plan remained the best available. He observed tersely, "Such an army as Sherman has (and with such a commander) is hard to corner or capture"—particularly if Hood's army had departed from the scene. This last consideration dominated Sherman's own thoughts. On October 16 he demanded to know at once when the evidence clearly showed "that Hood contemplates an invasion of Tennessee; invite him to do so." With heavy irony he added, "Send him a free pass in"—a joke that might have alarmed rather than amused the president. The farther west Hood traveled, the better Sherman's prospects, but his advance could not look as if Sherman had "lost" any territory or appeared careless. Even before he had written to reassure his political masters, Grant appeared to smile on Sherman's adventure. "On reflection, I think better of your proposition. It would be much better to go south than to be forced to come north." He approved of the destruction of Confederate war resources, especially railroad tracks and supplies; he also wanted to see the removal of horses, mules, and all stock, and he urged Sherman to arm freed slaves. He also accepted Sherman's view that his movement would "turn" Hood.[23]

During these busy days Sherman had to turn to personal administration, too. A whole series of letters from Ellen had piled up. She complained on October 19 that she had not heard from him for over a month. Ellen related proudly how she had become "quite a hero myself in the light of your reflected glory." Many gentlemen had called on her in Lancaster proffering "very pretty speeches complimenting you"; on a visit to Cincinnati, "everybody is ready to Serve me in anyway when they know me to be the wife of Gen'l Sherman"—a feeling that arose not just from admiration but from gratitude. After the important role she had played in saving her husband's military career, Ellen was entitled to feel more than a touch of satisfaction as the recipient of this praise. The approaching first anniversary of Willy's death cast a shadow over these bright feelings. Ellen still could not speak of him with composure, "so I keep him in my heart"; she had earlier pondered "how it changes the world to have a child like him laid in the cold bosom of the earth. My heart can never be fresh again." When she wrote on her birthday from Cincinnati, she reflected that "we have been taught the utter vanity of human ambition." Although Sherman had "won for yourself through merit a name which will be honored by the brave and true as long as history lasts," his eldest son, "the one to whom that name would have been most dear[,] is lying in the cold bosom of the earth deaf to all sound of human glory." Sherman agreed that Willy's loss could still not be borne. "I miss in him the only pride I could have in fame and success." For consolation, Sherman wrote to his daughter Minnie, revealing that one of the reasons he had objected to the girls' going to school in South Bend, Indiana, was that "there is no chance of my ever seeing you till you are out of school"; still, the time would pass quickly, "and we may then have a home."[24]

John Hill's time as Sherman's manservant had ended on July 19, but he had volunteered to stay on until the Atlanta campaign ended. Then, after the receipt of his full pay of $292, he departed for Illinois to visit his brother. "He was honest and faithful to the last." As agreed, Sherman wrote to Ellen asking her to send Hill a deed for one of the Fort Leavenworth, Kansas, lots, that had been made over to her by her father, though Sherman made it clear that neither of them could pay the taxes due once he became the owner—an anxiety shared by Ellen, who observed that "he will probably prefer to wait awhile before taking the deed and assuming the responsibility of the taxes." She felt confident that Hill would return to Sherman's service, for he "wants to stay with you for he told me he did when he was here." As indeed he did. In the interval, his successor had been briefed in detail—"a minute account of shirts with orders on all points." Sherman was confidently situated in Judge Lyon's house and had "a good mess."[25]

The other matter concerned a horse that the good citizens of Lancaster intended to purchase for him, which would cost $700 and be renamed

Atlanta. Ellen worried how he would receive the gift, as "there is no-one in L[ancaster] you like or care to hear about." He quickly wearied of any news about the place; for Ellen, Lancaster had one major attraction—Willy's grave. Whatever his private feelings, Sherman reacted gracefully to the news. "Of course I feel much gratified at this mark of honor and kindness on the part of my old Townsmen." He only specified that such a horse should not be "afraid of anything." He currently had seven horses, including one "very valuable" animal, Duke, who had been presented to him at Louisville. As he hoped to start on campaign shortly, he thought it best to hold the mount in "reserve" in Lancaster until the spring. It was on Duke that Sherman sat for a famous photograph taken before the defenses of Atlanta, looking much smarter than usual. He sent this to Ellen, along with two daguerreotypes of the burned-out locomotive house at Atlanta taken by the engineer officer on his staff, Captain Orlando M. Poe. The photograph on Duke "was very fine. He stood like a gentleman for his portrait, and I like it better than any I ever had taken." Eventually, Lancaster's leaders changed their minds and decided to "present a service of plate or something that you can hand to your children."[26]

Ellen also reported that "John Sherman is out making speeches & I am glad of it for it would be sham[e]ful to have the Butternut ticket succeed with that Hypocrite and weak coxcomb McClellan at its head." Ellen had never liked McClellan. "The Country would not be worth fighting for if placed in such miserable hands as that." McClellan had written Sherman a fulsome letter of praise on the conduct of his "remarkable" Atlanta campaign—that would ironically do more than anything else to prevent his election to the presidency. But he seemed to sense in Sherman a kindred spirit, especially after the publication of his letter to Spooner. His lavish praise could be construed as an approach, an effort to associate the hero of Atlanta with the Democratic Party. Soon enough reports began to surface in the newspapers that Sherman supported McClellan for president. A very worried John at once wrote to query this; Sherman replied almost as quickly to put his mind at rest. "I never said so, or thought so, or gave one the right to think so." Sherman might "despair of a popular Government, but if we must be so inflicted I suppose Lincoln is the best Choice, but I am not a voter." He also contacted Halleck so that he could reassure the president that he had not entered the camp of his political enemies. Sherman wrote frankly that he hated "to express a political opinion," particularly if tainted "by some dirty party platform."[27]

As Sherman stood on the cusp of launching his most famous ventures, the most celebrated or anathematized of his campaigns, it is appropriate to examine some of his ideas that governed their character. The first is their ambiguity, for his intent and indeed direction were only partly formed in his head.[28] The second is the supreme confidence that he had developed in himself. As a man of deeply conservative instincts, Sherman tended to be pessimistic about the future. Yet by 1864 he appeared utterly sanguine: no predicament would find him unable to overcome it; as the March proceeded he would find the most suitable expedient at the right time. As an experienced commander with nerves of finely tempered steel, Sherman had every faith in his fertile imagination. His mind would range as his troops wandered. Such restlessness was wholly characteristic of his mercurial disposition.

The experience of the Marches also brought a stronger identification of the commander with his men than had prevailed previously. A hint of what Sherman aimed at can be found in a letter to Ellen two weeks before the fall of Atlanta. "You know the cares and troubles of a family of six under your very eyes," he observed solemnly; "think of mine of over a hundred thousand with all the wants and cares of children. . . . Not only their wants but their hopes and fears, their ambitions and jealousies." He admitted he did not want to "perplex you with all these things," but Sherman's sentiment indicates the degree to which he wanted to take the relationship between the leader and the led further forward. Indeed, he sought to solemnize it and impart to it a spiritual dimension amid the moral challenges posed by incessant warfare. Sherman's treatment of this relationship is emblematic of his role as intellectual man of action—a "thought-deed man" of later generations. It was only ten years later while writing his *Memoirs* in more leisured times that Sherman could formulate the idea that armies could develop an individual, transcendental character. He reflected on the "atmosphere" that should be sensed, for any experienced commander "knows that difference between a willing and contented mass of men, and one that feels a cause of grievance." He thus accentuated the central point: "There is a soul to an army as well as to the individual man, and no general can accomplish the full work of his army unless he commands the soul of his men, as well as their bodies and legs."[29]

Victor Davis Hanson, in his fascinating survey of Epaminondas, Sherman, and Patton, is one of the few scholars to grasp that "all three were at the most basic level intellectuals, widely read in literature and the scholarship of war, and with a keen interest in questions metaphysical and philosophical"; he suggests "that most of their tirades and crudity were efforts to mask the embarrassment of such an aesthetic sense." Sherman was a warrior, not a scholar, but he thought deeply about the issues posed by the war. The Marches were to

Sherman fundamentally a moral expression of Union military power, even a moral equivalent of battle. That is to say, they were designed to humiliate the South and especially secessionist leaders, to humble its swaggering warriors, and to leave them in a state of despair contemplating unavoidable defeat. As the South had been humiliated, Northern arms should henceforth be treated with respect. The Marches thus sought a propaganda or moral victory aimed at the Confederate military and civil will. They would reveal to the world, not only to the South, that a tremendous change had occurred in the Civil War's military balance. Despite its redoubtable resistance throughout 1864, any Confederate success would prove transient—another road pointing to defeat.

The North had thus proved itself a "Military nation" that had demonstrated the desired martial qualities—steadfastness, grit, stamina, and skill to win, and win completely. That determination would be upheld by Lincoln's reelection in November. It cannot be stressed too heavily that Sherman's motives were not founded on any fury directed at the South, as has been suggested repeatedly, but were spurred more by his admiration for this "stupendous energy" demonstrated by the South's war effort and its ferocious resistance. Finally, as Hanson avers, the idea of "stasis" was alien to Sherman's nature. Not only did he need to keep moving himself, but so did his men if they were to retain their mettle and cohesion. As Sherman contemplated the first anniversary of Willy's death, he did not need to be reminded of the dangers of camp diseases to lolling Civil War soldiers, diarrhea and dysentery especially. Sherman determined to get his men back in the field, but that would require some drastic reorganization of the formations under his command.[30]

Sherman gave close attention to the form and structure of the force he was about to take into the field once more. Liddell Hart claimed that Sherman had transformed his formations into "a large 'flying column' of light infantry," which with an eye on the future he could only applaud. Sherman indeed placed emphasis on rapidity of marching rather than hard fighting. Liddell Hart pointed out the origins of armored warfare in such an approach, but like so many other efforts at linking Sherman's methods to the future, such claims are dubious. Liddell Hart's characterization should not mislead us to assume that Sherman intended to march this light infantry into the sunset without giving much thought to its logistical sustenance. On the contrary, Sherman's methods were not so much concerned with methods of fighting as with addressing supply and sustainability.

Sherman had available 62,000 officers and men (including the artillery) arranged in two wings: the right comprised the Army of the Tennessee under Oliver Howard, which fielded the 15th Corps, currently commanded by Major General P. J. Osterhaus, as Logan had taken a leave of absence to campaign for Lincoln, and Blair's 17th Corps; the left, under Henry Slocum, was drawn from the Army of the Cumberland, the 20th Corps under Alpheus Williams, and the 14th Corps under Jefferson C. Davis. Kilpatrick's cavalry of 5,500 officers and troopers received its orders directly from Sherman. Each unit received the attention of a fine-tooth comb, ridding it of sick, wounded, and slackers—only the youngest, keenest, and fittest soldiers were allowed to step forward. All garrisons in northern Georgia were withdrawn. Sherman did not exaggerate in his *Memoirs* when he described his troops proudly as "able-bodied, experienced soldiers, well equipped," who would display a strong and vigorous gait. Less than 2 percent of their number reported sick on any day over the next two months of winter.[31]

As Sherman did not expect to fight any big battles, he only took 65 artillery pieces with him (about one gun per thousand men), organized into batteries of four guns. The army was accompanied by 2,500 wagons, each pulled by six mules, and 600 ambulances, each pulled by two horses. The wagons were divided between the four corps, so each had an average of 800 horsed vehicles following behind. Therefore, even in this streamlined version, Sherman's forces hardly lacked a "tail"; it stretched back about 20 miles. The wagons transported comparatively small amounts of ammunition—a maximum of 200 rounds per man and 200 cannonballs per gun. His biggest deficiency, as before, was forage, though Sherman hoped it could be taken from the countryside. Aware that no amphibious operation could be mounted to help Sherman, and thus "your movements therefore will be independent of mine," probably until the fall of Richmond, Grant attempted to sustain him as much as he could from a distance. He ordered Halleck to send transports by sea to rendezvous with Sherman at Ossabaw Sound with ordnance, 200,000 rations of grain, 500,000 rations of provisions, and 300,000 rounds of ammunition. "Information should be got to Sherman of all preparations made to receive him on the Seaboard." This proved easier said than done, as Halleck did not know where that point might be.[32]

During this odd period, as Sherman prepared for a mission he still did not know for sure that he would be permitted to carry out, he increasingly disengaged from Hood. He took the opportunity to explain his venture further to Halleck as a means of spreading reassurance. "This movement is not purely military or strategic," he attempted to make clear, "but it will illustrate the vulnerability of the South." The main objective lay in striking at the Southern nervous system and provoking despair in the breasts of the most ardent secessionists, slaveholders especially. "They don't know what war means, but when the rice planters of the Oconee and Savannah see their fences and corn and hogs and sheep vanish before their eyes they will have something more than a mean opinion of the 'Yanks.'" He urged Halleck to send Thomas "all the troops you can spare of the new levies, that he may hold the line of the Tennessee during my absence of, say, 90 days." This asked a lot, so to Thomas he explained his mission concisely: "If you can defend the line of the Tennessee in my absence of three months, it is all I ask."

Sherman reported General P. G. T. Beauregard's arrival in the theatre to take control of operations in what remained of the Confederate West. But this was a minor matter: Hood largely ignored his new nominal chief. Far more trying were the ciphers that were "imperfect." Sherman needed clarification as to whether Savannah or Mobile was Grant's preferred objective. He also wanted clarification as to whether Grant wanted him to destroy Atlanta and its railroad. Grant replied crisply that supplies would be sent to Hilton Head and then transported to Savannah. "Destroy . . . all of military value in Atlanta."[33]

Without a line of supply running behind him, Sherman could not hope to begin a promenade with scant logistical support. He would have to carry a lot with him. He estimated his minimum requirements at 1.5 million rations of bread, coffee, sugar, and salt and 500,000 rations of salted meat. He had to lay in a reserve of food, a foundation, which any casual foraging in the countryside could supplement. On October 22 he gave Grant an explanation of all his preparations to protect his offensive movement. "I feel perfectly master of the situation here," he reported proudly. The Tennessee River was guarded by Union naval gunboats, and Thomas defended its line. Sherman planned to "push into Georgia and break up all its railroads and depots, capture its horses and negroes, make desolation everywhere, destroy the factories at Macon, Milledgeville, and Augusta, and bring up with 60,000 men on the seashore above Savannah or Charleston." He penciled in a start date of November 1 but still awaited Grant's permission to begin. As a prelude, he ordered Slocum to "preach this doctrine to men who go forth: 'If Georgia can afford to break our railroads, she can afford to feed us.'"[34]

On November 1, the provisional start date, he received a disappointing query from Grant. "Do you not think it advisable now that Hood has gone so far north to entirely settle him before starting on your proposed campaign?" Halleck all too earnestly rushed to concur with this view. Grant believed that the distance separating the two armies would encourage Hood to continue north rather than return the way he had come. "If you see the chance of destroying Hood's army, attend to that first and make your other secondary." Sherman replied that if he surrendered the initiative "the work of the last summer would be lost"; he then detailed the measures he had taken in Tennessee and trusted that Thomas would assume the offensive. "This is the best I can do and shall, therefore, when I get to Atlanta the necessary stores, move as soon as possible." Grant thought the matter over and on November 2 conceded that "I do not really see that you can withdraw from where you are to follow Hood, without giving up all we have gained in territory." He also accepted that Thomas should "be able to take care of Hood and destroy him." In his final flourish, Grant declared forthrightly, "I say go as you propose."[35]

While Grant blew successively hot and cold on Sherman's pet project, one final piece of the jigsaw of his preparations had to be inserted. He needed "two good pontoon bridges ready to move in five days," and he sent Orlando Poe to supervise the project. His timetable requirement was to cross the Ocmulgee River at Macon. It eventually became clear that his pontoon trains were the main reason he could never be held up by great, fast-flowing rivers, even in desolate country. This element of Sherman's success has rarely received the attention it deserves. The Army of the Cumberland's pontoons were light, portable, flexible, and easily assembled and dismantled. The idea behind them had originally been William S. Rosecrans's. Sherman owed him a great debt.[36]

Once Grant's authorization had been received, Sherman pushed on with the final arrangements and promised to inform Grant of the date of his departure. Slocum was given five days to remove all superfluous Union property from Atlanta; he urged that fire be used "freely, both on our own and the enemy's property." The date he finally selected was November 8–9. He justified this to Halleck on the grounds that he could then be certain that Thomas would be "prepared for any contingency," but he wanted to wait for news of Lincoln's reelection. He continued to urge that Canby abandon the line of the Mississippi and advance instead on the line of the Alabama River and Selma to "completely bewilder Beauregard, and he would burst with French despair." He then revealed to Halleck that he had not been motivated by revolutionary designs. His strategic concept was expressed in matter-of-fact terms. When he reached the sea, he would "be available for re-enforcing the Army in Virginia, leaving behind a track of devastation as well as a sufficient force to hold fast all that of pertinent value to our cause."[37]

Sherman's opinions in the first week of November do not convey the air of finality and confidence to be found in his *Memoirs*. On November 6 he confided to Grant some of the thoughts agitating "my busy brain"; he claimed with justice that Hood's peregrinations had not interrupted his supply line, but he admitted that he had experienced some uneasiness as to "whether I ought not to have dogged him far over into Mississippi, trusting to some happy accident to bring him to bay and to battle." But he remained steadfast in his faith in his calculations that his decision to divide his forces remained the correct one. Above all, he expressed the conviction that preventing Hood from seizing the initiative by "mere threats and maneuvers" would constitute no mean strategic success, and the Union could "derive all the moral advantages of a victory." But the exchange reveals he was under no illusion as to the risks he was taking. He also felt uneasiness at Grant's confidence in him: "He never speaks of himself but always says that Sherman is the man—I fear this, and would much rather occupy a lower seat." As he put it in the *Memoirs*, if successful the Marches would be accepted as "a matter of course," but if they failed, they "would be judged the wild adventure of a crazy fool." The "devil-may-care" attitude and casual acceptance of his measures by the men under his command also worried him. The ghostly call of past failures and humiliations never dissipated, but Sherman maintained a brave front.[38]

On November 6 Sherman issued a circular ensuring that all commanding officers addressed three matters: the presidential election, the payment of all troops (and the return to safekeeping of all the soldiers' money), and the rapid absorption of all new troops. As the morale of his own troops soared, Sherman calculated that the morale of the enemy would diminish. "I propose," he explained to Grant, "to act in such a manner against the material resources of the South as utterly to negative Davis's boasted threat and promises of protection." He then continued with a famous flourish, "If we can march a well-appointed army right through his territory, it is a demonstration to the world, foreign and domestic, that we have a power which Davis cannot resist." Sherman then proceeded to expound his grand strategic rationale. It is clear that this advance is viewed by him as complementary, not in competition with, Grant's and thus a substantial contribution to the overall attritional strategy. "This may not be war, but rather statesmanship; nevertheless it is overwhelming to my mind that there are thousands of people abroad and in the South who will reason thus: 'If the North can march an army right through the South, it is positive proof that the North can prevail in this contest,' leaving only open the question of its willingness to use that power." Further comment seems superfluous.[39]

Sherman judged that Lincoln's reelection, "which is assured," added the capstone to the arch of his strategic thinking. He had remained so tight-lipped that his staff could not guess as to his own preferences, and he ignored all discussion of the election. During these days he admitted a new officer on his staff into his confidence and mentioned his preference for Lincoln. This was Major Henry Hitchcock, the nephew of his old friend Major General Ethan Allen Hitchcock, and well known to many of his old St. Louis friends. Lincoln's triumph on November 8—212 votes in the electoral college to McClellan's 21, with 55 percent of the popular vote, including 77.5 percent of the soldiers' vote—provided the essential context that rendered the pursuit of a punitive strategy of attrition easier and the South's complete surrender possible. In his turn, Sherman's triumph at Atlanta had made it possible for him to play a larger, even decisive role in the Union's strategy-making.[40]

Sherman returned to Atlanta on the afternoon of November 14, at about the same time as the bulk of the fighting troops. Two days previously both the railroad and the telegraph lines had been broken. At least Sherman knew that the unfolding of his plans could not be interrupted by higher authority. But the boyish exuberance reported by some historians—most likely a much later retrospective report—cannot be found in his contemporary correspondence; it is not even mentioned in his *Memoirs*. Actually, he had intended to continue communicating with Thomas via the "main line," but this proved impossible. His contemporary thoughts are full of foreboding; Hitchcock found his new chief distracted and deep in thought, "but always [offered a] pleasant reply when addressed." Sherman had written to Minnie, Lizzie, and Tommy, but his letter to Ellen was terse and conveyed a disconcerting finality. "Write no more till you hear of me. Goodbye."[41]

On November 6 Sherman had sent Grant some discussion of the alternative avenues of advance open to him. This letter reveals the extent of Sherman's stage nerves. The day before the presidential election Grant replied with characteristic self-assurance, "I see no present reason for changing your plan. Should any arise you will see it or if I do will inform you." Grant expressed undiminished faith that "you will be eminently successful and at worst can only make a march less fruitful of results than is hoped for." The results exceeded both their expectations. The delay of a further week could be justified by Sherman's knowledge of the winter weather; Sherman hoped the heavy winter rains would be over by the end of the second week in November. His enterprise would be facilitated and he would be better able to keep to schedule in dry, fine weather.[42]

At long last, on November 14 Sherman's entire force "grouped by Atlanta" received its orders to march. The advance began the following morning. Howard's right wing set out for Jonesboro and McDonough, with instructions to cross the Ocmulgee River and feint strongly toward Macon while actually aiming to rendezvous at Gordon within seven days. Slocum's left wing departed via Decatur, ordered to tear up railroad track as far as Madison, burn the railroad bridge east of it across the Oconee River, then should turn south and enter Milledgeville, again within the week. Sherman did not leave Atlanta until November 16, accompanying Jefferson C. Davis's 14th Corps. On Bald Hill, the scene of desperate fighting on July 22, Sherman and his staff reined in, and "we naturally paused to look back upon the scene of our great battles." It was an auspicious moment redolent with war's grim and terrible beauty. "Behind us lay Atlanta, smouldering and in ruins, the black smoke arising high in air, and hanging over the ruined city." In the distance the last glimpses of the trains of Howard's right wing could still be seen. The 14th Corps marched before their commander "steadily and rapidly, with a cheery look and swinging pace, that made light of the thousand miles that lay between us and Richmond." The strains of "John Brown's Body" were struck up by a regimental band, and the entire corps burst out, "Glory, glory, hallelujah!" Sherman was impressed by this vigor of expression—"never before or since" had he heard "it done with more spirit, or in better harmony of time and place." Sherman's escort then "turned our horses to the east"; Atlanta disappeared "and became a thing of the past."[43]

During this campaign the staff became more important in the conduct of operations than hitherto because Sherman suffered from a painful frozen shoulder that rendered writing virtually impossible. The staff attributed this malady to his habit of wandering around the camps in the early hours of the morning in a nightshirt, checking picket lines and talking to soldiers. They numbered a dozen, but within a few days their most senior member, Brigadier General William F. Barry, the chief of artillery, was invalided home due to a painful skin infection resulting in the inflammation of his face. Heavy responsibility despite junior rank thus devolved upon the acting adjutant general, Dayton, who issued all orders and other directives to the wing commanders. Hitchcock took on the burden of drafting other correspondence and orders in addition to his duties as judge advocate. As a newcomer he was greatly impressed by Sherman. He frankly admitted that he recognized him "as a man of power more than any man I remember." It was the combination of thought and deed that so engaged him—"the sort of power which a flash of lightning suggests—as clear, as intense, and so rapid." Here was a man who loved music, literature, and the theater and could express himself lucidly and colorfully—and over a great range. Hitchcock admired "the wonderful range and celerity, and vigor of those thoughts. If ever a 'live man' has commanded any of our armies, he is one." Hitchcock found Sherman thoughtful and considerate and less gruff than he expected, though sometimes offhand. He talked to everybody—blacks and whites—in the same polite, frank, and unassuming way.[44]

Sherman's opponent, Beauregard, issued various proclamations that attempted to arouse resistance and stir efforts to destroy provisions and create a "scorched earth" that would halt Sherman's advance. One called on Georgians "to burn and destroy everything and assail him [Sherman] on all sides." When on November 18 Sherman arrived in Covington he could see scant evidence of any such ferocious resistance. A welcoming committee awaited him with an invitation to dinner. He missed this party, as he entered the town by an unanticipated route, though some enterprising Signal Corps officers were happy to take his place. Sherman rode on for another 4 miles and established his headquarters in the grounds of Judge John Harris's plantation. Here, accompanied by Hitchcock, he talked frankly with the "elders" among the newly freed slaves, pleading with them not to accompany his columns because adding innumerable mouths to feed from his restricted supplies "would simply load us down and cripples us in our great task." Such appeals enjoyed a mixed reception, as all slaves knew the arrival of Union troops meant the permanent shattering of their shackles. Sherman also encountered two other unwelcome features of the Marches, plundering and indiscipline. He met several soldiers laden down with plundered foodstuffs. Observing his stern expression, one cheeky fellow observed, "Forage liberally on the country." He found another group squabbling over a barrel of molasses. Sherman walked up to the barrel, scooped a sample, sucked his finger, and said simply: "Don't crowd, boys, there is enough for all."[45]

Sherman could take a joke against himself, and the contrast between his relaxed reaction to this indiscipline and behavior three years earlier in Kentucky represents an about-face. Yet his reaction highlights an issue that his modus operandi raised. The jocular reference to foraging was taken from Special Orders No. 120, issued on November 9 by Dayton. The two wings had indeed been enjoined to "forage liberally on the country during the march." But Sherman had intended this task to be entrusted to foraging parties designed to maintain a minimum of 10 days' supplies for each brigade so that this might be distributed equitably. The order expressly forbade soldiers from entering houses, and the phrase did not imply that soldiers should be allowed to wander about taking what they wanted when they felt like it. Such a permissive attitude would erode discipline and cohesion. Throughout, despite his conservative attitudes, Sherman remained tolerant of the destructive propensities of volunteer soldiers that were encouraged by punitive measures. Even before the March began, several pointless fires had been lit by willful soldiers. Hitchcock records Sherman observing of one group, "There are the men who do this. Set as many guards as you please, they will slip in and set fire. . . . I never ordered burning of any dwelling—didn't order this, but can't be helped. *I say Jeff. Davis burnt them.*"[46]

Sherman nevertheless did not need to be reminded that casual tolerance of indiscipline rested on a sharp knife's edge that could cut into his army's efficiency. For this reason he had stressed in Special Field Orders No. 119, issued the day before, that "the most important" duty that soldiers must attend to was to "keep their places and not scatter about as stragglers or foragers" vulnerable to being "picked up by a hostile people in detail." Howard, the right wing commander, distant from Sherman's presence, would have agreed with Hitchcock that "implicit instructions" and the well-worn phrase concerning foraging "caused irregularities almost beyond the power of control." He issued a series of restrictive orders and attempted to reduce the number of mills set ablaze, as they encouraged unauthorized freelance burnings; he also noticed that the number of mounted soldiers unaccountably increased correspondingly with the levels of pillaging. Sherman, alas, could only enforce discipline by the use of capital punishments, which he lacked the authority to sustain—and would, in any case, be bound to be reversed by his political chiefs. But even the threat of their introduction would have destroyed the enthusiasm felt by the soldiers for his venture and shattered the high morale and admiration for him on which its success rested. Sherman took a calculated risk in dealing with this issue by effectively turning a blind eye to it. It was worth taking in the sense that the fighting qualities of his troops were not seriously impaired by pillaging.

The harsh truth cannot be ducked that the longer destructive wars continue, the more indifferent the victors become toward individual destructive acts as their hearts harden. Sherman himself reflected this change of attitude;

he had not been in the vanguard of those calling for "war in earnest"—far from it—though he rationalized it more brilliantly than those who were. Hitchcock's increasing denunciation in his campaign diaries of levels of indiscipline reflects his comparatively callow attitudes and lack of previous experience, especially in dealing with a refractory civilian population or guerrilla action. This is revealed in a heated discussion he had with Dayton on the morning of November 16 during which Hitchcock argued for "self-restraint"—an argument made frequently in 1862, even by Sherman. Dayton replied coldly that "we should do whatever and as bad as the rebels, even to *scalping*." Hitchcock, a highly intelligent, slightly condescending, and somewhat opinionated man, considered Dayton's viewpoint "not important, save as typical." Valuable as his account of the Marches is, Hitchcock's limitation of experience distorts his depiction both of its architect and its conduct. But even Hitchcock expressed satisfaction "that horses are contraband of war by all international codes"—as many escaped slaves brought horses or mules (or both) when they arrived in Sherman's camps.[47]

Special Field Order No. 120 also specified an average daily march of 15 miles. The march rate would depend entirely on the weather, the maintenance of discipline in the ranks, and the absence of delays caused by incidents of pillaging and other infractions. Infringements that required lengthy halts were often waved aside by Sherman. Most formations managed to keep to schedule. On November 19 Hitchcock recorded a march of 15.5 miles. The total distance between Atlanta and Savannah is 250 miles; the direct distance proved to be only three-quarters to three-fifths of the total traversed. The total march might be estimated at 350 to 550 miles with an average of 12 to 15 miles per day. By comparison, Napoleon's Grande Armée took four months in 1805 to cover 1,000 miles (at 18 to 20 per day); Robert Crawfurd's Light Division marched 42 miles in 26 hours to reach Talavera in July 1809 during the Peninsular War; von Kluck's 1st Army in August 1914 marched 30 miles per day. The event that most closely resembles Sherman's March was the advance in 1704 of the Duke of Marlborough to the Danube covering 260 miles in 26 days—Sherman took 29—but Marlborough traversed friendly country and thus could insist on "very exact discipline."[48]

There were, in fact, four Marches each separated by about 10 miles, and Sherman could only accompany one at a time. Major George Nichols noted in December 1864 that Sherman's command marched in six columns. Maintaining the march rate, the commanding general arrived in Milledgeville on November 22. Kilpatrick's cavalry seized an important bridge over the

Oconee. The pace of the last days had slowed as the rains returned. Even Hitchcock began to grasp the subtlety of Sherman's design. "Evidently this movement had created a fearful panic ahead." Sherman had also succeeded in achieving his operational aim. As he explained in his report, the "first object" had been "to place my army in the very heart of Georgia, interposing between Macon and Augusta, and obliging the enemy to divide his forces to defend not only those points, but Millen, Savannah and Charleston."[49]

The afternoon prior to the entry into the state capital, Davis had selected for his bivouac an exposed and cold ridge. Fearing for his shoulder, Sherman rode on and found some shelter behind a clump of wild plum bushes. Thanks to the enticements of an elderly female slave, who insisted she "could find a better place," he inadvertently moved into a plantation house owned by Howell Cobb, a former Confederate secretary of state, then serving in the field at Macon in the rank of major general. On departing he ordered Davis with cold exactitude "to spare nothing." Here he set a pattern: the property of prominent, wealthy, slaveholding secessionists received particular attention from Union troops; Sherman also invited the slaves to help themselves. Once encouraged to loot and destroy, the soldiers did not need further orders to continue to do so.[50]

On the afternoon of November 23 Sherman entered Milledgeville and occupied the governor's mansion. He quickly established contact with the right wing, which had arrived at Gordon. He was pleased to hear that Charles C. Walcutt's 2nd Brigade had the day before disposed quickly of a militia assault at Griswoldville that had melted away before Union firepower, though Union troops were discomfited to discover a high proportion of adolescent boys and elderly men among the casualties. Walcutt lost 13 killed and 86 wounded to an estimated Confederate loss of 50 killed and 500 wounded. But Sherman had told Hitchcock that he had no choice but to "harden my heart": "to conquer . . . it must bring destruction and desolation, it must make the innocent suffer as well as the guilty, it must involve plundering, burning, killing." Such is the terrible logic of "*ceaseless war*." And as Sherman wrote mordantly, the Georgia militia "never repeated the experiment." Sherman had caught the enfeebled Confederate defense unawares operationally, and his subordinates were thus able to swat tactically its puny efforts at resistance. As the Marches proceeded, Sherman exploited fully all the advantages that accrued from seizing the initiative, so the defenders' efforts became correspondingly more fragile and ineffective; they were sometimes nonexistent.[51]

Fine weather succeeded the cold winds and heavy showers toward the last week of November. Sherman decided on an immediate resumption of the advance after some mischievous, lighthearted diversion in Milledgeville, during which a mock session of the Georgia legislature assembled, composed of Union officers who repealed the ordinance of secession; the more serious work of completing the destruction of all armories and public buildings that could be put to military use went on apace. But the destruction inflicted on Milledgeville was far from devastating, and all private property received due respect. That evening Sherman issued Special Field Orders No. 127 ordering the advance to restart on the 24th. It should follow up the "perfectly successful" first phase of the March. Kilpatrick should break up the railroad between Milledgeville and Millen and make every effort to release Union prisoners of war incarcerated at the latter since September. Alas, with surprising efficiency (which causes on the brink of defeat can sometimes find), these 10,000 men at Camp Lawton were spirited away in complete secrecy and its stockade destroyed days before Kilpatrick set out.[52]

The right wing should push on to Sandersville, destroying both the railroad and the telegraph; the left wing should proceed likewise "to the railroad opposite Sandersville," Sherman ordered, and destroy it "forward to the Ogeechee [River]." Sherman stressed that the destruction of communications remained "of vital importance to our cause." He had been growing unhappy at the careless and halfhearted attention given to this aspect and wanted to reverse it. Finally, Sherman took the opportunity to emphasize that "none but the regular organized foraging parties should be allowed to depart from the right and left of the road"; the wagon trains were streamlined, and all superfluous wagons, including those confiscated for foraging, he ordered destroyed. Units of prisoners were allotted to assist advance guards eager to construct temporary bridges or remove obstacles. Any efforts by Southern civilians to impede the advance should be dealt with "harshly"; if they attempted to burn corn or forage, then their houses, barns, and cotton gins should be likewise burned.

Sherman's painful arm and shoulder, despite constant massaging, continued to trouble him, and he still could not write. He remained with the 20th Corps and at Sandersonville found the bridge over Buffalo Creek burned. Though he was very annoyed, engineers were close at hand, and the delay amounted to only three to four hours. The town was occupied on November 26, with Howard's right wing to the south. Colonel Charles H. Howard, its commander's brother, reported the previous night. He stated that the citizens of Milledgeville admitted that the "Yankees treated them much better than expected." But the delay before Sandersonville, plus firing in the street, especially from the courthouse in the main square, which hit a dozen Union soldiers, put Sherman in a foul mood. At one point he threatened to burn Sandersonville. Hitchcock thought Sherman's policy on this matter was "right. He has his notions, and often says more than he means, but I have not seen a man . . . I think so near the right man to end this war." Hitchcock added that Sherman "was much troubled" by the ordeal of an elderly lady whose possessions were stripped by foragers, and he ordered "some coffee and other supplies sent her." So his conscience had not completely hardened after all. In the event, Sandersonville remained untouched, and Sherman pushed on the following day through pine forests to Tenniville Station (No. 13), while Slocum continued to destroy the railroad as far as Station No. 10 close to a crossing point over the Ogeechee.[53]

Sherman then transferred to the right wing and traveled with Blair's 17th Corps; he found Blair's knowledge and hospitality congenial. Howard traveled with Logan's 15th Corps pushed out on the outer flank a day's march

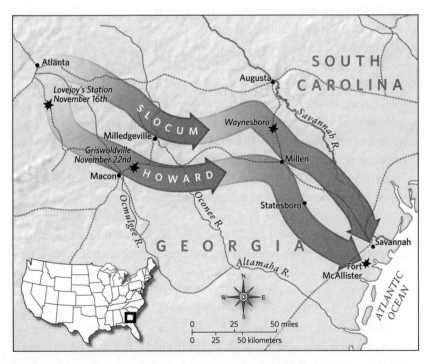

March to the Sea

ahead, ready to turn the flank of any Confederate opposition. Blair brought to Sherman's attention some of the more absurd reports in the Southern press concerning his "desperate retreat" to the Atlantic coast with an army of only 25,000 men. The staff chuckled over these, but Sherman put this information to good use. He realized that the Confederates, bewildered by the rapidity of his advance, had still failed to calculate his true objective and also underestimated his strength. Indeed, Beauregard persisted in treating this incursion as a minor raid and guessed at a force of 36,000. He needed to concentrate Confederate forces against Sherman but conspicuously failed to do so. Instead, he called for reinforcements, and Sherman left little time for them to arrive at the front. As Liddell Hart recognized, "Every gain in speed increases not only the attacker's security but the defender's insecurity." Sherman exploited these errors ruthlessly.[54]

Slocum received orders to shift to his left toward Lumpkin's Station and Jacksonboro. Kilpatrick's cavalry had already cut the Augusta Railroad near Waynesboro; Sherman instructed Kilpatrick to attack Wheeler and "to indulge him with all the fighting he wanted." Kilpatrick accomplished this mission at Thomas's Station, giving the impression of a full-blooded advance on Augusta. On November 30 the 17th Corps reached the Ogeechee River, and by December 3 it occupied Millen. Sherman's front at this point measured only 15 miles. As Wheeler's cavalry had been diverted northward, the narrow corridor between the Savannah and Ogeechee Rivers had been completely uncovered. Sherman could thus drive southeastward toward the city free of opposition. In any case, Augusta offered fewer enticements than Savannah, mainly because it was landlocked and Sherman needed to make contact with the coast. Halleck, once he had received confirmation that Sherman had crossed the Ogeechee, ordered the preparation of stores to be shipped to Hilton Head.

The area east of Millen formed the "Pine Barrens" or "Wire Grass" region, denoted by tall, slender, but tough grass unsuitable for forage—"except for Indian ponies," Sherman cut in during a discussion by his staff of its geography, revealing his detailed local knowledge. Nichols could not but express admiration for Sherman's "marvellous" memory and "acute powers of observation." The soil was sandy, darkened by cypress and live oak and palmetto trees; swamps and lakes provided shelter for alligators and snakes. Before setting out on the March, Sherman had a special map of the Georgian hinterland drawn based on the census of 1860, placing on each county a note of its population, numbers of livestock, and crop yields. This map provided valuable information, but its importance is apt to be exaggerated, as it could not determine his course. Sherman could not avoid the Pine Barrens just because he had this map in his possession.[55]

"The next movement will be on Savannah," Sherman informed Howard proudly on December 2, "your two corps moving along down the Ogeechee," with Blair's 17th Corps destroying the railroad while Logan's 15th Corps remained on the southwest bank "ready to cross over in case of opposition"; Sherman expressed delight that the Confederates were still uncertain of his ultimate objective. The left wing should keep synchronized with Blair, whose "progress you can rate by the smokes," while he attacked the railroad with "devilish" zeal—and therefore might be the target of opposition. Kilpatrick should continue to guard Slocum's rear and feint toward Waynesboro. Sherman was careful to ensure Dayton reminded Slocum that the commander's camp was located close to Buck Head Creek.[56]

Sherman's shoulder began to improve in the early days of December, allowing him to write a short note on December 3 and a longer one on December 4. He stressed to Slocum the need to fill all empty wagons as a precaution should the taking of Savannah be prolonged. Regaining the use of his right arm did not change his nocturnal habits. A few nights earlier Hitchcock was disturbed by somebody poking the fire and prowling about casting a "shadow on my tent" after 3:00 a.m. He got up to find the picturesque sight of the commanding general wandering about: "lower extremities—bare feet in slippers, red flannel drawers—as to upper, woollen shirt, over which his old dressing gown, and blue cloth (1/2 cloak) cape." Hitchcock then reflected, "He is proverbially the most restless man in the army at night—never sleeps a night through, and frequently comes out and pokes around in this style, disregarding all remonstrance as to taking cold." Sometimes disturbed by asthma, he made up the sleep deficit by snoozing during the day. His nocturnal meanders and his complete lack of pomp—he always rode on fields rather than forcing troops to make way for him—encouraged accessibility, not informality. Even private soldiers addressed him directly; increasingly they called him "Uncle Billy" to his face. He also exhibited an astonishing knowledge of his officers and NCOs. The feeling grew widespread among every man that "in a certain sense . . . Sherman had his eye on him." Banished forever was the stern, grumpy, unyielding curmudgeon of 1861. Instead there was the true, sympathetic leader who inspired trust—whom men followed willingly wherever he wanted to go—though he could still be stern when the occasion demanded it.[57]

Sherman had much to think about. The Pine Barrens presented a serious challenge given the ease with which felled trees could obstruct his advance.

Yet the engineer companies placed in the vanguard paid dividends, and all obstructions were removed "in an incredibly short time." Still, the risks to his advancing columns were by no means minor, because of the reduction in portable foodstuffs. If geography no longer favored him, however, his acute planning and forethought garnered countervailing advantages: he encountered no appreciable opposition until he got within 15 miles of Savannah. The troops were in fine fettle, as their life was a healthy one; even Hitchcock, new to camp and field, observed that "it is full of an independent and vigorous enjoyment"; the troops enjoyed foraging; the historian Lee Kennett remarks that it served as an "almost addictive source of pleasure." As Sherman's columns approached Savannah they were accompanied by more horses and mules, 35,000 in all, and more wagons, about 2,700, than they had started with. The seizure of horseflesh was excessive but ensured the horses retained their fitness. Riding made the March less strenuous. The craze for mounts spread across the infantry. "The 6th Iowa are plumb crazy on the horse question," an Illinois soldier observed.[58]

By December 8 the rhythm of Sherman's March began to change. That day he encountered a young officer of the 17th Corps who had been severely wounded by a mine. "This was not war, but murder, and it made me very angry," Sherman confessed. He immediately ordered a group of Confederate prisoners of war forward, with picks and shovels, "so as to explode their own torpedoes, or to discover and dig them up." Such an order is prohibited by the Geneva Convention; it was first signed in 1864, but the United States did not accede until 1882. The prisoners pleaded to be released from this duty, "but I reiterated the order, and could hardly stop laughing at their stepping so gingerly" along the path they were forced to tread. On December 10 Sherman went forward into the thick woods and espied a Confederate parapet, "with its deep ditches, canals and bayous, full of water; and it looked as though another siege was inevitable." His advance was restricted to five narrow causeways, "commanded by heavy ordnance" all too reminiscent of Chickasaw Bayou. Sherman quickly deduced that an assault would be "unwise," not least because "I had brought my army, almost unscathed, so great a distance"; any defeat at this stage would have disproportionate effects. Sherman reasoned he could win "by the operation of time." But time was not so bountiful: the logistical position was tricky, and a long siege appeared out of the question. The March to the Sea concluded with the sea just out of sight.[59]

Sherman, the author of the most famous and reviled of American campaigns, had relied entirely on himself. The scheme had been his, he had persuaded his skeptical chiefs to allow him to carry it out, and in doing so, he had taken a strategic gamble in Tennessee. Yet he had brought it off with aplomb. There can be no doubt that his freedom of maneuver and effortless progress was the product of a colossal Confederate error in permitting Hood's plunge toward Nashville. Hood's movement in the opposite direction also allowed Sherman's dispersed advance to gain momentum on a broad front. The moral opprobrium often lavished against Sherman, especially on the March to the Sea, was less marked at the time. Much of it is rooted in "the lies" of Confederate propagandists in the very final struggle for the moral high ground in waging this war. Many Southern voices can be found in the sources expressing surprise at how well they were treated. Sherman's style of war was far from novel. Correlli Barnett describes French columns in 1805 that resembled "migrating tribes of gypsies hung about with plunder, edible and otherwise." And they treated civilians far more harshly than Sherman's men did.[60]

If we accept the centrality of plunder as a motive for taking part in war, then it follows that the Southern pleading concerning the unique horrors to which they were subjected should be rejected. The criticism directed at Sherman is too personalized, as if he bears personal responsibility for every burning and act of vandalism. He has assumed a wholly false diabolic presence in this self-indulgent and self-serving folklore of victimhood. The further we move away from the actual events of November–December 1864, the blacker and sharper his presence is etched on Southern consciousness. Even contemporary critics of Sherman, including one on his own staff, Major Henry Hitchcock, tended to assume that if he had enforced his orders to the letter, then his soldiers would have instantly obeyed. Their behavior differs little from that of Union and Confederate troops on other fronts. Lee Kennett is undoubtedly correct in claiming that the soldiers, not their commanders, "fixed the parameters of desolation" in deciding what should be taken and what should be left, and this varied with units and individuals. "And had the saintly O. O. Howard commanded in Sherman's place," he notes shrewdly, "they would have done no differently."[61]

As for Sherman, he still had to bring this operation to a victorious conclusion, opening up supply lines to the US Navy waiting anxiously offshore. Once he had Savannah safely in his hands, he had to decide where to go, and what then? Would Grant call him to Virginia, or would he remain an independent commander? If the latter, what thoughts were agitating his "busy brain"?

14

Marching to Victory, December
1864–April 1865

The March to the Sea might be over, but Sherman had not yet reached the sea. He had managed to cross the Ogeechee River thanks to the reconstruction of King's Bridge "in an incredibly short time," but he still faced two thorny problems. First, he needed to make contact with the Union fleet. The Union signal station at a rice mill on the Cheeves plantation close to Ossabaw Sound had watched, searched, and signaled for two days but had found nothing. Sherman spent a lot of time gazing out to sea "watching for the appearance of the fleet." Second, he still needed to seize Savannah, a risky operation that had to be completed swiftly. It is true that Sherman encountered weak opposition and that the March had not pulled significant Confederate reinforcements to Savannah. Nonetheless, he lacked the equipment for a prolonged siege and might yet be seriously embarrassed. Savannah was defended and Ossabaw Sound covered by Fort McAllister, more than 30 miles south of the city. Logistical problems were growing worse. The variety of foodstuffs purloined previously had spoiled the men, who did not appreciate the predictable and dreary meals the cooks served up. But the main problem lay in the rapid diminution of fodder for the horses, mules, and herds of cattle. Sherman ordered his army commanders to besiege Savannah from the north and west while he gave his "personal attention" to operations farther south. Slocum was instructed, "Keep your men fresh, and devour large quantities of the potatoes and corn along the route."

Both Kirkpatrick's cavalry and scouts from the Army of the Tennessee searched for the Union fleet, as Sherman desired that the supplies it would bring should be transported to his camps via the Ogeechee River and then hauled from King's Bridge. A measure of Sherman's anxiety can be detected in his abrupt dismissal of an old prewar acquaintance, Confederate colonel Duncan L. Clinch, who had approached him personally, hoping to win favorable treatment. Sherman denounced him "in the sharpest talk I have heard lately," Hitchcock recorded, and though admitting that he still entertained the "kindest feelings for him personally," Sherman told him forcefully "that he must take the lot of a prisoner—that he could do nothing for him more than for any other, but he would be treated kindly, etc." [1]

The approach march to Fort McAllister had been sped up by the energy of Howard's engineers from the Army of the Tennessee. Sherman rode over to King's Bridge on the evening of December 12 to find that it was complete except for the handrail alongside the road. Feeling that men toppling over the edge was the least likely danger they might face, Sherman ordered that "health and safety" requirements should be ignored and that the bridge should be used without a handrail. The following day William B. Hazen's 2nd Division of the 15th Corps marched across the 2 miles of causeway over the rice fields to invest Fort McAllister from the west, south, and east. During this interval word arrived that masts might have been spotted out at sea, which convinced Sherman that the US Navy could not be looking for him after all. The stakes appeared to have risen. The tactical arrangements for Hazen's assault were not Sherman's concern, but should they fail, they would have far-reaching effects that might call into question the utility of his entire strategy. The commanding general gave Hazen his orders personally, as he commanded his old division. McAllister's garrison might be small, but it was strong in artillery, with 23 guns in barbette and one mortar. Hazen left the meeting under no illusion that Sherman believed "that on his action depended the safety of the whole army and the success of the campaign." Sherman and his staff then rode to the Cheeves plantation, where Sherman could simultaneously supervise attempts to find the US Navy and observe Hazen's progress. At about 1:00 p.m. the 2nd Division arrived before Fort McAllister's works, and four hours later it launched a simultaneous assault that overwhelmed them. Watching from Cheeves's rice mill, a relieved Sherman bore "testimony to the handsome manner in which it was accomplished."[2]

The fall of Fort McAllister permitted Sherman to concentrate his energies on establishing contact with the US Navy. Heartened by the success, he remained determined to make contact that night, and he remarks in his *Memoirs* that "I was dreadfully impatient." After receiving word of the sighting of a gunboat, he and Howard were rowed out on to Ogeechee by a small crew of volunteer officers; that evening Sherman inspected Fort McAllister and found a yawl, which he used to continue his journey down river a further 6 miles before he found the *Dandelion*. Sherman went aboard and wrote a series of letters to Secretary Stanton, Grant (via Halleck), and Major General John G. Foster, the commander of the Department of the

South. Sherman then returned on the same night to Hazen's makeshift head-quarters at Fort McAllister—only to be disturbed by Foster, who immediately offered him 600,000 rations and a dozen siege guns from Hilton Head. Despite his weariness he returned at once with Foster and by chance encountered Admiral John A. Dahlgren; Sherman's breezy enthusiasm and ebullience did much to revive Dahlgren's flagging spirits. Attending to a variety of arrangements kept Sherman occupied until he returned to Cheeves's Mill on December 15.[3]

With the additional support of siege guns, six 20-pounder Parrotts and six 30-pounder Parrotts loaned by Foster, Sherman turned to the problem of assaulting Savannah with fresh confidence. He determined to move on the city at the earliest opportunity; on December 17 he formally demanded its surrender. He attempted to intimidate Lieutenant General William J. Hardee, formally entrusted with the city's defense, by intimating that if left no alternative but to assault Savannah he would resort "to the harshest measures and shall make little effort to restrain my Army," thus exploiting for psychological effect the reputation he had gained. Hardee, however, called his bluff and rejected his demand. The swampy country around Savannah had complicated Sherman's tactical distribution, with his left resting on the Savannah River, 3 miles above the city, and the right on the Ogeechee at King's Bridge. He needed to assault either at one or two places over narrow causeways, though the arrival of the heavy ordnance had alleviated the predicament. The fates appeared to favor Sherman again: he went so far as to claim to Halleck that "their efforts thus far have been puerile, and I regard Savannah as already gained."[4]

Sherman had prevented Slocum from transferring an entire corps to the South Carolina side of the Savannah River, cutting the Union causeway, the sole remaining route out of the city. He estimated that Hardee's garrison amounted to 15,000 men, and he appeared excessively cautious in fearing that Slocum's men might be cut off from support. He mentions in his *Memoirs* a desire to avoid a Ball's Bluff–style disaster that had occurred along the banks of the Potomac, south of Washington, DC, in October 1861 when several hundreds of men, thrown into a panic, drowned in the river. More pertinent was Foster's fear that his forces were too weak to mount a second thrust from the east toward Slocum's corps. Sherman traveled to Port Royal to confer with Foster, and these deliberations used up more precious time. Hardee's defiance acted as a mask to disguise the preparations that he and his new nominal superior, General P. G. T. Beauregard, the commander of the Confederate Military Division of the West, were making to evacuate Savannah. During the night of December 20–21 Hardee's force slipped away while Sherman was still conferring with Dahlgren; on December 21 his adjutant, Dayton, got word to him that Union troops had occupied Savannah. On returning to Savannah Sherman rode straight to the Pulaski House, where he had once been a guest. Sherman was greatly disappointed the following day "that Hardee had escaped with his garrison"; other works are uniformly critical of what appears as yet another failure to bring this successful campaign to a triumphant conclusion. Sherman admitted to his foster father, Thomas Ewing Sr., that he should have caught Savannah's garrison on the Union causeway running north, "but if Hardee had given me two days I would have closed that also." Perhaps, but the issue is more complicated.[5]

Sherman played many roles; he was an operational as well as a tactical commander, and occasionally the tension between them conspired to frustrate him. During the planning of this operation Sherman had been distracted by the receipt before December 16 of two letters from Grant, one delivered personally by Colonel Orville Babcock of his staff. With no telegraph link, Grant had been forced to trace Sherman's progress by reading a digest of newspaper reports mainly drawn from the Richmond daily newspapers. His chief of staff, Rawlins, warned that taking so much notice of them might provoke complete censorship of Sherman's movements, but Grant ignored his advice. The first letter mainly presented for Sherman's benefit a concise *tour d'horizon* of overall progress on other fronts. Grant eschewed any idea of giving "directions for future action. But will state a general idea I have," and he awaited Sherman's views once "you have established yourself on the sea-coast." His main idea saw it as a paramount requirement "to get control of the only two through routes from east to west," which would be attained by taking Savannah or Augusta "or by holding any port east of Savannah. . . . If Wilmington falls, a force from there can cooperate with you." The letter concluded with some critical comments on George Thomas's conduct in Tennessee, especially his withdrawal into Nashville's defenses, which could not have made comfortable reading for Sherman.

The second letter, though much shorter, contained a very cogent statement of Grant's controlling idea: "I have concluded that the most important operation towards closing out the rebellion will be to close out Lee and his Army." It was also more prescriptive. Grant required Sherman to establish a fortified base on the coast that would continue to pose a threat to the region and distant Confederate forces, and "with the balance of your command come here by water with all dispatch." Grant remained emphatic that, though Sherman could select a subordinate to command the garrison left behind, "you I want in person." The removal of the bulk of his command to Virginia, Sherman remarked in his *Memoirs,* "was so complete a change from what I had supposed would be the course of events that I was very much concerned." The implications behind these two letters, especially the second, he admitted, "gave me great uneasiness"; however much he feared for his independent status, Sherman, the ever-loyal subordinate, at once began work on Grant's stipulations, sending Colonel Orlando Poe to Fort McAllister to study the ground. This site appeared at first glance the one most suitable to form the kernel of the fortification to shelter the garrison and its stores and equipment, as well as 2,500 wagons and "the vast herd of mules and horses" that would be left behind.[6]

Sherman sent a long statement of these preliminary preparations to Grant on December 16, proving once again why he was his most reliable subordinate. The backwash of Benjamin F. Butler's dismissal after his failure to seize Fort Fisher on December 24–25, 1864, had forced Grant to reappraise his strategic priorities after sending his two earlier letters. As these had not insisted that he take Savannah, Sherman had modified his plans and now ordered Slocum not to reinforce his left, a move that Sherman had initially favored. "But in view of the change of plan made necessary by your order of the 6th," Sherman assured Grant, "I will maintain things in *Status Quo* till I have got all my transportation for the troops you require at James River, which I will accompany and command in person." So his compliance with Grant's orders was the main reason for Sherman's tactical adjustment north of Savannah, not an incorrigible cautious tendency.

Naturally, he gave Grant a strong favorable impression of the March. He also sketched an alternative concept that he wanted to carry out should Savannah fall. Sherman intended "instantly to march to Columbia, S.C., thence to Raleigh, and thence to report to you." He calculated this would take six weeks, while he optimistically assumed that if the ships could be found he would arrive in Virginia by the middle of January.[7]

In his December 3 letter Grant, with his usual thoughtfulness, had suggested a possible visit to see Sherman and that Ellen might accompany him. Sherman wrote her a long letter the same night forewarning her that a trip to Georgia might be a possibility, "Await events and trust to fortune," he told her. "I'll turn up when and where you least expect me." He expressed pleasure at the continuing mild and pleasant weather but expected rain—he would not be disappointed—so had taken the precaution of corduroying the roads. On December 22 after the fall of Savannah, Sherman telegraphed Ellen announcing its capture. "We are all well." But Sherman's most famous communication that day was sent to President Lincoln: "I beg to present you as a Christmas gift the city of Savannah." The popular reaction to this act would influence Grant's decision-making, not least the dissipation of presidential anxiety over Sherman's marching techniques, coupled with a joint congressional resolution of thanks to Sherman and his troops for "their late brilliant movement through Georgia."[8]

Once contact with the US Navy had been firmly established, it brought some unexpected pleasures. Lieutenant Alfred Thayer Mahan, USN, the eldest son of Sherman's old teacher Dennis Hart Mahan, presented himself at Sherman's headquarters. He was received exuberantly. Sherman "broke into a smile all over, as they say," and shook his hand vigorously. Sherman permitted himself some warm reminiscence of his cadet days, recalling fondly that nothing brought him greater pleasure on leaving the blackboard after offering his solution than the unadorned compliment from his old teacher, "Very well done, Mr. Sherman."[9]

Mostly, though, the New Year brought vexation. The March wreaked havoc on his correspondence with Ellen. On November 8 she wrote warning that baby Charles had caught "a severe cold," and "I greatly fear he will never get over it but that it will end in consumption"; the doctor was also concerned about the consequences of his inherited asthmatic tendency. News of his son's death on December 4 came via John. Sherman had never laid eyes on the child and remained unaffected, though Ellen was not. She had endured the loss of two sons in 15 months, and the second calamity he could not share opened a chasm of misapprehension and misunderstanding in their relationship.[10]

A letter from Ellen did not arrive until the end of December and expressed a peevish tone. Although she had told her husband that she intended to stay with the children at South Bend, Indiana, during the holidays, he still sent his letter of December 16 to Lancaster. She refrained from inflicting on him an account of Charles's "long agony & my woe in witnessing and recalling it," though she felt relief "to have him safe with his heavenly Father." She hoped that his and Willy's prayers "may ensure my perseverance and obtain for you the gift of faith." Sherman continued to ignore these not so subtle hints that he should convert to Catholicism. His Christmas Day letter did not even mention Charley's death. Instead he commented, "My clothing is good yet and I can even afford a white shirt." He told Minnie the same day, "I have not even heard if the baby got well of the cold," but he did know by the New Year. He wrote to Ellen insensitively that "I cannot say that I grieve for him as I did Willy, for he was but a mere ideal, whereas Willy was incorporated with us, and seemed designed to perpetuate our Memories." Sherman remarked to Ellen that he felt that his wartime experience had rendered him "callous to death. It is so common, so familiar, that it no longer impresses me as of old."[11]

Another irritating distraction arrived on January 9, 1865: the secretary of war, Edwin M. Stanton. Stanton was a harsh, ruthless, and brusque man—blunt to the point of unpleasantness, utterly indifferent to the feelings of others. The ostensible reason for his visit concerned the respective jurisdiction of the War and Treasury Departments over expropriated cotton and who should profit from its disposal; on this matter Sherman held firm views. The priority allotted to cotton by Stanton served as a distraction from the real issue. Although an admirer of Sherman, Stanton had become exasperated by his attitudes toward the deployment of black troops. "He does not seem to appreciate the importance of this measure," Stanton wrote anxiously, "and appears indifferent if not hostile." Sherman's letter to Spooner had perturbed him. At the end of December Halleck warned Sherman that rising elements in the Republican Party claimed that "you have manifested an almost criminal dislike of the negro," displayed "contempt" toward the freedmen, and made no effort to recruit them into Union military service. The growing danger that they might be recruited by the Confederacy, moreover, required that every effort be made to ensure they could escape into Union lines. "These I know are the views of some of the leading men of the administration," Halleck concluded with his usual detached air, "and they now express dissatisfaction that you did not carry them out in your great raid."[12]

Once forewarned, Sherman sought to impress Stanton. He laid on a tour of Savannah and the troops' encampments. Stanton asked to meet 20 black leaders and on January 12 proudly asked them about their hopes and aspirations for life after the war. Then he asked Sherman to leave the room, which he did reluctantly, and inquired of the black leaders how Sherman had treated them. The account of this meeting in the latter's *Memoirs* is marked by an antipathy toward Stanton that Sherman did not feel that New Year's. He observed "that there is no doubt that Mr. Stanton when he reached Savannah shared these thoughts [of Sherman's critics]"; the evidence indicates that this claim is an exaggeration, though Stanton was perplexed by Sherman's behavior and sought reassurance. This he received from the black leaders, who regarded Sherman "as a man, in the providence of God, specially set apart to accomplish this work [of advancing their interests]." As for his treatment of them, "he did not meet the Secretary of War with more courtesy than he met us." They regarded Sherman as "a friend and gentleman." This pleased Stanton, and he invited Sherman and his staff to dinner with the admirals, where postwar issues were discussed at greater length. But both parties read into the conclusions what they wanted to find. A measure of insincerity had been expressed by both Sherman and Stanton—theirs was not a true meeting of minds. Stanton urged Sherman to bring the war to an end as quickly as possible. These misunderstandings laid the ground for a far worse final, almost disastrous rupture in their relations.[13]

Despite a measure of insincerity on both sides, Sherman had made a notable effort to reassure Stanton and the War Department. He strenuously attempted to make amends. On January 19, shortly after Stanton had left Savannah, on the pretext of returning a map that Stanton had mislaid ("I avail myself of the opportunity"), he wrote enclosing orders that had received the secretary's approval in draft form during his recent visit. These concerned the South Carolina Sea Islands and the 30-mile strip of abandoned rice fields "back from the sea" he had reserved for the settlement of the freedmen, though Special Field Orders No. 15 did not grant their permanent legal title. One of the most important directives of this order stipulated that youthful, able-bodied freedmen "must be encouraged to enlist as soldiers . . . to contribute their share toward maintaining their own freedom," thus "securing their rights as citizens of the United States." But Sherman was careful to rule out any form of compulsion. He expressed confidence that this order would help "create a schism in Jeff. Davis's dominions."[14]

Against the background of these anxieties and distractions was the incessant discussion of ideas about Sherman's next campaign. Grant's attitude had been influenced strongly by Sherman's hurried, even casual letter to Halleck written aboard the *Dandelion* after he had made contact with the US Navy. Here he had given a striking account of his March and intimated that "a similar destruction of roads and resources hence to Raleigh would compel General Lee to come out of his entrenched camp." He also revealed an inexhaustible enthusiasm for marching on Montgomery, Alabama, to slow Hood's progress in Tennessee if needed; he did not know then of Thomas's triumph at Nashville. Perhaps the Carolinas scheme had not been so firmly set in his mind as he suggests in his *Memoirs*. Within two days of its dispatch Grant ordered Halleck to inform Sherman that no troops from his command should be sent to Virginia "until plan of campaign is fully agreed upon." Sherman also received notification that the "whole matter of your future action should be left to your discretion." This was good news. Grant so liked Sherman's letter that he suggested to Stanton that a bowdlerized version of it be published: "It is refreshing to see a commander after a campaign of more than seven months' duration ready for still further operations, and without wanting any outfit or rest."[15]

Sherman's own advocacy of the concept of a continuing advance into South Carolina stressed the waste of military time consumed by the delays inherent in a voyage to Virginia. Grant conceded the strength of this argument. "I doubt whether you may accomplish more . . . where you are than if brought here; especially as I am informed . . . that it would take about two months to get you here with all the other calls . . . for ocean transportation." Grant also speculated that Lee "wants Richmond to be the last place surrendered. If he has such views it may be well to indulge him until we get everything else in our hands." In this regard, Sherman's concluding, punitive tone resonated with Grant. The former wrote passionately that the entire country "would rejoice to have this army turned loose on South Carolina to devastate that State, in the manner we have done in Georgia"; the psychological effect, Sherman calculated, "would have a direct and immediate bearing on your campaign in Virginia."[16]

Sherman's full statement of his plans, composed on Christmas Day 1864, ranks among his most lucid conceptual statements. As to their evolution, "I have thought them over so long that they appear as clear as daylight." He had deliberately left Augusta unoccupied because the Confederates could not tell whether this would be his next objective. Augusta was the home of a massive powder works, an extraordinary experiment in "state socialism" that in addition to munitions produced rifled muskets, shoes, and buttons. Augusta remained an inviting and vulnerable target, and its defense forced the Confederates to divide their skeletal forces between it and Charleston. Sherman intended to advance between them "on any curved line that gives me the best supplies," destroying railroads as he went to either Branchville or Columbia, South Carolina, occupying the latter (the state capital) and Camden. From there he would advance to cut the Charleston and Wilmington Railroad between the Santee and Cape Fear Rivers aiming for Wilmington, North Carolina, where contact could be reestablished with Dahlgren's ships. Once replenished, Sherman would head for Raleigh. "The game is up with Lee, unless he comes out of Richmond, avoids you, and fights me, in which event I should reckon on you being on his heels." Sherman expressed confidence that "I can handle him in open country."

One aspect of the plan that Sherman thought might be objectionable was his neglect of Charleston—"now a more desolated wreck, and is hardly worth the time it would take to starve it out." Sherman realized its symbolic importance and asked for guidance from Grant as to whether he should give it more attention. He preferred to avoid it "as a point of little importance," for its railroads to the interior had already been cut or destroyed. Nor had he neglected George Thomas. "I am gratified beyond measure at the result" of his victory at Nashville on December 15–16. He ordered him to pursue as far as Columbia, Mississippi, or Selma, Alabama, because he could subsist easily on the country. In sum, "Now that Hood is used up by Thomas, I feel disposed to bring the matter to an issue just as quickly as possible." And Grant felt disposed to let him do just this. On December 27 Sherman received orders that "you may make preparation to start on your Northern expedition without delay." He should destroy railroads in both Carolinas "and join the Armies operating against Richmond as soon as you can." The order concerning the destruction of railroads is significant, as some historians write as if Sherman had selected this objective for himself. Grant contemplated moving Sherman's troops to Virginia from North Carolina ports if an advance toward the rear of Petersburg should prove too difficult. He also made arrangements for the supply of his formations once he crossed the Roanoke River.[17]

Sherman had to give a great deal of thought to the logistical aspects of his next great challenge. The operational dimensions of the March across the Carolinas were more risky than they had been in Georgia. The distances were greater, as were the topographical barriers, especially the series of great rivers that he would need to cross, swollen by floodwaters, as Sherman was marching in the midwinter rains. In the first phase of the campaign, he would advance northward away from the coast. In Special Field Orders No. 139 Sherman issued instructions to shift "the grand depot of the army" to Savannah in order that "it may be supplied abundantly and well." On Christmas Day 1864 he wrote to the quartermaster general, Montgomery C. Meigs, agreeing emphatically that Union armies should be able to provide themselves with forage. He did not need more horses, except perhaps 400 to 500 "good artillery horses." He suggested that "my marches have demonstrated the great truth that armies, even of vast magnitude, are not tied down to bases." A day later, he assured Meigs, "You may rely upon me drawing from this country everything it affords for our wants, and adding as little as possible to the burdens of the Government."[18]

But even Sherman did not spend all Christmas working. He had accepted the invitation of Charles Green, a wealthy British banker, to move his headquarters to the latter's comfortable and elegant residence. On the evening of December 25, the staff held a "family dinner-party" and invited Generals Slocum and Corse to join them. After dining off Mr. Green's "handsome china and silver," the guests drank Sherman's health. Hitchcock thought it "as quiet and pleasant a Christmas dinner as one could wish—away from home."[19]

Back at his desk, Sherman continued his efforts to encourage trade. It is clear that he did not just requisition everything he needed but purchased some of it, as he laid down firm and clear procedures for all forms of trade. Still, gathering his stores remained a slow business. Though Blair's 17th Corps had taken Pocotaligo on January 15, getting Sherman's left wing up to Sister's Ferry had been delayed "by the non-arrival of our stores necessary to fill our wagons." But these tactical frustrations were reduced by greater cooperation. He waited intently for news of the renewed effort to take Fort Fisher, on which he had been briefed by Admiral Porter. Even if the assault failed once more and the garrison was pinned to its position, Sherman calculated, his engineers could "use that road back to Kinston and Goldsborough." He also wanted New Bern held strongly. "If Lee sees the points he may try and checkmate me there." Therefore, he urged Porter to "hold fast to New Bern with the tenacity of life." On January 21 Grant informed Sherman that Fort Fisher had fallen and explained that the 21,000 men of John Schofield's 23rd Corps, partners of old, would be sent either to Wilmington or New Bern. Sherman would assume the command of these troops again "as you come in communication with them."[20]

Grant also promised that should Sherman's progress be halted for any reason he would send two corps from Virginia to reinforce him. But Sherman reasoned that he was about to undertake a hazardous enterprise in which nature rather than the Confederates represented the greater threat. "I think the time has come now when we should attempt the boldest moves," he explained to Halleck, "and my experience is that they are easier of execution than most timid ones, because the enemy is disconcerted by them"—as they had been in Georgia. But his audacity rested on the finest of logistical calculations.

The aim of this March therefore needs further clarification, as Sherman and those who have written about him tend to stress the destruction inflicted on South Carolina as its ultimate validation. In further correspondence with Halleck he summarized his methods: he would "move rapidly to my objective, . . . striking boldly and quickly when my objective is reached. I will give due heed and encouragements to all peace movements, but conduct war as though it could only terminate with the destruction of the enemy and the occupation of all his strategic points." Destruction was necessary and far from unimportant in eroding the capacity of the Confederate war economy. However, as in Georgia, the main aim was the attack on Confederate resolve, morale, and reputation. He never expressed this aspect better than in his *Memoirs*. "My aim then was, to whip the rebels, to humble their pride, to follow them to their inmost recesses, and make them fear and dread us." He also wished to exploit the "undue fear of our western men" entertained by Southerners. Their trembling had led to many inventions of "such ghost-like stories of our prowess in Georgia, that they were scared by their own inventions." Sherman suspected that Southern morale had already been half subdued before he set out, and he would pile on further anguish.

On January 21 Sherman departed for Beaufort and then on arrival took a small group of his staff on a ride north to Pocotaligo, where they would "act as though [they] were bound for Charleston" about 50 miles eastward. Sherman knew this country well, having been stationed in Charleston in 1842–46. He had made some deliberately injudicious comments about his intentions earlier, and his moves were a convincing way of following them up. Howard was ordered to close up to the Salkehatchie River but not to cross it—though he was to give the impression that he intended to. "The next movement I want the enemy to feel is from the left flank." Here the floods produced by the "villainous" weather caused further delays, as Slocum's first pontoon bridge became submerged under floodwaters, and he had no choice but to advance farther upriver to Sister's Ferry, protected by a gunboat, the *Pontiac*, to lay another. Mercifully the rain abated, it turned cold and sunny, and the water levels fell. Sherman did not waste this unwanted additional time. He carried out a detailed reconnaissance of the entire area that convinced him of the wisdom of his chosen course of masking Charleston because of the immense difficulty of advancing on the city for so little reward.

Sherman desired that the right wing pivot on Pocotaligo and head north to Branchville, breaking the railroad from Augusta to Charleston. He hoped thereby to force the Confederates to withdraw behind the Edisto River. "I will then move in compact order," he informed General Foster in a detailed briefing, "and occupy that space of country lying in the triangle formed by

Kinston, Columbia, and Camden." He mentions that he might "devote some attention to Columbia and the railroads in that neighborhood." But he certainly does not offer the slightest evidence that he intended to devote any punitive attention to this region or that he intended to make a terrifying example of South Carolina's state capital. On the contrary, he hoped that sufficient forage and subsistence would be available to let him "move with rapidity to Florence" in an attempt to liberate the prisoners of war detained there. Earlier in private correspondence with Halleck, he had remarked irritably that he doubted whether he would "spare the public buildings there, as we did at Milledgeville." But this threat had been forgotten by the time he arrived at Columbia. He wished Foster, a cooperative and industrious officer with whom he enjoyed convivial relations who was now under his command, to do everything in his power to maintain the feint toward Charleston and distract Beauregard's attention as much as he could.

But the March could not begin until Sherman received word that Slocum had crossed the Savannah River. At last this arrived on January 29. Sherman had already set in motion a noisy diversion at Combahee Ferry and the railroad bridge over the Salkehatchie River to engage Confederate attention. But, as ever, preparing two or three stages ahead, he had alerted Foster to the need to arouse the garrison commanders at New Bern, Kinston, and Goldsboro to be ready to cooperate with him. He also relied on Foster to keep Admirals Dahlgren and Porter fully briefed on his movements and requirements. Sherman invariably placed the greatest importance on army-navy cooperation. He had already heard news of the fall of Wilmington, "which may modify matters somewhat, but the general principles above indicated will still be applicable and sufficient for your guidance."[21]

The March began on February 1, and Sherman was glad to be on the move again—"sallying forth," to use one of his favorite phrases. He and the staff that night lodged in Dr. Fielding Ficklin's house, initially minus their wagon train. This demanded sleeping on drafty floors, and on the first night Sherman was so cold that he got up several times to sit by the fire. This burned low, and to keep it alight he used an old mantel clock and parts of a bedstead, "the only act of vandalism that I recall done by myself personally during the war," he recalled wryly. The weather was cold and dry, though the previous weeks had witnessed "heavy and continuous rain" and the rivers had overflowed. As the country was "very low and intersected by creeks and points of salt marsh, making roads very bad," Sherman faced many disadvantages. Still, he hoped the Confederates would attempt to make a stand and block his progress. On the first day his troops covered 18 miles, a remarkable feat: Joseph Wheeler's cavalry had made the most of the delay to place obstructions and burn bridges, but the pioneer battalions were so efficient in removing them, Sherman wrote, "that obstructions seemed only to quicken their progress." Though Slocum's advance had been slower, the right wing hardly had a cake-walk. It had to cross swampy country in the cold; on February 3 two divisions of the 17th Corps crossed a swamp almost 3 miles wide, "with water varying from knee to shoulder deep," the two divisional commanders leading from the front, wading through the water with their men. The Confederate line along the Salkehatchie broke after a skirmish involving about 90 casualties. Sherman's most pressing worry remained supply, "but on this point I must risk a good deal"; he consoled himself "that where other people live we can, even if they have to starve or move away."[22]

Sherman resumed his previous practice of accompanying Blair's 17th Corps. On February 7–10 the right wing secured the line of the Charleston–Augusta Railroad and proceeded to destroy it; the left wing joined in the work on February 8–11. Sherman had succeeded in concentrating his force while Confederate forces remained divided; indeed, they were scattered from Branchville to Charleston and Aiken and Augusta. Moreover, Sherman continued to sow confusion by sending Kilpatrick's cavalry to the environs of Augusta again to threaten the city without being "drawn needlessly into a serious battle." On February 11 Sherman's entire force proceeded to Orangeburg, an important communications link between Charleston and Columbia, having crossed the South Fork of the Edisto River in the face of token resistance. The crossing did not go without a hitch, however, as parts of Blair's pontoon bridge flooded. All, including Sherman, trudged through water up to their waists; he stepped into deeper water, to general amusement, though soldiers rushed to rescue "Uncle Billy" and carried him across. He immediately realized that the Confederates could not hold Orangeburg and, with typical energy, waded back to his horse on the other side, rode to the pontoon bridge close to the town, almost repaired, and crossed to be one of the first to enter Orangeburg. This turned out to be a poor place, emitting, in Hitchcock's harsh opinion, a "general air of slovenliness, dirt and waste." The Edgefield Railroad and the Edisto Bridge soon drew the attention of Blair's troops. Sherman was as good as his word to Grant: "I will be sure that every rail is twisted." On February 14 he issued orders for both wings to rapidly march on Columbia, which he erroneously believed to be the focal point of a Confederate concentration. He wished to seize it before any concentration could be effected. As for supplies, "we find some hogs, bacon, and corn, but much has been carried off by Wheeler"—as Confederate cavalry "foraged liberally," too.[23]

The advance into South Carolina had been characterized by a certain violent relish, as buildings were set ablaze to give the cradle of secession a "warming"—actually, an initiation into the realities of war, which it had hitherto escaped, except along the coast. Sherman had expressed his views on the soldiers' feelings in graphic language. "They had," he wrote, "an insatiable desire to wreak vengeance upon South Carolina. I almost tremble at her fate, but feel she deserves all that seems in store for her." He had noted at Savannah "the submissiveness of its people," and this sense of powerlessness appears to have been exacerbated by the fumbling of Confederate commanders, who combined directed a force of rather fewer than 40,000 men but were reactive, dilatory, and completely outfoxed by Sherman's clever maneuvers, even though his swerve toward Columbia opened up a gap between his two wings of almost 40 miles.[24]

As Sherman's columns advanced, a significant proportion of the civilian population fled. Sherman observed harshly, "Vacant houses, being of no use to anybody, I care little about, as the owners have thought them of no use to themselves." The constant immersion of the men in cold water led to an increase in alcoholic consumption to warm themselves up, which contributed to wild, unchecked behavior—and many fires. Confederate efforts to burn cotton also led to many fires spreading. Sherman wrote to Wheeler encouraging him to "burn all cotton and save us the trouble. We don't want it, and it has proven a curse to our country." Orangeburg caught fire because of efforts to destroy cotton: Union troops there found themselves fighting rather than lighting fires and managed to save the Orphan Asylum of South Carolina, which housed about 300 children. Sherman's men were not always the guilty party. Indeed, the deliberate lighting of fires, especially in the woods, annoyed Sherman because it forced delay, as units had to locate alternative routes to avoid them. Foraging also became more protracted and hazardous, and more difficult, because of the army's slower pace—about 6 miles per day—over countryside already picked clean.[25]

Burnings were prevalent on Slocum's left wing front and therefore beyond Sherman's purview. At the beginning of the advance, several men were killed or maimed by "torpedoes"; Slocum's troops regarded them as "akin to poisoning a stream of water" and therefore did not regard their use "as fair or legitimate warfare." They exacted their revenge by burning empty houses, but Slocum's advance fell behind schedule, particularly once Sherman revealed that Columbia would be the main objective. Some accounts of the Marches give the impression that Sherman's soldiers spent all their time indulging in mindless vandalism. The eventual destruction of the novelist William Gilmore Simms's library at Woodlands, near Midway, en route to Columbia, appears to fit this philistine stereotype, but the burning of his library was carried out by later waves of troops, as initially it had been guarded by men of Charley Ewing's brigade. At Sherman's behest the fighting men were given many arduous tasks. Slocum's wing destroyed 60 miles of railroad. Howard's wing corduroyed expanses of dirt track; Hazen's division completed 17.6 miles and Force's division 15.8 miles. Despite random vandalism and the planned, systematic destruction, the actions of Sherman's men cannot be compared with later conflicts, such as the Eastern Front in World War II: accounts of pilfering were exaggerated, hardly any violence was directed against Southern civilians, and despite the removal of foodstuffs, no Southerner starved. As for the commanding general, for all his exposed rhetoric, he did not behave like the angel of death. The sometimes censorious Hitchcock observed him making "friends with the children, as usual, sharing his lunch with them, and greatly delighted a red-cheeked little girl of four or five years with a scarcely more rosy cheeked apple."[26]

On this operation Sherman abandoned the opportunism that had characterized the March through Georgia. The challenges he faced were so much greater, and he reverted to thinking out his plans well in advance in intricate detail. As early as January 1865 Sherman held that by advancing inland on Columbia, he gained the triangle between the Congaree and Wateree Rivers, tributaries of the Santee, "breaking up that great centre of the Carolina [rail] roads." He had sketched out this scheme the previous January: he would cross the boundary into North Carolina and "move straight for Goldsboro, via Fayetteville"; with Wilmington in Union hands, then "I can easily take Raleigh, when it seems that Lee must come out of his trenches or allow his army to be absolutely invested." Grant had approved this plan and gained Stanton's agreement to create a new Department of North Carolina under Schofield's command that he placed under Sherman's military division. He also encouraged Sherman that "the peace feeling within the rebel lines is gaining ground rapidly." Confederate vice president Alexander H. Stephens, R. M. T. Hunter, and J. A. Campbell were at Grant's headquarters waiting to be taken to a conference at Hampton Roads.

Grant had also touched on another delicate matter. Sherman had got wind of a congressional effort to pass a bill promoting him to lieutenant general. In his January 21 letter he denounced this as "mischievous." Sherman restated his loyal desire to serve under Grant, "for you and I now are in perfect understanding." Grant thanked Sherman for his "very kind letter" but reassured him that nobody "would be more pleased at your advancement than I, and if you should be placed in my position, and I put subordinate, it would not change our relations in the least." Grant would not object if he had to report to Sherman. The command relationship was strengthened throughout the campaign by this generosity of spirit on both sides. It would be able to bear the much greater storms that would lie ahead.[27]

The approach march to Columbia continued slowly over glutinous roads and rain-sodden swamp, cloaked by fog, with sinuous columns halted by mysterious delays. As the Confederates had been turned out of a strong entrenched position along the south bank of Congaree Creek, on February 15 the right wing closed up to the Congaree River and the state capital. Sherman could see through his binoculars "people running about the streets of Columbia, and occasionally small bodies of cavalry, but no masses." Union and Confederate artillery exchanged shots, which Sherman promptly stopped, though one of these set one of Columbia's railroad depots ablaze and prevented people from "carrying away sacks of corn and meal that we needed." This resistance persuaded Sherman that he might have to fight for Columbia. The right wing then encamped carelessly, with campfires that invited Confederate artillery fire that caused casualties and antagonized Union soldiers.

Confederate commanders soon realized that they were attempting to defend the indefensible. Firing on Union positions was especially foolish, as Columbia could not be declared an "open city." This term denotes that the defenders have abandoned its defense, and thus the attacker has no need to bombard it and take it by force. Columbia's chaotic, bungled, and last-minute evacuation compounded the problem, as large quantities of scarce war materials had to be abandoned. Sherman ordered Howard's right wing to advance on Columbia from the north over the Saluda River. This delay of a day before it was taken led to a complete disintegration of military discipline among the Confederates in Columbia, widespread pillaging by Confederate cavalry "as if they had been bred to the task," and belated, frantic steps to burn cotton that, due to contradictory orders, had been dumped in the streets in

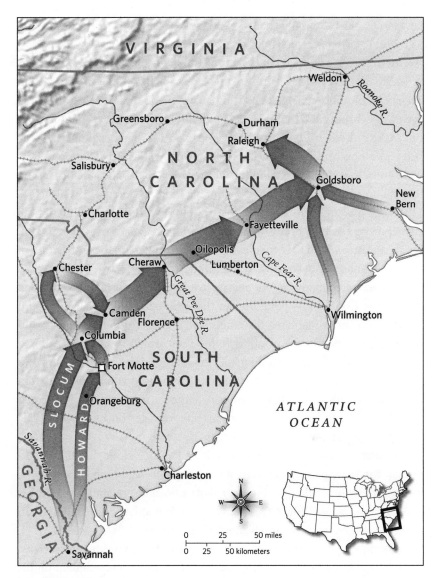

March through Carolinas

preparation for its removal; orders to burn it were only received at 7:00 a.m. on February 17. The Union army entered the city about three and a half hours later. Nichols for one admired its "graceful lines" and "noble contours."

But by 8:00 a.m. a considerable fire had already taken hold, and cotton fires are particularly tricky to extinguish. Nor was this the first of its kind. On

January 22, 1864, Columbia had already experienced a severe fire destroying $3 million worth of cotton and laying waste to property worth $400,000.[28]

This context is significant in evaluating the single most controversial event in Sherman's career—the burning of this state capital. If the Confederates had declared Columbia an "open city" and abandoned it a day earlier, then the events of February 17–18 might not have unfolded in the way that they did. But as the railroad bridge across the Congaree River had been burned, Blair laid a pontoon bridge close to it. Here Sherman waited to enter Columbia, sitting on a log while the engineers laboured. At about 10:00 a.m. he learned that the mayor had surrendered Columbia, and he entered it well before 11:00 a.m. Slocum's left wing lay close by, but his troops never entered the city. Howard received orders to occupy it with a segment of his command, but the balance would have their energies concentrated on the destruction of any public material pertaining to the Confederate war effort. In this regard Columbia offered many targets: at least five factories, as well as two railroad depots, the Confederate Note Bureau that printed its paper currency, and a series of offices organizing the commissary, conscription, ordnance, and the like. The loss of these would enfeeble Lee's army. Howard was ordered to "spare" all dwellings, including colleges, schools, asylums, and harmless private property. Special Field Orders No. 26 focused attention on the destruction of railroads and Columbia's manufacturing capacity. Sherman demanded "the fullest reports" from his subordinates on its progress. The city and its population were not his urgent concern.

Sherman reassured the mayor on at least two occasions that this would remain the case; peaceful citizens had nothing to fear. One such was the mother superior of the Ursuline convent, who had previously taught his daughter Minnie in Ohio. Charley Ewing was put at her disposal. Sherman also encountered some bedraggled escaped prisoners of war; one, S. M. H. Byers, sought him out later and gave him a poem he had written in captivity, "Sherman's March to the Sea." He was rewarded with an attachment on his staff. Then Sherman retired to his quarters at Blanton Duncan's house for an evening nap. But this was disturbed by the mayor bringing news of an old friend, Miss Mary Catherine Poyas, whose father's plantation he had visited while posted at Fort Moultrie in Charleston harbor years before. She had used an inscription in a book Sherman had given her to ensure that Union soldiers treated her property with respect. Even though she and other friends were not sure that "the terrible Sherman" and their old intimate were one and the same, he treated them all, especially the ladies, with great kindness.[29]

By the early evening Sherman could congratulate himself on restoring order in the city. But while riding through it he noticed a number of lolling, drunken soldiers. Columbia had become a center for the production or safekeeping of alcohol. In an effort to appease the "dreaded conqueror," citizens—"like idiots, madmen," complained Hitchcock—ladled out buckets of whiskey to soldiers as they arrived. There was even a measure of fraternization between Union soldiers and Columbia girls. The bulk of the 15th and 17th Corps marched through town. Perhaps 12,000 men dallied, though most returned to their camps; only 4,500 served as a provost guard. Columbia did not teem with soldiers for the simple reason that it was too small to accommodate them. Fires were still smoldering, though, and Sherman noticed cotton flying around in the wind like snow in a blizzard. He issued orders for the drunken soldiers to be cleared from the streets. When a fresh brigade arrived to carry these orders out, its commander, Brigadier General William B. Woods, diverted them to put the fires out. At about 8:00 p.m. the weather took over command from Sherman and Howard. All accounts stress the blustery conditions, and by evening a gale blew, with sparks floating in all directions beyond human control, spreading the fire southward and lighting the skyline with an eerie red glow. The poet Henry Reed ably captures its hideous, uncontrollable effect.

> The wind within a wind, unable to speak for wind;
> And the frigid burnings of purgatory will not be touched
> By any emollient.

The flames overwhelmed Columbia's small firefighting capacity, just as it had in January. The wind ensured that the fire would continue unchecked even if the drunken soldiers had been cleared from the streets.[30]

Some citizens of Columbia jumped to the conclusion that Sherman bore the responsibility for the conflagration and had intended the city's destruction all along. Rockets were spotted that signaled the timing of the incendiaries; drunken soldiers cut the hoses used by the firefighters; mobs obstructed all efforts to contain the blaze. In the ensuing mayhem, soldiers ordered to guard houses plundered them. Through it all, the "Great Satan," Sherman, rode about casually and untroubled, smoking a cigar and then tossing it onto the flames, adding to the fire. So said some residents, though there are always such personal touches in these yarns. He was "morally responsible"; "he alone is responsible for the terrible destruction."

There is not a jot of evidence to support these wild accusations, based on hearsay or fabrication. Far from being unconcerned, it could be argued, senior Union officers were too involved in Columbia: not just Sherman but Howard, Logan, Major General Charles R. Woods, and others were all in the streets issuing orders and contradicting one another; one brigadier should have been left to handle the job. But the damage and chaos were exaggerated. The fire burned itself out by 5:00 a.m., and the mob was dispersed or rounded up before then. There had been little violence; the only casualties were inflicted on the rioters, with two soldiers killed, 30 wounded, and 370 (including civilians and blacks) arrested. Though only four witnesses claimed to have observed Union soldiers cutting hoses, many others saw them protecting houses from plunderers or saving property from being consumed by the flames. If indeed there had been a conspiracy to destroy Columbia that ran straight down from the top, it would hardly have started with setting alight the building that housed Sherman's staff.[31]

As for the level of destruction, this, too, had been overstated by rash hyperbole. The flames took 265 private houses and 193 business and public structures, giving a total of 458, a third of the whole. The entire city had not been put to the sword and torch, as Mary Chesnut had predicted the previous November in her diary. But Columbia was very small, no more than a village of 8,502 people in 1860. This population had increased during the war, but many had fled on Sherman's approach, including Mrs. Chesnut. The damage that Columbia suffered cannot be compared with that endured by the burning of Moscow in 1812, a city with a population then of 270,000. There, just under 6,500 private houses, 8,251 shops and warehouses, and 122 of Moscow's 329 churches were lost; 12,000 perished, and there was wanton destruction of foodstuffs and materiél.[32]

The so-called Burning of Columbia—a misnomer for a series of fires lit by sundry parties rather than a single premeditated act—is significant as it represents Southerners' response to the success of Sherman's psychological assault on their powers of endurance. Mrs. Chesnut admitted she "gave way to abject terror" like so many others and fled to North Carolina. Southern accounts of the treatment of towns like Columbia paint a rosy picture of cozy, tranquil, and innocent places, trembling at the thought of the conqueror's heel, the depredations and chaos of the day before Sherman's arrival swept from the memory. The "burning" is represented as the appalling climax of "Yankee barbarism," with Sherman as its devilish anti-Christ, complementing the Christlike Robert E. Lee, suffering as his cause collapsed. The incidents of the "burning" were therefore reshaped in the propaganda war to fit a self-fulfilling prophesy best depicted by Mrs. Chesnut of "fire and sword and rapine and plunder." Such a depiction denotes, alas, the Confederate cause cloaked in a shroud of self-serving sentimental piety at odds with the reality of the war in 1865. According to Beauregard, Confederate citizens should have destroyed everything of value in the path of the invader; therefore, Confederates should have burned Columbia themselves. "*The people* are not destroying anything; what is burned," Hitchcock noted, "is done by Wheeler, and that not much." Southerers' failure to resist Sherman redounds to his credit, but their retrospective depiction of his Marches would eventually damage his reputation.[33]

Sherman's acquaintance with Columbia ended on February 21. The last two or three days were spent ensuring that all military-related installations "were properly destroyed by detailed working parties," as well as providing food and shelter for Columbia's population, and 100 rifled muskets were left behind for protection against deserters and vagabonds. This considerate treatment hardly accords with Mrs. Chesnut's depiction of it from afar. For almost the next two weeks Sherman traveled with Slocum's left wing; he messed with the 20th Corps. The left wing crossed the Saluda and Broad Rivers, reaching Winnsboro on February 21 and Rocky Mount on the Catawba River the following day. The weather broke, and torrential rain ensued, as the 20th Corps crossed the Catawba over a pontoon bridge, heading for Lancaster. Such a rapid movement took Beauregard by surprise again, and he fell back toward Charlotte, North Carolina. Sherman had also been apprised that the remains of Cheatham's corps of the Army of Tennessee had arrived, but the northward thrust of Sherman's wings had taken it unawares, and it, too, was in danger of being enveloped. Sherman wanted Slocum to mount a powerful thrust toward Charlotte with the aid of Kilpatrick's cavalry. He thought Jefferson C. Davis's 14th Corps "too slow," and it failed to cross the Catawba when the pontoon bridge collapsed in the rain and rush of floodwater. The 20th Corps halted until the 14th could catch up; Howard received orders to "march slow and in order." Slocum then received the benefit of what he later described as "some emphatic instructions from Sherman." Slocum's engineers did not let him down, either, and the 14th Corps finally crossed on February 27. The left wing united with the right at Cheraw on March 3, only a day behind. Here Sherman intended to issue "full orders" for the next stage of the advance. He was also determined, once again, to reduce the length and weight of his trains.[34]

His entry into Cheraw on his favorite horse, Duke, had been accompanied by drizzling rain. When he approached the town, he got directions from a newly freed slave who did not realize his identity; when informed of it he exclaimed, "Just look at that horse! ... He seemed to admire the horse more than the rider." Cheraw contained a great abundance of stores. When Sherman had observed earlier that it was "full of hospitals" but not much else, he could not have been more wrong, for it had been used by wealthy Charlestonians to store their luxury goods, including fine wines and carpets. The 17th Corps soon found the wine. Blair served Sherman "the finest Madeira I ever tasted," but he distributed wine evenly to all officers and men of both wings, ladling it into tin cups. Alcohol weakened disciplinary bonds once again, and some streets were pillaged, but not systematically. In any case, some periods were very quiet; most effort was directed toward the destruction of all military stores (24 guns, 2,000 muskets, and 3,600 barrels of gunpowder) and all transport and industrial installations, including the railroad, a branch line. Careless handling of the gunpowder led to an enormous explosion and some casualties—as at Columbia—among the Union troops. By comparison, however, with the citizens of Belgium in 1795, occupied by French revolutionary armies and subject to violence, forced requisitions on a great scale, forced payment of contributions, and the seizure of numerous hostages—"organized anarchy"—the citizens of South Carolina got off lightly.[35]

On March 6 Sherman put the two wings in motion toward Fayetteville, North Carolina. He had prepared this ground as early as January 21 when he had instructed the district commander, Innis M. Palmer, "not to attempt to hold more than you now have until you know I am near at hand, and you can discover the effect of my approach." Palmer should strengthen his grip on Morehead City and New Bern. The intervention of Schofield's Army of the Ohio and the fall of Wilmington gave added power to Union forces on the Atlantic coast. Goldsboro offered two railroads to supply Sherman, as well as a base from which he could drive on to Raleigh. But he still had to establish contact with Schofield and ascertain the precise location of other Union forces in the new Department of North Carolina. He had known for two weeks that Hardee had abandoned Charleston.[36]

During this time, as Sherman was preparing the last phase of his March, he became involved in another spat, this time with Wade Hampton, over the treatment of foragers. The issue had threatened to erupt from the day that Sherman had crossed into South Carolina. Prisoners taken from Slocum's wing had been murdered in the first week of February, as a result of the spiraling violence that had ensued after desperate Confederate use of "torpedoes." On February 23 Kilpatrick reported to Sherman that two of his foraging parties had been taken prisoner and then murdered; they were left adorned with labels warning "Death to all Foragers." Sherman ordered Kilpatrick to execute the same number of Confederate prisoners of war, "so that our enemy will see that for every man he executed he takes the life of one of his own." Howard received identical orders.[37]

Sherman wanted "the people of the South to realize the fact that they shall not dictate the laws of war or peace to us. If there is to be any dictation we want our full share." Accordingly, on February 24 he wrote a short letter to Hampton complaining of these outrages, though he doubted that Hampton had known of, let alone authorized, them. He indicated that "a similar number of prisoners in our hands [were] to be disposed of in like manner." As some Union soldiers had had their throats cut and two their skulls crushed, Sherman did not mean this literally, but rather intended that they should be placed before a firing squad. He had taken about 1,000 prisoners, and therefore we "can stand it as long as you" should there be a contest in retaliation. He explained to Howard that foraging constituted "our war right"; "Napoleon always did it, but could avail himself" of the civil authorities in occupied territories "to collect forage and provisions by regular impressments." Sherman might have added that the behavior of French troops was far more violent than that of Union troops and on a much greater scale. But apart from Savannah, Sherman found "no civil authorities who can respond to calls for forage or provisions[;] therefore [we] must collect directly of the people." He therefore exerted a right "as old as history." Though he admitted "much misbehavior" he could not "permit an enemy to judge, or punish with wholesale murder."[38]

Hampton replied at greater length three days later. "I do not, sir, question this right," he conceded at once in regard to foraging. But he proceeded to offer almost a blueprint for Confederate denunciations of Yankee "barbarity"—"even darker crimes than those crimes too black to be mentioned." These culminated at Columbia: "you laid the whole city in ashes, leaving amidst its ruins thousands of old men and helpless women and children"; Union soldiers were "more savage than the Indian" and burned the houses of those they robbed. Though he did not order the reprisals mentioned by Sherman, Hampton declared that he had ordered "my men to shoot down all of your men who are caught burning houses." He also threatened to shoot two Union prisoners for every Confederate executed. Yet despite the threats issued by both sides, Sherman's initial protest worked, and the killings of prisoners ended as quickly as they began. Both sides had ventured onto the treacherous ground of illegality. Lieber's Code only allowed retaliation "as a means of protective retribution, and moreover, cautiously and unavoidably"; neither side entered this dispute "after careful inquiry," and Sherman, the cautious lawyer, though he could plausibly plead the case of "protective retribution," makes no mention of this exchange in his *Memoirs*.[39]

As his troops filed out once more onto the road to Fayetteville on March 6, Sherman knew that his plans had been compromised. While visiting a house in Cheraw lately vacated by General Hardee, he discovered a recent copy of the *New York Tribune* that revealed his intention to advance on Goldsboro and be supplied from Morehead City—a prescient summary indeed. Sherman describes this report in his *Memoirs* as "mischievous," an understatement for him. In retrospect, this lucky accident appears as a blessing in disguise. If he had not found this copy, more recent than any that he had seen himself, then he might have pushed on in ignorance and blundered into an ambush. Overall the operation, despite Slocum's delay, had gone well; the army had been reunited and the Pee Dee River crossed without incident, despite the loss of the bridge. He even went so far as to exclaim, "I don't care what Beauregard does." But he realized that feints to the left were superfluous and that Hardee would attempt to unite with Cheatham's corps and three brigades of the Army of Northern Virginia recently arrived, whose presence had been reported by Schofield. Sherman ordered that his armies advance in echelon and in "compact masses." He knew before leaving Cheraw that Beauregard had been superseded by Joseph E. Johnston. The latter had received orders from the new Confederate general-in-chief, Robert E. Lee, to whom he reported, to concentrate "and drive back Sherman." Johnston had assumed command in the field on February 25. Sherman prepared for battle but remained confident: "If Joe Johnston wants to fight, I will fight him if he dares." Nevertheless, he warned Slocum to watch his left and assured him that he would "try and hold the Right Wing ready to turn to you in case Johnston attempts to strike you in flank"—though he doubted that Johnston would "try to concentrate his forces short of Raleigh."[40]

Sherman hastened to alter his tone once he crossed the state line between North and South Carolina. He notified Slocum that "a little moderation may be of political consequence to us in North Carolina." He also ordered that should no resistance be offered and the bridge at Fayetteville spared, "I wish the town to be dealt with generously." That is, all public stores and property would be destroyed, "but [we] will spare private houses." Fewer buildings were destroyed, but the great pine forests were set alight by arsonists. Heavy rainfall accompanied the drive on Fayetteville; Sherman divined a stiffening of resistance, and he expected Johnston to attempt to prevent its fall. Howard's wing had plunged into swamplands, which required being corduroyed before they could be crossed. Slocum received orders to feint to the northwest while Howard approached from the southwest. "Destroy nothing till I meet you, unless there be special reason that you know I will approve." Actually, Kilpatrick's cavalry sustained the only temporary loss inflicted on Sherman's forces during this advance. At daybreak on March 10, north of Solemn Grove, Hampton's cavalry took Kilpatrick by surprise, and he barely escaped in his nightshirt; first reports of this action perturbed Sherman, but he was relieved to hear that the cavalry recovered quickly and made a strong counterattack. But this action appeared ominous: Sherman's success in "interposing my superior army between the scattered parts of the enemy" seemed to be ending.[41]

His main priority remained to gain a bridgehead over the Cape Fear River, "lean towards the northeast," and reduce his trains by dispensing with the hordes of refugees, both black and white, that followed his columns; he also needed to establish contact with Wilmington and urged that a boat be sent up the Cape Fear. As the roads were so difficult, secure river lines were needed for the dispatch of "bread, sugar, and coffee. We have abundance of all else." On March 8 he finally gained confirmation that General Alfred H. Terry had taken Wilmington. Sherman received his first dispatch from Terry as he entered Fayetteville on March 11. He announced formal contact to his armies the following day. "I want everything concentrated at or as near Goldsboro as possible, with the railroad finished as near as possible."

On arrival in Fayetteville he wrote letters to both Stanton and Grant that offer important clues as to his thinking. He stressed that "the principles of the movement" were revealed in "the utter destruction of the enemy's arsenals at Columbia, Cheraw and Fayetteville"—installations that "were regarded as inaccessible to us, and now no place in the Confederacy is safe from the Army of the West." He then raised his sights. If Lee continued to hold Richmond regardless, he queried what value the Confederate capital could have. "He must come out and fight us on open ground, and for that we must ever be ready. Let him stick behind his parapets and he will perish." He concluded dryly that he thought he was "on the right road, though on a long one." He assured

Grant that "we are abundantly supplied" and "in splendid health, condition and spirit, although we have had foul weather"—and he badly needed shoes, stockings, sugar, coffee, and flour. But he got straight to the point that if he could occupy Goldsboro "without too much cost," he would "be in a position to aid you materially in the spring campaign." He anticipated "a junction with General Schofield in ten days." Johnston would "concentrate his scattered armies at Raleigh," he believed, "and I will be straight at him as soon as I get my men re-clothed and our wagons reloaded." But Lee, not Johnston, had become Sherman's ultimate enemy—and Richmond "our true destination."[42]

Sherman concentrated his efforts to unite with Schofield in the vicinity of Goldsboro, and he urged him "not to bring any" wagons, as he had enough for a force of 100,000 men. But Sherman feared that Johnston might yet concentrate an army of 40,000 to 45,000 men. He therefore had to make meticulous logistical preparations and make the most of the available fire-power, including distant and wasted garrisons at Charleston and Savannah. Sherman sought the cooperation of the US Navy to create an illusion that he strove to create a fake "base" at Fayetteville. But he urged on Terry the necessity of resupply by boat while he simultaneously divested himself of "20–30,000 useless mouths" either down the Cape Fear River or by road to Wilmington via Clinton. "We must not lose time for Joe Johnston to con-centrate at Goldsboro. We cannot prevent his concentrating at Raleigh, but he shall have no rest." He ordered that Schofield continue the building of the railroad from New Bern, and Terry from Wilmington. "If we can get the [rail]roads and secure Goldsboro by April 10, it will be soon enough, but every day now is worth a million of dollars." He also recognized the danger that Johnston might attempt to strike an isolated corps in flank, so "I will see that my army marches to Goldsboro in compact form." By exaggerating Johnston's potential strength he had invested in logistical overinsurance, but this would not be wasted, for Sherman would be disappointed by his slow progress in preparing and launching his ambitious plan for the final, culmi-nating advance toward Lee.[43]

Needless to say, he grasped that hitherto the Marches had been charac-terized by fighting "on a limited scale," usually by a single brigade, at most by one division; also, as so many men had spent prolonged periods wading through dirty water, clothing, stockings, shoes and underwear were "scarce." A tension had developed in his plans between the urgent need to resupply and the imperative to push on to prevent Johnston from enjoying the lei-sure to complete his concentration and prepare a counterstroke. Further, he needed to secure crossings over the Neuse River near Kinston and threaten Raleigh to ease the pressure on Schofield's Army of the Ohio as it advanced on Goldsboro—and he had to take account of Terry's movement to join him, too. But before "sallying forth" he destroyed the arsenal at Fayetteville. By driving his subordinates forward, he had both his armies except one division across the Cape Fear River by March 14. He thus set in motion the plan he had worked out two weeks before to advance in echelon, holding Howard back so that the right wing could pivot and rush to support the left should it be attacked by Johnston. "I want you to be as near in support as possible," he warned Howard. The country around Bentonville, covered in low woods, with proximity to roads and the railroad, posed dangers. "I do think it is Johnston's only chance to meet this army before an easy junction with Schofield can be effected." Consequently, he modified his plan by ordering Howard to get ahead of Slocum's wing, "so as, in case of action, to come up on his right." Sherman decided to stay "near Slocum" so that he could consolidate the movement and be ready to turn rapidly. On March 14 he overestimated Johnston's strength at 37,000 (minus his cavalry). It was all very well estimating Johnston's position and intentions, but Sherman had as yet no confirmation that Johnston's army lurked menacingly near his own.[44]

Ever since his departure from Fayetteville, Sherman had urged prudence and deliberation on Slocum. He made it clear that he would accept battle with Johnston but expressed a measure of tactical caution, for he "would not attack him in position until I make junction with General Schofield." Consequently, Sherman expressed delight when informed on March 16 that Schofield had occupied Kinston. He also indulged in more deception, as the naval forays up the Cape Fear River were made loudly "to make Joe Johnston believe that I have resupplied my wagons and can stand a thirty days campaign." Perhaps he might deter Johnston's attack until it suited him; at least the effort was worth making. He suggested that the tugboat *Eolus* stay at Fayetteville in case he needed to send urgent orders to Wilmington. He did not fear that he had lost the initiative; the whiff of imminent victory remained in his nostrils. He urged the new commander of the Department of the South, Quincy Gillmore, not to let his command "rest on its oars, but keep them going all the time" in the relentless war "to exhaust the enemy's country," because this "makes a soldier in Lee's and Johnston's army very anxious to get home to look after his family and property." On March 15 Grant indicated his overall agreement with Sherman's views, urging him to "get to Raleigh as soon as possible" so that he could "hold the railroad from there back." He waited impatiently for news of Sherman's junction with Schofield's and Terry's forces.

Johnston's resolve was amply demonstrated on March 16 in the skirmish at Averasboro, though this was an indeterminate encounter. Sherman mounted this thrust to gain "use of the Goldsboro road" and also to maintain the feint of an immediate advance on Raleigh, which he did not intend to mount until he had united with Schofield. Two successive Confederate positions were taken, although not the main line. Sherman initially estimated Slocum's loss at 300, yet such had been Confederate "pluck" here that it proved double this number. Hardee withdrew, but Slocum's advance along the Goldsboro road took him away from Howard, and Sherman told the latter: "You need not come over to Slocum unless you hear him engaged." The widening gap between the two wings convinced Johnston that his chance had come. He ordered a concentration at the crossroads town of Bentonville on Slocum's left. He planned a lightning strike to inflict a humiliating defeat on Slocum and give Sherman pause; at the very least he might gain the Confederacy some time.[45]

The Battle of Bentonville on March 19 enjoys the distinction of being the only general engagement fought during Sherman's Marches, and it was a small one. It serves to underline Sherman's success at fracturing Confederate military resources and resolve. He was not present on the field because, having traveled with Slocum on March 18, he decided to shift to the 17th Corps, an unfortunate but hardly fatal error. The business of fighting the battle was Slocum's, not his. Sherman had previously stressed the importance of Howard's mission in advancing on Goldsboro from the south—"and let your scouts strike out for Schofield at Kinston": linking up with Schofield remained his top operational priority. His thoughts ranged forward rather than drawing in to receive an attack. "I think you will find them [Johnston's troops] gone in the morning." He was wrong; Johnston's cavalry screen had done its job well. Johnston attempted to ambush Sherman's left wing using a technique he had employed before: block the Union advance, wait for Slocum to deploy, and trick him into attacking; once exposed, take the enemy by surprise by launching a counterattack in echelon against his exposed left flank. Slocum deployed 35,000 men, though his infantry strength was nearer 17,000. Johnston had scraped together 15,000 infantry and 4,200 cavalry, but found no use for the latter on the battlefield. Johnston enjoyed the tactical advantage of central position, but should Sherman succeed in uniting his two wings on the battlefield, Johnston would be staring disaster in the face. He demonstrated unwonted audacity by his decision to attack and "stand within his danger."[46]

As Sherman's prime role lay in operational direction and coordination, a detailed account of Bentonville is unnecessary. On March 20 initial success greeted the implementation of Johnston's plan. The main Confederate attack went in on Slocum's vulnerable left during a mild afternoon. Sherman at once informed Slocum that as he controlled Cox's crossroads and the bridge over the Neuse River at Goldsboro, "all of the Right wing will move at moonrise toward Bentonville." He gave instructions for Slocum to entrench "and hold your position to the last, certain that all the army is coming to you as fast as possible." Slocum demonstrated resolve, though ammunition was not plentiful. He stabilized the line and built a strong bastion manned by the 20th Corps in front of Reddick Morris's house just off the Goldsboro road. But local tactical gains did not amount to a Confederate operational triumph. Six Confederate assaults did not break through, even though the 14th Corps had been driven back a mile. Johnston committed a single error that stymied his slight hope for victory. He had reinforced the blocking force at the last minute at the expense of the assault. Slocum's firepower remained too strong, and the Confederate advance ground to a halt.

Sherman can certainly be criticized for neglecting the threat from the north until the late afternoon of March 19. He had been too preoccupied with logistical matters and linking up with Schofield. But when a courier arrived at Howard's tent near Falling Creek Church where Sherman took a nap that afternoon, he responded to the crisis with his usual energy and decisiveness. Rushing out to the campfire in his underwear, he nevertheless did not hesitate to give orders clearly and forcefully. Indeed, Major Hitchcock, champing at the bit to experience a battle, became irritated by Sherman's technique of giving general directions to Slocum: "Be ready to attack the enemy the moment you see signs of let go." Quite rightly, Sherman remained in the woods behind the front line, where he could easily be found and consulted. But given the strategic imperative issued by Grant, Sherman wished to contain the action at Bentonville. He grasped at once that a purely tactical success won over Johnston in North Carolina could have little direct effect on the truly decisive point in Virginia; he needed to conserve his strength for that. Any rapid consumption of ammunition or multiplication of casualties—all of whom would have to be transported and not left behind—could only serve to impede his movements and wear out his command before it could arrive at Richmond.[47]

During March 20 the Army of the Tennessee marched to Slocum's relief and by 3:00 p.m. came up on the right, with the 15th Corps contiguous and the 17th Corps on the right outer flank. The terrain lay heavily wooded, damp, and "spongy" and did not allay Sherman's doubts about fighting a general engagement at a place of the enemy's choosing and in "country different from what I expected." He also expressed surprise that though Johnston had been foiled in his main aim, he remained on the field when Sherman expected him to retreat. "I would rather avoid a general battle if possible, but if he insists on it, we must accommodate him." Sherman's supplies had run low, and he still lacked reliable intelligence as to Confederate strength. To gain a significant strategic success and complete the transfer of his three armies (including Schofield), Sherman only needed to avoid defeat, and this aim had already been achieved. He would gain nothing by hazarding his plans.

On March 21 Sherman issued orders to withdraw Mower's 1st Division of the 17th Corps from its current exposed position. Mower had rashly plunged forward through the Confederate gun line, and he might have cut off Johnston's line of retreat if supported by the whole of the right wing. Sherman admits twice in his *Memoirs* that he erred in showing such operational caution. Howard did not conceal his disappointment at this order, but the harsh criticism aimed at Sherman misses a fundamental point. Once united with Schofield, Sherman could do as he pleased, and Johnston would be powerless to resist him; the outcome of any tactical action thus appeared superfluous. In his report Sherman observed, "We had no object to accomplish by a battle, unless at an advantage," and he did not believe that the margin of advantage was great enough. Nathaniel Cheairs Hughes is one of the few historians to recognize that Sherman "never lost sight of his objective. He kept his operational priorities clear." Even the critical Howard later admitted "that there had been enough bloodshed already"; he eventually felt "glad that this last battle had not been pushed to an extremity." But Sherman took an even greater operational risk of a quite different order when he assumed that Johnston's army would not break up into guerrilla bands and continue the war using irregular means.[48]

By March 22 the remains of Johnston's army had withdrawn via Smithfield. He had sustained 240 killed and 1,700 wounded and left behind at least 1,500 prisoners. Sherman's casualties were slightly lower at 1,527 (194 killed, 1,112 wounded), but half of these fell on the 14th Corps alone. Johnston's loss was proportionately greater and, including prisoners, double Sherman's.[49]

Sherman found these figures satisfying. In notifying Grant of the battle on March 22 he observed that "Johnston's army was so roughly handled yesterday that we could march right on to Raleigh," and he had taken over 2,000 prisoners if those captured at Averasboro were included. He remarked, though, that the troops' exertions over the previous six weeks had left them ragged and dirty "and we must rest and fix up a little bit." He confided to Grant that he intended to deploy Terry at Faison's Depot and Schofield at Kinston in order to both defend the railroad and provide a screen behind which they could forage. He expressed irritation that the railroad links to the coast had yet to be restored. "I fear these have not been pushed with the vigor I expected, but I will soon have them both going." He also intended to reorganize his three armies. April 10 he marked down as the start date for the new advance on either Raleigh or Weldon. "Keep all parts busy," he had urged the week before, "and I will give the enemy no rest." These two letters, brimming with energy, enthusiasm, and confidence, reinforce why Sherman had become Grant's favorite subordinate, always pushing forward, never doubting or creating difficulties.

The force under his command now exceeded the 65,000 men, 40,000 animals, and 3,000 wagons he counted on departing Fayetteville. Though Sherman took great pains over his logistical arrangements, he perhaps underestimated the challenges of the task before him and the speed with which they could be overcome. He thought initially of organizing three armies of 25,000 men each, but this proved inadequate. He had also encouraged Schofield and Terry to leave their wagons behind, and for once he faced a shortage of horses and mules rather than a surplus. He had given his chief quartermasters, Brigadier Generals L. C. Easton and Amos Beckwith, a mission, he reflected grumpily to Grant, "purposely to make arrangements in anticipation of my arrival, and I have heard from neither, though I suppose them both at Morehead City." They were, and they had not let him down, but even these two admirable logisticians could not work miracles. They transferred the main supply base from Hilton Head to Morehead City, creating wharves and storehouses from nothing, plus a sawmill; all supplies were then sent up the Neuse River to Kinston. A complete set of 100,000 new uniforms was ready for Sherman's troops. Easton labored, moreover, to increase the number of available animals, but errors were made. The result of what Edward Hagerman calls "inadequate staff procedures," a serious blunder was committed in transporting locomotives and rolling stock for 5' gauge when only the existing 4'8½" was available (the standard British width). This led to the delays that Sherman complained of—but Easton's ingenuity surmounted every problem. By April 18 the failure to complete the railroad had been overcome.[50]

In the meantime, Sherman had been seized by the need to confer with Grant at City Point rather than wait until a later date. Sherman had always preferred "to stay with my troops. It gives me great power to share the days and nights." He revealed to Ellen that "soldiers have a wonderful idea of my knowledge and attach much of our continued success to it, and I really think they would miss me, if I were to go away for even a week." Although he kept complaining that he had no time to write letters, he still offered Grant on March 24 some initial thoughts on operations beyond the Roanoke. He was confident that they could "checkmate Lee, forcing him to unite Johnston with him in the defence of Richmond, or by leaving Richmond to abandon the cause. I feel certain if he leaves Richmond Virginia leaves the Confederacy." He also asked for detailed information about the Roanoke River "as to its navigability, how far up, and with what draft." This, he hoped, might be the final campaign. Sherman wanted to discuss all issues with Grant personally as he had the year before. No amount of correspondence could be as valuable as personal contact. It would be important to establish how their two forces should link up; there could be no misunderstandings. Sherman also had a personal motive: he wanted to share this moment on the cusp of victory with Grant. Eminence had its pitfalls, and he continued to complain that his fame led "silly people" to publish extracts of his hurriedly scribbled correspondence. He informed a St. Louis friend that as he was not running for any office, he remained "utterly indifferent whether they please or displease." His behavior remained obstinately inconsistent, for he could no longer afford to be as blunt as he pretended to be.[51]

An old St. Louis connection engaged him during these spring days and he found time to nurture it. He heard from Commodore Thomas Turner, USN, brother of his old friend Henry Turner, with whom he had ventured into business; since 1861 they had lost touch. Henry Turner's attitude to the war had been deeply equivocal: his two sons had joined up; one had fought for the Confederacy, the other for the Union, and both had been killed. Although Sherman acknowledged Turner's "bitter grief," he washed his "hands clean" as he had helped procure the Unionist son's commission and blamed Davis, Lee, and Johnston. Sherman wrote frankly that he professed himself "a better southern man, a truer friend to the People of the South," by defeating their "so-called Leaders," but he affirmed that he felt "the same personal friendship as ever." Henry Turner and Sherman restored contact.[52]

On March 26 Sherman handed over temporary command to Schofield and set out to visit Grant. He took the train to Morehead City and boarded the steamer *Russia* to City Point. On board he wrote to Ellen, assuring her in language that would have reassured Lincoln that we "must not let them [Confederates] have time to make new plans." When he reached City Point on the morning of March 27, he was "heartily" welcomed by Grant; one of the officers attending Grant, Horace Porter, left a memorable account of the meeting. As the *Russia* docked, they started down the wharf. "Before we reached the foot of the steps, Sherman had jumped ashore and was hurrying forward with long strides to meet his chief. As they approached Grant cried out, 'How do you do, Sherman!' 'How are you, Grant!' exclaimed Sherman; and in a moment they stood upon the steps with their hands locked in a cordial grasp, uttering earnest words of familiar greeting." Porter likened them to "two schoolboys coming together after a vacation" rather than "the meeting of the chief actors in a great war tragedy." Once they were sitting by the campfire, Sherman launched into an arresting account of the March to the Sea. "The story was the more charming," Porter observed, "from the fact that it was related without the manifestation of the slightest egotism." Porter added, "Never were listeners more enthusiastic; never was a speaker more eloquent."

After about an hour Grant indicated that the president was presently aboard a steamer, the *River Queen*, a short distance away and that they should both call on him. The two generals found Lincoln unattended in the aft-cabin. The candid and warm exchange between Sherman and Lincoln marked only their fourth meeting. It assumed a disproportionate importance in the latter's *Memoirs*. Sherman recalled that Lincoln revealed considerable anxiety over the security of his army in his absence and that he sought to reassure him. Lincoln's apprehension appears quite understandable after his earlier experience with overconfident or inert commanders; he did not wish Grant or Sherman to give the rebels any chance of gaining a second wind at a moment when he could sniff the tang of victory in the air.[53]

The next morning, Sherman received visits from George G. Meade and his old pal Edward O. C. Ord, commanders of the Armies of the Potomac and the James, respectively, and other senior officers, including Admiral David Dixon Porter. Grant, Sherman, and Porter then paid Lincoln another visit. Ostensibly they went to pay Mrs. Lincoln their respects, which the first two had failed to do the previous day, but she pleaded ill health and did not emerge. After this response, a "general conversation" ensued between the commander in chief and his senior commanders concerning the final phase of the Civil War. It can be construed as a kind of conference on strategy, but it was convened accidentally and conducted casually; it was really a social occasion that took an unexpectedly serious turn. Sherman's account in his *Memoirs* is self-serving and tendentious. Although it is supported in the *Journal* of Admiral Porter, who sent Sherman a relevant extract when he wrote it in 1866, the admiral's account is no less biased. It is more contemporaneous than Sherman's, but he muddled up some chronological details, and his presentation of events is overly influenced by spurious retrospective wisdom and loyalty to a friend. "It was, in fine," Porter concluded, "the President's policy and not his own that General Sherman carried out." Such a claim, however, cannot be sustained.

The main points that Sherman carried away from the meeting, which ended by noon, were, first, that Jefferson Davis might be allowed to flee abroad so long as the president had no direct knowledge of it; second, that Lincoln was prepared to tolerate—a view expressed in "full and frank" language, says Sherman—an immediate "civil reorganization of the South" on its surrender; and third, that full civil rights and the powers of the existing state governments would be restored in an effort to avoid anarchy once this surrender had been received. Such a scheme formed part of Lincoln's plan to bring the war to an immediate end. Sherman at long last might have grasped the full dimensions of Lincoln's greatness, but he disastrously misinterpreted Lincoln's ends and the means at his disposal. He blundered and trespassed on Lincoln's cardinal principle, namely, that no field commander should include political provisions in any surrender agreement offered to the enemy.[54]

Sherman started his return journey on the afternoon of March 28. At Old Point Comfort on the James River he took on board Senator John Sherman and Edwin L. Stanton, the secretary of war's son—another indicator of good relations at this date. On arrival, having established that the troops had been refitted and resupplied, he set about reorganizing them, which had been earlier approved by Grant and needed to be confirmed by Lincoln. He formally agreed to a change of name for Slocum's left wing to the Army of Georgia (a name used unofficially for some weeks), taking its place with the 14th and 20th Corps, the latter now commanded by the most thrusting of its divisional commanders, Joseph A. Mower. Schofield's Army of the Ohio took the center, currently composed of two corps, the 23rd under Jacob D. Cox and Alfred H. Terry's 10th Corps. Howard's Army of the Tennessee assumed its customary place on the right of the line. This reorganization raised two issues: first, Sherman acknowledged the harshness of replacing the competent Alpheus Williams of the 20th Corps so late in the day, but he had to anticipate a major challenge and calculated he needed Mower's drive and audacity; second, the formation of the Army of Georgia created a complication because half its troops belonged to Thomas's Army of the Cumberland. Sherman accurately predicted that Thomas would not be pleased by this new army's appearance "in the field." His letter to Thomas reveals his isolation because of his uncertainty whether "you are in my jurisdiction"; he could give him neither reinforcements nor orders, though Sherman did not think he was in need of either. But personal considerations had to be subordinated to winning the "most desperate" final encounter, perhaps against Lee and Johnston combined.[55]

Sherman intended on April 11 to advance on Burkeville, Virginia, with a feint toward Raleigh; all formations were to be ready to "perform a general left wheel" to protect the exposed flank. Sherman would travel with the center, close to his most senior subordinate, Schofield. That day Smithfield was occupied, and the engineers labored to repair the bridges over the Neuse to Raleigh, the state capital. On April 14 he received the gratifying news of Lee's surrender at Appomattox. He suspended the advance on Burkeville and settled instead on Raleigh. Johnston became his top priority again. He wished to capture or destroy his army before it could disperse into guerrilla bands and thus prolong the war for years. But his shortage of cavalry made this a tricky enterprise.

Fortunately, Lee's surrender had left Johnston bereft, and he, too, wished to end the war quickly, before it could take a guerrilla form. On the urging of North Carolina's governor, Zebulon B. Vance, Johnston sent a delegation to Sherman carrying a letter offering to meet him. Sherman replied encouragingly. The cavalry was at Durham Station and ordered "to keep up a show of pursuit"; Slocum's and Howard's commands had pushed through Raleigh while Schofield garrisoned it. Johnston lay at Hillsboro, and he and Sherman agreed to meet at an intermediate point between the picket lines at noon on April 17. Sherman had laid down the strict condition that Johnston maintain "the present position of your forces until each has notice of a failure to agree." He also indicated "a desire to save the people of North Carolina the damage they would sustain by the march through Central or Western parts of the state." Sherman had written to Grant two days before congratulating him on his victory and reassuring him that Appomattox would be his model—"magnanimous and liberal." The few days' delay did not concern him, as it allowed repairs to be completed on the railroad to Raleigh. He also asked for Sheridan's services: to do for Sherman what he had done for Grant—pursuing and fixing the enemy until the main body of the infantry came up, as Kilpatrick's cavalry was too weak to do this. If Johnston's army escaped into the backcountry, he would be powerless to stop it breaking up into guerrilla gangs. He confided to Ellen that this "is what I most fear." But he must have kept his intentions to himself throughout the negotiations. His motives remain a mystery, for his sudden shift from the course laid down by Grant cannot be explained. Even as late as April 10 he revealed doubts that the end of the war was truly approaching. He emphasized Davis's resolve to fight on. He will "sacrifice every man in the South and even his wife and child before he will give up his freedom." He continued candidly, "I know them like a Book. They cannot help it any more than Indians can their wild nature, but it is truth as disagreeable as many others in Nature." But over the next week he appears to have become seized by the idea that he, and he alone, could avoid this further bloodshed. He cast his battlefield caution aside. For once he remained silent, which would cost him dearly. Even Hitchcock predicted the evening before Sherman traveled to his last meeting with Johnston to formulate the final wording that the terms would be "the same as Grant's to Lee."[56]

On the morning of April 17, just as Sherman boarded the train to take him the 28 miles to Durham Station, he received word of Lincoln's assassination and the attempt on the life of Secretary of State William H. Seward; Vice President Andrew Johnson only escaped injury because his assassin lost his nerve. Sherman mistook its import, believing that Lincoln's assassination strengthened his hand in the effort to achieve a beneficent peace. He met Johnston—their first personal encounter—at 10:00 a.m. at James Bennett's house, five miles outside Durham Station on the Hillsboro road. At once he informed Johnston of Lincoln's demise, and the Confederate grasped its import immediately—and more accurately than Sherman. Johnston also admitted that a continuance of the war would be to commit the "highest possible crime." Sherman proposed that they "arrange terms of a permanent peace." When they resumed their deliberations on the following day at 2:00 p.m., Johnston urged that they both strive for peace "above party feeling" and that a statement guaranteeing the political rights of white Southerners be included in the agreement; this would, he said, "enable him to allay the natural fears and anxiety of his followers." The latter point Sherman conceded—unwisely. Johnston also claimed that he needed the assistance of John C. Breckinridge, Confederate secretary of war and a former vice president of the United States. Sherman committed another, even more serious error in conceding this, too, even though Breckinridge was admitted in his military role as a major general. Perhaps Sherman had been encouraged by the antiparty spirit, but he should not have been. In his report, he claimed that "to push an army whose commander had so frankly and honestly confessed his inability to cope with me were cowardly and unworthy [of] the brave men I led." Sherman thus considered his honor at stake, but his concessions ensured that he would be outgunned in political experience. The error was compounded by Sherman's agreement that the commanders should meet without their staffs, unlike Grant at Appomattox; Sherman sorely missed Hitchcock's legal expertise.

The eventual surrender document, "Memorandum, or Basis of Agreement" of April 18, went far beyond the provisions agreed at Appomattox. In effect Sherman had signed an armistice that he hoped would cover all other Confederate forces. Grant before Appomattox had forbidden Lee, who was, after all, Confederate general-in-chief, from negotiating such a general deal; Sherman encouraged Johnston to do so even though he lacked Lee's formal authority. In his report Sherman stressed his terms were a "basis." "It admitted of modification, alteration and change." He claimed that "at one blow" the "military power of the Confederacy which had threatened the national safety for years" would be ended. But the terms were inconsistent with what he claimed he would do, that is, parole and disarm Johnston's entire force and then permit the men to return to their homes. Sherman's final draft was derived from a paper submitted by John H. Reagan, the Confederate postmaster general, entitled "Basis of Pacification," handed to him by Breckinridge. Before Sherman began condensing its florid style, he produced a bottle of whiskey and offered the bibulous Breckinridge a glass, which he enthusiastically accepted. But Sherman was so preoccupied with his work he forgot to offer him another. Breckinridge was outraged. "General Sherman is a hog. Yes, sir, a hog," who lacked the manners of a Kentucky gentleman, he sputtered. Whatever their doubts about Sherman's claims to gentility, both Johnston and Breckinridge were well pleased with the final outcome. Sherman planned to disband Johnston's army but allow it to return to its constituent states, where its arms and property would be placed in state arsenals—in order to maintain order. "The several States" would be recognized once the oath of loyalty had been sworn; the federal authorities were not permitted "to disturb" former Confederates as long as they did not break the law, as a general amnesty would then be offered.[57]

Sherman explained to Grant that he had acted decisively to prevent Confederates "breaking up into Guerrilla Bands." He repeated a claim in his subsequent report that would become a lifelong mantra, namely, his faith in the certainty that "Lincoln would have approved, or at least not rejected [it] with disdain." This claim brought comfort but is irrelevant, for Sherman had seriously overreached himself. Even before his murder Lincoln had abandoned some of the views later attributed to him aboard the *River Queen*. He would never have tolerated such a document negotiated by a military man. In any case, the hysterical forces unleashed by the assassination, of which Sherman remained blithely ignorant, had completely changed the atmosphere in which decisions were made.[58]

On April 20 Sherman entrusted his precious memorandum to Hitchcock's disapproving hand. He was ordered to hand it only to the president. Hitchcock arrived in Washington the following afternoon and immediately entered an emotional maelstrom. He gave the document first to Grant, who immediately found Stanton, then much preoccupied in tracking down Lincoln's assassins and ensuring that the machinery of government continued to function. Stanton had become overwrought through overwork and grief. Stanton had also become persuaded by the belief that the assassination had been part of a gigantic political conspiracy; he determined to show no mercy to those associated with such villainy. He was far from pleased with Sherman's handiwork and quickly dictated a detailed refutation of the memorandum. He had also received information that Jefferson Davis had escaped from Richmond with a great treasure and wanted him tracked down and captured. An emergency meeting of the cabinet was called for that evening, and all parties, including Grant, were incredulous that Sherman had not done what he had promised. Stanton astutely noticed that the provisions concerning the protection of private property had not excluded slavery—even though Sherman himself had declared it dead. The document did not receive approval. Grant refrained from joining in the denunciation of Sherman, and he offered to go to Raleigh and take charge of the negotiations or any military operations that might result from their imminent breakdown. The new president, Andrew Johnson, quickly agreed that he should. Grant's calm presence probably saved Sherman from dismissal.[59]

Grant and Hitchcock arrived back at Morehead City on the evening of April 23. Hitchcock telegraphed ahead to say he would travel overnight but made no mention of Grant's presence, as the general-in-chief did not wish knowledge of his visit to spread. They arrived at Sherman's headquarters in Raleigh at 6:00 a.m., taking Sherman completely by surprise; his pleasure at seeing Grant again was short-lived when he was briskly informed that his terms had not been approved. As always in a crisis Sherman remained calm, too, and acted promptly, informing Johnston of Washington's disavowal of their efforts. Sherman makes the point in his *Memoirs* that he had not been superseded in command; nor did Grant "intimate it." He had, however, been officially warned—any other subordinate would have been dismissed. Grant's presence acted as a buffer that prevented this from happening; it was a skilful compromise that shielded Sherman from the consequences of his frightful blunder.

On April 26 Sherman met Johnston for a third time, and the latter agreed to surrender the forces under his immediate command on the same terms as Lee at Appomattox. Grant approved these and departed as swiftly as he had arrived. The matter might have ended there; Sherman planned to travel to Savannah so that he could coordinate effectively with James Harrison Wilson's cavalry thrust in Alabama. But in the meantime Stanton had maliciously leaked to the *New York Times* Sherman's memorandum, the numerous reasons why it had been rejected, and a dollop of innuendo as to why Sherman had allowed Davis to slip through his fingers, all garnished with the imputation that he had been bribed from the Confederate treasury to let him escape; it made for a deliciously provocative front-page story. Sherman was handed a copy of this newspaper just before he embarked for Savannah. It hardly improved his opinion of the journalistic trade, and he immediately postponed the voyage. He sent an outraged letter of complaint to Grant claiming that his distinguished service surely required the courtesy of being consulted before confidential documents were released to the press. But courtesy had never been Stanton's way.[60]

Further blows rained down on Sherman soon after. His old friend Henry W. Halleck had been shifted out of Washington after Appomattox, as he would have no role once Grant returned to Washington permanently. He took over the new Military Division of the James based in Richmond, Virginia, which included those parts of North Carolina not occupied by Sherman's troops. Their warm relations had continued as of old; shortly after Lincoln's murder Halleck sent him warning that a man called Clark was on his way to kill him, too. Sherman replied dryly in the covering letter sent with his memorandum, "He had better be in a hurry, or he will be too late." Halleck had been the source of the canard that Jefferson Davis had traveled with a great cache of gold. Instead of keeping out of the commotion surrounding his friend, Halleck, like all the other bureaucratic trimmers frustrated at no longer being at the center of Washington gossip and intrigue, felt compelled to make his own contribution, even though its source would inevitably be discovered by his target—his friend. He sent directives requiring other commanders to decline to obey Sherman's orders. Even after Grant repaired the damage, Halleck foolishly remarked that he "fear[ed] there is some screw loose [in Sherman] again." Halleck's subordinates echoed his views, suggesting Sherman was "crazy." A brutal reminder of the humiliations of November 1861 appeared cruel, even worse since they emanated from the old friend who had rescued him from them. Ellen's earlier warnings that Halleck had been all along shallow and insincere appeared vindicated. Sherman exploded in front of Admiral John Dahlgren, ignoring the latter's advice, endorsed by Grant, that he should calm down and ignore such spiteful remarks. Sherman sneered at Halleck's dubious military record, as he had never been near a bullet. Halleck remained oblivious of the hurt he had caused. The following week he invited Sherman to stay with him in Richmond. He received a chilly response: Sherman warned him he had no desire for "any friendly intercourse" and did not wish to meet him. With characteristic equivocation Halleck could only protest his warm admiration for Sherman and desire to continue their friendship. He explained feebly that he had only carried out the "wishes of the War Dept." and "deeply" regretted any offense caused. The matter remained in Sherman's hands—not his. Always a good hater, in this matter Sherman acted decisively: they would never meet again.[61]

However aggrieved he might have felt, only one author of his troubles could step forward—himself. He had a point, one emphatically restated, that he had received not "one word of instruction" on how to carry out the surrender negotiations. His own freely given statements of intent had rendered the issue of such documents unnecessary. Sherman had proved an impulsive and opinionated man with great faith in his own judgment—but on this occasion he had assumed too much. It is not an uncommon assumption in those who scorn "politics" that they have a ready answer to pressing problems. He could not resist the temptation to make an effort to find his own solution, buoyed by so much praise over the previous months and his wide experience drawn from "my past life and familiarity with the people and geography of the South." Sherman also claimed to enjoy the support of all his subordinates. Francis P. Blair Jr. undoubtedly agreed with Sherman, but opinion was not unanimous even among his staff. Hitchcock, for instance, thought Sherman's whole approach mistaken; Howard deplored Sherman's efforts, acknowledging he meant well but careful not to express a word of support. Even Ellen expressed shock at the terms he offered "perjured traitors"; she judged the memorandum "a great mistake" but thought the damage would be restricted. The only glimmer of approbation could be found in President Johnson's efforts to disassociate himself from Stanton's excesses. Johnson had not forgiven Sherman's ineffectiveness in East Tennessee in 1861, but over the ensuing weeks he cultivated Sherman. Yet these overtures remained small recompense for his essay in poor judgment. Another great moment, surely the crowning achievement of his career, had been sullied.[62]

PART IV

THINGS WILL NEVER BE THE SAME AGAIN: THE RECKONING

15

The Transition to Peacetime Soldiering, 1865–1869

As Sherman proceeded northward through Virginia toward Washington, DC, one question above all others agitated his mind—higher than getting even with Stanton: What on earth would he do when he got there? He had heard rumors about some kind of "grand review," but rapid demobilization of the 150,000 soldiers gathering there appeared more likely. No decision had been made as late as May 16. Grant still did not know whether or not there would be a parade, but his chief of staff, Brigadier General John A. Rawlins, advised Sherman to bring Ellen to Washington. He sent her a telegram asking her "if you would like to come and see the army before it is broken up." But Sherman only discovered there would be a review three days later when he found a report in a newspaper that stipulated that his troops would march on May 24. "I am old fashioned and prefer to see orders through some other channel," he wrote to Rawlins, "but if that be the new, so be it." A state of war continued to prevail, and the final Confederate units would not capitulate until June 1865. With several days' grace, Ellen managed to attend to her packing, get her own father organized, and get Tommy scrubbed. They all arrived safely in a hectic and crowded Washington on the afternoon of May 23 in the chaotic backwash of the first review of the Army of the Potomac. John Sherman met them and conveyed them to his house at 1321 K Street, situated next door to Mr. Stanton's.[1]

The arrival of "the Vandal Sherman," as he described himself, plus his troops, loud in threats that his Washington critics would have them "to reckon with," had led to significant developments even before his return to Washington—his first since the autumn of 1861. There had also been some wild talk, probably exaggerated in the retelling, of overthrowing the government. Stanton, perhaps sensing a matter he could exploit to his advantage, ordered both Grant and Sherman to testify before the congressional Joint Committee on the Conduct of the War on the issues surrounding the ill-fated memorandum of understanding reached between Sherman and Johnston the previous month. Due to his travels around the Carolinas, Sherman failed to receive the committee's summons and did not make his first appearance before it until May 22. Members of the committee initially sought to represent Sherman as a craven West Point defeatist, overly influenced by his Catholic wife, with a "natural leaning toward aristocracy . . . strengthened by the peculiar atmosphere created by hierarchic ideas, chiming in with the charms of his Louisiana home." But by the time he testified, they realized that defense of Stanton was an urgent priority. John Sherman had assured his brother that "the reaction has commenced, and you find some defenders." Within two weeks he calculated that "the feeling has so subsided and reacted that you can be calm and cautious," though this was rarely Sherman's way in such controversies. Sherman launched a preemptive assault based on the approach taken in his report, delivered with all his fluency and oratorical panache. He made no overtures to Stanton but instead denounced Stanton and Halleck's "act of perfidy" in instructing his subordinates not to obey his orders. It is a measure of Sherman's renewed popularity that the committee felt unable to challenge him even on points of detail. On leaving, Sherman felt vindicated—and less inclined to be reconciled with Stanton than ever.[2]

These discussions, however, transcend the Stanton-Sherman quarrel. In retrospect, the committee's failure to embarrass Sherman serves to underline the complete failure of Congress at this date to make any mark on Reconstruction policy. The ensuing great battle over this issue in 1866–67 would emerge as the defining momentous political contest of these years, and Sherman would be dragged unwittingly into its margins. The previous week he had sent Oliver O. Howard, who only a few days previously had agreed to head the new Freedmen's Bureau, a long, thoughtful letter about Reconstruction. Sherman's cogent remarks stand as one of the more lucid statements of a specific conservative point of view. He began by observing that "I cannot imagine that matters that may involve the future of 4,000,000 souls could be put in more charitable and more conscientious hands." But he cautioned, "God has limited the powers of man, and though in the kindness of your heart you would alleviate all the ills of humanity it is not in your power . . . to fulfill one-tenth part of the expectations of those who framed the bureau for the freedmen, refugees, and abandoned estates."

Sherman feared that agitation to give former slaves the vote for partisan purposes would disrupt the course by which they would acquire "freedom and political consequence to which [they are] or may be entitled by natural right"; he reminded Howard that blacks could vote in only three Northern states. It would require another "revolution, and as we have just emerged from one attempted revolution it would be wrong to begin another." Sherman contended that Southern whites would adapt to black freedom if "not harassed by 'confiscation' and political complication": "Many of them will sell or lease on easy terms part of their land to their former slaves," he predicted erroneously, "and gradually the same political state of things will result" as conditions that prevailed in Maryland, Kentucky, or Missouri. He did ultimately prove correct in claiming that taxpayers would rebel at the costs of maintaining "separate colonies of negroes, or the armies needed to enforce the rights of negroes dwelling in the Southern States in a condition antagonistic to the feelings and prejudices of the people." His views were invariably justified by virtue of his previous knowledge—"I know the people of the South even better than you do"—but their essence rather than their detail proved wrong-headed. White Southerners did not adapt but revealed a stubborn determination to keep freedmen in a state of permanent subordination and dependency. President Andrew Johnson seemed content to go forward on this basis. But by the end of 1865 even conservative Republicans in Congress who favored the "generous peace" proclaimed by Sherman had concluded that some guarantees were needed to defend the black population. It would take Sherman many years before he realized that the South's black citizens were the Union's most faithful allies. He never acknowledged his error.[3]

Sherman ended with a warning: "Don't let the foul airs of Washington poison your thoughts toward your old comrades in arms." Howard, of course, continued to enjoy warm relations with Stanton, but shortly before the grand review Sherman asked a great favor of him. Howard retained his rank and had not yet formally relinquished his appointment as commander of the Army of the Tennessee. Sherman asked him whether he would be prepared to stand aside and allow Logan to assume command prior to the review. Howard refused with "much feeling"; Sherman then cut in acknowledging Howard's right, "but it will be everything to Logan to have this opportunity." Sherman was sometimes more sensitive toward the feelings of others than his abrupt manner often conveyed. He genuinely admired Logan's powers of leadership and tactical ability; also, he must have discerned that Logan would be an influential postwar political figure. Any hurt that he might have felt at being passed over for army command in the summer of 1864 might be palliated by this gesture. Howard recalled Sherman "speaking very gently, as Sherman could, to one near him whom he esteemed," and he implored

Howard, "You are a Christian, and won't mind such a sacrifice." Howard then quickly agreed and made way for Logan. It was indeed a generous gesture, but Sherman would discover that it did not appease Logan.[4]

On May 23 preparations were made for the parade of Sherman's two armies. Their commander and his senior subordinates realized that they could not compete with the Army of the Potomac's smartness and "spit and polish," but they could make a virtue of the troops' scruffy but hardy, battle-worn look and workaday style, for the troops had made their reputation marching and would not let their commander down. The 24th dawned bright and sunny. Sherman, mounted on Duke, took his place at the head of the column that stretched back in company columns 20 men abreast interminably along Maryland Avenue to Long Bridge over the Potomac River and to their camps at Alexandria. The crowds were great and enthusiastic, the streets and public buildings colorfully decorated. On the stroke of 9:00 a.m. the signal gun was fired by the adjutant general, Major General E. D. Townsend, and Sherman led off the host down Pennsylvania Avenue. Sherman had insisted that Howard accompany him, and their joint staffs rode behind with the Army of the Tennessee, with Logan at its head. Sherman could not bring himself to turn around and check precision and deportment, but at the Treasury Building he paused and beheld a "magnificent" display. "The column was compact, and the glittering muskets looked like a solid mass of steel, moving with the regularity of a pendulum." The place where he stopped is now occupied by the equestrian statue of Sherman dedicated in 1903. At Lafayette Square he saluted Secretary of State William H. Seward, still recovering from injuries sustained in a previous carriage accident and the attempt on his life on April 13, who watched the occasion from his bedroom; he returned Sherman's salute. Sherman and the attendant officers then saluted the presidential reviewing stand in front of the White House with their swords. "All on his stand," Sherman recounted, "arose and acknowledged the salute." During his progress down Pennsylvania Avenue Sherman had been the recipient of not just "great applause" but, as a reporter noted, "many fine bouquets and wreaths," so many indeed that staff officers were summoned frequently "to take care of them." At the reviewing stand Sherman dismounted, greeted Ellen, her father, and Tommy, then shook hands with President Johnson, Grant, and members of the cabinet. Stanton approached and offered his hand, "but I declined it publicly, and the fact was universally noticed," Sherman recorded pointedly.

He then took his station on the president's left, and for more than six hours he stood and proudly took the salute "while the army passed in the order of the Fifteenth, Seventeenth, Twentieth and Fourteenth Corps." Sherman hailed it as "the most magnificent army in existence"; this was a true army in the full sense, well organized, well commanded, and disciplined, but it looked and comported itself very differently from what Sherman would have expected back in 1861. Sherman presents himself in his *Memoirs* as the spokesman and admirer of volunteer soldiers. They were more informal, more responsive, and more opinionated than browbeaten regulars, more swaggering and yet more practical. As the historian Margaret Leech observes, these were "frontier soldiers, taller and bonier than Eastern men." They had a more insistent, rolling rhythm, a forthright step. They put on a more picturesque show than the Easterners. Some divisions included not only their ambulances but also the baggage trains with goats, pack mules, cows, sheep, and even raccoons, dogs, and a monkey. Mary Ann "Mother" Bickerdyke, adored by the soldiery for her fearless defense of their interests, had accompanied the army from Belmont to Washington and rode sidesaddle in a calico dress—but with Logan's staff. Each division was preceded by its corps of black pioneers, and Sherman complimented them on "their perfect dress and step." Families of the freedmen also took part. Sherman judged the great review "a splendid success, and . . . a fitting conclusion to the campaign and the war." He and other observers strained to link this as a Western success conducted in a Western style, but in this zeal, they overlooked an important fact: that one-quarter of the troops were from the East.[5]

Sherman's gesture in snubbing Stanton left a sour taste in the mouth. He was taken to task by some newspapers, including the *New York Times*; despite his chilly nature, Stanton did not lack political allies. Grant had attempted to head Sherman off on May 19 when he intimated that he wanted to see Sherman soon: "I want to talk to you about matters upon which you feel sore." Before this discussion Sherman had written to Grant conveying the full extent of his outrage—and he was never one to understate a grievance. "No man shall insult me with impunity, even if I am an officer of the Army." When they did meet, none of Grant's blandishments could persuade Sherman to moderate his tone, and he seemed resolved on some kind of public gesture. He had written rashly and inaccurately that "I regard my military career as ended." But he had no clear-cut plans to return to civilian life, which had not treated him well, and he had just insulted his civilian boss. He warned Grant not to become a victim of Stanton, either. "The lust for power in political minds is the strongest passion of life," he wrote heatedly with Shakespearian analogies overflowing in his mind, "and impels Ambitious men (Richard III) to deeds of Infamy." Ellen, who witnessed the incident at close quarters, became perturbed at the possible consequences Sherman's petulant gesture might have on his postwar prospects.[6]

Sherman's hostility might not have abated, but there is evidence that Ellen sought to build bridges and make peace with Stanton. She had warned her husband not "to lay yourself liable or to compromise yourself." She believed Stanton "evidently wishes to conciliate. I do not care how harsh you are with him but I hope you will not give them the triumph of a court martial over you for breach of military etiquette." The attempted reconciliation was the scheme of Republican senator Solomon Foot of Vermont, who believed that "the country was interested in the preservation of friendly relations between them." Illinois senator Orville Hickman Browning enlisted Ellen as the key emissary. She sent Mrs. Stanton a bouquet. She asked Browning, an old friend of her father's and a supporter of Andrew Johnson—whom she liked and respected—to accompany her on a visit to pay her respects, as she had met Stanton but not his wife, and thus they were only slightly acquainted though staying just next door. The visit was convivial, "a very pleasant half hour," and Stanton stressed that he bore Sherman no ill will, and later indicated he would not try to interfere with his staff, as Sherman feared. But Stanton made it clear that he was not in the habit of making public amends, and, in any case, his dismissive view of the Sherman-Johnston accords had not changed. Little came of these efforts. Sherman wrote to Ellen in July that "Stanton is as vindictive as Old Satan and is so industrious and has the business of his office so complicated that Mr. Johnson fears to break with him, and Grant is not equal to his energy of thought and therefore will be kept back." Sherman admitted that "Stanton would be reconciled to me if I would"; but he could not tolerate "his aggrandizement and my abasement." The quarrel was personal on Sherman's side, but for Stanton personal considerations were of no account. His cold, indifferent response probably provoked Sherman's impotent fury. In March 1876 Sherman conceded that with greater age and experience he should have behaved with "more caution and prudence"—though he had never been one to overlook a slight. To Sherman Stanton would always symbolize the grasping, malign, and calculating party politician he so loathed.[7]

Other than some irritating rumors that Sherman should be nominated as the Democratic candidate for the presidency, the Shermans enjoyed their stay with John. It was followed by a trip to West Point. Ellen, who disliked the limelight, was pleased to see how unaffected her husband appeared. For all the praise lavished on him, he always remained blunt and humorous. Then they traveled to Chicago via South Bend, Indiana, where they visited the children at school at St. Mary's. During the welcome address, Sherman was touched by a reference to his two dead sons. He visited baby Charles's grave for the first time.

The Shermans arrived in Chicago for the opening on June 10 of the Great North-Western Sanitary Fair that aimed to raise money for impoverished soldiers and sailors. Ellen had first been approached by its organizers in December 1864, but she had been too overwhelmed with grief for Charles to get involved. By February 1865 she had changed her mind and agreed to preside at the Catholic Table with the bishop of Chicago, James Duggan. "So if you can send anything that will be either a curiosity or of value please do so," she implored her husband. Though rather snobbish at the thought of his wife selling things, Sherman was as good as his word and sent Ellen the rebel flag taken from Columbia and a Revolutionary seal. Grant also presented her with his horse, Jack, on whom he had ridden during most of his triumphs up to Vicksburg. Sherman formally opened the fair, and his fame brought in great crowds. On June 11 Grant arrived, too. The parade that Grant led through Chicago's streets was watched by 500,000 souls. He was asked to make a speech but declined; when the request was repeated the following day, Sherman offered to make it for him, but Grant joked, "I never ask a soldier to do anything I cannot do myself," and he uttered some laconic sentiments. It was at the fair that Sherman first heard from the general-in-chief, during a conversation in its margins, of his new command: the Military Division of the Mississippi. This time he would be based in St. Louis, a city he had always liked.[8]

Sherman took a short break back in Lancaster, and there he received Grant's directive, "You go to St. Louis to command the Military Division of the Mo [sic]. The order is out." Confusingly, Grant always referred to it as "the Missouri" before its formal change of name. Sherman replied the following day that he found his assignment "perfectly satisfactory." But he queried some details about the precise extent of his command, the forces assigned to him, and his subordinates. He had visited George Thomas in early July and found that though "a [Military] Division commander [he] now exercises much of the duties of a Departmental commander which may lead to confusion." Sherman, always acutely aware of the different talents required at the various levels of command, pointed out that in his previous command his mission had been specified as "to command the troops assembled for action leaving all the details to Dept. commanders." His aside revealed a certain insecurity "lest I may be neglecting something expected of me." He may even have been taking Ellen's advice and watching his back, but he had become convinced, in correspondence with both his brother and John Rawlins, Grant's chief of staff, "that I will be quietly left out in the cold." There is no evidence for this suspicion. He had crowned his return to a military career with a triumphal wreath, and though he flirted with leaving the army again, he had no serious plans to do so; he preferred this service to anything else. Finally, his duties focused on strategic direction and priorities and the ceaseless battle for more financial resources. He did not direct troops in the field personally again; this was done by his subordinates.[9]

The Military Division of the Mississippi, later redesignated Missouri, was geographically vast; it comprised about 25 percent of the continental United States. It stretched east-west from the Mississippi River to the Rocky Mountains and north-south from the 49th parallel to the Rio Grande. It included all the states in this region, plus the Idaho, Montana, Wyoming, and Dakota Territories in the North and the Utah, Arizona, and New Mexico Territories in the Southwest, as well as the Indian Territory north of Texas (now Oklahoma). It was divided into four departments: Dakota, Platte, Missouri, and Arkansas. In its previous incarnation his military division was large but had a lot of men; the new version was huge but had few men, and by the time he had inspected it they would become fewer. Grant's initial orders were that Sherman should "discharge all the troops that can possibly be dispensed with"; especially, he instructed, "reduce the Cavalry force as much as possible." Yet, despite such harsh reductions, Sherman's command might be the one most likely to be involved in military hostilities. Not only were the Sioux, Cheyenne, and other tribes troublesome, but Sherman had to be prepared in case Grant ordered an intervention to support the Mexican rebels led by Benito Juárez, opposed to the French-buttressed regime of the Emperor Maximilian. Should these be successful, then Sherman would have a good chance of succeeding Grant as general-in-chief.[10]

Yet, as in 1864–65, logistical anxieties came to the fore again; unlike in 1864–65, some of these were personal. In August 1865 his many St. Louis friends gave him $30,000 to acquire a house. Ellen was overjoyed: "at last a prospect of being with you permanently where we can have the children near us." Sherman had no choice but to turn to matters of personal administration before he could give his full attention to the affairs of his new command.

A move to St. Louis, Ellen pointed out, also raised the additional problem of schooling, especially for Minnie, "and I will send Minnie on first to convent school with the rest and take Lizzie with me." Then any house would have to be suitably furnished. "I would like to select the furniture but don't care a great deal, I hope you will get what is durable." Sherman settled all the family in the Planter's Hotel in St. Louis while he and Ellen concentrated on finding a house they liked. Sherman had also acquired, as Ellen proudly observed, "a fine carriage, a good driver and a handsome team of horses." She preferred a house in the suburbs to one in the town center. They selected a large, airy, redbrick house with a country feel, "the Nicolson place" on high ground, 912 Garrison Avenue, that he bought for $24,000; it had the advantage of being close to the center, and streetcars passed outside. All the family were delighted that, at last, they had a proper family home. Ellen liked St. Louis, and the shops were far superior to San Francisco's. They moved in on September 22 and spent the remainder of the month settling in, furnishing and improving their residence. Ellen then began the arrangements to purchase a lot in the Calvary Cemetery in St. Louis and transfer the remains of Willy and Charles there, after which "I can feel at home." In purchasing the house and in the intricate details of the move, Sherman abided by his wife's wishes.[11]

Despite greater domestic comfort, once he had returned to headquarters his other massive logistical problems had not eased. They were framed by the sheer enormity of his command, which posed insuperable difficulties. "Our plains resemble your seas," Sherman advised Admiral Porter, "and it will take some years of cruising for me to familiarize myself with all the interests and localities." He had 25,000 men at his disposal, but this force would be halved over the next year. Grant aimed to establish a regular army of 80,000 men, though he never came close to reaching this target. The US Army declined in strength during the Johnson years from 57,072 in 1866 to 36,953 after Grant became president in 1869. Sherman might receive reinforcements in the event of an Indian war, but the figures suggest he never enjoyed the resources to prevent its outbreak. He also faced another ineluctable difficulty. Despite the vastness of the West, the wilderness had become more accessible, and it lacked territories to which the Indian tribes could be "removed" and left undisturbed. Sherman sensed that the Indians might choose to make a ferocious "last stand" in defense of their hunting grounds. In October 1866 he would describe this as "one of those irreconcilable conflicts that will end only in one way[,] one or the other must be exterminated[,] and as Grant says[,] our tail is longest and [the] poor Indians in the end must go under."[12]

Even though he had been ordered to concentrate on reducing the number of his cavalry, he was reluctant to do so because this was his most valuable arm. The rapid construction of the Union Pacific Railroad Eastern Division toward Fort Riley, Kansas, permitted troops to be moved more rapidly, but railroads were vulnerable when left unguarded; he also had to protect 3,500 miles of stagecoach routes. Sherman had no choice but to concentrate his forces and depend on small forts as logistical bases from which he could advance into enemy territory when required via selected, protected routes. He believed passionately that settlers should be allowed to travel westward as far as they could farm; he long held that the "Western Desert," including Kansas, Nebraska, and the Dakotas, could not grow crops. He erroneously believed that the settlement problem would solve itself. Consequently, he deduced that westward migration should be restricted to a maximum of three routes that he could protect with the forces at his disposal: the Santa Fe Trail, the Oregon Trail, and the Smoky Hill route via Denver, Colorado. All other routes, he argued, should be closed and all remote, isolated settlements abandoned. All forts should be no more than 100 miles apart and equipped to support one another; they were expensive to maintain, however, and Grant wanted their numbers reduced. This effort to control westward movement was destined to fail, for over 100,000 people would attempt to travel during the summer of 1866. "We must not be surprised if some of them lose their lives, cattle and scalps," Sherman observed bluntly.[13]

As ever, he was incredibly restless and wanted to "sally forth" to inspect his command. He made his first trip in the autumn of 1865 to inspect the Union Pacific Railroad. He was so enthusiastic about the project that he advocated that it be given government aid, a matter that Grant immediately acted upon. He occasionally flared up irritably at the attentions of importunate admirers—the side effect of asthma, as niter papers had not been put in his luggage. The following year he undertook a more ambitious trip, accompanied part of the way by his brother John, to Fort Riley and from there to St. Paul and Minneapolis, Minnesota, and eventually Lake Superior, traveling "a distance of 160 miles of bad road" in an army ambulance that he called a "Dougherty," then pushing on to Detroit and then home. Such trips, he explained to Ellen, who missed him sorely, "enable[ ] me to study and understand most of the questions that daily rise in my business." By gaining first-hand knowledge, "I cannot be imposed on by interested parties."[14]

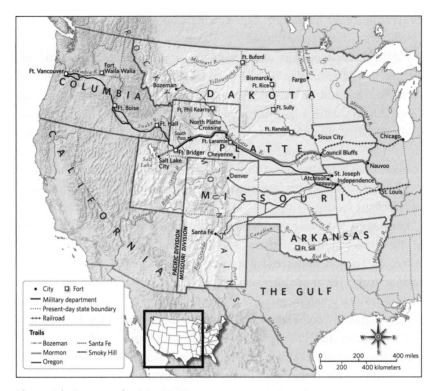

Sherman's Command, 1865–1868

In March 1866 the Department of the Missouri was divided into two departments, one with its headquarters at Leavenworth, Kansas, and the other at Omaha, Nebraska. Only Sherman and regular officers were left in post. Sherman pleaded with Grant to stay his hand in reducing his establishment further until he had received a "valuable Report submitted by General Pope." On the frontier John Pope had proved a perceptive officer of wide experience who earned Sherman's respect despite his calamitous defeat at the hands of Robert E. Lee at Second Bull Run in August 1862. He agreed with Pope's report, and so did Grant, and it served as the basis of the US Army's Indian policy, but further reductions went ahead. All three generals agreed on the need to treat the Indians more equitably "and to protect them from the encroachment of the Whites." To this end Grant supported Sherman's wish to channel westward travel, as by no means all Indians were hostile. "I think peace with the Indian can be secured in good part," Grant concluded, "by protecting them." Sherman agreed with this, too, but he disapproved of

Grant's choice for his second departmental commander, Philip St. George Cooke, whom he deemed too old.[15]

All the discussion, visits, and reports undertaken in 1866 made little difference to Indian affairs. The Department of the Interior's stranglehold on them could not be broken. Typically, two of its Indian commissioners, General Sam Curtis, whom Sherman respected, and Henry W. Reed, who dealt with the tribes of the Upper Missouri River, peremptorily demanded that the War Department feed them all during the winter. Sherman railed impotently at being lumbered with this expense at the last minute, deeming it a form of blackmail that suggested "evil consequences may arise" unless he provided the food.

On August 6 the title of his command changed to the Military Division of the Missouri. The Department of the Dakota was created and given to Alfred H. Terry, a volunteer lawyer who had managed to transfer into the regular army. The more Sherman saw of Terry, the more he came to admire his military judgment. Cooke's Department of the Platte was reduced in size, Winfield Scott Hancock was named to command the Department of the Missouri, and Sherman's old friend Ord was transferred to command the Department of Arkansas. Pleased by these changes, Sherman then traveled to inspect the Southwest. He was shocked by the pitiable state to which the Utes had been reduced and was determined to protect them so long as "they are not banded together in parties large enough to carry on war." In September at Fort Garland he parleyed formally with the Utes, employing Kit Carson, Indian agent in New Mexico and old California acquaintance, as his interpreter. He reiterated the essence of his policy when he urged the Utes to settle on the reservations. Many of the chiefs agreed but muttered excuses for their inaction, blaming the reluctance of "the young men." During the endless speeches, Sherman playfully picked up a young Indian boy; an anxious mother later found him snoozing in Sherman's lap. With no agreement in sight, Sherman got up and left the parley and said to Carson, "They will have to freeze and starve a little more, I reckon, before they will listen to common sense." He respected Carson, a devoted Unionist during the Civil War. "Kit is a good fellow," he observed to Ellen, "but getting old. He even talks about settling down." He did agree with Sherman, though, that the threat posed by the tribes in this quarter was greatly exaggerated. During the autumn Sherman had traveled 100 miles in three days, and "did not see or hear of an Indian . . . though we passed the whole length of the Cheyenne and Arapaho Reservation."[16]

By the end of the year Sherman clearly felt that he had got on top of his huge command and its manifold problems. Patience—hardly one of his virtues—and the railroad would go a long way to solve them. He knew that "difficulties were unavoidable," but he increasingly felt that he had them under control. The next step would be an effort to persuade the tribes to move to reservations—even the Sioux, whom he calculated might be content with the Black Hills of South Dakota. He issued orders to his subordinates to defend the lines of communication, confident that the Union Pacific Railroad would keep the Sioux and Cheyenne divided while he attempted to concentrate on their defense. "All the game is gone and the Indians must soon follow it. . . . Everybody wants an Indian War," he noted, because wars need soldiers to fight them and they bring money that growing businesses hanker after. Sherman's cynicism over the settlers' motives had become more pronounced during his travels. They were "resolved on trouble for the sake of profit." He was determined to resist this mischief.[17]

All Sherman's cogent assumptions were swept aside when 1866 concluded with a humiliating defeat. On December 21 an overconfident Brevet Lieutenant Colonel W. J. Fetterman allowed himself to be lured into a trap by the Sioux near Fort Phil Kearny, and his entire force of 81 officers and men, sent out to relieve some wood haulers who escaped safely, was annihilated. Sherman could only express bewilderment that the reverse—henceforth always referred to as the "Fetterman Massacre"—"could have been so complete." Grant requested a full report immediately on the affair; he acted decisively and, even before requesting Sherman's report and without consultation, dismissed Cooke and replaced him with Christopher Augur. Sherman hardly disapproved of these changes, but Cooke blamed him for this "cruel blow calculated to disgrace me" even though he had played no part in Cooke's removal. He thought the recent conflict had indeed revealed certain inefficiencies, but he "never supposed Gen[era]l Cooke was in the least to blame for the Phil Kearny massacre." The outlook appeared bleak: Sherman warned his brother John that he faced two Indian wars. Not just the Sioux but also the Cheyenne "will not settle down, and our people will force us to [do] it."[18]

Sherman sought to punish the Sioux for the humiliation at Fort Phil Kearny. In April 1867 he issued orders to Augur that aimed to "enforce and command that respect to our military power which alone enables us to fulfil our office." His policy rested on deterrence. He would protect peaceful, friendly tribes but strike hard at those, especially the Sioux, who had become "bold and insolent in the highest degree." It was urgent that Augur be well prepared, locate the vital ground, and be "on the spot" so that his troops could move rapidly and strike before the ponies of the Sioux had recovered from winter's ravages. He immediately realized that the Fetterman Massacre would ignite uproar and demands for military action from all quarters and all directions well beyond the resources he could muster. This concern underlined the need to remove friendly tribes, "for if they wander about at pleasure no matter how peacefully disposed they will be charged with the acts of others and be embroiled with the whites."[19]

Two events occurred that distracted Sherman from these pressing affairs. On January 10 he wrote to Grant informing him of the "event I have been waiting." The night before, Philemon Tecumseh Sherman, was born—dubbed "Cumpy," to distinguish him from his father. "Cump is much pleased with his boy," Ellen informed her father, "and well he may be, for the child is strong and healthy and just like him." The new baby boy was very much the center of attention in the Sherman household and much petted and cosseted. Ellen observed that even "Cump attempts to alter his tone of voice when he speaks to him (if there is no one about) and assumes a tender and persuasive tone, but" she joked, "he makes a horrible failure of it." She reported to her husband that "our baby is growing finely and continues in splendid health."[20]

The second eventuality was much more official and less welcome. On February 21 Sherman received orders to give all "assistance in your power to facilitate and make successful" the Indian Commission set up by the Johnson administration. Worse was to come. Although in April he had been ordered not to change his plans or allow the commission to interfere with their execution, in July he was informed that he had been nominated to serve on the commission. In the autumn two other commissioners joined him, the retired William S. Harney, whom he had encountered in Missouri in 1861, and Alfred H. Terry. "Harney even weaker than I had supposed—and Terry improves on close acquaintance," he noted. The commission's remit lay in seeking a peaceful resolution of frontier disputes by negotiating treaties. Sherman was skeptical that the hostile Sioux would treat with the commissioners and anxious that they might discover "the weakness and vulnerability of the steamboats" on the Missouri River. Settlers in the Department of the Platte endured a series of random raids, and Sherman fired off a lot of sound and fury, especially in Augur's direction. "So we must keep our hands off till the Indians become utterly uncontrollable, and then it will be too late." What good, he asked Grant, would come from talking to the friendly Sioux? He dismissed the commission's proceedings as "the same old senseless twaddle." However, he also admitted privately to Grant that as our "hauling contracts *all* failed this year," and as Augur had reinforced most of his advanced posts, he entertained serious doubts as to his ability to sustain operations against the Sioux, "as any expedition would have to haul its own food along the whole way." Allowing for pending railroad construction, he would "try to be better prepared next year." So he was not quite as disappointed by the appearance of the Indian Commission as he sometimes pretended to be.[21]

Sherman's real troubles lay in the political results of inflammatory rumors that grew in strength throughout 1867. The historian Robert Cook has characterized Western frontier society as "ethnically and racially plural but short on tolerance, equality, and stability." Clamors for protection could only be soothed at the expense of offensive movement. The exaggerated press stories that fed people's fears had another unwelcome by-product, the widening of the war. Sherman branded this "a mischievous design to precipitate hostilities by a series of false reports," and the chief troublemaker was known to him. Thomas F. Meagher, a lawyer who had served in the 69th New York in his brigade during the First Bull Run, had by a series of accidents ascended in the spring of 1867 to the position of acting governor of the Montana Territory. On April 9 he caused a commotion in the War Department by telegraphing a demand that regulars be sent to Montana, and on dubious authority he raised 800 volunteers, though they found no Indians to fight. Sherman dismissed him rightly as the instigator of a "stampede," but Stanton felt that the fears he voiced could not be ignored. Stanton had permitted the raising of the requested volunteers to placate and reassure anxious public opinion in the territories. Sherman issued a circular letter defining the procedure to be followed by the state and territorial governors. But Stanton, in a perfectly friendly correspondence, warned Sherman to be on his guard against "needless expense," and examples soon appeared. Of the 400 volunteers raised in Gallatin County, Montana, 100 were officers, including rather a lot of colonels.[22]

Fortunately, Meagher fell from the scene in July, quite literally. He tottered drunkenly along the deck of a river steamer moored near Fort Benton, misjudged the stern, and toppled into the Missouri River and drowned. News of Meagher's demise brought Sherman grim satisfaction. But all the territories from Montana to Colorado and the states in between implored Sherman for protection and were highly critical of his "cool, off-hand dubious pieces of advice." They predictably insinuated that although Sherman might have been "mad" in 1861, six years later he could only be called "half-crazy." But with military operations deferred, when he joined his fellow commissioners at Leavenworth he was remarkably relaxed and affable, even joking after an admirer stole his hat that it was easier to part with than his scalp. All who talked to him were impressed with his extraordinary knowledge of geography; one reporter called him a "walking dictionary." At North Platte, Nebraska, in September 1867 he met Sioux chiefs. The journalist and explorer Henry M. Stanley, who covered their deliberations, wrote that he talked to them bluntly but not unkindly, with "genial exhortations to the Indian to stand aside from the overwhelming wave of white humanity . . . and to take refuge in the Reservations"; though the tribes would receive all the help they needed if they acceded, a resort to war would be disastrous. But the Sioux had successfully, if temporarily, deterred further incursions into their hunting grounds around the Powder River and even enjoyed the right to hunt beyond them. Sherman's fellow commissioners concluded the Treaty of Medicine Lodge on October 21 without him, as he had been called to Washington, DC. This pact secured agreement in principle to the future assignment of a reservation for the Sioux, Cheyenne, and Arapaho.[23]

Sherman had managed to elude President Johnson's embraces, thanks to Grant's advice, and had avoided visits to Washington for some time. This unavoidable call highlights Sherman's relations with both the president and indeed a future president, Grant. These relations form a counterpoint to the issues he grappled with in the West. They occurred in parallel with his efforts on the frontier. Despite the War Department's slight irritation with his reluctance to reduce troop levels, Sherman's tour of command was deemed a success. Grant lacked firsthand knowledge of the region and relied heavily on his counsel. His friendship with Grant broadened and deepened during these years. They spoke and wrote to one another frankly. Grant visited the Shermans soon after they moved to St. Louis. He even encouraged Sherman to go on a long foreign trip with Minnie in the spring and summer of 1867, though given that this coincided with a crisis in Indian affairs, he was glad when Sherman decided not to go after all. Grant also revealed his ambivalence toward Washington; he dreaded returning to it but feared leaving it. Sherman, for his part, relied heavily on Grant's shrewd advice on political matters and made frequent protestations of loyalty and admiration, accepting that whatever might happen in the future, Grant would always remain the boss. He expressed his embarrassment and annoyance at some errors in a recently published book, *Sherman and His Campaigns* (1865), "whose publication I have long dreaded but could not avoid." Sherman and one of the authors, Samuel Bowman, had enjoyed a close relationship for more than a decade and had once shared the same roof. He had supported Bowman's literary efforts since April 1865 and had granted him some access to his papers. He harbored doubts about the project, but Bowman had persuaded him—while admitting that he wished to make money out of the book—"and I do not object," he observed, "for he says that others less capable will do the thing and make a botch of it." Eighteen months later, despite the book's blemishes, Sherman admired Grant's matter-of-fact reaction to it and his "calm stoicism which places you above all such petty annoyances"—a quality Grant evinced again in his reply.[24]

In January 1866 Grant briefed Sherman confidentially on the possibility he might be promoted to lieutenant general. Grant wished to make two nominations. He also wanted to nominate Sheridan and asked whether Sherman would support this "to ensure that a competent commander would be entrusted with future armies"; Sherman did and believed his youth an advantage. Sherman received notification of his promotion on July 25, 1866. His empathy with the president had not gone unnoticed. Earlier in May 1866 Radical congressman Thaddeus Stevens had attempted to veto any further advancement for Sherman by moving an amendment that froze any further promotions on the resignation or death of Winfield Scott, then ailing, and limited the number of lieutenant generals to one—Grant. This effort failed, which was just as well, since Scott died on May 29. Johnson insisted on presenting Sherman's commission as lieutenant general personally, and Sherman interrupted his summer tour of the West in 1866 to travel to Washington via Pittsburgh. His initial reaction to the promotion was rather flat. "I do not suppose the commissioning [of a] Lieutenant General will make any change to the present command. Yet it may—and it is well to contemplate it."[25]

Grant had not failed to notice Sherman's presidential favor, either. Sherman's stock had risen as Grant's fell, but Grant did not feel threatened by it. Of course, after Johnson's sudden elevation Sherman had quickly sent an encouraging letter, hoping that the new president would be successful. He explained in October 1866 that he especially applauded "his efforts to restore our country to political peace." Johnson asked Sherman whether he could publish this letter. Grant quickly warned Sherman that this could be a presidential maneuver to shore up his own design for Reconstruction, not least his faltering efforts to veto legislation to guarantee black rights, which

Stanton favored, and ultimately replace Stanton. He warned also that an important part of his plan would be "to have you in Washington either as Acting Secretary of War or in some other way." Grant also stressed the danger for the US Army should Sherman take "one or other side of the antagonistic political parties," which could hardly be exaggerated. The two generals intended to discuss the matter at a meeting of the Society of the Army of the Tennessee in Chicago in November, but in the event neither could attend. The content of their likely conversation might be inferred from the letters they exchanged before the meeting.[26]

There can be no doubt that Sherman held conservative views on Reconstruction policy. Orville Hickman Browning summed up Sherman's position neatly in his diary with some satisfaction: he "was fully conservative and utterly opposed to the unconstitutional and revolutionary measures of the radicals." In retrospect Johnson could see the similarities between what Sherman had attempted to do in his ill-fated memorandum of April 1865 with his own policy in 1866 of restoring a semblance of pre-1861 conditions in the Southern states as quickly as he could on his own authority; he also extended a conciliatory hand to the former Confederate leadership. Again, it was true, as Sherman declared to Ellen, that "I don't want the Extreme Radicals to govern the country and I did and do wish Mr. Johnson well in general terms," but he remained opposed to any "intermeddling with other people," and as he made clear to Grant, "I do not love a Rebel, or a Copperhead today one whit better than I did in 1864, nor do I approve of mob law in any manner, shape or form." The last was a reference to Ku Klux Klan attacks on black leaders, voters, and churches and violent outbreaks in New Orleans and elsewhere. He also had specific objections to serving soldiers sitting in the cabinet as secretary of war, because of the "mingling with other political questions and sharing the fate of the administration" like any other politician, "whereas we . . . must serve in succession every administration." He responded bluntly, "It is none of our business." Perhaps. Yet despite all that had passed between them—and the tone had become more cordial by the autumn of 1866—Stanton believed Sherman to be the man best equipped to run the War Department, should he be ousted, because the general knew it intimately and would know how to protect it.[27]

From the autumn of 1866 Stanton and Johnson began their furious duel as to who should control the War Department and thus the military direction of Reconstruction policy. Stanton refused to resign, but the man at the top of Johnson's list to replace him was Sherman. In October 1866 Sherman was called to Washington twice. Suitably briefed by Grant, he called on Johnson on October 6 and on October 26. Johnson could be obstinate and erratic, but he was devious and determined. On both occasions the president did not make an outright offer of the War Department but simply said how much he wanted Sherman to run it. This gambit permitted Sherman to sidestep the issue. Despite presidential blandishments, for once in his life, Sherman "kept very quiet." This was the signal point when Sherman refused to turn. If he had encouraged Johnson and then accepted a formal invitation to join his cabinet, he would indeed have become a full-time politician, available thanks to the ambidextrous character of the Johnson administration (both Johnson and Stanton, after all, were Democrats) to accept the presidential nomination of either party. He chose instead the loyal path of supporting his friend Grant.[28]

He had agreed to take Grant's place and accompany the administration's minister to Mexico, Lewis Campbell, in order to make contact with the Mexican resistance leader, Benito Juárez. Supporting the the anti-French resistance was a nominal priority of the Johnson administration. The mission was nothing more than an elaborate maneuver to remove Grant from the political scene in Washington, and he had refused to go; by accepting it, Sherman had affirmed his loyalty to the administration but at the price of wasted time. Campbell did not impress Sherman: "He drinks and loses all self-control when in that condition." Sherman received courteous invitations from Marshal François Achille Bazaine, the commander of French troops in Mexico, which he felt obliged to decline; he and Campbell failed to establish contact with Juárez, though they met one of his subordinates. Sherman returned in December to New Orleans, "where Bragg, Dick Taylor, R. O. Hébert and others visited"; then Campbell suddenly rejoined him. Sherman forced him to take the "pledge of abstinence . . . and [he] improved amazingly," but Sherman detected a relapse as he departed. More encouragingly, during his travels through the South back to St. Louis, the many Southerners involved were amicable; he "saw or heard nothing that was at all disagreeable." As for the Mexican trip, it certainly highlighted the huge chasm that yawned between the nominal importance of US–Latin American policy and the calibre of men like Campbell entrusted to execute it.[29]

In 1866-67 Sherman's incessant journeying took a toll on his marriage. Initially, Ellen accepted his trips sadly but stoically. But in the summer of 1866 when he suggested casually that he intended to take a long trip in a Dougherty with a tiny escort, she responded with horror, "You [Sherman] may be killed." Ellen relied on "my faith in God and His merciful protection"; though she agreed that the dry heat of the prairies was good for his asthma in a way that St. Louis was not, and accepted his need to escape, "I hope the long trip will be beneficial to your health." Characteristically, though she considered his instructions in the event of his death "kind," "I would not follow them to the letter"; she would remain in St. Louis, as it offered more opportunities for the children despite the periodic outbreaks of cholera in the summer. The following August, however, she complained, "The poor children are so disappointed at losing you for the summer when we anticipated so much happiness." After so long, Sherman had got used to living without his wife and family and cheerfully accepted the need for long trips away without a second thought. They provided him with a kind of release that his family did not.

The Ewings were strongly allied to Johnson, and Ellen liked him—especially for his support in the trying days in the autumn of 1861. In September 1867 she reported the arrival of the presidential party in St. Louis after the convention in Cleveland, Ohio, of the National Union movement. This was a third party composed of "moderates" on Reconstruction, which Johnson hoped to employ as a springboard for reelection in 1868. Thereafter he progressed on an ill-judged speaking tour known as "the swing around the circle," during which his Tennessee stump-speaking style, lubricated with copious bourbon, was ridiculed. Ellen put her finger on Johnson's difficulties, "as he exposes himself to insult by the undignified manner in which he speaks at the different points on the road." Johnson undoubtedly displayed a certain misguided tenacity. His own political position became more beleaguered: his Reconstruction schemes were replaced by congressional legislation, and his veto of the Fourteenth Amendment that protected the voting rights of former slaves failed. He determined to bring Sherman to Washington, as a military man's prestige, he was convinced, could shore up his administration.[30]

In March 1867, in order to protect Stanton, his allies in Congress passed the Tenure of Office Act, by which the president could not alter his cabinet without senatorial approval. In the summer Johnson asked Stanton to resign, but he refused—though he agreed to stand aside while the Supreme Court ruled on the constitutionality of the act. Grant reluctantly agreed to serve as secretary of war ad interim from August 1867. Grant explained his motives to Sherman at length. He revealed disillusion with the Johnson administration. The "romance . . . that men in high places . . . act only from motives of pure patriotism, and for the general good of the public has been destroyed," he wrote frankly. "An inside view proves too truly very much the reverse." He speculated about taking a break, perhaps going to Mexico, but if he did he wanted Sherman to take his place. He also underlined that he agreed to be what the historian Joan Waugh calls "his own boss" in order that the powers he had secured for the commanding general should not "revert again to the Secretary of War." This is a significant point when considering Sherman's disappointing legacy 18 months later. For the next six months Grant's relations with Johnson deteriorated, not just because he disapproved of his policy toward the War Department and Reconstruction but because he sought to distance himself from Johnson at the same time he was being courted by Republican bosses with the idea of nominating him as the Republican candidate for the presidency in 1868. Sherman found it difficult to believe that anything "would induce you to change your present commission for that of the presidency." But he was wrong; Grant was more intent on it than he seemed.[31]

Johnson remained determined to use Sherman as a counterweight to Grant. In October 1867 he once again dangled the prospect of the War Department before Sherman, who once more wisely declined; in any case, he would not seek to displace Grant. By the second week of January 1868 Sherman had returned to Washington in a more humble capacity, as the chairman of a board compiling a code of regulations and articles of war. On January 13 the Senate ruled that Johnson's action against Stanton could not be sustained. Grant had anticipated the Senate vote and had informed Sherman two days before that he could not possibly risk being prosecuted under the Tenure of Office Act, for if found guilty he would be imprisoned for five years and fined $10,000. The stakes were high because Grant's rivals for the Republican nomination in the Senate would not hesitate to use this weapon against him. He did not reveal this dimension of his thinking to Sherman. Grant stepped down as secretary of war ad interim on January 13.

Sherman's relations with Stanton were by now friendly, but as Grant's replacement he lobbied for Jacob D. Cox, an old subordinate who Sherman believed would "be acceptable to General Grant and the army generally." He urged this course on Johnson, but the latter remained noncommittal, for he was determined to use the issues provoked by the Tenure of Office Act to confront congressional usurpations of executive authority. Johnson assailed Grant at a cabinet meeting on January 14, calling him a duplicitous traitor, and friendly newspapers repeated the charge; thereafter they were permanently estranged. But Sherman and Grant remained committed to a further effort to persuade Stanton to resign for the good of the army. This effort predictably failed. Stanton returned to the War Department and took up permanent residence in his office. Sherman was also useful to Johnson because one of the president's most valued legal advisers was his father-in-law, Thomas Ewing Sr. Ewing agreed with Sherman that Cox might "have been wise as a peace offering," but Johnson had showed no interest in reconciliation because "it would have let off the Senate too easily from the effect of their arbitrary act." After the failure of his well-intentioned proposal, Sherman asked the president for leave to return to St. Louis. "For eleven years I have been tossed about so much that I really do want to rest, study, and make the acquaintance of my family."[32]

Sherman returned to St. Louis but could not escape the presidential tentacles for long. Johnson proposed to create a new Military Division of the Atlantic with its headquarters in Washington. Sherman recognized this as another maneuver "to remove Mr. Stanton from his office as Secretary of War, and have me discharge the duties." Of course, Sherman declared, Johnson's arrangement would be awkward because "it would put three heads to an army, yourself [Johnson], General Grant, and myself, and we would be more than human if we were not to differ. In my judgment it would ruin the army, and would be fatal to one or two of us." It would certainly have been fatal to his friendship with Grant. "Therefore," he concluded, with a powerful flourish, "with my consent, Washington never." But Johnson could not be dissuaded from this course. He issued the order for the Atlantic Military Division in February 1868 and began preparations to promote Sherman to brevet general. Sherman at once telegraphed John and urged him to oppose this in the Senate, as Sherman had consistently opposed promotions by brevet. "If I can't avoid coming to Washington," he added, "I may have to resign." In the background both Grant and Johnson maneuvered around an unspoken assumption of some kind of tribunal adjudicating on their activities, as yet undefined, and they began to gather detailed written accounts, especially relating to the dramatic days of January 11–14.

"Of course, I don't want to be drawn into the controversy," Sherman confided to Grant, "and should be almost drawn to resignation if the President should force me to come to Washington in any capacity likely to draw me into the vortex." In his response to Johnson, Sherman did not mince his words, indicating that he would not hesitate to resign if the president persisted with this plan. He excused Johnson's obduracy on the grounds that "our relations have always been most confidential and friendly" and he would not risk them, so that no "cloud of difficulty should arise between us," especially given their close family relations. Grant wrote quickly the same day to inform

Sherman that the order had been withdrawn, so the threats of resignation had worked. Sherman replied that he had "never felt so troubled in my life." He admitted that he felt "like Hamlet's Ghost": the looming, ominous threat of Washington political life "curdles my blood and mars my judgment." In revealing his relief to Grant, Sherman clearly perceived "the false position I would occupy as between you and the President." He was quick to emphasize the embarrassment such an unwanted position would expose him to. "Therefore I would be there with naked, informal and sinecure duties, and utterly out of place."[33]

What most perturbed Sherman was Washington's atmosphere "and the influences that centred here," which he found pernicious and detrimental to his equanimity. He could see how they had affected Grant, and if they disturbed "one so guarded and prudent as he is, what will be the result with me," he asked, "so careless, so outspoken as I am?" He could not live in a city with cycles of irresistible pressure; as only Sherman could put it, it was "enough to poison our minds and kindle into life that craving itching for fame which has killed more good men than bullets." It was not that Sherman lacked political skill, or even interest, but he was genuinely repelled by naked ambition, backstabbing, and intrigue for their own sake. Actually, he showed great good sense in rebuffing Johnson's overtures because acceptance would have drawn him onto the president's side and into the vortex of the president's impeachment. This great drama had been precipitated by Johnson's desperate efforts to rid himself of Stanton. The political process of impeachment began in February 1868, and the trial of Andrew Johnson started in March and ground on until his acquittal in May. Sherman remained on its margins, being asked to give testimony but not being called.[34]

Sherman succeeded in remaining on good terms with Johnson, not just to the end of his presidency in March 1869, which quickly assumed the form of a "lame duck," but until his death. He later recognized the great danger that Johnson had exposed him to in 1868. Sherman realized quickly that Johnson had been reduced to political impotence by congressional action. "He attempts to govern after he has lost the means to govern. He is like a general fighting without an army—he is like Lear roaring at the wild storm, bareheaded and helpless." Johnson's conduct could be dismissed as farcical "or meant mischief"—mainly the latter, because Sherman could only lose by the association. He managed to detach himself from Johnson while not alienating Grant. The latter referred to his "purest kindness, and a disposition to preserve harmony"; if Sherman had been tempted to stab Grant in the back, he would have tied himself to a loser rather than the coming man. He would not move back to Washington unless Grant became president.[35]

Sherman hastened back to the "vasty fields" of the West that meant "more to my family than Washington." Still, he could not escape entirely from the cycle of presidential electioneering. In early June he wrote to Grant congratulating him on his nomination on May 21, 1868, as Republican candidate for the presidency. "I feel a little strange though this was a foregone conclusion. If you want the office of course I want you to have it, and now that you have accepted the nomination of course you must succeed. It is a sacrifice on your part," he continued, "but one which I doubt you feel forced to make." Sherman at last realized he would have to commit himself to a move to Washington; he hoped it could be made during "the recess of schools" and asked for plenty of time to make his arrangements. "If there be anything you want me to do I feel certain you will not hesitate to let me know." Grant replied that Sherman need not move until November. He justified his course by not wishing to entrust national affairs to "mere trading politicians, the elevation of whom . . . would lose to us, largely, the results of this costly war which we have gone through." Reluctance and diffidence remained a habitual pose among that era's presidential aspirants, and Grant did not disclose that he wanted to be president. Their old comrade in arms, Grenville Dodge, urged Sherman to come out openly in support of Grant, but he believed it better to remain "neutral or silent," conscious of the rapidity with which parties succeeded one another in the White House. Sherman did make a suggestion that Grant come out West. "You could spend a month or two about the head of the Railroad, and if you go out one, you should come in by the other, thus seeing the effect of both."

Grant thought this an excellent suggestion, and so did his Republican campaign managers. At a time when presidential candidates traditionally did not deign to make speeches and solicit votes, this would be a fine way of attracting press attention without campaigning formally. Grant arrived in Leavenworth in July looking tired, a reporter noticed, while "Sherman looks remarkably well all over." They traveled extensively; at one point, Grant intervened decisively in a dispute between Dodge, now the chief engineer, and Thomas C. Durant, the owner of the Union Pacific, over the route to be taken. Sherman looked on approvingly as Grant supported Dodge. In Cheyenne, Wyoming Territory, the two celebrated commanders donned civilian clothes and sauntered about in an unaffected manner and "would not have been distinguished from any ordinary gentlemen strolling around the town." But later Sherman discovered that he did not like being heckled, as he was by

Democrats in St. Joseph, Missouri, on the return journey. "When you learn to behave yourself, I'll continue my speech," he snapped when intervening to support Grant.[36]

There remained much unfinished business on the frontier before he made any move to Washington. Military operations launched by Winfield Scott Hancock in Kansas had proved a public relations disaster, forcing Sherman's cooperation with the Peace Commission. The Treaties of Medicine Lodge and Laramie (April 23, 1868, with later accessions on May 25-26 and November 6) had reached agreement on the need to move friendly tribes to reservations; even the Sioux were given the western half of the Dakota Territory, but they remained defiant. Some hunting was permitted beyond the reservations by the Treaty of Medicine Lodge. All these provisions were bitterly denounced by frontier settlers. "Yet as I don't ask their votes," Sherman consoled himself, "I can stand their personal abuse." Contact between the settlers and the Cheyenne and Arapaho especially led to clashes, and 1868 witnessed an outbreak of raiding, especially on livestock in northwest Kansas. Sherman had only four regiments of cavalry available, but he still remained optimistic as to the ultimate outcome. That year the "golden spike" was hammered into the last rail that completed the Union Pacific Railroad at the bleak and windswept Promontory Point, Utah. "Time is helping us and killing the Indians fast, so that every year the task is less," he observed starkly. Sherman saw the Peace Commission as another way of killing time. Punitive military expeditions were pending: Grant hoped that this time they would "squelch" the Indians. Sherman explained that the aim of the operations was "to get the Indians out from the country between the Railroads, and we believe," he claimed toward the end of the year, "all are gone." In November 1868 at the Battle of the Washita against the Cheyenne, Arapahos and Kiowa, Lieutenant Colonel George A. Custer gained the necessary, though far from decisive, victory.[37]

After the Fetterman Massacre, historians have claimed, Sherman's attitude toward the tribes changed. There is indeed some loose talk of "extermination," and this is sometimes exploited to suggest that Sherman nursed genocidal intent. He did not mean genocide literally, nor did he ever seek it. The whole drift of his policy rested on a reluctance to fight the tribes unless attacked; he harbored resentment and sought punishment should they resort to violence, as he believed they bit the hand that fed them. His punitive attitudes hardened in 1872-73 with the murder of General E. R. S. Canby, an old West Point classmate and good friend, while attempting to negotiate the end of the Modoc War in the lava beds south of Tule Lake in northern California. Infuriated by the demise of his calm, decent, and well-intentioned subordinate, Sherman declared to reporters that "treachery is inherent in the Indian character." Sherman did represent the white triumphalist vision that hunter-gatherer societies must inevitably yield to an advanced, industrial society, but it was fundamentally humane in wishing to "remove" them from any unfair contest. His efforts in 1867 on behalf of the Utes and also the Navajos at Bosque Redondo— "a mere spot of green grass in the midst of wild desert," as he described it—when he allowed the latter to return to their homelands in northwest New Mexico, confirm this view emphatically. It is therefore a major error to link the supposed ruthlessness and brutality of the Marches with his frontier strategy to sustain an unbridled philosophy of "total war," wreaked without pity and intent on the complete destruction of the enemy. Yet Sherman's sympathy for the tribes should not be exaggerated. He respected their courage and martial skill in defense of what they believed in, and sometimes he linked their ferocity with the Confederates'. He admired, for instance, the "extraordinary," masterly retreat across Montana undertaken by the Nez Percé tribe before their eventual surrender in October 1877 but still ordered their pursuit "to the death, lead where they may," and wanted the leaders punished. Sherman did not admire the Indians in the same way that a later generation of their opponents, like Nelson A. Miles, did. He found them puzzling and unpredictable, and their passive inscrutability mystifying, as, so unlike him, they could sit for hours without betraying their thoughts. Yet his record is still a strong and liberal one and does not deserve obloquy.[38]

Nelson Miles, nakedly ambitious and desirous of extending his social connections, married into the Sherman family in June 1868. He had been introduced to John Sherman by Senators Henry Wilson and Charles Sumner and been invited to stay at John's home in Mansfield. There he met and courted Mary Hoyt Sherman, the eldest daughter of William and John's elder brother Charles Taylor Sherman, who had pursued a distinguished legal career in Cleveland, Ohio, and was currently a district court judge. Miles asked for Mary's hand in marriage, and after suitable soundings were taken, it was accepted. General Sherman decided to attend the marriage of his niece, though he expressed severe reservations over Miles's relentless self-promotion and shameless social climbing. Philip Sheridan served as best man at Cleveland's Trinity Church; all the military guests wore full dress uniform except for Sherman, a hint of disapproval. As the Ewings, even Ellen, had discovered and Miles would, too, the general was valueless as a "connection." Mary complained of her uncle's "peculiar sensitiveness about doing anything for a relation." Sherman found every excuse for not taking Miles onto his staff. For all that, the marriage was a happy one.[39]

General Sherman was by far the most famous of these three distinguished brothers gathered at a family wedding. Both the general and John would be deemed worthy of a presidential nomination, though neither won it—John tried, but the general did not. The marriage of Mary Hoyt Sherman to a rising star of the US Army, the attention it received in the newspapers, and the glittering array of guests underscored that the Shermans ranked among the first families of America. Sherman had traveled a long way up the path of ambition in a mere eight hectic years. His ambitions had been fulfilled, but could he rise higher?

16

Commanding General of the Army, 1869–1884

On November 3, 1868, Grant was elected to the presidency, leading to Sherman succeeding him as general-in-chief. Throughout Sherman had abstained from political activities, as "I have a deep-seated aversion to them from old experience in California," but he did express enthusiasm for Grant's win. He also made early preparations for the move to Washington. Anxieties were eased when Grant wrote to Ellen informing her that a group of wealthy admirers intended to buy his house for $65,000 and present it to his successor. Ellen doubted she would hear of the matter again but was quickly reassured when Grant's "beautiful letter" about 205 I Street NW arrived, describing the house as "large and the grounds [as] capacious." The whole business was concluded in about ten days. Sherman's only doubt related to one of the main donors, Daniel Butterfield, Hooker's old friend and former chief of staff, a rather slippery fellow: "I should much prefer that he should not be the chief party." But time would prove Butterfield's presence no impediment to Sherman's interest.[1]

Before Grant and Sherman's ascents to greater responsibility they were able to enjoy on December 15–16, 1868, one last wartime swan song with 2,000 former comrades at a joint reunion of the societies of the Armies of the Cumberland, Georgia, the Ohio, and the Tennessee in Chicago. At the meeting Grant and Sherman discussed the future structure of the army. Grant assured Sherman that he intended to make the arrangements he had introduced as general-in-chief permanent. The long duel between the commanding general and secretary of war waged since 1836 over who should direct the army would be finally decided in favor of the general-in-chief. Henceforth all orders would go out in the commanding general's name. Grant intended to keep John M. Schofield, who had succeeded Stanton earlier in 1868 as war secretary, to ensure these changes could not be dismantled. There is no reason to doubt Grant's sincerity, but taking the presidential oath of office changed both his perspective and his priorities.[2]

Sherman received the summons to Washington on February 24 and arrived two days later with Dayton and Audenried. On 4 March he listened to Grant's inaugural address, in which he promised "the greatest practicable retrenchment in expenditure, in every department of government." This pledge would have severe implications for the army. The same day, the president sent to the Senate his nomination of Sherman in the rank of General of the Army of the United States. The following day Schofield issued the executive order stipulating that Sherman would succeed as commanding general and that the chiefs of all departments, bureaus, and corps should report to him "and act under the orders of the general commanding the army." He would also serve as the channel by which all orders for presidential attention should first be sent to the secretary of war. The order authorized a major role for the commanding general, a title not mentioned in the Constitution and a rank that before 1861 had enjoyed a precarious existence. This measure of centralization might be considered a first step in embracing the "general staff revolution" that swept European armies in the 1860s. At the very least it created a forum for reforming the army. Such hopes would soon be dashed.[3]

Wasting not a second, that very same day Sherman issued General Orders No. 12 assuming command and named all the heads of the staff departments and bureaus as members of the commanding general's staff, plus his individual personal staff, which included two officers who would also work as the president's private secretaries, Horace Porter and Frederick T. Dent; this order appeared to give the general-in-chief significant influence within the executive branch. The heads of the bureaus immediately expressed disquiet, as they viewed themselves as part of the War Department, which, as Sherman pointedly observed, was part of "the civil branch of the Government which connects the army with the President and Congress." Here was the rub. Within less than 24 hours, Townsend, the adjutant general, wrote to Sherman that the president's March 5 order had "changed its form somewhat"; ominously, Schofield's services were not retained. The new secretary of war, John A. Rawlins, who was well known to Sherman, issued a new order on March 26, with Grant's approval, reversing all that they had previously agreed. Henceforth all orders and communications would be made through the secretary. Sherman sent off an incredulous note to the president pleading, "Please do not revoke your order of March 5 without reflection . . . because the Army and country would infer your want of confidence." Sherman could not understand why Grant had abandoned so hastily an idea they had both valued so highly. On visiting Grant, he was fobbed off with excuses about not wanting to upset the tubercular Rawlins, who indeed had only a few months to live. When Sherman pressed him, Grant snapped, "Well, if it is my order, I can rescind it, can't I?" At this, Sherman stood up, bowed, and replied stiffly, "Yes, Mr. President, you have the power to revoke your own order; you shall be obeyed. Good morning, sir."[4]

Sherman hoped that an accommodation might be reached with Rawlins. In practice this did not occur, though Rawlins made some effort to stay on good personal terms with him. The problem that Sherman could not overcome was that Grant now operated in a much broader field, and tussles in the War Department lay far down his list of priorities. The reassertion of executive authority after the Johnson impeachment appeared at the very top. Grant could not achieve his goal if he had to fend off accusations of "militarism," which were frequent at the beginning of his first term. He therefore downplayed his connections with other regulars: Schofield had to go, and so did his alliance with Sherman; here the latter's contemptuous views on politicians, so freely expressed, became a liability. Grant also had to fight off the congressional alliance of Benjamin F. Butler and John A. Logan, both of whom nursed personal grievances against Grant and Sherman, respectively. They argued that Sherman's order took away the secretary's "duties and powers devolved on him by Law, and that it changed the civil nature of the Department of War." To gain the greater objective Grant sacrificed Sherman (and the articles of war he, Sheridan, and Augur labored over in 1868). Sherman fumed that Grant gave the army up to what he called "political influence." He had learned a hard lesson in high politics, witnessed Grant's skill at it firsthand, and got scant return for his unconditional loyalty to Grant, but he was powerless to fight back.[5]

Sherman unwittingly became the architect of his further decline. When Rawlins died in September 1869, Grant attempted to make amends and asked Sherman to temporarily serve as secretary of war and then select his own successor—a golden opportunity, or so it seemed. James Harrison Wilson, who had served on Grant's staff, appeared a strong candidate, but Sherman discarded him because of his strong alliance with Rawlins. The other two names on the short list were Grenville Dodge and William W. Belknap. Belknap had commanded the 15th Iowa Volunteer Infantry and then the 3rd Old Iowa Brigade in 17th Corps. Grant favored Dodge, but Dodge felt he had a conflict of interest at Union Pacific and ruled himself out. That left Belknap, who had impressed Sherman as an orator at the recent Chicago reunion. As he had also served under Sherman, he unwisely inferred that Belknap might prove compliant. Sherman telegraphed him to offer the post, and then Grant invited him formally. Sherman then resigned, and Belknap succeeded him on October 25. This would not be a happy day for the general-in-chief.[6]

It turned out that Belknap shared Butler and Logan's interpretation of the civil-military relationship. He acted in a high-handed manner and issued orders directly not just to the bureaus but to the commands in the field, bypassing Sherman and leaving him completely ignorant of the most elementary administrative detail. Despite his title, Sherman did not command the army. The War Department lay outside his sphere, almost a competing institution. Sherman had no authority over all forms of supply, ordnance, and medical services—all vital to military operations. His protests were ignored, and he soon realized that his lot resembled the unenviable situation of Winfield Scott in the 1850s when he fought and lost a similar battle against Franklin Pierce's secretary of war, Jefferson Davis. Grant was indifferent, given the opportunity he had offered Sherman. Worse was to come. In February 1870 Logan introduced a bill to cut the military budget by $2 million. It comprised a series of draconian cuts to pay and pensions, coupled with compulsory retirements and demotions; the salary of the commanding general became a prime target for reduction at $19,000 per annum. Sherman found it galling that this attack had been mounted by a disaffected former subordinate, currently chairman of the House Military Affairs Committee. All of his efforts to mollify Logan for previous command disappointments had failed signally. Sherman stormed out of the public gallery when this act passed the House.[7]

Sherman then sought to block this legislation in the Senate. As always in a political crisis, he mobilized his allies with speed—not just John Sherman but the chairman of the Senate Military Affairs Committee, Henry Wilson. Through Wilson he submitted a detailed refutation of Logan's claims, though Wilson denied this had been made at his invitation. In the spring the House debated this letter, and then Sherman found another ally in Henry W. Slocum, currently the representative from New York's 3rd District. Logan deemed it "this most extraordinary and remarkable letter," a personal attack on both himself and the House. Sherman scored some debating points. It turned out that Logan's odd claim that the US Army had more staff officers than the French, Russian, or Prussian army was based on proportional measures. James A. Garfield observed that Logan's hatred for the regular army "amounts almost to insanity," and the tactless tone of Sherman's letter, with references to "demagogues," permitted Logan to denounce him for "dictating legislation," efforts that would sound "the death knell to our free institutions." To Sherman's protests that if his pay was cut he could not afford dinners or receptions, Logan retorted, "I do not care whether he can or not." He went on to vow to defend the country from dictation and aristocracy "in favor of republicanism," to cheers in the House. Sherman failed to block the bill's passage in the Senate, but it was amended so that savings could be made by retirement and death, and a cap was placed on recruitment over 30,000 enlisted men. Sherman's pay reduction left him with $13,500, on which, he grumbled, he could just about manage—though it remained a very substantial salary.[8]

Sherman found relief from political complications and unpleasantness by undertaking an inspection of the Texas frontier posts. On May 18, 1871, he crossed the Salt Creek Prairie under the watchful eye of a Kiowa war party about 100 strong led by Satank, Big Tree, Satanta, Eagle Heart, and Big Bear. The inspector general, Randolph B. Marcy, accompanied Sherman, as did a tiny escort. Their lives were saved by a Kiowa medicine man who predicted there were larger wagon trains to attack; the Kiowas slipped away and later ravaged a train of 10 wagons, killing eight and stealing 41 mules. Oblivious to their danger, Sherman arrived at Fort Richardson, and on hearing of the outrage ordered that the party be hunted down. He then pushed on northward to Fort Sill, which housed the Indian Agency. Lawrie Tatum, a Quaker, served as the agent for the Kiowas and Comanches, and did his conciliatory best. Both tribes could draw rations at Fort Sill, but the soldiers were not permitted to cross into Indian territory unless asked to do so by the agent. Benjamin H. Grierson, Sherman's favorite cavalryman, commanded the 10th Cavalry, a black "Buffalo" Regiment. Both Taylor and Grierson were unpopular with settlers and newspaper editors in neighboring Jacksboro, who complained bitterly that the tribes could take rest and sustenance at Fort Sill in between their raids on outlying farms and straggling wagon trains.

Sherman continued to believe that settlers deliberately exaggerated their ordeals to provoke military action from which they might profit, but on May 27 Satank and other chiefs arrived at Fort Sill for provisions and openly boasted to Tatum of their raid. The exasperated agent asked Grierson to arrest them. Sherman, furious at their effrontery, ordered Grierson to take Satank, Satanta, and Big Tree into custody. He then stalked out onto the porch of the commanding officer's quarters and confronted them himself. The details are confused, but the chiefs reached for their weapons, and possibly one fired an arrow; there must have been some prior planning, because Sherman then raised an arm, and the shutters of surrounding buildings at once opened, revealing black troopers with carbines cocked. This is the only recorded occasion when black troops served under Sherman's immediate command. A tense standoff with further scuffles ended with the three chiefs being incarcerated in chains. Satank was killed later trying to escape, and the other two received death sentences, which were commuted to life imprisonment, though neither served more than two years. When the Kiowas returned to raiding in 1873–74, Sherman's sympathies were challenged afresh. The experience also underlined that Ellen's long-standing fears for his safety were not overstated. During the Jacksboro Affair Sherman deliberately took unnecessary risks, almost as if he were determined to prove to himself that he was a warrior, not a bureaucrat.[9]

During this trying time Thomas Ewing Sr.'s health deteriorated rapidly. He had collapsed while addressing the Supreme Court and returned to Lancaster. Tom Jr. and his wife were now resident at the "house on the hill." As the old patriarch declined, all his family, including Sherman, gathered there. At first Ewing Sr. appeared to rally "and seem[ed] so well" that he and Ellen planned to return to Washington on October 11, but the recuperation did not last. Ewing Sr. had made admiring remarks about the Catholic Church during his last weeks and converted just before the end on October 26, 1871. His act brought Ellen much consolation, but it encouraged her to expect rather than to hope that Sherman would follow suit. Her less than subtle efforts would grate and provoke. The wall of Sherman's agnosticism proved impenetrable. As for his father-in-law, Ewing had played a major role in Sherman's advancement, having worked tirelessly on his behalf. But Sherman tended to associate him with the years of disappointment and humiliation and remembered, too, his part in keeping his family divided.[10]

As a way of escaping from his frustrations, in November 1871 Sherman at last took a lengthy trip to Europe. This combined sight-seeing with military observation. Accompanied by Joseph C. Audenried, Fred Grant, and other members of his staff, he traveled on the USS *Wabash* as a guest of Rear Admiral James Alden. He was seen off from New York by Ellen and Tommy. She thought he would enjoy the "congenial company and [be] free from encumbrance and care"; also, he would have more time to read. He landed at Cádiz and visited Gibraltar. Initially his asthma plagued him, but neither that nor the surprising cold and damp of a Spanish winter prevented him visiting, among others, Málaga, Seville, Toledo, and Madrid; his observations especially on Granada and Córdoba, which he visited on the anniversary of their seizure by the Spanish in 1492, betray a close reading of W. H. Prescott's three-volume *History of the Reign of Ferdinand and Isabella, the Catholic, of Spain* (1838). He then took a ship to Bordeaux, Marseilles, Toulon, and Nice; the latter was so "full of Americans . . . that we thought ourselves at home." Everywhere he visited he read voraciously on the history, geography, and culture of the region. From France he traveled to Genoa and Turin, Venice, Verona, and Florence, and then on to Rome, where he had an audience with the pope. He witnessed archaeological excavations at Pompeii before crossing the Mediterranean to Egypt via Malta. In Egypt he conversed with his old ally Charles P. Stone, a fellow West Pointer who, along with another 16 Americans and various Europeans, worked for the khedive of Egypt. Stone served, Sherman informed Turner, "as a sort of Adjutant General of the Egyptian army" and ensured that he had a long audience with the khedive, who turned out to be humorous and highly intelligent. From Alexandria he sailed to Constantinople, then Sevastopol, where he was joined by a small party headed by Governor Andrew Curtin of Pennsylvania, recently appointed as American minister to Russia. They journeyed east as far as the Sea of Azov before taking trains to Moscow and St. Petersburg. Then, with only Audenried for company, Sherman crossed central and then western Europe via Warsaw, Berlin, and Vienna, visiting S. M. H. Byers in Zurich, US consul general for both Italy and Switzerland. Sherman found Zurich "a most quiet agreeable Swiss town—easy of access and a central point." He thoroughly approved of the Swiss, "a good kind and virtuous people—clearly and industrious." Sherman confided to Byers the opinion, "Here in Europe so much is artificial." Using his good French and passable Spanish he spoke to everybody—whether they understood him or not.

There had been some amusing moments on this trip, particularly if they reflected cultural confusion. The sultan of the Sublime Porte at Constantinople assumed that one of Sherman's aides-de-camp, young Fred Grant, was the American "heir apparent," and to his perplexity Fred, "as a real prince," was ushered into the place of honor at breakfast rather than Sherman; when His Majesty discovered his error, Sherman was hurriedly invited back and had to postpone his departure—but greatly enjoyed the joke. The only sour note occurred in Berlin when, confused by the speed of his arrival, the imperial court was unprepared to receive him. As a result, the kaiser had not asked to see him—the formula Sherman had become accustomed to—so Sherman left the palace and traveled to another pressing and, in some ways, more important meeting. American journalists appeared determined to view this incident as a deliberate slight and attributed it to Sherman's pro-French sympathy in the Franco-Prussian War. Some biographers have accepted this view, but it lacks credibility. Certainly, Napoleon III in 1867 had sent salutations via John Sherman "that he considered you the genius of the Civil War." True, Sherman was an instinctive Francophile and enjoyed good relations with the French marshals, but he made no statements of overt sympathy. In any case, the Prussian high command had been subject to the ebullient pro-Prussian enthusiasm of Philip Sheridan. Even Elihu Washburne, who remained in Paris at the US embassy after all other diplomats had departed and basked in the admiration of the French people, received a gift of the kaiser's portrait. If Sherman had been regarded as a French stooge, he could not have gone to his next appointment with the man who had led the Prussian armies to victory—Field Marshal Helmuth Graf von Moltke the Elder.[11]

These two military intellectuals had much to discuss and established a convivial rapport, as Moltke spoke good English. Sherman thus received the benefit of a personal briefing from Moltke on the Prussian general staff and system of conscription. After he arrived in Paris, he wrote to Moltke thanking him for his kind hospitality and enclosing a photograph of himself and asking one of his Prussian host in return. Moltke expressed delight at his "honoured letter" which arrived while he was away. He "could only procure the photograph which you have the kindness to accept from me, after my return to Berlin. He tendered his "most sincere thanks" for Sherman's photograph; "it will always remind me," Moltke wrote enthusiastically, "of the most pleasant acquaintance with the celebrated leader of the troops of the USA."[12]

Sherman had arrived in Paris alone, having left Audenried to meet "some of his newly discovered relations," and initially stayed at the Grand Hotel. He then accepted an invitation to stay at an apartment in the rue de Presbourg overlooking the Arc de Triomphe, where Audenried rejoined him. His son Tom arrived on July 16 and then went off on his own trip to Geneva. At a breakfast party on July 26 hosted by Washburne, he met the explorer Henry M. Stanley, fresh from his success at finding Dr. Livingstone. Stanley confided that he had been one of the newspapermen who had covered the negotiations of the Indian Commission in 1868. He admitted that this experience had given him the confidence to undertake his African expeditions. Sherman reflected on the French defeats of 1870–71, putting them down to the "ease and luxuriousness" of French living that had "sapped the physical strength of the French people"; he came away unimpressed by threats of *revanche*. But he found firsthand discussion of such controversies enlightening. "The greatest advantage I expect from my tours of Europe will be that in after years I can understand current events and also comprehend perfectly what I read of past history."[13]

From Paris, Sherman crossed to Portsmouth, England. Later he would describe his trip to Britain as the high point of his foreign travels. It began on July 31 with a private visit of the Prince and Princess of Wales to the US squadron of five frigates anchored off Southampton Water. Admiral Alden hosted a lunch, with Sherman attending as the senior American guest. The prince carried a message to Sherman and Alden from Queen Victoria "of her desire to receive them" at Osborne House on the nearby Isle of Wight the following day. Sherman and the US minister, General Robert C. Schenck, lunched with senior courtiers before meeting the queen. According to the *New York World*, "The Queen was looking extremely well, and was in unusually good spirits"; this may have been due to Sherman's kindness to one of her sons on a visit to the United States two years before. Sherman was the first to be presented and then later met two younger members of the royal family, Prince Leopold and Princess Beatrice. For many years Sherman would demonstrate great admiration for Queen Victoria, whom he described as the perfect chief executive. He also exhibited impressive knowledge of the history of the royal family and insight into the strategic problems confronting the British Empire.[14]

Sherman and his son Tom arrived in London on August 4. They stayed at Fleming's Hotel, just off Piccadilly. Ellen had repeatedly urged him to visit the archbishop of Westminster, Cardinal Henry Manning, but Sherman expressed reluctance, mainly because such visits encouraged the erroneous assumption that he was a Catholic when he wished to avoid religious controversies. To his wife he expressed deep regret "that you always set your mind on things that do not chime with my preferences, or prejudices." Manning solved the problem by being absent for over a week and then calling on Sherman the day before he left London. Curiously, considering its proximity to the metropolis, Sherman did not make a pilgrimage to the Sherman ancestral home in Dedham, Essex. On August 9 he visited the Royal Arsenal at Woolwich, where he was given lunch at the splendid Royal Artillery mess. Afterward, as a gunner, he paid particular attention to experiments with gun cotton that took place in the nearby marshes. On August 13 he visited Oxford, hosted by Dr. Charles Mayo, dean of New College, Oxford. Sherman had met Mayo before; he was the kind of exotic adventurer to whom he was attracted. Unable to settle to the humdrum life of a British house surgeon at the city's

Radcliffe Infirmary, he had served in the Union army as staff surgeon-major and medical inspector of the 13th Corps during the Vicksburg campaign back in 1863, and in a similar capacity in the Prussian army in 1870–71. Mayo showed Sherman many of the artistic and archaeological treasures of Oxford. Thereafter the general traveled up to Edinburgh, Scotland, leaving for Stirling on August 20 and then Dundee, driving in procession through crowded streets before visiting the factories of the Baxter brothers. Among the greatest manufacturing centers in the world at that time, these factories produced tarpaulins, canvas wagon covers, sails, and heavy linens for army and navy uniforms.[15]

The trip concluded with a visit to Dublin, which Sherman relished, as he had numerous in-laws of Irish descent. He arrived back in America late on September 16, 1872, and was met by Ellen with Minnie and Elly. In the days that followed he was pestered by reporters wanting tho know whether Moltke had described Civil War armies as "armed mobs"—a likely apocryphal remark that had already gained wide circulation. "I have seen Moltke in person," Sherman barked. "I did not ask him the question because I did not presume that he was such an ass as to say that." He then stalked off.[16]

Some days later he accepted an invitation to be formally interviewed on his experiences by a chosen reporter, a rare concession. The comparisons he drew between European and American military methods were fascinating. Sherman believed the rank and file European soldier just as intelligent as the American but thought it took the latter a shorter time to become "a competent man." He had been impressed by the simplicity of European tactics—a lesson he took to heart. Having seen British army uniforms being mass produced, he concluded rightly that the British "would have to change the gaudy red uniforms," as French Zouaves "were mowed down as badly at Sedan as their New York prototypes at Bull Run." He believed the laminated Springfield the equal of any European weapon. He also predicted that the rapid spread of breechloaders would prevent cavalry attacks "in anything like the relative proportionate numbers at Waterloo."[17]

Sherman had returned to Washington by mid-October 1872 and found that nothing had changed. In 1873–74 the army was reduced to 25,000 men, and Sherman, increasingly despondent in these years of disappointment, decided to follow Scott's course and abandon Washington. But first he had to ensure that the nuptials of his eldest daughter, Minnie, were carried off with suitable aplomb. Minnie, who often deputized for Ellen as the principal hostess of 205 I Street NW, had through her poise, grace, and lively conversation emerged as a significant figure in Washington society. She had so impressed Prince Arthur, the third son of Queen Victoria, that he deemed her the most engaging girl he had met on his American trip of 1870. In February 1874 Minnie became engaged to Lieutenant Thomas W. Fitch, USN, whom she met in London, the scion of another Irish-American Catholic family. In October they married in a particularly grand ceremony at St. Aloysius Church in Washington. The khedive of Egypt's gift of a dazzling diamond necklace and matching earrings became the talk of the city.[18]

During the spring months of 1874 Sherman had gained the permission of both the president and Belknap to move his headquarters to St. Louis. He had considered this course since the summer of 1871. After a decade of warm intimacy and cooperation, his relations with Grant had become formal and distant. Sherman had approved of Grant's reelection in 1872 only on the grounds that his opponent, Horace Greeley, appeared even worse. Sherman had explained away Grant's course on the grounds that he was surrounded by sycophants. It was Ellen who maintained the diplomatic channels with the Grant family, as she had with Stanton. She paid frequent visits to the White House. During his European trip she reported that "I see Mrs. Grant and the president often and tell them all about your letters." Politically, though, Grant saw Sherman as a nuisance and was happy to see him depart. When Grant sought to suppress the White League uprising in Louisiana in 1874–75, he dealt directly with Philip Sheridan, bypassing the general-in-chief. Sherman sold his Washington house, and Ellen and the family were glad to head back to 912 Garrison Avenue. In December 1875 the Fitches were prevailed upon to share the house, though Mr. Fitch insisted on paying his share of the expenses. Through a series of exchanges Sherman also acquired another St. Louis property, in the Cote Brilliante suburb, as an investment.[19]

For somebody of Sherman's phenomenal energy and industry, the lack of any significant role, despite continuing as commanding general, was little short of torture. He confided yet again that "I regard my career as over, and propose to establish my children here because I have unbounded faith in the future of St. Louis," though others experienced difficulty in discovering where this lay. John urged him to keep a base in Washington, DC. In his new headquarters on the corner of 10th and Locust Streets with his small staff, he quickly found ways of filling his days. The most important project was finishing his *Memoirs*. Sherman could be discreet when it suited him, and he kept this project to himself, apart from a small circle, including his family and staff, though he did consult two historians, John Draper and

George Bancroft—but no important participants in the Civil War. It is likely that he had a full working draft ready by 1872, but he still had a lot of checking, revising, and amending to do, and he did not start looking for a publisher until 1874. Once accepted by Appleton he prepared the book for the press, and it appeared in two volumes in 1875. Sherman's book was a notable achievement as the first important account to appear by one of the Civil War's most celebrated commanders just over a decade after its end. Grant's own *Personal Memoirs* in two volumes appeared another decade later, in December 1885, and the flow of distinguished memoirs of the war began that year. Being first in the field brought advantages in establishing the parameters of the story, but it also brought certain handicaps, not least haste and perhaps the constricted perspective with which past events were viewed.[20]

Sherman's desire to write his account quickly arose principally from the need to establish a reliable record of his own experience as a source of verifiable knowledge that could inform postwar soldiers considering future warfare. Sherman's didactic intent was evident from its first page. Initially it began with his experiences in California in the 1850s and took the form of a Civil War book rather than a book about his life. It concluded with a series of reflections entitled "The Military Lessons of the Civil War," which he took the precaution of publishing earlier. Only in the second edition of 1886 did he add more personal material on his family background and early life. He also added a new concluding chapter on his post-1865 career. Few other Civil War commanders had so far attempted to appraise their experience and consider the military legacy of the war over the longer term. Sherman was without doubt, as the historian Russell F. Weigley observes, among the most cerebral commanding generals since Winfield Scott, not just in being able to comprehend his own experience but in looking to the future. He could take arguments to a new level while simultaneously linking them to the institutional development of the US Army. With the spread of professionalism in Western armies, the idea took root that the study of the past aided the refinement of future preparations for as yet unfought wars. The "lessons" that the past bequeathed were distilled in order to create a digest of useful knowledge for the purposes of study, education, and eventually the preparation of tactical manuals determining how the US Army would fight. These efforts germinated a significant body of fine military literature after 1865. This literary flowering ranks among Sherman's most significant contributions to the US Army.[21]

The literary qualities of Sherman's *Memoirs* are striking: the compelling narrative drive, vigor, brilliant turn of phrase and sardonic humour, and the concision of expression. His volumes, of course, are opinionated, exhibit strong prejudices, and occasionally pursue vendettas—McClernand and Stanton are prominent targets—and his accounts of military events exhibit the partiality, evasions, half-truths, and misrepresentations that are to be found in all such books, including Grant's. Sherman wrote at a time when many of his contemporaries were still alive, and some, especially the sensitive George H. Thomas, resented discussions of their shortcomings, however deserved. Another sensitive soul was Ambrose E. Burnside, who believed that he had been treated with excessive harshness as an unwitting recipient of Sherman's unnecessary exertions in pursuit of his unwanted relief in December 1863. A literary war broke out in 1875 involving the acolytes of both Grant and Thomas. Sherman's main critic was a Cincinnati journalist, Henry Van Ness Boynton. Boynton denounced Sherman in a polemic, *Sherman's Historical Raid* (1875), as a "false historian" because he stole the credit owed to others. Boynton had been given access to government archives, and Sherman convinced himself he was in Belknap's pay. His real sponsor turned out to be Orville E. Babcock, a West Pointer who had been a member of Grant's staff and head of his "backstairs" advisers in the White House. Sherman employed his brother-in-law Charles Moulton as his proxy. Moulton issued his response to Boynton, *The Review of General Sherman's Memoirs Examined*, later that year. Babcock pursued a wily course of his own. He briefly succeeded in lowering further the esteem in which Sherman held the president. Then, dramatically and unexpectedly, Grant cut the ground from under the feet of Sherman's critics by writing to the author an exceptionally sagacious letter.[22]

Grant admitted being influenced initially by the hostile reviews. "I did feel aggrieved," he admitted, supposing that their disagreements since 1869 might have influenced Sherman's presentation of their wartime partnership. Grant had begun "with the intention of writing the severest criticism in my power—not for publication" but for friends. However, having read the book, "I laid it down saying that if I had not read the criticisms I should have none of my own to make, except as your friend." Grant believed that Sherman could have avoided the hostile reception by seeking "friendly criticism before publication" and honing the rough edges of his style. Sherman delighted in Grant's central observation, namely, that "historically there is no more correct account of that portion of the war treated by you than is contained in *The Memoirs*." Grant had some small critiques. He thought it unnecessary to argue the case for the authorship of the plan to march to the sea, as "all history would have credited you with it without question." Grant's admirers, though, would continue to assert his claims to authorship of the March for another half century—even though he did not make them for himself. Grant also thought it an error "in attributing selfish motives to Blair and Logan for going into the war." He devoted more space to the case for Burnside, now a friendly Republican senator to whom he thought Sherman "unjust." Grant understood Sherman's exasperation at carrying out a long relief march for seemingly little gain, but he emphasized that at Knoxville he had forced James Longstreet's hurried withdrawal. Burnside painstakingly gathered an abundance of supplies he had not previously enjoyed "in honor of you who had opened the way for such supplies to reach his otherwise destitute command." Grant concluded warmly that he had written as a friend and was happy to admit error. "I believe on the whole the book does you great credit." Sherman was, of course, delighted to receive this letter. He reflected that many criticisms were aimed at points that are "not there. Still minds look at words in every possible shade of difference, as you know." This cordial exchange provided the basis on which their close friendship could be reestablished.[23]

A weakness of Sherman's treatment of the most important events of his life is a by-product of the pioneering furrow that he plowed. The accumulation of primary source material that contemporaries appreciated and historians have since exploited clogs up the book. Sherman performed a signal service in bringing so much of this material into the public record of the war, but at a cost: it lessens the impact of his own narrative and reduces the cogency and flow. The book also suffers from a further weakness that arises from omission rather than commission. Its remit is rather narrow by comparison with Grant's *Personal Memoirs*. In the summer of 1868 Sherman declared that "the War, no matter what its cause, or conduct was an epoch in our national history, that must be sanctified, and made to stand justified to future ages." But Sherman did not attempt this task, partly because such a sanctification did not interest observers as much in the 1870s as it did a decade later, and partly because of his own prime interest in the technical military dimensions of the war. It is this difference in perspective that accounts for the superiority of Grant's *Personal Memoirs* over Sherman's book. Grant's book is greater because of its sustained form and the skill with which he places his military account in the context of a defense of the Union cause. Grant's *Personal*

Memoirs are concerned only with his military rather than his political career. Yet he could not have written with such breadth of view had he not served two terms as president at a tumultuous time. Sherman increasingly realized the importance of upholding the Union cause in the 1880s, but by then it was too late to drastically change the structure of his *Memoirs*; it might have demanded another book, but if so, he never found the time to write it.[24]

All books, of course, are the product of the experience of authors at particular times reflecting their dominant interests at precise dates. Sherman's *Memoirs* reflected his priorities as general-in-chief. Therefore, their greatest importance is to the history of the US Army and the field of military thought. In his discussion of the "lessons" of the Civil War, needless to say, he devoted attention to siege craft, including field engineering, and to the railroads as a source of strategic mobility. But he reflected on five significant lessons that gave policy and organizational aspects a higher priority within the US Army:

(1) Preparedness was essential, as the federal government had failed to deter the outbreak of war in 1861.
(2) The commanding general must "be armed with the fullest powers of the executive."
(3) "The real difficulty was, and will be again, to obtain an adequate number of good soldiers."
(4) "The 'feeding' of an army is a matter of the most vital importance, and demands the earliest attention of the general intrusted with the campaign."
(5) "The value of the magnetic telegraph in war cannot be exaggerated."

As a general reflection on the indecisiveness of the war, Sherman attributed the failure to "take full advantage of a victory" to the presence of thick woods on American battlefields, as these provided a screen behind which the Confederates could escape and recover. He believed that breechloading weapons would "further 'thin out' the lines of attack" and result in future battles that would be short and decisive tactically. Here the experience of the Franco-Prussian War unduly influenced his thinking, but he quickly added that such tactical developments would not "affect the grand strategy, or the necessity for perfect organization, drill and discipline." They actually underlined the case for them.[25]

Sherman deduced from his analysis the vital importance of the organization that created the conditions under which future wars would be fought.

His priority had to be a consideration of the implications of what historians later called the "general staff revolution" that had brought Prussia rapid and overwhelming victory in the German Wars of Unification in 1866 and against France in 1870–71. To what extent should the United States adapt its military system to these new developments? Indeed, Sherman had discussed them with Moltke himself, their perfecting architect. Sherman clearly understood the system's implications, noting that "the general in actual command of the army should have a full staff, subject to his own command." But his attempt to create a "full staff" had failed in 1869, and later efforts to introduce even a diluted type of general staff were doomed to fail as well. Sheridan confirmed this reasoning by arguing that the idea of a general staff would be rejected by politicians and public opinion because it increased the political power of the army. Sherman thus declared that though the Prussian system remained "exactly adapted to their national traditions," it would be alien to American values. Thus he set his mind against trying to imitate any form of the German model.

The relative security of the United States and its low-level commitments on the frontier rendered continental-scale operations a remote contingency. But Sherman held that just because such wars were unlikely did not mean they would never happen. The Civil War and later conflicts of the nineteenth century indicated that future warfare would demand the mobilization of entire peoples and their resources. In such contests, Sherman suggested, "a higher order of intelligence and courage on the part of the individual soldier will be an element of strength." He concluded that the most effective way of achieving this efficiency would be to impart the ethos, methods, and usages of the regular army when training keen volunteers. The army should become the "school" of the nation. Sherman thus revived John C. Calhoun's idea from the 1820s of an "expansible army." In his 1879 report to the secretary of war Sherman recognized that as the regular army was small, in a future great war "we as a people must rely on the volunteer masses of soldiery." The expert knowledge of the regulars had to be disseminated "to the volunteer militia, on the shortest notice, . . . up to the moment of execution."[26]

Sherman's ambitions required significant reform of army educational institutions. A small but significant early step was the appointment in 1870 of the brooding, brilliant Emory Upton, the army's leading intellect of the younger generation, as commandant of cadets at West Point. Upton had already written a well-received tactical manual in 1868 and Sherman gave him the task of drawing up another that "assimilated" the tactics of the infantry, cavalry, and artillery using common terms, so that officers in one arm could easily command the other two, as frequently happened in 1861–65. Sherman did not wish to impose his own views on Upton, preferring that tactics should "conform strictly to your own opinions rather than mine." Here is a fine example of one intellect recognizing the qualities of another, more junior, and giving it free rein.[27]

Sherman also took some faltering steps in the direction of "postgraduate" military education. He tried to improve the education and training of middle-ranking officers for high command and staff appointments, even though the US Army lacked any form of staff course or training. Given his weak position, this effort had to be made piecemeal. In 1875 Sherman created the Artillery School of Application at Fort Monroe and re-established a similar engineer school at Fort Totten. In 1881 he took the crucial step of founding the School of Application for Infantry and Cavalry at Fort Leavenworth, Kansas, which slowly evolved toward the staff college model under another of Sherman's protégés, Arthur L. Wagner. Sherman even managed to persuade Congress to pay for an international trip that allowed Upton, Lieutenant Colonel George Forsyth, and Captain Joseph Sanger to observe British "small wars" techniques in India, Afghanistan, and elsewhere. Upton later became infatuated with German methods and styles, as evidenced in *The Armies of Asia and Europe* (1878). His advocacy helped Sherman less than he expected because the commanding general did not want to turn the US Army into a carbon copy of another, whether it be French or German, but create an *American* school of tactics. In this quest Sherman remained a resolute supporter of bodies such as the Military Service Institution of the United States, founded in 1878 and modeled on the Royal United Services Institute in London. In all these areas Sherman made a notable, positive, and sometimes pioneering contribution to the creation of a professional ethos for the US Army. He had succeeded in identifying this ethos with the regular army, and in 1885 he made this link explicit: "West Point and the Army are the only authority as to the use of words peculiar to the military profession. As Lawyers, Doctors and Divines are supposed to be experts in their phraseology."[28]

A negative dimension would later emerge from his efforts and the authority they imposed on later interpretations of American wars. Sherman read Upton's rather turgid analysis *The Military Policy of the United States* in draft after the author's suicide in March 1881; it was not published until 1904. They tended to share the same prejudices, especially the pernicious influence of politics and the incompetence and criminal waste that resulted from civilian control. Consequently, for half a century the achievements of the regulars were overpraised, and all the blunders and miscalculations were blamed on ignorant volunteers and hapless "political" generals. The Civil War confirmed Americans in their preexisting military prejudice. Here was a battle of ideas that Sherman won; this success reflected his strong partiality, sense of superiority, and venom.[29]

Sherman's achievements were made possible by a sudden improvement in his political position within the War Department. On March 2, 1876, Belknap hurriedly tendered his resignation, and that afternoon the House of Representatives voted to impeach him. By a vote of Congress in 1869, Sherman had lost the power exercised by Grant to appoint post traders, "sutlers," on the frontier and transferred it to the secretary of war. Belknap appointed relatives, friends, and helpful connections, including Grant's brother Orvil. The second Mrs. Belknap came to an arrangement in October 1870 whereby these positions could be "sold," particularly if the grateful recipient chose to be absent but still took the profits. Mrs. Belknap received half the payoff through a third party, and the money kept being paid after her death in December 1870. Belknap thereafter married her sister, Amanda "Puss" Bower. Given their lavish expenditure, such supplementary payments were welcome. Sherman had never suspected Belknap of corruption, always believing him to be an honest and brave soldier. Grant never departed from this view. The president's rapid acceptance of Belknap's resignation probably saved him from conviction. Sherman was also quick to insist that he had no prior knowledge of this scandal. "It was not my office to probe after vague rumors and whispers," he protested to John, "that had no official basis." He regarded Belknap as a casualty of a system that politicians had designed to suit themselves, and it remained intact in spite of the scandal.[30]

Grant's choice of a successor was Judge Alphonso Taft, the founder of the Ohio political dynasty. Taft lacked Belknap's military knowledge and needed Sherman's military advice and guidance. He wrote inviting Sherman to Washington. On April 6 Townsend issued orders announcing that army headquarters had returned to the capital. It stipulated that "all orders and instructions relative to military operations or affecting the military control of and discipline of the army required by its civil masters" should be issued by the commanding general. Sherman had been given direct authority over the adjutant general's department that dealt with "control and discipline," as well as appointments and promotions, but had been given none over the other staff bureaus that administered the army, whose heads continued to report directly to Taft. Sherman declared himself content with this compromise. He moved back to Washington, and after he rented a property on 15th Street, eventually his family rejoined him. Taft moved to the Justice Department in May 1876 and was succeeded by J. D. Cameron until the end of Grant's second term. Cameron's father had been killed under Sherman's command at First Bull Run. He abided by the arrangement agreed with Taft.[31]

The year 1876 turned out to be eventful. June brought the disaster at Little Big Horn and the annihilation of George Custer's command; September, the forced withdrawal of George Crook's advance along the Rosebud River. Sherman had mixed feelings about Custer, whom he regarded as "brave to the point of rashness" but selfish, self-absorbed, and lacking in sound judgment. Moreover, he underestimated his enemy. "Surely in grand strategy, we ought not to allow savages to beat us," Sherman complained, "but in this instance they did." Sherman offered to give Sheridan all the support he could muster. In August 1877 he carried out a tour of inspection in western Montana. He took his son Tom with him, as both parents were of the view the fresh air and exercise would do him good. Ellen worried that "you have not provided yourselves well against the Indians." "We are looking forward with great anxiety to your return," she wrote several weeks later. "I fear you have had too hard a trip for a man bordering on 60." But both father and son thoroughly enjoyed themselves, emerging not only unscathed but energized.[32]

The disputed presidential election of November 1876 between the Democrat Samuel J. Tilden, governor of New York, and Republican Rutherford B. Hayes, governor of Ohio, presented Sherman with the second great constitutional crisis of his lifetime. Tilden had a clear lead in the popular vote, 4,300,000 to Hayes' 4,036,000, but had 184 votes in the Electoral College—one short of outright victory—to Hayes's 165, with 20 more votes being contested. As the incumbent president until March 4, 1877, Grant assumed the responsibility of resolving the deadlock and ensuring a smooth succession. Sherman played a much more assured and sagacious part in 1876 than he had in 1861. The crisis was no less grave and carried the threat of provoking a second civil war. Sherman's priority was to defend Washington, DC, against marauding Democratic gangs who might try to force a decision in Tilden's favor. Both Grant and Sherman had received many warnings of the likelihood of such action. On November 16, Sherman wrote a memorandum called "Projet à la General Scott," recalling Winfield Scott's measures in 1861 to protect Washington from a secessionist coup. He sent eight companies of artillery "to make safe the most important personages and property necessarily here at the Capitol." In December Grant indicated that he might need "as many as 4000 men here [in Washington]," Sherman warned Sheridan, "and that is impossible without drawing from you"—just as Sheridan attempted to organize victory against the Sioux after the disaster at the Little Big Horn, Montana, the previous June. But the alarm passed, and so many troops were not needed. Sherman ordered that all officers be "extremely cautious and circumspect" in expressing political opinions. His main objective remained to support the process: "We must use our force and influence to sustain the authorities legally in existence and recognized." He feared that should the Democrats win, Southerners "may lord it over us who were their enemies. The passions and sorrows of war," he opined, "are not healed enough for us to bear too much." He hoped that Hayes would win, "for it will give more time for a change that may be inevitable." But on November 8 he reported that "everything thus reported indicates the election of Mr. Tilden. This will give us four years struggle for existence, and makes our positions insecure." The issue rested on a knife edge for several months.

The grave crisis brought Grant and Sherman together again in a common cause, and they quickly generated some of the old warmth. After controversial deliberations, in February 1877 to Sherman's relief, the bipartisan Joint Electoral Commission agreed to by Tilden awarded all the disputed electoral college votes to Hayes, but a filibuster by Democrats in the House of Representatives delayed the formal announcement of Hayes's victory until March 2. With Grant's tacit approval, on the following day Sherman modified the president's initial telegram to Stephen B. Packard, the Republican claimant to the disputed governorship of Louisiana, that indicated that "the obligations . . . to observe the status quo . . . was at an end." Grant thus signaled a desire to limit federal military activities in the former Confederate states only "to the mere preservation of peace in case of riot" rather than the maintenance of Republican governors. In other words, US troops would not be used to support Republican Reconstruction state governments in the South or to protect black voters. All reports emphasized the role of the White League, manned by former Confederate soldiers and sometimes equipped with artillery, in the violence designed to overthrow Republican regimes in the Southern states. Insurrectionists in the former Confederate states would quickly realize that Grant's policy had been altered. As Grant's letter was tantamount to a presidential order, Sherman claimed that he did not seek "to interpret the President's letter to Mr. Packard" but ordered Christopher Augur, commander of the Military District of Louisiana at New Orleans—a crucial state in the reexamination of electoral votes—to "keep the peace if possible, and . . . I believe you can prevent any material changes in the attitude of the contending parties till the new Administration can be fairly installed, and give the subject mature reflection." Although it was rumored that he had struck a deal to withdraw federal troops in return for the votes that had decided the disputed election, President-elect Hayes wished to slow the pace of this retreat and approved of Sherman's action.[33]

Sherman, too, approved of Hayes. He proved an open, high-minded, but pragmatic and astute politician and convivial company despite an attachment to temperance—alcohol was not served at the White House during his presidency. Sherman's brother John served as Hayes's secretary of the treasury, and both brothers had welcomed Hayes and his family to Washington on March 2, 1877. Hayes's struggle to get elected had delayed the composition of his cabinet. Sherman had some anxious moments as the new president considered the merits first of Simon Cameron, forever associated with the humiliation and failures of the autumn of 1861, then John Logan, and even Confederate general Joseph E. Johnston, as secretary of war, for Hayes searched for a nominal Southerner to promote "reconciliation," but he eventually chose George W. McCrary. An Iowa congressman, supporter of the railroad companies, and friend of Grenville M. Dodge, McCrary resigned in December 1879 to become a federal circuit court judge. Alexander Ramsey, formerly governor of Minnesota, took his place, and both were careful not to disturb the balance of relations with Sherman.[34]

The most significant legislative event of these years was the reforming efforts made by the Senate committee chaired by Ambrose E. Burnside. Mollified over his treatment in the *Memoirs*, Burnside aimed to centralize military decision-making and to strengthen the position of the commanding general. The sprawling 724-page report produced in 1878 accepted Sherman's view that he should enjoy "absolute power" over the staff bureaus, though it expressed this opinion in less colorful language. Its more guarded tone nevertheless provoked what William Marvel calls a "howl" of opposition from the staff bureaus. Its gargantuan size also presented serious difficulties in turning it into practicable legislation, and it endured numerous amendments. It was voted down by the House and then by the Senate.[35]

Sherman felt comfortable with the Hayes administration. Hayes gave a dinner at the White House in honor of Sherman and his staff in February 1878. Sherman even accepted invitations to Lucy Hayes's "sings" on a Sunday evening, booming out gospel songs. In September 1880 he organized a transcontinental railroad journey for the president, which took him out of Washington during the presidential election; Hayes had pledged when nominated that he would not be a candidate for reelection. Hayes soon realized that by traveling across the entire country with the ever-popular Sherman, he actually aided the Republican nominee, James A. Garfield. Hayes genuinely admired Sherman and had firmly turned down demands by Boynton—an early adviser on his presidential bid—for a court-martial to determine the merits of his complaints against Sherman's *Memoirs*. Yet at the end of his term Hayes admitted that his relations with the commanding general had soured. The reasons for this state of affairs all had to do with the prospects of others and not Sherman himself. First, he had proposed, and Sherman had opposed, a further military promotion for Grant. He wanted to create the rank of captain-general for him (in effect field marshal). There were no pensions for ex-presidents until 1953, and Grant would have to earn a living. Hayes considered this a kind of consolation prize for Grant after he had failed to win the Republican nomination for a third term as president in 1880. Sherman disapproved of this kind of special legislation for a better-paid position for an ex-president. He feared the proposal might stir up more political controversy in the officer corps. Hayes allowed the matter to drop. Second, Sherman resented the forced retirement of his friend Edward O. C. Ord when there were older candidates, like Irvin McDowell; he branded this "terrible discrimination." Sherman wanted to keep Ord's services—he had fallen on hard times and was "as poor as a rat"—while Hayes insisted on promoting William B. Hazen and Nelson Miles, whose services he did not want. Finally, he was annoyed that Hayes had dismissed Schofield as superintendent of West Point, the president having objected to the treatment of a pioneering black cadet, Johnson C. Whittaker. Sherman feared that the controversy might damage Schofield's prospects of succeeding as general-in-chief (it did not).[36]

Sherman knew Garfield, Hayes's successor, well and liked and respected him despite his long record of hostility to Grant, which Sherman had found more acceptable during the 1870s. Sherman expressed delight at receiving an invitation to be the grand marshal at the inauguration of Garfield and his vice president, Chester A. Arthur. The general became a frequent and conspicuous guest at the White House during Garfield's brief presidency, tending to hold court before worshipful groups of young ladies with a well-rehearsed repertoire of war stories. He established good working relations with the new secretary of war, Lincoln's eldest son, Robert Todd Lincoln, before Garfield's wounding on July 2, 1881. Garfield's assassin, Charles J. Guiteau, a deranged and disappointed office-seeker, sent Sherman a strange message after his arrest—though it was never received—on the dubious grounds that Sherman had been a lifelong supporter of Grant. "I am going to jail. Please order out your troops and take possession of the jail at once." Such a request convinced the general that Guiteau had lost his mind. Sherman initially believed that the president would recover, but over the following weeks Garfield's condition deteriorated fatally. As his successor, Arthur displayed good sense, serious application, and dignity and unexpectedly proved a highly competent administrator. Sherman's relations with the legislature were not so smooth. Periodically there were renewed assaults on his salary and further reductions during these years. Annoying and unfounded charges also surfaced in Congress concerning Sherman's supposedly palatial living, large expenses, and long trips "nominally to inspect posts, but really for pleasure." Without tours of inspection, Sherman complained, he could not command the army over such great distances or answer innumerable congressional inquiries. His travel expenses, he claimed, were no different from those of a lieutenant. If he traveled in luxurious cars, it was always as a guest of the railroad companies.[37]

In February 1884 Sherman would reach the age of 64. Having objected to the way in which Ord had been retired by presidential fiat, he had supported the passage of a law in 1882 requiring retirement at this age. Besides, after a disappointing debut, he had served longer than any other postwar commanding general. He believed that he bequeathed the army "in good shape and condition, well provided in all respects, and distributed for the best interests of the country." He was especially solicitous toward his staff, and though he formally retired on November 1, 1883, to ensure that his successor, Philip H. Sheridan, could establish himself before the new session of Congress, President Arthur retained their pay and rank until February 8, 1884. Dayton had married well in 1880 and had resigned to enter business in Cincinnati. Audenried served loyally in deteriorating health until his death that same year.[38]

Sherman's overall view of his tenure as commanding general appears highly positive. This view is justified, but a suspicion lurks that certain important questions were deferred rather than solved. The drama and magnitude of the events of 1861–65 should perhaps have required a thorough overhaul of American defense machinery. But the landscape remained unaltered. The prejudices, fears, and enmities that infused the prewar military system remained steadfast, perhaps had even grown keener, so that American institutions worked in the time-honored way. The relationship between the secretary of war and the general-in-chief is a notable example. The tussle between Scott and Jefferson Davis in the 1850s had settled nothing; nor, as Sherman was the first to discover, had the uneasy truce reached by Grant and Stanton before 1868. The compromise agreed by Sherman and Taft in 1876 was no more successful. This vexed relationship would not finally be clarified until the abolition of the rank of commanding general and the creation of a chief of staff of the army in 1903. Sherman had taken several important pioneering steps to establish a system that favored the commanding general. But for sound political reasons he did not embrace the "general staff revolution," because to do so appeared self-defeating. Sherman, despite all his outward bluster and lack of political finesse, advanced circumspectly in the suspicious and often hostile political environment in which he labored. He demonstrated that he could be as calculating as any professional politician.

Another issue is whether Sherman entertained more ambitious intentions but in 1869–70 had been forced to abandon them. Did he remain content with the existing system, happy with piecemeal improvements? Sherman's mission was surely to make the traditional, uneasy coalition of regulars and volunteers work more efficiently. He never succumbed entirely to the charms of the Prussian system, which introduced a corporate element into warfare. In his *Memoirs* Sherman candidly revealed, "I don't believe in a chief of staff at all, and any general commanding an army, corps, or division, that had a staff officer who professes to know more than his chief, is to be pitied." Sherman's entire outlook sought to conserve rather than to overturn. He sought above all an American compromise based on the Civil War experience and the fusion of regulars and volunteers—not to import a sterile and alien foreign system. Sherman's sustained, subtle, and delicate balancing act represents a formidable achievement.[39]

17

Retirement of a Kind, 1884–1891

In his 50s Sherman retained his rugged good looks and lithe athletic frame, making him an attractive and charismatic figure to women and to political bosses of both major parties. Lord Rosebery, the future British prime minister, met him in the winter of 1873. "I was particularly glad to see General Sherman who owns I think the finest face I have seen in America: a grand forehead and an iron mouth and chin." Sherman's vigor is conveyed in Gore Vidal's novel *1876* : "To the strains of some military march"—not "Marching through Georgia," Vidal assures us, as Sherman had come to hate it through repetition—"the erect figure of General William Tecumseh Sherman appeared. To much whistling and shouting, the General made his way to the empty presidential box." Vidal comments, too, on the coincidence that several of the founding fathers were red-haired—though Sherman would quickly go gray over the next decade. His lively reception is compared in the novel to the flat indifference or even outright cold hostility encountered by Grant.[1]

One of his biographers, Michael Fellman, is correct in thinking that part of Sherman's great passion for the theater had much to do with his own histrionic nature and charismatic presence. Whenever Sherman walked into a room, people noticed. The actress Mary Anderson, a devout Catholic, whose parents the Shermans had known in California, wrote a brief sketch of the general in 1935 in which she said, "General Sherman was the most striking person I have ever met." She compares him with the welter of royal personages and distinguished people she encountered in a long career, "but none have been quite as splendid as that tall, slender, erect and rugged soldier, with eyes like the Thracian eagle, and fearless and courage in his looks, his words and gestures. His presence was an inspiration: he stands quite apart in my memory." Such reflections, of course, are concerned with Sherman's exterior, but they are not uncommon in recollections of him. And in any consideration of the potential of candidates for high office put before the electorate of a mass democracy, external characteristics were of supreme importance. A successful candidate had to be both available and appealing, two of Sherman's highest qualifications—and the allure of men in uniform remained insatiable. Yet Sherman's intent seemed much more doubtful. Did he really want to be president? If he did not, could he be persuaded, in spite of his better judgment, to forsake his reservations for the good of the country?[2]

Sherman combined an abundance of "public service" with attractive self-made qualities; he also served as an insuperable symbol of the country and of the Union cause, a champion of freedom without appearing too radical. Sherman's instincts were deeply conservative and could be presented as reassuring. "If ever a country was too much governed, ours is," he had pointedly observed. Even Sherman's scathing opinions of politicians and the feebleness and venality of the political system could be turned to his advantage, as a deep prejudice against party spirit and the dirty tricks of politicians consistently resurfaced after 1865. By contrast, a military hero could fill the pail drawn from the well of hope; he could, in the historian Michael Heale's words, "touch instincts deep in the American psyche." He could personify "the American destiny in a way which was beyond mere politicians." Sherman had identified himself with the most important part of that mission—the settlement of the West. The great respect with which he was held, despite his vicissitudes, and his enduring popularity across all sections of the country were unique assets.[3]

Sherman had been mentioned on several occasions in 1864–65 as presidential timber and again in 1871 when the New York Herald came "out in full blast" on behalf of his possible candidacy in 1872. Sherman refused to challenge Grant, though his brother John stressed that "I have seen nothing in the course of the Republican Party unfriendly to you. . . . You have hosts of friends in our party. " Moreover, in the 1870s Sherman demonstrated more open support for the Republicans than he had the decade before. He acknowledged the party as a bulwark of the Union cause. Still, in 1876 when Ellen wrote to mark her pleasure at his triumph "over the petty malice and strong party machinations of your enemies—and pretended friends," Sherman replied promptly, advancing the line he repeated consistently over the next decade. "You need never fear that I will ever be infested with the poison of Presidential aspiration, on the contrary, the place has no temptations, but quite the contrary." He wished to leave this unpleasant fate to those "trained in that school of scandal and abuse," like Ellen's cousin James G. Blaine and other Republican spoils men like Roscoe Conkling and Benjamin H. Bristow.[4]

Despite these swipes against Republican spoils men, Sherman's attacks on the Democrats increased in bitterness. He expressed to Ellen a disgust on hearing Southern Democrats "on the floor of Congress" boasting "of having fought against the Government, and intimat[ing] they will do so again." Sherman's forthright views were a response to a thoughtful letter from Ellen. She urged him "not to give the Democrats so much political capital as you do." Hitherto, she recorded, "you have had the respect and confidence of the people of the whole United States of all parties and in a marked degree." But Ellen feared that he had adopted a partisan tone. He invariably supported Republican presidential candidates as guardians of the Union flame. "The Republicans are glad to make use of you—John Sherman as well as the rest of them." She reassured him that "I am not arraigning you nor reproaching you . . . but I must pay you the respect and the kindness to warn you here." Sherman responded that he drew a distinction between types of political activity. "Politics of party are one thing, politics affronting the existence of the government is another." Still, Ellen's parting shot on a delicate matter from "one outside of all politics," namely, "You once were above party—would that you were now you would be happier," hit home. He made a firmer effort to conciliate Democrats.[5]

Sherman needed all his resolve in 1884 when the Republican Party made a determined effort to nominate him as its candidate for the presidency. Sherman expressed no interest, though John noticed that naming him served "to crowd off other candidates"; in any case, nomination did not guarantee election. "The chances are for the Democrats," John counseled, "but for their proverbial blundering." But the sheen of Sherman's celebrity did not diminish. The mail brought an avalanche of requests "for autographs, photographs, donations, tokens, such as saddles, swords, muskets, buttons, etc., etc., which I used in the war—many letters predicting that I will be the next president, and that the writer foresaw it and was the first to conceive the thought." By March he believed his name had been gradually dropped, and he expressed relief—though greatly mistaken. During these months he had been impressed by Postmaster General Walter Q. Gresham, "as honest, outspoken, judicious a man as I know among my old soldiers," but the contest for the nomination looked deadlocked between Secretary of State James G. Blaine, and the incumbent, President Chester Arthur. Blaine was superficially the more glamorous candidate, known as the "Plumed Knight." Quicksilver in word and deed, both theatrical and facile, Blaine had inherited a certain Irish charm and rhetorical versatility that many feared veiled a rogue. Without doubt, his winning ways and stained elegance promoted widespread distrust. Arthur had proved an unexpected success after Garfield's assassination. Highly competent, grave, and dignified, he enjoyed strong support. Yet in 1882 he had been diagnosed with Bright's disease (a kidney disease that in its chronic form often proved terminal in the nineteenth century), and his doctors only gave him a few more years to live. He issued orders that bewildered his followers, as his condition remained a closely guarded secret: "I do not want to be re-elected. Go to your friends and get them to stop their activities."[6]

The likelihood of a deadlocked convention was thus far more apparent than real, but Blaine did not know that. As the front-runner, he looked vulnerable. John Sherman warned his brother that if Blaine failed at the first fence, "a movement will be made for your nomination, and if entered upon will go like wild fire"; John advised that if these events beyond the general's control should come to pass, "unsought and with cordial unanimity, you ought to acquiesce." He pointed out that under these dramatic circumstances, Blaine should be prepared to transfer his delegates to General Sherman. John had entered the lists, too, as he had in 1880, though he lacked his brother's affability and appealing record; he admitted his chances were poor, but General Sherman's way to the nomination was "easy."[7]

Sherman, though, found many of these requests for him to run, especially from his old soldiers, tantamount to moral blackmail. They exploited ties of affection forged during the Civil War. He rejected them on two grounds: first, "that it would be the height of folly to allow any false ambition to allow the use of my name for any political office"; second, that it was not for others to take a decision for him that would so disrupt his private life. Why, he asked, should a prosperous contented man of 65 who enjoyed "the universal respect of my neighbors and countrymen, embark on the questionable game of politics?" As the United States basked "in a state of absolute peace," it required sober and sensible administration and did not need the expertise of a military man.[8]

Unaware of Arthur's illness, when delegates met at the Republican convention in Chicago in June the pressure on Sherman was compounded. Just before the convention the crafty Blaine wrote to Sherman urging him to accept the nomination as a patriotic duty. He put pressure on Sherman by saying, "You can no more refuse than you could have refused to obey an order when you were a lieutenant in the army. . . . It would in such an event injure your great fame as much as to decline *as it would for you to seek it*." Blaine had not given up his own candidacy; he probably sought to put Sherman on the spot and force a premature declaration because he suspected that Sherman's support might crumble. He could then dispose of Sherman's candidacy by persuading him to complacently rest on his laurels while Blaine worked to undermine him. Alternatively, Blaine might have hoped for an emphatic rejection; if the latter, he was not disappointed. In his reply of May 28 Sherman repeated that "I will not in any event entertain or accept a nomination as a candidate for president by the Chicago Republican Convention, or any other convention for reasons personal to myself." He carefully slipped through Blaine's clutches by asserting that "I ought not to subject myself to the cheap ridicule of declining what is not offered. I will not tamely place destiny in the hands of friends," in which category he placed Blaine. But the preelection pantomime through which all candidates had undergone—literally in Arthur's case—solemnly denying ambition and desire for high office, came back to kick Sherman. The more emphatic the rejection, the more likely were delegates to assume the exact opposite.

Sherman's clear-cut rejection had the unfortunate effect of galvanizing some anti-Blaine delegates into thinking that Sherman was preparing to run. Sherman's neighbor the former Missouri senator J. B. Henderson acted as his spokesman. He came under increasing pressure to make an announcement. He began to rather enjoy the role of *eminence grise* and began to encourage Blaine's critics. A Democrat busybody, Senator James R. Doolittle, wrote to Sherman on June 3 calling on him to accept the nomination. Sherman and Doolittle had worked together on Andrew Johnson's Indian Peace Commission of 1867 and disagreed then; Sherman was no more likely to heed his advice on this matter. Henderson sent him a telegram pleading that he should accept because he had no other choice. His son Tom stood by side his when this telegram arrived and witnessed a memorable scene. Sherman was talking in the family's St. Louis home. "Without taking his cigar from his mouth, without changing his expression," Tom recalled later, "... my father wrote the answer, 'I will not accept if nominated and will not serve if elected.'" When the declaration was read out on the floor of the convention it provoked a great roar of knowing laughter.[9]

Sherman showed real wisdom in standing aloof from the convention's machinations. Blaine's instinct had not misled him: Sherman's support might have been enthusiastic but lacked ballast. Sherman's appeal rested on two contradictions that could be easily exploited. Because he was a non-politician, all sides on every issue took it for granted he would side with them, or, as they did not know his views, agreed that he would find a solution satisfactory to all. The other and more significant problem lay in the sobering reality that the convention would not be deadlocked. Arthur had done respectably on the first ballot, but his supporters were not able to advance his cause. Consequently, on the fourth ballot on June 7 Blaine won outright, with John A. Logan elected as his running mate. Any Sherman candidacy would have faced severe difficulties under these unfavorable conditions. There was an additional consideration that had little to do with the calculations of party delegates: his wife's outspoken Catholic advocacy would have proved a hazard at a time of rising anti-Catholic prejudice over schools, when an anti-Catholic diatribe by Rev. Josiah Strong, *Our Country: Its Possible Future and Present Crisis*, sold more than half a million copies. In the event, the crucial moment in the campaign that torpedoed Blaine's candidacy occurred in New York, when a Republican supporting Presbyterian minister Samuel D. Burchard denounced the Democrats as the party of "Rum, Romanism, and Rebellion," thus alienating mainly Irish voters; had Sherman been the candidate instead of Blaine, it is doubtful that Ellen would have remained silent, causing dismay in Republican ranks. Ellen, in any case, would never have been persuaded to serve as "first lady," a title first bestowed on Lucy Hayes. She had informed her husband well before the convention that she "rejoiced that you are so positive in rejecting all advances of politicians to secure you for the Presidency." She expressed confidence he could beat both Blaine and his brother John for the nomination. "I would do nothing for either of them nor for you because I would have no consideration in return." So he knew her position well in advance. The public brickbats exchanged in this underhanded, vicious, and hard-fought election that focused on the personal weaknesses of the candidates would have upset his family and infuriated the thin-skinned Sherman, a man unaccustomed to political mudslinging. His candidacy, Ellen affirmed, would be "the ruin of your family, so I am thankful that you do not contemplate it." Finally, no candidacy can prosper if the candidate does not wish to be president. In March 1869, when approached to influence the composition of Grant's cabinet, Sherman had replied with incredulity that "I can't see what can tempt any gentleman who has accumulated some property to come here [Washington] as a cabinet minister." He also observed of presidential politics, "Fifty men lose reputation in luck or station when one gains it." He did not depart from these views to his dying day.[10]

There was much sound and fury behind the bid to get Sherman nominated in 1884, but of a negative kind—to block Blaine—and few positive impulses. It is sometimes suggested that the young Theodore Roosevelt had agreed to announce Sherman's candidacy, but there is no evidence to support the claim, as he remained loyal to his preferred candidate, George F. Edmunds of Vermont. Sherman replied to Doolittle's letter on June 10. It is a wonderful letter, full of self-knowledge and good sense—and concern for the Republican Party. He observed that he entertained "old-fashioned ideas of freedom and the right of every man to shape his own destiny"; if forced, he feared he might have answered "in terms which would damage it [the Republican Party] as well as myself." He also wrote to Blaine on June 7 a teasing letter of congratulation. He admitted he had been a candidate of a "negative kind," mainly because certain "injudicious friends were determined to use my name," but he had been equally determined to stop them. He also used the letter to build bridges with Logan, who had "spasms of generosity as well as hatred, and I will be only too happy to aid his canvas by being a full witness to his good qualities." His public praise for Blaine was more guarded. "He is talented, as all admit, and as honest as the time calls for." But Blaine's critics were right. Whoever won the state of New York won the election, and the Democrat, Grover Cleveland, took it by fewer than 1,000 votes and emerged the winner. Former president Hayes thought the Republicans would have won if they had picked a better candidate, like General Sherman, or even his brother John.[11]

Amid all the dissimulation surrounding the curious episode of the 1884 election, Sherman's sincerity and frankness stand out. In 1889 John Sherman acknowledged these qualities. "You are living the life proper for your position and services—everywhere welcome, all you say and do applauded, and secure in a competence and independent in all things." Not running allowed him to retain that life. Throughout, Sherman allowed himself to be guided by his perception of Grant's unhappy time in the White House, though it is by no means certain that Grant shared it. "Not a single person has been president in our time without having been, in my judgment," Sherman averred, "the most abused, if not the most miserable man in the whole community." Sherman, a highly strung and sensitive man, avoided this fate; he liked being admired.[12]

By the time Sherman had reached his final verdict on these matters, his friend Grant had died and been placed in his temporary tomb. Grant's last 18 months had exposed him to a series of humiliating calamities. In early

1884 he discovered that he had been swindled out of the fortune he had poured into an investment bank, Grant and Ward, by the managing partner. Ferdinand Ward had the gall to urge Grant to raise fresh moneys to "rescue" the bank and then placed these in his own personal account. A further disaster followed with the default of the Wabash Railroad, in which the trust fund raised by Grant's admirers in 1866, a further $250,000, was lost. The Grants were left poverty-stricken, initially surviving on donations volunteered by friends. Grant's predicament agitated Sherman's perennial money worries; if it could happen to Grant it could happen to him, too. In July 1884 Grant explained that he could no longer speak at the annual reunion of the Society of the Army of the Tennessee. But he reported that he had taken up writing to ease his money worries and had agreed to write articles for the *Century Magazine* on the Battle of Shiloh and the Vicksburg campaign. Sherman put the very best gloss he could on their chief's absence from the reunion. Grant, he explained, had been overtaken by a financial "blizzard, a very cyclone" of a type not uncommon on Wall Street. Sherman also expressed confidence that Grant still had "years of useful and happy life" ahead of him, a prediction that proved mistaken.[13]

In the summer of 1884 Grant experienced sharp pain while trying to swallow a mouthful of peach. Three months passed before he consulted a doctor; his condition, quickly diagnosed as cancer of the tongue, had in the meantime spread to the throat and become inoperable. He deteriorated rapidly, being unable to eat, sleep, or swallow. Sherman's reaction to the grim news showed a measure of confusion. "I am sure that Dr. Douglas told me that there was no cancer—but Dr. Alexander says it *is* cancer." He adjusted to reality with his customary frankness, however: "He will gradually waste away and die." But Grant mounted a valiant rearguard action and devoted himself to work on his *Personal Memoirs*. "I think it is a matter of vital importance," Sherman reflected, "that he should complete his Memoirs."[14]

Sherman had periodically expressed regret that though his amicable relations with Grant had been restored, they lacked the easy intimacy of 1863–69. But regular visits to see the ailing Grant soon brought back the old ease and familiarity. Sherman's breezy, witty, and ebullient personality acted as a tonic to the pain-racked Grant. Sherman proudly announced to Ellen on Christmas Eve 1884 that "Grant says my visits have done him more good than all the doctors." He continued to visit after Grant and his family moved in June 1885 to a pleasant house on Mount McGregor, near Saratoga Springs, New York, that had been lent to him. But he still wrote sadly to Grant's eldest son, Fred, that "I am older than your father and of a shorter-lived race than he, therefore never dreamed of outliving him." The stream of invitations that Sherman received to write articles about Grant irritated him: "As to money in this connection the very thought is revolting."[15]

Grant died on July 23, 1885, four days after completing his *Personal Memoirs*. Shortly afterward Sherman received a treasured invitation to attend the private funeral service along with Horace Porter, a former member of Grant's wartime staff and staunch political ally. Grant resembled Sherman in being an agnostic who approved of many Christian injunctions on life and conduct. Sherman had also been named a pallbearer at the state funeral, along with Philip Sheridan; at Fred Grant's request, President Grover Cleveland named Joseph E. Johnston and Simon Bolivar Buckner as former Confederate pallbearers, and they were paired with Sherman and Sheridan, respectively. Their appearance bolstered the Lost Cause outlook, which profited from the reconciliation of Northern and Southern whites that rested on shared values that ignored slavery and emancipation. Sherman had acted kindly toward his former antagonists; indeed, he had treated Johnston with respect in his *Memoirs*. Johnston believed he owed Sherman a debt and would attend his funeral, too, as an honorary pallbearer. Sherman had also been generous in his support of poverty-stricken John B. Hood's petition to be paid $20,000 for his military papers. After Hood's death in 1879 he had even kept them safe for two years. Lost Cause values were celebrated at Grant's state funeral on August 8, 1885. "Such a funeral never before occurred in America," Sherman assured Julia Grant, "and never will again." But encouraging Lost Cause messages undercut Sherman's efforts to defend the Union cause after Grant's death.[16]

Sherman also intervened decisively in the debates over Grant's permanent resting place. Both Sheridan and Logan argued in favor of a Washington, DC, location. Sherman supported the family in arguing for a permanent tomb on the banks of the Hudson River in New York City. He made this case in a powerful speech at the 18th Annual Reunion of the Army of the Tennessee in Chicago in September 1885, underlining his support for a "strong, solid, simple monument, characteristic of the man, over his grave on the banks of the Hudson." After all, this was "the spot selected by his son, approved by the entire family, and accepted by all who had a right to be consulted." New York had been Grant's last home, and Sherman's advocacy had a profound influence on those from the West who accused New Yorkers of bossily appropriating Grant and his memory.[17]

Indeed, Sherman became the guardian of Grant's historical legacy and a champion of his fundamental greatness. The war had nourished their friendship, which the latter's biographer Adam Badeau deemed "among the most beautiful and remarkable in history." It revived once Sherman had published his own *Memoirs* because he had devoted this book to the war rather than use it as a platform to attack Grant the politician. Social invitations from Grant had quickly followed its publication. During his voyage around the world Grant gave a series of interviews to the journalist John Russell Young in which Sherman featured. In the summer of 1878 he remarked, "There is no man living for whose character I have a higher respect than for that of Sherman. He is not only one of the best men living, but one of the greatest we have had in our history." Sherman had reciprocated with similar tributes, but beyond extolling Grant's virtues, he bequeathed the most singular theme that has permeated the Grant literature ever since. In his most thoughtful assessment he dwelt on the enigma posed by Grant's character. He confided to Mrs. Edwin F. Hall that "he is a strange character. Nothing like it is portrayed by Plutarch or the many who have striven to portray the great men of ancient or modern times." Viewing Grant from many angles, he concluded, "Yet to me he is a mystery, and I believe he is a mystery to himself."[18]

For a decade after Appomattox the conduct of the Civil War had sparked little interest. Sherman's *Memoirs* had stirred a preliminary skirmish, but Grant's death and the tremendous commercial success of his *Personal Memoirs* began an obsessive trend of every incident being picked over and reconsidered. Grant's historical forays in the mid-1880s eventually involved Sherman in a heated controversy that degenerated into a personal and unedifying feud over the role of the Army of the Cumberland (formerly Ohio) at the Battle of Shiloh. At the same time, James B. Fry, formerly Don Carlos Buell's chief of staff, published a defense of his stubborn and quarrelsome chief, *Operations of the Army under Buell* (1884). The writing of Grant's article on Shiloh preceded it, and Buell had been annoyed by its neglect of his own contribution to the victory. At the outset, all appeared calm and even-tempered. Fry placed much of the blame for Buell's laggard progress, especially in Tennessee, on Halleck. Grant and Sherman both agreed years later that his orders tended to be "cautionary," that is, designed to deflect any blame on others "in case of disaster."

Before his death Grant had agreed to write four articles for the new series in the *Century Magazine*. The editors contacted Sherman, hoping he would write on the March to the Sea. He declined but eventually wrote an acute analysis of Union strategy in 1864–65. All these articles were later compiled and published as *Battles and Leaders of the Civil War* (1887), a work that did much to nourish the popular appetite for the war. Sherman applauded Grant's efforts to clarify persistent misconceptions about Shiloh. He also argued that it is "far better that it should be done by those who saw most and knew of the plans and purposes." Buell had not arrived on the Shiloh battlefield until the late afternoon and had missed its greatest crisis. "I am sure you will set right some of the mistakes into which history has drifted by the perseverance and repetitions of people who love to appear in print," Sherman told Grant before his death. Indeed, a week later he declared that he did not blame Fry for making the best case he could for Buell. "But," he observed shrewdly, "Buell did not create *results*." Alas, the tone of the dispute would quickly change.[19]

Given their mutual admiration, it is hardly surprising that Grant and Sherman shared a very similar view of the Civil War. It did not result from collusion and was true of specific points as well as general themes. Neither would accept that the Army of the Tennessee had been taken by surprise at Shiloh. In their wider perspective they had not the slightest doubt concerning the paramount need for Union strategy to develop a punitive dimension: to strike with ruthlessness at civilian morale by means of the destruction of public and private property to win a complete victory. Their aim had been to reach beyond the battlefield and subdue the civilian population that supported the maintenance of the Confederacy. Shiloh, again, had assumed enormous significance in their thinking as a signpost that indicated a need for more drastic methods. Buell, by comparison, deplored what he considered to be ill-disciplined ravages in Georgia and the Carolinas. On the destruction of property, Sherman admitted that "I know that in the beginning I too had the old West Point notion that pillage was a capital crime and punished it severely." But he retorted that Buell's view was "a one-sided game of war"; Sherman aimed to "subdue the enemy," and in this quest, he candidly declared, "they [the Confederates] deserved all they got and more." He thus recapitulated the argument made frequently in 1864–65; he put any depredations down "to the account of Rebels who had forced us into the war."[20]

Sherman assured Fry of his continuing warm regard for both him and his old friend Buell. He alluded to his "almost unlimited respect for his [Buell's] personal courage and real ability as a soldier," but he warned that when Buell "questioned the motives of others his equals if not superiors he transcended the limits of friendly criticism." Here Sherman referred to

Buell's furious reaction to Grant's article in the *Century Magazine* on Shiloh. Sherman thought his essay was "invaluable, direct, simple and will carry conviction" and had told Grant so before his death. Buell thought otherwise and believed it to be a travesty. The central point at issue provoked a series of violent exchanges. Sherman realized that Buell shared all those "persistent misconceptions" that Sherman had urged Grant to dispose of once and for all. The only persuasive part of Buell's indictment was his belief that both Grant and Sherman had been surprised, but thereafter he veered off the rails of historical reality. As a latecomer to the battlefield, all he could remember was the fear, chaos, and confusion he had found in the rear areas. He concluded erroneously that Grant had been defeated on the first day and been "rescued" by the Army of the Ohio; further, he believed that "a fresh division" from Buell's army had shattered Confederate cohesion and brought victory on the second day, at a cost of over 2,000 casualties. Buell's views appeared in 1886 and percolated into public print mainly via his acolytes, notably Fry. Sherman's bitter exchanges were with the latter, and he had no direct contact with his former friend. Buell remarked sourly that the accounts of Shiloh in Sherman's *Memoirs* and in later exchanges were essays in vanity and self-glorification.[21]

Sherman had warned Fry early on, "I was in hopes this absurd claim of having 'saved us' would have been dropped—if renewed I think both Buell and you will regret it." He reported to Grant in the autumn of 1884 that Fry "took exception to my assertion that Buell's approach to the battlefield was not such as to entitle him to the claim of having rescued us from distruction [*sic*]. He seemed desirous to draw me into a controversy for publication but this I would not." Unfortunately, Sherman did not maintain this course, and an acrimonious exchange followed. "We held our ground all day," he wrote to Grant proudly, "till reinforcement came—which ought to have come *sooner.*" He would not allow Fry to besmirch this achievement, but its reiterations became more venomous. The columns of words that Sherman directed toward his literary enemies were often more audaciously deployed than the troops he had once sent forward in battle. There were some grounds for outrage in the Buell camp, not least Sherman's claim that Buell had not been "over-anxious to share our danger. . . . *And you know it.*" Such recklessness led him into foolish exaggeration—if not contradiction, if he had been sincere in praising Buell's courage—and he apologized and asked for the letter back; his luck held, and this spat remained private. But in a later, even more petty skirmish, Fry entrapped Sherman when he claimed that Sherman had suggested "that

Grant would have disappeared to history" had General C. F. Smith not died shortly after the fall of Donelson in April 1862. Despite his age, Smith had always remained subordinate to Grant, but at key difficult points in Grant's military career he might have presented an attractive, reliable alternative. All Sherman had to do was acknowledge this hypothetical possibility. Sherman, though, adamantly denied that he had written any such thing, but Fry revealed a damning copy of a letter containing Sherman's verdict sent to the editors of the *Official Records*, which he had forgotten he had ever composed. Sherman's talent for the arresting phrase, coupled with an overwhelming, argumentative passion, had led to an embarrassing blunder.[22]

The rawness of Sherman's nerves could be explained by the recent loss of his friend Grant. Their relationship had experienced ups and downs both at its start and nearer the end, but its essential integrity remained solid. Despite his protestations to the contrary, Buell's dogmatic and exaggerated views were an attack on both Grant and Sherman. Sherman felt it his duty to rebut them with all the vigor he could muster. Buell's prejudices had not changed since the afternoon of April 6, 1862. His view that Grant had really been defeated contributed to the powerful Southern myth that somehow Shiloh constituted a "lost victory." The ground at Shiloh could be treacherous—and it has been claimed that this thwarted the Confederates—but topography unaided rarely defeats an enemy. Buell, a narrow-minded, self-righteous man, had once liked Sherman but had always disliked Grant. He displayed unconscious envy and implied that their reputations had fraudulent foundations. No modern historian has sustained Buell's interpretation of Shiloh. He deployed only 17,918 men on April 7 and suffered 2,103 casualties, 17 percent of those engaged against the 22 percent *total* loss of Grant's army. Far from being exaggerated, Sherman's contribution to the victory had been underrated: he drew more than half the Confederate army to his sector, mounted a counterattack, and withdrew twice intact under fire, inflicting more casualties than any other division. Buell's disregard of all this is indeed a travesty.[23]

One central question remains unanswered. Why did Sherman invest so much effort in defending his record at Shiloh? He provided one answer in the spring of 1884 just after the publication of volume 10 of the *Official Records*, dealing with operations in Tennessee during that fateful spring. He noted with pleasure that "the truths of the events of the Battle of Shiloh are pretty well understood," then went on to observe, "There were two battles of Shiloh and Pittsburg Landing April 6–7, 1862." One was fought "with cannon and muskets—resulting in a victory for the Union cause—the other fought with pens, by the fugitives and correspondents who at a Safe distance invented their own facts and hastily published them, Sustaining a Shameless defeat." This reference explains but does not excuse the invective thrown at Buell operating "at a safe distance." He had every confidence that his own vantage point would be regarded as the true one. "The Public is at perfect liberty to choose between them." But his response hits out at many of his own pet scapegoats and makes no reference to himself. Perhaps, as usual, Ellen put it best when she wrote some years earlier: "This is the anniversary of the battle of Shiloh—the most important and the most interesting to me of the whole war for it was on this day that you had the opportunity to reassert yourself after the calumnies of your enemies had nearly ruined you. From that day, I laid aside all anxiety about you." For the entire Sherman family, the name Shiloh summoned up redemption, the beginning of his successful military career. Attacks on his record there threatened to uproot all he had achieved. His response became heated and unguarded, though it was far from unjustified.[24]

In the ceaseless war of the memoirs, Sherman found dealing with fellow Union generals difficult enough, but in the later 1880s a new front opened with former Confederates and their admirers advancing in support of the Lost Cause. In 1886 Sherman wrote to George Townsend to say he had been reading his romantic Civil War novel *Katy of Catoctin*, published that year by Appleton. Sherman revealed that he had recommended it to John A. Logan, who had responded warmly to the olive branch proffered during his ill-fated foray as Blaine's vice-presidential running mate two years earlier. Sherman reported that Logan had expressed displeasure at the special pleading advanced on behalf of Confederate leaders. His complaint gave point to Sherman's increasing frustration at the many excuses that had been fashioned on behalf of the Lost Cause. "Now that the Rebels are contesting for political power lost by this foolish Rebellion—a conspiracy and Rebellion not a 'War Between the States' as is now claimed," he added emphatically, "the whole truth should now come out."

He aimed his conspiracy thesis against the conspirator-in-chief, Jefferson Davis, and matters did not turn out well. After the publication of Davis's dreary apologia, *The Rise and Fall of the Confederate Government* (1881), Sherman initially thought it so tedious as not to be worth any exegesis, but in 1884 he reintroduced his conspiracy theory when addressing the audience at the opening of the new headquarters of the Grand Army of the Republic in St. Louis. Other newspapers picked up the story from the *St. Louis Republican*, and the issue spilled onto the floor of the Senate. The main evidence for Sherman's accusation that Davis had led a well-laid conspiracy against the US government lay in a series of Davis's letters and reports detailing the activities of an underground Northern secessionist movement called the Knights of the Golden Circle, whose nefarious activities had been much exaggerated during the war itself. But all the claimed documentation had either been lost or destroyed in the Great Chicago Fire of 1871. Such unsatisfactory evidence permitted the legalistic Davis to mount an insulting attack on Sherman to which he was powerless to reply.[25]

A later skirmish had a happier outcome. In the spring of 1887 Sherman reported that General Garnet Wolseley, Victorian Britain's foremost soldier, had written "a most interesting article" about Robert E. Lee. While a lieutenant colonel in January 1861, Wolseley had been sent to Toronto as an assistant quartermaster general; the following year he spent two months in the Confederacy and had met Lee. In March 1863 he published an article in *Blackwood's Magazine* entitled "A Month's Visit to Confederate Headquarters." He described Lee "as being a splendid specimen of an English gentleman," handsome, kindly, but reserved. In this second, much later article, "General Lee," that appeared in the *North American Review,* Wolseley's mature reflections resulted in an even more favorable depiction. For Wolseley Lee was "the most perfect man I ever met." From his youth Lee had been "a model of all that was noble, honourable and manly." He likened Lee to the Duke of Marlborough, not just in military ability but also in charm and affability. In his depiction Wolseley drew upon several aspects of the Lost Cause tradition. For instance, he put Lee's defeat down to his being "beaten down by sheer force of numbers." But he likened Lee not to Grant but to Lincoln, "the far-seeing statesman," "each is representative of the genius that characterized his country." Lee, Wolseley claimed, would come to be regarded "as the great American of the nineteenth century" worthy of comparison with George Washington.[26]

All this proved too much for Sherman. "I am compelled to join issue with General Wolseley in his conclusion, while willing to admit nearly all his premises." On this occasion Sherman could express "the highest respect and admiration" for Wolseley. And it is clear that his high regard for Wolseley, as they had been friends for more than a decade, troubled Sherman, and he hesitated to publish his rejoinder. But he persevered in the hope that Wolseley's verdict on Lee "will not be accepted by the military world as conclusive and final."[27]

It is likely that Wolseley and Sherman were introduced during Sherman's visit to London in the summer of 1872, as Wolseley served in the War Office in Whitehall from 1871 as assistant adjutant general before he departed for West Africa and the Ashanti War in 1873. They shared similar views on the "curse" of the party spirit and a dedication to a professional military ethos. The two generals exchanged a friendly correspondence from the early 1880s. In December 1882 Wolseley wrote to Sherman via the British legation in Washington, DC, thanking him for some favorable remarks that Sherman had made concerning the "neatness" and "despatch" with which Wolseley had settled his Egyptian campaign. Sherman expressed pleasure at Wolseley's compliments, not supposing that "the hero of England would have paused to notice my brief allusion." In 1883 Sir Garnet and Lady Wolseley traveled across the United States, and Sherman's daughter Rachel met them at a dinner party held in their honor in St. Louis. She invited them to afternoon tea at 912 Garrison Avenue, so they met most of the Sherman family. Sherman had already departed on his very final tour of the West as general-in-chief, and his enjoyment of this trip was marred by missing his British friends. Sherman often wrote to Wolseley asking him to help other Americans visiting London, including the actor Lawrence Barrett.[28]

Such friendly exchanges did not inhibit the sweep of Sherman's criticism of Wolseley's view of Lee. His prime target was Wolseley's presentation of Lost Cause mythology. Once "the smoke and confusion of battle" had cleared, Sherman agreed that Lincoln "was the great civil hero of the war" but asserted that Grant, not Lee, was its "chief military hero." Sherman might have sustained this view by reference to the outpouring of grief that had emanated from the South at Grant's death. Instead, he deployed specific arguments against Lee. He made some critical points about his conduct during the secession crisis that qualified Wolseley's hero worship. Sherman's assessment was not unrelentingly critical. He thought Lee too much "a typical American" to succumb to "the temptations of military dictatorship"; "he was unquestionably right" to subordinate himself to the Confederate president. But when placed in the balance, Sherman found Lee wanting when compared either to Grant or his fellow Virginian George H. Thomas.[29]

Sherman's arguments underwrote the Union case in the controversies that raged over Civil War generalship for the next century. Ellen encouraged him in this quest, as she considered his "a very fine article," and "the Rebs ought not to have the entire field," but she warned him to "buckle on the armor of indifference," for his criticisms would bring the "malice [of] your enemies north and south . . . down on you." He did not mince his words. Lee's "sphere of action," Sherman contended, "was . . . local. He never rose to the grand problem which involved a continent and future generations. His Virginia was to him the world." His defense of Richmond was valiant, but "he stood on the front porch battling with the flames whilst the kitchen and house were burning, sure in the end to consume the whole." Then, after reflecting on Lee's disappointments at Antietam and Gettysburg, he reached the following withering conclusion: "As an aggressive soldier Lee was not a success, and in war that is the true and proper test." By comparison, Grant's thoughts "straddled a continent"; he assumed the greatest burden in 1864 and "began a campaign equal in strategy, in logistics, and in tactics to any of Napoleon, and grander than any contemplated by England." True, he enjoyed a numerical superiority, but "nothing like the disproportion stated by General Wolseley." In elevation and range Grant was Lee's superior. The final salute to Grant's greatness could be found in the terms he offered Lee at Appomattox—"so liberal as to disarm all criticism."[30]

Sherman also paid just tribute to Thomas, who had died of a stroke in 1870. He believed that Thomas "holds a higher plane in the hearts and affections of the American people than General Lee." Thomas was also "a better soldier of equal intelligence"; further, he excelled Lee "in the moral and patriotic line of action at the beginning of the war." When Thomas died, James A. Garfield had been selected to deliver the oration at a memorial service before the veterans of the Army of the Cumberland at Cleveland, Ohio. Sherman was anxious lest old Confederates like Fitzhugh Lee, the general's nephew, try to paint him as a conditional Unionist who in 1861 "leaned to the South," and he urged Garfield to reject this scenario. Garfield's oration turned out a great success, and Sherman quoted from it liberally in his essay. On Thomas's Unionism, Sherman could not have been more emphatic: "He remained true to his oath and his duty, always, to the very last minute of his life." As only Providence or war could have eradicated slavery, Sherman concluded positively, "we . . . are the better for it," and he observed proudly "that the war was worth to us all it cost in life and treasure."[31]

Finally, Sherman contended that the British preoccupation with Lee and the Army of Northern Virginia exposed a one-dimensional attitude to American affairs. The British appeared "not to realize that the strength of our country lies to the west of the Appalachians." He also chided Wolseley that Americans did not need "advice from abroad" on their heroes, a riposte that threw a bucket of cold water over Wolseley's idolatry. Wolseley wrote a good-natured letter agreeing to disagree. Sherman's forthright article forms one of the earliest and most influential refutations of Lee as a national, as distinct from a Southern, symbol.[32]

Sherman did not spend all his time writing. When not brandishing the quill, he read voraciously. In his time as general-in-chief Sherman had Colonel Audenried, a thoughtful and cultured man, organize a Headquarters Library. Sometimes it found books for Ellen and lent them to her. Sherman often read the books she requested. These reveal his continuing interest in art. In the late 1870s he acquired the works of John Ruskin, read John Addington Symonds's *The Renaissance in Italy* (7 volumes, 1875–86) and J. R. Green's *A Short History of the English People* (4 volumes, 1877–80). Sherman's long friendship with the artist George Healy provides further evidence that his interest in art had not been extinguished. He had introduced Healy to Grant in 1868 and encouraged his design to paint an evocation of Lincoln, Grant, Sherman, and Admiral Porter aboard the *River Queen* in 1865, one of his most successful works. Healy also painted portraits of both Sherman and Ellen. In his painting of the general, Healy managed to capture both his athleticism and determination but also his reflective nature. Healy had hosted Sherman in Rome in 1872 and had arranged his visit to the Vatican. Sherman also read works that touched upon his time as commanding general, such as P. S. Michie, *Life and Letters of General Emory Upton* (1885). In the summer of 1885 Ellen and the family visited his old staff officer Colonel J. E. Tourtelotte near Lake Minnetonka in Minnesota. This trip turned into a staff reunion, as Orlando Poe and his family joined them and so did John Hammond, who had served Sherman so faithfully in 1861–62. Sherman now served as their librarian, as Ellen wrote to him requesting that he pack Michie's book so that Tourtelotte could read it; alas, the pleasant prospect of a holiday in Minnesota ended with Grant's untimely death. At the end of 1885 Sherman also read *The Story of Archer Alexander* by William Greenleaf Eliot, which revealed much of Missouri's early history and included material on the Blairs and John C. Frémont. Sherman found it "so interesting . . . that it commanded my admiration . . . and [desire] to underlie the lessons which it teaches." Sherman's attitude to knowledge remained incorrigibly utilitarian.[33]

Ellen refers in her letter from Minnesota to the family's sorrow at leaving him behind on his own looking after 912 Garrison Avenue, which "will keep you busy when you are not at your book." This turned out to be a detailed account of his overseas travels in 1871–72, amounting to 300 foolscap pages. It was written to keep his grandchildren in prosperity. He asked Mark Twain for his candid opinion on the manuscript, attracted by the terms Twain had offered Grant for his *Personal Memoirs* and his success at selling them. Twain rejected it, thinking it too flabby and lacking sinew and the muscular qualities so evident in his *Memoirs*. He believed that the second book would be compared adversely with them. Sherman took these criticisms in good spirit, but Twain's harshness discouraged any further large-scale literary ventures. Ellen had urged him to write a third volume of his *Memoirs* on the post-1865 years, but he did not do so, only adding another chapter to the second edition of 1888. But a portion of the diary on which the second, stillborn book was based eventually appeared posthumously.[34]

Sherman's days were filled not only with writing and disputation but also with significant domestic upheavals. In June 1886 the Shermans sold their house on Garrison Avenue in St. Louis and moved to New York. Both Minnie and Thomas Fitch and Elly and her husband (she had married Lieutenant Commander Alexander Thackara, USN, in May 1880) had moved to Pennsylvania the year before; Cumpy attended Yale University. So the metropolis became a convenient staging post for keeping in touch with the family. Mary Audenried and other friends had found Sherman's preference for St. Louis puzzling, and John Sherman especially expressed a wish that he return to the East Coast. Sherman, Ellen, Rachel, and Lizzie all moved into the Fifth Avenue Hotel (on the corner of 32nd Street) before he bought a comfortable house at 75 West 71st Street.

Over the preceding eight years Sherman's marriage had experienced some stress. He could be gruff, astringent, and tartly unsympathetic, particularly toward Ellen's growing fears for her health, which he tended to dismiss as "imaginary." He was also a perennial absentee. Ellen, though a powerful personality, clever and shrewd, and sometimes a better judge of events than her husband, had become increasingly elusive, preoccupied—especially with her devotions—ethereal, and unpredictably volatile. During these years she turned against her brothers Tom Jr. and Charley because she considered their attitude to the Church too casual. Her animus toward Tom dated from Willy's death. Ellen judged him in 1864 "a supremely selfish man [who] has failed in my affliction to treat me as an ordinary friend." She forbade her husband to discuss their affairs with him. As for John Sherman, she feared his growing influence and dreaded being beholden to him after her husband's death. Until the 1870s it was she who dispensed patronage, as she knew everybody. With the advent of the Hayes presidency followed by Garfield-Arthur, she knew nobody. She was jealous of the influence of the Sherman clan and complained she had been rendered "friendless"—"a washer woman should receive the same consideration that I do." Until 1884 she remained at 912 Garrison Avenue, "where I can be independent," while Sherman rented a house on 15th Street in Washington, DC. Since 1878 she had been given a house rent-free in Lancaster. She needed independence from her husband and had her own money. Sherman disliked her independence, sometimes scolded her severely, but then wanted her advice. In November 1877 she retorted, "You have told me you do not like sentiment—nor many other things to which I am prone"—but he was the first to complain when she did not write.[35]

Sherman tended also to dismiss her religious distractions as "superstition." Most of his life Sherman had demonstrated considerable tolerance of Catholicism and mixed happily with Catholics, even though—despite his wife's hopes—he knew he could never be a Catholic "from the nature of my mental organization" and questioning nature. His lodestones were reason and science, not faith. Still, they managed to coexist, but an explosion occurred in May 1878 that resulted in aftershocks for almost a decade. Tom had quickly taken his brother Willy's place in Sherman's affections, though he could never supplant him, and they had spent much time together. Tom sometimes appeared brooding and preoccupied like his mother, but he was clever, talented, diligent, and much liked. Sherman entrusted him with his business affairs in St. Louis and took a close interest in his education, planning it very carefully; he showed progressive attitudes in persuading Tom his studies should be based on natural law, engineering, and modern science. Tom attended the Sheffield Scientific School at Yale, and Sherman intended he should next attend Washington University's law school in St. Louis before entering Colonel Henry Hitchcock's law practice. Sherman calculated Tom could then provide for the family after he had passed away. This grand paternal plan fell apart in May 1878 when Tom wrote to his father informing him that he had plans of his own, and they could not be less welcome. Tom had decided to become a Jesuit priest and would soon depart for an English seminary.[36]

Sherman's reaction to this "great calamity" showed him at his choleric, ranting worst. He raged against "that insidious whispering set of priests" that had persuaded Tom to desert him, leaving his hopes in ruins. Ellen had only learned about Tom's ambition the week before. She approved of it, of course, but recognized "the terrible disappointment this must be" to her husband. Yet, though lacking the faith to see Tom's yearning for such a solemn duty, "you nevertheless have the stern principle which will eventually cause you to feel that he must act according to his convictions." She also deflated the rhetoric underlying his lamentations of woe: "No disgrace or 'ruin' can befall you except by your own act." In the event, the grand scheme that Sherman nursed for Tom, redolent of his deep-seated insecurity, proved superfluous— for all his daughters married well, and his family did not fall into penury, as he so often feared. Ellen naturally defended her son, but her letters lack the gloating attributed to them by Michael Fellman. She warned her husband not to "wound the heart of the son who loves you above everything on this earth." Sherman would only endure unhappiness, she went on, until he thought kindly of him. Ellen was right again. Father and son were reconciled on Tom's return to the United States in August 1880.[37]

A cooling in Sherman's relations with Ellen followed the falling-out in 1878, almost entirely on his side. Ellen was left alone to look after the St. Louis house with its "boxes of books," Sherman's gun collection, and innumerable other trophies safely stored away. She moved near Baltimore. Her correspondence remained warm and friendly. "I fear you are very lonely dear Cump, without the girls. Come out to us as soon as you can. I am very anxious about you, but I keep distracted by the moving." But Sherman came to believe that Ellen had played a part in traducing Tom from his true loyalty, and nothing could persuade him otherwise. His antagonism toward the Catholic Church did not abate, though it became less vitriolic. These developments inform the background to another aspect of Sherman's private life in these later years, a series of affairs with younger women. In reality Sherman was far from lonely.[38]

Relationships with women other than his wife were a postwar fancy, undoubtedly a by-product of his fame. It is said that power constitutes the ultimate aphrodisiac, but in Sherman's case he did not ascend to the presidency but remained perpetually available to fill it—even in 1888—and this added to his appeal. Sherman invariably found himself surrounded by groups of admiring young ladies. He played up to the idea that he served as their avuncular guide in life. He acknowledged the age difference, but in the nineteenth century it was not uncommon for young women to marry men well into later middle age. His relations were flirtatious, with the exchange of many kisses. But Sherman would exploit these if he sensed an opportunity. Mildred Hazen, the young wife of William B. Hazen, found his "off-hand" attentions tiresome and when cornered called a halt to them.[39]

Sherman's interest in the theater brought him into contact with several attractive, clever, and cultivated actresses. Ellen disliked theaters almost as much as steamships, and her seclusion offered Sherman opportunities to meet new people. The Shermans had re-created their long-distance marriage of 1857–65. This arrangement had worked—though they did not think so then—and would do so again. But this time Sherman added to it. Michael Fellman's description of this arrangement as a trial or informal separation in a "bitterly discordant marriage" is an exaggeration. The Shermans discovered late in life that their marriage had worked best when they communicated at a distance. The term "separation" suggests that the marriage had ended, but there is no evidence of any such finality in their prolific correspondence. Both continued to write intimately and confide in one another—notwithstanding tensions and disagreements—as they had before.[40]

Sherman's relationship with other women tended to reflect his intellectual and artistic interests. Many of the women also resembled Ellen in their intelligence and forthright characters. Among the actresses he admired were Adelaide Ristori and Ada Rehan. Fellman adds Mary Anderson to the list, but she was a devout Catholic, so it is more likely that they enjoyed a guardedly flirtatious, bantering relationship of the kind common among very close friends. The relationship that was most important to Sherman during the frustrating 1870s was with the sculptor Vinnie Ream, whose talent he admired and with whose "long tresses" he toyed. In 1878 she married an army officer, Lieutenant Richard Hoxie, an engineer; Sherman attended the wedding and, unusually for him, sometimes attempted to aid Hoxie's career. Vinnie and Sherman continued to correspond until 1887. She appealed to the bohemian and creative side of the complex nature of this soldier who had once loved to paint. But when she tried to revive their relationship in the mid-1880s, Sherman knew that it was over, insisting "the old times will *never* come back . . . *we* change."[41]

The other significant younger woman in his life was Mary Audenried. She was the widow of his loyal staff officer Colonel Joseph Audenried, who had suffered from a serious but undiagnosed illness (possibly multiple sclerosis) since 1876 and died in 1881. Mary hailed from a distinguished Philadelphia mercantile family and thus had money of her own; Sherman initially gave her emotional and not financial support. The same ambiguous pattern emerged as with Vinnie Ream. Sherman sought to give Mary avuncular advice but gradually became embroiled in a romantic attachment. In 1881–82 he implored her to marry again: "You should marry a man your own age." The affair continued in this vein until Sherman retired from the army and prepared to return to St. Louis. Mary had a complicated relationship with the Sherman family because she had known them all so well for many years. The children had stayed with her and had befriended her spoiled and wilful daughter, Florence. Florence had a marked interest in young men who were usually deemed unsuitable; she was no more likely to listen to Sherman's advice than her mother's. In 1884 Mary paid an ill-starred visit to the Sherman house in St. Louis, where she quarreled with Ellen and Lizzie over Catholicism; Fellman speculates that mother and daughter might have guessed as to the changed relationship between Mary and Sherman. Afterward a dispute erupted between Florence and her school over one of her many dalliances, and Mary took her daughter's side. Ellen had opened one of her letters to Sherman on the matter and waded into the controversy, criticizing Mary for endangering her daughter's immortal soul. Sherman expressed fury at Ellen's unwanted intrusion but remained conscious of the risks of exposure and destroyed the more incriminating correspondence. Ellen protested that she had opened the letter in error.

Although this relationship brought Sherman illicit pleasure as well as upset, Mary's own personality—married elder men were her preferred quarry—imposed strict limits on any entanglements. They continued to exchange playful and sexually charged letters until 1890. This was a consensual and convenient arrangement, but there is no reason to believe that Sherman wanted to substitute it for the marriage that had anchored his life since 1850. Like so many other men who pursue extramarital affairs, Sherman wanted both, family stability and sexual adventure, but the latter could be more easily sacrificed. As he frankly admitted to Mary in 1884, "I do honestly want to live out the balance of my days in peace." He faced the ineluctable reality that even should he want one—a highly questionable claim—Ellen would have been utterly horrified at even the suggestion of divorce.[42]

The emphasis placed by some of Sherman's biographers on his intimate relationships with the fair sex is apt to conceal that he gained most satisfaction from male company. His yearning for it explains much of his restlessness and absence from his family. Lord Rosebery first met him at "what Americans call a 'stag party' that is a party without ladies." The comradeship of soldiers of all ranks, not just officers, brought him contentment. On retirement he devoted much time to veterans' organizations, such as the Society of the Army of the Tennessee (his favorite) and the Grand Army of the Republic. An immensely strong reciprocal bond of affection tied Sherman and his veterans together. Sherman assured a confidant "that the consciousness of this feeling towards me on the part of the Old Soldiers, especially of the Army of the Tennessee is a source of infinite pride and satisfaction in these my declining years." He also concerned himself with the young, being much in demand for West Point graduations ceremonies. His diary bulged with commitments. He cried off from attending his West Point class reunion in May 1886. "I find myself overtaxed with promises," he explained, "which I cannot neglect. I must be in Chicago May 29, at Indianapolis June 2, and at San Francisco August 3—during which time I must transfer my household to New York City." Sherman also took on a heavy burden of entertainment at home, with lunch at 11:00 a.m. and dinner at 6:00 p.m. He also dined out a good deal. In the autumn of 1890, he attended a dinner party in honor of the Comte de Paris, author of a highly regarded *Histoire de la guerre civile en Amérique* (1883).[43]

Still so active and prominent on the social scene, Sherman remained perennially a favored candidate with Republican power brokers, who had approached him yet again in 1888, via his daughter Rachel, to run for the presidency but had received an abrupt refusal. Sherman expected Grover Cleveland to be reelected, but he went down before the Republican Benjamin Harrison, another of Sherman's old subordinates.

His sociability laid a heavy burden on an asthmatic man in his late 60s, and sometimes Sherman succumbed. In 1884 he reported that "I am recently back from Washington and New York, bringing with me as usual a severe cold for which I must nurse myself for some weeks." For asthmatics, colds and coughs were a far worse ordeal, as blocked tubes added to the difficulties of breathing. But his overall health appeared good, though his teeth decayed badly in the 1880s. He had lost a front tooth in 1876, and the rest were taken out in 1887 and replaced with dentures; the process was unpleasant, "and I hope," Ellen sympathized, "the dentist will not be too slow about it." Although Sherman found wearing dentures a "trial," he persevered and did not discourage invitations.[44]

A portent of mortality came suddenly with news of Philip H. Sheridan's sudden death at the end of 1888. Sheridan was 11 years Sherman's junior; the news came as a great shock, and Sherman was deeply affected at Sheridan's funeral in Arlington Cemetery. A memorial service was organized for March 1889 in Albany, New York, with General Wager Swayne, who had served in the 16th and 17th Corps and was a distinguished New York lawyer, invited to give the oration. Sherman initially declined to attend because of a severe cold and only agreed eventually to go if he could travel to Albany and back on the same day. Despite these hesitations, Sherman delivered that day one of his marvelous short, seemingly unprepared tributes that outshone Swayne's longer, more ponderous effort. He later had difficulty coping with requests for "copies," as there were none. He could not remember what he had said and had to reconstruct it using a stenographer's notes taken down on the day. He joked that he could not issue an affidavit claiming "it even approaches what I actually spoke."[45]

Sherman had become sensitive to the obligation to pay respect to Sheridan's memory because the wings of the Angel of Death had flapped in his own home. In 1882 at Ellen's home in Oakland, Maryland, the Shermans had lost two of their Fitch granddaughters, Katie and Maria, Maria a new-born and Katie just 2 years old, both having succumbed to typhoid. Sherman had telegraphed frantically to doctors but to no avail. "I feel dreadfully for poor Minnie," Ellen wrote to her husband, "for I know by experience what the anguish is." Sherman knew, too, for the event brought back painful memories of Willy's loss to the same ailment almost twenty years before. Then death crept closer. In the summer of 1886 Ellen believed she had contracted malaria, which Sherman dismissed as hypochondria. But the tone of her correspondence changed: "I am not now certain but that you will outlive me." She then wrote to confirm that the doctor had diagnosed heart disease and that her breathing difficulties were caused by "cardiac asthma." She could no longer dress herself because she could not lift her arms; defensive about her weight, she reported that it had not increased since she had left St. Louis at 165 pounds, though she remained stout and experienced growing lameness as a result. In January 1888 Ellen had been staying with Minnie, but by the autumn she decided to move to Manhattan, "to our own home which I shall be slow to leave."[46]

Their New York City home had been established by her husband, and she agreed not to try to take it over. "You can continue to be 'Boss' . . . as long as you choose, so you need not dread our coming." Ellen did not have the energy to make any such effort, and after she celebrated her 64th birthday on October 4, 1888, her health rapidly deteriorated. On November 7 she endured a severe heart attack; a second followed on November 25. Sherman felt such anxiety that he gave up his bedroom so that the doctor could attend to Ellen's needs and still take rest next door. He took personal charge of her care. Ellen murmured to him, "You must think of yourself, Cump," but he replied, "I can think only of Ellen." The end came peacefully on November 28,

1888. The death of the most significant person in Sherman's life left him prostrate for a month, though he insisted on supervising all the arrangements for Ellen's funeral in St. Louis, where she was buried next to Willy.[47]

Despite their long periods of agreed, amicable separation, Ellen had far more than a periodic walk-on role in their marriage. Arguably, for all of Sherman's outward bluster, she remained the dominant partner. Ellen had a strong, self-willed character, the exact opposite of the submissive, obedient wife. She was a shrewd counselor, often more sensible and less petulant than her husband, though ferocious if crossed. She had forceful opinions, especially relating to her devout religious beliefs, and rarely gave way if challenged. Though he was loath to admit it, Sherman preferred his wife to be confident and articulate. Thanks to her father, Ellen exerted formidable powers of patronage, though this declined later. Sherman owed the salvation of his career in the disastrous winter of 1861–62 to her, when she consolidated his position by writing a series of letters to his military friends in positions of authority. Ellen made a substantial contribution to Sherman's intellectual development, broadening his interests, widening his horizons, and thus shaping the direction of his career. Sometimes this influence was felt in a negative way, such as bolstering his resistance to a presidential nomination. Even their aggravating tensions over money and Ellen's spendthrift ways were overcome. In April 1887 Sherman wrote to Ellen worried that she and the family thought him "close"—that he might appear ungenerous and his pocketbook firmly shut. If there had been bitter recrimination between them, as claimed by Michael Fellman, then this would have been the time for it to erupt. On the contrary, Ellen observed, "You like to growl a little, but you have never questioned me or held me to strict account." And she repeated, "You have always been most liberal in your dealings with me in supplying me with money at all times and all the children feel as I do about it." Fellman's portrait of ceaseless haggling—"they tortured one another to the grave"—seems inaccurate. They needed one another, but Ellen cherished her independence, so by trial and error they worked out an unconventional arrangement that suited both their needs. There is no reason to doubt the sincerity of Sherman's mourning. Their son Tecumseh summed up the situation best. Their differences never interfered "with unwavering mutual respect, consideration and affection."[48]

Ellen's death forced Sherman to contemplate his mortality. Recalling the controversy over Grant's tomb—still unresolved in 1888—he expressed a desire to avoid any "unseemly scramble for my worthless body"; he insisted that he "be buried by Mrs. Sherman's side with a simple but tasty [tasteful] headstone." He also insisted that it be constructed of granite, not marble, and wanted it to be modeled on the headstone of his loyal staff officer and companion Audenried, who lay in the West Point cemetery, though minus "its ornaments and inscriptions." His idea of a memorial was remarkably modest by comparison with those of his contemporaries. He allowed himself one indulgence. He contrived his own epitaph: "Faithful and Honorable." It has strong West Point echoes and did him justice, for loyalty shines as one of his most notable qualities inherited from his father.[49]

During these last years Sherman glimpsed the final curtain. Even before retiring, he realized that the years of achievement had passed. "It is hard for me to realize," he admitted to his British friend Wolseley, "that I am too rapidly passing into the category of the Old Fogy, and that a new Race of young men is fast treading on our heels, looking to past successes for examples, and past failures for warnings—such alas is the truth"; he had become an object of study. He had led a worthwhile life, but it had quickly receded into the past. Occasionally he mentioned a premonition: "I feel death reaching out for me." After Sheridan's death he started calling himself "the Last of the Mohicans" as the last senior general of the Union cause, and one so interested in literature. Although incredibly busy, he enjoyed these last years. His membership of the Union League Club in Manhattan brought him great pleasure, and he spent many evenings there.[50]

On January 31, 1891, he dined at the Press Club in honor of the Welsh-American explorer Henry M. Stanley, whom he had known for more than twenty years. Sherman had been asked to move the vote of thanks and offer a toast. Stanley enjoyed seeing Sherman again, noting that he was "in an exceedingly amiable mood"—also that he sported "a rubicund complexion," an early symptom of his last illness. They "exchanged pleasant compliments to each other in our after-dinner speeches." Sherman warmed to the theme of the "Old Army" of which he remained the shining exemplar. Stanley "recognized an oratorical power few men not knowing him would have suspected." He reflected on Sherman's technique during this last lyrical coda. "He had the bearing of one who could impress, also those easy gestures which fix the impression, and the pathos which charms the ear, and affects the feelings."[51]

On the evening of Wednesday, February 4, Sherman accompanied a group of friends to a production at the Casino Theatre; the following afternoon he attended a wedding. By Friday he had developed a harsh cold and cough and a sore throat. He felt so ill he had to cancel a dinner engagement at the Union

League Club with his old friend the actor Lawrence Barrett. By Saturday the symptoms of erysipelas were marked—a contagious virus leading to redness of the skin that could be contracted via the tear duct. The ailment often leads to painful swelling of the throat and sometimes delirium but is rarely fatal. In Sherman's case, however, it opened the way for pneumonia. The redness spread to his neck, and he could hardly speak. On Sunday he read Charles Dickens's *Great Expectations*, but thereafter he grew weaker each day, and movement was painful. By February 11 regular bulletins on his health were issued in the newspapers. An anxious crowd of admirers gathered outside his house on West 71st Street, just as they had gathered outside Grant's house. His preferred doctor, Charles J. Alexander, an army surgeon, moved into the house and battled to arrest his patient's decline. On February 12 Sherman seemed to rally as the symptoms of erysipelas subsided, but this only concealed the greater threat. He left his bed and clambered to a chair close by; he uttered a few indistinct words, reputedly "faithful and honorable." He expired on Sunday, February 14, at 1:50 p.m. as his lungs filled with mucus . He was surrounded by his children, except Tom, who was returning from Britain, his two sons-in-law, Fitch and Thackara, his younger brother John, and his brother-in-law Tom Ewing Jr.[52]

Sherman's life had often been led amid controversy and tumult, which did not ebb as death approached. An unseemly dispute broke out after a story appeared in the *New York Times* detailing how his children took advantage of John Sherman's brief absence to smuggle a Catholic priest into his bedroom. He administered extreme unction, and thus Sherman, at long last, could be claimed for the Church. In reply John observed that his brother would have permitted such an act if conscious; moreover, John would have allowed it even if present because his brother had been "too good a Christian and too human a man to deny his children the consolations of their religion." Sherman's daughters Rachel and Lizzie had indeed emphatically insisted their father be given the last rites. Most of his life had been conducted with impressive tolerance of Catholicism; his diatribes of 1878–80 were exceptional rather than the rule—and greatly upset old Catholic friends like Henry Turner. So John's observations were more firmly representative of his lifelong attitude than the innuendo of the *New York Times*, which summoned up anti-Catholic bigotry and images of underhand designs. But the controversy rumbled on.

Contrary to Sherman's wishes, his body lay in state at his home and received two grand funerals, one in New York, comparable with Grant's, and another in St. Louis; both were massive affairs watched by countless thousands who filled the streets. Many others turned out by the railroad line as his coffin traveled across the country to Pittsburgh, traversed Ohio, Indiana, and Illinois, and then headed southwest to St. Louis on the west bank of his beloved Mississippi River. At both funerals Father Tom Sherman officiated, and grumbles were heard at the Catholic character of the rites. Then at long last, at the Calvary Cemetery outside the city that had been his home for many years, they were stilled. Sherman's coffin was lowered next to the graves of Ellen, Willy, and Charley. Volleys were fired by soldiers of his old regiment, the 13th Infantry. Of the huge number of tributes from home and abroad, former president Rutherford B. Hayes, who attended both ceremonies, captured his vital character best. Sherman was, quite simply, "the most interesting and original character in the world."[53]

Conclusion

Weighed in the Balance and Not Found Wanting

Though William T. Sherman did not live a long life, he remained active until the very end. He did not have to endure a prolonged decline or loss of his faculties, but because he outlived even his younger contemporaries, he appears to be longer-lived than he was. Yet a man of such drive and energy bequeathed a significant legacy of achievement.[1]

Several of his achievements are not controversial; two of them are indisputable. First, Sherman ranks alongside Abraham Lincoln and Ulysses S. Grant as one of the three prime architects of Union victory in the Civil War. He played a major role—though subsidiary to Lincoln and Grant—in restoring the Union and thus setting the United States on the path to global preeminence: a goal that could be glimpsed in 1891. The nature of that contribution, however has sparked controversy. Whatever view might be taken of it, there can be little dispute that Sherman had become an icon of the Union cause and had become—and remains—world famous. "The March [to the Sea] was a great drama," two scholars of Civil War mythology reflect, "its leading man born to the role, whether or not we like the story line." Second, though Sherman's most resounding acts occurred during the Civil War, he achieved significant things afterward, the most notable being his connection with the "winning" of the West and his identification with it. He understood what the novelist Willa Cather calls the "enigma" of the sprawling country of infinite variation. She suggests a pioneer must have imagination and should be able to enjoy the idea of things as well as the things themselves. Sherman imbibed the idea of the frontier after 1866, taking in its epic scale and unfathomable beauties. Cather refers to the "Genius of the Divide, the great, free spirit which breathes across it"; Sherman found liberation from professional frustrations and constricting domestic routine there.[2]

Sherman is usually ranked among the greatest of American generals, though he has never lacked critics. A notable one is the British writer Lieutenant Colonel A. H. Burne, who certainly acknowledges Sherman's qualities. He argues that Sherman's record exhibits "imagination, resource, versatility, broadness of conception and genuine powers of leadership," but he also contends that "the war was won in Virginia in April, and it would in all probability have been won there, and then, had Sherman's men not rifled a house nor burnt a barn in the whole of the Confederacy." Many of Burne's criticisms anticipated those of Albert Castel. Castel has argued—and the point has been made many times—that "never once . . . did he engage or even try to engage the enemy with his full available strength" and attempt to inflict a crippling blow on Confederate military power deployed in the field. "He was, in short," Castel concludes, "a general who did not like to fight." However, in 1865 the young Lieutenant Stephen B. Luce, who had been supporting Sherman's operations in the Carolinas, came ashore to confer with Sherman's staff and met their commander for the first time. Luce was astounded not just by the depth of Sherman's grasp of the operational dimensions but by its breadth, how all the parts of the whole fitted together in one coherent whole. The "scales fell from my eyes," Luce later recalled; he counted this one of the key moments in his education as a naval officer. His experience seems to highlight a key question that needs an answer, namely: To what extent did Sherman's well-known tactical caution qualify his abilities as an orchestrator of campaigns and as a strategist?[3]

Military analysts have provided the tools by which the abilities of commanders can be assessed. Military activity is pursued at three interconnected levels, which are not necessarily interdependent, though they usually build on one another: first, the tactical, that is, the art of fighting; second, the operational, the series of stepping-stones that contributes to successful campaigns that secure both intermediate and ultimate objectives; third, the strategic, the overall objective that aims at the defeat of the enemy. Strategy is of two types: military strategy, the direction, coordination, and maintenance of armed forces, as equipment and supply form its lifeblood; and grand strategy, which fulfills governmental policy aims and must embrace important nonmilitary factors, such as foreign policy, diplomacy, propaganda, economics, finance, and industrial production. It should also be stressed that it is widely acknowledged that even the most brilliantly successful of commanders, except for Alexander the Great, have not revealed equal aptitude at all three of these levels, at any rate simultaneously.[4]

Sherman is an unusual figure because he was present at the first great battle of the Civil War and at the last great act in April 1865. He thus had incomparable experience of the war stretching from the Arkansas River to the Potomac River in Virginia. He had been present at four repulses—First Bull Run, Chickasaw Bluffs, Tunnel Hill, and Kennesaw Mountain. The tactical indecisiveness and the primacy of the defense exhibited in the war had impressed themselves on his mind. His experience therefore dovetailed with his temperamental inclinations, and he tended to pursue strategic and operational offensive aims by defensive means. He did not employ this combination as consistently or as neatly codified as Sir Basil Liddell Hart would later present his campaigns. Nonetheless, his designs did have a detrimental effect on the enemy by drastically weakening a numerically inferior foe. In reaching his conclusions, Sherman brought superb mental qualities to bear on the complex challenges he faced. Yet despite his intellectual curiosity, reflective bent, and wide reading, his successes were not the result of mere cleverness and book-learning, though these did give his ideas coherence and structure. Major General J. F. C. Fuller argued that once a soldier "has experienced something it has changed his nature by becoming part of himself. Experience is therefore the highest form of study." Sherman also brought other qualities to the task than intellect: the ability to reduce a problem to its essentials; to differentiate between what is important and what is not and remain abreast of those essentials; to make decisions under pressure, particularly when things went wrong—perhaps in spite of it—as setbacks sometimes resulted from his errors; to display moral courage and determination as well as physical courage, for he was a true leader; and last, but by no means least, to benefit from luck. In short, he brought true instincts and understanding of the needs of the hour—what Dennis Hart Mahan had called "common sense"—and did not deviate from his chosen course.[5]

His style of warfare was by no means new in the nineteenth century. It is one particularly favored in the English-speaking world because its military traditions render the raising and maintenance of large armies difficult, and once raised they cannot be replaced effortlessly. Sherman continually complained about such handicaps, but to no avail. He also faced a further complication. The environment in which he operated revealed treacherous features that demanded skill to traverse them successfully. The historian Earl Hess has argued that the degree to which Civil War armies prospered logistically depended on the level of infrastructure they enjoyed. Once he left Chattanooga, Sherman plunged into terrain that lacked substantial towns or lines of communication, save on the coast, with the signal exception of Atlanta. He had to rely on his own resources, a single-track railroad, and the North's command of the sea—though Chattanooga lay a long way from the coast. Geography, therefore, had to be overcome, as well as the Confederate army. In succeeding against both, Sherman took the best elements of his old West Point training, with its orderly, systematic, and meticulous methods and its emphasis on detail, and transferred it to a more unruly, unpredictable, threatening environment that worked on a scale beyond the ken of his teachers. Sherman's synthesis ranks among his most important achievements, mainly because it elevated the neglected art of logistics.[6]

Logistics, not numbers, was the golden key that unlocked Confederate defenses for Sherman and enabled him to organize successfully his advances into the Southern hinterland. That his chosen style of warfare had long historical roots can be shown by reference to the similarity of Sherman's campaign with those of the fifteenth-century English king Henry V, who waged war in France during the Hundred Years' War. Henry, too, exhibited a sense of order, understood the need for detailed planning and organization, and recognized the value of the command of the sea. Finally, Henry V, like Sherman, aimed to reduce the impact of war's ravages and limit his casualties; though civilians might have found the visits of Sherman's troops deeply unpleasant and distressing, they were not accompanied by savage violence or mistreatment of individuals. Amid highly colored Southern descriptions of their ordeals, the absence of violence on Sherman's Marches needs to be underlined. And so does the absence among the Southern population of large-scale famine of the type that broke out in later wars.[7]

Logistics and operational planning were based on depth of preparation. Sherman's diligence conferred a tight grip over both the composition of plans and the gathering of the means to support them, and no detail would be left to chance. Sherman might not have used his staff in innovative ways, but they worked as messengers that placed the vast quantities of detail at his disposal in an easily digestible form. Sherman did not allow himself to become swamped by detail or be hypnotized by it. George B. McClellan sought refuge in detail from the responsibilities that he craved but found perplexing; Sherman did not. He became more decisive as he grew in seniority, not less. Perhaps no man is a hero to his valet, but Sherman's staff worked more effectively than McClellan's because they worked as a team. Many of his staff, Hammond, Dayton, Audenried, Tourtelotte, and Hitchcock, among others, became lifelong friends. Sherman did employ them tentatively as his agents, though they had no more authority than any other Union staff officer. A remark by Moltke is worthy of Sherman, whom he admired: "Luck in the long run is given only to the efficient."[8]

Given the range of Sherman's talents. it is all too evident that the tactical level reveals him at his least impressive. There were extenuating circumstances even if it is admitted at once that Sherman cannot be hailed as a great tactician, for he did lack the killer instinct. He commanded in 1864-65 a conglomeration of armies of different sizes on which he succeeded in imposing some order and coherence. Their clumsy structure did place all kinds of constraints on him, especially of time, as bigger units came up to support the smaller; he had an ad hoc grouping at his disposal, not an army group. Yet Sherman tried to do too much, and he became enmeshed in military operations at too many different levels simultaneously. At Chattanooga he served as a de facto corps commander when he should have supervised a subordinate. He tried to revert to a directing role during the Atlanta campaign but experienced frustration in dealing with the Army of the Cumberland, whose corps commanders could be inert and contrary. Joseph Hooker provided a further complication, as his self-serving, domineering manner threatened to sideline George H. Thomas and annoy all Sherman's senior subordinates.

Did the four repulses that Sherman participated in or direct have any significant harmful effects? At First Bull Run in July 1861, Sherman's inexperience matched that of his contemporaries, but he compensated for it by his cool judgment in the retreat, extricating his brigade intact—often the acid test for fine generalship. At Chickasaw Bluffs in December 1862, a battle that Sherman had never expected to fight unsupported, his failure on December 27-29 tends to detract unjustly from the impeccable judgment he displayed throughout the first Vicksburg campaign. At Tunnel Hill during the Battle of Chattanooga, efforts to delegate were complicated by Francis P. Blair's absence on political business; Sherman's luck for once turned against him, but his frustrations were embarrassing rather than harmful to the progress of Union arms. Finally, at Kennesaw Mountain in June 1864, the error was less the decision to attack than the place selected. Once again Sherman's decision had been shaped by the inescapable reality that the best-placed formation, Schofield's Army of the Ohio, lacked the strength to inflict a decisive defeat on the Confederates. Sherman's repulse made no difference to the outcome, pace, or direction of the Atlanta campaign.

That said, Sherman often sought victory in battle, did not consciously seek to avoid it, but failed to gain a significant major offensive victory. Resaca stands as an exception in May 1864, an inspired example of tactical improvisation but halfhearted in its outcome. This latter tendency can only be explained by reference to Sherman's fundamental weakness: he proved too slack in the organization and combination of the tactical offensive, whereas he excelled at tactical defensive arrangements. Sherman regarded a tactical triumph as a bonus, not a necessity, but his campaigns were still successful without one: a "decisive victory" never served as a prerequisite for operational success. Sherman felt that Union generals were too eager to seek tactical decisions that hazarded their operational plans rather than fulfilled them. Perhaps, but Sherman enjoyed the luxury that Grant's great campaign in Virginia, hammering away at Lee remorselessly, took this burden from his shoulders. Liddell Hart is therefore wrong to deduce that Sherman's record reveals that battle is unnecessary.[9]

The second category, the operational level, is the enabling function in war. It fulfils the aims of campaigns that contribute to a successful strategic plan. Sherman's experience in 1862–63 offered him a valuable apprenticeship. He learned how to maintain and sustain deep strategic penetrations of Confederate territory. He succeeded in mounting long drives without exhausting the men, most of whom marched on their feet. Sherman was by no means the first commander to understand the psychologically paralyzing effect of strategic advances into an enemy's hinterland, for Napoleon's campaigns presented resounding models in the nineteenth century, but he perfected the technique, thanks to his logistical skill. Under Grant's tutelage he learned how to live off the country; later he learned how to assess the distance he could march without overstraining his lines of communications or endangering resupply. His advance across Mississippi and Alabama to Chattanooga, Tennessee, in the autumn of 1863 in terrible weather, plus the subsequent relief of Knoxville the following December, taught him much, though at the time he was disappointed with both. Sherman thus grasped a tremendously potent psychological weapon. The great spaces of Confederate territory could no longer present an unassailable challenge to Union military power. Indeed, Sherman would turn this weapon against those who once boasted of its power to thwart invasion.

Sherman revealed two other strengths. First, his skill at river crossings had been evident as early as First Bull Run; he brought it to a pitch of perfection at the Chattahoochee three years later. Successfully crossing the great rivers of the South, whether opposed or not, turned out to be a vital factor in sustaining the momentum of his campaigns, particularly in the Carolinas. Second, the adaptability of his logistical measures requires renewed emphasis. He pared back the size of his fighting echelons, thus ensuring that they were mobile and light and their consumption frugal. Sherman maintained that foraging remained a historic right, though Confederate authorities were rarely present to assist in the organization of regular impressments, and his foragers had to take what they needed, often wastefully. It is significant that towns where Sherman met the mayor were better treated than those whose officials had fled. Sherman's successes depended not at all on great numbers of men or the quality of their weapons but on his ability to keep them in the field and his ruthless exploitation of naked Confederate weakness. Whatever rigors his soldiers endured, Napoleon spared no effort to ensure that they were paid regularly, and Sherman did likewise. His soldiers regarded plunder as payment in advance, as did their successors in the two world wars.[10]

Despite his logistical preoccupations, Sherman did not become obsessed by them and got the relationship between operational art and logistics right. The speed and dexterity of his maneuvers were not determined but facilitated by them. Thanks to his foresight and power of decision, he grew stronger as his opponents grew weaker. Sherman's exploitation of surprise and deception prevented any "driving" of the country, the creation of a "desert" by a systematic "scorched earth" policy. As the British discovered in 1803–4 while preparing for a Napoleonic invasion, and the Confederates found to their cost in 1864, such measures require time. Southern complacency was compounded by a fatal underestimation of the scale of Sherman's endeavor. Sherman made deception look easy, and his later campaigns offer textbook examples of how to mislead an enemy: switching to concentrate on his prime objective only after the enemy had moved in the wrong direction. Though his numbers were not great and his equipment was light, Sherman managed to present an image of an irresistible juggernaut.[11]

The third area, that of strategy, is the most important but also the most controversial of Sherman's contributions to both Union victory and the overall legacy to American military practice and theory. First, to achieve the erosion of support for the Confederate war Sherman had to strike at public opinion in the Deep South, where the secessionist heart beat strongest. Second, he aimed to shatter the foundations of Confederate military power by inflicting blows on its communications network, factories, and administrative structures; that is, he subjected public property to systematic destruction. He aimed to fatally undermine confidence in Confederate leadership and its chosen direction, its ability to wage war, and its fragile international prestige. Sherman expressed his aims cogently in a letter of November 1864

when he affirmed he would "act in such a manner against the material resources of the South as utterly to negative Davis's boasted threat and promises
of protection."[12]

Sherman's main aim was thus psychological: to create fear and damage the
Confederacy's prestige and self-respect, as well as the esteem in which it was
held abroad; to demonstrate in the most humiliating fashion the incompetence and impotence of the Confederate government and its generals; and
to show that the Confederacy had no right to exist. Sherman's strategy made
an immensely significant contribution to the psychological dimensions of
Union strategy and the propaganda war because of its "zero-sum" character.
As Southern enthusiasm for war diminished, the confidence and pride of
Northern opinion soared. If Confederate defeat resulted from the superior
power of the North, then the strength of Northern support for war has been
underestimated as a factor in the Confederate collapse of 1865. So, too, has
Sherman's role in boosting that support, especially by his taking of Atlanta
and his courage in launching the Marches when surrounded by doubt.[13]

Sherman sought nothing less than to turn the South's self-righteous arrogance and pride—manifest in its newspapers and political speeches—against
it. The historian Lee Kennett suggests that "in a sense" Sherman made war "on
the southern mind," but this is too nebulous an objective, though he did attack its powers of endurance. In the winter of 1864-65 Jefferson Davis talked
boldly of throwing back Sherman's advance into Georgia, transforming it into
a "retreat from Moscow"; other officials, both military and civil, talked loudly
of destroying all the supplies in Sherman's path. All this verbiage proved
empty. But Sherman advanced toward and contiguously with the Atlantic
Ocean and made the most of Union naval dominance. The sea delimited
his advance neatly and prevented any temptation to overreach himself. As
most of South and North Carolina had been virtually untouched by the war,
Sherman calculated shrewdly that panic and exaggeration would do his job
for him, and he was proved right. The hysterical edge of opinion in the Deep
South released fears of murder and rapine once associated with emancipation that were quickly transferred to Sherman and his troops. This com-
pound reinforced Sherman's desired image of an unstoppable omnipotent
juggernaut trampling over Confederate resistance. During the Marches, destruction served as the means to achieve a strategic end, not the end. Though
the plantations of the Southern ruling class were targeted, the amount of private property—as opposed to public property—destroyed has been greatly
exaggerated. Even Liddell Hart's praise for the "physical and moral" effect of

the Marches, which resulted in "unchecked progress," relies on Confederate accounts that stressed the destruction of private property rather than on a grasp of the true subtlety of Sherman's psychological attack.[14]

The suggestion that Sherman's strategy was primarily aimed at civilians and their property accounts for the controversy that has besmirched his reputation. Harsh judgments are misplaced because the idea of "civilians" as a "distinct category" had only emerged at the beginning of the nineteenth century; questions of what boundaries defined "civilians" and what protections they enjoyed were not acknowledged until the century's end. Francis Lieber does not use the term "civilian" in his famous code, which Sherman faithfully followed. "The citizen or native of a hostile country," he writes, "is thus an enemy, as one of the constituents of a hostile state or nation, and as such is subjected to the hardships of the war." In short, Lieber argued that they could not somehow opt out of the war in which they were involved.[15]

Why, then, should perpetual negative judgment be expressed in the court of public opinion when dealing with Sherman's actions and legacy? Such a negative reaction can only be explained by reference to what Matthew Carr calls the "elevated moral aura" that so often surrounds American warmaking. This has involved complex issues of military law and ethics. A complicating tendency is the persistent influence of the Southern intellectual movement known as the Lost Cause that posits a gallant, chivalrous, nimble Confederacy ground down by the overwhelming legions of a ruthless, soulless industrial machine that overcame the more noble cause—a refined form of historical sentimentalism. John B. Walters's *Merchant of Terror: General Sherman and Total War* (1973) exemplifies the genre. His is an unfailingly critical work that ends with the burning of Columbia. Sherman, concludes Walters, "set himself up to judge what constituted right and wrong." He expounded "a terrorist philosophy" and employed "a mode of warfare which transgressed all ethical rules and showed an utter disregard for human rights and dignity." Under his tutelage, Union soldiers learned "to direct their hatred against the people of the South."[16]

Numerous Sherman admirers have linked him with the successful conduct of "total war" in the twentieth century. But revulsion against the conduct of the Vietnam War broadened the appeal of Walters's denunciations of Sherman and total war waged against the South at a time when "total war" appeared to be an "inevitable" phase in war's evolution. What James Reston Jr. found reprehensible was Sherman's "intellectual justification for it [total war], his lack of remorse at it, his readiness to distort the record for psychological advantage." His malign intent planted "the Sherman seed for the Agent Orange and Agent Blue programs of food deprivation in Vietnam." And he did this and so much else all by himself. But ultimately the identification of Sherman with "total war" has damaged his reputation because of an erroneous assumption that "total war" and morality are incompatible. It accounts for Sherman's identification in folklore with Ivan the Terrible, and the harder ideological edge of neo-Confederate apologists has led to greater venom being thrown at Sherman in the twenty-first century than ever during his lifetime, as a "barbarian, a hooligan and a war criminal."[17]

What is striking about these indictments is their lack of context, the neglect of the legacy of the guerrilla war in Missouri, and the attribution to Sherman of actions he did not undertake. Sherman's veterans did not need him to teach them how to punish rebels. Furthermore, the concept of "total war" is deeply flawed, an imprecise label that at best describes the two world wars but is of dubious relevance to the US Civil War. For all the vivid descriptions of desolation in *Merchant of Terror* implying that the entire states of Georgia and South Carolina were devastated, depicting conditions akin to a nuclear winter, Walters fails to explain why so few of the residents of these states were killed or even seriously assaulted. The conduct of French troops in Calabria, Italy, in 1806–11 was far worse, with mass executions and deportations on a scale not witnessed in 1861–65. Nor did the citizens of Atlanta suffer a fraction of the privations, pain, and heartbreak endured during the siege of Genoa, Italy, in 1800, where 15,000 starved to death. And compared with the treatment of the residents of Georgia, who Walters admitted were permitted to act as "individuals," reluctant to destroy their own property, in Portugal in 1810 and Russia in 1812 people were forced to destroy their crops and property by their own side.[18]

Although Sherman's biographers have done much to improve understanding of the context in which he operated, they have done so only through the lens of the American experience when comparison with foreign wars is equally important. Walters's assertion that "the persons of non-combatants were considered inviolate under the rules of war" before 1861 is rendered absurd by such comparisons. Significantly, Sherman never claimed that his Marches were major, innovative departures from historical practice. No matter how "total" we might consider them, they should not be regarded as clear-cut alternatives to Grant's methods but as subordinate, complementary, attritional acts. Sherman could reduce his casualties and mount his dazzling maneuvers only because of John B. Hood's impulsive gamble of mounting an invasion of Tennessee. Had he not done so, Sherman would have had little choice but to continue to advance on Savannah, slowly, step by step, regardless of increased casualties, as he had done when capturing Atlanta. He could have been overthrown on the famous Marches if Confederate commanders had shown more skill in defense.[19]

When Sherman's strategy is judged by the standards of the mid-nineteenth century, free of so much didactic and distorting polemical encrustation, what is his final achievement? He made a massive contribution to Union victory. "His plan," the historian Donald Stoker recognizes, "was strategy at its grandest." The greatest risks that Sherman took were strategic. He struck directly at the Confederacy's ability to wage war and concentrated on bringing the war to a rapid and decisive end. His philosophy of war appears more restrained than he has been given credit for. Even his postwar operations reflect this tendency. He always attempted to deter conflict and acted only to punish those who had broken the peace. Once he had set out to punish the Confederates, his strategy exhibited three outstanding features. First and foremost, it worked. Once Atlanta fell, Sherman quickly turned Confederate defiance into a stupor of hopelessness. Second, he rapidly grasped—mainly thanks to his reading on the Napoleonic Wars and Napier's *History*—that the Enlightenment laws of war had been rendered otiose. They had been replaced by a vague ethic of "humanitarian constraint" because it was assumed that issues of "justice" could not be resolved once armies took the field. The status of "civil wars" as a distinct category long remained ambiguous and understudied. Such wars had not been included under the rubric of the initial Geneva Convention of 1864. Sherman confronted this ambiguity; was he dealing with disruptive violence, rebellion, revolution, or war? By the summer of 1862 he deduced that if "humanitarian constraint" were offered unconditionally, winning any war would be immensely difficult. Third, he treated these complex issues as one central question that demanded a synthesis rather than a series of ad hoc responses. He hoped to reduce overall casualties and suffering, though his method appears provoking: for "the more awful you can make war the sooner it will be over." Yet his interpretation of "awfulness" had been defined by Lieber's Code and "military necessity"—the paramount need for the Union to attain an overwhelming and complete victory. Still, it would be a mistake to believe that his governing idea required the abandonment of morality. To suggest otherwise is patent nonsense. It smugly assumes the maintenance of what the legal historian John Fabian Witt calls "the easy nostrums of restraints in wartime" when they had been overtaken by overall levels of violence on both sides.[20]

Sherman's responses to the vagaries of civil war indicate the power and acuity of his intellect and an ability to focus on key issues and synthesize them into a coherent and practicable military solution. Yet for all these qualities, Sherman's great contribution remains both subordinate and subsidiary to Grant's. Sherman could enfeeble the Confederacy by his chosen method but not bring it tumbling down. This would only occur once its premier and redoubtable field army, Lee's Army of Northern Virginia, had been pursued and forced to capitulate. The historian T. Harry Williams's verdict has stood the test of time: "Sherman was not the man to deliver the last great blow."[21]

How did Sherman recollect his prolonged experience of warfare? His most frequently quoted declaration is "War is hell." Sherman's son P. Tecumseh Sherman denied that he had ever said it and suggested that it was a "popular version" of his response to the mayor of Atlanta in September 1864: "War is cruelty and you cannot refine it." The provenance of Sherman's remark is complicated because the phrase does not survive in his own hand. As an accomplished public speaker, he rarely used a prepared text. He did have a consistent and well-thought-out message that he adapted to cater to individual audiences. He quickly forgot the detail of what had been said, and we are often reliant on reporters' accounts or the conversations recorded long after the event. Tecumseh Sherman did concede the possibility that these words were used in one of his father's "many unprepared speeches," and this seems the most likely source of the phrase.[22]

Whatever Sherman's precise words, there can be little doubt that he expressed a sentiment that is frequently admitted by experienced soldiers. Though Sherman repeated himself, the source that is rather arbitrarily given an authority over all other occasions is the meeting of the Grand Army of the Republic held at the Ohio State Fair Grounds, in Columbus, on August 11, 1880. This visit was part of Rutherford B. Hayes's trip to the West during which Sherman accompanied the president. Hayes was the guest speaker, and he was pleased with his speech, which he delivered well before a large, rain-drenched crowd, with 5,000 veterans placed at the front; he thought the affair "very successful," but he had no idea that anything memorable had been said. The veterans called for Sherman, and his remarks were brief. He joked about the weather not deterring his old soldiers. He referred to himself as "Uncle Billy" and admitted his love for them "as his own flesh and blood." His key phrase came quickly. "There is many a boy here today who looks at war as all glory, but boys, it is all hell." The year before, Sherman said something similar at the Michigan Military Academy graduation ceremony. There he commented that "it is only those who have never fired a shot nor heard the shrieks and groans of the wounded who cry aloud for blood, more vengeance, more desolation. War is hell." There can be little doubt that this is an individual and authentic sentiment. But Sherman did not mean that war lacked utility or purpose; quite the contrary. At Columbus he added: "I look upon war with horror"—which was true, for he revealed something less than enthusiasm for war in 1861—"but if it has to come I am here."[23]

Sherman referred to the experience of combat of individual soldiers, not to war's general nature or purpose. His prime target was the thick layer of sentimentality that had been applied to battle in novels and plays by writers with no military experience, neglecting its harsh realities and unendurable suffering. By the 1880s, as the military analyst Theo Farrell has observed, war had "become an entertainment in its own right." War had been recast as an exciting, colorful adventure sold by the spurious glamor that Sherman at the Michigan Military Academy had derided as "moonshine." Death, dirt, boredom, exhaustion physical and moral, gnawing and all-pervasive fear, and disease, the greatest killer of all, were more likely to overbear the soldier. Sherman had seen it all. But a positive outcome could be attained. The young simply had to face facts and learn from Civil War veterans while they still could. Sherman urged attendance at the Grand Army of the Republic's campfires, which he extolled, to discover the true reason why the Union "owe[s] its debt of gratitude" to its veterans. What Sherman did not offer was a catchall justification or description of the nature of war that sanctioned any lack of restraint. As Matthew Carr rightly observes, those who intone "war is hell" most frequently are those determined to make it so, and far more hellish than anything experienced on the Marches.[24]

This man of achievement was in many respects a sympathetic character, likable and much liked, who enjoyed extraordinary restless energy, but he could be choleric, impulsive, and vindictive if crossed. Like many another fiery cuss, he mellowed with age. Sherman had always been a turbulent spirit with strong partialities and prejudices, laced with humor of the teasing, hyperbolic Western kind. He could be a harsh judge of character—as successful generals must be—and if he once lost respect, even for a friend, such as Halleck, that respect could never be regained. Sherman also allowed passion to get the better of his judgment. His dislike of reporters continued into old age long after he had been courted by them, and his harshness toward them ranks among his most incorrigible and foolish errors. Some of his worst strictures were made on paper late at night after the odd glass of bourbon when overtired and unable to sleep because of asthma. Then matters always appear more lamentable than they truly are.[25]

Though he was accused by some of his biographers of narcissistic tendencies, the bedrock of his life and actions was an unchallenged integrity never tainted by disappointment and failure. He always inspired trust. William M. Thackeray, one of his favorite authors, claims that "scandal almost always does master people: especially good and innocent people." Though occasionally Sherman skated on thin ice, it never mastered him. He could be vain and succumb to overconfidence, as in his ill-fated negotiations with Joseph E. Johnston in April 1865. Yet he could also reveal pellucid self-knowledge. He refused to try to supplant Grant in 1867 and resisted all later efforts to make him a presidential candidate. Sherman's view that he had always been too highly strung and voluble to make a good president should be regarded as the correct one. He did not allow ambition or vainglory to tempt him. Some of his outbursts against the inertia and inefficiency of democratic institutions during a prolonged period of national crisis have led to overheated interpretation. He has been accused of preferring dictatorship and showing "dictatorial" tendencies himself. His "ego seemed boundless," says his biographer Michael Fellman, with absurd hints that he masqueraded as a proto-fascist. These are grave imputations but can be dismissed without hesitation. In the spring of 1862 Sherman wrote to his foster father, "I contend we are fighting for the supremacy of *Written* Law, as against the rule of mere party and popular prejudice." He denigrated the shifting moods and whims of popular opinion and its "cupidity"—but then so did many of his contemporaries. He only regarded dictatorship negatively in the Roman sense, "to restrain the excesses" of popular anxiety at times of crisis and to defend constitutional freedom. Such opinions and fears of the "wild, terrible despotism of mobs, vigilante committees or any species of irresponsible crowds" denote the terrible and lasting scars inflicted on Sherman's character by his experiences in California in 1856. They do not represent an exact ideological choice.[26]

Edmund Burke once commented that good government required two qualities, wisdom and virtue. Sherman had plenty of the latter but was deficient in the former, lacking balance and patience. He always needed a boss to advise him and save him from his errors, usually Grant. His understanding of this need ultimately explains why he did not want to be president. It should also be recalled that expressions in favor of dictatorship were surprisingly common during the crises of 1862-63.[27]

He might have relied on instinct and sometimes less consistently on good sense, but the place of the intellect had a high priority in his life. Sherman may be numbered among the ranks of the most prominent nineteenth-century American intellectuals in the sense of being interested in the pursuit of ideas and having an intrinsic respect for them. He had an insatiable intellectual curiosity and omnivorous appetite for books, not just in literature but in the law, history, geography, and the natural sciences. Sherman's most important gifts were his synthetic mental faculties: the power to think creatively and reflect on war profoundly but in the round, not just particular aspects of it. He could also adapt his thinking to the circumstances in which he operated. Though his assumptions could be faulty—he could never understand that the strength of Northern public opinion underwrote his successes, for instance—his deductions were often sound and sometimes inspired. He developed his plans combining the dimensions of both thought and practice. What did he want to do and how did he intend to carry his design out? Though he was superficially less learned than Halleck, his thinking was less derivative and pedantic and more original. Only Sherman could have carried out the Great Marches, no matter how much he owed to others on the way. The combination of thought and practice explains Sherman's infinite superiority over Halleck in his power to make things happen.

Intellectuals display sensitivity, a quality that Lee Kennett believes Sherman lacked "in the same way most of us [do]." However, an excess of it, as exhibited by George B. McClellan, especially in 1862, leads to hesitation and mental confusion. Architects of victory, like revolutionaries, require sterner qualities, not sentimentality. Sherman focused remorselessly on his objective. John B. Walters argues that Sherman had a "butterfly mind." He flitted from one idea to another lightly and inconsequentially. This claim, based on the reminiscences of his old Louisiana friend David Boyd that Sherman's mind moved like "lightning to its conclusions," suggests rapidity of thought rather than superficiality. All of Sherman's writings, correspondence, reports, and published works are cogent, well organized, and skilfully argued; none are diffuse. Not for nothing is Sherman the most quoted American after Lincoln. He was a dazzling literary stylist.[28]

But Sherman's thoughts on the thousands of slaves he freed are rarely supportive and sometimes, in private, scornful. His short-sightedness toward African Americans is usually agreed to be a serious blemish on his record and deserves attention. In 1888 he made up for his previous attitude with a remarkable essay, "Old Shady, with a Moral," a reference to a freed slave employed as a cook by James McPherson in the Vicksburg campaign who gave his name to a song he composed, "his own song of deliverance from the bonds of slavery." After retirement Sherman gave more thought to the role of slavery in the coming of the war and the role of black Americans in it. He had always shown pride in his claim that he had freed more slaves than any other commander. Now the scales fell from his eyes, and they did so at a propitious time—just on the cusp of the concerted effort to write the black contribution to the war out of the historical record. Michael Fellman considers this essay an act of redemption, but it is more important as an effort to bring his public views more in line with his private behavior. It is also a lucid statement of the nature of the Union cause and its everlasting symbolic significance. Sherman realized that this was in danger of being submerged by Confederate views as the nostrums of the Lost Cause gained wide acceptance in both North and South. The essay also has attractive perversity. Just at a time when the "solid South" sought to defraud and intimidate blacks out of their voting rights and Northerners neglected their pleas for justice, Sherman announced, "I confess that I feel partial to the colored people of the United States."[29]

The essay contains some mature reflections on the slave system that Sherman had defended in 1859-60. In the second edition of his *Memoirs*, published in 1886, he freely asserted that slavery was the Civil War's "chief cause." He also declared that the field hands were "treated like animals" and expressed incredulity "that such things could be." He paid tribute to those "lovely people who toiled in the fields to raise corn" to feed Confederate armies "whom they knew to be employed to perpetuate their own bondage." He also praised their unconditional support during the war, sheltering prisoners of war, succoring fleeing or lost Union soldiers, and providing valuable information. Even as the Confederacy crumbled, they "did *not* resort to the torch and dagger" as Caribbean slaves had done during uprisings. He warned the South that it played with fire again and might ignite another civil war. Then he made his clarion call with no thought of personal gain: "Let the Negro vote and count his vote honestly." His final plea placed him astride the main current of Union liberalism. "Let us freely accord to the Negro his fair share of influence and power, trusting the perpetuity of our institutions to the everlasting principles of human nature which tolerate all races and all colors." Lincoln and Grant could not have put it better, but within three years he had joined them in death, that restless pen thrown down forever, and despite its abundant sincerity, the message and the moral of "Old Shady" went unheeded. This change of sentiment had come far too late.[30]

Sherman's attitude to race forms a blind spot rectified belatedly. The fusion of thought and practice in other areas galvanized his military conduct. He proved himself a highly successful general but did not lack faults. He never won an offensive battle, except Resaca, and his period of independent command seems short, less than a year, compared with the Duke of Wellington's seven years in the Peninsular War or the Duke of Marlborough's decade in the Low Countries. But his strengths greatly outweighed his weaknesses. He made a pioneering contribution to the American interpretation of strategy and the operational level of war that would gain in authority after his death and determine a revised version of the laws of war. In the last phase of his career he made a positive contribution to debates over the role, structure, and doctrine of the US Army in peacetime. Equally significant, in his *Memoirs* and other writings, he discussed the overall significance of the Civil War and reviewed what could be learned from it and the transcendent nature of its legacy.

Sherman's importance is indisputable, as icon, hate figure, or moral scapegoat—the one to blame for all the aspects of the United States of their time of which so many diverse writers have disapproved. This latter role sometimes has scant connection with the reality of what he achieved and how he went about achieving it in his own life. But the good greatly outweighed the ill. Sherman had the courage of his convictions, despite his early failures and humiliations and hesitant false start in 1861. He never lost faith in the destiny of the United States and fulfilled a promise to help make it one again and then remake it.

Notes

Introduction

1. Mark E. Neely Jr., *The Civil War and the Limits of Destruction* (Cambridge, MA: Harvard University Press, 2007), 2, 201; he believes, on the contrary, that the war revealed "remarkable . . . traditional restraint" (106–7, 108, 197). The latter phrase is Major General J. F. C. Fuller's; see *The Conduct of War, 1789–1961* (London: Eyre and Spottiswoode, 1961), 107.
2. Roger Spiller, *An Instinct for War* (Cambridge, MA: Belknap Press of Harvard University Press, 2005), 243.
3. Roger H. Nye, *The Challenge of Command* (Wayne, NJ: Avery, 1986), 27.
4. Brian Holden Reid, "How Were American Civil War Armies Kept in the Field?" in *Raise, Train and Sustain* , ed. Peter Dennis and Jeffery Grey (Loftus, NSW: Australian Military History Publications, 2010), 17–18.
5. See the wise discussion in A. P. Wavell, *Generals and Generalship* (Harmondsworth: Penguin, 1941), 27, 25.
6. Nye, *Challenge of Command*, 81. My interpretation diverges markedly from that of Michael Fellman, *Citizen Sherman: The Life of William Tecumseh Sherman* (New York: Random House, 1995), 122–23, 146, 182–83, which emphasizes a sweeping mood swing that unleashes "destructive rage" on the South.
7. T. Harry Williams, *McClellan, Sherman and Grant* (New Brunswick, NJ: Rutgers University Press, 1962), 67; for a dissenting view, see Michael Fellman, *Citizen Sherman* (New York: Random House, 1995), 73n.
8. Richard Hofstadter, *Anti-Intellectualism in American Life* (London: Jonathan Cape, 1964), 27.
9. The difference is highlighted by a remark made in 1986 by the historian Michael Biddis, later president of the Historical Association (1991–94) and joint vice president of the Royal Historical Society (1995–99), at a seminar I gave at the University of Reading on the relationship of history to contemporary strategic studies: "the duty of the historian is to ask the right *questions*, not provide the answers." Such a view is anathema to the military intellectual.
10. Hofstadter, *Anti-Intellectualism in American Life*, 145–46. The populist tendency, as Hofstadter observes, elevated "inborn, intuitive, folkish wisdom over the cultivated, oversophisticated, and self-interested knowledge of the literati and the well-to-do" (154). For Grant's habit of concealing his knowledge and views, see Michael B. Ballard, *U. S. Grant: The Making of a General, 1861–1863* (Lanham, MD: Rowan and Littlefield, 2005), 3; "Speech to the 166 Ohio Regiment," August 22, 1864, in

The Collected Works of Abraham Lincoln, ed. Roy P. Basler, 9 vols. (New Brunswick, NJ: Rutgers University Press, 1953), 7:512.

11. Sherman to Henry W. Halleck, January 12, 1865, in *Correspondence*, 795.

12. Seymour Martin Lipset and Earl Raab, *The Politics of Unreason: Right-Wing Extremism in America, 1790-1970* (London: Heinemann, 1971), 34–71.

13. Fellman, *Citizen Sherman*, 182–83, gives the opposite view and refers to Sherman's "considerable terrorist capacities.... Sherman's vision was the most explicit as well as the most inhumane about the meanings of war."

14. See Edith Wharton, *Hudson River Bracketed* (1929; London: Virago, 1986), 113, where the heroine observes, "You see, books have souls, like people."

Chapter 1

1. The name Sherman means a "shearer of woollen cloth"; see P. H. Reaney, *A Dictionary of British Surnames* (London: Routledge and Kegan Paul, 1958), 292. Only Stanley P. Hirshson, *The White Tecumseh: A Biography of William T. Sherman* (New York: Wiley, 1997), 1–2, deals with the Sherman line.

2. B. H. Liddell Hart, *Sherman* (London: Ernest Benn, 1930), 11; Anthony Bailey, *John Constable: A Kingdom of His Own* (London: Chatto and Windus, 2006), 4, 6–7, 119; Jean Goodman, "Munnings, Sir Alfred James (1878–1959)," *Oxford Dictionary of National Biography*, 64 vols. (Oxford: Oxford University Press, 2004), 39:761–64 (hereafter *ODNB*).

3. Norden quoted in William Hunt, *The Puritan Moment: The Coming of Revolution in an English County* (Cambridge, MA: Harvard University Press, 1983), 5, 10–11, 317n1; *A History of the County of Essex*, vol. 10, *Lexden Hundred (Part)*, ed. Janet Cooper (London: Victoria County History, 2001), 157, 173, 174 (hereafter *VCH Essex*); wills of July 31, 1599, 45/24 and January 20, 1590, 34/51 in F. G. Emmisson, *Elizabethan Life: Wills of Essex Gentry Merchants* (Chelmsford: Essex County Council, 1978), 308–9.

4. Hunt, *Puritan Moment*, 144–48; *VCH Essex*, 180; Jason Yiannikkou, "Rogers, John (ca. 1570-1636)," *ODNB* 47:562–63; Patrick McGrath, *Papists and Puritans under Elizabeth I* (London: Blandford, 1967), 210–11; on the Puritan passion for learning, see David Hackett Fischer, *Albion's Seed: Four British Folkways in America* (New York: Oxford University Press, 1989), 133–34.

5. *VCH Essex*, 160; Hunt, *Puritan Moment*, 202–3; *Memoirs* (1889) 1:9; Christopher Hill, *The Century of Revolution, 1603-1714* (London: Thomas Nelson, 1961), 54–55. Billeting was prohibited by the Petition of Right (1628), to which Charles I had acceded. For a defense of the king's policy, see Kevin Sharpe, *The Personal Rule of Charles I* (New Haven, CT: Yale University Press, 1992), 40–42.

6. Hunt, *Puritan Moment*, 248, 252, 253–55, 260–61; N. A. M. Roger, *The Safeguard of the Sea: A Naval History of Britain, 660-1649* (New York: Norton, 1997), 342; Hill, *Century of Revolution*, 56–57; Sharpe, *Personal Rule of Charles I*, 605–8.

7. Hooker, quoted in Hunt, *Puritan Moment*, 243, and also see 163–64, 277; Conrad Russell, "Hampden, Sir John (1594-1643)," *ODNB* 24:976–84; Fischer, *Albion's*

Seed, 25, 26, 27–28, 39–40. There was a reciprocal relationship between Dedham and Emmanuel College, as its students traveled there to hear "Roaring" Rogers; see *VCH Essex*, 180. Christopher Hill, *God's Englishman: Oliver Cromwell and the English Revolution* (London: Weidenfeld and Nicolson, 1970), 40–41; "John Sherman," in John Eliot, *A Biographical Dictionary: Containing a Brief Account of the First Settlers* (Salem, MA: Cushing and Appleton, 1809), 427–28; Sharpe, *Personal Rule of Charles I*, 720–30, 756–57; see also Joke Kardux and Edward van der Bilt, *Newcomers in an Old City: The American Pilgrims in Leiden, 1609–1620*, 3rd rev. ed. (Leiden: Uitgeverij and Niermans, 2007), 26–27, on the intermediate refuge before traveling to the New World.

8. Marcus Cunliffe, *In Search of America* (New York: Greenwood Press, 1991), 34; *Memoirs* (1889) 1:9. The most prominent was Roger Sherman, who signed all the great documents of the Continental Congress, culminating in the Constitution (1787). See "Sherman, Roger, 1722–1793," in Mark M. Boatner, *Cassell's Biographical Dictionary of the American War of Independence* (London: Cassell, 1973), 1003–4; John Sherman, *Recollections of Forty Years in the House, Senate and Cabinet*, 2 vols. (Chicago: Werner, 1895), 1:26–27.

9. Daniel J. Boorstin, *The Americans: The Colonial Experience* (New York: Random House, 1958), 20; Michael Kammen, *People of Paradox: An Inquiry concerning the Origins of American Civilization* (New York: Alfred A. Knopf, 1972), 29, 42, 43, 45–46, 47. On anxieties over "the singular charm" of Indian life, its "most perfect freedom, the ease of living, and the absence of those cares and corroding solicitudes" of civilized being, see J. Hector St. Jean de Crevecoeur, *Letters from an American Farmer*, ed. Albert E. Stone (1782; Harmondsworth: Penguin, 1981), 213–14; these attracted the young especially (see 215–25). John Sherman gives a clear and fuller summary of the family tree than his brother, though he confuses the first two Edmund Shermans mentioned in this chapter (*Recollections* 1:5); so, too, does "The Sherman Family," *New York Times*, February 19, 1865.

10. *Memoirs* (1889) 1:9–10; John Sherman, *Recollections* 1:12–14; Richard Hofstadter, *America at 1750: A Social Portrait* (London: Jonathan Cape, 1972), 148–51; Mark V. Krasny, *Washington's Partisan War, 1775–1783* (Kent, OH: Kent State University Press, 1996), 243–46, 276–77, 308–11, 314–15. It is well to recall that 30,000 Loyalists fought for the British and 80,000 went into exile; Esmond Wright, *Fabric of Freedom, 1763–1800* (London: Macmillan, 1965), 126. On the Revolution as a civil war, see Cunliffe, *In Search of America*, 41.

11. Charles Sellers, *The Market Revolution: Jacksonian America, 1815–1846* (New York: Oxford University Press, 1991), 16, 18–19; John Sherman, *Recollections* 1:15; Henry Adams, *History of the United States during the Administrations of Thomas Jefferson*, 4 vols. (1889; New York: Library of America, 1986), 1:7, 9, 12, evokes the challenges of traveling across the wilderness.

12. John Sherman, *Recollections* 1:16–18; J. W. Fortescue, *A History of the British Army*, 13 vols. (London: Macmillan, 1917), 8:529–31; Harry L. Coles, *The War of 1812* (Chicago: University of Chicago Press, 1965), 50–56; John Sugden, *Tecumseh: A Life* (New York: Henry Holt, 1997), 304.

13. Anna McAllister, *Ellen Ewing: Wife of General Sherman* (New York: Benziger, 1936), 4–5, 5–6; Ella Lonn, *Salt as a Factor in the Confederacy* (1933; Tuscaloosa: University of Alabama Press, 1965), 19, 20; Lloyd Lewis, *Sherman: Fighting Prophet* (1932; New York: Harcourt Brace, 1958), 3–17, 24; Sellers, *Market Revolution*, 74.

14. Fischer, *Albion's Seed*, 62–68; McAllister, *Ellen Ewing*, 7; *Memoirs* (1889) 1:11; Carl R. Schenker Jr., "'My Father Named Me William *Tecumseh*': Rebutting the Charge That General Sherman Lied about His Name," *Ohio History* 115 (2008): 50, 61, 62–66, and on Lewis's sources, see 71, 72, 73; Lewis, *Sherman*, 33–34; Michael Fellman, *Citizen Sherman: A Life of William Tecumseh Sherman* (New York: Random House, 1995), 6–9.

15. *Memoirs* (1889) 1:11; Sugden, *Tecumseh*, 391–93, on his Canadian status; on his strengths and weaknesses, 9, 65, 96, 127, 314, 354, 358; on his hostility to the US, 178, 187, 212, 266; by not accompanying his regiment, Charles Sherman denied himself a chance of seeing his later hero—a prisoner of war at Detroit described him as "one of the finest looking men I have ever seen" (306). Note also British admiration in 1939-45 for Erwin Rommel; see Desmond Young, *Rommel* (1950; London: William Collins, 1972), 23.

16. *Memoirs* (1889) 1:12–13; John Sherman, *Recollections* 1:24; Lewis, *Sherman*, 27–28.

17. Duke of Saxe-Weimar, *Travels through North America during the Years 1825 and 1826*, 2 vols. (Philadelphia: Carey, Lea, and Carey, 1828), 2:152, and for his view of the wretchedness of Indiana, see 126; Lewis, *Sherman*, 26–29, evokes Sherman's childhood beautifully. Also see Michael F. Holt, *The Rise and Fall of the Whig Party* (New York: Oxford University Press, 1999), 5–11; Corwin quoted in William R. Brock, *Parties and Political Conscience: American Dilemmas, 1840-1850* (Millwood, NY: KTO Press, 1979), 10; for an allusion to "King Andrew I," see the cartoon opposite 556 in Holt's *Whig Party*.

18. *Memoirs* (1889) 1:13–14; John Sherman, *Recollections* 1:28–29 ("Everybody was kind," he recalls). Lampson was adopted by another distinguished lawyer, Charles Hammond of Cincinnati.

19. John Sherman, *Recollections* 1:30,32; McAllister, *Ellen Ewing*, 10; Lewis, *Sherman*, 39–40; but see John F. Marszalek, *Sherman: A Soldier's Passion for Order* (New York: Free Press, 1993), 15, who develops a plausible case that Sherman remained "apart" being caught "in the middle" between two families. But this reaction depends on the circumstances. My maternal grandparents informally adopted a young adult woman in 1942. She then cut herself off completely from her natural family, of whom I knew nothing until after her death in 2006.

20. Lewis, *Sherman*, 39–40; McAllister, *Ellen Ewing*, 12, 13, 14.

21. See the allusions in Marszalek, *Sherman*, 12–13; John Sherman, *Recollections* 1:32–33, 34.

22. McAllister, *Ellen Ewing*, 17.

23. *Memoirs* (1889) 1:14–15, 16; McAlister, *Ellen Ewing*, 17.

24. *Memoirs* (1889) 1:16–17; Charles Dickens, *American Notes* (1892 ed.; London: Granville, 1985), 147–49. The 1840 class was typical; see Stephen E. Ambrose, *Duty, Honor, Country: A History of West Point* (Baltimore: Johns Hopkins

University Press, 1966), 83. James L. Morrison, *"The Best School in the World": West Point, 1833-1866* (Kent, OH: Kent State University Press, 1986), 64 (hereafter *Best School*); the average pass rate 1833-54 stood at 48.1 percent (106).

25. Marcus Cunliffe, *Soldiers and Civilians: The Martial Spirit in America, 1775-1865*, 3rd ed. (London: Gregg, 1993), 162–63, 164, 166; Morrison, *Best School*, 61–62, 66, 73: many, like Sherman, sprang from "rural small towns" and were members of the rising middle class rather than an "aristocracy."

26. Though Sherman, as usual, in 1872 hurried to underline that he was not "a Sunday school cadet"; see Lewis, *Sherman*, 56 . On the syllabus, see John W. Brinsfield, "The Military Ethics of General William T. Sherman: A Reassessment," in *The Parameters of War*, ed. Lloyd Matthews and D. E. Brown (New York: Pergamon-Brassey's, 1989), 89–92; and Morrison, *Best School*, 23–24, 113, especially on "the Chaplain's Course," though its elements could be found in any civilian college of the period.

27. Ambrose, *Duty, Honor, Country*, 63–69, 90, 166; Hirshson, *White Tecumseh*, 15; Correlli Barnett, "The Education of Military Elites," in *Governing Elites: Studies in Training and Selection*, ed. Rupert Wilkinson (New York: Oxford University Press, 1969), 204; Morrison, *Best School*, 31, 35, 59–60, 91, 100, 105, 144–15, notes many contemporary criticisms of a mathematical bias and the resistance of the scientific faculty to any changes to their approach; Sherman to Ellen Ewing, May 13, July 10, 1837, CSHR 9/19 UNDA.

28. *Memoirs* (1889) 1:16; Morrison, *Best School*, 49, 50–51, 52–53; John F. Marszalek, *Commander of All Lincoln's Armies: A Life of General Henry W. Halleck* (Cambridge, MA: Belknap Press of Harvard University Press, 2004), 25–26; Hirshson, *White Tecumseh*, 15; Oliver O. Howard, *Autobiography*, 2 vols. (New York: Baker Taylor, 1904), 1:55–56, offers a shrewd assessment of Bartlett; Ambrose, *Duty, Honor, Country*, 91–96, 99–102.

29. Ambrose, *Duty, Honor, Country*, 80; Sherman to Ellen Ewing, July 10, 1837 CSHR 9/19 UNDA; Walter H. Hebert, *Fighting Joe Hooker* (Indianapolis: Bobbs-Merrill, 1944), 21; Marszalek, *Halleck*, 26; Freeman Cleaves, *Rock of Chickamauga: The Life of General George H. Thomas* (1948; Norman: University of Oklahoma Press, 1978), 9–10; on West Point food and Benny Haven's Tavern, see Morrison, *Best School*, 77–78.

30. Sherman to Ellen Sherman, February 20, 1838, CSHR 9/19 UNDA.

31. Sherman to John Sherman, December 6, 1837, January 9, 1839, in *The Sherman Letters*, ed. Rachel Sherman Thorndike (New York: Scribner's, 1894), 3, 6–7; Sherman to Ellen Ewing, November 24, 1838, January 22, 1839, CHSR 9/19, UNDA.

32. Sherman to Ellen Ewing, October 22, 1837, December 10, 1838, May 4, August 21, 1839, CSHR 9/19 UNDA; Sherman to John Sherman, September 15, 1838, *Sherman Letters*, 5.

33. The dispute over 12,000 square miles was settled by the Webster-Ashburton Treaty of 1842 60:40 in the United States' favor; see William Earl Weeks, *The New Cambridge History of American Foreign Relations*, vol. 1, *Dimensions of the Early American Empire, 1754-1865* (New York: Cambridge University Press, 2013), 154–55; Sherman to Ellen Ewing, November 1, 1839, CSHR 9/19 UNDA; Sherman to John Sherman, April 13, 1839, January 14, 1840, *Sherman Letters*, 8.

34. An edition translated by Captain John O'Connor was published by J. Seymour in New York in 1817. See Paul D. Casdorph, *Confederate General: R. S. Ewell* (Lexington: University Press of Kentucky, 2004), 14; Alan Schom, *Napoleon Bonaparte* (New York: HarperCollins, 1997), 375, 381–83.

35. See Mahan's letter of March 8, 1866, to the *New York Evening Post*, March 10, 1866, reprinted in the *Army and Navy Journal* 3 (March 31, 1866), 124–26; Ian C. Hope, *A Scientific Way of War: Antebellum Military Science, West Point, and the Origins of American Military Thought* (Lincoln: University of Nebraska Press, 2015), 124–26; Colonel Hope also makes a persuasive argument that Mahan did not act as a conduit for Baron Jomini's thought, see Ibid., 153, 155–56; Morrison, *Best School*, 49, 96, 153.

36. Sherman to Ellen Ewing, December 10, 1838, CSHR 9/20 UNDA; Morrison, *Best School*, 40–41.

37. Sherman to Ellen Sherman, June 5, 1840, CSHR 9/20/22 UNDA, in which he warned her that Judge Irvin was dying; *Memoirs* (1889) 1:16–17; Hirshson, *White Tecumseh*, 16–17, details these unfortunate closing episodes. Also see Stephen D. Engle, *Don Carlos Buell: Most Promising of All* (Chapel Hill: University of North Carolina Press, 1999), 17.

38. Adams, *History* 1:60, quotes the opinion of George Cabot that democracy leads to the "government of the worst." On Daniel Sherman as the source of his great-grandson's humorous bent, see the *New York Times*, February 19, 1865.

39. See Morrison's excellent comments in *Best School*, 153, for this and the following paragraph.

40. See Barnett, "Education of Military Elites," 198, on mathematics and West Point's machinelike efficiency—until the requirement changed; on the "indoctrination" of tradition, see the editor's "Elites and Effectiveness," in Wilkinson, *Governing Elites*, 223; Sherman to John Sherman, March 7, 1840, *Sherman Letters*, 12.

Chapter 2

1. Brooks D. Simpson, *Ulysses S. Grant: Triumph over Adversity, 1822–1865* (Boston: Houghton Mifflin, 2000), 9; Marcus Cunliffe, *Soldiers and Civilians: The Martial Spirit in America, 1775–1865*, 3rd ed. (London: Gregg, 1993), 127, 130. The 1970s was the only other period when USMA graduates resigned as soon as they could; see Ward Just, *Military Men* (London: Michael Joseph, 1972), 32; James L. Morrison Jr, *"The Best School in the World": West Point, 1833–1866* (Kent, OH: Kent State University Press, 1986), 10; Sherman to Ellen Ewing, April 7, 1842, CSHR 9/22 UNDA.

2. *Memoirs* (1889) 2:18–19, 20–22.

3. Sherman to John Sherman, March 30, 1841, in *The Sherman Letters*, ed. Rachel Sherman Thorndike (New York: Charles Scribner's Sons, 1894), 14 (hereafter *SL*); Sherman to Ellen Ewing, September 7, 1841, CSHR 9/22 UNDA.

4. Sherman to John Sherman, January 16, March 30, 1841, *SL*, 14–15; *Memoirs* (1889), I, 25–27

5. Sherman to John Sherman, February 15, 1842, *SL*, 21; the unlucky might have to wait 34 years (see Cunliffe, *Soldiers and Civilians*, 131). Sherman to Ellen Ewing, January 13, 1842, CSHR 9/22 UNDA; *Memoirs* (1889) 1:27–28.

6. See James Lee McDonough, *William Tecumseh Sherman: In the Service of My Country* (New York: Norton, 2016), 69; Russell F. Weigley, *A Great Civil War: A Military and Political History* (Bloomington: Indiana University Press, 2000), xiv–xvii; *Memoirs* (1889) 1:27.

7. Sherman to Ellen Ewing, April 7, 1842, CSHR 9/22 UNDA; *Memoirs* (1889) 1:28.

8. *Memoirs* (1889) 1:28–29; Sherman to Ellen Ewing, November 28, 1842, March 12, 1843, CSHR 9/22/23 UNDA; Sherman to John Sherman, May 23, 1843, *SL*, 23. Compare Sherman's description of his painting technique with another artist's: "It was the bursting effort to concentrate that impressed his subjects. The studio seemed to throb with an electric energy as he worked. But somehow the moment of finishing never quite arrived." Michael Holroyd, *Augustus John*, 2 vols. (London: Heinemann, 1974–75), 2:105.

9. Sherman to Ellen Ewing, September 7, 1841, November 28, 1842, CSHR 9/22 UNDA; *Memoirs* (1889) 1:29; Anna McAllister, *Ellen Ewing: Wife of General Sherman* (New York: Benziger, 1936), 36–37.

10. John L. Stephens, *Incidents of Travel in Central America, Chiapas and Yucatan*, 10th ed., 2 vols. (London: John Murray, 1842); Sherman to Ellen Ewing, February 8, 1844, CSHR 9/23 UNDA.

11. The historical context of the Etowah mounds is established in Alan Taylor, *American Colonies* (New York: Viking, 2001), 16; *Memoirs* (1889) 1:30, 31–32; Sherman to John Sherman, January 19, 1844, *SL*, 24–25; Sherman to Ellen Ewing, November 28, 1842, CSHR 9/22 UNDA; on Anderson, see Ezra J. Warner, *Generals in Blue* (1964; Baton Rouge: Louisiana State University Press, 1989), 7–8.

12. Sherman to Ellen Ewing, February 8, 1844, CSHR 9/23 UNDA.

13. Sherman to Ellen Ewing, June 14, 1844, CSHR 9/23 UNDA; Sherman to John Sherman, March 7, 1840, *SL*, 12. John Sherman had been discouraged by their elder brother, Taylor, too; Lieutenant Sherman's doubts might have been informed by Taylor's tongue-tied diffidence before a jury. See John Sherman, *Recollections*, 2 vols. (Chicago: Weiner, 1895), 1:35, 49–50.

14. Sherman to Ellen Ewing, September 17, 1844, in *Home Letters of General Sherman*, ed. M. A. de Wolfe Howe (New York: Scribner's, 1909), 27; Sherman to John Sherman, October 24, 1844, *SL*, 26. John had been a loyal Whig since he was 16; see *Recollections* 1:45, 92–93. Sherman to Ellen Ewing, April 7, 1842, CSHR 9/22 UNDA; Ellen Ewing to Sherman, July 2, 1844, CSHR 9/30 UNDA.

15. John W. Brinsfield, "The Military Ethics of General William T. Sherman: A Reassessment," in *The Parameters of War*, ed. L. J. Matthews and D. E. Brown (New York: Pergamon-Brassey's, 1989), 88, 90–91. John Sherman followed a similar course of reading; see *Recollections* 1:50. Geoffrey Best, *Humanity in Warfare* (London: Weidenfeld and Nicolson, 1980), 40. The sixth edition of Vattel was published in Philadelphia by T. and J. W. Johnson in 1844. *A Normative Approach to War: Peace, War and Justice in Hugo Grotius*, ed. Yasuaki Onuma (Oxford: Clarendon

516 NOTES TO PAGES 42–46

Press, 1993), 58; John Fabian Witt, *Lincoln's Code: The Laws of War in American History* (New York: Free Press, 2012), 51, 72, 75, 76–77. Witt is rightly skeptical (85–86) on the depth of these studies at West Point; witnesses tend to assume that Sherman drew only upon his cadet reading in later disputes over military law. See Oliver O. Howard, *Autobiography*, 2 vols. (New York: Baker and Taylor, 1907), 1:57.

16. See Robert Wooster, *Nelson A. Miles and the Twilight of the Frontier Army* (Lincoln: University of Nebraska Press, 1993), 268; Grady McWhiney, *Braxton Bragg and Confederate Defeat*, vol. 1 (1969; Tuscaloosa: University of Alabama Press, 1991), 30, 34–35; *Memoirs* (1889) 1:32–33; Sherman to Ellen Ewing, June 9, 1845, January 30, 1846, *Home Letters*, 30, 31, though he told his brother "that if it [his chance] slides by . . . I must remain contented with my present commission." Sherman to John Sherman, January 4, 1846, *SL*, 30.

17. *Memoirs* (1889) 1:38–40; Sherman to Ellen Ewing, June 30, 1846, *Home Letters*, 34. Of his property, he wrote, "My bookcase is my pet and will, I trust, receive a few caresses from you." It did; the bookcase, "carefully locked up," was kept in her bedroom. McAllister, *Ellen Ewing*, 51. On early regrets, see Sherman to Elizabeth Reese, November 10, 1846, *SL*, 35.

18. Vincenzo Bellini's *Beatrice di Tenda* (1833); *Memoirs* (1889) 1:40; Sherman to Ellen Ewing, July 12, August 3, September 12, 16, 18, 1946, *Home Letters*, 36–37, 40, 42, 49, 52–53, 59, 63, 68. Theatrical display of all kinds has always been a vital part of Hispanic culture and, combined with the relative ease with which Brazil adapted to independence without revolutionary upheaval, led to a conservative intellectual life that Sherman found congenial. See Edwin Williamson, *The Penguin History of Latin America* (Harmondsworth: Penguin, 1992), 156–57, 296–98. *The Wandering Jew* is a medieval travelogue and book of fables.

19. Sherman to Elizabeth Reese, November 10, 1846, *SL*, 31: "waves such as I had never seen before." Sherman to Ellen Ewing, November 6, 24, 26, December 5, 1846, January 27, March 12, 1847, in *Home Letters*, 68, 69, 72, 73, 77, 81, 86, 87; *Memoirs* (1889) 1:46–47.

20. *Memoirs* (1889) 1:48–49, 50, 55, 57; Sherman's later reflections on Frémont tend to be more critical (see 53); on Carson, see 74–75. He thought Stockdale "talks too much and does too little." See Sherman to Ellen Ewing, March 12, July 11, 1847, in *Home Letters*, 87–88, 92. For a defense of Frémont, see Allan Nevins, *Frémont: Pathmarker of the West*, 2nd ed. (New York: Longmans Green, 1955), 310–16.

21. Sherman to Ellen Ewing, April 25, 1847, February 3, 1848, *Home Letters*, 102, 108, 109, 111; *Memoirs* (1889) 1:53; on Warner's death, see 1:107–8.

22. He always underrated the value of the Mexican acquisitions of 1848; see *Memoirs* (1889) 1:58–66; Sherman to Ellen Ewing, September 16, 1846, *Home Letters*, 61. "The people of the United States," he observed to Ellen, seemed "determined to possess north Mexico, regardless of the principles involved."

23. *Memoirs* (1889) 1:75, 78, 86; for Mason's attempts to control desertion, see 84–85, 100, 106; on Mason's report to the Adjutant General, see 85–86; Ellen Ewing to Sherman, January 1, 1849, CSHR 9/31 UNDA; Sherman to Ellen Ewing, August 28, 1848, *Home Letters*, 117.

24. Ellen Ewing to Sherman, January 1, May 19, 1849, CSHR 9/31 UNDA; Sherman to Ellen Ewing, March 5, 1849, CSHR 9/24 UNDA; McAllister, *Ellen Ewing*, 60; *Memoirs* (1889) 1: 86–87. Nineteenth-century "popular editions" of Macaulay's *History* were never less than two volumes, so their weight was hardly inconsiderable.

25. Ellen Ewing to Sherman, February 5, 1849 CSHR 9/31 UNDA; Sherman to Ellen Ewing, March 5, 1849, CSHR 9/24 UNDA; *Memoirs* (1889) 1:85, 90–91, 101, 105; Michael Fellman, *Citizen Sherman* (New York: Random House, 1995), 25

26. Ellen Ewing to Sherman, February 12, 1845, February 5, May 19, May 22, 1849, CSHR 9/30/31 UNDA; Sherman to Ellen Ewing, March 5, 1849, CSHR 9/24 UNDA; McAllister, *Ellen Ewing*, 58.

27. *Memoirs* (1889) 1:101–102, 105, 109–10; Ellen Ewing to Sherman, 22 May 1849 CSHR 9/31 UNDA; Elbert B. Smith, *The Presidencies of Zachary Taylor and Millard Fillmore* (Lawrence: University of Kansas Press, 1988), 53–54, 58.

28. Ellen Ewing to Sherman, May 22, 1849, CSHR 9/30 UNDA; Sherman to Ellen Ewing, March 27, 29, 1850, CSHR 9/24 UNDA. I am delighted to acknowledge the guidance I have received on these medical points from Professor Sir Robert Lechler. Sir Robert raised another intriguing possibility: that Sherman suffered from another respiratory malady that was diagnosed by nineteenth-century doctors as asthma. But as he cannot examine Sherman this can only be a guess.

29. *Memoirs* (1889) 1:115; "heavy in the extreme" was how Sherman remembered Webster's famous speech. Robert E. Curran, *A History of Georgetown University*, vol. 1, *From Academy to University, 1789–1889* (Washington, DC: Georgetown University Press, 2010), 130–31; McAllister, *Ellen Ewing*, 62–64; Lloyd Lewis, *Sherman: Fighting Prophet* (1932; New York: Harcourt Brace, 1958), 84–85; Sherman to John Sherman, June 16, 1850, Sherman Papers, Library of Congress.

30. "Merchant" is John Sherman's euphemism (see his sunny description of Reese in his *Recollections* 1:23–24), but both Elizabeth and William had been supportive at difficult times in her younger brothers' youth. Lewis, *Sherman*, 82; Ellen Sherman to Sherman, July 21, 1855 (addendum of July 30), CSHR 9/32 UNDA; Sherman to Ellen Ewing, March 27, 1850, CSHR 9/24 UNDA.

31. *Memoirs* (1889) 1:117–20; Sherman to Ellen Sherman, May 21, September 30, December 2, 1852, *Home Letters*, 124, 128, 130–31. John was equally surprised by his mother's death; *Recollections* I:94. Family Trees, Library of Congress, https://www.loc.gov/collections/william-t-sherman-papers/articles-and-essays/family-trees/.

Chapter 3

1. *Memoirs* 1:120–23; *Home Letters of General Sherman*, ed. M. A. de Wolfe Howe (New York: Scribner's, 1909), 133; T. J. Stiles, *The First Tycoon: The Epic Life of Cornelius Vanderbilt* (New York: Alfred A. Knopf, 2009), 180–82, 186, 195–96, 205–6.

2. *Memoirs* (1889) 1:123–28; Dwight L. Clarke, *William Tecumseh Sherman: Gold Rush Banker* (San Francisco: California Historical Society, 1969), 17 (hereafter *Gold Rush Banker*).

3. Sherman to Ellen Sherman, June 30, 1853, *Home Letters*, 135-36; Clarke, *Gold Rush Banker*, 3, 18–21. Miss Montez later settled in California.

4. Clarke, *Gold Rush Banker*, 20, 22, 26, 41. The bank building survived the 1906 earthquake and stands to this day; for later photographs and memorials, see the web page "Site of the Bank of Lucas, Turner and Co." at https://www.hmdb.org/Marker. asp?Marker-33402. Sherman to Ellen Sherman, June 30, 1853, *Home Letters*, 137; Ellen Sherman to Sherman, June 23, 1853, May 13, 1855, CSHR 9/31 UNDA. Ellen added that her father had "every confidence in yr. judgment and coolness of decision." McAllister, *Ellen Ewing*, 85–86; *Memoirs* (1889) 1:129.

5. *Memoirs* (1889) 1:130; McAllister, *Ellen Ewing*, 92–93, 94–97.

6. Clarke, *Gold Rush Banker*, 27, 51, 60, 61–63, 96, 101, 120, 173, 179.

7. Clarke, *Gold Rush Banker*, 22, 28, 31, 34, 56.

8. McAllister, *Ellen Ewing*, 95–98; Clarke, *Gold Rush Banker*, 28, 35, 36, 53, 63, 92, 96–97, 170. As Sherman admitted (see Clarke, *Gold Rush Banker*, 179), "I piled my troubles and sorrows on you a little too thick."

9. Clarke, *Gold Rush Banker*, 65, 68–69, 95, 119, 168; *Memoirs* 1:133–35. Meiggs's total debts were just short of $1 million, though he lived in Chile "like a prince," Sherman wrote indignantly—but he did eventually pay some of his debts.

10. This discussion rests on Sherman's contemporary account sent to Turner, quoted in full by Clarke, *Gold Rush Banker*, 107–11; *Memoirs* (1889) 1:140–42.

11. Clarke, *Gold Rush Banker*, 107, 110–11; *Memoirs* (1889) 1:143–44. The later recollection is much more hostile to Folsom as it is contrasted with Hammond's boundless generosity; but Folsom did raise the loan, though Sherman claimed he failed to do so, and Sherman does not point out that Hammond was very generous with public funds, not his own money .

12. Clarke, *Gold Rush Banker*, 112–13, 114, 115, 193; *Memoirs* 1:114. Hammond, who got the money back was later prosecuted for his "noble act" but acquitted.

13. McAllister, *Ellen Ewing*, 118–20; Ellen Sherman to Sherman, April 21, 23, 28, 29, 1855, the last including a long account of her ordeal, CSHR 9/32 UNDA; Ellen Sherman to Mrs. Bowman, April 22, 1855, CSHR 9/32 UNDA; Sherman to Ellen Sherman, May 8, 16, 31, 1855, *Home Letters*, 138–40 (quoted). The friendship with Bowman developed despite his "high" charges: they "make me squirm at times," he confided to Turner. See Clarke, *Gold Rush Banker*, 52.

14. *Memoirs* (1889) 1:146.

15. *Memoirs* 1:146–48; Clarke, *Gold Rush Banker*, 145, 185, 203–7; Sherman to Turner, May 18 (with an addendum dated May 20), 1856, printed in full in Clarke, *Gold Rush Banker*, 206–17 with an edited version in "Sherman and the San Francisco Vigilantes: Unpublished Letters of General William T. Sherman," *Century Magazine* 56 (December 1891): 296–301 (hereafter "Unpublished Letters"), and an unpaginated version on the internet at http://www.militarymuseum.org/Sheman2.html; Sherman to Thomas Ewing Sr., May 21, 1856, "Unpublished Letters," 301. For earlier examples of the militia siding with vigilantes, see Brian Holden Reid, "A Survey of the Militia in Eighteenth Century America," *Army Quarterly* 110 (January 1980): 52.

16. Sherman to Thomas Ewing, May 21, June 16, 1856, "Unpublished Letters," 300–302; Clarke, *Gold Rush Banker*, 209–13, 215, 217. Casey and Cora were executed a few days later, "suspended," Sherman recorded, "from beams projecting from the windows of the committee's rooms without other trial than could be given in secret, and by night." *Memoirs* 1:152.

17. Wool to Johnson, June 5; Sherman to Wool, June 7; Sherman to Thomas Ewing, June 16, 1856, "Unpublished Letters," 303, 305–6; *Memoirs* (1889) 1:153–56, indicates a rather less clear-cut assurance but one issued all the same. On Washington inertia, see Sherman to John Sherman, July 7, 1856, in *The Sherman Letters*, ed. Rachel Sherman Thorndike (New York: Charles Scribner's Sons, 1894), 59 (hereafter *SL*).

18. Sherman to Thomas Ewing, May 21; Sherman to Turner, July 2; Sherman to John Sherman, July 7, August 3, 1856, "Unpublished Letters," 302, 306–8; Clarke, *Gold Rush Banker*, 225, 242.

19. For his advocacy of Stone and closing the bank down, see Clarke, *Gold Rush Banker*, 93, 170–71, 185–86, 254, 256, 265, 278, 336, 354, though Stone's imprimatur received a blemish when Sherman discovered that he had been swindled out of $40,000 by a clerk.

20. Sherman to Ellen Sherman, July 29, October 6, 1857, *Home Letters*, 148, 152; Ellen Sherman to Sherman, June 16, August 29, September 15, 1855, July 12, September 1, 1857, CSHR 9/32/33 UNDA.

21. Ellen Sherman to Sherman, August 31, September 7, 12, 23, October 1, 1858, June 3, 20, 1859, CSHR 9/34/35 UNDA; Sherman to Ellen Sherman, July 29, 1857, April 18, 1859, *Home Letters*, 149, 157; Ellen Sherman to Sherman, November 30, 1857, September 27, 1858, CSHR 9/33/34 UNDA; on Sherman's failed applications for a commission, see Sherman to John Sherman, November 21, 1857, December 6, 1857, Sherman Papers, Library of Congress.

22. Mason Graham was the half brother of his old commander R. B. Mason. See D. C. Buell to Sherman, June 17; *Louisiana Democrat*, June 20, 1859; Sherman to Gov. Wickcliffe, July 1; Graham to Sherman, August 3, 1859, in *General W. T. Sherman as College President: A Collection of Letters, Documents, etc.*, ed. Walter L. Fleming (Cleveland, OH: Arthur H. Clark, 1912; London: Forgotten Books, 2015), 22–23, 24, 26, 33 (hereafter *College President: Letters*).

23. "Statement," May 10, 1859; Sherman to Thomas Ewing Sr., November 27; Sherman to Ellen Ewing, November 12, December 2; Sherman to Graham, November 21; McClellan to Sherman, October 23, 1859, in *College President: Letters*, 19–21, 46, 48, 59, 64, 40–42. Marcy was McClellan's father-in-law; see Ethan S. Rafuse, *McClellan's War* (Bloomington: Indiana University Press, 2005), 81–82.

24. Sherman to Graham, December 2; Sherman to Ellen Sherman, December 16; Sherman to Boyd, November 27, 1859, in *College President: Letters*, 72–73, 69; Ellen Sherman to Sherman, December 5, 11, 1859, CSHR 9/35 UNDA; Board of Supervisors' Announcement, MS copy, November 17, 1859, Sherman Papers, USMA Special Collections.

25. Sherman to George W. Cullum, September 5, 1859, Sherman Papers, USMA Special Collections; Cullum's compilation appeared as *Biographical Register of Officers and*

Graduates of the US Military Academy at West Point, NY, 2 vols. (New York, 1868). Sherman approved his later revised entry as "Very good—dates all right and perfectly satisfactory to the subject." Sherman to Cullum, June 21, 1866, Sherman Papers, USMA Special Collections. Perry Miller, *The Life of the Mind in America* (London: Gollancz, 1966), 63, 69, 316-18; a desire for "practical religion" also made itself felt (65).

26. Miller, *Life of the Mind*, 7, 14, 88-93, 165-66, quoting D. T. Blake of Columbia University; Rafuse, *McClellan's War*, 80; Baron Jomini, *The Art of War* (London: Greenhill, 1992), 17, 48, 321; Allan Nevins, *The State Universities and Democracy* (Urbana: University of Illinois Press, 1962), 270; Sir William Napier, *History of the War in the Peninsula and in the South of France, 1807-1814*, 6 vols. (1834; London: Constable, 1993), 4:305; Paddy Griffith, *Military Thought in the French Army, 1815-51* (Manchester: Manchester University Press, 1989), 69; Address before the Young Men's Lyceum of Springfield, Illinois, January 27, 1838, in *The Language of Liberty: The Political Speeches and Writings of Abraham Lincoln*, ed. Joseph R. Fornieri (Washington, DC: Regency, 2003), 33.

27. Barrett made his New York debut in 1857. See Attilio Favorini, "Barrett, Lawrence (April 4, 1838-March 20, 1891)," in *American National Biography*, 26 vols., ed. John A. Garraty and Mark C. Carnes (New York: Oxford University Press, 1999; supps. 2002, 2005), 2:234; Clarke, *Gold Rush Banker*, 330; Alden T. Vaughan and Virginia M. Vaughan, *Shakespeare in America* (New York: Oxford University Press, 2012), 2-3, 4, 29-30, 36. The Vaughans emphasize Shakespeare's "neutrality" for the participants of the crisis of 1775-83, and this argument seems equally apposite to 1850-61 or even 1861-65; also see 43, 51, 55, 66, 72-74, 86, 182. See Ellen Sherman to Sherman, July 2, 1844, CSHR 9/30 UNDA, when she suggests a future trip to Britain, "whose proud sons you so much admire." The quotation from Burns is from a poem, "To a Louse on Seeing One on a Lady's Bonnet at Church" (1786).

28. Sherman to Graham, December 25, 1859, January 6, February 8, March 5, 30, April 12, 1860; Sherman to Ellen Sherman, January 4, November 25, 1860; Sherman to Thomas Ewing Sr., February 12, 1860; Graham to T. O. Moore, February 9, 1860; Sherman to Board of Supervisors, March 1, 1860, in *College President: Letters*, 101-2, 301, 91, 153, 161, 155, 153, 182-83, 185, 192, 193, 198.

29. John Sherman to Sherman, December 24, 1859; Sherman to John Sherman, January 16, 1860, *SL*, 78-79; Allan Nevins, *The Emergence of Lincoln*, 2 vols. (New York: Scribner's. 1950), 1:210; Bragg to Sherman, December 16, 1859; Graham to Sherman, January 15; Sherman to Graham, February 16, 1860, in *College President: Letters*, 81, 122-24, 168.

30. Sherman to Ellen Sherman, July 10, 1860, October 29, 1859; Sherman to Boyd, April 4, 1861, in *College President: Letters*, 43, 44-45, 241, 376.

31. Sherman to Graham, January 1, 24, 30, February 2, 6, 8, 10, August 30, 1860; Sherman to Ellen Sherman, February 3, 1860; Memorandum by G. Mason Graham (Summer 1860); Annual Report of the Superintendent (January 1861), in *College President: Letters*, 99, 128-29, 137-42, 142-44, 145-47, 262-64, 266-67, 324.

32. Sherman to Graham, December 25; Bragg to Sherman, December 26, 1860, in *College President: Letters,* 317–18, 319; on the vacuous nature of secessionist pressures, see Brian Holden Reid, *The Origins of the American Civil War* (New York: Addison Wesley Longman, 1996), 264–67, and on the Sumter Crisis, 332–34.

33. Sherman to Moore, January 18 (twice); Resolution of the Board of Supervisors, February 14; Sherman to Dr. S. A. Smith, February 19, 1861, in *College President: Letters,* 341–42, 343–44, 363. Louisiana favored secession less than other states of the Deep South: although 80 secessionists were elected to the state convention, so were 44 "cooperationists" who were more cautious; but the ordnance still passed 113 to 17. See Holden Reid, *Origins of the American Civil War,* 274.

34. Sherman to Minnie Sherman, December 15, 1860, in *Sherman's Civil War: Selected Correspondence of William T. Sherman, 1860–1865* (Chapel Hill: University of North Carolina Press, 1999), 18; Sherman to Boyd, April 23, 1861, in *College President: Letters,* 476; William L. Barney, "Rush to Disaster: Secession and the Slaves' Revenge," in Robert Cook et al., *Secession Winter* (Baltimore: Johns Hopkins University Press, 2013), 10–11, 26–33.

35. Sherman to Ellen Sherman, February 13, 1860, in *College President: Letters,* 164.

36. Ellen Sherman to Sherman, April 13, 1859, CSHR 9/35 UNDA; Sherman to Boyd, May 13, 1861, *College President: Letters,* 382.

Chapter 4

1. *Memoirs* 1:66–67; Sherman to Ellen Sherman, February 25, 1861, in *Sherman's Civil War: Selected Correspondence of William T. Sherman, 1860–1865* (Chapel Hill: University of North Carolina Press, 1999), 58 (hereafter *Correspondence*).

2. Sherman to John Sherman, March 9, 21, 1861, *Correspondence,* 61, 62.

3. Ellen Sherman to Sherman, January 16, 1861, CSHR 9/37, UNDA.

4. This term is used occasionally by both Northerners and Southerners to describe the United States before 1861.

5. Sherman to John Sherman, March 9, 1861, *Correspondence,* 61–62.

6. *Memoirs* 1: 67–68; Sherman to John Sherman, March 9, 21, 22, April 18; Sherman to David Boyd, April 4, 1861, *Correspondence,* 62, 63, 64, 65, 69; Lloyd Lewis, *Sherman: Fighting Prophet* (1932; New York: Harcourt Brace, 1958), 149–50; Michael Fellman, *Citizen Sherman: A Life of William Tecumseh Sherman* (New York: Random House, 1995), 85–86; for the reasons behind Lincoln's studied optimism, see Brian Holden Reid, *The Origins of the American Civil War* (London: Addison Wesley Longman, 1996), 251, 331–33, 339–40.

7. Sherman to John Sherman, March 22, April 8, 18; Sherman to Thomas Ewing Jr., May 23, 1861, *Correspondence,* 63–64, 67, 69, 91.

8. Proclamation Calling Militia and Convening Congress, April 15. 1861, in *The Collected Works of Abraham Lincoln,* ed. Roy P. Basler, 9 vols. (New Brunswick, NJ: Rutgers University Press, 1953), 4:331–32; Sherman to John Sherman, March 22, 1861, *Correspondence,* 64.

9. Sherman to John Sherman, April 8, 18, 1861, *Correspondence*, 67, 70; *Memoirs* 1:168; Fellman, *Citizen Sherman*, 86.

10. Sherman to John Sherman, April 8, 22; Sherman to David Boyd, April 4, 1861, *Correspondence*, 68, 71, 66; Marcus Cunliffe, *Soldiers and Civilians: The Martial Spirit in America, 1775–1865* (London: Eyre and Spottiswoode, 1969), 298.

11. B. H. Liddell Hart, *Sherman: Soldier, Realist, American* (New York: Dodd, Mead, 1929), 78; Sherman to John Sherman, April 4, 1861, *Correspondence*, 67.

12. Sherman to John Sherman, March 21, April 4, 22; Sherman to David Boyd, April 4, 1861, *Correspondence*, 63, 65, 66, 72.

13. Sherman to John Sherman, April 22, 1861, *Correspondence*, 71.

14. Sherman to John Sherman, April 22, 25, 26; Sherman to Simon Cameron, May 1, 1861, *Correspondence*, 72–73, 74, 75, 76, 78, 79; for similar views marked by a lack of eagerness for war, see Brian Holden Reid, "General McClellan and the Politicians," *Parameters* 17, no. 3 (September 1987): 102–3.

15. *Memoirs* 1:171.

16. Sherman to John Sherman, May 11; Sherman to Thomas Ewing Sr., May 11, 1861, *Correspondence*, 74, 79–80, 81–82; *Memoirs* 1:174.

17. *Memoirs* 1:172; Sherman to John Sherman, April 25; Sherman to David Boyd, May 13, 1861, *Correspondence*, 74, 83.

18. Sherman to Thomas Ewing Sr., May 1; Sherman to John Sherman, April 18, 26, 11, May 20; Sherman to David Boyd, May 13, 1861, *Correspondence*, 77, 70, 84, 76, 88; Charles E. Vetter, *Sherman: Merchant of Terror, Advocate of Peace* (Gretna, LA: Pelican, 1992), 77, offers sensible comment on his "opportunism."

19. Sherman to David Boyd, April 4, May 13; Sherman to Thomas Ewing Sr., May 1; Sherman to John Sherman, May 20, 1861, *Correspondence*, 66, 83, 84, 89, 77.

20. Proclamation Calling for 42,034 Volunteers, May 3, 1861, in Lincoln, *Collected Works* 4:353.

21. Sherman to John Sherman, April 22, 25, May 20, 24, June 8; Sherman to Thomas Ewing Sr., May 17; Sherman to Ellen Sherman, June 8, 1861, *Correspondence*, 72, 76, 87, 98–99, 100; *Memoirs* 1:174–75.

22. Sherman to John Sherman, June 8, 20; Sherman to Ellen Sherman, June 8, 12, 17, 1861, *Correspondence*, 100, 102, 104.

23. Sherman to John Sherman, May 20, 24, 1861, *Correspondence*, 88, 92.

24. In his *Memoirs* Sherman misspells his name as "Quimby."

25. Sherman to Ellen Sherman, July 3, 1861, *Correspondence*, 106; for the interconnections and details of Sherman's regiments, see Cunliffe, *Soldiers and Civilians*, 6–7, 11; *Memoirs* 1: 180.

26. John F. Marszalek, *Sherman: A Soldier's Passion for Order* (New York: Free Press, 1993), 147–48; *Memoirs* 1:180; Sherman to Minnie Sherman, July 14; Sherman to Ellen Sherman, July 6, 7, 1861, *Correspondence*, 109–10, 108.

27. Sherman to John Sherman, July 3, 15, 1861, *Correspondence*, 104, 106, 107, 108, 115.

28. Sherman to Ellen Sherman, June 12, July 3, 6, 15, 1861, *Correspondence*, 102, 107, 108, 115, 116.

29. Sherman to Ellen Sherman, July 3, 15, 16, 1861, *Correspondence*, 107, 117.

30. Sherman to Maria Sherman, July 14, 28; Sherman to Ellen Sherman, July 15; Sherman to Charles Ewing, June 20, 1861, *Correspondence*, 110, 125, 111, 105; David Detzer, *Donnybrook: The Battle of Bull Run, 1861* (New York: Harcourt, 2004), 142–43.

31. Sherman to John Sherman, July 19, 1861, *Correspondence*, 120; on "masked batteries," see Detzer, *Donnybrook*, 120–21.

32. *OR*, ser. 1, 2:310; Sherman to John Sherman, July 19; Sherman to Ellen Sherman, July 19, 1861, *Correspondence*, 120, 118–19; Detzer, *Donnybrook*, 164–65; William C. Davis, *Battle at Bull Run* (New York: Doubleday, 1977), 114–24. As for "ducking," the writer George Orwell recalled of his first action in the Spanish Civil War (1936–39) that he was annoyed he ducked, "but the movement appears to be instinctive and almost everybody does it at least once." See *Homage to Catalonia* (1938; London: Penguin, 2000), 22.

33. Davis, *Battle at Bull Run*, 74, 102, 154.

34. Sherman to John Sherman, July 19; Sherman to Ellen Sherman, July 19, 28, 1861, *Correspondence*, 121, 119, 129; Detzer, *Donnybrook*, 187–88.

35. *OR*, ser. 1, 2:349, 368; Sherman to Ellen Sherman, July 28, 1861, *Correspondence*, 122–23; Cunliffe, *Soldiers and Civilians*, 15–16.

36. *OR*, ser. 1, 2:369; Sherman to Ellen Sherman, July 28, 1861, *Correspondence*, 123; see Cunliffe's observation, *Soldiers and Civilians*, 8: "They postured because they knew of no other way of behaving."

37. For a critical view of Hunter, see Detzer, *Donnybrook*, 260; *OR*, ser. 1, 2:369; Sherman to Ellen Sherman, July 28, 1861, *Correspondence*, 123. Until 10.30 or 11:00 a.m. Beauregard intended to attack to the east at Mitchell's Ford, which would have aided McDowell's plan and exposed Confederate lines of communication further. See Davis, *Bull Run*, 189–92.

38. This is the term used in his report (*OR*, ser. 1, 2:369), and it should not be confused with the higher formation. For a definition, see Robert Horne, *A Précis of Modern Tactics* (London: Stationery Office, 1873), 7, 10; Sherman's knowledge of the deployment is derived from William J. Hardee, *Rifle and Infantry Tactics* (Philadelphia: J. B. Lippincott, 1861), 18.

39. *OR*, ser. 1, 2:369–70; Sherman to Ellen Sherman, July 28, 1861, *Correspondence*, 124; Davis, *Bull Run*, 208–13, 215–19; Emory M. Thomas, *Bold Dragoon: The Life of J .E. B. Stuart* (New York: Harper and Row, 1986), 80–81.

40. Sherman to Ellen Sherman, July 28, 1861, *Correspondence*, 124.

41. *OR*, ser. 1, 2: 370; Thomas, *Bold Dragoon*, 81.

42. *OR*, ser. 1, 2:350, 370–71; Detzer, *Donnybrook*, 422–23.

Chapter 5

1. *Memoirs* 1:182; *OR*, ser. 1, 2:371; Sherman to Ellen Sherman, July 28, 1861, in *Sherman's Civil War: The Selected Correspondence of William T. Sherman, 1860–1865*, ed. Brooks D. Simpson and Jean V. Berlin (Chapel Hill: University of North Carolina Press, 1999), 124 (hereafter *Correspondence*); Tyler's report, *OR*, ser. 1,

524 NOTES TO PAGES 98–106

2:351, gives a slightly smaller loss of 581; William C. Davis, *Battle at Bull Run* (Baton Rouge: Louisiana University Press, 1977), 253.

2. Sherman to Ellen Sherman, August 3, 1861, *Correspondence*, 126; Charles E. Vetter, *Sherman: Merchant of Terror, Advocate of Peace* (Gretna, LA: Pelican, 1992), 96.

3. Sherman to Ellen Sherman, July 28, August 3, 1861, *Correspondence*, 124–25, 127.

4. Sherman to Ellen Sherman, August 3, 1861, *Correspondence*, 126, 127–28.

5. Sherman to Ellen Sherman, July 24, 28, August 3, 1861, *Correspondence*, 125, 126.

6. Sherman to Ellen Sherman, July 28, August 3, 22, 1861, *Correspondence*, 125, 127, 129. McClellan was right; see T. Harry Williams, *P. G. T. Beauregard: Napoleon in Gray* (1955; Baton Rouge: Louisiana State University Press, 1989), 89. Like his counterparts, Sherman overlooked the important contribution of General Joseph E. Johnston to the Confederate victory.

7. *Memoirs* 1:187–89.

8. *Memoirs* 1:189–91; Sherman misdates the visit as July 26. John F. Marszalek, *Sherman: A Soldier's Passion for Order* (New York: Free Press, 1993), 152, quotes some details from the speech that Sherman mentioned in an address delivered in 1872.

9. Sherman to Ellen Sherman, July 24, August 17, 19; Sherman to Thomas Ewing Sr., September 15, 1861, *Correspondence*, 121, 130, 132, 137.

10. Sherman to Ellen Sherman, August 17, 1861, *Correspondence*, 130–31; *Memoirs* 1:192.

11. Sherman to Ellen Sherman, August 20–27, 1861, *Correspondence*, 135; *Memoirs* 1:192–92. For the reasons why the Union had difficulty in fielding very large armies, see Brian Holden Reid, *America's Civil War: The Operational Battlefield, 1861–1863* (Amherst, NY: Prometheus Books, 2008), 402–4.

12. Sherman to Ellen Sherman, September 9, 1861, *Correspondence*, 136; *OR*, ser. 2, 2:125–26, 920; *OR*, ser. 1, 4:307.

13. Sherman to Ellen Sherman, August 20–27; Sherman to John Sherman, September 9, 1861, *Correspondence*, 135–36; *Memoirs* 1:194; also see William B. Hesseltine, *Lincoln and the War Governors* (New York: Alfred A. Knopf, 1955), 173–74.

14. Allan Nevins, *Frémont: Pathmarker of the West*, 2nd ed. (New York: Longmans, Green, 1955), 473, 476–77, 493–97; *Memoirs* 1:194–97; Sherman to Ellen Sherman, September 8, 1861, *Correspondence*, 138–40; Dwight L. Clarke, *William T. Sherman: Gold Rush Banker* (San Francisco: California Historical Society, 1969), 116, 121.

15. Nevins, *Frémont*, 499–505; Holden Reid, *America's Civil War*, 51; Sherman to Thomas Ewing Sr., September 15; Sherman to Ellen Sherman, September 18, 1861, *Correspondence*, 137–38; *OR*, ser. 1, 4:301, 347.

16. *Memoirs* 1:197–200; Sherman to Thomas Ewing Sr., September 30, 1861, *Correspondence*, 141; Marszalek, *Sherman*, 158–59.

17. Sherman to Thomas Ewing Sr., September 30, 1861, *Correspondence*, 141–42.

18. Sherman to Thomas Ewing Sr., September 30; Sherman to John Sherman, October 5, 1861, *Correspondence*, 141–42, 143–44.

19. Sherman to Ellen Sherman, October 10, 1861, *Correspondence*, 149; *Memoirs* 1:199.

20. *OR*, ser. 1, 4: 300, 306–7, 308; also see Sherman to Lincoln, October 10, 1861, *Correspondence*, 146. Sherman apologized for his impertinence in Sherman to Salmon P. Chase, October 14, 1861, *Correspondence*, 150; *Memoirs* 1:200.

21. *OR*, ser. 1, 4:308–9, 548–49; *Memoirs* 1:200–203; Marszalek, *Sherman*, 162; Sherman to Ellen Sherman, November 1, 1861, *Correspondence*, 155.

22. *OR*, ser. 1, 4: 315–16, 317; Sherman to Salmon P. Chase, October 14, 1861, *Correspondence*, 149.

23. *OR*, ser. 1, 4:325, 332–33, 335–36, 340–41, 350; *OR*, ser. 2, 2:920; Sherman to Ellen Sherman, October 26, 1861, *Correspondence*, 152, 153, 155.

24. Ellen Sherman to Sherman, October 4, 1861, CSHR 9/37, UNDA; Sherman to Ellen Sherman, October 6, 1861; Sherman to John Sherman, January 8, 1862, *Correspondence*, 145, 178–79; *OR*, ser. 1, 4:324–25; for the East Tennessee fury directed at Sherman, see Hans L. Trefousse, *Andrew Johnson* (New York: Norton, 1989), 147.

25. *OR*, ser. 1, 3:547. Frémont's allies complained that Thomas had a record of hostility toward their hero; see Nevins, *Frémont*, 537. Lloyd Lewis, *Sherman: Fighting Prophet* (1932; New York: Harcourt, Brace, 1958), 196.

26. *OR*, ser. 2, 2: 125–26; *OR*, ser. 14: 253–54, 312, 316, 337, 353; Sherman to Ellen Sherman, November 1; Sherman to William Dennison, November 6, 1861, *Correspondence*, 155, 157.

27. *OR*, ser. 1, 4, 359; Sherman to Anderson, November 21, 1861, *Correspondence*, 159; Sherman added: "You know with what reluctance I entered on my command and have always felt that somehow or other I would be disgraced by it." Ellen Sherman to Sherman, August 22, November 18, 1861, CSHR 9/37 UNDA; Sherman to Ellen Sherman, October 6, 1861, *Correspondence*, 145; Ellen Sherman, Diary 1861, entries November 8–16, 1861, CSHR 5/15, UNDA.

28. Marszalek, *Sherman*, 163–64; idem, John F. Marszalek, *Commander of All Lincoln's Armies: A Life of General Henry W. Halleck* (Cambridge, MA: Belknap Press of Harvard University Press, 2004), 56, 95–96; Ellen Sherman, Diary 1861, entries November 26–December 3, 1861, CSHR 5/15 UNDA.

29. I am grateful to Sir Simon Wessely for a discussion of these points. Also see Roy Porter, *Madness: A Brief History* (Oxford: Oxford University Press, 2002), 118–20, 147–53.

30. Ellen Sherman to John Sherman, November 10, 1861, *Correspondence*, 156; Marszalek, *Sherman*, 163, 167; *Memoirs* 1:205, 214–15.

31. Lewis, *Sherman*, 200; Marszalek, *Sherman*, 165, 169; Fellman, *Citizen Sherman*, 99n; James Lee McDonough, *William T. Sherman: In the Service of My Country* (New York: Norton, 2016), 294, is sensibly more equivocal and sees a mix of mental and physical factors.

32. See above, chap. 4.

33. *Oxford Textbook of Psychiatry*, an electronic publication that can be accessed at http://www.oxfordreference.com/view/10.1093/acref/9780199657681.001.0001/acref-9780199657681, 776. I am grateful to Sir Simon Wessely for this reference.

34. Sherman to Ellen Sherman, October 6, November 11; on his health, see letters to her and John Sherman on September 18, October 5; sleeplessness, October 7, October 12, 1861; Sherman to John Sherman, January 4, 1862, *Correspondence*, 140, 143, 145, 147, 154–55, 174; Lewis, *Sherman*, 197 *OR*, ser. 1, 4:350; Lewis, *Sherman*, 197, 200. The relationship between depression and suicide is emphasized in Richard Gabriel, *The Painful Field: The Psychiatric Dimension of Modern War* (New York: Greenwood Press, 1988), 9.

35. *Cincinnati Commercial*, December 11, 1861; available also in Lewis, *Sherman*, 201; Ellen Sherman, Diary 1861, entry for December 11, CSHR 5/15, UNDA; also see Fellman, *Sherman*, 165. Sherman had imprisoned the *Cincinnati Commercial* reporter in Louisville for ignoring his instructions not to visit his camps; see Sherman to Halleck, December 12, 1861, *Correspondence*, 165. If anything, prejudice against those who have suffered mental illness has got worse, and it is worth speculating whether Sherman would have been allowed to continue serving in wars of a later date. The reaction to the revelation in 1972 that the Democratic vice presidential candidate, Senator Tom Eagleton of Missouri, had been treated for mental illness years before and put it behind him is a startling example. The animus toward Eagleton among George McGovern's staff, their suspicion of his "frailty," and the way they succumbed to fear of "the stigma of a deranged mind" is as notable as the attacks of Republican critics on McGovern's choice of running mate. See Theodore H. White, *The Making of the President 1972* (London: Jonathan Cape, 1974), 201, 203.

36. Sherman to Thomas Ewing Sr., December 12, 1861, *Correspondence*, 161, 163; Fellman, *Citizen Sherman*, 103–4.

37. Sherman to Halleck, December 12, 1861, *Correspondence*, 165.

38. *OR*, ser. 1, 2.1:200–201; Ellen Sherman, Diary 1861, entry for December 18, CSHR 5/15, UNDA.

39. Marszalek, *Halleck*, 113–14; Lewis, *Sherman*, 203–4; Ellen Sherman, Diary 1861, entry for December 20, CSHR 5/15, UNDA; *Memoirs* 2:218.

Chapter 6

1. *OR*, ser. 1, 7:609; Sherman to Ellen Sherman, February 17, 1862, in *Sherman's Civil War: Selected Correspondence of William T. Sherman, 1860–1865*, ed. Brooks D. Simpson and Jean V. Berlin (Chapel Hill: University of North Carolina Press, 1999), 191 (hereafter *Correspondence*). Halleck had published *Elements of Military Art and Science*, essentially a compilation, in 1846.

2. *Memoirs* 1:219–20.

3. *OR*, ser. 1, 10.2:50–51.

4. Sherman to Ellen Sherman, February 21; Sherman to John Sherman, February 23, 1862, *Correspondence*, 192, 193; *Memoirs* 1:221. Colonel William B. Hazen recalled the meeting as bad-tempered; see Lloyd Lewis, *Sherman: Fighting Prophet* (1932; New York: Harcourt Brace, 1958), 212–13.

5. Order of Battle Prepared by W. T. Sherman Brig. Gen. Comdg Div.—Sherman's Division at Shiloh Old Meeting House, 2½ miles west of Pittsburg Landing, Tennessee, William T. Sherman Papers, Chicago History Museum Research Center; Sherman to John Sherman, February 23; Sherman to Charles Ewing, February 27, 1862, *Correspondence*, 192–93, 194; for a description of the sympathy the POWs received—and outright support later in St. Louis—see Flavel C. Barber, *Holding the Line: The Third Tennessee Infantry, 1861–1864*, ed. Robert H. Ferrell (Kent, OH: Kent State University Press, 1994), 37, 39.

6. Sherman to Ellen Sherman, March 6, 1862, *Correspondence*, 195.

7. Sherman to Ellen Sherman, March 12, 1862, *Correspondence*, 196; *Memoirs* 1:221;John F. Marszalek, *Commander of All Lincoln's Armies: A Life of Henry W. Halleck* (Cambridge, MA: Belknap Press of Harvard University Press, 2004), 119, defends him from charges of envy.

8. *OR*, ser. 1, 10.1:8; *Memoirs* 1:226. Worthington continued to be a source of irritation; see Sherman to Philemon B. Ewing, May 16, 1862, *Correspondence*, 221.

9. Sherman to Ellen Sherman, March 12, 1862, *Correspondence*, 196; *Memoirs* 1:225, 227.

10. *OR*, ser. 1, 10.1:22.

11. *Memoirs* 1:219; Sherman to Ellen Sherman, March 17/18, April 14; Sherman to Thomas Ewing Sr., April 4, 1862, *Correspondence*, 197–98, 200, 203; *OR*, ser. 1, 10.1:28, 33.

12. Sherman to Thomas Ewing Sr., April 4; Sherman to Ellen Sherman, April 3, 1862, *Correspondence*, 199–200, 201–2.

13. Sherman to Ellen Sherman, March 12, April 3; Sherman to Thomas Ewing Sr., April 4, 1862, *Correspondence*, 196, 198, 200.

14. Sherman to Ellen Sherman, April 3, 1862, I *Correspondence*, 198.

15. Sherman to Ellen Sherman, April 3, 1862, *Correspondence*, 198; *OR*, ser. 1, 10.1:89; T. Harry Williams, *Lincoln and His Generals* (New York: Alfred A. Knopf, 1952), 85.

16. James Lee McDonough, *Shiloh: In Hell before Night* (Knoxville: University of Tennessee Press, 1977), v; *Memoirs* 1:215.

17. *Memoirs* 1:229; *OR*, ser. 1, 10.1:83; the last possibility is suggested by B. H. Liddell Hart, *Sherman: Soldier, Realist, American* (New York: Dodd, Mead, 1929), 131.

18. McDonough, *Shiloh*, 7, 11, 22, 30–36, 40, 59–60, 68–69, 76–85; Thomas L. Connelly, *Army of the Heartland: The Army of Tennessee, 1861–1862* (Baton Rouge: Louisiana State University Press, 1967), 109–13, 130–42; for a defense of Johnston, Brian Holden Reid, *America's Civil War: The Operational Battlefield, 1861–1863* (Amherst, NY: Prometheus Books, 2008), 137, 141.

19. *OR*, ser. 1, 10.2:94; on surprise, see Shelford Bidwell, *Modern Warfare: A Study of Men, Ideas and Weapons* (London: Allen Lane, 1973), 6, 91–92, 199–200, 212–13.

20. *OR*, ser. 1, 10.1:89–90, 248; *Memoirs* 1:228–30; McDonough, *Shiloh*, 56.

21. *OR*, ser. 1, 10.1:248, 264; Sherman to Ellen Sherman, April 11; Sherman to John Sherman, May 7; Sherman to Thomas Ewing Sr., May 3, 1862, *Correspondence*, 201, 214–15, 216.

22. *OR*, ser. 1, 10.1:249–50; McDonough, *Shiloh*, 109; O. Edward Cunningham, *Shiloh in the Western Campaign of 1862*, ed. Gary D. Joiner and Timothy B. Smith (New York: Savas Beattie, 2001), 149n10, 151, 154, 166, 167n7, 171.

23. *OR*, ser. 1, 10.1:250–51; McDonough, *Shiloh*, 114, 116; Cunningham, *Shiloh*, 373–75n42; Sherman to Ellen Sherman, April 11, 14, 1862, *Correspondence*, 201, 204; he told Ellen on April 11 (*Correspondence*, 202): "You must learn to live without money, as that is going to be a scarce commodity."

24. "Grant's Pertinacity," *Army and Navy Journal* 31 (December 30, 1893): 317.

25. *OR*, ser. 1, 10.1:250–51; Sherman to Ellen Sherman, April 11, 1862, *Correspondence*, 201–2; Stephen D. Engle, *Don Carlos Buell: Most Promising of All* (Chapel Hill: University of North Carolina Press, 1999), 224, 228; *Memoirs* 1:245–46; Larry J. Daniel, *Days of Glory: The Army of the Cumberland, 1861–1865* (Baton Rouge: Louisiana State University Press, 2004), 80, stresses Buell's "perverse pleasure" at Grant's predicament.

26. *OR*, ser. 1, 10.1:251–52; Sherman to Ellen Sherman, April 11, 1862, *Correspondence*, 202; Daniel, *Days of Glory*, 81.

27. *OR*, ser. 1, 10.1:104, 252, 253–54, 640.

28. *OR*, ser. 1, 10.1:252, 253. Sherman had proved most cooperative in anticipating and responding to the problems of others. In his report, McClernand acknowledged Sherman's zeal for cooperation but made no reference to any reliance on his judgment (122). This is not surprising, as McClernand spent a lifetime celebrating nobody's qualities save his own. Hurlbut frankly admitted that "he received his instructions" and carried them out (203); on Sherman giving orders to 1st Division, see 240 and Sherman to Thomas Ewing Sr., April 27, 1862, *Correspondence*, 213. This evidence contradicts Albert Castel's contention that Sherman invented this dominant role in "exaggerations, equivocations and fabrications": *Victors in Blue* (Lawrence: University of Kansas Press, 2011), 91.

29. Michael Fellman, *Citizen Sherman: A Life of William T. Sherman* (New York: Random House, 1995), 408, 353.

30. Sherman to Ellen Sherman, May 26, 1862, *Correspondence*, 227–28; *OR*, ser. 1, 10.2:102; *OR*, ser. 1, 10.1:743.

31. Sherman to John Sherman, April 23; Sherman to Ellen Sherman, April 14; Sherman to Thomas Ewing Sr., April 27; Sherman to Philemon B. Ewing, May 16, 1862, *Correspondence*, 206–207, 203–4, 211–12, 223.

32. Fellman, *Citizen Sherman*, 117.

33. Sherman to Ellen Sherman, April 11, April 24; Sherman to John Sherman, April 19, 1862, *Correspondence*, 204, 205, 208–10.

34. Thomas L. Livermore, *Numbers and Losses in the Civil War in America, 1861–1865*, 2nd ed. (Boston: Houghton Mifflin, 1901), 79. Later research has multiplied these figures by at least 10 percent; in some units they were 20 percent larger. Cunningham, *Shiloh*, 376n44.

35. Sherman to Ellen Sherman, May 24, 1862, *Correspondence*, 224–25; William B. Hesseltine, *Lincoln and the War Governors* (New York: Alfred A. Knopf, 1955),

194–95. On April 19 Governor Harvey drowned when he fell into the Tennessee River in a boating accident.

36. Sherman to Philemon B. Ewing, May 16, 1862, *Correspondence*, 221–24; Grant to Sherman, April 15, 1862, *Grant Papers* 5:45, 323.

37. *Memoirs* 1:255–56; Sherman to Grant, June 6, 1862, *Correspondence*, 232–33.

38. *Memoirs* 1:250; Sherman to John Sherman, May 7, 1862, *Correspondence*, 215–16; Bruce Tap, *Over Lincoln's Shoulder: The Committee on the Conduct of the War* (Lawrence: University of Kansas Press, 1998), 46.

39. On measures since leaving Shiloh, see *OR*, ser. 1, 10.1:645–46; *OR*, ser. 1, 10.2:100, 102–4, 136; Sherman to Ellen Sherman, April 14, June 16, 1862, *Correspondence*, 203, 235.

40. *OR*, ser. 1, 10.1:839–41, 741–42, 743–44, 667, 674, 738–40, 681; *Memoirs* 1:253; Sherman to Ellen Sherman, June 6, 1862, *Correspondence*, 234–35.

41. Sherman to Ellen Sherman, May 26; Sherman to John Sherman, May 31, 1862, *Correspondence*, 226–28, 231–32; for a defense of Halleck's caution based on a lack of logistical capacity, see Earl J. Hess, *The Civil War in the West: Victory and Defeat from the Appalachians to the Mississippi* (Chapel Hill: University of North Carolina Press, 2012), 49–54.

42. Sherman to John Sherman, May 12; Sherman to Ellen Sherman, June 6, 1862, *Correspondence*, 234–35.

Chapter 7

1. Sherman to P. B Ewing, July 13, November 2, 1862, in *Sherman's Civil War: The Selected Correspondence of William T. Sherman, 1860-1865*, ed. Brooks D. Simpson and Jean V. Berlin (Chapel Hill: University of North Carolina Press, 1999), 251, 253, 319 (hereafter *Correspondence*).

2. Sherman to Ellen Sherman, October 4, 1862, *Correspondence*, 313.

3. *Memoirs* 1:205. Two of Sherman's earlier biographers, John F. Marszalek, *Sherman: A Soldier's Passion for Order* (New York: Free Press, 1993), 195, and Michael Fellman, *Citizen Sherman: A Life of William T. Sherman* (New York: Random House, 1995), 142, note the ambivalent transition but conclude that the result is a penchant for unleashing unbridled violence.

4. *OR*, ser. 1, 17.2:72, 201; Sherman to P. B. Ewing, July 13, 1862, *Correspondence*, 250–51.

5. Lloyd Lewis, *Sherman: Fighting Prophet* (1932; New York: Harcourt Brace, 1958), 243–48.

6. *OR*, ser. 1, 17.2:156–57; Sherman to John Park, July 27, 1862, *Correspondence*, 258; Stanley P. Hirshson, *White Tecumseh: A Biography of General William T. Sherman* (New York: Wiley, 1997), 129–30. Also see Phillip S. Paludan, *The Presidency of Abraham Lincoln* (Lawrence: University Press of Kansas, 1994), 127, 145–46.

7. Sherman to Minnie Sherman, August 6, 1862, *Correspondence*, 262.

8. Sherman to Ellen Sherman, July 31, 1862, *Correspondence*, 260. In 1863 the Second Confiscation Act was extended to cover all presidential and congressional

measures taken against slavery. Employment and the continuance of business activities depended on signing the oath. See Peter J. Parish, *The American Civil War* (London: Eyre Methuen, 1975), 509, 519, 524.

9. Sherman to E. S. Plummer and Other Surgeons, July 23; Sherman to Ellen Sherman, July 31, 1862, *Correspondence*, 261.

10. Sherman to Ellen Sherman, July 21; Sherman to Thomas Ewing Sr., August 10; Sherman to Thomas Tasker Gantt, September 23; Sherman to John Sherman, November 24, 1862, *Correspondence*, 260, 263–64, 303, 337; *OR,* ser. 1, 17. 2:158, 159.

11. Sherman to Gideon J. Pillow, August 14, 1862, *Correspondence*, 274–75. Sherman still had not seen the provisions of the Confiscation Acts six weeks later; see Sherman to Gantt, September 23, 1862, *Correspondence*, 303. Also see Sherman to John A. Rawlins, August 14, 1862, in *Freedom: A Documentary History of Emancipation, 1861-1867*, Series 1, I, *The Destruction of Slavery,* ed. Ira Berlin et al. (Cambridge: Cambridge University Press, 1985), 291n.

12. Sherman to Thomas Hunton, August 24, 1862, *Correspondence*, 285–86; also see Brian Holden Reid, "William T. Sherman and the South (Peter J. Parish Memorial Lecture, 2009)," *American Nineteenth Century History* 11, no. 1 (March 2010): 1–16.

13. Sherman to U. S. Grant, August 17; Sherman to Thomas Ewing Sr., August 10; Sherman to John Sherman, September 3, October 1, 1862, *Correspondence*, 278–80, 263, 293, 309–10.

14. Sherman to Andrew Johnson, August 10, 1862, *Correspondence*, 265.

15. Sherman to Ellen Sherman, July 31, 1862, *Correspondence*, 260; see Craig Symonds, *Lincoln and His Admirals* (New York: Oxford University Press, 2008), 283–88.

16. *OR*, ser. 1, 17.2:200; Sherman to Isaac F. Quimby, August 15; Sherman to Grant, August 17; Sherman to Ellen Sherman, August 20; Sherman to John A. Rawlins, August 14, 1862, *Correspondence*, 276, 278, 279, 283.

17. Sherman to Rawlins, August 14; Sherman to Halleck, August 18, 1862, *Correspondence*, 276, 281.

18. Sherman to Rawlins, August 14; Sherman to Minnie Sherman, October 4; Sherman to Grant, August 17, 1862, *Correspondence*, 276, 279, 315.

19. Sherman to Halleck, August 18; Sherman to Ellen Sherman, August 20; Sherman to Editors of Memphis *Bulletin* and *Appeal*, September 28, 1862, *Correspondence*, 307–8; *OR*, ser. 1, 17.2:205.

20. *OR*, ser. 1, 17.2:201; Sherman to Hindman, October 17; Sherman to Ellen Sherman, September 25; Sherman to Memphis Editors, September 21, 1862, *Correspondence*, 300–301, 305, 316, 317.

21. Sherman to Ellen Sherman, September 25; Sherman to Hindman, October 17; Sherman to Miss P. A. Fraser, October 22, 1862, *Correspondence*, 305, 316–17, 318; Mark Grimsley, *The Hard Hand of War: Union Military Policy Toward Civilians, 1861-1865* (New York: Cambridge University Press, 1995), 114–17. Grimsley treats this episode within its proper context of the war, especially after the methods employed in Missouri, and reduces therefore Sherman's role, frequently exaggerated, in the introduction of punitive methods. This tradition was given scholarly respectability by John

B. Walters, "General William T. Sherman and Total War," *Journal of Southern History* 14, no. 4 (1948): 447–80, esp. 459–67.

22. Sherman to Ellen Sherman, July 31; Sherman to William H. H. Taylor, August 25; Sherman to John Sherman, August 26, 1862, *Correspondence*, 260, 287, 291; Holden Reid, "Sherman and the South," 4–6.

23. Sherman to New York Gentlemen, September 17; Sherman to John Sherman, September; Sherman to Ellen Sherman, September 12, 1862, *Correspondence*, 295, 296, 299, 301.

24. Sherman to John Sherman, October 1; Sherman to Ellen Sherman, August 20; Sherman to Miss P. A. Fraser, October 22, 1862, *Correspondence*, 281, 310, 318–19.

25. Sherman to Ellen Sherman, October 1, 14; Sherman to Halleck, November 17, 1862, *Correspondence*, 328–29.

26. Grant to Sherman, November 14, 1862, *Grant Papers* 6: 310–11; *Memoirs* 1:179.

27. *OR*, ser. 1, 17.2:347–48; for the background, see Brian Holden Reid, *America's Civil War: The Operational Battlefield, 1861–1863* (Amherst, NY: Prometheus Books, 2008), 316–17.

28. Sherman to John Sherman, November 24, 1862, *Correspondence*, 337: "The truth is he is in Springfield Illinois trying to be elected to the US Senate."

29. Sherman to P. B. Ewing, July 13, 14; Sherman to Thomas Tasker Gantt, September 23, 1862, *Correspondence*, 253, 254, 303.

30. Sherman to John Sherman, November 24, 1862, *Correspondence*, 236–37; *OR*, ser. 1, 17.2:209; *Memoirs* 1:284–85.

31. *OR*, ser. 1, 17.2:217, 348, 361, 374, 396, 402–3.

32. Grant to Sherman, December 8, 1862, *Grant Papers* 6:406–7.

33. *OR*, ser. 1, 17.2:397; Sherman to Ellen Sherman, December 14, 1862, *Correspondence*, 343.

34. Sherman to John Sherman, December 6, 1862, *Correspondence*, 339; Sherman appears unaware that Nathaniel P. Banks had been named to replace Butler. Hans L. Trefousse, *Ben Butler: The South Called Him Beast* (New York: Twayne, 1957), 132–33.

35. *OR*, ser. 1, 17.2:374–75, 392; *OR*, ser. 1, 17.1:616.

36. *OR*, ser. 1, 17.2:2, 392, 396; *OR*, ser. 1, 17.1:603.

37. *OR*, ser. 1, 17.2:392, 407; Grant to Sherman, December 7, 1862, *Grant Papers* 6:404.

38. *Memoirs* 1:289; Sherman to John Sherman, December 6; Sherman to Irving McDowell, December 14, 1862, *Correspondence*, 339, 341; on McDowell's abstinence, see T. Harry Williams, *Lincoln and His Generals* (New York: Alfred A. Knopf, 1952), 19.

39. *OR*, ser. 1, 17.2:409–10; *OR*, ser. 1, 17.1:602–3, 610; Sherman to Ellen Sherman, December 14, 1862, *Correspondence*, 342; *Memoirs* 1:289.

40. *OR*, ser. 1, 17.2:424, 426; *OR*, ser. 1, 17.1:604, 610; David J. Eicher, *The Longest War: A Military History of the Civil War* (New York: Simon and Schuster, 2001), 389–90.

41. *OR*, ser. 1, 17. 2:424–26.

42. *OR*, ser. 1, 17.1:605–6, 613; *Memoirs* 1:289–90.

43. *OR*, ser. 1, 17.1:606.

44. *OR*, ser. 1, 17.1:607; *Memoirs* 1:200.

45. *OR*, ser. 1, 17.1:607, 613.

46. *OR*, ser. 1, 17.1:608; *Memoirs* 1:292; Morgan's response is in "The Assault on Chickasaw Bluffs," in *Battles and Leaders of the Civil War*, ed. Robert U. Johnson and Clarence C. Buel, 4 vols. (New York: Century, 1974), 3:462–70.

47. Thomas L. Livermore, *Numbers and Losses in the Civil War in America, 1861–1865*, 2nd ed. (Boston: Houghton and Mifflin, 1901), 96–97; *OR*, ser. 1, 17.1:609.

48. B. H. Liddell Hart, *Sherman: Soldier, Realist, American* (New York: Dodd, Mead, 1929), 164; Marszalek, *Sherman*, 206–7, 208; Richard M. McMurry, *John Bell Hood and the War for Southern Independence* (1982; Lincoln: University of Nebraska Press, 1992), 45–50. Morgan evokes an air of an "impracticable" operation doomed inevitably to defeat as justification for his failure; see Morgan, "Assault on Chickasaw Bluffs," 466–67.

49. *OR*, ser. 1, 17.2:532; Fellman, *Citizen Sherman*, 127; Hirshson, *White Tecumseh*, 139–41.

50. *OR*, ser. 1, 17.1:606, 610.

51. It was at Zela during the Pontic War that the utter destruction of Pharnaces' army inspired Caesar to observe, "Veni, vidi, vici": "I came, I saw, I conquered"; see Suetonius, *Divus Julius* 37. *OR*, ser. 1, 17.1:613; Sherman to John Sherman, January 6, 1863, *Correspondence*, 351–52.

52. *Memoirs* 1:293.

Chapter 8

1. Sherman to Ellen Sherman, January 4, 24, 1863, in *Sherman's Civil War: Selected Correspondence of William T. Sherman, 1860–1865* (Chapel Hill: University of North Carolina Press, 1999), 349, 363 (hereafter *Correspondence*); Ellen Sherman to Sherman, January 19, 1863, CSHR 9/39 UNDA.

2. Sherman to Ellen Sherman, January 4; Sherman to John Sherman, January 6, 1863, *Correspondence*, 350, 352; *Memoirs* 1:296.; Richard L. Kiper, *Major General John A. McClernand: Politician in Uniform* (Kent, OH: Kent State University Press, 1999), 157–62, makes the case for him but does not persuade except to show how well he exploited the knowledge of other commanders.

3. Sherman, *Memoirs* 1:296–97. His account is corroborated by Porter in his MS Private Journal No. 1, Ac 4948A, completed in Annapolis on October 16, 1866, 3, 390–92, 396, 485–87, 610, Container 22, David Dixon Porter Papers, Manuscript Division, Library of Congress (hereafter DDPP, LC). This substantial work of almost 1,000 MS pages was used by Porter to quarry out his memoirs and naval history of the war; it is modeled on his father David Porter's *Journal of a Cruise* (1815, 1822; Annapolis, MD: Naval Institute Press, 1986).

4. Porter, Private Journal No. 1, 489, 490, DDPP, LC; *Memoirs* 1:296–97; *OR*, ser. 1, 17.1:700–701, gives 31,753; Thomas L. Livermore, *Numbers and Losses in the Civil War in America, 1861–1865*, 2nd ed. (Boston: Houghton Mifflin, 1901), 98, gives

28,944, which I have followed; Sherman to Ellen Sherman, January 4; Sherman to John Sherman, January 17, 1863, *Correspondence*, 351, 361.

5. See Sherman to Ellen Sherman, January 28, 1863, *Correspondence*, 378, for his views on the initial surprise achieved; *Memoirs* 1:298; all other details from Sherman's report of January 17, 1863, in *OR*, ser. 1, 17.1:754–55.

6. *OR*, ser. 1, 17.1:755–57; *Memoirs* I:238–301. Ellen was very fond of Dayton, too: "I enjoy his letters exceedingly. He is very clever." Ellen Sherman to Sherman, January 30, 1863, CSHR 9/39 UNDA.

7. *OR*, ser. 1, 17.1:757; Sherman to Thomas Ewing Sr., January 16; Sherman to John Sherman, January 17, 1863, *Correspondence*, 354, 361; Ellen Sherman to Sherman, January 30, 1863, CSHR 9/39 UNDA; Livermore, *Numbers and Losses*, 98; *OR*, ser. 1, 17.2:570–71; McClernand to Grant, January 11; Grant to McClernand, January 13, 1863, *Grant Papers* 7:217, 220. Kiper, *McClernand*, 168–69, 173–79, documents Porter's detestation of McClernand. His claim that Porter and Sherman combined as "instigators" to place "McClernand in an unfavourable light" seems overdrawn; Sherman would surely have exploited Grant's anger more directly if he had conspired in this way. In his letter of January 11 cited above McClernand claimed that Porter "cooperated brilliantly."

8. Sherman to John Sherman, January 6, 1863, *Correspondence*, 352. Ellen had been ill since December 23, 1862, probably brought on by intense anxiety over her husband: "My hand is weak & nervous & I can scarcely write"; Ellen Sherman to Sherman, January 14, 1863, CSHR 9/39 UNDA. U. S. Grant, *Personal Memoirs*, 2 vols. (London: Sampson Low, 1885), 1:339–40; Grant to McClernand, January 13, 18, 1863, *Grant Papers* 7:220, 340.

9. Sherman to Ellen Sherman, January 16, 1863, *Correspondence*, 358–59; *OR*, ser. 1, 17.2:572.

10. Sherman to Ellen Sherman, January 4; Sherman to Grant, January 17, 1863; *OR*, ser. 1, 17.1: 476, 570–71; *OR*, ser. 1, 17.2:432–33, 461; *OR*, ser. 1, 24.1:9 (telegram).

11. Sherman to Ellen Sherman, January 16; Sherman to John Sherman, January 17, 1863, *Correspondence*, 358–59. Kiper, *McClernand*, 183, refers to a "poisonous relationship," but this does not extend to professional intercourse. For the literary allusion, see William Shakespeare, *Julius Caesar*, act 1, scene 2, where Cassius opines, "I know that virtue be in you, Brutus / As well as I do know your outward favor."

12. Sherman to Ellen Sherman, January 24, 1863, *Correspondence*, 363–64.

13. Grant to Halleck, January 20; Grant to Colonel John C. Kelton, February 11, 1863, *Grant Papers* 7:234, 274.

14. *OR*, ser. 1, 17.2:571; Sherman to John Sherman, January 25; Sherman to Ellen Sherman, January 24; Sherman to Stephen A. Hurlbut, , March 16, 1863, *Correspondence*, 371–72, 364, 423.

15. Sherman to Ellen Sherman, January 24, January 28; Sherman to John Sherman, January 25, 1863, *Correspondence*, 364, 372-73, 378; *Memoirs* 1:305; *OR*, ser. 1, 24.3:9–10; *OR*, ser. 1, 17.2:568. During his absence Sherman kept Grant supplied with newspapers and intelligence reports "from rebel sources that Banks approaches Port

Hudson." Grant to Halleck, Grant to Julia D. Grant, January 25, 28, 1863, *Grant Papers* 7: 249; on Porter's aims, see Private Journal No. 1, 508, DDPP, LC.

16. *OR*, ser. 1, 24.3:10, 36–37, 38; Sherman to John Sherman, January 25, 1863, *Correspondence*, 372.

17. Sherman to Ethan A. Hitchcock, January 25, 1863, *Correspondence*, 369; Porter, Private Journal No. 1, 479, DDPP, LC.

18. Sherman to Ellen Sherman, January 28; Sherman to David D. Porter, February 1, 1863, *Correspondence*, 378, 380–81; Ellen Sherman to Sherman, January 19, February 8, CSHR 9/39 UNDA; Sherman to Thomas Ewing Sr., January 16; Sherman to John Sherman, January 31, 1863, *Correspondence*, 361, 354; John F. Marszalek, *Sherman's Other War: The General and the Civil War Press*, rev. ed. (1981; Kent, OH: Kent State University Press, 1999), 139.

19. Sherman to John Sherman, January 31, 1863, *Correspondence*, 379; Ellen Sherman to Sherman, February 11, 1863 CSHR 9/39 UNDA; Marszalek, *Sherman's Other War*, 132–35, 139–40; Porter, Private Journal No. 1, 477, DDPP, LC.

20. Knox's report had appeared on January 17; see Marszalek, *Sherman's Other War*, 136–37, 137–38, 140. Ellen Sherman to Sherman, February 4, 8, 1863, CSHR 9/39 UNDA.

21. Sherman to John Sherman, January 17, 31; Sherman to Thomas Ewing Sr., January 16, 1863, *Correspondence*, 254–55, 362, 379. As Sherman warned Murat Halstead, "they shall not insult me with impunity in my own camp" *OR*, ser. 1, 17.2:897.

22. Sherman to Ellen Sherman, January 28, 1863, *Correspondence*, 378; *OR*, ser. 1, 17.2:588, 896.

23. *OR*, ser. 1, 17.2:896; on the youth of field reporters, see Marszalek, *Sherman's Other War*, 52.

24. See above, p. 177.

25. Sherman to John Sherman, January 31; Sherman to Blair, February 2, 1863, *Correspondence*, 379, 381–82; *OR*, ser. 1, 17.2:582, 584, 586; Blair to Sherman, February 3, 1863, in S. M. H. Byers, "Some War Letters," *North American Review* 144, no. 364 (March 1887): 294.

26. *OR*, ser. 1, 17.2:587–88, 589–90.

27. On Thayer's legal and volunteer background, see Ezra J. Warner, *Generals in Blue* (1964; Baton Rouge: Louisiana State University Press, 1988), 499–500. Sherman had offered an example of Knox's articles appearing in southern newspapers in *OR*, ser. 1, 17.2:588. See also Sherman to John Sherman, February 12, 1863, *Correspondence*, 396; Marszalek, *Sherman's Other War*, 144–52, offers excellent coverage. On Ellen's fears, see Ellen Sherman to Sherman, February 14, 22, 24, March 4, 1863, CSHR 9/39 UNDA.

28. Sherman to Thomas Ewing Sr., February 17; Sherman to Rawlins, February 23; Sherman to John Sherman, April 3; Sherman to Knox, April 7, 1863, *Correspondence*, 398–99, 408, 438, 440; *OR*, ser. 1, 17.2:892–93; Ellen Sherman to Sherman, February 22, 24, 1863, CSHR 9/39 UNDA; Marszalek, *Sherman's Other War*, 155–59, 161.

29. Michael Fellman, *Citizen Sherman* (New York: Random House, 1995), 128–35; Marzsalek, *Sherman's Other War*, 160–61; Sherman to John Sherman, February 4; Sherman to Grant, April 8; Sherman to Halstead, April 8, 1863, *Correspondence*, 389,

441, 442–43; *OR*, ser. 1, 17.2:233–34, 895. Sherman was explicit in his statement to Halstead: "I am no enemy to freedom of thought, freedom of the 'Press' and speech."

30. *OR*, ser. 1, 17.2:896; Sherman to John Sherman, January 25, 1863, *Correspondence*, 372; *OR*, ser. 1, 24.3:69–70. Throughout March, Thomas Ewing Sr. supported Sherman's wish to sue the Cincinnati *Gazette* and the Missouri *Republican* and began preparations, though they petered out. Ellen Sherman to Sherman, March 7, 9, 23, 1863, CSHR 9/39 UNDA.

31. *OR*, ser. 1, 24.3:36; Sherman to Ellen Sherman, February 6; Sherman to E. O. C. Ord, February 22, 1863, *Correspondence*, 393, 406; Ellen Sherman to Sherman, February 8, 10, 11, 14, March 26, 1863, CSHR 9/39 UNDA.

32. Sherman to Ellen Sherman, February 26; Sherman to Edwin M. Stanton, January 25, 1863, *Correspondence*, 411, 375–76.

33. Sherman to John Sherman, January 25, February 18; Sherman to P. B. Ewing, March 3; Sherman to David Tod, March 12, 1863, *Correspondence*, 373–75, 403–5, 413–14, 416.

34. *OR*, ser. 1, 24.3:158.

35. Sherman to P. B. Ewing, March 3; Sherman to Minnie Sherman, March 15, 1863, *Correspondence*, 414, 422.

36. Sherman to S. A. Hurlbut, March 16, 1863, *Correspondence*, 423; Grant to Sherman, March 16, 1863, *Grant Papers* 7:423–24; *OR*, ser. 1, 24.3:114, 437; *OR*, ser. 1, 24.1:433–434.

37. *OR*, ser. 1, 24.1:432–34, 434–35, 436, 458; *OR*, ser. 1, 24.3:436–37; Grant to Sherman, March 22, 1863, *Grant Papers* 7:455; *Memoirs* 1:307–11; Porter, Private Journal No. 1, 542–43, DDPP, LC, quickly skates over this incident and the "ridiculous position" it put him in.

38. Sherman to John Sherman, April 3, 1863, *Correspondence*, 437, 439.

39. Sherman to Ellen Sherman, April 10; Sherman to John Sherman, April 10, 1863, *Correspondence*, 446, 450; Brooks D. Simpson, *Ulysses S. Grant: Triumph over Adversity, 1822–1865* (New York: Houghton Mifflin, 2000), 173–79, 218; Brian Holden Reid, "The Commander and His Chief of Staff: Ulysses S. Grant and John A. Rawlins," in *Command and Leadership in War*, ed. G. D. Sheffield, rev. ed. (1997; London: Brassey's, 2002), 25–26.

40. John Keegan, *The Mask of Command* (London: Jonathan Cape, 1987), 198; *Memoirs* 1:315.

41. *OR*, ser. 1, 24.3:179–80; Sherman to Rawlins, April 8, 1863, *Correspondence*, 443–45; *Memoirs* 1:315–16; Porter, Private Journal No. 1, 559, DDPP, LC, had been impressed by Grant's abstemiousness. Kiper, *McClernand*, 206–7, refers darkly to "a conspiracy" against McClernand, before detailing his underhand actions that so appalled Sherman and others. On the drunken incident he related to Lincoln attempting to defame Grant, see Brian Holden Reid, *America's Civil War: The Operational Battlefield, 1861–1863* (Amherst, NY: Prometheus Books, 2008), 324.

42. Sherman to John Sherman, April 10; Sherman to Ellen Sherman, April 10, 1863, *Correspondence*, 449–51, 445–48; Ellen remained suspicious that John "has espoused the quarrel against me" or that he "has had his mind poisoned in some way." Ellen Sherman to Sherman, February 10, 22, March 26, April 2, 4, 7, 13, 1863 CSHR 9/

39 UNDA. Also see Allan G. Bogue, *The Earnest Men: Republicans of the Civil War Senate* (Ithaca, NY: Cornell University Press, 1981), 36–37.

43. Sherman to Ellen Sherman, April 23, 1861, *Correspondence*, 455, 456; *OR*, ser. 1, 34. 1:751; *Memoirs* 1:317–18, though the tone of the retrospective account is shaded more optimistically than his contemporary correspondence; Porter, Private Journal No. 1, 572–73, DDPP, LC.

44. *OR*, ser. 1, 24.1:752; Porter, Private Journal No. 1, 584–88, 589, DDPP, LC; Sherman to John Sherman, April 3, 26, 1863, *Correspondence*, 439, 462; Grant to Sherman, April 24, *Grant Papers* 7:117–18. Grant, increasingly aware of the extent of Sherman's doubts, concluded this missive: "I leave the management of affairs at your end of the line to you."

45. Grant to Sherman, April 27, 1863, *Grant Papers* 7:122; *OR*, ser. 1, 24.1:752, 577; Sherman to Ellen Sherman, May 2, 1863, *Correspondence*, 466; Porter, Private Journal No. 1, 605–7, 608, DDPP, LC; Ellen Sherman to Sherman, April 7, 1863, CSHR 9/ 39 UNDA.

46. *OR*, ser. 1, 24.:577, 752–53; Sherman to Ellen Sherman, May 6, 1863, *Correspondence*, 468. Sherman claimed that the distance marched by Fifteenth Corps totaled 83 miles; see Sherman to Ellen Sherman, May 9, 1863, *Correspondence*, 470.

47. Sherman to Ellen Sherman, May 6, 1863, *Correspondence*, 468–69; *Memoirs* 1:320–21.

48. Sherman to Ellen Sherman, May 6, 9, 1863, *Correspondence*, 469, 470; Grant to Sherman, May 3, 4, 9, 1863, *Grant Papers* 8:151–52, 158–59, 178–79, 183–84; *OR*, ser. 1, 24.1:752–53.

49. *OR*, ser. 1, 24.1:754.

50. *OR*, ser. 1, 24.1:; see his later reflections on the hotel incident in *Memoirs* 1:322. The owner might have antagonized Union soldiers by curtly rejecting payment with greenbacks, and later they exacted a malicious revenge.

51. *OR*, ser. 1, 24.1:754–55; *Memoirs* 1:323–24.

52. Lloyd Lewis, *Sherman: Fighting Prophet* (1929; New York: Harcourt Brace, 1958), 277, is the best evocation; see also U. S. Grant, *Personal Memoirs*, 2 vols. (London: Sampson Lowe), 1885), 1:528, 542n.

53. *OR*, ser. 1, 24.1:755–56; Sherman to Ellen Sherman, May 19, 1863, *Correspondence*, 471. For an example of skeptical discussion, see Rowena Reed, *Combined Operations in the Civil War* (1978; Lincoln: University of Nebraska Press, 1993), 239, 255.

54. *OR*, ser. 1, 24.1:756; for Grant's optimistic expectations of the attack, see Bruce Catton, *Grant Moves South* (Boston: Little, Brown, 1960), 450–52.

55. Sherman to Ellen Sherman, May 19, 1863, *Correspondence*, 471; *Memoirs* 1:471; Ellen Sherman to Sherman, May 22, 1863, CSHR 9/39 UNDA.

56. *OR*, ser. 1, 24.1:756; *Memoirs* 1:325–26; General Field Orders, May 21, 1863, *Grant Papers* 8:245–46.

57. Sherman to Ellen Sherman, May 25, 1863, *Correspondence*, 471–73; *OR*, ser. 1, 24.1:756; Porter, Private Journal No. 1, 662–68, DDPP, LC.

58. *OR*, ser. 1, 24.1:756–57.

59. *OR*, ser. 1, 24.1:757–58; *Memoirs* 1:326–27; Sherman to Ellen Sherman, May 25, 1863, *Correspondence*, 472; Livermore, *Numbers and Losses*, 472; on McClernand's comparative success, see Kiper, *McClernand*, 260–62.

60. *OR*, ser. 1, 24.1:758; *Memoirs* 1:328; Sherman to Ellen Sherman, May 25, 1863, *Correspondence*, 472; Porter, Private Journal No. 1, 662–68, DDPP, LC.

61. Sherman to Ellen Sherman, May 25, 1863; Sherman to John Sherman, May 29, 1863, *Correspondence*, 472, 479.

62. For McClernand's brash General Order No. 72 of May 29, 1863, see *OR*, ser. 1, 24.1:160–61, and for Sherman and McPherson's responses, see 162–64; Stanley P. Hirshson, *The White Tecumseh: A Biography of William T. Sherman* (New York: John Wiley, 1997), 157, also stresses Blair's role; Porter, Private Journal No. 1, 659–60, DDPP, LC.

63. Grant to McClernand, June 17, 1863, *Grant Papers* 8:384–85; *OR*, ser. 1, 24.1:103, 157, 159, 161–62, 164–65, 165–67, 167–68, 168–69. The only politician who supported McClernand was Richard Yates, the governor of Illinois, who on June 30 did not ask for his reinstatement but suggested he be put in command in Pennsylvania. On McClernand's illusions concerning his influence in Lincoln's administration, see Kiper, *McClernand*, 270–71, 273, 275–77. McClernand died in September 1900.

64. Sherman to Ellen Sherman, July 5, 1863, *Correspondence*, 501. See Grant's comment (*OR*, ser. 1, 24.1:159) that he had attempted "to do the most I could with the means at my command which ... made me tolerate General McClernand long after I thought the good of the service demanded his removal." For a favorable review of his record, see Kiper, *McClernand*, 304.

65. Grant to Sherman, June 22, 1863, *Grant Papers* 8:408; Sherman to John McArthur, n.d., William T. Sherman Papers, ALS 72.397, Box 1, Special Collections and Preservation Division, Chicago Public Library (hereafter SP, CPL).

66. For these operations, see *OR*, ser. 1, 24.2:245–48, 532–33, and Sherman to McArthur, July 2, 1863, ALS 72.402, Box 1, SP, CPL. By June 30 he had become "uneasy" about Lee's invasion of Pennsylvania, news of which he had picked up from the St. Louis newspapers.

67. *OR*, ser. 1, 24.2:533–34, 520–21; *Memoirs* 1:329. He remarked sarcastically of Klein, "This boy of Ohio birth is not very loyal." Mr. Klein's son was serving in Vicksburg. See Sherman to Ellen Sherman, June 27; Sherman to John Sherman, June 27; Sherman to Grant, July 4, 1863, *Correspondence*, 491, 495, 497.

68. Sherman to Ellen Sherman, June 27, 1863, *Correspondence*, 491; *OR*, ser. 1, 24.2:525, 528, 534, 540; Craig Symonds, *Joseph E. Johnston* (New York: Norton, 1992), 211, estimates Johnston's strength at "nearly 23,000 men."

69. *OR*, ser. 1, 24.2,:535–36, 521–22, 523, 525–27. Lauman did not serve in the field again. Ezra J. Warner, *Generals in Blue* (1964; Baton Rouge: Louisiana State University Press, 1988), 276.

70. *OR*, ser. 1, 24.2:524, 526, 535, 539, 541–42; Sherman to John Sherman, July 19, Sherman to Porter, July 19, 1863 *Correspondence*, 507, 505. The latter also reveals that Sherman's generals attended a supper at the governor's mansion in which "the 'Army and Navy *forever*' was sung with a full and hearty chorus." For a

misconceived criticism of Sherman's decision not to pursue (it was not a cavalry raid), see James Harrison Wilson, *Under the Old Flag*, 2 vols. (New York: Appleton, 1912), 1:234–36.

71. *OR*, ser. 1, 24.2:537–38, 530–31, 540; Sherman to John Sherman, August 3 ("I am sick and tired of the plundering and pilfering that marks our progress"); Sherman to John A. Rawlins, August 4, 1863, *Correspondence*, 515, 518–19.

72. *OR*, ser. 1, 24.2:532; Sherman to John Sherman, July 28, 1863, *Correspondence*, 509.

73. Sherman to Thomas Ewing Sr., August 13; Sherman to Grant, July 4, August 15; Sherman to Wallace, August 27, 1863, *Correspondence*, 522, 523, 496, 527.

74. Sherman to P. B Ewing, August 5; Sherman to John Sherman, September 9, 1863, *Correspondence*, 520, 521, 539; Ellen Sherman to Sherman, February 20, 22, April 13, 28, June 26, July 1, 26, October 16, 1863, CSHR 9/39 UNDA.

75. Ellen Ewing Sherman, "Recollections of Willie Sherman" (1863), CSHR 4/64 UNDA, 1, 3, for this and the previous paragraph; *Memoirs* 1:348; Sherman to Grant, October 4, 1863, *Grant Papers* 9:274; Sherman to Charles C. Smith, October 4, MS copy, ALS 72.402, Box 1, SP, CPL; Sherman to Ellen Sherman, October 6, 28, 1863, *Correspondence*, 553, 568. The best account of the Shermans' deep mourning is Michael Fellman, *Citizen Sherman: The Life of William T. Sherman* (New York: Random House, 1995), 199–212. The ultimate standard is Queen Victoria's grief at Prince Albert's passing in 1861; see Adam Rappaport, *Magnificent Obsession: Victoria, Albert and the Death That Changed the Monarchy* (London: Hutchinson, 2011), 146–47, 150–53, 156–60.

76. Sherman to Ellen Sherman, July 5, April 27; Sherman to David Stuart, August 1, 1863, *Correspondence*, 499, 453, 512.

77. Sherman to John Sherman, July 28; Sherman to Stuart, August 2; Sherman to P. B. Ewing, August 5; Sherman to Wallace, August 27; Sherman to Tuttle, August 20, 1863, *Correspondence*, 510, 512, 520, 527, 525. See Fellman, *Citizen Sherman*, 146, 172, for a discussion of Sherman's supposed "release of anger," especially at Jackson in July 1863, which "had let loose a ferocity from within himself toward Southern civilians that he had formerly reserved for newspapermen and then had extended to guerrillas." See also *OR*, ser 2, 5:672.

Chapter 9

1. On these complex issues I have followed Paul Griffiths, "The Distinction between Innate and Acquired Characteristics," in *The Stanford Encyclopaedia of Philosophy*, Fall 2009 ed., ed. Edward N. Zalta, https://plato.stanford.edu/entries/innate-acquired/. Brian Holden Reid, "Command and Leadership in the Civil War," in *Themes of the American Civil War*, 2nd ed., , ed. Susan-Mary Grant and Brian Holden Reid (2000; New York: Routledge, 2010), 100–123; B. H. Liddell Hart, *Sherman: The Genius of the Civil War* (London: Ernest Benn, 1930); J. F. C. Fuller, *Grant and Lee: A Study in Personality and Generalship*, 2nd ed. (Bloomington: Indiana University Press), 1, remains seminal on the personal factor.

2. On the humanity "of the great," see Gamaliel Bradford, *Lee the American* (London: Constable, 1912), 281: "They laugh as we, suffer as we, fail as we" and are often "astonished at triumphing as we should be." Sherman to Grant, October 4, 1863, *Grant Papers* 9:274.

3. An amusing description of a junior officer standing up to McClernand's bullying can be found in James Harrison Wilson, *Under the Old Flag*, 2 vols. (New York: Appleton, 1912), 1:182–83, though one suspects the anecdote has been improved; the memoir itself is consistently hostile to Sherman. On Pike, see *Memoirs* 1:274. Pike died later in a pistol accident in Oregon that "probably saved him from a slower but harder fate."

4. In this frankness, Sherman resembled the character in Voltaire, *Candide; or, Optimism* (1759; Ware, Herts: Wordsworth Editions, 1999), 41.

5. General Fuller observes, "Now, in a crowd of men, the faculty of humour is more highly developed than those of intellect and reason." Amusement thus aids the speed of their training. See his *Training Soldiers for War* (London: Hugh Rees, 1914), 39. For the view that true leadership is not imposed but desired, see Correlli Barnett, *The Lords of War: From Lincoln to Churchill, Supreme Command, 1861-1945* (Barnsley: Praetorian Press, 2012), xlix.

6. *OR*, ser. 1, 17.2:434–35.

7. General Fuller cites the example of the French Revolutionary War general Charles Dumouriez (1739-1823), who "won the hearts of his men. How? By unrelenting work among them" (*Training Soldiers for War*, 87).Oliver O. Howard, *Autobiography*, 2 vols. (New York: Baker and Taylor, 1907), 1:474, 482; Elizabeth Sherman Cameron to Liddell Hart, February 10, 1930, Liddell Hart Papers 9/7/7, Liddell Hart Centre for Military Archives, King's College London.

8. Stow Persons, *The Decline of the American Gentility* (New York: Columbia University Press, 1973), vi–vii, 55, 57–59. On courage, note Clausewitz's dictum: "War is the realm of danger; therefore, *courage* is the soldier's first requirement"; *On War*, ed. Michael Howard and Peter Paret (Princeton, NJ: Princeton University Press, 1976), I, iii, 101. Wilson, *Under the Old Flag* 1:160–61; at the time Wilson's views were less pompously expressed than here, where he positions himself as the "real" author of Grant's triumph.

9. Sherman to George Hoyt, April 23, 1881, Sherman Papers, USMA Special Collections, Box 1, for the sentiments expressed in the previous two paragraphs. As Wellington did not publish any memoirs, the second book is probably J. M. Tucker, *The Life of the Duke of Wellington; compiled from despatches* (London: J. Blackwood, 1880).

10. Sherman to P. B. Ewing, October 24, 1863, in *Sherman's Civil War: Selected Correspondence of William T. Sherman, 1860-1865*, ed. Brooks D. Simpson and Jean V. Berlin (Chapel Hill: University of North Carolina Press, 1999), 564 (hereafter *Correspondence*).

11. Shelford Bidwell, *Modern Warfare: A Study of Men, Theories and Weapons* (London: Allen Lane, 1973), 18; this book is a sustained refutation of Liddell Hart's strategy of "the indirect approach." Sherman to Hoyt, May 27 , 1882, Sherman Papers, USMA Special Collections, Box 1.

12. Liddell Hart, *Sherman*, 297–98.

13. Robert Jackson, A *Systematic View of the Formation, Discipline and Economy of Armies* (London: Stockdale, 1804), 229, says a commander's character stands before his army like "a mirror." He continues that a commander's "original genius ... commands attention, and it gives a covering of protection, in reality or idea, which proves a security against the impressions of fear." Martin Van Creveld, *Command in War* (Cambridge, MA: Harvard University Press, 1985), 2, 10–11, 75, 115, 142–43, 147, explores the theme of the "span of command via the theme of the "directed telescope"—the ability of a commander to acquire information "tailored to meet ... momentary (and specific) needs." Note General Fuller's criticisms of Wellington in *The Decisive Battles of the Western World*, 3 vols. (London: Eyre and Spottiswoode, 1954–56), 2: 492–94.

14. Sherman Papers, USMA Special Collections, Box 1,17.2:435; Brian Holden Reid, *America's Civil War: The Operational Battlefield, 1861–1863* (Amherst, NY: Prometheus Books, 2008), 149–50, 233–34, 364–66.

15. Grant to Lincoln, July 22, 1863, *OR*, ser. 1, 24.3, 541; S. M. H. Byers, "Some War Letters," *North American Review* 144, no. 364 (March 1887): 295.

16. Sherman to Rawlins, September 17, 1863, *Correspondence*, 551.

17. Sherman to Halleck, September 17, 1863, *Correspondence*, 44, 545, 547, 549; Lloyd Lewis, *Sherman: Fighting Prophet* (1932; New York: Harcourt Brace, 1958), 306; *The Collected Works of Abraham Lincoln*, ed. Roy P. Basler, 9 vols. (New Brunswick, NJ: Rutgers University Press, 1953), 7:51–56.

18. Sherman to Halleck, October10; Sherman to Major J. M. Wright, October 19, 1863, *Correspondence*, 556, 561–62.

19. *OR*, ser. 1, 30.1:161; *OR*, ser. 1, 31.2:569; *Memoirs* 1:350–51.

20. *OR*, ser. 1, 30.4:234–35; *OR*, ser. 1, 31.2:569–70; Sherman to Halleck, October 10, 1863, *Correspondence*, 555–56; Wilson's hostile account in *Under the Old Flag* 1:290–91 implies that Sherman had a free hand to choose his route and that he had commanded the Army of the Tennessee for the two months prior to the battle, when he did not.

21. *OR*, ser. 1, 30.4:354, 355, 356, 380; *OR*, ser. 1, 31.2:570; Sherman to Ellen Sherman, October 12, 1863, CSHR 2/07, UNDA; Sherman to Ellen Sherman, October 14, 1863, *Correspondence*, 558, 559–60.

22. *OR*, ser. 1, 31.4:356; Sherman to Ellen Sherman, October 14, 1863, *Correspondence*, 559.

23. Sherman to Ellen Sherman, October 12, 1863, CSHR 2/07 UNDA; Sherman to Ellen Sherman, October 14, 1863, *Correspondence*, 560–61; *OR*, ser. 1, 31.2:570; *OR*, ser. 1, 30.4:354, 473; Wilson, *Under the Old Flag* 1:290.

24. *OR*, ser. 1, 30.4:355, 357, 359–60; *OR*, ser. 1, 31.2:570; *OR*, ser. 1, 30.4:354, 473; Wilson, *Under the Old Flag* 1:290.

25. *OR*, ser. 1, 30.4:380, 382–83, 384–85.

26. *OR*, ser. 1, 30.4:403–4, 451, 476; Sherman to P. B. Ewing, October 24, 1863, *Correspondence*, 564.

27. *OR*, ser. 1, 30.4:475–76, 452, 407, 357; *OR*, ser. 1, 31.3:99–100.

28. *OR*, ser. 1, 32.2:307, 451; *OR*, ser. 1, 31.2:570–71; *OR*, ser. 1, 31.3:100–101; *OR*, ser. 1, 32. 2:451; on the delegated departmental powers in his absence, see Sherman

to McPherson, November 18, 1863, *Correspondence*, 573–74: "Suppress all riots, disorders and irregularities ... [and do] not bother yourselves about the rights and wrongs growing out of differences between Masters and Servants, the employer and the employed."

29. Sherman to Ellen Sherman, November 8, 14, CSHR 2/09 UNDA; *OR*, ser. 1, 31.2:29, 571; Howard, *Autobiography* 1:473–74; *Memoirs* 1:361.

30. Sherman to Ellen Sherman October 19, 1863, CSHR 2/07; Ellen Sherman to Sherman, October 16, 23, CSHR 9/39; also see Ellen Sherman to Sherman, October 17, 19, 21, November 9, 25, 30, 1863, CSHR 9/39, UNDA. Wilson, *Under the Old Flag* 1:295, claims the movements of the Army of the Tennessee "were disjointed, desultory, and abortive, while those of the enemy were coherent and effective."

31. *Memoirs* 1:363–64; *OR*, ser, 1, 31.2:37, 39, 41; Wilson, *Under the Old Flag* 1:290–91; Byers, *Some War Letters*, 293; Steven E. Woodworth, *Six Armies in Tennessee* (Lincoln: University of Nebraska Press, 1998), 173.

32. *Memoirs* 1:364; of the more critical biographies, see Lee Kennett, *Sherman: A Soldier's Life* (New York: HarperCollins, 2001), 215–16.

33. *OR*, ser. 1, 31.2:28, 31–32, 33, 572; *OR*, ser. 1, 31.3:216; U. S. Grant, "Chattanooga," in *Battles and Leaders of the Civil War*, 5 vols., ed. Robert C. Underwood and Clarence C. Buel (New York: Century, 1890), 3:692–93; Horace Porter, *Campaigning with Grant* (New York: Century, 1897), 4–11; my interpretation generally follows Peter Cozzens, *The Shipwreck of Their Hopes: The Battles for Chattanooga* (Urbana: University of Illinois Press, 1994), 112–16, 124, though my emphases are very different.

34. Howard is quoted in Cozzens, *Shipwreck of Their Hopes*, 113; *OR*, ser. 1, 31.2: 31–32, 572; Osterhaus's report on his contribution to Hooker's success is in *OR*, ser. 1, 31.2:598–601.

35. *OR*, ser. 1, 31.2:33, 572–73; Grant, "Chattanooga," 701; S. M. H. Byers, "Sherman's Attack at the Tunnel Hill," in *Battles and Leaders of the Civil War*, 5 vols., ed. Robert C. Underwood and Clarence C. Buel (New York: Century, 1890), 3:712; Steven E. Woodworth, *Nothing but Victory: The Army of the Tennessee, 1861–1865* (New York: Alfred A. Knopf, 2005), 467.

36. See Cozzens's comment on spreading "a bit of deserved tarnish on the lustrous image of Sherman's genius" (*Shipwreck of Their Hopes*, 154).

37. *OR*, ser. 1, 30.4:73, 433–34; *OR*, ser. 1, 30.3:73; Grant to Blair, August 23, 1863, *Grant Papers* 9:199, permitted the extension and thanked Blair for defending Grant; Allan G. Bogue, *The Congressman's Civil War* (Cambridge: Cambridge University Press, 1989), 93–94; Herman Belz, "The Etheridge Conspiracy of 1863: A Projected Conservative Coup," *Journal of Southern History* 36, no. 4 (November 1970): 549, 551–52; Lewis, *Sherman*, 318; Sherman to Ellen Sherman, November 17, 1863, *Correspondence*, 572–73.

38. Byers, "Sherman's Attack on Tunnel Hill," 712; *OR*, ser. 1, 31. 2:32, 573.

39. *OR*, ser. 1, 31.2:33, 745–46.

40. *OR*, ser. 1, 31.2:33, 43–44, 574, 596; Cozzens, *Shipwreck of Their Hopes*, 220; Grant, "Chattanooga," 704.

41. *OR*, ser. 1, 31.2:574–75, 747–48.

42. *OR*, ser. 1, 31.2:574–75; Woodworth, *Nothing but Victory*, 470–73; Cozzens, *Shipwreck of Their Hopes*, 205–10.

43. *OR*, ser. 1, 31.2:75, 752; Woodworth, *Nothing but Victory*, 476–77.

44. Cozzens, *Shipwreck of Their Hopes*, 241, argues that Sherman was "in over his head," the opposite of the truth: he was dabbling in matters well beneath his command ceiling. Woodworth, *Six Armies in Tennessee*, 192; Carl Schurz, *Reminiscences*, 3 vols. (New York: Doubleday, Page, 1908), 3: 75; *OR*, ser. 1, 31.2:34.

45. Grant's report supported his loyal lieutenant on this point. Sherman's assault, he wrote, "caused the enemy to mass heavily against him." *OR*, ser. 1, 31.2:34.

46. Cozzens, *Shipwreck of Their Hopes*, 575, 752; Woodworth, *Nothing but Victory*, 476–77; *OR*, ser. 1, 31.2:34–35, 575–76, 596; Woodworth, *Six Armies in Tennessee*, 193.

47. *OR*, ser. 1, 31.2:35, 576–77, 581.

48. *OR*, ser. 1, 31.2:589; Cozzens, *Shipwreck of Their Hopes*, 157; Edward Hagerman, *The American Civil War and the Origins of Modern Warfare* (Bloomington: Indiana University Press, 1988), 221; Craig Symonds, *Stonewall of the West: Patrick Cleburne and the Civil War* (Lawrence: University Press of Kansas, 1997), 161–64.

49. There are parallels between Chattanooga and the Battle of Toulouse in 1814. At the latter, the Duke of Wellington sought to cross a river and seize high ground, and two British assaults were repulsed. See the analysis in Michael Glover, *Wellington as Military Commander* (London: Batsford, 1968), 141–47; Field Marshal Viscount Montgomery of Alamein, "Wellington Memorial Lecture," *RUSI Journal* 114, no. 656 (December 1969): 9–10, 13.

50. Sherman to John Sherman, December 29, 1863, *Correspondence*, 576–77; *OR*, ser. 1, 31.2:45, 575, 580–81,752; Thomas L. Livermore, *Numbers and Losses in the Civil War in America, 1861–1865*, 2nd ed. (Boston: Houghton Mifflin, 1901), 107; Liddell Hart, *Sherman*, 290–91; Cozzens, *Shipwreck of Their Hopes*, 391–92.

51. *OR*, ser. 1, 31.2:577; Schurz, *Reminiscences* 3:78; Wilson, *Under the Old Flag* 1:307.

52. *OR*, ser. 1, 31.3:297.

53. *OR*, ser. 1, 31.2:577–58, 579; *Memoirs* I1:367–68; Howard is keen in his *Autobiography* to point out that he accompanied Sherman into Knoxville, not Granger, as claimed by their commander (1:492).

54. Ellen Sherman to Sherman, November 25, 30, 1863, CSHR 9/39; Sherman to Ellen Sherman, January 25, 1864 (misdated 1863), CSHR 2/10, UNDA; Ezra J. Warner, *Generals in Blue* (1964; Baton Rouge: Louisiana State University Press, 1988), 146.

55. *OR*, ser. 1, 32.1:173–74; *OR*, ser. 1, 32.2:201; on Meridian's broader significance in a supposed "strategy of raids," see Richard Beringer, Herman Hattaway, Archer Jones, and William N. Still Jr., *Why the South Lost the Civil War* (Athens: University of Georgia Press, 1986), 310–14.

56. MS copy, December 7, 1863, Sherman Papers, Chicago History Museum Research Center; *OR*, ser. 1, 3.3:353–54.

57. *OR*, ser. 1, 32.2:201; *OR*, ser. 1, 32.1:174; Sherman to Ellen Sherman, February 2, 1864, CSHR 2/11 UNDA.

58. *OR*, ser. 1, 31.1:182, 185–86; Sherman to John Sherman, December 29, 1863, *Correspondence*, 578.

59. *OR*, ser. 1, 32.1:174–75, 181–82.
60. *OR*, ser. 1, 32.1:179–81, 183–84; also see Woodworth, *Nothing but Victory*, 479–81.
61. *OR*, ser. 1, 32.1:175–76, 221.
62. *OR*, ser. 1, 32.1:176–77; *Memoirs* 1:394–95; Sherman to Ellen Sherman, February 29, 1864, CSHR 2/11 UNDA.
63. Albert Castel, *Decision in the West: The Atlanta Campaign of 1864* (Lawrence: University Press of Kansas, 1992), 55; these claims are repeated in Castel, *Victors in Blue* (Lawrence: University Press of Press, 2011), 250.
64. *OR*, ser. 1, 32.1:177; Sherman to Ellen Sherman, October 12, 1863, CSHR 2/07 UNDA.

Chapter 10

1. See Lieutenant General Sir John Kiszely's discussion, "The British Army and Approaches to War since 1945," in *Military Power: Land Warfare in Theory and Practice*, ed. Brian Holden Reid (London: Frank Cass, 1997), 179–206.
2. Sherman to James B. Brigham, January 26, 1864, in *Sherman's Civil War: Selected Correspondence of William T. Sherman, 1860–1865*, ed. Brooks D. Simpson and Jean V. Berlin (Chapel Hill: University of North Carolina Press, 1999), 591 (hereafter *Correspondence*); John Fabian Witt, *Lincoln's Code: The Laws of War in American History* (New York: Free Press, 2012), 15, 27, 36, 51, 58–69, 70, 71, 72, 75, 169.
3. Sherman to Roswell M. Sawyer, January 31, 1864, *Correspondence*, 599.
4. Sherman to Sawyer, January 31, Sherman to Joseph Holt, April 6, 1864, *Correspondence*, 599, 615; Sherman to Ellen Sherman, April 26, 1864, CSHR 2/13 UNDA; Witt, *Lincoln's Code*, 268, stresses that the "overwhelming majority of prosecutions" were for spying.
5. Sherman to Sawyer, January 31, 1864, *Correspondence*, 600–602.
6. Sherman to Ellen Sherman, March 12; Sherman to John Sherman, April 5, 1864, *Correspondence*, 609, 613. The idea that the sectional dispute "can only be solved by War" was a centerpiece of the earlier "essay" Halleck wanted to publish; see Sherman to Halleck, September 17, 1863, *Correspondence*, 547.
7. Sherman to Sawyer, January 31; Sherman to Minnie Sherman, January 12, 1864, *Correspondence*, 587.
8. Grant to Sherman, March 4, 1864, *Grant Papers* 10:186–87; on Grant's desire for trustworthy subordinates, see Albert Castel, *Victors in Blue* (Lawrence: University Press of Kansas, 2011), 137, 202, 248, 304.
9. Sherman to Grant, March 10; Sherman to Ellen Sherman, March 12, 1864, *Correspondence*, 603, 608.
10. Sherman to John Sherman, March 24, 1864, *Correspondence*, 610; for a restatement of the view that "to a large degree, the Union victory in the Civil War was a Western victory in more than one sense of the term," see Earl J. Hess, *The Civil War in the West* (Chapel Hill: University of North Carolina Press, 2012), xiii.
11. Grant to Sherman, March 4, 1864, *Grant Papers* 10:190. Indeed, in his personal letter to Sherman, Grant had stipulated that he would not accept any appointment which required making "that city my H[ea]d Q[ua]r[ter]s" (187).

12. Sherman to Ellen Sherman, March 10, 1864, *Correspondence*, 604, 606, 607; Ellen Sherman to Sherman, March 8; Sherman to Ellen Sherman, January 25, February 28, 1864, CHSR 2/10/11 UNDA.

13. And not to be confused with a division of troops, a formation that had emerged during the eighteenth century. See B. H. Liddell Hart, *The Ghost of Napoleon* (London: Faber and Faber, 1933), 45–47, 65–67.

14. Sherman to Ellen Sherman, March 10, 12; Sherman to Brayman, April 2, 1864, *Correspondence*, 605, 608, 609; Sherman to Ellen Sherman, April 18, 1864, CSHR 2/13 UNDA; John F. Marszalek. *Sherman's Other War: The General and the Civil War Press*, rev. ed. (1991; Kent, OH: Kent State University Press, 1999), 176–78, 184.

15. *Memoirs* 2:5–7; U. S. Grant, *Personal Memoirs*, 2 vols. (London: Sampson Low, 1886) 2:119, 126; Sherman to Fry, April 10, 1864, *Correspondence*, 616. Stanton disliked Buell not least for his efforts to exploit the press; Benjamin P. Thomas and Harold H. Hyman, *Stanton: The Life and Times of Lincoln's Secretary of War* (New York: Alfred A. Knopf, 1962), 260.

16. Ellen Sherman to Sherman, January 21, 29, February 8, 1864, CSHR 9/40 UNDA; Sherman to John Sherman, March 24, 1864, *Correspondence*, 609; Grant to Sherman, March 4, 1864, *Grant Papers* 10:190, 251–53.

17. See Major General J. F. C. Fuller, *Lectures on FSR II* (London: Sifton Praed, 1931), 6, 165. The role of conferences, Fuller avers, should be the "explanation of an idea ... not a seeking for an idea and letting people do what they please." They should never be called "to pick the brains of subordinates."

18. *Memoirs* 2:7–9; for his report, see *OR*, ser. 1, 38.1: 59.

19. Sherman to Ellen Sherman, March 24; Sherman to John Sherman, March 24, April 11; Sherman to Grant, April 2, 1864, *Correspondence*, 609, 619, 611; on the unanimity over Palmer, see Sherman to Grant, April 10, 1864, *Correspondence*, 617.

20. *OR*, ser. 1, 32.3:221, 276; *Memoirs* 2:13–14; Sherman to Grant, April 2, 1864, *Correspondence*, 611.

21. Sherman to Grant, April 2, 1864, *Correspondence*, 611; *Memoirs* 2:15.

22. Stephen Z. Starr, *The Union Cavalry in the Civil War*, 3 vols. (Baton Rouge: Louisiana State University Press, 1979–85), 3:393–99,, for his discussion of "the grim catalogue of avoidable and unavoidable difficulties that kept a large percentage of the Union cavalry dismounted at any given moment."

23. Sherman to Grant, April 10, 1864, *Correspondence*, 617; *Memoirs* 2:27–29.

24. Sherman to Grant, April 10, 1864, *Correspondence*, 618; Sherman to Ellen Sherman, October 19, 1863, CSHR 2/08 UNDA.

25. Sherman to Grant, April 10, 1864, *Correspondence*, 618. This is a reference to Jackson's campaign during the First Seminole War of 1817–18 when he departed Fort Scott, Georgia, on March 10, 1818, and crossed into Florida on the east bank of the Apalachicola River with less than three days' rations of parched corn and pork to feed 3,000 troops and 2,000 Indian allies. As the supplies ran out, Jackson spotted supply boats sailing up from Alum Bluffs, Liberty County, Florida. See Robert Remini, *Andrew Jackson: The Course of American Empire* (1977; Baltimore: Johns Hopkins University Press, 1998), 352.

26. The previous three paragraphs are based on Sherman to Ellen Sherman, April 18, 1864, CSHR 2/13 UNDA; Sherman to John Sherman, April 5, 1864; *OR*, ser. 1, 32.3:279–80, 420, respectively; *OR*, ser. 1, 38.4:3; Sherman to Grant, April 10, 1864, *Correspondence*, 617.

27. For Sherman's uplifting appeal, see *Memoirs* 2:11–12, but in *OR*, ser. 1, 38.4:74–75, Sherman makes an attractive business case: "Your [rail]road will double and quadruple as the Cumberland falls and your road can well profit ... by enlarging its capacity."

28. For Banks's orders from Grant in the 1864 campaign, see *OR*, ser. 1, 34.1:11.

29. Sherman to Grant, April 10; Sherman to John Sherman, April 11, 1864, *Correspondence*, 618, 619-20; *OR*, ser. 1, 38.4:25, 74.

30. *OR*, ser. 1, 38.1:59; *OR*, ser. 1, 38.4:125.

31. Sherman to Ellen Sherman, April 27, 1864; Sherman to Thomas Ewing Sr., April 18, 1864, *Correspondence*, 623, 631–32; Ellen Sherman to Sherman, April 11, 15, 1864, CSHR 9/40 UNDA; *OR*, ser. 1, 38.4:23–24; *Memoirs* 2:22. Sherman indicates that the staff in Nashville "were empowered to give orders in my name" but not to take decisions in their commander's name.

32. Sherman to Minnie Sherman, May 2; Sherman to Ellen Sherman, May 4, 1864, *Correspondence*, 632–34.

33. *OR*, ser. 1, 38.4:3, 5, 11. My interpretation is the reverse of Albert Castel, *Decision in the West: The Atlanta Campaign of 1864* (Lawrence: University Press of Kansas, 1992), 90–91. Castel argues that Sherman's plan "violates the spirit if not the letter of Grant's instructions." Sherman, according to this view, made Atlanta, not Johnston's army, the prime objective of the campaign because he disliked battles. Grant appears not to have noticed this disobedience.

34. *OR*, ser. 1, 38.4:56, 64, 65.

35. *Memoirs* 2:31; Sherman refers here to the "shelter tent," made of cotton and sometimes rubber, erected by two muskets driven into the ground joined by a guy rope, over which the tent was pitched. Liddell Hart's view that Sherman had grasped the style of modern mobile warfare is repeated in his theoretical works, but most conveniently in his introduction to an abridged version of Sherman's *Memoirs* called *From Atlanta to the Sea*, ed. B. H. Liddell Hart (London: Folio Society, 1961), 11–12. Liddell Hart devoted much labor to this centenary project, as indicated by the correspondence in the Liddell Hart Papers 9/17/13, Liddell Hart Centre for Military Archives, King's College London.

36. *OR*, ser. 1, 38.4:82–83, 84, 89, 99, 98, 120.

37. *OR*, ser. 1, 38.4:88, 111, 121; Castel, *Decision in the West*, 121, 123, 135, 138–39; Steven E. Woodworth, *Nothing but Victory: The Army of the Tennessee, 1861–1865* (New York: Alfred A. Knopf, 2005), 495–96; *Memoirs* 2:32–34. McPherson faced some 4,000 raw and bedraggled Confederate troops.

38. *OR*, ser. 1, 38.4:111, 112, 113, 114.

39. *OR*, ser. 1, 38.4:112, 121, 122, 125; *Memoirs* 2:34. See the President's Message to the House of Representatives, April 28, 1864, asking that he be allowed to return to the field, in *The Collected Works of Abraham Lincoln*, ed. Roy P. Basler, 9 vols. (New Brunswick, NJ: Rutgers University Press, 1953), 7:39.

40. *OR*, ser. 1, 38.1:59, 139–41; Craig L. Symonds, *Joseph E. Johnston: A Civil War Biography* (New York: Norton, 1992), 277–81; Woodworth, *Nothing but Victory*, 496–97; Sherman's remark to McPherson is quoted in Castel, *Decision in the West*, 150.

41. Oliver O. Howard, "The Struggle for Atlanta," in *Battles and Leaders of the Civil War*, 4 vols., ed. Robert C. Underwood and Clarence C. Buel (New York: Century, 1890), 4:301; *OR*, ser. 1, 38.4:184; *OR*, ser. 1, 38.1:59.

42. *OR*, ser. 1, 38.4:184.

43. *OR*, ser. 1, 38.1:141–42; *Memoirs* 2:34–35; for a detailed account with an emphasis very different from mine, see Castel, *Decision in the West*, 153–55, 169–71, 180–81; on Johnston's retreat, Thomas L. Connelly, *The Autumn of Glory: The Army of Tennessee, 1862–1865* (Baton Rouge: Louisiana State University Press, 1971), 342–43.

44. The casualty figures are estimates; the casualty returns for this campaign are consolidated in Sherman's report to August 1864, *OR*, ser. 1, 38.1:85; Thomas L. Livermore, *Numbers and Losses in the Civil War in America, 1861–1865,* 2nd ed. (Boston: Houghton Mifflin, 1901), 119n1; *Memoirs* 2:36; Sherman to Ellen Sherman, May 20, 22, 1864, *Correspondence*, 636, 638.

45. Sherman to Ellen Sherman, May 22; Sherman to John Sherman, May 26, 1864, *Correspondence*, 638, 639, 640.

46. Thomas uses the term "pursuit" in his report: *OR*, ser. 1, 38.1:142.

47. Sherman to Ellen Sherman, May 22, 1864, *Correspondence*, 639; *OR*, ser. 1, 38.4:60; *Memoirs* 2:37.

Chapter 11

1. *OR*, ser. 1, 38.4:216–17, 29.

2. *OR*, ser. 1, 38.1:66; *OR*, ser. 1, 38.4:219. Sherman's contemporary correspondence does not reveal knowledge of Johnston's projected counterstroke at Cassville, which he did not learn of until their accidental meeting in autumn 1865 aboard a river steamer sailing from Memphis to Cairo. So this knowledge does inform the account in *Memoirs* 2:37–39.

3. *OR*, ser. 1, 38.4:220, 223, 224, 233.

4. *OR*, ser. 1, 38.4:233, 242–43.

5. *OR*, ser. 1, 38.4:242–43, 249. Thomas, unaware of the true reason for Johnston's departure—the disruption of his planned counterstroke—proudly reported that the enemy must have been "demoralized" by his "unexpected" advance (263). Sherman's critical inference is found in his report, *OR*, ser. 1, 38.1:65.

6. *OR*, ser. 1, 38.4:248–49, 261, 272.

7. *OR*, ser. 1, 38.4:260–61, 262.

8. *OR*, ser. 1, 38.4:261; Benjamin P. Thomas and Harold M. Hyman, *Stanton: The Life and Times of Lincoln's Secretary of War* (New York: Alfred A. Knopf, 1962), 294; William B. Hesseltine, *Lincoln and the War Governors* (New York: Alfred A. Knopf, 1948), 321, 350.

9. *OR*, ser. 1, 38.4:275, 282, 294, 295.

10. *OR*, ser. 1, 38.4:248, 262, 278, 288–89.

11. *OR*, ser. 1, 38.4:294, 260, 266. But Sherman would have rejected Liddell Hart's contention that "the direct battle-lusting strategy" governing Grant's Virginia campaign "mortally damaged" the prospects for Union victory. B. H. Liddell Hart, *Sherman* (London: Ernest Benn, 1930), 9.

12. Sherman to Ellen Sherman, May 22, 1864, in *Sherman's Civil War: Selected Correspondence of William T. Sherman, 1860–1865*, ed. Brooks D. Simpson and Jean V. Berlin (Chapel Hill: University of North Carolina Press, 1999), 639 (hereafter *Correspondence*); *Memoirs* 2:39, 42; "Descendants of Allen Martin and Related Families," https://wc.rootsweb.com/cgi-bin/igm.cgi?op=GET&db=bfhawkins&id=I45259 (accessed December 13, 2013).

13. *OR*, ser. 1, 38.1:65; *OR*, ser. 1, 38.4:272.

14. *OR*, ser. 1, 38.4:271, 274, 285–86; *OR*, ser. 1, 38.1:65, 72–73.

15. *OR*, ser. 1, 38.4:288; Craig L. Symonds, *Joseph E. Johnston: A Civil War Biography* (New York: Norton, 1992), 296–97.

16. *OR*, ser. 1, 38.1:66, 143.

17. *OR*, ser. 1, 38.4:299.

18. *OR*, ser. 1, 38.4:317; Walter H. Hebert, *Fighting Joe Hooker* (Indianapolis, IN: Bobbs Merrill, 1944), 277.; Albert Castel, *Decision in the West: The Atlanta Campaign of 1864* (Lawrence: University Press of Kansas, 1992), 225–26.

19. Hebert, *Hooker*, 278.

20. For harsh comments the year before on "the common clay out of which many of our new Generals are made," especially Hooker, see Sherman to Ellen Sherman, April 17, 1863, *Correspondence*, 452.

21. *OR*, ser. 1, 38.4:312, and for similar instructions to Thomas, 316.

22. Stephen E. Woodworth, *Nothing but Victory: The Army of the Tennessee, 1861–1865* (New York: Alfred A. Knopf, 2005), 509–10; *Memoirs* 2: 44; *OR*, ser. 1, 38.4:321.

23. *OR*, ser. 1, 38.1:66; *OR*, ser. 1, 38.4:322, 323.

24. *OR*, ser. 1, 38.1:66; for Castel's criticisms, see *Decision in the West*, 231, 235, 241; on Grant's errors, see Gary Gallagher, ed., *The Spotsylvania Campaign* (Chapel Hill: University of North Carolina Press, 1998), 33, 35, 36, 57; anxiety over manpower and reinforcements is revealed in *OR*, ser. 1, 38.4:343.

25. Sherman to Ellen Sherman, May 28, June 1, 1864, CSHR 2/14/15 UNDA; Sherman to Ellen Sherman, June 8, 1864, *Correspondence*, 644n3.

26. *OR*, ser. 1, 38.4:326–27, 339; *OR*, ser. 1, 38.1:66.

27. *OR*, ser. 1, 38.1:66; *OR*, ser. 1, 38.4:331–32, 333, 338–39; Woodworth, *Nothing but Victory*, 511–14.

28. *OR*, ser. 1, 38.4:346–47; Sherman to Ellen Sherman, June 1, 1864, CSHR 2/15 UNDA; *Memoirs* 2:45; see also Thomas's reference to "an almost hidden foe" in his report, *OR*, ser. 1, 38.1:144.

29. *OR*, ser. 1, 38.4:346, 343, 342.

30. *OR*, ser. 1, 38.4:347, 385–86, 388–92, 395–97, 407.

31. *OR*, ser. 1, 38.4:401, 403–4, 405–6, 427.

32. *OR*, ser. 1, 38.4:408–10, 413–14, 418, 420, 422, 425, 427; Part 1, 67.

33. *OR*, ser. 1, 38.1:66; Castel, *Decision in the West*, 261.

34. Shimon Naveh, *In Pursuit of Military Excellence* (London: Frank Cass, 1997) covers these issues well. My understanding of them has been greatly enhanced by numerous discussions with Major General Julian Thompson, CB.

35. Castel acknowledges these points (*Decision in the West*, 261–62); Livermore, *Numbers and Losses*, 119–20.

36. *OR*, ser. 1, 38.4:427, 428, 439, 443–44, 453.

37. *OR*, ser. 1, 38.4:444, 449, 452, 453, 455–56, 471–72; *OR*, ser. 1, 38.1:68; Richard M. McMurry, *Atlanta 1864: Last Chance for the Confederacy* (Lincoln: University of Nebraska Press, 2000), 100–101.

38. *OR*, ser. 1, 38.1 :67–68; *Memoirs* 2:53–54. Sherman in the latter refers to the Lost Cause legend that he fired the shot personally.

39. On the resentment, see Castel, *Decision in the West*, 112.

40. *OR*, ser. 1, 38.4:486–88, 492, 496, 498–99; also see 534–35: "Instead of turning on Kennesaw we shall ignore it and move against Johnston, merely watching Kennesaw." Forrest's determination is impressive in comparison with his timorous opponents, as at Brice's Crossroads he collapsed with exhaustion. See John W. Martin, "Fighting under Forrest at Brice's Crossroads," in *New Annals of the Civil War*, ed. Peter Cozzens and Robert I. Girardi (Mechanicsburg, PA: Stackpole, 2004), 369, 377.

41. *OR*, ser. 1, 38.4:529–30, 558; *OR*, ser. 1, 38.1:68.

42. *OR*, ser. 1, 38.1:68; Oliver O. Howard, *Autobiography*, 2 vols. (New York: Baker and Taylor, 1907) 1:576; *Memoirs* 2:57–59: "In years, former rank and experience, he thought he was our superior"—indeed repeatedly said so; Hebert, *Hooker*, 279–81; Castel, *Road to Atlanta*, 297–99, stresses a personal motive; McMurry, *Atlanta 1864*, 106, is also disapproving.

43. *OR*, ser. 1, 38.4:535; Symonds, *Johnston*, 309; *OR*, ser. 1, 38.1: 68 (my italics).

44. *OR*, ser. 1, 38.4:534–35, 544, 582; on the rain, see 544; on forage and consumption, 543; on the sutlers, see *Two Germans in the Civil War: The Diary of John Deuble and Letters of Gottfried Rentscher*, ed. and trans. Joseph R. Reinhart (Knoxville: University of Tennessee Press, 2004), 134–35. The sutlers were not explicitly mentioned in these orders, but their access to rail transport had previously been restricted and fell into all the categories criticized.

45. For Garrard's unedifying bleating, see *OR*, ser. 1, 38.4:555.

46. *OR*, ser. 1, 38.4:507–8; Jack D. Welsh, *Medical History of Union Generals* (Kent, OH: Kent State University Press, 1997), xii, shows that Stoneman suffered from hemorrhoids; Castel, *Decision in the West*, 284–85; for Grant's problems in the east, see Michael C. C. Adams, *Our Masters the Rebels: A Speculation on Union Military Failure in the East, 1861–1865* (Cambridge, MA: Harvard University Press, 1978), 152–61.

47. "If Johnston fights for Marietta we must accept battle, but if he give[s] ground we must be most active." *OR*, ser. 1, 38.4:566; Howard, *Autobiography* 1:566–67.

48. *OR*, ser. 1, 38.1:68; *OR*, ser. 1, 38.4:34.

49. Albert Castel, *Tom Taylor's Civil War* (Lawrence: University of Kansas Press, 2000), 131–32; on Sherman's frantic efforts to concentrate his cavalry and create more couriers and orderlies, see *OR*, ser. 1, 38.4:54, 542, 569.

50. *OR*, ser. 1, 38.4:582, 588, 589, 592, 596–97; Howard, *Autobiography* 1:588.

51. Ambrose Bierce, *In the Midst of Life and Other Tales*, ed. with an afterword by Marcus Cunliffe (New York: New American Library, 1961), 10, 67.

52. Sherman to Ellen Sherman, June 9, 1864, *Correspondence*, 642; *OR*, ser. 1, 38.1:69, 151; Livermore, *Numbers and Losses*, 120–21; Woodworth, *Nothing but Victory*, 525; *OR*, ser. 1, 38.4:590, 609; *Memoirs* 2:61.

53. *OR*, ser. 1, 38.4:616–19, 622, 629; on the reaction to the repulse, see 610–12; McMurry, *Atlanta 1864*, 109–10; and Charles Royster, *The Destructive War* (New York: Alfred A. Knopf, 1991), 296–97, 300–301, 304–6, 307, 311, 315–17.

54. *OR*, ser. 1, 38.4:629, 630–32, 635–36, 637, 644–45; on Sherman's anxiety for his lines of communication back to Chattanooga and Nashville, see 647–48.

55. *OR*, ser. 1, 38.4:644, 646–47; *OR*, ser. 1, 38.5:30; *Memoirs* 2:62; Joseph E. Johnston, "Opposing Sherman's Advance to Atlanta," *Battles and Leaders of the Civil War* (1887; Edison, NJ: Castle, 1987), 4:273. His bewilderment at the sterility of his success at Kennesaw is conveyed by the absurd claim that the battle had inflicted 6,000 casualties on Sherman.

56. *OR*, ser. 1, 38.5:21–22, 30–33, 34; Howard, *Autobiography* 1:593–95; Sherman admitted to "being terribly angry" at Marietta (*Memoirs* 2:65).

57. *OR*, ser. 1, 38.5:37–38, 42, 46; *Memoirs* 2:66; Symonds, *Johnston*, 316–18.

58. *OR*, ser. 1, 38.5:50, 54; *Memoirs* 2:66; Howard, *Autobiography* 1:597.

59. *OR*, ser. 1, 38.5:50, 55–56, 59, 61–62, 65–66.

60. *OR*, ser. 1, 38.1:69; *OR*, ser. 1, 38.5:68–69, 70, 71–72, 76, 82, 123. Garrard was informed that if he wished "to hang the wretch who sought to hide under a neutral flag" Sherman would "approve the act beforehand" (5:76). The workforce of almost 500 women was eventually moved to Indiana (5:104).

61. *OR*, ser. 1, 38.5:76–78, 80, 85, 89.

62. *OR*, ser. 1, 38.5:75, 98, 99.

63. *OR*, ser. 1, 38.4:1:70; *OR*, ser. 1, 38.5:104, 107–8; for Thomas's reconnaissance of Johnston's *tête-de-pont* that Sherman had so skilfully evaded, see 5:108.

64. *OR*, ser. 1, 38.5:109, 112, 120–21, 141; Dodge had kept 1,000 men working on the bridge every 24 hours. His spirit appealed to Sherman, assuring him that "not one minute shall be lost in pushing it forward" (119).

65. *OR*, ser. 1, 38.5:108, 113, 114, 123, 124.

66. *OR*, ser. 1, 38.5:114, 124, 125, 127, 128.

67. *OR*, ser. 1, 38.5:131, 133, 134, 137–38, 139–40.

68. *OR*, ser. 1, 38.5:142–43.

69. *OR*, ser. 1, 38.5:143, 144, 149, 150, 154; for a critical discussion of Johnston's conduct, see Thomas L. Connelly, *The Autumn of Glory: The Army of Tennessee, 1862–1865* (Baton Rouge: Louisiana State University Press, 1969), 361–71, 392–421; Judith Lee Hallock, *Braxton Bragg and Confederate Defeat*, vol. 2 (Tuscaloosa: University

of Alabama Press, 1991), 192–99, demonstrates Bragg's hostility toward Johnston; Symonds, *Johnston*, 322–23, is more sympathetic in dealing with his predicament.

70. *OR*, ser. 1, 38.5:5, 147, 154, 158, 159; Stoneman complained of the difficulties of keeping his operations secret, "women as well as men acting as scouts and messengers" (145); *OR*, ser. 1, 38.1:71.

71. *OR*, ser. 1, 38.5:150.

72. For Canby, see *OR*, ser. 1, 38.5:85. Liddell Hart, like virtually all Sherman's later biographers, takes the success of the crossing for granted, as does Woodworth, *Nothing but Victory*, 527–28; Castel, *Decision in the West*, 341, ever ready to damn with faint praise, considers it "his best, as well as his easiest, move of the campaign." Howard, *Autobiography* 1:607; Sherman to Ellen Sherman, July 9, 1864, *Correspondence*, 663.

Chapter 12

1. W. B. Yeats, "The Song of Wandering Aengus," in *The Poems*, ed. Daniel Albright (London: J. M. Dent, 1992), 77, line 18; *OR*, ser. 1, 38.5:167.

2. *OR*, ser. 1, 38.5:170, 176, 180–81.

3. *OR*, ser. 1, 38.5:182, 183; on Johnston's removal on July 17–18, see Albert Castel, *Decision in the West: The Atlanta Campaign of 1864* (Lawrence: University Press of Kansas, 1992), 352–58, 360–65.

4. Sherman to Philemon B. Ewing, Hugh B. Ewing, July 13, 1864, in *Sherman's Civil War: Selected Correspondence of William T. Sherman*, ed. Brooks D. Simpson and Jean V. Berlin (Chapel Hill: University of North Carolina Press, 1999), 665, 666–67 (hereafter *Correspondence*).

5. Ellen Sherman to Sherman, July 7, 9, 16, 20, August 1, 1864, CSHR 9/40 UNDA. The latter comments on the expense of living in Lancaster with 21 servants and "over 24 to each meal—chance, visitors etc etc." Lloyd Lewis, *Sherman: Fighting Prophet* (1932; New York: Harcourt Brace, 1958), 364. Sherman gave his assent to the move in a telegram of June 10 (see CSHR 2/15 UNDA), but in Sherman to Ellen Sherman, July 29, 1864, *Correspondence*, 676, he argues for her staying put and the girls remaining at school in Cincinnati.

6. Ellen Sherman to Sherman, July 16, 1864, CSHR 9/40, UNDA; Sherman to Ellen Sherman, July 29, 1864, *Correspondence*, 677.

7. Charles de Gaulle, *War Memoirs: The Call to Honour, 1940–1942* (London: Collins, 1955) 1:119; here he refers to M. Boisson, Vichy governor-general of French West Africa. Major General J. F. C. Fuller, *Lectures on FSR II*, with endnotes by Albert Castel (London: Sifton Praed, 1931), 6; *Memoirs* 2:72; A. H. Burne, *Lee, Grant, and Sherman* (1939; Lawrence: University Press of Kansas, 2000), 101–3, 110–12; Castel, *Road to Atlanta*, 412–13, rightly criticizes Hood's tendency to blame his subordinates for his errors, which General Fuller considers "inexcusable." Hood's faults are dissected in Richard M. McMurry, *John Bell Hood and the War for Southern Independence* (1982; Lincoln: University of Nebraska Press, 1992), 128–30, 132, 139, 148–51.

8. *OR*, ser. 1, 38.5:185–86, 188, 193–95.

9. *OR*, ser. 1, 38.5:195, 297, 211; *OR*, ser. 1, 38.1:71; *Memoirs* 2:73; W. T. Sherman, "The Grand Strategy of the Last Year of the War," in *Battles and Leaders of the Civil War*, ed. Robert U. Johnston and Clarence C. Buel (1887; Edison, NJ: Castle , 1987), 4:253, gives 4,796 Confederate casualties; Castel, *Decision in the West*, 380–81, suggests Union losses nearer 1,900. See Thomas L. Livermore, *Numbers and Losses in the Civil War in America, 1861–65*, 2nd ed. (Boston: Houghton Mifflin, 1901), 122–23.

10. As usual, the more junior the officer, the more scathing he was toward those "who had the power [but] had not the nerve, the *spirit* and *dash* to order forward march!" Albert Castel, *Tom Taylor's Civil War* (Lawrence: University Press of Kansas, 2000), 140–41; for historians' criticisms, see McMurry, *Atlanta 1864*, 152; Castel, *Decision in the West*, 378–79; Steven E. Woodworth, *Nothing but Victory: The Army of the Tennessee, 1861–1865* (New York: Alfred A. Knopf, 2005), 532–33.

11. *OR*, ser. 1, 38.5:5, 209, 218, 231; *OR*, ser. 1, 38.1:72; *Memoirs* 2:75.

12. *OR*, ser. 1, 38.5:195, 218, 232; Woodworth, *Nothing but Victory*, 542–43; *Memoirs* 2:75–76. Sherman's evocation is an elaboration of Sherman to Lorenzo Thomas, July 23, 1864, *Correspondence*, 670–71.

13. *OR*, ser. 1, 38.5:222, 223, 225, which also reveal, "I hate to base any calculations on the cavalry."

14. A highway, the West McPherson Highway at East Maple Street, now runs close to the cemetery containing McPherson's grave at Clyde, Ohio. It is marked by an equestrian statue subscribed by the members of the Society of the Army of the Tennessee—now much unvisited. The author paid homage there in April 2006. *Memoirs* 2:77–78; Stanley P. Hirshson, *The White Tecumseh: A Biography of William T. Sherman* (New York: Wiley, 1997), 230–31; Lewis, *Sherman*, 384–87; Sherman to Emily Hoffman, August 5, 1864, *Correspondence*, 682–83.

15. Woodworth, *Nothing but Victory*, 559–63, 565–67; *OR*, ser. 1, 38.5:235–37; *OR*, ser. 1, 38.1:157; Livermore, *Numbers and Losses*, 123; Sherman gives similar figures in *OR*, ser. 1, 38.5:241.

16. Sherman to L. Thomas, July 23, 1864, *Correspondence*, 671; *OR*, ser. 1, 38.5:241; Ellen Sherman to Sherman, July 25, 1864, CHSR 9/40 UNDA.

17. Sherman to Ellen Sherman, July 26, 1864, *Correspondence*, 671–72.

18. *OR*, ser. 1, 38.5:240–41; *Memoirs* 2:67–72.

19. Oliver O. Howard, *Autobiography*, 2 vols. (New York: Baker and Taylor, 1907), 2:16–17; *OR*, ser. 1, 38.5:260–61, 266.

20. *OR*, ser. 1, 38.5:248, 259–60, 271–74, 523; Walter H. Hebert, *Fighting Joe Hooker* (Indianapolis, IN: Bobbs-Merrill, 1944), 284–89. In September 1864 he received command of the Northern Department, having in August predicted Sherman's failure.

21. *OR*, ser. 1, 38.5:266, 272, 522–23; Sherman to Logan, July 27, 1864, *Correspondence*, 675; Marcus Cunliffe, *Soldiers and Civilians: The Martial Spirit in America, 1775–1865* (London: Eyre and Spottiswoode, 1969), 281.

22. *OR*, ser. 1, 38.5:238, 243, 247–48, 255–56.

23. *OR*, ser. 1, 38.5:238, 243, 247, 255–56, 272.

24. *OR*, ser. 1, 38.5:275; Howard, *Autobiography* 2:14; Castel, *Decision in the West*, 414.

25. Thucydides, *History of the Peloponnesian War*, trans. C. F. Smith, Loeb Classical Library, 4 vols. (Cambridge, MA: Harvard University Press, 1923), 7:xix, 2; *OR*, ser. 1, 38.5:247.

26. Howard, *Autobiography* 2:18. Livermore, *Numbers and Losses*, 124, estimates Confederate losses at 4,300 (including "missing"). Most historians rightly consider this figure too high; see McMurry, *Atlanta 1864*, 157, and Castel, *Decision in the West*, 434; *OR*, ser. 1, 38.5:285, 289.

27. Ambrose Bierce, "One Kind of Officer," in *Civil War Stories* (New York: Dover, 1994), 107, 109–10; Castel, *Tom Taylor's Civil War*, 151.

28. *OR*, ser. 1, 38.5:301, 303, 309, 310–11, 314, 320–21; Sherman wrote of Stoneman's raid on Andersonville: "It was a bold and rash adventure, but I sanctioned it and hope for its success from its very rashness" (340).

29. *OR*, ser. 1, 38.5:327, 328–29, 330, 333, 333; *OR*, ser. 1, 38.1:158.

30. *OR*, ser. 1, 38.5:334–35, 336, 340, 341, 352, 355–56, 370–71, 383–85, 391; *OR*, ser. 1, 38.1:79; Sherman to Ellen Sherman, August 2, 1864, *Correspondence*, 681. Palmer was a competent enough "political general" and proficient at division-level operations. He was later a Republican governor of Illinois before returning to the Democratic fold. Ezra J. Warner, *Generals in Blue* (Baton Rouge: Louisiana State University Press, 1964), 358–59.

31. *OR*, ser. 1, 38.5:390–91; Sherman to John Sherman, July 31; Sherman to Ellen Sherman, August 2, 1864, *Correspondence*, 679, 681; Sherman to Ellen Sherman, August 6, 1864, CSHR 2/17 UNDA.

32. Sherman to Emily Hoffman, August 5, 1864, *Correspondence*, 682–83; Chaucer, *Canterbury Tales*, "General Prologue," line 72.

33. *OR*, ser. 1, 38.5:445.

34. Sherman to Halleck, June 27, 1864, *Correspondence*, 659; *OR*, ser. 1, 38.5:445.

35. *OR*, ser. 1, 38.5:350, 390–91, 393, 399, 407–9, 412, 434, 450, 457; *OR*, ser. 1, 38.1:79.

36. *OR*, ser. 1, 38.5:409.

37. *OR*, ser. 1, 38.5:411, 417, 418–19, 423–24, 436, 456, 482, 488.

38. *OR*, ser. 1, 38.5:447, 451, 452–54, 460–61, 463–64, 481, 482, 489, 497, 526–27, 537–38, 540, 546; the order is misdated in *Memoirs* 2:103 *OR*, ser. 1, 38.1:79.

39. *OR*, ser. 1, 38.5:548, 549, 550, 551, 555, 557, 569–70, 573–74, 621–22, 628–29, 641; *OR*, ser. 1, 38.1:79–80; *Memoirs* 2:103–4.

40. *OR*, ser. 1, 38.5:471, 488, 521, 569.

41. *OR*, ser. 1, 38.5:705–6, 717–18, 734; *OR*, ser. 1, 38.1, 80; McMurry, *Hood*, 148; Howard, *Autobiography* 2:34–37; Woodworth, *Nothing but Victory*, 579–80.

42. *OR*, ser. 1, 38.5:718–19, 726, 731, 734–35, 746; *OR*, ser. 1, 38.1:82; Howard, *Autobiography* 2:39; Livermore, *Numbers and Losses*, 125; Castel, *Decision in the West*, 506–57, 518, 521.

43. *OR*, ser. 1, 38.5:719, 746, 763, 794; Livermore, *Numbers and Losses*, 126; McMurry, *Atlanta 1864*, 175–76; *Memoirs* 2:109.

44. *OR*, ser. 1, 38.5:764, 771, 773–74, 777.

45. Order of Thanks to William T. Sherman and Others, in *The Collected Works of Abraham Lincoln*, ed. Roy P. Basler, 9 vols. (New Brunswick,

NJ: Rutgers University Press, 1953), 7:523.; Brian Holden Reid, "The Military Significance of the 1864 Presidential Election," in *Reconfiguring the Union: Civil War Transformations*, ed. Iwan W. Morgan and Philip John Davies (New York: Palgrave Macmillan, 2013), 77–99; Sherman to Thomas Ewing Jr., September 17, 1864, *Correspondence*, 715.

46. Sherman to Thomas Ewing Sr., August 11, 1864, *Correspondence*, 689; election figures are from Harold M. Hyman, "Election 1864," in *History of American Presidential Elections*, 5 vols., ed. Arthur M. Schlesinger Jr. and Fred Israel (New York: Chelsea House, 1985), 3:168–69.

Chapter 13

1. *OR*, ser. 1, 38.5:789–90, 794; Sherman to Halleck, September 4, Sherman to Grant, September 10, 1864 in *Sherman's Civil War: Selected Correspondence of William T. Sherman, 1860–1865* (Chapel Hill: University of North Carolina Press, 1999), 705, 697 (hereafter *Correspondence*).

2. Sherman to John B. Hood, September 7; Sherman to Ellen Sherman, September 17, 1864, *Correspondence*, 704, 717; *OR*, ser. 1, 39.2:414–15.

3. See Martin Crawford, "Jefferson Davis and the Confederacy," in *Themes of the American Civil War*, rev. 2nd ed., ed. Susan-Mary Grant and Brian Holden Reid (New York: Routledge, 2010), 162; for Hood's letter of September 9, see *OR*, ser. 1, 39.2: 415.

4. Sherman to Hood, September 10; Sherman to James M. Calhoun et al., September 12, 1864, *Correspondence*, 706–7; the Council Members' letter is in *OR*, ser. 1, 39.2:417–18. On the issues, see Charles Guthrie and Michael Quinlan, *Just War: The Just War Tradition, Ethics in Modern Warfare* (London: Bloomsbury, 2007), 23. Richard M. McMurry, *John Bell Hood and the War for Southern Independence* (1982; Lincoln: University of Nebraska Press, 1992), 157, considers the correspondence "undignified"; I do not consider such an eloquent statement of the Union case lacking in dignity.

5. John Fabian Witt, *Lincoln's Code: The Laws of War in American History* (New York: Free Press, 2012), 232–37, 250–52; *Memoirs* 2:117–28 (quotation, 122); Sherman to Hood, September 14, 1864, *Correspondence*, 710–11; Hood's letter of September 12 is in *OR*, ser. 1, 39.2:420–22 (quotation, 420).

6. For these paragraphs, see Sherman to Ellen Sherman, August 6, 1864, CSHR 2/17 UNDA; Sherman to Eugene Casserly, September 17; Sherman to John A. Spooner, July 30; Sherman to Thomas Ewing Sr., September 15, 1864, *Correspondence*, 713, 677–78, 712; John F. Marszalek, *Sherman's Other War: The General and the Civil War Press*, rev. edi. (1981; Kent, OH: Kent State University Press, 1999), 176–78, 181–83; Michael C. C. Adams, *Living Hell: The Dark Side of the Civil War* (Baltimore: Johns Hopkins University Press, 2014), 34.

7. *OR*, ser. 1, 38.5:791–94; also Sherman to Halleck, September 4, 1864, *Correspondence*, 698–701, especially on his erroneous view of the élan of black troops (700).

8. *OR*, ser. 1, 38.5:794; Sherman to Thomas Ewing Sr., September 17; Sherman to Ellen Sherman, September 17, 1864, *Correspondence*, 716, 717.

9. Grant to Sherman, September 12, 1864, *Grant Papers* 13:144; Sherman to Grant, September 12; Sherman to Edward Everett, September 17; Sherman to Lincoln, September 17, 1864, *Correspondence*, 705, 714, 716; *Memoirs* 2:137–40, 142. Although open to approach, both Stephens and Brown envisaged merely a convention of states as a way forward, relegated "to the realms of wildest dreams" by Lincoln's reelection and Sherman's March. See Joseph H. Parks, *Joseph E. Brown of Georgia* (Baton Rouge: Louisiana State University Press, 1977), 296–99, on their essential caution.

10. Grant to Sherman, September 12, 1864, *Grant Papers* 12:154–55; Horace Porter, *Campaigning with Grant* (New York: Century, 1897), 288, 289–90.

11. Porter, *Campaigning with Grant*, 290–91, 293–94.

12. Sherman to Grant, September 20, 1864, *Correspondence*, 722.

13. T. Harry Williams, *McClellan, Sherman, and Grant* (New Brunswick, NJ: Rutgers University Press, 1962), 69–70.

14. Sherman to Grant, September 20, 1864, *Correspondence*, 723–24; *OR*, ser. 1, 38.5:793.

15. The first attempt to feature Sherman as a character in fiction concerned the siege of Allatoona: *Allatoona* (1875), a five-act "corny romance" cowritten by Judson Kilpatrick and J. Owen Moore. See Edward Caudill and Paul Ashdown, *Sherman's March in Myth and Memory* (Lanham, MD: Rowman and Littlefield, 2008), 130.

16. For this and the previous two paragraphs, see Steven E. Woodworth, *Jefferson Davis and His Generals* (Lawrence: University Press of Kansas, 1990), 291; Sherman to Lincoln, September 28; Sherman to Grant, October 1; Sherman to Ellen Sherman, October 1, 1864, *Correspondence*, 726–28; *Memoirs* 2:140–44. Grant had counseled him that Davis remained in Richmond on September 22; see Grant to Sherman, September 26, 1864, *Grant Papers* 12:212.

17. *Memoirs* 2:145–50; Steven E. Woodworth, *Nothing but Victory: The Army of the Tennessee, 1861–1865* (New York: Alfred A. Knopf, 2005), 585–86; A. H. Burne, *Lee, Grant, and Sherman* (1939; Lawrence: University Press of Kansas, 2000, foreword and endnotes by Albert Castel), 136–38.

18. Grant to Sherman, September 28, *Grant Papers* 11:227; Sherman to Grant, October 1864, *Correspondence*, 731.

19. *OR*, ser, 1, 39.3:729–30; Sherman to Thomas, October 2, 9; Sherman to Halleck, September 4, 1864, *Correspondence*, 729–30, 731, 700–701; *OR*, ser, 1, 39.3:365; Grant to Sherman, September 26, October 11, 1864, *Grant Papers* 12:211, 289–90.

20. Sherman to Grant, October 10, 11, 1864, *Correspondence*, 732–33.

21. Sherman to A. W. Plattenbury, November 13, 1887, Sherman Papers, Chicago History Museum Research Center; T. Harry Williams, *Lincoln and His Generals* (New York: Alfred A. Knopf, 1952), 339–40; Peter J. Parish, *The American Civil War* (New York: Holmes and Meier, 1975), 478–79.

22. *OR*, ser, 1, 39.2:222; Brian Holden Reid, "The Military Significance of the Presidential Election of 1864," in *Reconfiguring the Union: Civil War Transformations*, ed. Iwan Morgan and Philip John Davies (New York: Palgrave Macmillan, 2013), 91–93.

23. *OR*, ser, 1, 39.3:311; Grant to Stanton, October 13; Grant to Sherman, October 12, 1864, *Grant Papers* 12:302, 298.

24. Ellen Sherman to Sherman, September 4, October 4, 7, 19, CSHR 9/40; Sherman to Ellen Sherman, October 29, CSHR 2/18 UNDA; Sherman to Minnie Sherman, September 18, 1864, *Correspondence*, 721. Ellen complained on October 16 it was "unnatural" to write so many unanswered letters, as they "might as well be addressed to a myth," CSHR 9/40).

25. Sherman to Ellen Sherman, September 17, 29, 1864, *Correspondence*, 718; Ellen Sherman to Sherman, August 16, 1864 (two letters), CSHR 9/40 UNDA.

26. Ellen Sherman to Sherman, September 17, August 9, CSHR 9/40 UNDA; Sherman to Minnie Sherman, September 18; Sherman to Thomas Ewing Sr., September 23; Sherman to Ellen Sherman, October 1, 1864, *Correspondence*, 721, 725, 728.

27. Ellen Sherman to Sherman, September 17, 1864, CSHR 9/40 UNDA; McClellan to Sherman, September 26, 1864, in *The Civil War Papers of George B. McClellan: Selected Correspondence*, ed. Stephen Sears (New York: Da Capo Press, 1992), 604; Sherman to John Sherman, October 11, 1864, *Correspondence*, 733; *OR*, ser, 1, 39.3:203.

28. See Ovid, *Metamorphoses* 2.170–71, "He knows not . . . where the road is."

29. Sherman to Ellen Sherman, August 15, 1864, CSHR 9/40 UNDA; *Memoirs* 2:387. I am indebted here to the insights of Victor Davis Hanson, *The Soul of Battle* (New York: Free Press, 1999), 5, 10–11 (quotation). Though I disagree with the way the argument develops, I consider his claim that volunteer or conscripted mass armies, "great democratic militias[,] are by definition armies of a season and of a particular spirit" a keen insight (57). See also 59, 60.

30. See Brian Holden Reid, "William T. Sherman and the South," *American Nineteenth Century History* 11, no. 1 (March 2010), esp. 6, 10–11, 14; Hanson, *Soul of Battle*, 134–35. Even in 1864 cases of diarrhea and dysentery were numbered in the hundreds of thousands; see Adams, *Living Hell*, 44–45.

31. B. H. Liddell Hart, *Sherman: Soldier, Realist, American* (1929; New York: Praeger, 1958), 330–31, 381; Liddell Hart, *Memoirs*, 2 vols. (London: Cassell, 1965), 1:167–68; Sherman's report is in *OR*, ser. 1, 44:7; *Memoirs* 2:167–68, 172; Joseph T. Glatthaar, *Sherman's March to the Sea and Beyond* (New York: New York University Press, 1985), 19–20.

32. Grant to Sherman, October 11; Grant to Halleck, October 13, *Grant Papers* 12:290, 304–5; *Memoirs* 2:176–77; Stephen E. Ambrose, *Halleck: Lincoln's Chief of Staff* (1962; Baton Rouge: Louisiana State University Press, 1990), 184–86.

33. *OR*, ser. 1, 39.3:220, 222, 305, 324, 357–58, 365; T. Harry Williams, *P. G. T. Beauregard: Napoleon in Gray* (1955; Baton Rouge: Louisiana State University Press, 1989), 241–44.

34. *OR*, ser. 1, 39.3:370–71, 394–95, 406.

35. *OR*, ser. 1, 39.3:576–77, 594. These messages crossed one another on November 1–2, but it is best to present them in the order in which they were written.

36. *OR*, ser. 1, 39.3:577; Philip L. Shiman, "Engineering and Command: The Case of William S. Rosecrans, 1862–1863," in *The Art of Command in the Civil War*, ed. Stephen E. Woodworth (Lincoln: University of Nebraska Press, 1998), 100, 107.

37. *OR*, ser. 1, 39.3:577, 578, 594–95, 613–14.

38. *OR*, ser. 1, 39.3:657–58, 658–59; Sherman to P. B. Ewing, November 10, 1864, *Correspondence*, 755; *Memoirs* 2:179.

39. *OR*, ser. 1, 39.3:660–61; Sherman to Grant, November 6, 1861, *Correspondence*, 751.

40. Henry Hitchcock, *Marching with Sherman* (New Haven, CT: Yale University Press, 1927), 29; Holden Reid, "Military Significance of 1864 Presidential Election," 91.

41. *Memoirs* 2:171, 177; Sherman to Thomas, November 11; Sherman to Ellen Sherman, November 12, *Correspondence*, 757–58; Hitchcock, *Marching with Sherman*, 43, 60; N. A. Trudeau, *Southern Storm: Sherman's March to the Sea* (New York: HarperCollins, 2008), 46, but this is based on Earl Schenck Miers, *The General Who Marched to Hell* (New York: Alfred A. Knopf, 1951), 218, which is full of errors and unreliable on detail.

42. Grant to Sherman, November 7, 1864, *Grant Papers* 12:394; Hitchcock, *Marching with Sherman*, 23, 40, 42, 44, mentions discussions of the weather. Hitchcock complained on November 9 that it "rains almost all the time since I joined." On a vital but overlooked factor in military history, see Harold A. Winters et al., *Battling the Elements* (Baltimore: Johns Hopkins University Press, 1998), 8–9.

43. *OR*, ser. 1, 44:7–8, 460–61; *Memoirs* 2:171, 177, 178–79. When the Confederates returned to Atlanta after his departure, they estimated that its communications could not be repaired before February 1865. See Earl J. Hess, *The Civil War in the West* (Chapel Hill: University of North Carolina Press, 2012), 262.

44. *Memoirs* 2:178; Hitchcock, *Marching with Sherman*, 23, 29, 30, 31, 34, 66–67, 71.

45. G. W. Nichols, *The Story of the Great March* (London: Sampson and Low, 1865), 30–31 (entry for November 24, 1864); Trudeau, *Southern Storm*, 127, 128, 136–37; Hitchcock, *Marching with Sherman*, 68–72; *Memoirs* 2:180–81.

46. As Sir John Fortescue writes: "In truth war, an ugly thing at the best of times, is rarely so inhuman as when waged by amateurs." See his *A History of the British Army*, 13 vols. (London: Macmillan, 1899–1930), 9:349; *OR*, ser. 1, 39.3:, 713-14; Hitchcock, *Marching with Sherman*, 27, 52–53, 62, 75; Trudeau, *Southern Storm*, 124; *Memoirs* 2:174–75.

47. In addition to references in note 46 that cover the last three paragraphs, see *OR*, ser. 1, 39.2:713, and Oliver O. Howard, *Autobiography*, 2 vols. (New York: Baker and Taylor, 1901), 2:77–78; for Hitchcock's additional criticisms of Sherman's failure to enforce discipline, see *Marching with Sherman*, 86–87.

48. Hitchcock, *Marching with Sherman*, 76–77; Edward Hagerman, *The American Civil War and the Origins of Modern Warfare* (Bloomington: Indiana University Press, 1988), 341n26; Richard Holmes, *Firing Line* (London: Jonathan Cape, 1985), 116; for Marlborough's efforts, see Richard Holmes, *Marlborough* (London: HarperCollins, 2008), 260–62.

49. Nichols, *Great March*, 47 (entry for December 3, 1864); Hitchcock, *Marching with Sherman*, 81–83; *OR*, ser. 1, 44:8.

50. *Memoirs* 2:184–88; Hitchcock, *Marching with Sherman*, 184–85; Glatthaar, *Sherman's March to the Sea and Beyond*, 141, points out that many soldiers did not differentiate between rich and poor.

51. *Memoirs* 2:187–88, 190; Hitchcock, *Marching with Sherman*, 77; *OR*, ser. 1, 44:8, 519; Trudeau, *Southern Storm*, 193–215; Liddell Hart, *Sherman*, 350–52. Having passed the two-thirds mark "without a hitch," Liddell Hart remarks, "the army might have been engaged on a peaceful route march" (351).

52. Sherman was not present at the mock vote but "enjoyed the joke" (see *Memoirs* 2:190); Trudeau, *Southern Storm*, 190; Anne J. Bailey, *War and Ruin: William T. Sherman and the Savannah Campaign* (Wilmington, DE: Scholarly Resources, 2003), 44, 81, 111; *OR*, ser. 1, 44: 527–28.

53. Oliver Howard witnessed a massage session; see "Sherman's Advance from Atlanta," *Battles and Leaders of the Civil War*, 4 vols. (1887; Edison, NJ: Castle, 1987), 4:663; *OR*, ser. 1, 44:8, 527; Hitchcock, *Marching with Sherman*, 87, 96–97.

54. *OR*, ser. 1, 44:9; Howard, "Sherman's Advance from Atlanta," 108–9; Williams, *Beauregard*, 246–47; B. H. Liddell Hart, *The British Way in Warfare*, 3rd ed. (Harmondsworth: Penguin, 1942), 33.

55. *OR*, ser. 1, 44:9, 555, 581–82, 592–93; Liddell Hart, *Sherman*, 351–54; Nichols, *Great March*, 75; Woodworth, *Nothing but Victory*, 600–602; Hitchcock, *Marching with Sherman*, 114–15; Lee Kennett, *Sherman: A Soldier's Life* (New York: HarperCollins, 2001), 263.

56. *OR*, ser. 1, 44:263 602–3, 606, 609, 611.

57. *OR*, ser. 1, 44:616, 624; Hitchcock, *Marching with Sherman*, 112–13; Daniel Oakey, "Marching through Georgia and the Carolinas," in *Battles and Leaders of the Civil War*, ed. Robert U. Johnson and Clarence C. Buel, 4 vols. (1887; Edison, NJ: Castle, 1987), 4:671–72.

58. *OR*, ser. 1, 44:9–10; *Memoirs* 2:193; Hitchcock, *Marching with Sherman*, 105; Lee Kennett, *Marching through Georgia* (New York: HarperCollins, 1995), 269–70, 282; Hagerman, *American Civil War and the Origins of Modern Warfare*, 286.

59. *Memoirs* 2:194–95; *OR*, ser. 1, 44:10; Woodworth, *Nothing but Victory*, 602–3.

60. Correlli Barnett, *Bonaparte* (London: Allen and Unwin, 1978), 108.

61. Kennett, *Marching through Georgia*, 287; on the frequency of looting in all wars, see Holmes, *Firing Line*, 353–55.

Chapter 14

1. Sherman's report is in *OR*, ser. 1, 44:10–11, 489, 676–77, 718; G. W. Nichols, *The Story of the Great March* (London: Sampson Low, 1865), 56 (entry for December 13, 1864); John G. Barrett, *Sherman's March through the Carolinas* (Chapel Hill: University of North Carolina Press, 1956), 25; Noah Andre Trudeau, *Southern Storm: Sherman's March to the Sea* (New York: HarperCollins, 2008), 406, 409, 412–13; Henry Hitchcock, *Marching with Sherman* (New Haven, CT: Yale University Press, 1927), 173–74, 176. Clinch was Robert Anderson's brother-in-law.

2. *OR*, ser. 1, 44:11; *Memoirs* 2:195–96; Trudeau, *Southern Storm*, 417–34; Steven E. Woodworth, *Nothing but Victory: The Army of the Tennessee, 1861–1865* (New York: Alfred A. Knopf, 2005), 603–5.

3. *OR*, ser. 1, 44:11; *Memoirs* 2:197, 200–203; on Confederate efforts to keep Sherman's progress secret, see Roswell Lamson to Kate, December 5, 1864, in *Lamson of the Gettysburg: The Civil War Letters of Lieutenant Roswell Lamson, USN*, ed. James M. McPherson and Patricia R. McPherson (New York: Oxford University Press, 1997), 213; Robert J. Schneller, *A Quest for Glory: A Biography of Rear Admiral John A. Dahlgren* (Annapolis, MD: Naval Institute Press, 1996), 301.

4. *OR*, ser. 1, 44:11, 694, 718, 719–20, 737–38; Sherman to Halleck, December 13; Sherman to Hardee, December 17, 1864, in *Sherman's Civil War: Selected Correspondence of William T. Sherman, 1860–1865*, ed. Brooks D. Simpson and Jean V. Berlin (Chapel Hill: University of North Carolina Press, 1999), 762, 768–69 (hereafter *Correspondence*).

5. Sherman to Halleck, December 13; Sherman to Thomas Ewing Sr., December 31, 1864, *Correspondence*, 762, 782; Trudeau, *Southern Storm*, 475–77, 480, 485–86; Hitchcock, *Marching with Sherman*, 187, 198; A. R. Chisolm, "The Failure to Capture Hardee," in *Battles and Leaders of the Civil War*, ed. Robert U. Johnson and Clarence C. Buel (1887; Edison, NJ: Castle, 1987), 4:679–80.

6. Grant to Sherman, December 3, 6, 1864, *Grant Papers* 13:56–57, 72–73; *OR*, ser. 1, 44:506–7; *Memoirs* 2:204–6.

7. Sherman to Grant, December 16, 1864, *Correspondence*, 763–64, 765; *OR*, ser. 1, 44:718. On Fort Fisher, see Rowena Reed, *Combined Operations in the Civil War* (1978; Lincoln: University of Nebraska Press, 1993), 351–54; Horace Porter, *Campaigning with Grant* (New York: Century, 1897), 360–63, remarks (360) on Sherman's "prompt and enthusiastic letter." Butler attempted to stir up political trouble for Grant before the Joint Committee on the Conduct of the War; see Bruce Tap, *Over Lincoln's Shoulder: The Committee on the Conduct of the War* (Lawrence: University Press of Kansas, 1998), 236–41.

8. Sherman to Ellen Sherman, December 16; Sherman to Lincoln, December 22, 1864, *Correspondence*, 767–68, 772; Sherman to Ellen Sherman, December 22, 1864 (telegram), CSHR 2/19 UNDA; David Herbert Donald, *Lincoln* (London: Jonathan Cape, 1995), 553; *Memoirs* 2:229.

9. A. T. Mahan, *From Sail to Steam: Recollections of a Naval Life* (New York: Harper, 1907), 191–92.

10. Ellen Sherman to Sherman, November 8, 1864, CSHR 9/40 UNDA. For a moving observation that no woman "gets over" the "loss of a child," see Mary Soames, *Clementine Churchill* (London: Cassell, 1979), 202.

11. Ellen Sherman to Sherman, December 29, 1864, CSHR 9/40 UNDA; Sherman to Ellen Sherman, December 25, 31; Sherman to Minnie Sherman, December 25, 1864, *Correspondence*, 778, 779, 785.

12. *OR*, ser. 1, 44:809; *OR*, ser. 1, 47.2:99: "All the cotton in Savannah was the prize of war and belonged to the United States, and nobody should recover a bale of it with my consent. . . . All cotton became tainted with treason since 1860"; *OR*, ser. 1, 47.2:16; *OR*, ser. 1, 44:836.

13. A record of this meeting by E. D. Townsend is in *OR*, ser. 1, 47.2:31–42 (at 42); Benjamin P. Thomas and Harold M. Hyman, *Stanton: The Life and Times of Lincoln's*

Secretary of War (New York: Alfred A. Knopf, 1962), 343–45; Stanley P. Hirchson, *The White Tecumseh: A Biography of William T. Sherman* (New York: Wiley, 1997), 271–74; *Memoirs* 2:242–49 (quotation at 248).

14. *OR*, ser. 1, 47.2:60–61, 87–88. For his affable manner toward ex-slaves, see Nichols, *Great March*, 64 (entry for January 1, 1865); in *Memoirs* 2:249–50, Sherman defended his record on black recruitment, pointing out his consistency in preventing compulsion, but it was typical of the hostility he felt toward Stanton in the 1870s that he suggested that the secretary's motives were mixed being "not of pure humanity but of politics."

15. *OR*, ser. 1, 44:701–2, 715, 729, 754.

16. *OR*, ser. 1, 44:742–43; Grant to Sherman, December 18, 1864, *Grant Papers* 13:130.

17. C. L. Bragg et al., *Never for Want of Powder: The Confederate Powder Works in Augusta, Georgia* (Columbia: University of South Carolina Press, 2007); *OR*, ser. 1, 44:793, 797–98; Grant to Sherman, December 27, 1864, *Grant Papers* 13:168–70. Sherman did not receive this missive until January 2, 1865 (see *Grant Papers* 13:171).

18. *OR*, ser. 1, 44:793, 799, 807, 811; *Memoirs* 2:257–58.

19. *Memoirs* 2:218; Hitchcock, *Marching with Sherman*, 201.

20. In his reply that day, Sherman wrote of his joy at Fisher's fall "because it silences Butler's direct, mean and malicious attack on you" in his final address to his troops, "and I admired the patience and skill by which you relieved yourself and the country of him." *OR*, ser. 1, 47.2:103.

21. *OR*, ser. 1, 47.1:18–19; *OR*, ser. 1, 44, 842-43; 47.2:52-53, 59, 62, 67-68, 69-70, 82, 96–97, 104; *Memoirs*, II, pp. 249, 253, 254; Sherman to Halleck, December 24, 1864, *Correspondence*, 777.

22. His reference to himself is significant because of the innumerable other (invented) references in Lost Cause literature to acts committed by Sherman. See also Hitchcock, *Marching with Sherman*, 218, 223, 233, 236; *OR*, ser. 1, 47.1:19; *OR*, ser. 1, 47.2:136, 194–95.

23. *OR*, ser. 1, 47.1:20; *OR*, ser. 1, 47.2:155, 203, 343, 383; *Memoirs* 2:275–76; Hitchcock, *Marching with Sherman*, 239; Woodworth, *Nothing but Victory*, 612; on "Wheeler's work," that is, plunder, see Nichols, *Great March*, 57 (entry for December 6, 1864).

24. Sherman to Halleck, December 24, 1864, *Correspondence*, 776; Woodworth, *Nothing but Victory*, 606–7, 613; Charles Royster, *The Destructive War* (New York: Alfred A. Knopf, 1991), 330–31; T. Harry Williams, *P. G. T. Beauregard: Napoleon in Gray* (1955; Baton Rouge: Louisiana State University Press, 1989), 249–50.

25. *OR*, ser. 1, 47.2:342; Woodworth, *Nothing but Victory*, 608–13.

26. Barrett, *Sherman's March through the Carolinas*, 54–58; Henry W. Slocum, "Sherman's March from Savannah to Bentonville," in *Battles and Leaders of the Civil War*, ed. Robert U. Johnston and Clarence C. Buel, 4 vols. (1887; Edison, NJ: Castle, 1987), 4:684–85; Woodworth, *Nothing but Victory*, 609, 614–15; Hitchcock, *Marching with Sherman*, 242; Nichols, *Great March*, 77, confirms that Sherman's headquarters became a "playground for children."

27. *OR*, ser. 1, 47.2:154–55, 183–84, 193–94; on Sherman's possible promotion, see 103–4, 194.

28. *OR*, ser. 1, 47.1:20–21; *OR*, ser. 1, 47.2:401, 429; Nichols, *Great March*, 112 (entry for February 17, 1865); Oliver O. Howard, *Autobiography*, 2 vols. (New York: Baker and Taylor, 1907), 2:117–19; Marion B. Lucas, *Sherman and the Burning of Columbia* (College Station: Texas A&M University Press, 1976), 22, 42–43, 47, 51, 57–59, 60–62, 65–66, 68.

29. *OR*, ser. 1, 47.2:444–45; Lucas, *Sherman and the Burning of Columbia*, 27–28, 29, 30, 60–62, 78, 86–88; Jacqueline G. Campbell, "'The Most Diabolical Act of All Barbarous War': Soldiers, Civilians and Burning of Columbia," *American Nineteenth Century History* 3, no. 3 (Fall 2002): 55.

30. Campbell, "Burning of Columbia," 56; Hitchcock, *Marching with Sherman*, 269; Lucas, *Sherman and the Burning of Columbia*, 25, 75, 80–81, 92–93; on drunken troops, see 85, 93; on the wind, 95–96, 165–66; Lucas is probably too censorious toward Howard's role. In *OR*, ser. 1, 47.1:21, Sherman reported a "perfect tempest of wind was raging." Howard, *Autobiography* 2:121, recalled "a hurricane" blew. Henry Reed, "Chard Whitlow," in *The Oxford Book of Twentieth Century English Verse*, ed. Philip Larkin (Oxford: Oxford University Press, 1973), 477.

31. *OR*, ser. 1, 47.1:21–22; Lucas, *Sherman and the Burning of Columbia*, pp. 102, 108, 110–11, 117, 121, 141, 154. On the entry of the "cutting hoses" yarn into the scholarly literature, see Barrett, *Sherman's March through the Carolinas*, 78–79: "On occasions the men went so far as to destroy the engines themselves." On the "hellish images," see Campbell, "Burning of Atlanta," 57, 59–60, 61.

32. Lucas, *Sherman and the Burning of Columbia*, 126–27; Dara Olivier, *The Burning of Moscow* (London: George Allen and Unwin, 1966); *Mary Chesnut's Civil War*, ed. C. Vann Woodward (New Haven, CT: Yale University Press, 1981), 671 (entry for November 17, 1865); the figures on Moscow are derived from Ivan Katayev, "The Burning of Moscow," in *Patriotic War and Russian Society* (1911; Jubilee Ed., 2005), www.museum.ru/1812/Library/sitin/book4_10.html, n.p.—a work published in Russian, and I am grateful to Major General Mungo Melvin, CB, OBE, for helping me with the translation.

33. David G. Chandler, *The Campaigns of Napoleon* (1967; London: Weidenfeld and Nicolson, 1995), 814–15; *Mary Chesnut's Civil War*, 702, 715 (entries for January 1865, and February 16, 1865); Hitchcock, *Marching with Sherman*, 250.

34. Lucas, *Sherman and the Burning of Columbia*, 122–25; Howard, *Autobiography* 2:124–27; *OR*, ser. 1, 47.1:22; *OR*, ser. 1, 47.2:513, 518–19, 547, 556, 573, 582, 603; Slocum, "Sherman's March from Savannah to Bentonville," 687. Sherman had expressed concern that Slocum's Left Wing lacked pontoon capacity on February 16; see *OR*, ser. 1, 47.2:445, 668.

35. *Memoirs* 2:290, 291–92; Barrett, *Sherman's March through the Carolinas*, 108–11; Peter M. R. Stirk, *A History of Military Occupation from 1792 to 1914* (Edinburgh: Edinburgh University Press, 2016), 62–64.

36. *OR*, ser. 1, 47.2:111–12; *OR*, ser. 1, 47.1:23; *Memoirs* 2:289; though his knowledge of Wilmington's fall was based on "vague rumours." One of his informants was the son of Richard Bacot, whom he had known at West Point.

37. *OR*, ser. 1, 47.2:537; Nichols, *Great March*, 124–25 (entry for February 24, 1865); Woodworth, *Nothing but Victory*, 625–27.

38. *OR*, ser. 1, 47.2:544, 537. The Lieber Code justifies foraging for "the subsistence and safety of the army"; see General Orders No. 100, *OR*, ser. 2, 5:672.

39. *OR*, ser. 1, 47.2:596–97. Indeed, the killing of Union foragers was invariably justified by some "dastardly deed" like the age-old excuse "shot while trying to escape." See Barrett, *Sherman's March through the Carolinas*, 103–5; Howard, *Autobiography* 2:130–31; Woodworth, *Nothing but Victory*, 626–27, estimates that three Confederate prisoners were shot by March 1 (but two of these were found in Union uniforms); General Orders No. 100, *OR*, ser. 2, 5:673.

40. *OR*, ser. 1, 47.2:670–71, 672, 676, 691–92, 703–4; *OR*, ser. 1, 47.1:23–24; Craig L. Symonds, *Joseph E. Johnston: A Civil War Biography* (New York: Norton, 1992), 342–43; Brian Holden Reid, *Robert E. Lee: Icon for a Nation* (London: Weidenfeld and Nicolson, 2005), 231.

41. *OR*, ser. 1, 47.2:704, 754–55, 763–64, 779, 788; *OR*, ser. 1, 47.1:23; Barrett, *Sherman's March through the Carolinas*, 125–30. The forest fires contributed to a growing international shortage of turpentine and resin; see *The Age* (Melbourne), December 14, 1864, and *Brisbane Courier*, January 14, 1865. Thank you, Arthur Lucas.

42. *OR*, ser. 1, 47.2:801, 803, 805, 817; in his correspondence Sherman frequently spells Goldsboro "Goldsborough." I have continued to use the abbreviated modern form.

43. *OR*, ser. 1, 47.2:790–91, 794, 800–801, 803, 804, 813, 817.

44. *OR*, ser. 1, 47.2:876, 692, 795, 821–22, 835, 857, 867.

45. *OR*, ser. 1, 47.2:845, 857, 860; Ibid., Part 1, 24; Barrett, *Sherman's March through the Carolinas*, 152–55; Symonds, *Johnston*, 348.

46. *OR*, ser. 1, 47.2:885, 886, 904; *Memoirs* 2:303; Howard, *Autobiography* 2:145–46, recognized the technique from the Battle of Fair Oaks in the Peninsular Campaign of 1862; Nathaniel Cheairs Hughes, *Bentonville: The Final Battle of Sherman and Johnston* (Chapel Hill: University of North Carolina Press, 1996), 46, 47, 56; Thomas L. Livermore, *Numbers and Losses in the Civil War in America, 1861–65*, 2nd ed. (Boston: Houghton Mifflin, 1901), 134–35, overestimates Johnston's infantry strength on the field at 16,895; William Shakespeare, *The Merchant of Venice*, act IV, scene 1, line 179, ed. John Drakakis (London: Arden Shakespeare, 3rd ser., 2010).

47. *OR*, ser. 1, 47.2:905, 906–7, 909, 918; Slocum, "Sherman's March from Savannah to Bentonville," 695; Hughes, *Bentonville*, 112–14; Barrett, *Sherman's March through the Carolinas*, 166, 177; Hitchcock, *Marching with Sherman*, 304, 306.

48. *OR*, ser. 1, 47.2:941; *OR*, ser. 1, 47.1:26; Howard, *Autobiography* 2:148, 150; Woodworth, *Nothing but Victory*, 629–31; *Memoirs* 2304, 306; Hughes, *Bentonville*, 230.

49. *OR*, ser. 1, 47.2:941; Howard, *Autobiography* 2:148, 150; Woodworth, *Nothing but Victory*, 629–31; *Memoirs* 2:304, 306; Hughes, *Bentonville*, 230.

50. *OR*, ser. 1, 47.2:950, 822, 951; Sherman to Grant, March 23, 1865, *Correspondence*, 827–28; Edward Hagerman, *The American Civil War and the Origins of Modern Warfare* (Bloomington: Indiana University Press, 1988), 287–88, 292.

51. Sherman to Ellen Sherman, March 23; Sherman to Grant, 24 March; Sherman to Frederick F. Low, 24 March; Sherman to William M. McPherson, March 24, 1865, *Correspondence*, 828–29, 830, 832; Nichols, *Great March*, 98–99 (entry for February 10, 1865).

52. Sherman to Thomas Turner, March 25, 1865, *Correspondence*, 835–36n6.

53. Sherman to Ellen Sherman, March 26, 1865, *Correspondence*, 836; Sherman's report (*OR*, ser. 1, 47.1:28), dates his arrival on the "evening of the 27th of March," but this must be a slip corrected in *Memoirs* 2:324–25; Horace Porter, *Campaigning with Grant* (New York: Century, 1890), 417–18.

54. *Memoirs* 2:326–28; Porter, *Campaigning with Grant*, 419–20, 422–24, confirms Sherman's chronology; Porter's account from his neatly hand-written Private Journal No. 2, Ac4948A, in the David Dixon Porter Papers, Manuscript Division, Library of Congress, quoted also in *Memoirs* 2:328–31. T. Harry Williams, *Lincoln and His Generals* (New York: Alfred A. Knopf, 1952), 352, notes Sherman's "misreading" of Lincoln's priorities. Donald's *Lincoln*, 572–74, stresses Lincoln's determination "to keep control" of any negotiations. Also see William C. Harris, *Lincoln's Last Months* (Cambridge, MA: Belknap Press of Harvard University Press, 2004), 197–98.

55. *OR*, ser. 1, 47.2:28, 29; *Memoirs* 2:333.

56. *OR*, ser. 1, 47.1:30–32; Sherman to Johnston, April 14; Sherman to Grant, April 12; Sherman to Ellen Sherman, April 22, 1865, *Correspondence*, 861, 859, 872; Barrett, *Sherman's March through the Carolinas*, 211–16; Mark L. Bradley, *This Astounding Close: The Road to Bennett Place* (Chapel Hill: University of North Carolina Press, 2000), 91, 94–95, 103, 108–14, 126–28; Sherman to Ellen Sherman, April 10, 1865, CSHR 2/23 UNDA; Hitchcock, *Marching with Sherman*, 302.

57. The Agreement is enclosed with Sherman to Grant, April 18, 1865, 863–65; *OR*, ser. 1, 47.1:32–33; Symonds, *Johnston*, 353–55; Bradley, *Bennett Place*, 163–65, 170–71.

58. Sherman to Grant, April 18, 1865, *Correspondence*, 863–64; *OR*, ser. 1, 47.1:33.

59. *OR*, ser. 1, 47.1:33; *OR*, ser. 1, 47.3:263; *Memoirs* 2:357; Elizabeth Leonard, *Lincoln's Avengers* (New York: Norton, 2004), 8–11; Hitchcock, *Marching with Sherman*, 302–3; Thomas and Hyman, *Stanton*, 405–7.

60. *Memoirs* 2:357–59, 363–67; U. S. Grant, *Personal Memoirs*, 2 vols. (London: Sampson Low, 1885–86), 2:515–17; Brooks D. Simpson, *Let Us Have Peace: Ulysses S. Grant and the Politics of War and Reconstruction* (Chapel Hill: University of North Carolina Press, 1991), 98–101.

61. *OR*, ser. 1, 47.3:221, 243–44, 276–77, 311–12, 380, 435, 446, 478, 955, 968; John F. Marszalek. *Commander of All Lincoln's Armies: A Life of General Henry W. Halleck* (Cambridge, MA: Belknap Press of Harvard University Press, 2004), 222–23, 224–25. Halleck shared Lieber's suspicion of armistices; see Thomas and Hyman, *Stanton*, 409.

62. *OR*, ser. 1, 47.1:33, 36–37; Hitchcock, *Marching with Sherman*, 304; Howard, *Autobiography* 2:158–59; Ellen Sherman to Sherman, April 26, 1865, CSHR 9/41 UNDA; Hans L. Trefousse, *Andrew Johnson: A Biography* (New York: Norton, 1989), 210–11.

Chapter 15

1. *OR*, ser. 1, 47.3:507; Sherman to Rawlins, May 19, 1865, *Sherman's Civil War: Selected Correspondence of William T. Sherman, 1860–1865*, ed. Brooks D. Simpson and Jean V. Berlin (Chapel Hill: University of North Carolina Press, 1999), 902 (hereafter *Correspondence*); Sherman to Ellen Sherman, May 17, 1865, CSHR 2/24 UNDA; Anna McAllister, *Ellen Ewing: Wife of General Sherman* (New York: Benziger Brothers, 1936), 304–5; Gary W. Gallagher, *The Union War* (Cambridge, MA: Harvard University Press, 2011), 8–9.

2. John Sherman to Sherman, May 2, 16, 1865, Sherman Papers, Library of Congress; Charles Royster, *The Destructive War* (New York: Alfred A. Knopf, 1991), 349–50; Benjamin P. Thomas and Harold M. Hyman, *Stanton: The Life and Times of Lincoln's Secretary of War* (New York: Alfred A. Knopf, 1962), 415; Bruce Tap, *Over Lincoln's Shoulder: The Committee on the Conduct of the War* (Lawrence: University Press of Kansas, 1998), 247, 249–51.

3. Sherman to Howard, May 17, 1865, *Correspondence*, 899–900; Oliver O. Howard, *Autobiography* (New York: Baker and Taylor, 1907), 2:207–10; William R. Brock, *An American Crisis: Congress and Reconstruction, 1865–1867* (London: Macmillan, 1963), 46, still has much wisdom on this contest.

4. Howard, *Autobiography* 2:210–11.

5. Steven E. Woodworth, *Nothing but Victory: The Army of the Tennessee, 1861–1865* (New York: Alfred A. Knopf, 2005), 638–39; *Memoirs* 2:378–79; Howard, *Autobiography* 2:211–12; Gary W. Gallagher, *The Union War* (Cambridge, MA: Harvard University Press, 2011), 14, 26, 169n14; Royster, *Destructive War*, 408–15; Jane E. Schultz, *Women at the Front* (Chapel Hill: University of North Carolina Press, 2004), 119, 137, 167–68; Robert G. Athearn, *William T. Sherman and the Settlement of the West* (Norman: University of Oklahoma Press, 1956), 5–6; Margaret Leech, *Reveille in Washington, 1860–1865* (London: Eyre and Spottiswoode, 1942), 416–17.

6. Grant to Sherman, May 19, 1865, *Grant Papers* 15:73, 74, 75; Sherman to Grant, May 10, 1865, *Correspondence*, 894, 895; *Memoirs* 2:376.

7. Ellen Sherman to Sherman, May 17, 1865, CSHR 9/41 UNDA; Thomas and Hyman, *Stanton*, 417; Orville Hickman Browning, *Diary*, 2 vols., ed. Theodore C. Pease and James G. Randall (Springfield: Illinois State Historical Library, 1925), 2:30, 40 (entries for May 20, July 26, 1865); Sherman to Ellen Sherman, July 16, 1865, CSHR 2/25 UNDA; *Grant Papers* 15:75, quoting Adam Badeau, *Military History of U. S. Grant*, 3 vols. (New York: Appleton, 1881), 3:710.

8. McAllister, *Ellen Ewing*, 307–8; Ellen Ewing to Sherman, February 15, 1865, CSHR 9/41, UNDA; Sherman to Ellen Sherman, March 23, 1865, *Correspondence*, 829; Grant to Ellen Sherman, May 31, 1865, *Grant Papers* 15:117, 118; Jean Edward Smith, *Grant: A Biography* (New York: Simon and Schuster, 2001), 419.

9. Grant to Sherman, June 29, 1865; Sherman to Rawlins, June 25, 1865, *Grant Papers* 15:231–32. On the "desire to be rid of me," see Sherman to John Sherman, August 9, November 4, 1865, Sherman Papers, Library of Congress.

10. Sherman to Grant, July 20, 1864; Grant to Sheridan, July 1, 1865, *Grant Papers* 15:276, 235; on US belligerence toward Mexico, see Brian Holden Reid, "Power, Sovereignty and the Great Republic: Anglo-American Relations in the Era of the Civil War," *British Foreign Policy, 1865–1965*, ed. Erik Goldstein and B. J. C. McKercher (London: Frank Cass, 2003), 59–60.

11. Ellen Sherman to Sherman, August 14, 18, 19, 24, 1865, CSHR 9/41 UNDA; McAllister, *Ellen Ewing*, 312–18; Stanley P. Hirshson, *The White Tecumseh: A Biography of William T. Sherman* (New York: Wiley, 1997), 323. The Sherman Testimonial Fund of Ohio had also given him $9,696.10, which he had invested in interest-bearing bonds.

12. Athearn, *Sherman and the Settlement of the West*, 13–14, 29; Grant to Stanton, October 20, 1865, *Grant Papers* 15:358; Russell F. Weigley, *History of the United States Army* (London: Batsford, 1968), 566; Sherman to Ellen Sherman, October 26, 1866, CSHR 2/26 UNDA.

13. Athearn, *Sherman and the Settlement of the West*, 27, 31, 33, 36–38, 40, 42–43.

14. Sherman to Rawlins, October 23, 1865; Grant to Sherman, October 31, 1865, January 26, 1867, *Grant Papers* 15:377–78, 380–83, 17:30–31; Sherman to Ellen Sherman, May 26, 1866, CSHR 2/26 UNDA. Ellen blamed herself for mislaying the nitre papers on his first trip; see Ellen Sherman to Sherman, October 12, 1865, CSHR 9/41 UNDA: "I ought to have put it in."

15. Grant to Sherman, March 3, 1866, *Grant Papers* 16:92–93, 93–97; Grant to Sherman, March 14, 1866, *Grant Papers* 16:116–17, 118–20; Athearn, *Sherman and the Settlement of the West*, 40, 49, 70, 97–102, 189–90. Cooke, a Virginia Unionist, was J. E. B. Stuart's father-in-law.

16. Sherman to Grant, May 24, 1866, *Grant Papers* 16:159; Athearn, *Sherman and the Settlement of the West*, 49–50; Sherman to Ellen Sherman, September 20, 1866, CSHR 2/25 UNDA; Sherman to Rawlins, September 30, 1866, *Grant Papers* 16:334–35. Carson died in 1868.

17. Athearn, *Sherman and the Settlement of the West*, 96–97; Sherman to John Sherman, October 20, 1866, Sherman Papers, Library of Congress; Sherman to Ellen Sherman, September 20, 1866, CSHR 2/25 UNDA.

18. Grant to Sherman, January 8, 14; Sherman to Grant, January 8, 1867; Cooke to Sherman, January 8, 1867 (Grant also refused to permit Cooke to go before a Court of Inquiry); Sherman to Dodge, January 22, 1867, *Grant Papers* 17:16, 18–19, 31; Sherman to John Sherman, December 30, 1866, Sherman Papers, Library of Congress. For an account of the Fetterman Massacre, see Robert M. Utley, *Frontier Regulars: The United States Army and the Indian 1866–1891* (New York: Macmillan, 1973), 103–7.

19. Sherman to Rawlins, January 11, 1867; Sherman's endorsement, March 30, 1867, on Augur's request for "suitable" reservations, *Grant Papers* 17:25, 57; his April orders are quoted in Athearn, *Sherman and the Settlement of the West*, 130, 199–200.

20. Sherman to Grant, January 10, 1867, *Grant Papers* 17:14; McAllister, *Ellen Ewing*, 317; Ellen Sherman to Sherman, September 1, 1867, CSHR 9/43 UNDA.

21. Grant to Sherman, February 21, April 10, 1867, *Grant Papers* 17:56, 110; Sherman to Grant, July 25, September 25, 1867, *Grant Papers* 241, 345; Athearn, *Sherman and the Settlement of the West*, 106, 113, 149–51, stresses his annoyance.

22. Robert Cook, *Civil War America: Making a Nation, 1848–1877* (London: Longman, 2003), 290; Athearn, *Sherman and the Settlement of the West*, 116–21, 133–39, 140–45; Grant to Sherman, May 17; Stanton to Sherman, May 16, 1867, *Grant Papers* 17:146–47, 148, 150; Meagher's telegram is in *Grant Papers* 17:106–7.

23. Athearn, *Sherman and the Settlement of the West*, 125, 150, 156–58, 165–68, 173–75, 178–79; H. M. Stanley, *The Autobiography of Sir Henry Morton Stanley GCB*, ed. Dorothy Stanley (London: Sampson Low, 1909), 26–27.

24. Grant to Sherman, July 22, 28, August 21, September 10, October 31, 1865; Grant to Stanton, August 12, 1865, *Grant Papers* 15:281, 287, 305–6, 317, 377, 296; Sherman to Grant, October 30; Grant to Sherman, November 5, 1865, *Grant Papers* 15:393–94; Grant to Sherman, January 13, 15, 1867; Grant to Sherman April 29, 1867; Sherman to Grant, March 21, April 20, 29, 1867; Grant to Sherman May 23, 1867, *Grant Papers* 17:13, 23–24, 131–32, 132–34, 157–58. The book that slightly distorted Sherman's opinions is Col. S. M. Bowman and Lt. Col. R. B. Irwin, *Sherman and His Campaigns* (New York: Charles B. Richardson, 1865); see also Sherman to Ellen Sherman, April 5, 1865, *Correspondence*, 846.

25. Grant to Sherman, January 16; Sherman to Grant, January 22, 1866, *Grant Papers* 16:22–24; *Memoirs* (1889) 2:413; Sherman to Ellen Sherman, July 29, 1866, CSHR 2/27 UNDA; *Congressional Globe*, 39th Congress, 1st Sess., pt. 2, 2393: the amendment was defeated 78-50, with 55 abstentions. Sheridan's nomination had to wait until 1869.

26. Grant to Sherman, October 18, 1866, January 13, 1867; Sherman to Grant, October 19,; Rawlins to Manning Force, November 9; Grant to Manning Force, November 11, 1866, *Grant Papers* 16:337–38, 339, 377, 378, 17:13–14.

27. Browning, *Diary* 2:163 (October 9, 1867); Sherman to Grant, October 19, 1866, *Grant Papers* 16:339; Hans L. Trefousse, *Andrew Johnson: A Biography* (New York: Norton, 1989), 216, 226–27; Sherman to Ellen Sherman, September 1, 1866, CSHR 2/25 UNDA; Thomas and Hyman, *Stanton*, 470. Sherman certainly noticed the similarity between his memorandum with Joseph E. Johnston and Johnson's policy; see Sherman to John Sherman, November 4, 1865, in *The Sherman Letters*, ed. Rachel Sherman Thorndike (New York: Charles Scribner's Sons, 1894), 257 (hereafter *SL*).

28. Sherman to Ellen Sherman, October 26, 1866, CSHR 2 UNDA; Trefousse, *Johnson*, 298; Thomas and Hyman, *Stanton*, 503; Sherman, *Memoirs* (1889) 2:414–15; on the first visit, see *Grant Papers* 17:347; on the second, John Sherman to Sherman, October 26, and Sherman to John Sherman, October 31, 1866, Sherman Papers, Library of Congress.

29. Sherman to Grant, October 19, December 30, 1866, *Grant Papers* 16:339, 422–23. Sherman was one of the voices urging Grant not to go; *Memoirs* (1889) 2:415–20; Gordon Connell-Smith, *The United States and Latin America* (London: Heinemann, 1974), 14.

30. Ellen Sherman to Sherman, August 16, 1866, CSHR 9/42 UNDA; see Mark Twain's view of a "wild sense of freedom" in *Roughing It* (Hartford, CT: American Publishing, 1972), 48; Brock, *American Crisis*, 262–63. Sure enough, his remarks at St. Louis formed part of Article 10 of the Articles of Impeachment; see *Supplement to the Congressional Globe*, 40th Congress, 2nd Sess., *The Trial of Andrew Johnson* (Washington, DC: F. and J. Rives and George Bailey, 1868), 4.

31. Grant to Sherman, September 18, 1867, *Grant Papers* 17:343. Johnson later attempted to persuade Sherman that he had helped Grant in consolidating his authority as general-in-chief; see Sherman to Grant, January 27, 1868, *Grant Papers* 18:108; Joan Waugh, *U. S. Grant: American Hero, American Myth* (Chapel Hill: University of North Carolina Press, 2009), 117; Sherman to Grant, September 25, 1867, *Grant Papers* 17:346. Grant would deny that he was a candidate, "but suppose the people insist on making me one, what can I do? ... And Mrs. Grant would decidedly object to my giving any such promise." Quoted in Jean Edward Smith, *Grant: A Biography* (New York: Simon and Schuster, 2011), 430.

32. Sherman, *Memoirs* (1889) 2:420–22, 423–25; Grant to Sherman, January 19; Sherman to Grant, January 27, 1868, *Grant Papers* 18:105, 106–7; Waugh, *Grant*, 117–18; Thomas and Hyman, *Stanton*, 559–60, 565, 567–74.

33. *Memoirs* (1889) 2:426–27, 429, 430–32; Grant to Sherman, January 19, February 10, 1868; Sherman to Grant, January 27, February 10, *Grant Papers* 18:105, 106–7, 109, 138–39, 140–41.

34. *Memoirs* (1889) 2:427; Michael Les Benedict, *The Impeachment and Trial of Andrew Johnson* (New York: Norton, 1973), 140; Allan J. Lichtman, *The Case for Impeachment* (New York: HarperCollins, 2017), 8, 18.

35. *Memoirs* (1889) 2:430; Sherman to John C. Busch et al., September 11, 1875, Sherman Papers, Chicago History Museum Research Center; Sherman to Thomas Ewing Sr., February 14, 1868, in *The Home Letters of General Sherman*, ed. M. A. deWolfe Howe (New York: Scribner's, 1909), 373; Sherman to Grant, February 10; Grant to John Sherman, February 22, 1868, *Grant Papers* 18:109, 173. He also enjoyed the benefit of the many warnings issued by his brother concerning Johnson's character; see John Sherman to Sherman, October 26, 1866, February 23, 1868, *SL*, 278, 311.

36. The Shakespearian echoes are to the "vasty fields of France"; see *Henry V* (London: Arden Third Series, ed. T. W. Crake, 1995), Prologue, 120, line 12; Sherman to John Sherman, March 14, 1868, Sherman Papers, Library of Congress; Sherman to Grant, June 7, 24; Grant to Sherman, June 21, 1868, *Grant Papers* 18:292–94; Waugh, *Grant*, 118–21; Athearn, *Sherman and the Settlement of the West*, 212–17; on Grant's pose, see John A. Carpenter, *Ulysses S. Grant* (New York: Twayne, 1970), 74: "Grant had done nothing to gain the nomination. But he did nothing to discourage those who were seeking it for him."

37. Sherman to John Sherman, June 11, 1868, Sherman Papers, Library of Congress; Sherman to Grant, June 7, September 27, November 18; Grant to Sherman, September 25, 1868, *Grant Papers* 18:259, 19:45–46, 81; Athearn, *Sherman and the Settlement of the West*, 196, 202, 206, 217–18, 227–28; Robert M. Utley, *Cavalier in Buckskin: George Armstrong Custer and the Western Military Frontier* (Norman: University of

Oklahoma Press, 1988), 53–54, 64–75. Sherman's only contribution to these operations was to persuade Grant that Custer's 1867 court-martial suspending him from
duty for a year should be remitted; Sherman to Grant, September 27, 1868 (telegram),
Grant Papers 19:45.

38. For an example of more illiberal attitudes of one who agreed that Indian affairs
should be transferred to the War Department, see Allan Peskin, *Garfield* (1978; Kent,
OH: Kent State University Press, 1990), 297–99; Athearn, *Sherman and the Settlement
of the West*, 84, 87, 131, 160, 202–3, 229, 235, 237, 298–301; for Miles, see *Personal
Recollections and Observations of Nelson A. Miles*, 2 vols. (1896; Lincoln: University
of Nebraska Press, 1992), 1:107–8; on annihilation, see Russell F. Weigley, *The
American Way of War* (1973; Bloomington: Indiana University Press, 1977), 153, 156,
158, 163, and Lance Janda, "Shutting the Gates of Mercy: The American Origins of
Total War," *Journal of Military History* 59, no. 1 (January 1995), 7–26; Utley, *Frontier
Regulars*, 309.

39. Sherman to Grant, June 24, 1868, *Grant Papers* 18:294; Robert Wooster, *Nelson
A. Miles and the Twilight of the Frontier Army* (Lincoln: University of Nebraska Press,
1993), 50–51; Peter R. DeMontravel, *A Hero to His Fighting Men: Nelson A. Miles,
1839–1925* (Kent, OH: Kent State University Press, 1998), 59–61. Judge Taylor
Sherman, who died in 1879, is buried in Lake View Cemetery, Cleveland, overlooking
the Rockefeller Monument.

Chapter 16

1. Marcus Cunliffe, *American Presidents and the Presidency*, 2nd ed. (London: Fontana,
1972), app. 1, 320; Grant to Ellen Sherman, February 2, 1869, *Grant Papers*
19:122-23; Ellen Sherman to Sherman, February 4, 8, 1869, CSHR 9/45 UNDA;
Sherman to Grant, September 28, 1868; Grant to Sherman, January 5, February 12;
Sherman to John Sherman, February 21, 1869, *Grant Papers* 19:46, 122–23, 128; but
on Butterfield's desire to increase his influence, see Jean Edward Smith, *Grant: A
Biography* (New York: Simon and Schuster, 2001), 420.

2. *Memoirs* (1889) 2:437–38.

3. Grant, Inaugural Address, March 4; To the Senate, March 4, 1869, *Grant Papers*
19:140, 143.

4. *Memoirs* (1889) 2:441, 442; Townsend to Sherman, March 6; Sherman to Grant,
March 26, 1869, *Grant Papers* 19:144; Lloyd Lewis, *Sherman: Fighting Prophet* (1932;
New York: Harcourt Brace, 1958), 601.

5. Sherman to Schofield, March 29, 1869, *Grant Papers* 19:145; Smith, *Grant*, 477–79,
shows how torn Grant was between two friends, then decisively selecting the most
politically helpful option.

6. Sherman's appointment was not formally styled *ad interim*; Sherman to Belknap,
October 12; Grant to Belknap, October 18; Sherman to Grant, October 18, 1869,
Grant Papers 19:259, 260, 261–62, 263; *Memoirs* (1889) 2:443–44.

7. *Memoirs* (1889) 444–45, 446–51.

8. *Congressional Globe*, House of Representatives, 41st Congress, 2nd Sess., pt. 3, 2275–76, 2277–78, 2279, 2280; Allan Peskin, *Garfield* (1978; Kent, OH: Kent State University Press, 1999), 300; on his pay, see John F. Marszalek, *Sherman: A Soldier's Passion for Order* (New York: Free Press, 1993), 431. By comparison, the vice president and members of Congress earned $5,000 per annum.

9. A detailed account of this affair is found in Robert Utley, *Frontier Regulars: The United States Army and the Indian, 1866-1891* (New York: Macmillan, 1973), 206–13.

10. Sherman to Philip Sheridan, October 10, 1871, Sherman Papers, Chicago History Museum Research Center; Anna McAllister, *Ellen Ewing: Wife of General Sherman* (New York: Benziger, 1936), 330–32; James M. McDonough, *William Tecumseh Sherman: In the Service of My Country* (New York: Norton, 2016), 673, notes the religious divergence; the *Memoirs* do not mention his father-in-law's demise, though he pays tribute to him in "General Sherman's Tour of Europe," *Century* 35 (1909): 729.

11. "General Sherman's Tour," 729–30, 732, 734, 735, 736; Sherman to John Sherman, April 16, 1872, in *The Sherman Letters*, ed. Rachel Sherman Thorndike (New York: Charles Scribner's Sons, 1894), 337 (hereafter *SL*); on Napoleon III's view, see *SL*, 290, 292; *The Times*, July 16, 1872; McDonough, *Sherman*, 676, repeats the journalists' view; on Sheridan, see Alistair Horne, *The Fall of Paris: The Siege and the Commune, 1870-71* (London: Macmillan, 1965), 52–53, 209; on Washburne, see Smith, *Grant*, 471n.

12. For this and previous paragraphs on the trip, see, for the itinerary, Sherman to John Sherman, December 21, 1871, *SL*, 234; Ellen Sherman to Sherman, November 30, 1871, April 15, 1872, CSHR 9/45 UNDA; McAllister, *Ellen Ewing*, 333–36; *Memoirs* (1889) 2:451–52; Lewis, *Sherman*, 612; McDonough, *Sherman*, 674–77; Moltke to Sherman, September 29, 1872, Sherman Papers, USMA Special Collections.

13. Sherman to Ellen Sherman, July 7, 16, 24, 1872, CSHR 9/29 UNDA.

14. The next president, Rutherford B. Hayes, records a discussion when Sherman dilated at length on the consequences of the death of Princess Alice, the Second Afghan War, and routes to India and Australia. See *Hayes: The Diary of a President, 1875-1881*, ed. T. Harry Williams (New York: David McKay, 1964), 176 (entry for December 16, 1878). Princess Alice was the second daughter of Queen Victoria.

15. Ellen Sherman to Sherman, April 15, 1872, CSHR 9/45; Sherman to Ellen Sherman, July 26, 1872, and an (undated) note by his granddaughter Eleanor Sherman Fitch, CSHR 9/29 UNDA. Fleming's Hotel has survived intact from both aerial attack, 1940–45, and the attention of developers; see *The Times*, August 1, 5, 10, 16, 22, September 5, 1872. On Mayo, see his *Oxford Dictionary of National Biography* entry by C. H. Mayo, revised by James Mills, 37:616. Mayo was one of the first Union officers to enter Vicksburg on July 4; see Amanda Foreman, *The World on Fire* (London: Allen Lane, 2016), 495–96, who calls him an "old friend."

16. McAlister, *Ellen Ewing*, 336–37; Jay Luvaas, "The Influence of the German Wars of Unification on the United States," in *On the Road to Total War: The American Civil War and the German Wars of Unification, 1861-1871*, ed. Stig Forster and Jorg Nagler (Cambridge: Cambridge University Press, 1997), 605. The full version of Moltke's remark usually reads, "two armed mobs chasing each other around the country, from which nothing could be learned." See J. F. C. Fuller, *The Generalship of Ulysses*

S. Grant (London: John Murray, 1929), 19–20. It served a two-edged polemical use, highlighting European condescension and willful ignorance of the war's true historical significance. But he never said it.

17. "From Our American Correspondent," *The Times*, October 2, 1872. Scarlet jackets were last worn at the Battle of Gennis in the Sudan in 1885. See Edward M. Spiers, "The Late Victorian Army, 1868-1914," in *The Oxford History of the British Army*, ed. David G. Chandler (Oxford: Oxford University Press, 1996), 193.

18. Born in 1850, Prince Arthur had been named after his godfather, the Duke of Wellington, and pursued a military career. The Shermans entertained him at a reception in February 1870, and Sherman presented him with a Winchester rifle mounted in gold. Cecil Woodham-Smith, *Queen Victoria: Her Life and Times* (London: Hamish Hamilton, 1972) 1:310; McAllister, *Ellen Ewing*, 325–27, 338–40.

19. Sherman to Ellen Sherman, June 13, 1872, *Home Letters*, 381; Ellen Sherman to Sherman, April 5, May 14, 1872, CSHR 9/45 UNDA; McAllister, *Ellen Ewing*, 340, 342–43.

20. Sherman to Thomas B. Bryan, March 1, 1876, Sherman Papers, Chicago History Museum Research Center; *Memoirs* (1889) 2:453–54; Lee Kennett, *Sherman: A Soldier's Life* (New York: HarperCollins, 2001), 317.

21. Later editions focused on the "lessons" then deemed relevant; the most celebrated is *From Atlanta to the Sea*, ed. with an introduction by B. H. Liddell Hart (London: Folio Society, 1961), 10–16, and see the correspondence in the Liddell Hart Papers 9/7/13, Liddell Hart Centre for Military Archives, King's College London; also see Brian Holden Reid, "'A Signpost That Was Missed?' Reconsidering Lessons from the American Civil War," *Journal of Military History* 70, no. 2 (April 2006): 386–87, 406–7, and "Civil Military Relations and the Legacy of the Civil War," in *Legacy of Disunion: The Enduring Significance of the American Civil War*, ed. Susan-Mary Grant and Peter J. Parish (Baton Rouge: Louisiana State University Press, 2003), 158–60.

22. Michael Fellman, *Citizen Sherman* (New York: Random House, 1995), 325–26; Carpenter, *Grant*, 121–23.

23. Regarding credit for the March, Adam Badeau, *Military History of U. S. Grant*, 3 vols. (New York: Appleton, 1882) 3:42–48, 64–65, would take up Babcock's cudgel. Fuller, *Generalship of Grant*, 5, 436–38, and B. H. Liddell Hart, *Sherman* (London: Eyre and Spottiswoode, 1930), 328–43, battle it out, and the issue permeates the correspondence of the two most important writers who revived the reputation of northern generalship before 1945. See Fuller to Liddell Hart, June 14, December 4, 1929; Liddell Hart to Fuller, May 20, 1929, Liddell Hart Papers 1/302169/175/189. The remainder of this paragraph is based on Grant to Sherman, January 29, and Sherman to Grant, February 2, 1876, *Grant Papers* 27:16–19; also see the correspondence between Babcock and Boynton on 19.

24. Sherman to Grant, June 24, 1868, *Grant Papers* 18:294; Joan Waugh, "Ulysses S. Grant, Historian," in *The Memory of the Civil War in American Culture*, ed. Alice Fahs and Joan Waugh (Chapel Hill: University of North Carolina Press, 2004), 5, 15, 17–19, 20–21, 26, 28, 30–31.

25. *Memoirs* (1889) 2:382, 386, 389, 394–95, 398.

26. *Memoirs* (1889) 2:443; Luvaas, "Influence of German Wars of Unification," 601, 605; Holden Reid, "Civil Military Relations," 160–62; Russell F. Weigley, *Towards an American Army: Military Thought from Washington to Marshall* (New York: Columbia University Press, 1962), 84–85; Mark Grandstaff, " 'Preserving the Habits and Usages of War': William Tecumseh Sherman, Professional Reform in the US Officer Corps, 1865-1881, Revisited," *Journal of Military History* 62, no. 3 (July 1998): 521–45.

27. J. P. Clark, *Preparing for War: The Emergence of the Modern US Army, 1815-1917* (Cambridge, MA: Harvard University Press, 2017), 103–6; Perry D. Jamieson, *Crossing the Deadly Ground: United States Army Tactics, 1865-1899* (Tuscaloosa: University of Alabama Press, 1994), 9–10; Sherman paid tribute to Upton's contribution in *Memoirs* (1889) 2:466.

28. Sherman to John DeWitt Mullin, June 8, 1885, Sherman Papers, USMA Special Collections; Weigley, *History of US Army*, 273–77; Jamieson, *Crossing the Deadly Ground*, 3.

29. Weigley, *Towards an American Army*, 125; Marcus Cunliffe, *Soldiers and Civilians: The Martial Spirit in America, 1775-1865* (London: Eyre and Spottiswoode, 1969), 434.

30. *Memoirs* (1889) 2:445–46; William S. McFeely, *Grant: A Biography* (New York: Norton, 1982), 427–29; Carpenter, *Grant*, 153–57; Robert G. Athearn, *William T. Sherman and the Settlement of the West* (Norman: University of Oklahoma Press, 1956), 267–68; Sherman to John Sherman, March 10, 1876, Sherman Papers, Library of Congress. The Senate voted 36 to convict and 25 for acquittal, but of the latter 22 voted on the technicality that Belkap's resignation took him beyond the Senate's jurisdiction.

31. Ari Hoogenboom, *Rutherford B. Hayes: Warrior and President* (Lawrence: University Press of Kansas, 1995), 256, 257; *Memoirs* (1889) 2:454–55; Sherman to John Sherman, March 10, 1876, postscript, *SL*, 239. Ellen's sensitivity to the ailing friendship with Grant led her to misinterpret Cameron's appointment "as a move of Grant against you"—the nephew of the hated Simon Cameron of the autumn of 1861; Ellen Sherman to Sherman, May 22, 1876, CSHR 9/46 UNDA.

32. Report of General W. T. Sherman, July 8, 1876: "General Crook returned to Fort Laramie in a measure unsuccessful so far as the main purpose was concerned." Submitted by the President, to the Senate, July 8, 1876, *Grant Papers* 37:169, 170–71; Athearn, *Sherman and the Settlement of the West*, 132, 314; Ellen Sherman to Sherman, August 12, September 7, 17, 1877, CSHR 9/47 UNDA.

33. Robert Wooster, "John M. Schofield and the Multipurpose Army," *American Nineteenth Century History* 7, no. 2 (June 2006):181; Sherman to Ellen Sherman, November 2, 1876, *Home Letters*, 386; Sherman to Sheridan, November 8, 1876, *Grant Papers* 28:18; Grant to Sherman, November 12, 1876; Grant to J. D. Cameron, March 3; Sherman to Augur, March 3, 1877, *Grant Papers* 28:164, 166; on Sherman's memorandum, see 28:37; for reports of Democratic paramilitary activity, see 28:34–36; Sherman to Schofield, January 19, 1877, in 28 :149; see a range of reports in 28:107–112.

34. *Hayes: The Diary of a President,* 235, 257 (entry for July 7 and Hayes to McCrary, December 13, 1879); Hoogenboom, *Hayes*, 296, 306–8, 440.

35. *Hayes: The Diary of a President, 1875–1881*, ed. T. Harry Williams (New York: David McKay, 1964), 235; Hoogenboom, *Hayes*, 296, 306–8, 440; "John M. Schofield," 182; William Marvel, *Burnside* (Chapel Hill: University of North Carolina Press, 1993), 423; C. Vann Woodward, *Reunion and Reaction: The Compromise of 1877 and the End of Reconstruction* (Boston: Little Brown, 1951), 176–77.

36. *Hayes: Diary of a President*, 121, 176, 183, 269, 271 (entries for February 20, December 16, 1878, January 4, 1879, April 11, 1880, January 23, 1881); Hoogenboom, *Hayes*, 345, 424–25, 427, 456; Utley, *Frontier Regulars*, 350, 366–67n26; Cunliffe, *American Presidents and the Presidency*, 170; Sherman to John Sherman, April 15, 1882, *SL*, 356. Whittaker had demanded a court-martial to clear him of accusations of trumped-up stories of assault and self-inflicted wounds in order to avoid examinations, charges the court accepted. Hayes would only discharge him on grounds of academic weakness. This sorry saga confirmed Sherman's prejudice that "I do not believe West Point is the place to try the experiment of social equality." See Stephen E. Ambrose, *Duty, Honor, Country: A History of West Point* (Baltimore: Johns Hopkins University Press, 1966), 235–36.

37. Sherman to C. T. Christenson, December 1, 1880, Sherman Papers, USMA Special Collections; Ira Rutkow, *James A. Garfield* (New York: Henry Holt, 2006), 89; Sherman to John Sherman, July 3, 4, 13, 1881, February 28, 1882, *SL*, 350–52, 353–55.

38. *Memoirs* (1889) 2:459–61.

39. William B. Skelton, "The Commanding Generals and the Question of Civil Control in the Antebellum US Army," *American Nineteenth Century History* 7, no. 2 (June 2006): 166; Clark, *Preparing for War*, 117; *Memoirs* (1889) 2:402.

Chapter 17

1. *Lord Rosebery's North American Journal, 1873*, ed. A. R. C. Grant with Caroline Combe (London: Sidgwick and Jackson, 1967), 117 (entry for December 9, 1873); Gore Vidal, *1876* (New York: Random House, 1976), 221, 224–25; Edward Caudill and Paul Ashdown, *Sherman's March in Myth and Memory* (Lanham, MD: Rowman and Littlefield, 2008), 140–41, on that "blasted tune" composed in early 1865 and, of course, not sung by Sherman or his veterans.

2. Quoted in Anna McAllister, *Ellen Ewing: Wife of General Sherman* (New York: Benziger, 1936), 363. Mary Anderson was a virtually self-taught actress who specialized in Shakespearian roles; she befriended the Prince of Wales, later Edward VII, and other members of the royal family in 1883-84 during her successful seasons in London; see *Cambridge History of American Theatre*, vol. 2, *1870–1945*, ed. Don B. Wilmeth and Christopher Bigsby (Cambridge: Cambridge University Press, 1999), 456–57.

3. Michael J. Heale, *The Presidential Quest: Candidates and Images in American Political Culture, 1787–1852* (London: Longman, 1982), 18, 132–40, and esp. 141–42, 168.

4. John Sherman to Sherman, July 16, 1871, Sherman Papers, Library of Congress; Ellen Sherman to Sherman, May 2, 1876, CSHR 9/46 UNDA; Sherman to Ellen Sherman, May 13, 1876, in *The Home Letters of General Sherman*, ed. M. A. deWolfe Howe (New York: Scribner's, 1909), 383–84.

5. Sherman to Ellen Sherman, August 1; Ellen Sherman to Sherman, July 29, 1878, CSHR 9/48 UNDA.
6. Gresham had commanded a division in 17th Corps and been wounded at the Chattahoochee; see Stephen E. Woodworth, *Nothing but Victory: The Army of the Tennessee, 1861-1865* (New York: Alfred A. Knopf, 2005), 531–32. Thomas C. Reeves, *Gentleman Boss: The Life of Chester Alan Arthur* (New York: Alfred A. Knopf, 1975), 317–18, 372, 373–74.
7. John Sherman to Sherman, January 9, May 4, 1884, Sherman Papers, Library of Congress.
8. Sherman to John Sherman, March 7, May 7, 1884, Sherman Papers, Library of Congress.
9. For Blaine's maneuver and Sherman's response, see Mark D. Hirsch, "Election of 1884," in *History of American Presidential Elections*, 5 vols., ed. Arthur M. Schlesinger and Fred L. Israel (New York: Chelsea House and McGraw-Hill, 1971) 4:1562–63; Tom Sherman's recollection is in Lloyd Lewis, *Sherman: Fighting Prophet* (1932; New York: Harcourt Brace, 1958), 638. The reaction of the convention delegates to the famous telegram was noted by an eyewitness, his niece. See Elizabeth Sherman Cameron to Sir Basil Liddell Hart, February 10, 1930, Liddell Hart Papers 9/7/7, Liddell Hart Centre for Military Archives, Kings College London.
10. Richard White, *The Republic for Which It Stands: The United States during Reconstruction and the Gilded Age, 1865-1896* (New York: Oxford University Press, 2017), 316–20, 472–73. The controversy erupted over the desire of the Third Plenary Council of the Catholic Church to increase the number of its schools; see Robert Wiebe, *The Search for Order, 1877-1920* (London: Macmillan, 1967), 44, 58, 110; Hirsch, "Election of 1884," 1566–67, 1570–71, 1572, 1577–80, 1595–98; Sherman to J. E. Williams, March 25, 1869, Sherman Papers, ALS 86.40.17, Chicago Public Library; Ellen Sherman to Sherman, September 20, 1883, CSHR 9/53 UNDA.
11. Sherman to James G. Blaine, June 7, 1884, in the Appendix of Documents, Hirsch, "Election of 1884," 1599; "Why General Sherman Declined the Nomination in 1884," *North American Review* 171, no. 525 (August 1900): 243–45. Sherman approved of Blaine's financial dealings with the transcontinental railroads, but these were probably corrupt; see Ari Hoogenboom, *Rutherford B. Hayes: Warrior and President* (Lawrence: University Press of Kansas, 1995), 483; White, *Republic for Which It Stands*, 474. Edmund Morris, *The Rise of Theodore Roosevelt*, 2nd ed. (New York: Random House, 2010), 241, 258–59 vividly captures the bitter and overheated atmosphere at the Chicago convention.
12. John Sherman to Sherman, July 21, Sherman to John Sherman, July 22, 1890, in *The Sherman Letters* (New York: Scribner's, 1894), 380–81; see J. Enoch Powell, *Joseph Chamberlain* (London: Thames and Hudson, 1977), 151, for the view that all political careers end in failure.
13. Grant to Sherman, July 31, August 9, 1884; W. T. Sherman, Speech to the Society of the Army of the Tennessee, August 13, 1884, *Grant Papers* 31:181–82.
14. Quoted in William S. McFeely, *Grant: A Biography* (New York: Norton, 1981), 495–96, 504, Grant had consulted Dr. John H. Douglas first; Alexander fell among "the

battery of specialists" consulted later. See Jean Edward Smith, *Grant: A Biography* (New York: Simon and Schuster, 2001), 624; also see Mark Perry, *Grant and Twain* (New York: Random House, 2004), 64–67.

15. Sherman to Ellen Sherman, December 24, 1884, quoted in Lewis, *Sherman*, 638.

16. Joan Waugh, *Ulysses S. Grant: American Hero, American Myth* (Chapel Hill: University of North Carolina Press, 2009), 230, 235 (quoted), 246; Craig L. Symonds, *Joseph E. Johnston* (New York: Norton, 1992), 370, 380; Richard M. McMurray, *John Bell Hood and the War for Southern Independence* (1982; Lincoln: University of Nebraska Press, 1992), 201–2.

17. Waugh, *Ulysses S. Grant*, 280. The new tomb was not dedicated until 1897.

18. Badeau to Sherman, February 28, 1877; Grant to Sherman, November 12, 1876; Interview, July 6, 1878, *Grant Papers* 28:39, 42, 425; "General Sherman's Opinion of General Grant," *Century Magazine* (April 1897): 821; his correspondent is identified in *Century Magazine* 70 (1905): 316–18.

19. Grant to Sherman, September 8, 1884; Sherman to Grant, September 3, 10, 1884, *Grant Papers* 30:201–2; Clarence C. Buel to Sherman, August 15, 1884, *Grant Papers* 30:188.

20. Russell F. Weigley, *Towards an American Army: Military Thought from Washington to Marshall* (New York: Columbia University Press, 1962), 92–93, 95; Sherman to Fry, September 3, 1884, *Grant Papers* 30:203.

21. Sherman to Fry, September 3, 1884; Sherman to Grant, February 5, 1885, *Grant Papers* 31:203, 268; Grant's article, "The Battle of Shiloh," eventually appeared in *Battles and Leaders of the Civil War*, 4 volumes, ed. Robert U. Underwood and Clarence C. Buel (1887; Edison, NJ: Castle, 1987) 1:465–536; Stephen D. Engle, *Don Carlos Buell: Most Promising of All* (Chapel Hill: University of North Carolina Press, 1999), 358.

22. Sherman to Fry, September 3; Sherman to Grant, October 22, 1884, *Grant Papers* 31:204, 228; Engle, *Buell*, 354–58; John F. Marszalek, *Sherman: A Soldier's Passion for Order* (New York: Free Press, 1993), 475–76. Grant had been deeply saddened by Smith's demise; see Jean Edward Smith, *Grant: A Biography* (New York: Simon and Schuster, 2001), 208.

23. For Buell's aspersions, see "Shiloh Reviewed," *in Battles and Leaders of the Civil War*, ed. Robert U. Johnson and Clarence C. Buel (1887; Edison, NJ: Castle, 1987), 1:536; I am indebted to Larry J. Daniel, *Days of Glory: The Army of the Cumberland, 1861–1865* (Baton Rouge: Louisiana State University Press, 2004), 80, 83–84, and James Lee McDonough, *William Tecumseh Sherman: In the Service of My Country* (New York: Norton, 2016), 12–16.

24. Sherman to Col. A. I. Harding, March 30, 1884, Sherman Papers, Chicago History Museum Research Center (hereafter CHMRC); Ellen Sherman to Sherman, April 6, 1878, CSHR 9/48 UNDA.

25. Sherman to George A. Townsend, November 21, 1886, Sherman Papers, USMA Special Collections; Townsend published three other novels. The term "War between the States" only became fashionable in the mid-1880s; see Gaines Foster, *The Ghosts of the Confederacy* (New York: Oxford University Press, 1987), 118.

26. These two articles and other writings are reprinted in Garnet Wolseley, *The American Civil War: An English View*, ed. James A. Rawley (1964; Harrisburg, PA: Stackpole Books, 2002), 30–31, 53, 55, 56, 61, 66, 68, 70. The linking of Lee with Lincoln became a powerful theme in British writing; see Dom David Knowles, *The American Civil War* (Oxford: Clarendon Press, 1926), ix, "I will yield to no American in my admiration for both Lincoln and Lee."

27. W. T. Sherman, "Grant, Thomas, Lee," *North American Review* 144, no. 366 (May 1887): 437–38; Sherman to Ellen Sherman, April 2, 1887, CSHR 2/56 UNDA.

28. On the similarity of Sherman and Wolseley's opinions, see Garnet Wolseley, *The Soldier's Pocket-Book*, 5th ed. (London: Macmillan, 1886), 5; Alfred Vagts, *A History of Militarism*, rev. ed. (London: Hollis and Carter, 1959), 419; Sherman to Henry Howard [to forward to Wolseley], December 3, 1882; Sherman to Wolseley, February 25, 1884, Wolseley Papers, Hove Public Library, East Sussex, England; Ellen Sherman to Sherman, October 27, 1883, CSHR 9/52 UNDA; Sherman to Lawrence Barrett, February 25, 1884, Sherman Papers, USMA Special Collections. Barrett also acted as a mentor to Beaumont Smith, the son of Sherman's former subordinate A. J. Smith. He was one of the leading American actors of his day and shared some of Sherman's glowering impetuosity. See *Cambridge History of American Theatre* 2:454–55.

29. Elizabeth R. Varon, "'Save in Defence of My Native State': A New Look at Robert E. Lee's Decision to Join the Confederacy," in R. J. Cook et al., *Secession Winter* (Baltimore: Johns Hopkins University Press, 2013), 34–57; Sherman, "Grant, Thomas, Lee," 439–41.

30. Sherman, "Grant, Thomas, Lee," 442–43; Ellen Sherman to Sherman, April 4, 1887, CSHR 9/55 UNDA.

31. Sherman, "Grant, Thomas, Lee," 442–45, 449, 450; for his advice to Garfield, see Sherman to Garfield, August 4, 1870, in "Unpublished Letters of General Sherman," *North American Review* 152, no. 412 (March 1891): 371.

32. Sherman, "Grant, Thomas, Lee," 450; Harold Nicolson, *Good Behaviour: Being a Study of Certain Types of Civility* (London: Constable, 1955), 1, has interesting observations on exemplars, like Lee; Eric Foner, "The Making and Breaking of the Legend of Robert E. Lee," *New York Times*, August 28, 2017 believes the legend "needs to be retired."

33. Sherman to Grant, January 17, 1868; Grant to Sherman, March 18, 1868, January 19, 1869; Grant to Porter, May 25, 1868, *Grant Papers* 17:204, 262, 19, 109–10. Healy made effective use of photography in portrait painting; see Lois Marie Fink, "Healy, George Peter Alexander," in *American National Biography* 10:454–56; "General Sherman's Tour of Europe," *Century* 35 (1899): 734 (entry for February 11, 1872); Ellen Sherman to Sherman, July 9, August 9, 1885 CSHR 9/54 UNDA; Sherman to William Greenleaf Eliot, December 1885, William Greenleaf Eliot Papers, Missouri History Museum, Washington University, St. Louis.

34. Ellen Sherman to Sherman, July 9, 1885, CSHR 9/54 UNDA; Lewis, *Sherman*, 640; "General Sherman's Tour of Europe," *Century* 35 (1899): 729–40.

35. Ellen Sherman to Sherman, n.d. [March 1864], March 15, August 27, November 5, 1877, August 21, 1881, CSHR 9/47/48/51/61, UNDA.

36. Sherman to Ellen Sherman, July 7, 1872, CSHR 9/29 UNDA.

37. For his "forbearance," see Sherman to Ellen Sherman, July 7, 1872, CSHR 9/29 UNDA; for Sherman's fulminations against the Catholic Church, see McDonough, *Sherman*, 680–82; Ellen Sherman to Sherman, May 29, June 7, June 9, July 5, 1878, CSHR 9/48 UNDA; Fellman's overdrawn interpretation is in *Citizen Sherman*, 381–82.

38. Ellen Sherman to Sherman, June 27, July 2, 1878, CSHR 9/48 UNDA.

39. See her account quoted in Marszalek, *Sherman*, 417.

40. Fellman, *Citizen Sherman*, 347–49. Fellman suggests sexual tensions between them, Sherman's "unceasing demands" versus Ellen's preference for abstinence as a form of "birth control" (347), but this can only be speculation. Fellman agrees that any separation—if it occurred—soon ended with a "general truce" (351).

41. Fellman, *Citizen Sherman*, 355–58.

42. Fellman, *Citizen Sherman*, 358–70; Ellen Sherman to Sherman, May 2, 1876, CSHR 9/46, describes some of Audenried's symptoms; for visits of the family, especially Rachel to Mary's house, see Ellen Sherman to Sherman, August 5, 1880, January 24, 1881, CSHR 9/49 UNDA; Marszalek, *Sherman*, 419–21. Mary Audenried continued another affair simultaneously with the former Confederate general Albert Pike, who was more than a decade older than Sherman.

43. Rosebery, *North American Journal* 117 (entry for December 9, 1873); Sherman to Colonel A. I. Harding, March 30, 1884, CHMRC; Sherman to Charles Baden, May 9, 1886; Sherman to Brig. General William C. Brown, July 29, 1889; Sherman to R. Butler, September 26, 1890, Sherman Papers, USMA Special Collections. The Orleanist dynasty should have been restored and the Comte de Paris crowned in 1873 but for the obstruction of the legitimist Bourbon claimant, the Comte de Chambord; see Alfred Cobban, *A History of Modern France*, 3 vols. (Harmondsworth: Penguin, 1965), 3:12–17.

44. Sherman to William V. Jacobs, January 28, 1884, Sherman Papers, CHMRC. He was still complaining of a lingering cough nine months later. On other aspects of his health, see Ellen Sherman to Sherman, May 9, 1876, September 20, 1885, CSHR 9/46/54, and Sherman to Ellen Sherman, May 17, 1887, CSHR UNDA. On presidential persistence, see Ellen Sherman to Sherman, April 11, 1887, CSHR 9/55, and Sherman to Ellen Sherman, December 15, 1887, CSHR UNDA; his view of Cleveland's prospects is in Sherman to Ellen Sherman, June 24, 1888, *Home Letters*, 400.

45. Sherman to N. M. Curtis (Chairman, Sheridan Memorial Service), March 30, April 5, 16, 18, 19, 20, 1889, Sherman Papers, CHMRC.

46. McAllister, *Ellen Ewing*, 357–59; Ellen Sherman to Sherman, August 6/7, 1882, and Sherman's telegram; note by Eleanor Sherman Fitch, (their elder sister), on the same, August 30, 1936; Sherman to Dr. Morris, August 6, 1882. Ellen revealed that she and Julia Grant had been weighed in 1869 at 150 and 175 pounds respectively. Ellen Sherman to Sherman, July 20, 1886, April 4, 11, 30, May 3, 1887, CSHR 9/52/54/55 UNDA.

47. On Ellen's decline and death, see Ellen Sherman to Sherman, July 25, August (ca.) 15, 1887, September 17, 1888, CSHR 9/55 UNDA; McAllister, *Ellen Ewing*, 366–68.

48. Ellen Sherman to Ethan Allen Hitchcock, April 25, May 13, 29, 1862, Sherman Papers, USMA Special Collections; Fellman, *Citizen Sherman*, 370; P. Tecumseh Sherman,

foreword to McAllister, *Ellen Ewing*, vii; nevertheless, this biography presents a too cozy view of their marriage, more consistent with social norms before ca. 1980 than it really was.

49. Sherman to William C. Brown, July 22, 1889, Sherman Papers, USMA Special Collections.

50. Sherman to Wolseley, December 3, 1882, Wolseley Papers, Hove Public Library. The reference, of course, is to James Fenimore Cooper's famous novel published in 1826.

51. H. M. Stanley, *The Autobiography of Henry Morton Stanley, GCB*, ed. Dorothy Stanley (London: Sampson Low, 1909), 426.. Stanley returned to Britain permanently and renaturalized as a British subject in 1892.

52. Lawrence Barrett survived his friend by a mere five weeks, dying on March 20, 1891. An obsession with the last utterances of the great developed in the 19th century. Given Sherman's difficulties talking, "faithful and honorable" might be a convenient retrospective reconstruction.

53. *New York Times*, February 13, 1891; the argument that both "the admirably conducted" Catholic services were "a comfort to his children" is repeated by Oliver O. Howard, *Autobiography*, 2 vols. (New York: Baker and Taylor, 1907), 2:553; Stanley P. Hirshson, *The White Tecumseh: A Biography of William T. Sherman* (New York: Wiley, 1997), 365–66, 387–88, 390, exaggerates the significance of the "religious squabbling"; Marszalek, *Sherman*, 491–99, gives the most detailed account of the last days and funerals; Hayes's tribute is quoted in Hoogenboom, *Hayes*, 525.

Conclusion

1. Compare with the succession of strokes that incapacitated Marlborough: Richard Holmes, *Marlborough: England's Fragile Genius* (London: HarperPress, 2008), 472.

2. Edward Caudill and Paul Ashdown, *Sherman's March in Myth and Memory* (Lanham, MD: Rowman and Littlefield, 2008), 183; Willa Cather, *O Pioneers!* (1913; London: Virago Press, 1983), 17, 37, 50.

3. A. H. Burne, *Lee, Grant, and Sherman* (1939; Lawrence: University Press of Kansas, 2000), with endnotes by Albert Castel, 200–201; Albert Castel, *Decision in the West: The Atlanta Campaign of 1864* (Lawrence: University Press of Kansas, 1992), 565; Luce is quoted in J. P. Clark, *Preparing for War: The Emergence of the Modern US Army, 1817-1917* (Cambridge, MA: Harvard University Press, 2017), 164.

4. Further elucidation can be found in Brian Holden Reid, *America's Civil War: The Operational Battlefield, 1861-1863* (Amherst, NY: Prometheus Books, 2008), 441–45; Clayton R. Newell and Michael D. Krause, eds., *On Operational Art* (Washington, DC: US Army Center of US Military History, 1994), 9–10, though this assumes knowledge.

5. Victor Davis Hanson, *The Soul of Battle* (New York: Free Press, 1999), 224, stresses his wide experience; see J. F. C. Fuller's reflections on its importance in *Sir John Moore's System of Training* (London: Hutchinson, 1925), 91.

6. Earl Hess, *The Civil War in the West* (Chapel Hill: University of North Carolina Press, 2012), xi–xii, xiii, 129–31, 134, 231, 319. On Sherman's fusion of the old and the new, see Russell F. Weigley, *Towards an American Army* (New York: Columbia University Press, 1962), 81.

7. Christopher Allmand, *Henry V* (London: Eyre Methuen, 1992), 189, 218, 219, 221. Catastrophe in 1944-45 was averted in the Netherlands, but 16,000 people still starved to death; see M. R. D. Foot, "Netherlands," in *The Oxford Companion to the Second World War*, ed. I. C. B. Dear and M. R. D. Foot (New York: Oxford University Press, 1995), 783.

8. Quoted in Alfred Vagts, *A History of Militarism*, rev. ed. (London: Hollis and Carter, 1959), 469.

9. Liddell Hart rightly argues "that strategy is ... the master of tactics" but is too dogmatic in concluding "that to pursue it [battle] single-mindedly is to chase a will-o'-the wisp," that is, a mirage. B. H. Liddell Hart, *Sherman* (London: Ernest Benn, 1930), 440, 441.

10. Brian Holden Reid, "How Were Civil War Armies Kept in the Field?" in *Raise, Train and Sustain*, ed. Peter Dennis and Jeffrey Grey (Sydney: Australian Military History Publications, 2010), 14, 18, 24; on Napoleon, see David Kaiser, *Politics and War*, enlarged ed. (Cambridge, MA: Harvard University Press, 2000), 256; on looting in 1914-18 and 1939-45, see Richard Holmes, *Firing Line* (London: Jonathan Cape, 1985), 354. In May 1945 Field Marshal Erich von Manstein had his baton "lifted" by a British soldier; see Mungo Melvin, *Manstein: Hitler's Greatest General* (London: Weidenfeld and Nicolson, 2010), 431.

11. See Richard Glover, *Britain at Bay: Defence against Bonaparte, 1803-1814* (London: George Allen and Unwin, 1973), 54; the 1801 memorandum advocating the "driving" of Southern England is published in Fuller, *Sir John Moore's System of Training*, 48–57, at 50, 57.

12. Sherman to Grant, November 6, in *Sherman's Civil War: Selected Correspondence of William T. Sherman, 1860-1865*, ed. Brooks D. Simpson and Jean V. Berlin (Chapel Hill: University of North Carolina Press, 1999), 751 (hereafter *Correspondence*).

13. Peter J. Parish, "The Will to Write and the Will to Fight: Some Recent Books on the American Civil War," *Journal of American Studies* 32, no. 2 (August 1998): 302.

14. Lee Kennett, *Sherman: A Soldier's Life* (New York: HarperCollins, 2001), 348; Matthew Carr, "General Sherman's March to the Sea," *History Today* 64 (November 2014): 31; Donald Stoker, *The Grand Design: Strategy and the US Civil War* (New York: Oxford University Press, 2010), 382–83; B. H. Liddell Hart, *Strategy: The Indirect Approach*, 4th ed. (London: Faber and Faber, 1967), 151–52.

15. General Orders No. 100, Section 1, Article 21, *OR*, ser. 2, 5:672; Lawrence Freedman, *The Future of War: A History* (London: Allen Lane, 2017), 32.

16. Matthew Carr, *Sherman's Ghosts: Soldiers, Civilians, and the American Way of War* (New York: New Press, 2015), 5; on "moral retrogression," see Major General J. F. C. Fuller, *The Conduct of War, 1789-1961* (London: Eyre and Spottiswoode, 1961), 107; John B. Walters, "General William T. Sherman and Total War," *Journal of Southern History* 14, no. 4 (November 1948): 447–80, at 466; John B. Walters, *Merchant of Terror* (Indianapolis, IN: Bobbs-Merrill, 1973), 128, 78, 82.

17. James Reston Jr., *Sherman's March and Vietnam* (New York: Macmillan, 1984), 91, 111, is strongly influenced by Walters: compare 110–11 with *Merchant of Terror*, 58, 190–94. James M. McPherson, *This Mighty Scourge* (New York: Oxford University Press, 2007), 123; Charles E. Vetter, *Sherman: Merchant of Terror, Advocate of Peace* (Gretna, LA: Pelican, 1992), 161.

18. Milton Finley, *The Most Monstrous of Wars: The Napoleonic Guerrilla War in Southern Italy, 1806–11* (Columbia: University of South Carolina Press, 1994), 75, 105; Geoffrey Best, *War and Society in Revolutionary Europe, 1770–1870* (Leicester: Leicester University Press, 1982), 101; see *Merchant of Terror*, 160–61, 182–83. Rory Muir observes that the Portuguese had a "tradition of stripping the countryside" during invasions and did so without coercion in 1810 because of their memories of the "horrors" of 1807–9, systematic "terror, pillage and extortion" never matched by Sherman's soldiers in 1864–65; see his *Wellington: The Path to Victory, 1769–1814* (New Haven. CT: Yale University Press, 2013), 361–62.

19. On its meaninglessness, see Eugenia C. Kiesling, "'Total War, Total Nonsense,' or the Military Historian's Fetish," in *Arms and the Man: Military History Essays in Honor of Dennis Showalter* (Leiden: Brill, 2011), 215–41; Theo Farrell, *The Norms of War* (Boulder, CO: Lynne Reiner, 2005), 70–71; Brian Bond, *War and Society in Europe, 1870–1970* (Leicester: Leicester University Press, 1984), 168, considers it "just as much a myth as total victory or total peace." Walters, *Merchant of Terror*, 138; his interpretation of Lieber's concept of "military necessity" is narrow (see "General Sherman and Total War," 447). Steven E. Woodworth persists in the view that Sherman's methods offered an alternative to Grant's in an otherwise fine biography, *Sherman* (New York: Palgrave Macmillan, 2009), 119; also see Vegetius, *De re militarii* 3.v for the view that armies are more exposed on the march than in battle.

20. Stoker, *Grand Design*, 381; Freedman, *Future of War*, 37; David Armitage, *Civil Wars: A History in Ideas* (New Haven, CT: Yale University Press, 2017), 169–72; John Fabian Witt, *Lincoln's Code: The Laws of War in American History* (New York: Free Press, 2012), 279, 280. Walters criticizes Sherman for "generalization" instead of "investigating individual cases"; see *Merchant of Terror*, 74.

21. T. Harry Williams, *McClellan, Sherman and Grant* (New Brunswick, NJ: Rutgers University Press, 1962), 77.

22. On the numerous misquotations and false attributions that occurred within 25 years of Sherman's death, see *New York Times*, September 8, 1914; for Tecumseh Sherman's views, see *Army and Navy Journal* 45, no. 37 (May 16, 1908): 995; for the view that the phrase is apocryphal, see *Army and Navy Journal* 48, no. 30 (March 25, 1911): 880.

23. *Hayes: The Diary of a President, 1875–1881*, ed. T. Harry Williams (New York: David McKay, 1964), 291, 292–93 (entries for August 5 and 14, 1880); John F. Marszalek, *Sherman: A Soldier's Passion for Order* (New York: Free Press, 1993), 476–77; quotations from the June 19, 1879, speech are from *Words on War*, ed. Jay M. Shafritz (New York: Prentice Hall, 1990), 457.

24. Farrell, *Norms of War*, 74–75; Shafritz, *Words on War*, 457; W. T. Sherman, "Camp Fires of the GAR," *North American Review* 147, no. 384 (November 1888): 497–502.

Sherman worried lest "the wise man stays at home and leaves the fool to take the buffets and kicks of war"; see Carr, *Sherman's Ghosts*, 288.

25. He complained of the "great liberties" taken by the press in describing his move to New York in 1886; see W. T. Sherman, "An Unspoken Address to the Loyal Legion," *North American Review* 142, no. 352 (March 1886): 295.

26. W. M. Thackeray, *The Virginians*, 2 vols. (1857; London: Dent, 1937), 1:235; Kennet, *Sherman*, 352; Michael Fellman, *Citizen Sherman* (New York: Random House, 1995), 130–33; Sherman to Ellen Sherman, August 3, 1861, September 12, 1862; Sherman to Thomas Ewing Sr., June 7, 1862; Sherman to John Sherman, September 3, 1862, August 3, 1863, April 5, 1864; Sherman to John T. Swayne, June 11, 1863; Sherman to David Stuart, August 1, 1863, in *Correspondence*, 126, 295, 239, 293–94, 516, 613, 480, 512.

27. Burke's comment is in *The Works of the Rt. Hon. Edmund Burke*, 12 vols. (London: John C. Nimmo, 1888) 3:297. Richard H. Dana was exasperated with the president and Congress: "[Lincoln] is an unutterable calamity to us where he is. Only the army can save us. Congress is not a council of state"; see Charles Francis Adams Jr., *Richard Henry Dana: A Biography*, 2 vols. (New York: Houghton Mifflin, 1890) 2:265.

28. Kennett, *Sherman*, 352; Ronald Syme, *The Roman Revolution* (1939; London: Folio Society, 2009), 329, 503; Walters, *Merchant of Terror*, 40, 42–44, 72–73.

29. "Old Shady, with a Moral," *North American Review* 147, no. 383 (October 1888): 362, 366; Fellman, *Citizen Sherman*, 409.

30. *Memoirs* (1889) 1:36. These sentiments fly in the face of contemporary social Darwinism, with which Sherman was acquainted; see "Old Shady, with a Moral," 364, 365, 366, 367, 368. But as William R. Brock has shown, Darwinism invariably gave way if the achievements of the Union victory of 1865 seemed endangered: *Investigation and Responsibility* (Cambridge: Cambridge University Press, 1984), 25–26, 42, 251–52, 259–60.

Bibliography

Manuscript Sources

William Greenleaf Eliot Papers, Missouri History Museum, Washington University, St. Louis

Sir Basil Liddell Hart Papers, Liddell Hart Centre for Military Archives, King's College London

David Dixon Porter Papers, Manuscript Division, Library of Congress, Washington, DC

William T. Sherman Family Papers, Archives of the University of Notre Dame, Notre Dame, Indiana 46556

William T. Sherman Papers, Chicago History Museum Research Center

William T. Sherman Papers, Chicago Public Library

William T. Sherman Papers, Manuscript Division, Library of Congress, Washington, DC

William T. Sherman Papers, United States Military Academy, Special Collections, Jefferson Hall, West Point, NY

Garnet Joseph Wolseley Papers, Hove Public Library, East Sussex, England

Published Primary Works

Browning, Orville Hickman. *Diary.* 2 volumes. Edited by Theodore C. Pease and James G. Randall. Springfield: Illinois State Historical Library, 1925.

Buell, D. C. "Shiloh Reviewed." In *Battles and Leaders of the Civil War.* 4 volumes. Edited by Robert U. Johnson and Clarence C. Buell. 1887; Edison, NJ: Castle, 1987, 1:465–536.

Burke, Edmund. *The Works of the Rt. Hon. Edmund Burke.* 12 volumes. London: John C. Nimmo, 1888.

Byers, S. M. H. "Sherman's Attack at the Tunnel." In *Battles and Leaders of the Civil War.* 4 volumes. Edited by Robert U. Johnson and Clarence C. Buel. 1887; Edison, NJ: Castle, 1987, 3:712–13.

Byers, S. M. H. "Some More War Letters." *North American Review* 144, no. 364 (March 1887): 374–80.

Chesnut, Mary. *Mary Chesnut's Civil War.* Edited by C. Vann Woodward. New Haven, CT: Yale University Press, 1981.

Chisolm, A. R. "The Failure to Capture Hardee." In *Battles and Leaders of the Civil War.* 4 volumes. Edited by Robert U. Johnson and Clarence C. Buel. 1887; Edison, NJ: Castle, 1987, 4: 679–80.

Dueble, John. *Two Germans in the Civil War: The Diary of John Deuble and Letters of Gottfried Rentscher.* Edited and translated by Joseph R. Reinhart. Knoxville: University of Tennessee Press, 2004.

Flavel, C. Barber. *Holding the Line: The Third Tennessee Infantry, 1861–1864*. Edited by Robert H. Ferrell. Kent, OH: Kent State University Press, 1994.

Grant, U. S. "The Battle of Shiloh." In *Battles and Leaders of the Civil War*. 4 volumes. Edited by Robert U. Johnson and Clarence C. Buel. 1887; Reprint, Edison, NJ: Castle, 1987, 2: 465–86.

Grant, U. S. "Chattanooga." In *Battles and Leaders of the Civil War*. 4 volumes. Edited by Robert U. Johnson and Clarence C. Buel. 1887; Edison, NJ: Castle, 1987, 3:692–93.

Grant, U. S. *The Papers of Ulysses S. Grant*. Edited by John Y. Simon. 31 volumes. Carbondale: Southern Illinois University Press, 1967–2009.

Grant, U. S. *Personal Memoirs*. 2 volumes. London: Sampson Lowe, 1885.

"Grant's Pertinacity." *Army and Navy Journal* 31 (December 30, 1893), n.p.

Hitchcock, Henry. *Marching with Sherman*. New Haven, CT: Yale University Press, 1927.

Howard, Oliver O. *Autobiography*. 2 volumes. New York: Baker and Taylor, 1907.

Howard, Oliver O. "Sherman's Advance from Atlanta." In *Battles and Leaders of the Civil War*. 4 volumes. Edited by Robert U. Johnson and Clarence C. Buel. 1887; Edison, NJ: Castle, 1987, 4:663–66.

Howard, Oliver O. "The Struggle for Atlanta." In *Battles and Leaders of the Civil War*. 4 volumes. Edited by Robert U. Johnson and Clarence C. Buel. 1887; Edison, NJ: Castle, 1987, 4:293–325.

Johnston, Joseph E. "Opposing Sherman's Advance to Atlanta." In *Battles and Leaders of the Civil War*. 4 volumes. Edited by Robert U. Johnson and Clarence C. Buell. 1887; Edison, NJ: Castle, 1987, 4:260–73.

Lamson, Roswell. *Lamson of the Gettysburg: The Civil War Letters of Lieutenant Roswell Lamson, USN*. Edited by James M. McPherson and Patricia R. McPherson. New York: Oxford University Press, 1997.

Lincoln, Abraham. *The Collected Works of Abraham Lincoln*. 9 volumes. Edited by Roy P. Basler. New Brunswick, NJ: Rutgers University Press, 1953–55.

Lincoln, Abraham. *The Language of Liberty: The Political Speeches and Writings of Abraham Lincoln*. Edited by Joseph R. Fornieri. Washington, DC: Regency Publishing, 2003.

Mahan, A. T. *From Sail to Steam: Recollections of a Naval Life*. New York: Harper, 1907.

Martin, John W. "Fighting Under Forrest at Brice's Crossroads." In *New Annals of the Civil War*. Edited by Peter Cozzens and Robert I. Girardi. Mechanicsburg, PA: Stackpole, 2004, 363–80.

McClellan, George B. *The Civil War Papers of George B. McClellan: Selected Correspondence*. Edited by Stephen Sears. New York: Da Capo Press, 1992.

Morgan, George W. "The Assault on Chickasaw Bluffs." In *Battles and Leaders of the Civil War*. 4 volumes. Edited by Robert U. Johnson and Clarence C. Buell. 1887; Edison, NJ: Castle, 1987, 3:462–70.

Nichols, G. W. *The Story of the Great March*. London: Sampson and Low, 1865.

Oakey, Daniel. "Marching through Georgia and the Carolinas." In *Battles and Leaders of the Civil War*. 4 volumes. Edited by Robert U. Johnson and Clarence C. Buell. 1887; Edison, NJ: Castle, 1987, 4:671–79.

Porter, David. *Journal of a Cruise*. 1815, 1822; Annapolis, MD: Naval Institute Press, 1986.

Porter, Horace. *Campaigning with Grant*. New York: Century, 1897.

Schurz, Carl. *Reminiscences*. 3 volumes. New York: Doubleday, Page, 1908.

Sherman, John. *Recollections of Forty Years in the House, Senate and Cabinet*. 2 volumes. Chicago: Werner, 1895.

"The Sherman Family." *New York Times*, February 19, 1865.

Sherman, P. Tecumseh. *Army and Navy Journal* 14, no. 37 (May 16, 1908): 995; 48, no. 30 (March 25, 1911): 880.

Sherman, W. T. "Camp Fires of the GAR." *North American Review* 147, no. 384 (November 1888): 497–502.

Sherman, W. T. *From Atlanta to the Sea*. Edited by B. H. Liddell Hart. London: Folio Society, 1961.

Sherman, W. T. "General Sherman's Opinion of General Grant." *Century Magazine* 53, no. 6 (April 1897): 821; 70 (1905): 316-18.

Sherman, W. T. "General Sherman's Tour of Europe." *Century Magazine* 35 (1899): 729-40.

Sherman, W. T. "The Grand Strategy of the Last Year of the War." In *Battles and Leaders of the Civil War*. 4 volumes. Edited by Robert U. Johnson and Clarence C. Buel. 1887; New York: Century, 1890, 4:247–59.

Sherman, W. T. "Grant, Thomas, Lee." *North American Review* 144, no. 366 (May 1887): 437–50.

Sherman, W. T. *Home Letters of General Sherman*. Edited by M. A. de Wolfe Howe. New York: Scribner's, 1909.

Sherman, W. T. *Memoirs*. 2 volumes. London: Henry King, 1875.

Sherman, W. T. *Memoirs*. 2nd revised edition. 2 volumes. New York: Appleton, 1889.

Sherman, W. T. "Old Shady, with a Moral." *North American Review* 147, no. 383 (October 1888): 361-68.

Sherman, W. T. "Sherman and the San Francisco Vigilantes: Unpublished Letters of General William T. Sherman." *Century Magazine* 56 (December 1891): 296-301.

Sherman, W. T. *The Sherman Letters*. Edited by Rachel Sherman Thorndike. New York: Charles Scribner's Sons, 1894.

Sherman, W. T. "Sherman on Grant." *North American Review* 140 (January 1886): 111-13.

Sherman, W. T. "Unpublished Letters of General Sherman." *North American Review* 152, no. 412 (March 1891): 371-75.

Sherman, W. T. "An Unspoken Address to the Loyal Legion." *North American Review* 142, no. 352 (March 1886): 295-308.

Sherman, W. T., and J. R. Doolittle. "Why General Sherman Declined the Nomination in 1884." *North American Review* 171, no. 525 (August 1900): 243-45.

Sherman, W. T. *General W. T. Sherman as College President: A Collection of Letters, Documents etc.* Edited by Walter L. Fleming. Cleveland, OH: Arthur H. Clark, 1912; London: Forgotten Books, 2015.

Sherman, W. T. *Sherman's Civil War: Selected Correspondence of William T. Sherman, 1860-1865*. Chapel Hill: University of North Carolina Press, 1999.

Slocum, Henry W. "Sherman's March from Savannah to Bentonville." In *Battles and Leaders of the Civil War*. 4 volumes. Edited by Robert U. Johnson and Clarence C. Buel. 1887; Edison, NJ: Castle, 1987, 4:681-95.

The Trial of Andrew Johnson. Supplement to the *Congressional Globe*, 40th Congress, 2nd Session, Washington, DC: F. and J. Rives and George Bailey, 1868.

War of the Rebellion: A Compilation of the Official Records of the Union and Confederate Armies. 70 volumes in 128 parts. Washington, DC: Government Printing Office, 1880-1901.

Wilson, James Harrison. *Under the Old Flag*. 2 volumes. New York: Appleton, 1912.

Secondary Works

Adams, Charles Francis, Jr. *An Autobiography.* 1916; New York: Chelsea House, 1983.

Adams, Charles Francis, Jr. *Richard Henry Dana: A Biography.* 2 volumes. New York: Houghton Mifflin, 1890.

Adams, Henry. *History of the United States during the Administrations of Thomas Jefferson.* 4 volumes. 1889; New York: Library of America, 1986.

Adams, Michael C. C. *Living Hell: The Dark Side of the Civil War.* Baltimore: Johns Hopkins University Press, 2014.

Adams, Michael C. C. *Our Masters the Rebels: A Speculation on Union Military Failure in the East, 1861-1865.* Cambridge, MA: Harvard University Press, 1978.

Allmand, Christopher. *Henry V.* London: Eyre Methuen, 1992.

Ambrose, Stephen E. *Duty, Honor, Country: A History of West Point.* Baltimore: Johns Hopkins University Press, 1966.

Ambrose, Stephen E. *Halleck: Lincoln's Chief of Staff.* 1962; Baton Rouge: Louisiana State University Press, 1990.

Armitage, David. *Civil Wars: A History in Ideas.* New Haven, CT: Yale University Press, 2017.

Athearn, Robert G. *William T. Sherman and the Settlement of the West.* Norman: University of Oklahoma Press, 1956.

Badeau, Adam. *Military History of U. S. Grant.* 3 volumes. New York: Appleton, 1881.

Bailey, Anne J. *War and Ruin: William T. Sherman and the Savannah Campaign.* Wilmington, DE: Scholarly Resources, 2003.

Bailey, Anthony. *John Constable: A Kingdom of His Own.* London: Chatto and Windus, 2006.

Ballard, Michael B. *U. S. Grant: The Making of a General, 1861-1863.* Lanham, MD: Rowan and Littlefield, 2005.

Barnett, Correlli. *Bonaparte.* London: Allen and Unwin, 1978.

Barnett, Correlli. *The Lords of War: From Lincoln to Churchill, Supreme Command, 1861-1945.* Barnsley: Praetorian Press, 2012.

Barney, William L. "Rush to Disaster: Secession and the Slaves' Revenge." In *Secession Winter,* edited by Robert Cook et al. Baltimore: Johns Hopkins University Press, 2013, 10-33.

Barrett, John G. *Sherman's March through the Carolinas.* Chapel Hill: University of North Carolina Press, 1956.

Belz, Herman. "The Etheridge Conspiracy of 1863: A Projected Conservative Coup." *Journal of Southern History* 36, no. 4 (November 1970): 549-67.

Benedict, Michael Les. *The Impeachment and Trial of Andrew Johnson.* New York: Norton, 1973.

Beringer, Richard, Herman Hattaway, Archer Jones, and William N. Still Jr. *Why the South Lost the Civil War.* Athens: University of Georgia Press, 1986.

Best, Geoffrey. *Humanity in Warfare.* London: Weidenfeld and Nicolson, 1980.

Best, Geoffrey. *War and Society in Revolutionary Europe, 1770-1870.* Leicester, UK: Leicester University Press, 1982.

Bidwell, Shelford. *Modern Warfare: A Study of Men, Ideas and Weapons.* London: Allen Lane, 1973.

Bierce, Ambrose. *Civil War Stories.* New York: Dover, 1994.

Bierce, Ambrose. *In the Midst of Life and Other Tales*. Edited and with an afterword by Marcus Cunliffe. New York: New American Library, 1961.

Boatner, Mark M. *Cassell's Biographical Dictionary of the American War of Independence*. London: Cassell, 1973.

Bogue, Allan G. *The Earnest Men: Republicans of the Civil War Senate*. Ithaca, NY: Cornell University Press, 1981.

Bond, Brian. *War and Society in Europe, 1870–1970*. Leicester, UK: Leicester University Press, 1984.

Boorstin, Daniel J. *The Americans: The Colonial Experience*. New York: Random House, 1958.

Bowman, S. M., and R. B. Irwin. *Sherman and His Campaigns*. New York: Charles B. Richardson, 1865.

Bradford, Gamaliel. *Lee the American*. London: Constable, 1912.

Bradley, Mark L. *This Astounding Close: The Road to Bennett Place*. Chapel Hill: University of North Carolina Press, 2000.

Bragg, C. L., et al. *Never for Want of Powder: The Confederate Powder Works in Augusta, Georgia*. Columbia: University of South Carolina Press, 2007.

Brinsfield, John W. "The Military Ethics of General William T. Sherman: A Reassessment." In *The Parameters of War*, edited by L. J. Matthews and D. E. Brown. New York: Pergamon-Brassey's, 1989, 87–103.

Brock, William R. *Investigation and Responsibility*. Cambridge: Cambridge University Press, 1984.

Brock, William R. *Parties and Political Conscience: American Dilemmas, 1840–1850*. Millwood, NY: KTO Press, 1979.

Brooke, Christopher. *From Alfred to Henry III*. London: Thomas Nelson, 1962.

Burne, A. H. *Lee, Grant, and Sherman*. 1939; Lawrence: University Press of Kansas, 2000, with endnotes by Albert Castel.

Cambridge History of American Theatre, volume 2, *1870–1945*. Edited by Don B. Wilmeth and Christopher Bigsby. Cambridge: Cambridge University Press, 1999.

Campbell, Jacqueline G. "'The Most Diabolical Act of All Barbarous War': Soldiers, Civilians and Burning of Columbia." *American Nineteenth Century History* 3, no. 3 (Fall 2002): 53–72.

Campbell, Jacqueline G. *When Sherman Marched North from the Sea: Resistance on the Confederate Home Front*. Chapel Hill: University of North Carolina Press, 2003.

Carpenter, John A. *Ulysses S. Grant*. New York: Twayne, 1970.

Carr, Matthew. "General Sherman's March to the Sea." *History Today* 64 (November 2014): 29–35.

Carr, Matthew. *Sherman's Ghosts: Soldiers, Civilians, and the American Way of War*. New York: New Press, 2015.

Castel, Albert. *Decision in the West: The Atlanta Campaign of 1864*. Lawrence: University Press of Kansas, 1992.

Castel, Albert. *Tom Taylor's Civil War*. Lawrence: University Press of Kansas, 2000.

Castel, Albert. *Victors in Blue*. Lawrence: University Press of Kansas, 2011.

Cather, Willa. *O Pioneers!* 1913; London: Virago Press, 1983.

Catton, Bruce. *Grant Moves South*. Boston: Little, Brown, 1960.

Caudill, Edward, and Paul Ashdown. *Sherman's March in Myth and Memory*. Lanham, MD: Rowman and Littlefield, 2008.

Chandler, David G. *The Campaigns of Napoleon.* 1967; London: Weidenfeld and Nicolson, 1995.

Chisholm, Anne. "Lady Great Heart." *Times Literary Supplement*, March 10, 2017.

Clark, J. P. *Preparing for War: The Emergence of the Modern US Army, 1815-1917.* Cambridge, MA: Harvard University Press, 2017.

Clarke, Dwight L. *William Tecumseh Sherman: Gold Rush Banker.* San Francisco: California Historical Society, 1969.

Clausewitz, Carl von. *On War.* Edited by Michael Howard and Peter Paret. Princeton, NJ: Princeton University Press, 1976.

Cobban, Alfred. *A History of Modern France.* 3 volumes. Harmondsworth, UK: Penguin, 1965.

Coffman, Edward M. *The Embattled Past: Reflections on Military History.* Lexington: University of Kentucky Press, 2014.

Coles, Harry L. *The War of 1812.* Chicago: University of Chicago Press, 1965.

Connell-Smith, Gordon. *The United States and Latin America.* London: Heinemann, 1974.

Connelly, Thomas L. *Army of the Heartland: The Army of Tennessee, 1861-1862.* Baton Rouge: Louisiana State University Press, 1967.

Connelly, Thomas L. *The Autumn of Glory: The Army of Tennessee, 1862-1865.* Baton Rouge: Louisiana State University Press, 1971.

Cook, Robert. *Civil War America: Making a Nation, 1848-1877.* London: Longman, 2003.

Cozzens, Peter. *The Shipwreck of Their Hopes: The Battles for Chattanooga.* Urbana: University of Illinois Press, 1994.

Crawford, Martin. "Jefferson Davis and the Confederacy." In *Themes of the American Civil War.* Revised 2nd edition, edited by Susan-Mary Grant and Brian Holden Reid. New York: Routledge, 2010, 98-117.

Crevecoeur, J. Hector St. Jean de. *Letters from an American Farmer.* Edited by Albert E. Stone. 1782; Harmondsworth, UK: Penguin, 1981.

Creveld, Martin Van. *Command in War.* Cambridge, MA: Harvard University Press, 1985.

Cullum, G. W. *Biographical Register of Officers and Graduates of the US Military Academy at West Point, NY.* 2 volumes. New York, 1868.

Cunliffe, Marcus. *American Presidents and the Presidency.* 2nd edition. London: Fontana, 1972.

Cunliffe, Marcus. *In Search of America.* New York: Greenwood Press, 1991.

Cunliffe, Marcus. *Soldiers and Civilians: The Martial Spirit in America, 1775-1865.* 3rd edition. 1968; London: Gregg, 1993.

Cunningham, O. Edward. *Shiloh and the Western Campaign of 1862.* Edited by Gary D. Joiner and Timothy B. Smith. New York: Savas Beattie, 2007.

Curran, Robert E. *A History of Georgetown University*, volume 1, *From Academy to University, 1789-1889.* Washington, DC: Georgetown University Press, 2010.

Daniel, Larry J. *Days of Glory: The Army of the Cumberland, 1861-1865.* Baton Rouge: Louisiana State University Press, 2004.

Davis, William C. *Battle at Bull Run.* New York: Doubleday, 1977.

Dawson, Joseph G., III. *Doniphan's Epic March.* Lawrence: University Press of Kansas, 1999.

Dawson, Joseph G., III, ed. *The Late 19th Century Army: A Research Guide.* New York: Greenwood Press, 1990.

Dawson, Joseph G., III, ed. *The Louisiana Governors: From Iberville to Edwards.* Baton Rouge: Louisiana State University Press, 1990.

De Gaulle, Charles. *War Memoirs*. 3 volumes. London: Collins/Weidenfeld and Nicolson, 1955-60.

DeMontravel, Peter R. *A Hero to His Fighting Men: Nelson A. Miles, 1839-1925*. Kent, OH: Kent State University Press, 1998.

Detzer, David. *Donnybrook: The Battle of Bull Run, 1861*. New York: Harcourt, 2004.

Dickens, Charles. *American Notes*. 1892 edition; London: Granville, 1985.

Doctorow, E. L. *The March: A Novel*. New York: Random House, 2005.

Donald, David Herbert. *Lincoln*. London: Jonathan Cape, 1995.

Eicher, David J. *The Longest War: A Military History of the Civil War*. New York: Simon and Schuster, 2001, 389-90.

Eliot, John. *A Biographical Dictionary: Containing a Brief Account of the First Settlers*. Salem, MA: Cushing and Appleton, 1809.

Emmisson, F. G. *Elizabethan Life: Wills of Essex Gentry Merchants*. Chelmsford, UK: Essex County Council, 1978.

Engle, Stephen D. *Don Carlos Buell: Most Promising of All*. Chapel Hill: University of North Carolina Press, 1999.

Fahs, Alice, and Joan Waugh, eds. *The Memory of the Civil War in American Culture*. Chapel Hill: University of North Carolina Press, 2004.

Farrar-Hockley, Anthony. *The Edge of the Sword*. London: Frederick Muller, 1954.

Farrell, Theo. *The Norms of War*. Boulder, CO: Lynne Reiner, 2005.

Favorini, Attilio. "Barrett, Lawrence (April 4, 1838-March 20, 1891)." *American National Biography*. Edited by John A. Garraty and Mark C. Carnes. 26 volumes. New York: Oxford University Press, 1999; supplements 2002, 2005.

Fellman, Michael. *Citizen Sherman*. New York: Random House, 1995.

Fellman, Michael. *Inside War: The Guerrilla Conflict in Missouri during the American Civil War*. New York: Oxford University Press, 1989.

Fink, Lois Marie. "Healy, George Peter Alexander." *American National Biography*. Edited by John A. Garraty and Mark C. Carnes. 26 volumes. New York: Oxford University Press, 1999; supplements 2002, 2005.

Finley, Milton. *The Most Monstrous of Wars: The Napoleonic Guerrilla War in Southern Italy, 1806-11*. Columbia: University of South Carolina Press, 1994.

Fischer, David Hackett. *Albion's Seed: Four British Folkways in America*. New York: Oxford University Press, 1989.

Foner, Eric. "The Making and Breaking of the Legend of Robert E. Lee." *New York Times*, August 28, 2017.

Foot, M. R. D. "Netherlands." In *The Oxford Companion to the Second World War*. Edited by I. C. B. Dear and M. R. D. Foot. New York: Oxford University Press, 1995.

Foreman, Amanda. *The World on Fire*. London: Allen Lane, 2016.

Fortescue, J. W. *A History of the British Army*. 13 volumes. London: Macmillan, 1899-1930.

Foster, Gaines. *The Ghosts of the Confederacy*. New York: Oxford University Press, 1987.

Freedman, Lawrence. *The Future of War: A History*. London: Allen Lane, 2017, 32.

Fuller, J. F. C. *The Conduct of War, 1789-1961*. London: Eyre and Spottiswoode, 1961.

Fuller, J. F. C. *The Decisive Battles of the Western World*. 3 volumes. London: Eyre and Spottiswoode, 1954-56.

Fuller, J. F. C. *The Generalship of Ulysses S. Grant*. London: John Murray, 1929.

Fuller, J. F. C. *Grant and Lee: A Study in Personality and Generalship*. 2nd edition. Bloomington: Indiana University Press, 1957.

Fuller, J. F. C. *Lectures on FSR II*. London: Sifton Praed, 1931.

Fuller, J. F. C. *The Military Papers and Correspondence of Major General J. F. C. Fuller, 1916-1933*. Edited by Alaric Searle. History Press for the Army Records Society, 2017.

Fuller, J. F. C. *Sir John Moore's System of Training*. London: Hutchinson, 1925.

Fuller, J. F. C. *Training Soldiers for War*. London: Hugh Rees, 1914.

Gabriel, Richard A. *The Painful Field: The Psychiatric Dimension of Modern War*. New York: Greenwood Press, 1988.

Gallagher, Gary, ed. *The Spotsylvania Campaign*. Chapel Hill: University of North Carolina Press, 1998.

Gallagher, Gary. *The Union War*. Cambridge, MA: Harvard University Press, 2011.

Glatthaar, Joseph T. *March to the Sea and Beyond*. New York: New York University Press, 1985.

Glover, Michael. *Wellington as Military Commander*. London: Batsford, 1968.

Glover, Michael. *Wellington's Peninsular Victories*. London: Batsford, 1963.

Glover, Richard. *Britain at Bay: Defence against Bonaparte, 1803-1814*. London: George Allen and Unwin, 1973.

Goodman, Jean. "Munnings, Sir Alfred James (1878-1959)." *Oxford Dictionary of National Biography*. 64 volumes. Oxford: Oxford University Press, 2004, 39:761-64.

Grandstaff, Mark. "'Preserving the Habits and Usages of War': William Tecumseh Sherman, Professional Reform in the US Officer Corps, 1865-1881, Revisited." *Journal of Military History* 62, no. 3 (July 1998): 521-45.

Griffith, Paddy. *Military Thought in the French Army, 1815-51*. Manchester, UK: Manchester University Press, 1989.

Grimsley, Mark. *The Hard Hand of War: Union Military Policy towards Civilians, 1861-1865*. New York: Cambridge University Press, 1995.

Guthrie, Charles, and Michael Quinlan. *Just War: The Just War Tradition, Ethics in Modern Warfare*. London: Bloomsbury, 2007.

Hagerman, Edward. *The American Civil War and the Origins of Modern Warfare*. Bloomington: Indiana University Press, 1988.

Hallock, Judith Lee. *Braxton Bragg and Confederate Defeat*. Volume 2. Tuscaloosa: University of Alabama Press, 1991.

Hanson, Victor Davis. *The Soul of Battle*. New York: Free Press, 1999.

Hardee, William J. *Rifle and Infantry Tactics*. Philadelphia: J. B. Lippincott, 1861.

Harris, William C. *Lincoln's Last Months*. Cambridge, MA: Belknap Press of Harvard University Press, 2004.

Hayes, Rutherford B. *Hayes: The Diary of a President, 1875-1881*. Edited by T. Harry Williams. New York: David McKay, 1964.

Heale, Michael J. *The Presidential Quest: Candidates and Images in American Political Culture, 1787-1852*. London: Longman, 1982.

Hebert, Walter H. *Fighting Joe Hooker*. Indianapolis, IN: Bobbs Merrill, 1944.

Hess, Earl J. *The Civil War in the West: Victory and Defeat from the Appalachians to the Mississippi*. Chapel Hill: University of North Carolina Press, 2012.

Hesseltine, William B. *Lincoln and the War Governors*. New York: Alfred A. Knopf, 1955.

Hill, Christopher. *The Century of Revolution, 1603-1714*. London: Thomas Nelson, 1961.

Hill, Christopher. *God's Englishman: Oliver Cromwell and the English Revolution*. London: Weidenfeld and Nicolson, 1970.

Hirsch, Mark D. "Election of 1884." In *History of American Presidential Elections*. Edited by Arthur M. Schlesinger and Fred . Israel. 5 volumes. New York: Chelsea House and McGraw Hill, 1971.

Hirshson, Stanley P. *The White Tecumseh: A Biography of William T. Sherman.* New York: Wiley, 1997.

A History of the County of Essex, vol. 10, *Lexden Hundred (Part).* Edited by Janet Cooper. London: Victoria County History, 2001.

Hofstadter, Richard. *America at 1750: A Social Portrait.* London: Jonathan Cape, 1972.

Hofstadter, Richard. *Anti-Intellectualism in American Life.* London: Jonathan Cape, 1964.

Holden Reid, Brian. *America's Civil War: The Operational Battlefield, 1861–1863.* Amherst, MA: Prometheus Books, 2008.

Holden Reid, Brian. "Civil Military Relations and the Legacy of the Civil War." In *Legacy of Disunion: The Enduring Significance of the American Civil War.* Edited by Susan-Mary Grant and Peter J. Parish. Baton Rouge: Louisiana State University Press, 2003, 151–70.

Holden Reid, Brian. "Command and Leadership in the Civil War." In *Themes of the American Civil War,* 2nd edition. Edited by Susan-Mary Grant and Brian Holden Reid. 2000; New York: Routledge, 2010.

Holden Reid, Brian. "The Commander and His Chief of Staff: Ulysses S. Grant and John A. Rawlins." In *Command and Leadership in War.* Edited by G. D. Sheffield. Revised edition. 1997; London: Brassey's, 2002.

Holden Reid, Brian. "General McClellan and the Politicians." *Parameters* 17, no. 3 (September 1987): 101–12.

Holden Reid, Brian. "How Were American Civil War Armies Kept in the Field?" In *Raise, Train and Sustain.* Edited by Peter Dennis and Jeffery Grey. Loftus, NSW: Australian Military History Publications, 2010.

Holden Reid, Brian. "The Military Significance of the 1864 Presidential Election." In *Reconfiguring the Union: Civil War Transformation.* Edited by Iwan W. Morgan and Philip John Davies. New York: Palgrave Macmillan, 2013.

Holden Reid, Brian. *The Origins of the American Civil War.* New York: Addison Wesley Longman, 1996.

Holden Reid, Brian. "Power, Sovereignty and the Great Republic: Anglo-American Relations in the Era of the Civil War." In *Power and Stability: British Foreign Policy 1865–1965.* Edited by Erik Goldstein and B.J.C. McKercher. London: Frank Cass, 2003, 45–76.

Holden Reid, Brian. "'A Signpost That Was Missed'? Reconsidering Lessons from the American Civil War." *Journal of Military History* 70, no. 2 (April 2006): 386–407.

Holden Reid, Brian. *Studies in British Military Thought.* Lincoln: University of Nebraska Press, 1998.

Holden Reid, Brian. "A Survey of the Militia in Eighteenth Century America." *Army Quarterly* 110 (January 1980): 52.

Holden Reid, Brian. "William T. Sherman and the South (Peter J. Parish Memorial Lecture, 2009)." *American Nineteenth Century History* 11, no. 1 (March 2010): 1–16.

Holmes, Richard. *Firing Line.* London: Jonathan Cape, 1985.

Holmes, Richard. *Marlborough.* London: HarperCollins, 2008.

Holroyd, Michael. *Augustus John.* 2 volumes. London: Heinemann, 1974–75.

Holt, Michael F. *The Rise and Fall of the Whig Party.* New York: Oxford University Press, 1999.

Hoogenboom, Ari. *Rutherford B. Hayes: Warrior and President.* Lawrence: University Press of Kansas, 1995.

Hope, Ian C. *A Scientific Way of War: Antebellum Military Science, West Point, and the Origins of American Military Thought.* Lincoln: University of Nebraska Press, 2015.

Horne, Alistair. *The Fall of Paris: The Siege and the Commune, 1870-71.* London: Macmillan, 1965.

Horne, Robert. *A Précis of Modern Tactics.* London: Stationery Office, 1873.

Howard, Michael. *Liberation or Catastrophe? Reflections on the History of the Twentieth Century.* London: Continuum, 2007.

Howe, Daniel Walker. *The Political Culture of the American Whigs.* Chicago: University of Chicago Press, 1979.

Hughes, Nathaniel Cheairs. *Bentonville: The Final Battle of Sherman and Johnston.* Chapel Hill: University of North Carolina Press, 1996.

Hunt, William. *The Puritan Moment: The Coming of Revolution in an English County.* Cambridge. MA: Harvard University Press, 1983.

Hyman, Harold M. "Election 1864." In *History of American Presidential Elections.* Edited by Arthur M. Schlesinger Jr. and Fred Israel. 5 volumes. New York: Chelsea House, 1985.

Jackson, Robert A. *Systematic View of the Formation, Discipline and Economy of Armies.* London: Stockdale, 1804.

Jamieson, Perry D. *Crossing the Deadly Ground: United States Army Tactics, 1865-1899.* Tuscaloosa: University of Alabama Press, 1994.

Janda, Lance. "Shutting the Gates of Mercy: The American Origins of Total War." *Journal of Military History* 59, no. 1 (January 1995),:7-26.

Jomini, Baron de. *The Art of War.* 1862; London: Greenhill, 1992.

Just, Ward. *Military Men.* London: Michael Joseph, 1972.

Kaiser, David. *Politics and War.* Enlarged edition. Cambridge, MA: Harvard University Press, 2000.

Kammen, Michael. *People of Paradox: An Inquiry concerning the Origins of American Civilization.* New York: Alfred A. Knopf, 1972.

Kantor, Mackinlay. *If the South Had Won the Civil War.* 1960; New York: Tom Doherty Associates, 2001.

Kardux, Joke, and Edward van der Bilt. *Newcomers in an Old City: The American Pilgrims in Leiden, 1609-1620.* 3rd revised edition. Leiden: Uitgeverij and Niermans, 2007.

Keegan, John. *The Mask of Command.* London: Jonathan Cape, 1987.

Kennett, Lee. *Marching through Georgia.* New York: Harper Collins, 1995.

Kennett, Lee. *Sherman: A Soldier's Life.* New York: HarperCollins, 2001.

Kiesling, Eugenia C. "'Total War, Total Nonsense,' or the Military Historian's Fetish." In *Arms and the Man: Military History Essays in Honor of Dennis Showalter.* Leiden: Brill, 2011, 215-42.

Kiper, Richard L. *Major John A. McClernand: Politician in Uniform.* Kent, OH: Kent State University Press, 1999.

Kiszely, John. "The British Army and Approaches to War since 1945." In *Military Power: Land Warfare in Theory and Practice.* Edited by Brian Holden Reid. London: Frank Cass, 1997, 179-206.

Knowles, Dom David. *The American Civil War.* Oxford: Clarendon Press, 1926.

Krasny, Mark V. *Washington's Partisan War, 1775-1783.* Kent, OH: Kent State University Press, 1996.

Leech, Margaret. *Reveille in Washington, 1860-1865.* London: Eyre and Spottiswoode, 1942.

Lewis, Lloyd. *Sherman: Fighting Prophet.* 1932; New York: Harcourt Brace, 1958.

Lichtman, Allan J. *The Case for Impeachment.* New York: HarperCollins, 2017.

Liddell Hart, B. H. *The British Way in Warfare*. 3rd edition. Harmondsworth, UK: Penguin, 1942.

Liddell Hart, B. H. *The Ghost of Napoleon*. London: Faber and Faber, 1933.

Liddell Hart, B. H. *Sherman*. London: Ernest Benn, 1930. US edition: *Sherman: Soldier, Realist, American*. New York: Dodd Mead, 1929.

Liddell Hart, B. H. *Strategy: The Indirect Approach*. 4th edition. London: Faber and Faber, 1967.

Lipset, Seymour Martin, and Earl Raab. *The Politics of Unreason: Right-Wing Extremism in America, 1790–1970*. London: Heinemann, 1971.

Livermore, Thomas L. *Numbers and Losses in the Civil War in America, 1861–1865*. 2nd edition. Boston: Houghton Mifflin, 1901.

Lonn, Ella. *Salt as a Factor in the Confederacy*. 1933; Tuscaloosa: University of Alabama Press, 1965.

Lord, Francis A. *Civil War Collector's Encyclopaedia*. New York: Castle, 1965.

Lord Rosebery's North American Journal, 1873. Edited by A. R. C. Grant with Caroline Combe. London: Sidgwick and Jackson, 1967.

Lucas, Marion B. *Sherman and the Burning of Columbia*. College Station: Texas A&M University Press, 1976.

Luvaas, Jay. "The Great Military Historians and Philosophers." In *A Guide to the Study and Uses of Military History*. Edited by John E. Jessup and Robert W. Coakley. Washington, DC: US Army Center for Military History, 1988, 59–88.

Luvaas, Jay. "The Influence of the German Wars of Unification on the United States." In *On the Road to Total War: The American Civil War and the German Wars of Unification, 1861–1871*. Edited by Stig Förster and Jörg Nagler. Cambridge: Cambridge University Press, 1997, 597–619.

Luvaas, Jay. *The Military Legacy of the Civil War: The European Inheritance*. Chicago: University of Chicago Press, 1959.

Marszalek, John F. *Commander of All Lincoln's Armies: A Life of General Henry W. Halleck*. Cambridge, MA: Belknap Press of Harvard University Press, 2004.

Marszalek, John F. *Sherman: A Soldier's Passion for Order*. New York: Free Press, 1993.

Marszalek, John F. *Sherman's Other War: The General and the Civil War Press*. Revised edition. 1981; Kent, OH: Kent State University Press, 1999.

Marvel, William. *Burnside*. Chapel Hill: University of North Carolina Press, 1993.

Mayo, C. H. Revised by James Mills. "Charles Mayo (1837–77)." *Oxford Dictionary of National Biography*. 63 volumes. Oxford: Oxford University Press, 2004, 37:616.

McAllister, Anna. *Ellen Ewing: Wife of General Sherman*. New York: Benziger, 1936.

McDonough, James Lee. *Shiloh: In Hell before Night*. Knoxville: University of Tennessee Press, 1977.

McDonough, James Lee. *William Tecumseh Sherman: In the Service of My Country*. New York: Norton, 2016.

McFeely, William S. *Grant: A Biography*. New York: Norton, 1982.

McGrath, Patrick. *Papists and Puritans under Elizabeth I*. London: Blandford, 1967.

McMurry, Richard M. *John Bell Hood and the War for Southern Independence*. 1982; University of Nebraska Press, 1992.

McMurry, Richard M. *Atlanta 1864: Last Chance for the Confederacy*. Lincoln: University of Nebraska Press, 2000.

McPherson, James M. *This Mighty Scourge*. New York: Oxford University Press, 2007.

McWhiney, Grady. *Braxton Bragg and Confederate Defeat.* Volume 1. 1969; Tuscaloosa: University of Alabama Press, 1991.

Melvin, Mungo. *Manstein: Hitler's Greatest General.* London: Weidenfeld and Nicolson, 2010.

Miers, Earl Schenck. *The General Who Marched to Hell.* New York: Alfred A. Knopf, 1951.

Miles, Nelson A. *Personal Recollections and Observations of Nelson A. Miles.* 2 volumes. 1896; Lincoln: University of Nebraska Press, 1992.

Miller, Perry. *The Life of the Mind in America.* London: Gollancz, 1966.

Montgomery, Bernard. "Wellington Memorial Lecture." *RUSI Journal* 114, no. 656 (December 1969): 8-13.

Morris, Edmund. *The Rise of Theodore Roosevelt.* 2nd edition. New York: Random House, 2010.

Morrison, James L. *"The Best School in the World": West Point, 1833-1866* (Kent, OH: Kent State University Press, 1986.

Muir, Rory. *Wellington: The Path to Victory, 1769-1814.* New Haven, CT: Yale University Press, 2013.

Napier, William. *History of the War in the Peninsula and in the South of France, 1807-1814.* 6 volumes. 1834; London: Constable, 1993.

Naveh, Shimon. *In Pursuit of Military Excellence.* London: Frank Cass, 1997.

Neely, Mark E., Jr. *The Civil War and the Limits of Destruction.* Cambridge, MA: Harvard University Press, 2007.

Nevins, Allan. *The Emergence of Lincoln.* 2 volumes. New York: Scribner's, 1950.

Nevins, Allan. *Frémont: Pathmarker of the West.* 2nd edition. New York: Longmans, Green, 1955.

Nevins, Allan. *The State Universities and Democracy.* Urbana: University of Illinois Press, 1962.

Newell, Clayton R., and Michael D. Krause, eds. *On Operational Art.* Washington, DC: US Army Center of US Military History, 1994.

Nicolson, Harold. *Good Behaviour: Being a Study of Certain Types of Civility.* London: Constable, 1955.

Nye, Roger H. *The Challenge of Command.* Wayne, NJ: Avery, 1986.

Olivier, Dara. *The Burning of Moscow.* London: George Allen and Unwin, 1966.

Onuma, Yasuaki, ed. *A Normative Approach to War: Peace, War and Justice in Hugo Grotius.* Oxford: Clarendon Press, 1993.

Orwell, George. *Homage to Catalonia.* 1938; London: Penguin, 2000.

Paludan, Phillip S. *The Presidency of Abraham Lincoln.* Lawrence: University Press of Kansas, 1994.

Parish, Peter J. *The American Civil War.* London: Eyre Methuen, 1975.

Parish, Peter J. "The Will to Write and the Will to Fight: Some Recent Books on the American Civil War." *Journal of American Studies* 32, pt. 2 (August 1998): 302.

Parks, Joseph H. *Joseph E. Brown of Georgia.* Baton Rouge: Louisiana State University Press, 1977.

Perry, Mark. *Grant and Twain.* New York: Random House, 2004.

Persons, Stow. *The Decline of the American Gentility.* New York: Columbia University Press, 1973.

Peskin, Allan. *Garfield.* 1978; Kent, OH: Kent State University Press, 1990.

Porter, Roy. *Madness: A Brief History.* Oxford: Oxford University Press, 2002.

Powell, J. Enoch. *Joseph Chamberlain.* London: Thames and Hudson, 1977.

Rafuse, Ethan S. *McClellan's War*. Bloomington: Indiana University Press, 2005.

Rappaport, Adam. *Magnificent Obsession: Victoria, Albert and the Death That Changed the Monarchy*. London: Hutchinson, 2011.

Reaney, P. H. *A Dictionary of British Surnames*. London: Routledge and Kegan Paul, 1958.

Reed, Rowena. *Combined Operations in the Civil War*. 1978; Lincoln: University of Nebraska Press, 1993.

Reeves, Thomas C. *Gentleman Boss: The Life of Chester Alan Arthur*. New York: Alfred A. Knopf, 1975.

Remini, Robert. *Andrew Jackson: The Course of American Empire*. 1977; Baltimore: Johns Hopkins University Press, 1998.

Reston, James, Jr.. *Sherman's March and Vietnam*. New York; Macmillan, 1984.

Roger, N. A. M. *The Safeguard of the Sea: A Naval History of Britain, 660-1649*. New York: Norton, 1997.

Royster, Charles. *The Destructive War*. New York: Alfred A. Knopf, 1991.

Russell, Conrad. "Hampden, Sir John (1594-1643)." *Oxford Dictionary of National Biography*. 64 volumes. Oxford: Oxford University Press, 2004, 24:976-84.

Rutkow, Ira. *James A. Garfield*. New York: Henry Holt, 2006.

Saxe-Weimar, Duke of. *Travels through North America during the Years 1825 and 1826*. 2 volumes. Philadelphia: Carey, Lea, and Carey, 1828.

Schafritz, Jay M., ed.. *Words on War*. New York: Prentice Hall, 1990.

Schneller, Robert J. *A Quest for Glory: A Biography of Rear Admiral John A. Dahlgren*. Annapolis, MD: Naval Institute Press, 1996.

Schultz, Jane E. *Women at the Front*. Chapel Hill: University of North Carolina Press, 2004.

Sellers, Charles. *The Market Revolution: Jacksonian America, 1815-1846*. New York: Oxford University Press, 1991.

Sharpe, Kevin. *The Personal Rule of Charles I*. New Haven, CT: Yale University Press, 1992.

Shiman, Philip L. "Engineering and Command: The Case of William S. Rosecrans, 1862-1863." In *The Art of Command in the Civil War*. Edited by Stephen E. Woodworth. Lincoln: University of Nebraska Press, 1998, 84-117.

Simpson, Jeffrey. *Officers and Gentlemen: Historic West Point in Photographs*. Tarrytown, NY: Sleepy Hollow Press, 1982.

Skelton, William B. "The Commanding Generals and the Question of Civil Control in the Antebellum US Army." *American Nineteenth Century History* 7, no. 2 (June 2006): 153-72.

Simpson, Brooks D. *Let Us Have Peace: Ulysses S. Grant and the Politics of War and Reconstruction*. Chapel Hill: University of North Carolina Press, 1991.

Simpson, Brooks D. *Ulysses S. Grant: Triumph over Adversity, 1822-1865*. Boston: Houghton Mifflin, 2000.

Smith, Elbert B. *The Presidencies of Zachary Taylor and Millard Fillmore*. Lawrence: University Press of Kansas, 1988.

Smith, Jean Edward. *Grant: A Biography*. New York: Simon and Schuster, 2001.

Soames, Mary. *Clementine Churchill*. London: Cassell, 1979.

Spiers, Edward M. "The Late Victorian Army, 1868-1914." In *The Oxford History of the British Army*. Edited by David G. Chandler. Oxford: Oxford University Press, 1996, 187-210.

Spiller, Roger. *An Instinct for War*. Cambridge, MA: Belknap Press of Harvard University Press, 2005.

Spiller, Roger. "Six Propositions." In *Between War and Peace: How America Ends Its Wars.* Edited by Matthew Moten. New York: Free Press, 2011, 1-20.

Stanley, H. M. *The Autobiography of Sir Henry Morton Stanley G.C.B.* Edited by Dorothy Stanley. London: Sampson Low, 1909.

Starr, Stephen Z. *The Union Cavalry in the Civil War.* 3 volumes. Baton Rouge: Louisiana State University Press, 1979.

Stephens, John L. *Incidents of Travel in Central America, Chiapas and Yucatan.* 10th edition. 2 volumes. London: John Murray, 1842.

Stiles, T. J. *The First Tycoon: The Epic Life of Cornelius Vanderbilt.* New York: Alfred A. Knopf, 2009.

Stirk, Peter M. R. *A History of Military Occupation from 1792 to 1914.* Edinburgh: Edinburgh University Press, 2016.

Stoker, Donald. *The Grand Design: Strategy and the US Civil War.* New York: Oxford University Press, 2010.

Sugden, John. *Tecumseh: A Life.* New York: Henry Holt, 1997.

Syme, Ronald. *The Roman Revolution.* 1939; London: Folio Society, 2009.

Symonds, Craig. *Joseph E. Johnston: A Civil War Biography.* New York: Norton, 1992.

Symonds, Craig. *Lincoln and His Admirals.* New York: Oxford University Press, 2008.

Symonds, Craig. *Stonewall of the West: Patrick Cleburne and the Civil War.* Lawrence: University Press of Kansas, 1997.

Tap, Bruce. *Over Lincoln's Shoulder: The Committee on the Conduct of the War.* Lawrence: University Press of Kansas, 1998.

Taylor, Alan. *American Colonies.* New York: Viking, 2001.

Terraine, John. *The Smoke and the Fire.* London: Sidgwick and Jackson, 1980.

Thackeray, W. M. *The Virginians: A Tale of the Last Century.* 2 volumes. 1859; London: J. M. Dent, 1937.

Thomas, Benjamin P., and Harold H. Hyman. *Stanton: The Life and Times of Lincoln's Secretary of War.* New York: Alfred A. Knopf, 1962.

Thomas, Emory M. *Bold Dragoon: The Life of J. E. B. Stuart.* New York: Harper and Row, 1986.

Thucydides. *History of the Peloponnesian War.* Translated by C. Foster Smith. Loeb Classical Library. 4 volumes. Cambridge, MA: Harvard University Press, 1919.

Trefousse, Hans L. *Andrew Johnson.* New York: Norton, 1989, 147.

Trefousse, Hans L. *Ben Butler: The South Called Him Beast.* New York: Twayne, 1957.

Trudeau, Noah A. *Southern Storm: Sherman's March to the Sea.* New York: HarperCollins, 2008.

Tucker, J. M. *The Life of the Duke of Wellington; compiled from despatches.* London: J. Blackwood, 1880.

Twain, Mark. *Roughing It.* Hartford, CT: American Publishing Company, 1872; New York: Hippocrene, 1988.

Utley, Robert M. *Cavalier in Buckskin: George Armstrong Custer and the Western Military Frontier.* Norman: University of Oklahoma Press, 1988.

Utley, Robert M. *Frontier Regulars: The United States Army and the Indian, 1866-1891.* New York: Macmillan, 1973.

Vagts, Alfred. *A History of Militarism.* Revised edition. London: Hollis and Carter, 1959.

Varon, Elizabeth R. "'Save in Defense of My Native State': A New Look at Robert E. Lee's Decision to Join the Confederacy." In *Secession Winter.* Edited by R.J. Cook et al. Baltimore: Johns Hopkins University Press, 2013, 34-57.

Vaughan, Alden T., and Virginia M. Vaughan. *Shakespeare in America.* New York: Oxford University Press, 2012.
Vetter, Charles E. *Sherman: Merchant of Terror, Advocate of Peace.* Gretna, LA: Pelican, 1992.
Vidal, Gore. *1876: A Novel.* New York: Random House, 1976.
Voltaire. *Candide; or, Optimism.* 1996; Ware, Herts: Wordsworth Editions, 1999.
Walters, John B. "General William T. Sherman and Total War." *Journal of Southern History* 14, no. 4 (November 1948): 447-80.
Walters, John B. *Merchant of Terror: General Sherman and Total War.* Indianapolis, IN: Bobbs-Merrill, 1973.
Warner, Ezra J. *Generals in Blue.* 1964; Baton Rouge: Louisiana State University Press, 1989.
Watt, Robert N. "Apaches Without and Enemies Within: The US Army in New Mexico." *War in History* 18, no. 2 (April 2011): 1-36.
Watt, Robert N. "'Horses Worn to Mere Shadows': The Ninth US Cavalry's Campaigns against the Apaches in New Mexico Territory, 1879-1881." *New Mexico Historical Review* 86, no. 2 (Spring 2011): 197-222.
Watt, Robert N. "Victorio's Military and Political Leadership of the Warm Springs Apaches." *War in History* 18, no. 4 (November 2011): 457-94.
Waugh, Joan. "Ulysses S. Grant, Historian." In *The Memory of the Civil War in American Culture.* Edited by Alice Fahs and Joan Waugh. Chapel Hill: University of North Carolina Press, 2004, 5-38.
Waugh, Joan. *U. S. Grant: American Hero, American Myth.* Chapel Hill: University of North Carolina Press, 2009.
Wavell, A. P. *Generals and Generalship.* Harmondsworth, UK: Penguin, 1941.
Weigley, Russell F. *A Great Civil War: A Military and Political History.* Bloomington: Indiana University Press, 2000.
Weigley, Russell F. *History of the United States Army.* London: Batsford, 1968.
Weigley, Russell F. *Towards an American Army: Military Thought from Washington to Marshall.* New York: Columbia University Press, 1962.
Welsh, Jack D. *Medical History of Union Generals.* Kent, OH: Kent State University Press, 1997.
West, Rebecca. *The Meaning of Treason.* Revised edition. 1949; London: Pan, 1956.
Wharton, Edith. *Hudson River Bracketed.* London: Virago, 1986.
White, Richard. *The Republic for Which It Stands: The United States during Reconstruction and the Gilded Age, 1865-1896.* New York: Oxford University Press, 2017.
White, Theodore H. *The Making of the President 1972.* London: Jonathan Cape, 1974.
Wiebe, Robert. *The Search for Order, 1877-1920.* London: Macmillan, 1967.
Williams, T. Harry. *Lincoln and His Generals.* New York: Alfred A. Knopf, 1952.
Williams, T. Harry. *McClellan, Sherman, and Grant.* New Brunswick, NJ: Rutgers University Press, 1962.
Williams, T. Harry. *P. G. T. Beauregard: Napoleon in Gray.* 1955; Baton Rouge: Louisiana State University Press, 1989.
Williamson, Edwin. *The Penguin History of Latin American.* Harmondsworth, UK: Penguin, 1992.
Winters, Harold A., et al. *Battling the Elements.* Baltimore: Johns Hopkins University Press, 1998.
Witt, John Fabian. *Lincoln's Code: The Laws of War in American History.* New York: Free Press, 2012.

Wolseley, Garnet. *The American Civil War: A British View*. Edited by James A. Rawley. 1964; Harrisburg: Stackpole Books, 2002.

Wolseley, Garnet. *The Soldier's Pocket-Book*. 5th edition. London: Macmillan, 1886.

Wolseley, Garnet. *Wolseley and Ashanti*. Edited by I. F. W. Beckett. Stroud, Gloucestershire: History Press for the Army Records Society, 2009.

Woodham-Smith, Cecil. *Queen Victoria: Her Life and Times*. London: Hamish Hamilton, 1972.

Woodward, C. Vann. *Reunion and Reaction: The Compromise of 1877 and the End of Reconstruction*. Boston: Little, Brown, 1951.

Woodworth, Steven E. *Jefferson Davis and His Generals*. Lawrence: University Press of Kansas, 1990.

Woodworth, Steven E. *Nothing but Victory: The Army of the Tennessee, 1861–1865*. New York: Alfred A. Knopf, 2005.

Woodworth, Steven E. *Sherman*. New York: Palgrave Macmillan, 2009.

Woodworth, Steven E. *Six Armies in Tennessee*. Lincoln: University of Nebraska Press, 1998.

Wooster, Robert. *Nelson A. Miles and the Twilight of the Frontier Army*. Lincoln: University of Nebraska Press, 1993.

Wooster, Robert. "John M. Schofield and the Multipurpose Army." *American Nineteenth Century History* 7, no. 2 (June 2006): 173–91.

Wright, Esmond. *Fabric of Freedom, 1763–1800*. London: Macmillan, 1965.

Yiannikkou, Jason. "Rogers, John (ca. 1570–1636)." *Oxford Dictionary of National Biography*. 64 volumes. Oxford: Oxford University Press, 2004, 47:562–63.

Young, Desmond. *Rommel*. 1950; London: William Collins, 1972.

Websites

Descendants of Allen Martin and Related Families. http://wc.rootsweb.ancestry.com

Griffiths, Paul. "The Distinction between Innate and Acquired Characteristics." In *The Stanford Encyclopaedia of Philosophy*. Edited by Edward N. Zalta. Fall 2009. http://plato.stanford.edu/archives.fall2009/innate-acquired/

Katayev, Ivan. "The Burning of Moscow." In *Patriotic War and Russian Society* (in Russian). Originally published 1911; Jubilee Edition, 2005), n.p. http://www.museum.ru/1812/Library/sitin/book4_10.html

Site of the Bank of Lucas, Turner and Co. https://www.hmdb.org/Marker.asp?Marker-33402

Oxford Textbook of Psychiatry. http://www.oxfordreference.com/view/10.1093/acref/9780199657681.001.0001/acref-9780199657681

Index